THE BOAT BUYER'S GUIDE TO
Express and Sedan Cruisers

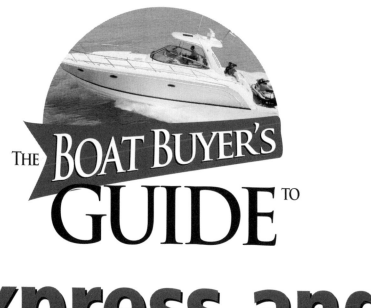

THE BOAT BUYER'S GUIDE TO

Express and Sedan Cruisers

ED MCKNEW

INTERNATIONAL MARINE / McGRAW-HILL

CAMDEN, MAINE · NEW YORK · CHICAGO · SAN FRANCISCO · LISBON · LONDON · MADRID · MEXICO CITY · MILAN · NEW DELHI · SAN JUAN · SEOUL · SINGAPORE · SYDNEY · TORONTO

The **McGraw·Hill** Companies

1 2 3 4 5 6 7 8 9 10 DOC DOC 9 8 7 6

Originally published by American Marine Publishing, Inc.
488 Bay East Road
Traverse City, MI 49686
231-933-0827
E-mail: info@powerboatguide.com
www.powerboatguide.com

Library of Congress Cataloging-in-Publication Data
McKnew, Ed.
  The boat buyer's guide to express and sedan cruisers / Ed
McKnew.
      p. cm.
  Includes index.
  ISBN 0-07-147353-X (alk. paper)
  1. Motorboats—United States—Catalogs. 2. Motorboats—
Prices—United States—Catalogs. 3. Used boats—United
States—Catalogs. 4. Used boats—Prices—United States—
Catalogs. 5. Motorboats—Purchasing. I. Title.
  VM349 .M338 2006
  623.82/31402973—dc22   2006041726

Questions regarding the ordering of this book should be
addressed to
The McGraw-Hill Companies
Customer Service Department
P.O. Box 547
Blacklick, OH 43004
Retail customers: 1-800-262-4729
Bookstores: 1-800-722-4726

www.internationalmarine.com

Photographs courtesy the author.

Contents

Contents

Contents

Flybridge Cruisers

Contents

Contents

Runabouts

Introduction

The introduction in 1989 of the *PowerBoat Guide* provided yacht brokers and dealers with the first comprehensive handbook ever produced covering late-model powerboats from 27 to 80 feet long. Designed specifically for marine industry professionals, the *PowerBoat Guide* quickly became an annual publication, and in 1995 the editors made the book an even more popular resource with the addition of retail high-low appraisal values for new and used boats. Compiled and edited by an experienced broker, no other publication offers such a wealth of information on current and out-of-production express cruisers, trawlers, motor yachts, and sportfishing boats. Over the years, the *PowerBoat Guide* has grown to become a standard tool within the yacht sales community, with users found in most every brokerage office in the country. Often called the "Yacht Broker's Bible," it is easily one of the most-quoted publications in the business.

Even as the *PowerBoat Guide* has matured, the boat-buying marketplace has become more diverse and fragmented. The Internet makes more information available to boat shoppers than ever before, but paradoxically it provides no context or comparisons for that information, and as a result the consumer winds up feeling overwhelmed by unprocessed data. We believe this state of affairs is bad for everyone. Boat buyers can't be sure of finding the right boat at a fair price, and boat brokers lose sales. It is time, therefore, to give consumers broader access to the same information brokers have. These considerations have prompted us to offer the *PowerBoat Guide*'s reviews and appraisals to consumers for the first time.

In doing so, we've had to confront the fact that the *PowerBoat Guide* has grown to almost 2,000 pages, making it too big and too expensive for a consumer audience. Working with the editors of International Marine, we have therefore divided it into three consumer editions: *The Boat Buyer's Guide to Express and Sedan Cruisers* (which you now hold in your hands), *The Boat Buyer's Guide to Motor Yachts and Trawlers*, and *The Boat Buyer's Guide to Sportfishing Boats*.

The Boat Buyer's Guide to Express and Sedan Cruisers covers hundreds of the most popular family cruisers, sportboats, flybridge yachts, and family sedan powerboats built since 1980. These are the boats most people turn to for weekend entertaining, family outings, and close-to-home cruising. Including both domestic and imported brands, many of these yachts offer an impressive blend of exciting performance and state-of-the-art styling. Others, with their spacious interiors and posh accommodations, place the focus on luxury and eye-popping sex appeal.

This unique publication with its pictures, factory specifications, prices, and concise reviews for hundreds of powerboat models will give you the essential information you need to make a smart buying decision. And the book is not just for buyers; boatowners and boating enthusiasts alike will find it a valuable addition to their boating libraries for its insightful comments, hard-to-find production information, and real-world performance data.

From the inexpensive 27-foot midcabin express to the high-powered, high-priced 75-foot Mediterranean sport cruiser, *The Boat Buyer's Guide to Express and Sedan Cruisers* covers the entire range of day cruisers and sportboats in a single comprehensive and easily referenced volume that is unique in the marine industry. We believe it will make shopping for a boat a much more enjoyable and rewarding experience.

Frequently Asked Questions

In an effort to clear away some of the confusion regarding the purchase of a new or used boat, we have listed below some of the most common questions asked by boat buyers. The answers presented to these questions reflect the thinking of the author. We believe the information presented here will address several important issues confronting buyers of boats listed in this publication.

Q. Beam is important to us since we want as much interior volume as possible in a boat. Some models we've been aboard recently seem cavernous inside, and their beams were unusually wide. The question is, how much is too much beam?

A. Although modern production boats clearly have more beam than their predecessors, many yacht designers still consider 1 foot of beam for each 3 feet of length close to the ideal length-to-beam ratio for yachts under 55 feet. Having said that, the fact is that most modern production boats have beams that exceed that 3:1 ratio. It's not unusual, for example, to see a 36-footer with a 13-foot beam or, say, a 45-footer with a 16-foot beam.

Q. Should I be looking for a boat with diesel engines?

A. In many cases the answer is going to be yes. In the last few years diesels have become much more common in smaller boats than in the past. It used to be that you seldom saw diesels in anything under 35 feet, but that's changed since the price of diesel engines has come down. They're also getting smaller (and lighter), which allows them to be installed in smaller boats. With gas prices escalating, we may see more and more express cruisers with diesels.

Range is often a factor in a cruising yacht, and diesels can deliver up to 50 percent more of it than the same boat with gasoline engines. It should be noted, however, that gas-powered express and sedan cruisers are still common and make great boats.

Indeed, in a smaller aft-cabin cruiser, there is still much to recommend gas. The added expense of diesels in a 35-foot boat could easily add up to a quarter of the purchase price. But, again, diesels are becoming more affordable now as new technology allows manufacturers to reduce both the size and weight of diesel engines while increasing their performance.

In resolving this question, keep in mind that the resale value of a diesel-powered boat will often go a long way toward justifying the added up-front expense.

Q. I know that engine hours are important, but what constitutes a lot of hours on a particular set of motors?

A. This is always a hard question to answer, so we'll just offer up some general guidelines. When it comes to gas engines (inboards and I/Os), most dealers and brokers figure those with over 1,000 hours are probably tired. With turbocharged diesels 3,500 hours is a lot of running time, and with naturally aspirated diesels it's not uncommon to pile up 5,000 hours before an overhaul is required.

Unfortunately, a good many of today's ultra-high-performance diesels never see 2,000 hours before an overhaul is required. Sometimes this is a manufacturer problem, but premature marine diesel death usually results from improper owner care and maintenance. Lack of use and poor exercise habits may be the number-one killer. Humidity (moisture) on cylinder components can be avoided with regular running and engine heaters. Diesel engines should be run under a load whenever possible. If your mechanical surveyor suggests new oil, fuel, or water hoses, do it. Trying to save money here can be very expensive in the long run.

Having said that, it's important to note that there are far too many variables to make any buying decisions based upon engine hours alone. It's imperative to have the diesels in a used boat surveyed just as you have the boat itself professionally examined before reaching a final decision. It's not quite so critical with gas engines since they cost far less to rebuild than diesels; however, it's always worth the small expense of having a compression test done on gas engines just to see what you're getting into.

Determining the actual hours on an engine (or a set of engines) can be difficult. There are generally hour meters installed in boats over 25 feet (that may or may not be operating properly), but they're not always found in smaller gas-powered boats. Even if you have access to all the service records, we strongly suggest that you rely on an expert to evaluate the engines in any boat you have a serious interest in owning.

Q. I'm looking at a boat with propeller tunnels in the hull. What are the advantages and disadvantages?

A. Propeller tunnels (commonly called prop pockets) are often employed by designers to reduce shaft angles and draft requirements. Manufacturers like Sea Ray and Phoenix have used them for years, and they're a common characteristic in the hull designs of many European models.

While reduced shaft angles and draft requirements offer significant advantages in many hulls, there are some potential downsides to their use. Among them is loss of lift at the stern, which may result in a bow-high running attitude, poor high-speed steering, and an increased turning radius. Finally—and this applies primarily to fishing boats—prop-pocket hulls generally require more finesse in tight-quarter handling.

We know of no trawlers using propeller tunnels in the hull. In motor yachts (or convertibles), prop pockets are often used in conjunction with V-drives. (Without prop pockets, the shaft angles resulting from a V-drive installation would be prohibitively steep.) It's worth noting that many of the high-performance European-built yachts reviewed in this book use propeller tunnels. In most cases, we believe the advantages inherent in a well-designed prop-pocket hull can outweigh the potential disadvantages mentioned above.

Q. Should I reject a boat with bottom blisters?

A. Generally, no. Blisters can almost always be repaired, although the process can require a fair amount of time and expense. With that in mind, it is rare indeed to see a blistering problem so severe that it actually affects the integrity of the hull.

While some boats tend to re-blister again and again, most bottoms properly dried and protected should remain blister-free for five years or longer.

Q. Can I rely on the boat tests that I read in the national magazines?

A. Yes, they're usually accurate as far as they go. For example, the performance figures—speeds at various rpms, fuel burn data, etc.—are quite reliable, although it's always wise to keep in mind that these are new boats with light loads and plenty of factory preparation. Don't look for a lot of hard-hitting criticism in these tests, however, because boating magazines (including ours) depend upon boat manufacturers for a major part of their advertising revenues.

We've read a lot of boat tests over the years. In our opinion, the best and most comprehensive are conducted by *Boating* magazine. *Sea* and *Sport Fishing* also have some excellent reviews.

Q. How important is a lower helm?

A. That depends upon your location. A lower helm is a great convenience—a luxury, actually—when you're getting an early start on a chilly morning or trying to stay dry on a wet, windy day. For visibility, however (and to avoid seasickness), most skippers prefer the bridge station for heavy weather running in spite of the physical discomforts.

Aside from the added expense (which can be considerable), a lower helm takes up valuable room in the salon, which would otherwise be devoted to living space. Not surprisingly, inside helms are most commonly seen in northern climates, especially in the Great Lakes and the Pacific Northwest. On the other hand, a lower helm in Florida (or along the Gulf Coast) is often a hindrance to a boat's resale value since it may be viewed as a useless and unnecessary feature.

Note that lower helms are often a standard feature in trawlers and also in many most motor yachts over 50 feet in length.

Q. Should I hesitate before purchasing a Taiwan boat? Several dealers and brokers I've met have been very critical of their quality.

A. Today's Taiwan imports no longer enjoy the huge price advantage over their U.S. counterparts that they had in the 1970s and 1980s. While it's true that many of the boats imported from Taiwan during that period were cheaply built and suffered from poor quality control, others were surprisingly well built and represented long-term excellent values. The Taiwanese unquestionably had the skills to turn out a first-rate product, but most of their clients were U.S. importers whose only objective was a fat profit back home. Asked to turn out cheap boats in volume, the Taiwanese responded by flooding the market with waves of inexpensive trawlers and sailboats, usually with an abundance of interior and exterior teak woodwork.

The big price advantages Taiwan products had in

the American market began to dry up several years ago, and today their exports must compete on a level playing field with our own domestic yachts. There's been a big shakeout in the boatbuilding business in Taiwan in the past decade and many of the smaller, less productive yards have shut down. Those remaining are generally experienced boatbuilders with modern facilities, state-of-the-art technology and highly skilled, well-paid workers. Many of these yards have successfully sold their products into the European market.

The 1970s and '80s were the heyday of the trawler-style Taiwan import. They were affordably priced (thanks to a very favorable U.S.-Taiwan exchange rate), and their handsome all-teak interiors and economical operation appealed to North American boaters tired of plain-Jane fiberglass interiors and/or the high operational expenses associated with gas-powered motor yachts. (Remember, those were the days of oil embargoes and increasing fuel costs.) Trawlers are still in demand, but the Taiwanese dollar has increased dramatically in the past decade, and the cost of today's Taiwan-built trawler is comparable to what an American-built model might cost. Consequently, those imported during the seventies and eighties have held their resale values as well as or better than their U.S. counterparts—a good indication of their continuing popularity on the used market. Many of the Taiwan motor yachts currently being imported into this country are completely modern boats with plenty of high-tech construction and customer appeal, and practically all of today's trawler-style boats are being produced in Taiwan. We can think of no reason to avoid them.

Q. Are freshwater boats really worth more?

A. Sure, no question about it. Salt water is hard on a boat, especially the gelcoat, electronics, paint, metalwork, and engine room components. And while nearly all diesel-powered boats have closed cooling systems, the same is not always true of gas engines. In a saltwater environment it's wise to look for a boat with a closed cooling system since it usually lengthens engine life.

Another reason freshwater boats often bring a premium price has to do with the fact that they generally have fewer engine hours. The boating season in most freshwater regions is shorter than many of the largest saltwater boating areas. Furthermore, the majority of freshwater vessels spend their winters out of the water—many in a protected environment with reduced exposure to the corrosive effects of sun, wind and rain.

As might be imagined, a well-maintained saltwater vessel is probably a better investment than a poorly maintained freshwater boat. One final factor that equalizes the values between the two is equipment. An East or West Coast saltwater boat is often fitted out with better cruising equipment and more elaborate electronics than a similar Great Lakes or inland waters vessel.

Q. Should I avoid a boat if the manufacturer has gone out of business or is currently undergoing hard times?

A. Emphatically, no. There are plenty of good used boats on the market from manufacturers who couldn't survive the poor economy of the past several years. The parts you will need from time to time are always available from catalog outlets or suppliers. Engine parts, of course, are easily secured from a number of sources. Generally speaking, there are no components used in a production model that cannot be replaced (or repaired) by a good yard.

Note that many of the most popular models on today's brokerage market were built by companies now out of business.

Q. For resale, should I only consider a brand of boat with big-name market recognition?

A. There is no question that certain popular brands have consistently higher resale values. There are, however, many designs from small or regional builders that are highly sought after by knowledgeable boaters. Often, the market for these models is tighter and generally less saturated than the high-production designs—a factor that often works to a seller's advantage.

Q. If I decide to buy a used boat, should I use a broker?

A. If you have plenty of time on your hands, you could locate a good boat at a fair price without a broker. Unless you find a boat for sale by owner, you end up working with a broker anyway—the listing agent.

Do your homework and end up with an agent who has your long-term interests at heart. You're not paying for his time and expertise until you purchase a boat through him. Keeping several brokers in competition against one another often results in no one giving you the time that you'll require.

About the Prices

Retail High and Retail Low

The *Retail High* is the average selling price of a clean, well-maintained boat with light-to-moderate equipment. This boat will show little wear and tear, and all systems and equipment will be in good working order. Note that boats with an exceptional equipment list—or those showing very little use—will often sell at a figure higher than the published Retail High.

The *Retail Low* is the average selling price of a boat with modest equipment and below-average maintenance. This boat may need attention to various equipment and cosmetic issues, but in most respects she should be seaworthy and ready to use.

Condition Price Adjustments

Boats that are in truly outstanding condition and loaded with optional equipment may sell for as much as 15 percent over the published Retail High. Similarly, boats that require extensive yard work to put them into serviceable condition can be expected to sell for well below the published Retail Low figure.

Geographical Price Adjustments

The prices published in this guide apply to boats found on the East Coast, Florida, and the Gulf of Mexico. To adjust the price for another region, please use the following guide:

Great Lakes & Midwest: . . . . +10%
Pacific Northwest: . . . . +15%
Inland Rivers & Lakes: . . . . +5–10%
California: . . . . +15%

Freshwater vs. Saltwater Boats

Boats that have been used exclusively in fresh water are nearly always worth more than those used in a saltwater environment. The saltwater environment is hard on boats—both cosmetically and mechanically—and they require considerably more maintenance than freshwater boats. Great Lakes boats offer the added advantage of having been used for only a few months each year rather than year-round. (Indeed, many are stored during the winter months.)

Depreciation

Determining depreciation is a complex process with many factors to take into consideration. Some boats hold their prices better than others, some drop rapidly in value, and local economic conditions can often play a part in determining a boat's market value. In the final analysis, there is no consistent depreciation formula we know of that can be applied with any degree of accuracy.

Insufficient Data

A series of asterisks (******) indicates that the editors were unable to obtain enough resale information on a particular model to come up with dependable resale price estimates.

For price updates after January 1, 2007, call 800-832-0038.

Important Notes

For the most part, the contents of this book are straightforward and easily understood. Before launching into the pages, however, we strongly suggest that you take a few moments and review the following points. Failure to do so is likely to result in some confusion and misunderstanding.

Factory Specifications

The specifications listed for each model are self-explanatory although the following factors are noted:

1. *Clearance* refers to bridge clearance, or the height above the waterline to the highest point on the boat. Note that this is often a highly ambiguous piece of information since the manufacturer may or may not include such things as an arch, hardtop, or mast. Use this figure with caution.
2. *Weight* is a factory-provided specification that may or may not be accurate. Manufacturers differ in the way they compute this figure. For the most part, it refers to a dry boat with no gear.
3. *Designer* refers to the designer of the hull only.
4. *NA* means that the information is not available.

Performance Data

Whenever possible, performance figures have been obtained from the manufacturer or a reliable dealer or broker. When such information was unavailable, the author has relied upon his own research together with actual hands-on experience. The speeds are estimates and (in most cases) based on boats with average loads of fuel, water, options and gear.

All speeds are reported in knots. Readers in the Great Lakes or inland waterways may convert knots to miles per hour by multiplying a given figure by 1.14.

Cruising Speeds, Gas Engines

Unless otherwise noted, the cruising speed for gas-powered inboard (or sterndrive) boats is calculated at 3,000–3,200 rpm.

Cruising Speeds, Diesel Engines

The cruising speeds for diesel-powered boats are calculated as follows:

1. Detroit (two-stroke) Diesels: about 200–250 rpm off the top rpm rating.
2. Other (four-stroke) Diesels: about 350–400 rpm off the manufacturer's maximum rpm rating.

Cruising Speeds, Outboard Engines

The cruising speeds for outboard-powered boats is generally figured at 4,000 rpm.

Useful Terms

Abaft—behind

Athwartships—at a right angle to the boat's length

Bulkhead—an upright partition separating compartments in a boat

Bulwark—a raised portion of the deck designed to serve as a barrier

Chine—the point at which the hullsides and the bottom of the boat come together

cid—referring to the cubic inch displacement of an engine, e.g., 454-cid gas engine

Coaming—vertical surface surrounding the cockpit

Cuddy—generally refers to the cabin of a small boat

Deadrise—the angle from the bottom of the hull (not the keel) to the chine

Deep-V Hull—a planing hull form with at least 18 degrees of deadrise at the transom and a fairly constant "V" bottom shape from stem to stern

Displacement Hull—a hull designed to go through the water and not capable of planing speed

Forefoot—the underwater shape of the hull at the bow

Freeboard—the height of the sides of the hull above the waterline

gph—gallons per hour (of fuel consumption)

Gunwale (also gunnel)—the upper edge of the sheerline

Hull Speed—the maximum practical speed of a displacement hull. To calculate, take the square root of the waterline length (LWL) and multiply by 1.34.

Knot—1 nautical mile per hour. To convert knots to statute mph, multiply by 1.14.

Modified-V Hull—a planing hull form with (generally) less than 18 degrees of transom deadrise

Nautical Mile—measurement used in salt water. A nautical mile is 6,076 feet.

Planing Speed—the point at which an accelerating hull rises onto the top of the water. To calculate a hull's planing speed, multiply the square root of the waterline length by 2.

Semi-Displacement Hull—a hull designed to operate economically at low speeds while still able to attain planing speed performance

Sheerline—the fore-and-aft line along the top edge of the hull

Sole—a nautical term for floor

Statute Mile—measurement used in fresh water. A statute mile equals 5,280 feet.

Express and Sedan Cruisers

Express Cruisers

Design Assets
Generous cockpit seating, family-friendly cabin accommodations

Design Limitations
Poor weather protection, modest range

Price Leaders
Larson, Bayliner, Maxum, Rinker, Monterey, Doral

Quality Leaders
Chaparral, Sea Ray, Regal, Formula, Sunseeker, Four Winns, Viking Sport Cruisers, Tiara

Albin 27 Family Cruiser

Albin 28 Tournament Express

Length Overall . . . . 26'9"	Headroom . . . . 6'2"
Length WL . . . . 24'4"	Water . . . . 40 gals.
Beam . . . . 9'8"	Fuel . . . . 72/100 gals.
Draft . . . . 2'6"	Hull Type . . . . Semi-Disp.
Weight . . . . 6,500#	Designer . . . . Joe Puccia
Clearance . . . . NA	Production 1983–95

Length w/Pulpit . . . . 29'11"	Fuel, Std . . . . 132 gals.
Hull Length . . . . 28'4"	Fuel, Opt. . . . . 192 gals.
Beam . . . . 9'9"	Water . . . . 36 gals.
Draft, I/Os . . . . 1'10"	Hull Type . . . . Modified-V
Draft, Inboard . . . . 3'2"	Deadrise Aft . . . . 16°
Weight . . . . 7,500#	Production 1993–Current

The Albin 27 Family Cruiser is a descendant of the Swedish-built Albin 25 Cruiser, one of the best-selling small craft ever produced. The 27 was an extremely popular model for Albin thanks to her fuel-efficient operation, affordable price, and sturdy, solid fiberglass construction. A full-length keel provides sure-footed tracking when the seas pick up, and a shallow draft makes the 27 ideal for cruising the Intracoastal or inland lake regions. While her twin-cabin accommodations are necessarily basic (she is, after all, only a 27-footer), they are nonetheless adequate for the cruising couple or an undemanding small family. The forward cabin features a good-sized double berth, full galley, dinette, hanging locker, and a surprising amount of storage. Perhaps the best feature of the Albin 27 is her center-cockpit layout with its inboard seating and protected helm. Built in the U.S., Albin 27s require relatively little maintenance and they handle a chop quite well for a small boat. Several small diesel engines were available over the years, all of which consume only 2–3 gph at a cruising speed of 10–12 knots. Note that a bow thruster and additional fuel were standard in later models.

The Albin 28 Tournament Express is a sturdy fishboat/family cruiser with a practical deck layout, a skeg-protected rudder and cabin accommodations for four. The 28 is a rather traditional-looking boat with a hint of Downeast styling, and her foam-cored hull boasts a prop-protecting skeg for increased tracking and stability. While the centerline engine box dominates the cockpit (standard power is a single V-drive inboard), there's still enough working space for a couple of undemanding anglers. A hardtop (optional) with sliding side windows provides weather protection for the helm, and a drop curtain or optional bulkhead door encloses it completely. Belowdecks, the compact interior is accented with mica cabinets, teak trim, and a classy teak-and-holly sole. A wide quarter berth extends beneath the bridgedeck, and a bow thruster is standard. Note that for 2003 a Flush Deck option moved the engine forward, under the wheelhouse, narrowing the quarter berth but opening up the cockpit. Among several engine choices, a single 300hp Yanmar (or Cummins) diesel will cruise at 18 knots with a top speed of 22–23 knots.

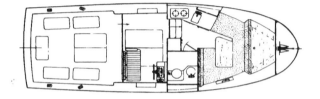

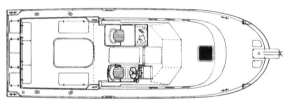

Albin 30 Family Cruiser

Length Overall . . . . 31'5"	Fuel . . . . 126 gals.
Length WL . . . . 26'8"	Water . . . . 26 gals.
Beam . . . . 10'0"	Waste . . . . 18 gals.
Draft . . . . 3'2"	Hull Type . . . . Modified-V
Weight . . . . 9,800#	Deadrise Aft . . . . 19°
Clearance, Arch . . . . 8'3"	Production 2004–Current

Introduced in 2004, the Albin 30 Family Cruiser is the successor to the company's popular 27 Family Cruiser manufactured from 1983–95. This is an ideal small cruiser for the family whose priorities include economical operation, easy handling, and—perhaps most important of all—an affordable price. The hull of the Albin 30 is solid fiberglass, and a skeg-mounted rudder provides protection for the running gear in the event of grounding. Her split-plan layout offers sleeping accommodations for five adults in two separate cabins. The galley and head are in the forward cabin where a convertible U-shaped dinette and portside quarter berth will sleep three, and twin single berths in the aft cabin can be converted into a queen bed. The cockpit is deep enough to keep youngsters safe and secure, and visibility from the semi-enclosed helm is excellent. A hatch between the helm and companion seats provides good access to the engine. Additional features include an in-floor cockpit storage well, wide side decks, a total of ten opening ports, and a bow pulpit. A single 300hp Perkins diesel will cruise the Albin 30 Family Cruiser at 16–17 knots and reach a top speed of around 22 knots.

Albin 31 Tournament Express

Length w/Pulpit . . . . 33'0"	Clearance, Hardtop . . . . 9'3"
Hull Length . . . . 31'8"	Fuel . . . . 300 gals.
Beam . . . . 12'4"	Water . . . . 73 gals.
Draft, Single Engine . . . . 3'10"	Hull Type . . . . Modified-V
Draft, Twin Engines . . . . 3'3"	Deadrise Aft . . . . 14°
Weight, Twin Engines . . . . 14,000#	Production 1995–Current

Based on the smaller Albin 28 Tournament Express, the Albin 31 TE is a distinctive Downeast-style fisherman whose spacious interior allows her to double as a capable family cruiser. She's built on a modified-V hull with a fairly wide beam for a 31-footer, and the single-engine version comes with a bow thruster and skeg-protected prop. In her standard mode, the Albin 31 has a three-sided pilothouse enclosure with the bridgedeck open to the cockpit, although a pair of optional doors can make the wheelhouse a fully enclosed cabin. The cockpit comes with a transom baitwell and fish box, and a transom door is standard along with in-deck storage and rod holders. The interior sleeps four with an athwartships double berth aft of the galley and a convertible dinette/double berth forward. There's a separate stall shower in the head—a big plus on any small boat with cruising aspirations. Additional features include easy access to the engines, wide side decks, an opening windshield, transom shower, and raw-water washdown. Among several engine options, a single 370hp Cummins diesel will cruise at 16 knots, and twin 315hp Yanmar diesels will cruise at 22–24 knots.

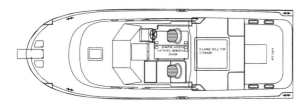

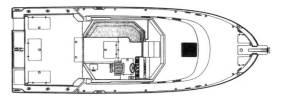

Bridgedeck

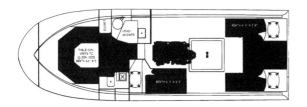

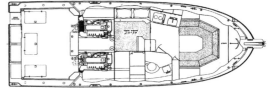

Interior

See Page 294 for Pricing Information

See Page 294 for Pricing Information

Albin 35 Tournament Express

Length w/Pulpit	36'11"	Fuel	370 gals
Hull Length	34'11"	Water	160 gals.
Beam	12'4"	Cockpit	80 sq. ft.
Draft	3'0"	Hull Type	Modified-V
Weight	18,000#	Deadrise Aft	13°
Clearance	11'0"	Production	1995–Current

The Albin 35 Tournament Express is a hardtop version of the Albin 35 Convertible. She's a moderately priced family cruiser/weekend fisherman with roomy accommodations and a cockpit that's large enough to meet the needs of weekend anglers. Built on a fully cored hull with moderate beam, a flared bow and a shallow keel, the solid, workmanlike construction of the Tournament Express is noteworthy. Buyers have a choice of interior layouts. The standard version has a single-stateroom with the galley down, and the alternate floorplan moves the galley into the salon and adds a second stateroom on the lower level. Either way, the interior of the Albin 35 is bright and cheery and the wraparound cabin windows provide excellent helm visibility in all directions. Additional features include wide side decks, six opening cabin ports and opening salon windows, transom door, integral bow pulpit, and a separate stall shower in both floorplans. Among several single- and twin-screw engine options, a pair of 370hp Cummins diesels will cruise the 35 Tournament Express at an economical 24 knots and reach a top speed of just under 30 knots.

Single-Stateroom Layout

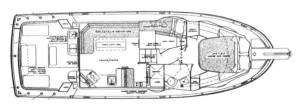

Two-Stateroom Floorplan

See Page 294 for Pricing Information

Atlantic 34 Sportsman

Length	34'0"	Fuel	300 gals.
Beam	12'0"	Cockpit	NA
Draft	3'0"	Hull Type	Modified-V
Weight	13,500#	Deadrise Aft	16°
Clearance	8'0"	Designer	J. Scopinich
Water	40 gals.	Production	1988–92

Until the 34 Sportsman came along, Atlantic Yachts of Palatka, FL (which went out of business in the early 1990s), had been known primarily for their line of Hargrave-designed trawlers and motor yachts. It came as a surprise, then, to see the company's first new design in years fall into the sportfishing category. A popular and good-selling model, the 34 Sportsman was built on a solid fiberglass hull with a modified-V bottom, a wide beam, and generous flare at the bow. Her large bi-level cockpit was offered in several deck configurations for use as an express cruiser or sportfisherman. A centerline hatch on the bridgedeck provides trouble-free access to the motors. Below, the cabin accommodations are laid out in the conventional manner with V-berths forward, an enclosed standup head with shower, small galley, and a dinette seating area. Standard 454-cid big-block gas engines will cruise the Atlantic 34 Sportsman at a comfortable 25 knots and reach top speeds in the neighborhood of 31–32 knots. Optional 300hp GM 8.2 diesels cruise around 27 knots and reach 31 knots top. A total of 77 Atlantic 34s were built before production ended in 1992.

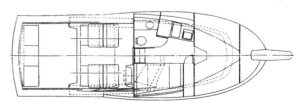

See Page 295 for Pricing Information

Bayliner 2755 Ciera Sunbridge

Length	27'0"	Fuel	78 gals.
Beam	8'6"	Water	28 gals.
Draft, Up	1'8"	Waste	13 gals.
Draft, Down	3'3"	Hull Type	Deep-V
Weight	5,200#	Deadrise Aft	20°
Clearance	7'2"	Production	1989–93

The 2755 Ciera Sunbridge was the biggest trailerable model ever built by Bayliner. There are trade-offs in a boat like this; the narrow 8-foot, 6-inch beam of the 2755 results in a rather confining interior compared with other 27-footers, most of which have wider beams and are therefore not trailerable. The cockpit is small as well, and at just over 5,000 pounds the 2755 is a relatively light boat for her size. Conversely, the narrow beam makes for a more easily driven hull, and the 2755 provides a good turn of speed with just a single sterndrive I/O. Built on a solid fiberglass deep-V hull, the midcabin interior sleeps four (two adults, two kids) and comes with a removable dinette table, a small galley pod, four opening ports and a standup head with sink and shower. Visibility from the raised helm is excellent, and the cockpit comes with an L-shaped lounge forward, transom gate, a transom seat, entertainment table and a cockpit sink with storage under. Lacking side decks, a walk-through windshield provides access to the bow. Among a couple of engine choices available during her production years, a single 300hp 7.4L I/O will cruise at 25 knots and reach a top speed of around 35 knots.

Bayliner 2850/2855 Sunbridge

Length	27'5"	Fuel	120 gals.
Beam	10'0"	Water	30 gals.
Draft, Up	1'11"	Headroom	6'2"
Draft, Down	3'3"	Hull Type	Deep-V
Weight	5,775#	Deadrise Aft	NA
Clearance	6'8"	Production	1983–89

Bayliner has had their share of popular boats over the years and the 2850/2855 Ciera Sunbridge was certainly one of them. Introduced in 1983 as the 2850 Contessa Sunbridge (and becoming the 2855 Ciera Sunbridge in 1988 when the floorplan was updated), she was marketed as a budget-priced family cruiser with sleek styling, a wide beam, and a spacious midcabin layout. This is a roomy boat below for a 28-footer with good headroom thanks to her raised foredeck and elevated helm. Berths for six are provided together with a standup head compartment, decent counter space, and a full-size galley. The cockpit has plenty of lounge seating for guests, and visibility from the helm position is excellent. Note that when she became the Ciera Sunbridge in 1986, the deckhouse was redesigned and raised slightly, and the interior was completely rearranged with a U-shaped dinette to port replacing the previous dinette forward. Built on a lightweight hull, most were sold with a single 260hp Volvo sterndrive engine. She'll cruise easily at 18 knots and reach a top speed of 26–27 knots. it's important to note that the 2855 Ciera Sunbridge name was applied to two later Bayliner models in the 1990s (see following pages).

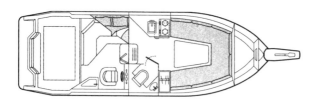

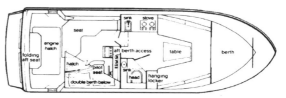

Contessa Floorplan (1983–87)

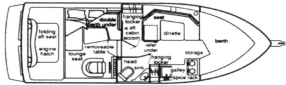

Ciera Floorplan (1988–89)

See Page 296 for Pricing Information

5

See Page 296 for Pricing Information

Bayliner 2855 Sunbridge (1991–93)

Length	28'1"	Fuel	102 gals.
Beam	9'6"	Water	35 gals.
Draft, Up	1'8"	Hull Type	Deep-V
Draft, Down	3'3"	Deadrise Aft	18°
Weight	6,510#	Designer	Bayliner
Clearance	9'2"	Production	1991–93

The 2855 Ciera Sunbridge is a practical family cruiser with a midcabin floorplan and a rather innovative salon layout. Bayliner engineers designed a wraparound dinette lounge for this model with a removable jump seat for access to the V-berth—a great entertaining arrangement with pit-style seating for a crowd. The dinette converts in the normal fashion to a double berth, and both the forward and midcabin sleeping areas are fitted with privacy curtains. Topside, a big L-shaped lounge seat (with removable table) provides guest seating opposite the helm. A shower is built into the transom, and a fold-down ladder is available for swimmers. Hull construction is solid fiberglass and a wide 9-foot, 6-inch beam results in a rather roomy boat both above and below. While she's fairly light compared with other similar boats her size, she rides quite well in a chop thanks to her moderately deep-V hull design. The standard 230hp MerCruiser I/O will cruise at 17 knots (around 25 knots top), and the optional 300hp motor will deliver 19 knots at cruise and about 30 knots wide open. With only 100 gallons of fuel capacity, don't plan on any long trips.

Bayliner 2855 Sunbridge (1994–99)

Length w/Pulpit	30'3"	Fuel	109 gals.
Beam	9'7"	Water	33 gals.
Draft, Up	1'8"	Hull Type	Deep-V
Draft, Down	3'4"	Deadrise Aft	22°
Weight	6,510#	Designer	Bayliner
Clearance	8'6"	Production	1994–99

The 2855 Ciera Sunbridge pictured above is actually a makeover of an earlier Bayliner 2855 Ciera Sunbridge model (1991–93) with a more contemporary profile and an updated interior with a larger galley and improved storage. The hull is basically the same as the earlier 2855 with an extra inch of beam and a little more deadrise at the transom. While she's definitely on the light side compared with similar boats her size, she rides quite well in a chop thanks to her deep-V hull design. The midcabin floorplan of the 2855 Sunbridge is arranged with double berths fore and aft and a convertible dinette, which can sleep two kids. Privacy curtains separate both sleeping areas and headroom is adequate throughout most of the cabin. Outside, a big U-shaped lounge (with a removable table) is opposite the helm. Lacking side decks, a windshield walk-through provides access to the foredeck. Additional features include a slide-out jump seat behind the companion lounge, a transom door, a sport arch, and colorful hull graphics. A light boat with limited fuel capacity, a single 300hp sterndrive will cruise at 20 knots and reach 30+ knots wide open.

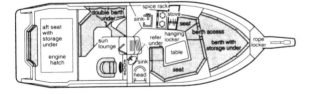

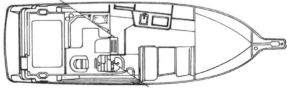

See Page 296 for Pricing Information

See Page 296 for Pricing Information

Bayliner 285 Cruiser

Length	29'6"	Fuel	102 gals.
Beam	9'10"	Water	33 gals.
Draft, Up	1'8"	Waste	20 gals.
Draft, Down	3'1"	Hull Type	Deep-V
Weight	7,185#	Deadrise Aft	21°
Clearance	9'1"	Production	2000–Current

The Bayliner 285 (called the 2855 Ciera Sunbridge in 2000–02) is similar to previous 28-foot Bayliner express boats in her contemporary styling, roomy accommodations, and a very affordable price. Built on a solid fiberglass deep-V hull with a relatively wide beam, the midcabin floorplan of the 285 is arranged with a V-berth forward with privacy curtain and the owner's stateroom aft with a solid privacy door and plenty of storage. The dinette will seat four comfortably, and three overhead deck hatches provide ventilation and additional lighting. A full galley, standup head, and generous storage round out the interior. In the cockpit, Bayliner introduced a unique L-shaped lounge seat in the 285 that converts into a sun pad or an aft-facing bench seat. A fold-down bench seat is installed at the transom, and a transom door opens to an extended swim platform. Lacking side decks, an opening panel in the windshield provides access to the foredeck. Among several engine options, a single 300hp MerCruiser sterndrive will cruise the Bayliner 285 at 20 knots and reach a top speed of just over 30 knots.

Bayliner 2859 Classic Cruiser

Length	27'9"	Fuel	102 gals.
Beam	9'9"	Water	36 gals.
Draft, Drive Up	1'7"	Waste	30 gals.
Draft, Drive Down	3'0"	Hull Type	Modified-V
Weight	7,597#	Deadrise Aft	15°
Clearance	9'1"	Production	1993–2004

Originally called the Super Classic 28 (1993–95) and later the 2859 Ciera Express (1996–2002), the Bayliner 2859 Classic Cruiser is a conservatively styled hardtop cruiser whose modest price and practical layout have great appeal to budget-minded buyers. The layout of this boat is similar to most hardtop models her size with the helm and sofa on the bridgedeck and the dinette, galley and V-berth on the lower level. What sets the 2859 apart from the norm is her amidships berth (located beneath the bridgedeck), an arrangement that brings the total sleeping capacity to six. A privacy curtain separates the forward berth from the salon, and there's a handheld shower in the head compartment. While the cockpit of the 2859 Express is fairly small, it's still large enough for a couple of light-tackle anglers or a couple of folding deck chairs. Additional features include a well-equipped galley with plenty of storage, a swim platform and boarding ladder, and a transom door. Among several sterndrive engine options offered over the years, a single 310hp MerCruiser will cruise at an economical 22 knots and reach a top speed of around 30 knots. Note the small fuel capacity.

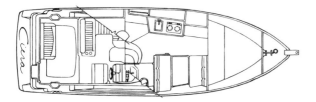

See Page 296 for Pricing Information

7

See Page 296 for Pricing Information

EXPRESS CRUISERS

Bayliner 2950/2955 Avanti Sunbridge

Length	28'8"	Fuel	120 gals.
Beam	10'6"	Water	30 gals.
Draft, Drives Up	2'0"	Waste	13 gals.
Draft, Drives Down	3'6"	Hull Type	Deep-V
Weight	7,400#	Deadrise Aft	20°
Clearance	9'6"	Production	1988–90

Introduced in 1988 as the 2950 Avanti (she became the 2955 Avanti in 1989), this roomy express is yet another example of why Bayliner so dominates the market for entry-level boats. Fully equipped (there were no options except air conditioning), a new 2955 Avanti Sunbridge delivered for about $50,000 in 1989/90—far less than competitive boats. Not surprisingly, a lot of 2955s were sold during her production run and they are quite common on today's aftermarket. With a wide 10-foot, 6-inch beam, the accommodations are quite spacious for a 29-footer. The midcabin floorplan will sleep four adults and two kids and includes an enclosed standup head with shower and a small mini-galley. Note the absence of a privacy door in the forward stateroom—a not uncommon configuration in a boat of this type where some models even do without a bulkhead to separate the cabins. Too, the swim platform is a bolt-on affair rather than a modern integral design. A single 340hp I/O was standard (16 knots cruise and 28 top), and twin 260hp MerCruisers were optional (21–22 knots cruise/33 top). Note that the engine compartment is a tight fit with twin engines.

Bayliner 3055 Ciera Sunbridge

Length	30'7"	Fuel	125 gals.
Beam	10'0"	Water	36 gals.
Draft, Drives Up	1'6"	Hull Type	Modified-V
Draft, Drives Down	3'0"	Deadrise Aft	14°
Weight	8,000#	Designer	Bayliner
Clearance	8'9"	Production	1991–94

The Bayliner 3055 Ciera Sunbridge (called the 3055 Avanti Sunbridge in 1991) was a very popular model for Bayliner during her early-1990s production years. A 10-foot beam is about average for a modern 30-footer, so the 3055 Sunbridge isn't a notably roomy boat below for her length although the accommodations are certainly adequate. She has a fairly straightforward midcabin floorplan with a convertible dinette, a small galley (the refrigerator is placed under the dinette seat), and an enclosed standup head with shower. Both staterooms have curtains for privacy. The cockpit is well arranged with lounge seating opposite the helm and a wet bar behind the helm seat. The engine access hatch in the cockpit has gas-assist springs, and the transom platform has a folding swim ladder and a built-in shower. Like all Bayliner products, most everything was standard in the 3055 Sunbridge (except air conditioning), and there were practically no options. While the detailing and finish are basic, the low price continues to attract budget-minded buyers on the used market. A single 300hp I/O will cruise at 17 knots and reach a top speed of 26–27 knots.

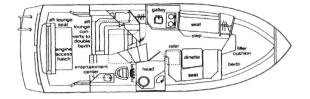

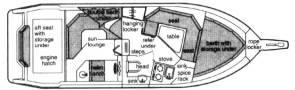

Bayliner 305 Cruiser

Length Overall . . . . 31'6"	Fuel . . . . 148 gals.
Beam . . . . 11'0"	Water . . . . 35 gals.
Draft, Drives Up . . . . 1'9"	Headroom . . . . 6'5"
Draft, Drives Down . . . . 2'9"	Hull Type . . . . Modified-V
Weight . . . . 11,857#	Deadrise Aft . . . . 17°
Clearance, Arch . . . . 7'10"	Production 1999–Current

The affordably priced Bayliner 305 (called the 3055 Ciera Sunbridge from 1999–2002) is an entry-level family cruiser with several very attractive features. With a wide 11-foot beam, the 305 is a roomy boat both inside and out, and while the mediocre finish reflects her low price, there is still much to admire from the standpoint of comfort and practicality. Headroom—well over 6 feet—is excellent in this boat, and the generous beam results in a surprisingly expansive cabin layout. The midcabin floorplan is arranged in the conventional manner with double berths fore and aft, an enclosed head to port, adequate storage, and a well-equipped galley. In the cockpit, a U-shaped lounge features a removable table and converts to a sun pad. A wet bar/entertainment center is to port, and a transom door opens to the integral swim platform with its retractable swim ladder and built-in shower. Lacking side decks, a walk-through windshield provides access to the bow. A pair of 220hp MerCruisers sterndrives will cruise in the low 20s (about 30 knots top), and later models with a pair of 300hp Mercs will cruise in the high 20s and top out at over 40 knots.

Bayliner 3255 Avanti Sunbridge

Length w/Platform . . . . 35'2"	Fuel . . . . 180 gals.
Hull Length . . . . 32'11"	Water . . . . 35 gals.
Beam . . . . 11'0"	Clearance . . . . 11'0"
Draft, Drives Up . . . . 2'0"	Hull Type . . . . Modified-V
Draft, Drives Down . . . . 3'0"	Deadrise Aft . . . . 17°
Weight . . . . 10,261#	Production 1995–99

Introduced in 1995 and remaining in production for the next four years, the Bayliner 3255 Avanti Sunbridge is a conservative family express whose major attractions were an affordable price and generous cabin accommodations. Built on a lightweight, solid fiberglass hull with a relatively wide beam and moderate transom deadrise, the reverse arch of the 3255 is her most prominent styling feature. The midcabin floorplan is arranged in the conventional manner with double berths fore and aft and a full galley, enclosed head and shower, convertible dinette, and a good-size hanging locker in the salon. (Note that an accordion pocket door separates the forward stateroom from the salon.) On deck, a U-shaped settee (with a removable table) is opposite the helm in the bi-level cockpit. The side decks are narrow and getting around the arch to access the side decks isn't easy. Additional features include a cockpit wet bar, transom door, integral bow pulpit, swim platform, and a foredeck sun pad. Optional 310hp MerCruiser sterndrives will cruise the Bayliner 3255 Avanti Sunbridge at 19–20 knots and deliver top speeds of around 32 knots.

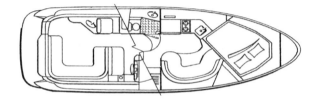

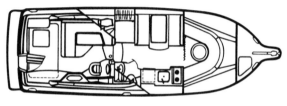

Bayliner 3450/3485/3785 Sunbridge

Length w/Pulpit	36'7"	Fuel	205 gals.
Hull Length	33'9"	Water	50 gals.
Beam	12'10"	Waste	34 gals.
Draft	3'0"	Hull Type	Modified-V
Weight	13,150#	Deadrise Aft	NA
Clearance	9'6"	Production	1987–90

Bayliner's marketing people had a field day with this late-1990s sportcruiser giving her three different names in the four years she was in production. She was introduced as the 3450 Avanti Sunbridge in 1987; for 1988–99 she was called the 3485; and in 1990 (when she gained a new integrated swim platform) she was known as the 3785. While she might have been considered "racy" in the late 1990s with her bold graphics, raked arch and Med-style bow rail, by today's standards the 3450/3485 is downright garish with little to recommend her other than a low price and a big interior. Built on a beamy modified-V hull, the midcabin floorplan is arranged with a U-shaped galley opposite the galley in the salon. A privacy door separates the forward stateroom from the salon, and there's enough room is the aft stateroom for two adults. The decor is cheap and poorly finished. On deck, a settee opposite the helm provides plenty of guest seating, and additional bench seating is built into the transom. Hatches in the aft cockpit floor provide good access to the engines and V-drive units. Standard 330hp gas engines will cruise the Avanti around 20 knots with a top speed of 27–28 knots.

Bayliner 3250/3255/3555 Sunbridge

Length	34'7"	Fuel	205 gals.
Beam	11'5"	Water	50 gals.
Draft, Drives Up	2'4"	Waste	34 gals.
Draft, Drives Down	3'8"	Hull Type	Deep-V
Weight	10,200#	Deadrise Aft	19°
Clearance	9'0"	Production	1988–94

Because they change their model designations so often, it's always confusing to follow any Bayliner product that stays in production for more than a few years. Here's the story of this boat: Introduced in 1988 as the 3250 Avanti Sunbridge (with a 31-foot, 6-inch LOA), the name was changed to 3255 Avanti in 1989. She became the 3555 Avanti Sunbridge (pictured above) in 1990 when a new integral swim platform added some length and sex appeal to her lines. This was a popular model for Bayliner during her production years, and aside from some minor decor updates from year to year, her floorplan remained essentially unchanged from the original. A convertible U-shaped dinette is opposite the galley in the salon, and it's notable that the forward stateroom is fitted with a privacy door rather than just a curtain. As midcabins go, the one in the 3555 isn't as cramped as most, and ventilation—two opening ports and an escape hatch—is very good. On deck, there's guest seating opposite the helm, and a pair of hatches in the cockpit sole provide good access to the motors. Among several engine options, twin 250hp MerCruiser I/Os will cruise efficiently at 22 knots and reach a top speed of around 28–29 knots.

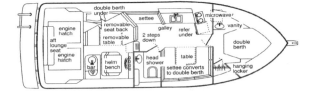

Bayliner 3685 Avanti Sunbridge

Length Overall . . . . 39'4"	Water . . . . 65 gals.
Beam . . . . 13'0"	Waste . . . . 48 gals.
Draft . . . . 3'7"	Headroom . . . . 6'5"
Weight . . . . 21,000#	Hull Type . . . . Modified-V
Clearance, Arch . . . . 12'11"	Deadrise Aft . . . . 15°
Fuel . . . . 244 gals.	Production 1998–99

The 3685 Avanti Sunbridge is a straightforward family express whose principal attraction was her very affordable price tag. Indeed, the Avanti was quite a value considering her long list of standard equipment although the fit and finish left something to be desired. A very contemporary late-1990s design with her reverse arch and integral swim platform, the Avanti was constructed on a solid fiberglass hull with a relatively wide beam and moderate transom deadrise. The midcabin floorplan is standard in boats of this type with staterooms fore and aft (each with a double berth), a full galley, convertible dinette, and an amidships head with shower. On deck, a U-shaped settee abaft the helm converts into a spacious sun pad. A removable cocktail table stores beneath the sole, and a large gas-assist hatch provides easy access to the engines. Additional features include a foredeck sun pad, doublewide helm seat, transom door, a recessed windlass locker, and a cockpit refreshment center. On the downside, the side decks are quite narrow. Among several V-drive engine options, twin 310hp gas engines will cruise at 18 knots, and 330hp Cummins diesels cruise at 21–22 knots. Note the brief two-year production run.

Bayliner 4085 Avanti Sunbridge

Length . . . . 42'0"	Water . . . . 77 gals.
Beam . . . . 13'5"	Waste . . . . 45 gals.
Draft . . . . 3'5"	Hull Type . . . . Modified-V
Weight . . . . 22,100#	Deadrise Aft . . . . 16°
Clearance, Arch . . . . 12'11"	Designer . . . . Bayliner
Fuel . . . . 330 gals.	Production 1997–99

Bayliner has built a loyal following among entry-level boaters over the years with their series well-designed family boats at super-competitive prices. The 4085 Avanti was a good example of Bayliner's market prowess—what brokers like to call a lot of boat for the money. Built on a solid fiberglass modified-V hull with a relatively wide beam, her midcabin floorplan is arranged with double berths in both staterooms and a convertible U-shaped lounge and full galley in the salon. Note that each stateroom has a privacy door (rather than curtains), and the head is fitted with a separate stall shower. The amidships lounge/stateroom has a small sofa and partial standing headroom at the entrance. On deck, there's a doublewide seat at the helm followed by a large circular settee aft (with a removable table) and a full wet bar to port. The Avanti's deep swim platform can store a personal watercraft. Additional features include a gas-assist engine room hatch, side-dumping exhausts and a reverse arch. Standard 310hp V-drive MerCruiser inboards will cruise at a modest 15–16 knots (about 25 knots top), and optional 315hp Cummins diesels will cruise around 25–26 knots.

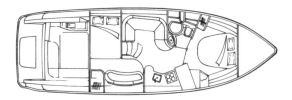

Bertram 28 Moppie

Length	28'6"	Water	27 gals.
Beam	11'0"	Cockpit	85 sq. ft.
Draft	2'7"	Hull Type	Deep-V
Weight	10,400#	Deadrise Aft	23°
Clearance	7'1"	Designer	D. Napier
Fuel	234 gals.	Production	1987–94

The last in a series of Bertram 28-footers, the 28 Moppie is a well-styled inboard runabout with the quality engineering and rugged construction one expects in a Bertram product. She's built on a beamy, solid fiberglass deep-V hull with a steep 23 degrees of transom deadrise. Aside from her superb handling characteristics, the Moppie's primary attraction remains her expansive and versatile bi-level cockpit layout. The lower level has plenty of room for a fighting chair, and the low freeboard adds significantly to her fishability. In an unusual design twist, the Moppie's galley is on deck, concealed in molded lockers abaft the helm and companion seats. Twin hatches in the bridgedeck sole provide excellent service access to the engines. Belowdecks, the compact cuddy cabin includes a head with a foldaway cover, a sink and V-berth. Additional features include a vented windshield, a painted bow rail and windshield, and teak interior trimwork. A good performer with standard 260hp MerCruiser gas engines, the 28 Moppie will cruise around 24 knots and reach 31–32 knots top. Optional 230hp Volvo diesels cruise at 28 knots.

Bertram 30 Moppie

Length	30'6"	Water	30 gals.
Beam	11'3"	Cockpit	64 sq. ft.
Draft	3'1"	Hull Type	Deep-V
Weight	13,200#	Deadrise Aft	18.5°
Clearance	7'3"	Designer	Bertram
Fuel	275 gals.	Production	1994–97

A versatile boat designed to accommodate the needs of weekend cruisers as well as hard-core anglers, the Bertram 30 Moppie is a well-styled inboard express whose upscale price reflected her quality construction and superior engineering. Built on a beamy, solid fiberglass deep-V hull, the Moppie's clean lines exude sex appeal even without the integral swim platform and molded bow pulpit common to most modern express boats. Three deck plans made her adaptable to fishing, cruising, or daytime activities. The standard layout has only a helm seat on the bridgedeck; the Sport Cruiser features a large L-shaped settee opposite the helm; and the Sportfish version comes with a companion seat, bait-prep center, washdowns and rod holders. The interior is the same for all three versions with a double berth forward, a small galley, convertible dinette, and a standup head with shower. Access to the motors, below the bridgedeck, is very good, and a transom door was standard. Twin 310hp gas engines will cruise the Moppie at 22 knots and reach 30+ knots top. Optional 300hp Cummins (or Cat) diesels will cruise at 27 knots (31 top), and 340hp Cats will cruise about 29–30 knots and reach 33 knots wide open.

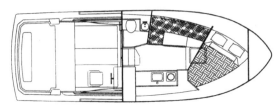

Standard Deck Layout

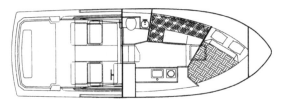

Sportfish Layout

See Page 298 for Pricing Information

See Page 298 for Pricing Information

Bertram 36 Moppie

Length . . . . 35'10"	Water. . . . . 75 gals.
Beam . . . . 13'0"	Cockpit . . . . 97 sq. ft.
Draft. 3'8"	Headroom . . . . 6'4"
Weight. . . . . 18,700#	Hull Type . . . . Deep-V
Clearance. . . . . 8'0"	Deadrise Aft. . . . . 17.5°
Fuel . . . . 400 gals.	Production 1996–2000

The Bertram 36 Moppie is an upscale express whose classic good looks and rugged construction will appeal to anglers seeking a premium open sportfisherman or a capable weekend cruiser. Heavily built on a solid fiberglass deep-V hull with a relatively wide beam, the Moppie could be configured with different cockpit layouts for fishing or cruising (see floorplans below). Bertram engineers did an excellent job in designing a wide-open and comfortable cabin layout. There's a separate stall shower in the head (a real plus), the sofa converts to upper and lower berths, the galley is fitted with stove, microwave and refrigerator, and the forward queen berth can be separated from the salon with a privacy curtain. Outside, the entire bridgedeck can be raised on hydraulic rams for engine access. Additional features include a cockpit transom door, maple interior woodwork, and a bow pulpit. Among several engine options, twin 420hp Cummins diesels will cruise the 36 Moppie at 26 knots and deliver a top speed in the neighborhood of 30 knots. Note that the Moppie was dropped from the lineup in 1998 but reintroduced with a slightly revised interior the following year.

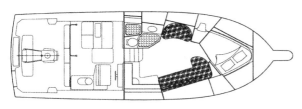

Sportfish Layout

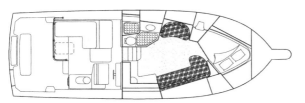

Cruising Layout

See Page 298 for Pricing Information

Bertram 43 Moppie

Length . . . . 43'4"	Cockpit . . . . 106 sq. ft.
Beam . . . . 15'0"	Clearance. . . . . 9'1"
Draft. 4'8"	Hull Type . . . . Deep-V
Weight. . . . . 38,290#	Deadrise Aft . . . . 17°
Fuel . . . . 546 gals.	Designer . . . . Bertram
Water. . . . . 160 gals.	Production 1995–96

Express fishermen over 40 feet have become popular in recent years with hard-core anglers, and the Bertram 43 Moppie was pitted against some very tough competition when she was introduced in 1995. (Too tough as it turned out; production lasted only two years.) Like all Bertrams, the 43 was heavily constructed on a deep-V hull with a relatively wide beam and a well-flared bow. Two different deck layouts were available: the cruising version has a radar arch and wraparound seating in the cockpit, and the sportfishing version has a completely unobstructed cockpit with a transom fish box, direct cockpit access to the engine room, rod storage, and a transom door and gate. Belowdecks, the Moppie's maplewood interior is arranged with a huge galley, berths for four adults, and a spacious head with separate stall shower. Additional features include a molded bow pulpit, a doublewide helm seat with lounge seating opposite, and fairly wide side decks. A good performer, the 43 Moppie will cruise at a fast 27 knots with standard 550hp 6V92 diesels and reach 30+ knots top. Those powered with 625hp DDEC 6V92s will cruise at an honest 28 knots with a full tower and load.

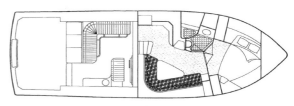

Sportfishing Version

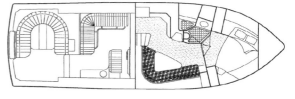

Cruising Version

See Page 299 for Pricing Information

Bertram 46 Moppie

Length . . . . 46'0"	Water. . . . . 135 gals.
Beam . . . . 14'11"	Cockpit . . . . 106 sq. ft.
Draft. 4'8"	Hull Type . . . . Deep-V
Weight. . . . . 42,000#	Deadrise Aft . . . . .17°
Clearance. . . . . .9'1"	Designer. . . . . Dave Napier
Fuel . . . . 650 gals.	Production 1993–96

Introduced in 1993, the Bertram 46 Moppie was built on a stretched version of the proven Bertram 43 Convertible hull with cored hull-sides, a wide beam, and a relatively steep 17 degrees of transom deadrise. This was one of the bigger express cruisers produced in the early 1990s, and like previous Moppies the 46 was aimed at the market for both serious anglers and upscale cruisers alike. Offered with several interior layouts, the single-stateroom floorplan (with two heads—very unusual) appealed more to the sportfish market while the two-stateroom layout is more suited for cruising activities. Either way, there's seating on the bridgedeck for a small crowd, and the sportfish version came with molded tackle centers in the cockpit. Until 1995, the Moppie had reversed engines with V-drive-like shaft couplers; thereafter, the engine installations were straight inboards. Also in 1995, the genset was moved from under the cockpit into the more protected environment of the engine room. A good-running boat and a comfortable ride in a chop, a pair of 735hp 8V92s will cruise the Bertram 46 Moppie at a fast 28–29 knots and reach top speeds in the neighborhood of 32 knots.

Californian 44 Veneti

Length w/Pulpit . . . . 47"10"	Fuel . . . . 400 gals.
Hull Length. . . . . 44'0"	Water. . . . . 190 gals.
Beam . . . . 15'2"	Hull Type . . . . Modified-V
Draft. . . . . 4'0"	Deadrise Aft . . . . .15°
Weight. . . . . 30,000#	Designer . . . . J. Marshall
Clearance. . . . . 10'0"	Production 1988–89

Increasingly dated by today's Euro-style sportboats, the Californian 44 Veneti remained a fairly popular boat on the used market for several years after she went out of production in 1989. Interestingly, she was one of the first American sportcruisers to employ an integrated swim platform—something just about every express-boat builder embraced by the early 1990s. Belowdecks, the Veneti's floorplan is arranged with two private staterooms and two full heads—still an unusual layout since most 40–45-foot express boats have a single stateroom and one head. Consequently, the salon dimensions are much smaller than one expects to find in boat this size. While visibility from the elevated helm is good, the console—with its various levels of gauges and switches—is best described as confusing. Additional features include a big engine room, a bow pulpit, a cockpit wet bar, wide side decks, radar arch, and good storage. Note that the Veneti's original hull design made for a wet ride until spray rails were added early in 1989. No racehorse in spite of her sleek profile, twin 375hp Caterpillar diesels will cruise the Californian 44 Veneti at 20–21 knots and reach a top speed of about 24 knots.

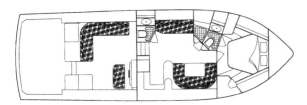

Single Stateroom with Sportfish Options

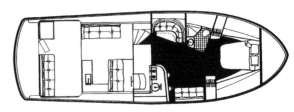

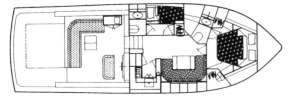

Two Staterooms with Cruising Options

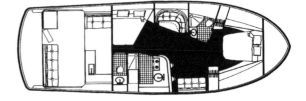

See Page 299 for Pricing Information

See Page 302 for Pricing Information

Carver 27/530/300 Montego

Length w/Platform	29'2"	Headroom	6'2"
Hull Length	27'3"	Fuel	120 gals.
Beam	10'0"	Water	41 gals.
Draft	2'10"	Hull Type	Modified-V
Weight	6,900#	Deadrise Aft	8°
Clearance	9'0"	Production	1986–93

A good-selling model for Carver, the 27 Montego underwent a couple of name changes following her introduction in 1986, becoming the Carver 530 Montego during 1991–92 and the 300 Montego in 1993, her final year of production. Carver designers packed an impressive amount living space into this 27-foot hull, but an elevated foredeck and high freeboard gave her a rather ungainly, high-profile appearance. The Montego's midcabin floorplan is furnished with a circular dinette/double berth forward, a compact galley, a standup dressing area in the entryway to the midcabin, and a double-entry head compartment. Outside, the cockpit is quite spacious for a 27-footer with bench seating at the transom and a walk-through to the swim platform. Note that the Montego's original swim platform was replaced in 1990 with a more elaborate bolt-on unit. A bow pulpit and trim tabs were standard. On the downside, the Montego's detailing and finish are less than impressive. A stiff ride in a chop, twin 205hp V-6 sterndrives (among several engine packages) will cruise the 27 Montego at 22–23 knots and deliver 30+ knots wide open.

Carver 28 Riviera

Length	28'0"	Fuel	160 gals.
Beam	11'1"	Water	52 gals.
Draft	2'10"	Hull Type	Modified-V
Weight	8,900#	Deadrise Aft	10°
Clearance	9'3"	Designer	R. MacNeill
Cockpit	NA	Production	1983–89

The Carver 28 Riviera is a compact family cruiser whose affordable price and unusual twin-cabin layout struck a responsive chord with a good many budget-minded boaters in the 1980s. Needless to say, there are only a handful of 28-footers with two staterooms (the Albin 27 comes to mind) and not everyone will be satisfied with the Riviera's cramped accommodations. Heavily built on a solid fiberglass hull with a wide beam, the best part about this boat is her open-air center cockpit with its wraparound windshield. Visibility from the helm is excellent, the side windshields provide some protection from the weather, and there's seating for six around the dinette table and jump seat. When the weather turns sour owners can snap on the camper-style canvas enclosure panels and keep on going. Below, the galley is forward and shares cabin space with the convertible dinette and the enclosed head compartment. Aft, the full-width guest stateroom can sleep three in decidedly confined quarters. A notably wet boat and a seriously hard ride in a chop, twin 220hp gas engines will cruise the Carver 28 Riviera at 18 knots with a top speed in the neighborhood of 27 knots.

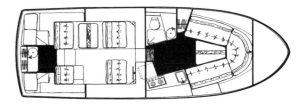

See Page 303 for Pricing Information

See Page 303 for Pricing Information

Carver 280 Mid-Cabin Express

Length Overall	29'10"	Water	25 gals.
Length w/Platform	28'0"	Fuel	100 gals.
Beam	9'6"	Waste	18 gals.
Draft	3'3"	Hull Type	Deep-V
Weight	5,900#	Deadrise Aft	19°
Clearance	8'9"	Production	1988–98

The 280 Mid-Cabin Express began life in 1988 when she was introduced as the Carver 25 Montego, an affordable midcabin cruiser with modern lines and, for just a 25-footer, very spacious accommodations. Built on a solid fiberglass deep-V hull with a wide beam and an integral swim platform, Carver redesigned this boat for 1993, dropping the Montego designation and reintroducing her as the 280 Mid-Cabin Express. The hull remained the same, but the 280 has a redesigned deckhouse, a more stylish curved windshield, and a new, much improved cabin layout with the head aft—rather than in the middle of the cabin as before—and a starboardside dinette. The level of finish is a bit disappointing. Where the original 25 Montego slept four, the 280 Express can sleep six. The cockpit didn't change much during her production years: a cutout in the transom leads to the swim platform, and a bench seat and table were standard. Available with single or twin sterndrives, a 280 Express fitted with a single 300hp Volvo Duoprop gas engine will cruise at 23 knots and reach 33–34 knots top. Twin engines were optional. Note that she was called the 528 Montego in 1991 and 1992.

Carver 29 Monterey

Length w/Pulpit	32'9"	Fuel	200 gals.
Hull Length	28'8"	Water	52 gals.
Beam	11'1"	Headroom	6'1"
Draft	2'10"	Hull Type	Modified-V
Weight	10,000#	Deadrise Aft	10°
Clearance	10'8"	Production	1985–86

Obviously dated by today's sportboat standards, the Carver 29 Monterey was an inexpensive entry-level family express with a roomy interior and a surprisingly spacious cockpit. The Monterey differs from most express boats her size in that she's powered by straight inboard engines, a setup that will appeal to many cruisers who prefer the dependability only inboards can provide. This is notable because the vast majority of modern express boats under 30 feet have sterndrive power, which—with the engines aft in the hull—permits a more spacious midcabin interior layout. Built on a solid fiberglass hull, the Monterey's wide beam together with her modest transom deadrise results in a rather harsh ride in a chop. Her bi-level cockpit is arranged with a wet bar and bench seating forward while the entire aft section of the cockpit is wide open. Below, there are berths for four in the cabin along with a compact galley, removable dinette table, and a small head with shower. Lacking side decks, a walk-through windshield provides access to the bow. Twin 270hp Crusader gas engines will cruise at 18 knots and reach a top speed of around 28 knots. Note the short 2-year production run.

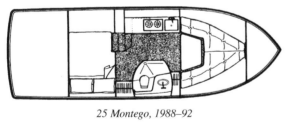

25 Montego, 1988–92

1993–98

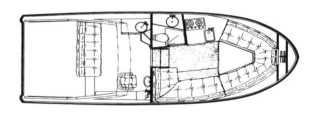

See Page 303 for Pricing Information

16

See Page 303 for Pricing Information

Carver 30 Allegra

Length Overall . . . . 34'0"	Fuel . . . . 150 gals.
Hull Length . . . . 30'8"	Water . . . . 51 gals.
Beam . . . . 11'0"	Waste . . . . 37 gals.
Draft . . . . 3'1"	Hull Type . . . . Modified-V
Weight . . . . 10,950#	Deadrise Aft . . . . 18°
Clearance . . . . 8'5"	Production 1989–90

When she was introduced in 1989, the Carver 30 Allegra was considered a rather sporty boat with colorful hull graphics and a fairly bold appearance. That, combined with a roomy interior and a low price, made the Allegra an altogether attractive package for entry-level day cruisers. She was built on a solid fiberglass hull with moderate beam and a steep 18 degrees of deadrise aft. There's a lot of cockpit space in the Allegra—more than many express boats her size—which makes this a fun boat for daytime family activities. A wet bar was standard, and a U-shaped lounge aft is big enough for a small crowd. The interior of the Allegra provides sleeping accommodations for four. The master stateroom—which has a solid door rather than a privacy curtain—has an offset double berth, and of course the dinette/lounge converts to a double berth in the usual way. On the downside, the Allegra's uneven fit and finish reflects her low price. Additional features include a cockpit transom door, a swim platform, and a foredeck sun pad. Twin 235hp Volvo sterndrives were standard in the Allegra. She'll cruise at 20 knots and reach a top speed of around 33 knots. Note the brief two-year production run.

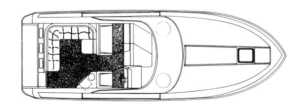

Carver 310 Mid-Cabin Express

Length Overall . . . . 33'5"	Fuel . . . . 180 gals.
Length w/Platform . . . . 31'3"	Water . . . . 56 gals.
Beam . . . . 10'10"	Waste . . . . 28 gals.
Draft . . . . 2'8"	Hull Type . . . . Modified-V
Clearance, Arch . . . . 10'11"	Deadrise Aft . . . . NA
Weight . . . . 11,400#	Production 1995–97

Carver designers applied some unusual styling features to the 310 Mid-Cabin and the result is a hull and deck mold with more dips and curves than most anything else on the market. Hull construction is solid fiberglass, and a wide beam and relatively high freeboard combine to provide a very roomy interior. Two floorplans were available in the 310. The standard layout had a spacious salon with an extra-large L-shaped lounge aft that converts to private sleeping quarters with privacy curtain. The alternate floorplan offered a midcabin stateroom at the expense of a smaller salon. Outside, the cockpit has a doublewide helm seat with a wet bar opposite. The wraparound seating aft of the helm converts to a sun lounge. Additional features include a foredeck sun pad, walk-through windshield, side exhausts, and radar arch. Available with V-drive or sterndrive power, optional 5.8-liter Volvo I/Os will cruise at 25 knots (about 42 knots top), and 5.7-liter Crusader (or MerCruiser) inboards cruise at 24 knots (about 34–35 knots top). This model, with some changes, became the Trojan 320 Express in 1998. (Note that Carver produced Trojans for a few years following their purchase of the company in 1993).

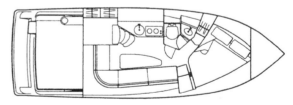

Standard Floorplan

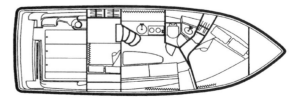

Alternate Floorplan

Carver 32 Montego

Length	32'3"	Fuel	192 gals.
Beam	12'4"	Water	92 gals.
Draft	2'9"	Waste	20 gals.
Weight	13,000#	Hull Type	Modified-V
Clearance	9'0"	Deadrise Aft	6°
Headroom	6'4"	Production	1987–91

Carver's 32 Montego sportcruiser was built using the hull originally designed for the Carver 32 Mariner—a wide, flat-bottom affair with a broad entry, shallow keel, and solid fiberglass construction. While not known as an especially efficient design, it does have the advantage of offering considerable interior volume with which to work. The Montego combines a sportboat profile with a comfortable interior layout, and the result was a practical and affordable weekend family cruiser. Her full-width floorplan is spacious for a boat of this type and features a mid-stateroom beneath the bridgedeck. The galley is forward in the salon, and a double-entry head with stall shower provides private access from the forward stateroom. The cabin is decorated with textured wall coverings, Formica counters, and inexpensive fabrics. Overall, the level of finish is very mediocre. A hard-riding boat, standard 270hp gas engines (with V-drives) will cruise the Carver 32 Montego around 15–16 knots, and the optional 350hp Crusaders will cruise in the neighborhood of 20 knots and reach 29–30 knots wide open. Note that in her final production year she was called the 534 Montego.

Carver 538 Montego/380 Express

Length	38'5"	Water	91 gals.
Beam	13'2"	Cockpit	NA
Draft	3'4"	Hull Type	Deep-V
Weight	16,000#	Deadrise Aft	19°
Clearance	15'11"	Designer	Carver
Fuel	250 gals.	Production	1990–94

A boat of many names (she was introduced as the Carver 35 Monterey in 1990, and during 1991–92 she was called the Carver 538 Montego), the 380 Express was a fairly popular bridgedeck cruiser with an early-1990s sportboat profile and a roomy midcabin interior. Because she rides on a deep-V hull (Carvers are generally built on low-deadrise bottoms), the 380 is a reasonably comfortable boat in a chop. A wide beam combined with a single-level floorplan makes the Montego a spacious boat below with lots of living space in the salon/galley area. Headroom is good throughout thanks to the elevated foredeck, but small cabin windows result in a dark, slightly claustrophobic interior, and the absence of natural lighting is immediately apparent. On deck, an L-shaped lounge is opposite the helm on the bridgedeck level and bench seating is built into the transom on the cockpit level. The Montego's most significant downside is her unattractive bolt-on swim platform—it just looks cheap. A bow pulpit, fender storage racks, and a wet bar were standard and a radar arch was a popular option. Twin 350hp gas inboards with V-drives will cruise the 380 Express at 16–17 knots and reach a top speed of 25 knots.

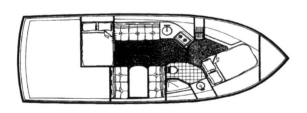

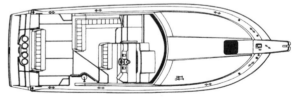

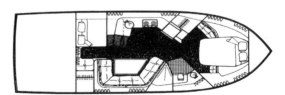

See Page 303 for Pricing Information

See Page 304 for Pricing Information

Celebrity 285/290/310 Sport Cruiser

Century 300 Grande

Length w/Pulpit	31'0"	Clearance	9'0"
Hull Length	28'5"	Fuel	137 gals.
Beam	10'4"	Water	22 gals.
Draft, Down	3'3"	Hull Type	Modified-V
Draft, Up	2'5"	Deadrise Aft	18°
Weight	8,800#	Production	1989–96

Length	29'1"	Water	23 gals.
Beam	10'6"	Waste	30 gals.
Draft	2'10"	Hull Type	Modified-V
Weight	8,360#	Deadrise Aft	14°
Clearance	NA	Designer	Century
Fuel	144 gals.	Production	1984–89

Introduced in 1989 as the 285 Sport Cruiser, Celebrity engineers completely reworked the boat in 1990 with a new deckhouse and interior as well as a new redesigned bottom when it became evident that the boat had some shortcomings that needed fixing. The revised 290 Sport Cruiser, with a much-improved profile, lasted for four years (1990–93) until she was again updated in 1994 with a new integral swim platform replacing the bolt-on platform of the 290. Called the 310 Sport Cruiser from 1994–96, she's a fairly conventional family express with a midcabin floorplan and a roomy cockpit. Hull construction is solid fiberglass, and her 10-foot, 4-inch beam is about average for a 30-footer. The 290/310 floorplan remained essentially unchanged over the years aside from decor and hardware upgrades. Both staterooms can be separated from the main cabin with privacy curtains, and headroom is about 6 feet, 4 inches. Outside, there's seating for six in the bi-level cockpit. Note that the side decks are narrow on this boat and foredeck access is not easy. Twin 350-cid MerCruiser sterndrives will cruise the Celebrity 290/310 at 22–23 knots and reach a top speed of 35+ knots.

The largest boat in the Century fleet for several years during the late 1980s, the 300 Grande was a popular model in her day thanks to her then-modern styling and comfortable interior accommodations. Hull construction is solid fiberglass, and it's worth noting that the Grande was built with foam flotation for an added measure of safety. Several midcabin floorplans were utilized during her production run, and all provided berths for six along with a full-size galley and enclosed head compartment with sink and shower. Folding curtains separate the sleeping areas from the main salon and the convertible dinette will seat four adults comfortably. Outside, the cockpit seats six and includes a folding transom seat, a double aft-facing companion seat, and a swivel bucket seat at the helm. A bow pulpit and a teak swim platform were standard, and a radar arch and trim tabs were popular options. Among several single- and twin-engine sterndrive options offered during her production years, a pair of 260hp MerCruiser I/Os will cruise at 23 knots and reach a top speed of around 32 knots. (Note that twin V-drive inboards were also available.)

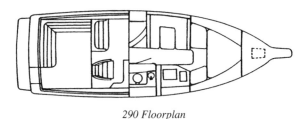

290 Floorplan

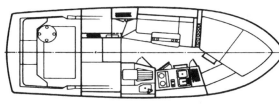

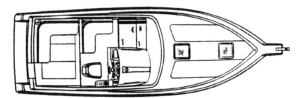

310 Floorplan

Chaparral Signature 26/27/270

Chaparral Signature 270

Length w/Pulpit	28'5"	Fuel	105 gals.
Beam	9'0"	Water	25 gals.
Draft, Up	2'1"	Waste	25 gals.
Draft, Down	2'9"	Hull Type	Modified-V
Weight	6,249#	Deadrise Aft	20°
Clearance	9'8"	Production	1992–2000

Length w/Platform	29'3"	Max Headroom	6'3"
Hull Length	26'5"	Fuel	100 gals.
Beam	9'6"	Water	30 gals.
Draft, Up	1'6"	Hull Type	Modified-V
Draft, Down	2'9"	Deadrise Aft	20°
Weight	8,200#	Production	2003–Current

Called the Signature 26 when she was introduced in 1992 and the Signature 27 from 1993 to 1999, Chaparral renamed this model the Signature 270 for the year 2000. This was the second of three Chaparral products to carry the Signature 27 model designation; the original Signature 27 (1988–1991) was trailerable with a narrower beam. Featuring good-quality materials and solid construction, the 27/270 was priced slightly above the average for sportcruisers her size. An elevated foredeck provides marginal headroom below at the expense of a somewhat top-heavy exterior appearance. The cabin layout is arranged with a circular dinette/V-berth forward, a compact galley and head, and a snug midcabin stateroom aft. Outside, an L-shaped lounge is opposite the helm, and a hideaway bench seat is fitted at the transom. With no windshield opening and narrow side decks, foredeck access is difficult. Additional features include an integral bow pulpit, anchor locker, transom door, and a removable cockpit table. Among several single and twin sterndrive engine options, a single 300hp 7.4-liter MerCruiser sterndrive will cruise at 25 knots and reach a top speed of 34–35 knots.

There are plenty of midsize family cruisers to choose from, but Chaparral's Signature 270 stands apart for her quality construction and roomy accommodations. Unlike several 27-foot cruisers with their trailerable 8-foot, 6-inch beams, the 270's generous 9-foot, 6-inch beam insures a more livable interior as well as a larger cockpit. A handsome boat on the outside, the interior of the Signature 270 sleeps six: two in the forward V-berth, two in the aft cabin, and two more when the dinette is converted. The galley is a little light on storage and counter space; the head, on the other hand, is surprisingly roomy. Privacy curtains separate the sleeping areas from the main cabin, and the upscale decor is a blend of cherry cabinetry, designer fabrics, and vinyl wall coverings. In the cockpit, the helm has a tilt wheel and dual flip-up seating. Lacking side decks, a walk-through windshield provides access to the foredeck. Additional features include a transom storage locker, cockpit entertainment center, radar arch, and a well-designed engine room with a push-button lift. Engine options include single and twin gas sterndrives to 540 hp. A pair of 225hp Volvos will top out at close to 40 knots.

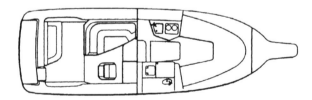

See Page 306 for Pricing Information

See Page 306 for Pricing Information

Chaparral Signature 27/278 XLC

Length	26'6"	Water	22 gals.
Beam	8'2"	Headroom	6'2"
Draft	2'8"	Hull Type	Modified-V
Weight	5,100#	Deadrise Aft	20°
Clearance	NA	Designer	Chaparral
Fuel	140 gals.	Production	1984–91

A popular model, the 278 XLC was for a time the largest boat in the Chaparral fleet. (Note that Chaparral called her the Signature 27 during her last three years of production.) Like most trailerable cruisers in this size range, the 278 XLC is a midcabin design although her narrow 8-foot, 2-inch beam results in a more compact interior than other trailerable models with a full 8-foot, 6-inch beam. The floorplan provides berths for six and includes double berths fore and aft, a convertible dinette, a small galley and a standup head compartment with shower. The 278's dark teak interior remained unchanged until 1988 when a new designer motif with lighter fabrics and Formica cabinetry was introduced. The cockpit—also updated in 1988—will seat six to eight people and came with a bench seat at the transom. A hatch in the sole provides easy engine access, and the side decks—while narrow—are at least wide enough for bow access. Additional features include some colorful hull graphics, a teak bow pulpit and swim platform, and teak handrails on the foredeck. Among several engine options, a single 330hp MerCruiser sterndrive will cruise in the low 20s and reach a top speed of 30+ knots.

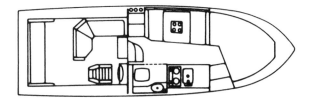

Chaparral Signature 28/29

Length w/Pulpit	31'11"	Clearance	9'4"
Hull Length	29'3"	Fuel	121 gals.
Beam	9'9"	Water	30 gals.
Draft, Up	1'11"	Hull Type	Modified-V
Draft, Down	2'9"	Deadrise Aft	20°
Weight	8,200#	Production	1991–2000

A popular boat with a 9-year production run, the Chaparral Signature 29 (called the Signature 28 in 1991–92) stood apart from most other family cruisers during the 1990s for her quality construction and good all-around performance. The 29 was considered a gracefully designed boat when she was introduced, and a generous 9-foot, 9-inch beam results in a very spacious interior. The layout is different from most midcabin designs: a V-berth area is forward, followed by an aft-facing wraparound dinette that spans the full width of the interior. A high/low table converts the dinette into a double berth, while the aft cabin is separated from the main salon with a privacy door rather than just a curtain. The cockpit is arranged in two sections: a three-person bench seat stows away in the transom, and a large U-shaped settee is forward, opposite the helm. On the downside, the side decks are quite narrow. As many as six people can be seated comfortably in the cockpit, and visibility from the helm is excellent. A bow pulpit, radar arch, and cockpit wet bar were all standard. Twin 190hp MerCruiser sterndrives will cruise the Signature 28 in the mid 20s and reach a top speed of around 35 knots.

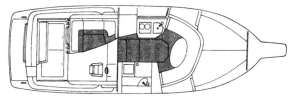

See Page 306 for Pricing Information

See Page 306 for Pricing Information

Chaparral Signature 280/290

Length w/Platform	30'8"	Fuel	115 gals.
Hull Length	28'2"	Water	25 gals.
Beam	10'0"	Waste	25 gals.
Draft, Down	2'9"	Hull Type	Modified-V
Weight	8,500#	Deadrise Aft	18°
Headroom	6'4"	Production	2001–Current

It's surprising what manufacturers can put into a 28-foot boat these days. The Chaparral Signature 280 (called the Signature 290 in 2004) is a case in point: with extra freeboard to provide standing cabin headroom, the Chaparral has a sleeping capacity of six in a floorplan that few will find cramped. With a generous 10-foot beam, Chaparral designers used the space well. The layout is similar to most boats of this type with a convertible dinette forward, U-shaped cabin dinette (also convertible), and a double berth in the aft cabin, which, incidentally, has a privacy door rather than just a curtain. Galley storage is very good due to the large storage locker in the galley floor, and the decor is a blend of cherry cabinetry, designer fabrics, and vinyl wall coverings. Note that the cabin entryway is quite narrow. The cockpit has wraparound seating aft, built-in entertainment center, and a spacious storage locker under the portside passenger seat. Additional features include a transom storage locker, walk-through windshield, extended swim platform, and a radar arch. Several sterndrive engine options are available. Among them, twin 190hp MerCruisers will deliver a top speed in the neighborhood of 35 knots.

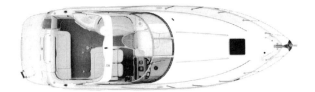

Chaparral Signature 300

Length w/Platform	31'3"	Fuel	153 gals.
Beam	10'3"	Water	30 gals.
Draft, Up	2'1"	Headroom	6'7"
Draft, Down	2'9"	Hull Type	Modified-V
Weight	9,800#	Deadrise Aft	20°
Clearance, Arch	11'0"	Production	1998–2003

The Signature 300 is good-quality family cruiser with a well-arranged cockpit and an upscale, very comfortable interior. Like many Chaparral cruisers, she's constructed on a modified-V hull with a solid fiberglass bottom, moderate beam and an integral swim platform. While the Signature's midcabin interior is similar to many other 30-footers, the quality of the hardware, woodwork and upholstery is immediately evident. The roomy aft cabin, with its convertible settee and removable dinette table, is definitely the master stateroom in this boat with far more amenities than the forward berth. The cockpit seats six and includes a double helm seat, a U-shaped settee aft (which converts into a big sun pad), and a wet bar. The aft bench seat can be folded away to free up some cockpit space, and a gas-assist hatch provides easy access to the engine compartment. Additional features include a transom shower, walk-through windshield (there are no side decks), cockpit lighting and five opening ports. Among several engine options, twin 250hp Volvo sterndrive gas engines will cruise the Signature 300 in the mid to high 20s and reach a top speed of around 40 knots.

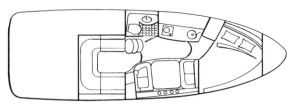

See Page 306 for Pricing Information

See Page 306 for Pricing Information

Chaparral Signature 30/31

Length w/Pulpit	33'2"	Clearance	9'4"
Hull Length	30'6"	Fuel	150 gals.
Beam	10'9"	Water	40 gals.
Draft, Up	1'11"	Hull Type	Modified-V
Draft, Down	2'9"	Deadrise Aft	17°
Weight	9,750#	Production	1990–97

Chaparral has a reputation for quality products, and the Signature 31 (called the Chaparral Signature 30 from 1990–92) was one of the more sophisticated express cruisers in her size range during the 1990s. Like all Chaparral models of her era, she was built on a modified-V hull with moderate beam and a solid fiberglass bottom. Her midcabin interior is arranged in the conventional manner with double berths fore and aft and a convertible dinette in the salon. Both sleeping areas are fitted with privacy curtains, and it's worth noting that the galley can best be described as compact. On deck, the cockpit floor is flush from the transom forward—rare in a midcabin cruiser. The L-shaped lounge opposite the helm converts (with the aid of an insert) into a sun pad, and the bench seat at the transom folds away into the transom bulkhead when not in use. The helm console was updated in 1993 (among a few other upgrades). Additional features include plenty of cockpit storage, a hidden swim ladder, reasonably wide side decks, and a radar arch. A good performer, twin 230hp MerCruiser (or 250hp Volvo) sterndrives will cruise the Signature 31 at 18 knots and reach 30+ knots wide open.

Chaparral Signature 310

Length w/Platform	33'4"	Headroom	6'5"
Beam	10'7"	Fuel	147 gals.
Draft, Up	2'1"	Water	29 gals.
Draft, Down	2'9"	Hull Type	Modified-V
Weight	11,375#	Deadrise Aft	17°
Clearance	11'2"	Production	2004–Current

An impressive blend of modern styling and first-rate accommodations, Chaparral's Signature 310 is a well-built weekend cruiser for those willing to pay a little extra for a quality product. Chaparral builds a good boat, and the 310 stands apart from other cruisers her size for her excellent tooling and above-average finish. Built on a modified-V hull with cored hullsides and a solid fiberglass bottom, the midcabin interior sleeps six in a layout typical of most boats in this class. Cherry cabinetry, designer fabrics, and upscale furnishings highlight the entire cabin, and the galley is notable for its generous storage. Note also that both of the 310's hanging lockers are cedar lined—a thoughtful touch. At the helm, the tiered, non-glare dash includes space for flush-mounting a full array of electronics. As many as eight can be seated in the cockpit where a full wet bar, transom shower, and portable cooler are standard. Additional features include a transom storage locker, extended swim platform, walk-through windshield, double helm seat with bolsters, and foredeck sun pad. A good open-water performer, twin 280hp Volvo sterndrives will cruise the Chaparral 310 in the mid 20s and reach a top speed of about 35 knots.

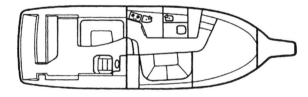

Chaparral Signature 330

Chaparral Signature 350

Length w/Platform . . . . 35'0"	Headroom . . . . 6'5"
Beam . . . . 11'3"	Fuel . . . . 170 gals.
Draft, Up . . . . 2'1"	Water . . . . 29 gals.
Draft, Down . . . . 3'2"	Hull Type . . . . Modified-V
Weight . . . . 13,400#	Deadrise Aft . . . . 19°
Clearance . . . . 11'2"	Production 2003–Current

Length w/Platform . . . . 37'0"	Fuel . . . . 240 gals.
Beam . . . . 11'10"	Water . . . . 35 gals.
Draft, Up . . . . 2'1"	Headroom . . . . 6'7"
Draft, Down . . . . 2'9"	Hull Type . . . . Modified-V
Weight . . . . 15,000#	Deadrise Aft . . . . 18°
Clearance . . . . 11'2"	Production 2001–Current

Crisp styling, tasteful cabin accommodations, and excellent performance are the hallmarks of Chaparral's Signature 330 (called the Signature 320 in 2003). This is an upscale family cruiser whose quality features and exemplary fit and finish are apparent to even inexperienced boaters. Built on a modified-V hull with cored hullsides and generous beam, the 330's main cabin is an appealing blend of cherrywood cabinetry, designer fabrics, and vinyl overheads. A wraparound lounge with a table forward converts to a big V-berth, and the 330's private midcabin is notable for its partial standing headroom, entryway door, and built-in vanity with sink, mirror, and upholstered seat. The galley, with its faux-granite surfaces and stainless steel sink, has enough storage for a long weekend. In the cockpit, the centerline boarding door aft allows for an unusually guest-friendly seating layout. Additional features include a cockpit wet bar, dual transom lockers, a tiered, non-glare dash, generator, and an extended swim platform. Twin 300hp MerCruiser sterndrives deliver a top speed in the range of 40 knots. Note the small anchor locker and limited fuel capacity.

Mid-size family cruisers have always been a popular breed in the American market, and with so many to choose from it's often difficult to tell one from another. Chaparral's Signature 350 stands out, however, thanks to her better-than-average finish and a very innovative helm arrangement. Chaparral has always built good boats and the 350 is certainly no exception. Constructed on a beamy modified-V hull, the cherrywood interior of this Signature is one of the most luxurious to be found in a boat her size. In a departure from the norm, a pocket door separates the forward berth from the salon—a privacy feature of genuine value to most cruisers. The galley is also well designed with plenty of counter space, and the aft cabin is very spacious with a dinette and privacy door. The 350's elevated helm platform, with its U-shaped settee and doublewide helm seat, is unique. Additional features include a walk-through windshield, a transom storage locker, excellent engine access, foredeck sun pad, and a cockpit wet bar. Among several sterndrive or inboard options, twin 315hp Volvo sterndrives will cruise in the low 20s and reach a top speed of over 35 knots.

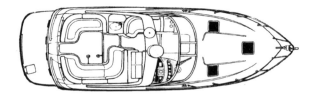

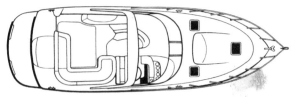

Chris Craft 258/268/27 Concept

Length . . . . 27'0"	Water. . . . . 20 gals.
Beam . . . . 9'0"	Waste . . . . 20 gals.
Draft. 3'0"	Hull Type . . . . Deep-V
Weight. . . . . 5,000#	Deadrise Aft . . . . 20°
Clearance . . . . NA	Designer . . . . Chris Craft
Fuel . . . . 80/97 gals.	Production 1992–96

The Chris Craft 258/268/27 Concept is best described as part cruiser and part performance boat. (Note that she was called the 258 Concept in 1992, the 268 during 1993–94 and the 27 Concept in 1995–96.) A good-looking, non-trailerable cruiser with attractive sportboat lines, the Concept was built on a deep-V hull with moderate beam and a relatively steep 20 degrees of deadrise at the transom. She's a good open-water performer capable of going fast through some rough water. Since the aim of the Concept is outdoor entertainment, most of her length is devoted to an expansive cockpit layout with wraparound lounge seating for a crowd (the seat bottom pulls out to form a sun pad). A hideaway ladder folds down over the companionway door and allows access through the windshield to the foredeck—very resourceful. Below, her compact cabin features a standup head and a convertible dinette. A single 310hp sterndrive will cruise the Concept at 22 knots (36 knots top). Twin 5.0-liter sterndrives will cruise at 28–29 knots (40+ knots top), and optional 5.8-liter Volvos cruise at a fast 38 knots and deliver a top speed of around 50 knots. Note that the fuel was increased to 97 gallons in 1995.

See Page 307 for Pricing Information

Chris Craft 272/282/30 Crowne

Length w/Pulpit . . . . 31'6"	Clearance. . . . . 9'6"
Hull Length. . . . . 29'5"	Fuel . . . . 100 gals.
Beam . . . . 10'0"	Water. . . . . 25 gals.
Draft, Up . . . . 1'10"	Hull Type. . . . . Modified-V
Draft, Down . . . . 3'2"	Deadrise Aft . . . . 16°
Weight. . . . . 8,400#	Production 1991–97

The introduction of the Crowne series in 1991 was an effort by Chris Craft to resurrect the company's declining family cruiser sales. A distinctive boat with high freeboard, the 30 Crowne (note that she was called the 272 Crowne in 1991–92, the 282 Crowne in 1993–94, and the 30 Crowne from 1995–97) owes her graceful appearance to a molded bow pulpit, a curved wraparound windshield, circular foredeck hatches, and an integrated swim platform. Belowdecks, the companionway stairs are a series of welded steps that create a more open look than the usual molded stairs. The midcabin accommodations will sleep four, and the elevated foredeck provides good headroom in the Crowne's main cabin. The U-shaped cockpit lounge can seat six, and the stylish helm console is a real eye-catcher. A wet bar was standard, and fender racks are built into the swim platform. Additional features include a foldaway helm seat, walk-through windshield, and radar arch. Twin 351-cid sterndrives will cruise the 30 Crowne at 17 knots (33–34 knots top), and optional 454-cid I/Os will cruise at 20 knots and top out around 40 knots. Note the rather limited fuel capacity.

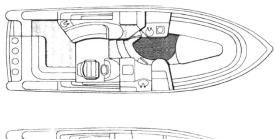

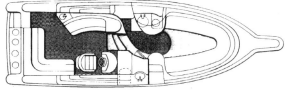

See Page 307 for Pricing Information

Chris Craft 280/284 Amerosport

Length w/Pulpit . . . . 31'3"	Fuel . . . . 150 gals.
Hull Length . . . . 27'9"	Water . . . . 25 gals.
Beam . . . . 10'2"	Hull Type . . . . Deep-V
Draft . . . . 2'9"	Deadrise Aft . . . . NA
Weight . . . . 8,214#	Designer . . . . Chris Craft
Clearance . . . . 9'0"	Production 1987–90

Introduced in 1987 when Euro-style express cruiser sales were really beginning to heat up, the Chris 284 Amerosport's bolt-on swim platform and unattractive hull graphics did little to distinguish her from the more upscale sportboat competition. Hull construction is solid fiberglass, and a fairly wide beam gave the 284 a spacious interior for a 28-footer. Her midcabin floorplan is arranged in the conventional manner with double berths fore and aft, a convertible dinette, and a good-sized galley with good storage. Like other Chris Craft Amerosport models of her era, the interior fixtures, hardware, and decor items are below average in quality. With the companionway offset to port, guest seating in the forward part of the cockpit is limited to the doublewide helm seat—a not-uncommon arrangement in express boats this size. A tubular radar arch became optional in 1989, and in 1990 (her last year of production) the SE model had a traditional swim platform rather than the bolt-on appendage of earlier models. A good-running boat, twin Volvo 271hp Duoprop I/Os will cruise the 284 Amerosport at a fast 27 knots and deliver 40 knots wide open.

Chris Craft 280/281 Catalina

Length . . . . 28'11"	Fuel, Twin . . . . 125 gals.
Beam . . . . 10'9"	Water . . . . 25 gals.
Draft . . . . 2'5"	Hull Type . . . . Modified-V
Weight . . . . 7,000#	Deadrise Aft . . . . 15°
Clearance . . . . 8'6"	Designer . . . . Chris Craft
Fuel, Single . . . . 100 gals.	Production 1977–85

The 280/281 Catalina formed the backbone of Chris Craft's presence in the small family-cruiser market for many years. She was inexpensive to buy and easily maintained, and her interior provided berths for six long before the advent of today's V-drive, midcabin designs. Hull construction was solid fiberglass, and a generous beam resulted in a fairly roomy boat for a 28-footer. The 28 Catalina was offered in two versions: the single-engine 280 model and the twin-engine 281 version. The single-level cabin accommodations are arranged with the galley and head aft, next to the companionway where they're convenient to the cockpit. Large cabin windows provide excellent natural lighting and ventilation, and there's plenty of storage under the settee and berths. Performance with a single 230hp gas inboard is 17–18 knots at cruise and 25 knots wide open. With twin inboards, speeds increase to around 21 knots at cruise and 30 knots top. Note that the 280 carries a 100-gallon fuel capacity while the 281 has 125 gallons. Additional features include wide side decks, good engine access, and a swim platform. A sistership, the 291 Catalina Bridge, is basically the same boat with a small two-person flybridge.

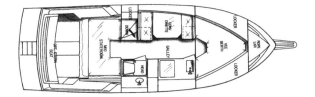

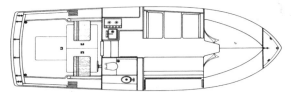

Chris Craft 300/308 Express Cruiser

Length	32'10"	Water	41 gals.
Beam	10'6"	Waste	35 gals.
Draft	2'6"	Headroom	6'1"
Weight	10,000#	Hull Type	Deep-V
Clearance	7'3"	Deadrise Aft	21°
Fuel	150 gals.	Production	1999–2003

The Chris Craft 308 Express Cruiser (called the 300 Express in 1999) is a capable, entry-level family cruiser with a contemporary profile and surprisingly spacious interior accommodations. This is a boat designed to satisfy the needs of a growing family looking to move up from their too-small trailerable weekender—a full-size mid-cabin cruiser with good accommodations and respectable performance at an affordable price. Built on an easy-riding deep-V hull with moderate beam, a well-flared bow and reverse chines, the original midcabin interior of the 300 Express—a poorly designed layout with the refrigerator under the island berth—was completely updated for the year 2000 when she became the 308 Express. This major revision also eliminated the side decks, which permits a roomier cockpit with improved seating. Additional features of the 308 include a walk-through windshield, transom door and shower, cockpit wet bar and a well-arranged galley with adequate storage. Among several sterndrive engine options, twin 5.0-liter I/Os will cruise around 20 knots (34–35 knots top), and twin 5.7-liter engines will cruise at 26 knots (37–38 knots wide open).

Chris Craft 320/322 Amerosport Express

Length w/Pulpit	34'7"	Fuel	200 gals.
Hull Length	31'11"	Water	50 gals.
Beam	11'11"	Hull Type	Deep-V
Draft	2'7"	Deadrise Aft	NA
Weight	12,000#	Designer	S. Leonard
Clearance	10'9"	Production	1987–90

The Chris Craft 320 Amerosport Express (called the 322 Amerosport in 1989 and the 320 Express Cruiser in 1990) is a fairly generic express cruiser with a traditional sportboat profile and spacious interior accommodations. Hull construction is solid fiberglass, and her 12-foot beam is wide for a 32-footer. Surprisingly, the 320/322 Amerosport lacks the midcabin floorplan seen in most other express cruisers her size. The galley and head are aft (where they're easily accessed from the cockpit), and a curtain provides privacy in the stateroom. Outside, the single-level cockpit is arranged with elevated helm and companion seats with bench seating at the transom. A centerline hatch in the cockpit sole provides good access to the motors, and molded cockpit steps port and starboard make boarding easy. Note the unattractive bolt-on reverse swim platform. A radar arch and bow pulpit were standard. Standard 270hp Crusader inboard gas engines (without the V-drives required in midcabin designs) will cruise the 320/322 Express at 19 knots (29–30 knots top). Optional 350hp Crusaders will cruise at 22 knots and reach 33–34 knots wide open.

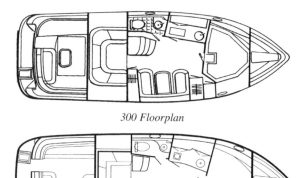

300 Floorplan

308 Layout

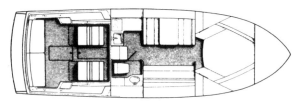

See Page 307 for Pricing Information

27

See Page 307 for Pricing Information

EXPRESS CRUISERS

Chris Craft 320/328 Express Cruiser

Length	32'0"	Water	41 gals.
Beam	11'10"	Waste	35 gals.
Draft	3'2"	Headroom	6'2"
Weight	12,000#	Hull Type	Deep-V
Clearance	9'7"	Deadrise Aft	21°
Fuel	210 gals.	Production	1997–Current

Largest boat in the Chris Craft fleet at the turn of the millennium, the 328 Express Cruiser (called the 32 Crowne in 1997 and the 320 Express in 1998–99) is a contemporary midcabin family cruiser whose moderate price will appeal to budget-minded buyers. Chris Craft enthusiasts haven't had much to cheer about in recent years when it comes to well-styled boats, but the 328 combines several nice design touches wrapped up in a conservative but still-contemporary package. She's constructed on a solid fiberglass deep-V hull with a wide beam, and her centerline helm position (as opposed to the traditional starboardside console) is somewhat unique. Belowdecks, the midcabin floorplan is quite spacious for a boat this size. The layout is fairly conventional with double berths fore and aft, a small galley and a head with shower. The Crowne's anchor arrangement is pretty slick—a concealed windlass lowers the self-stowing anchor through an opening beneath the bow. Additional features include a walk-through windshield, an electric engine compartment hatch, and transom door. Among several engine options, twin 5.7-liter Volvo I/Os will cruise at 23 knots and reach a top speed of 36–37 knots.

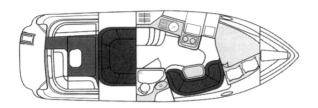

Chris Craft 332 Express

Length	33'0"	Water	50 gals.
Beam	12'1"	Cockpit	NA
Draft	2'9"	Hull Type	Deep-V
Weight	11,560#	Deadrise Aft	18°
Clearance	7'11"	Designer	Chris Craft
Fuel	250 gals.	Production	1981–86

A popular boat for Chris Craft in the early 1980s, the 332 Express (called the 332 Amerosport in 1986) is unusual in that she was built on a true deep-V hull—a rare platform for a dedicated family cruiser. Deep-V hulls tend to roll a lot in a beam sea (especially at slow speeds), and they aren't noted for their fuel efficiency, but they do have superb rough-water handling qualities—a characteristic that quickly sets the 332 apart from most of the competition. Note that this is a pure express boat with a flush cockpit and straight inboard power. She underwent several updates over the years including the addition of a radar arch in 1983, and in 1986 the floorplan was slightly rearranged and a bolt-on swim platform was added at the transom. While her interior isn't unusually roomy for a 33-footer, the 332 has one of the larger cockpits to be found in a boat this size—large enough for a couple of anglers to do some serious fishing. (Indeed, the oversize cockpit more than compensates for the somewhat compact cabin accommodations.) With big-block 454-cid inboard gas engines, she'll cruise comfortably around 21–22 knots and reach a top speed in the neighborhood of 30 knots.

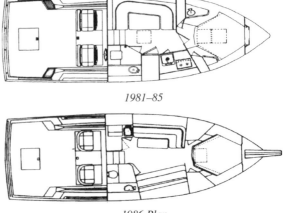

1981–85

1986 Plan

Chris Craft 336 Mid-Cabin Express

Length	33'0"	Fuel	250 gals.
Beam	12'1"	Water	50 gals.
Draft	2'9"	Hull Type	Deep-V
Weight	12,360#	Deadrise Aft	18°
Clearance	7'11"	Designer	Chris Craft
Cockpit	NA	Production	1983–87

The growing popularity of midcabin family cruisers in the early 1980s prompted Chris Craft to rework the interior of their 332 Express in order to create the look-alike 336 Mid-Cabin Express. Indeed, it's difficult to tell the difference between the two boats until you step aboard and confront the raised bridgedeck in the cockpit of the 336. The interior dimensions are about average for a 33-footer, and there were no significant changes to the midcabin layout over the years other than cosmetic updates. Both staterooms are fitted with privacy doors rather than curtains—something you never see anymore in modern midcabin cruisers—and a vanity is fitted in the forward stateroom. A bench seat in the aft cockpit will seat four and it's notable that the 336 did not have a transom door. Three removable hatches in the cockpit sole provide excellent engine access (although the bench seat must first be removed). The side decks are wide enough for secure foredeck access. A good open-water performer thanks to her deep-V hull, 340hp gas engines will cruise the Chris 336 at 21 knots and reach a top speed of around 30 knots. Note that she was called the 336 Amerosport in 1987.

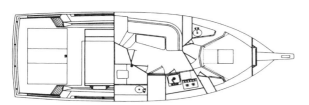

Chris Craft 33/34 Crowne

Length w/Pulpit	34'10"	Weight, 33	9,500#
Hull Length	32'8"	Fuel	180 gals.
Beam	11'0"	Water	35 gals.
Draft, 34	2'11"	Hull Type	Deep-V
Draft, 33	3'2"	Deadrise Aft	18°
Weight, 34	10,000#	Production	1991–97

Try to follow this: Introduced as the sterndrive 302 Crowne (1991–92), Chris Craft offered an inboard option in 1993—the sterndrive model then became the 322 while the inboard version was called the 340. In 1995, the designations were again changed with the sterndrive becoming the 33 Crowne and the inboard model now called the 34 Crowne. All were built on solid fiberglass hulls with moderate beam and a fully integrated swim platform and bow pulpit. A centerline companionway leads down into the Crowne's spacious interior where the midcabin floorplan will sleep six adults. A curved settee—elevated from the salon sole—dominates the main cabin, and the fore and aft sleeping areas both have privacy curtains. In 1996, Chris Craft designers rearranged the cockpit, eliminating the U-shaped lounge aft of the helm in favor of a bench seat at the transom. Additional features include a cockpit wet bar, a wide swim platform with fender racks, oval ports, and (in the 340/34 model) side-dumping exhausts. The 302/322/33 Crowne, with twin 235hp OMC (or 230hp Volvos) sterndrives, will cruise in the low 20s, and the 340/34 Crowne with 300hp Volvo inboards will cruise at about 25 knots.

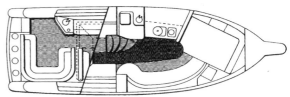

Original Floorplan

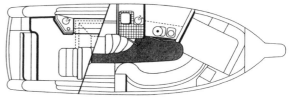

Updated Layout

See Page 308 for Pricing Information

See Page 308 for Pricing Information

Chris Craft 36 Roamer

Length	36'3"	Fuel	286 gals.
Beam	12'6"	Water	54 gals.
Draft	3'1"	Waste	30 gals.
Weight	17,220#	Hull Type	Modified-V
Clearance	12'10"	Deadrise Aft	17°
Headroom	6'6"	Production	2003–Current

The 36 Roamer is proof that innovative styling and quality construction are once again synonymous with the Chris Craft name. With her flawless gelcoat and graceful lines, the Roamer is an unusually distinctive boat in a world of look-alike fiberglass cruisers. She rides on a conventional modified-V hull with a well-flared bow, moderate transom deadrise, and a generous 12-foot, 6-inch beam. Belowdecks, the Roamer's elegant interior is a blend of cherrywood cabinetry, Ultraleather upholstery, and maple flooring. A sofa bed in the salon, an island bed in the bow, and another bed aft will sleep six, and the head includes a separate shower stall. The galley, which occupies the entire port side of the salon, is notable for its excellent storage and Corian counters. Topside, the helm is on the centerline with a double bench seat that is open to the cockpit on both sides. A sun lounge is to port, and the L-shaped cockpit seating can accommodate several guests. Engine access is excellent: the entire aft cockpit rises at the flip of a switch. A cockpit wet bar and walk-through transom are standard. Optional 370hp Yanmar diesels will cruise the 36 Roamer in the mid 20s and reach close to 30 knots wide open.

Deck Plan

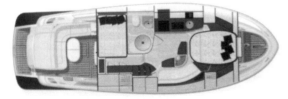

Interior Plan

See Page 308 for Pricing Information

Chris Craft 360 Express

Length	38'7"	Water	50 gals.
Beam	13'0"	Cockpit	NA
Draft	3'0"	Hull Type	Deep-V
Weight	15,000#	Deadrise Aft	18°
Clearance	NA	Designer	D. Fletcher
Fuel	300 gals.	Production	1988–92

The Chris Craft 360 Express (called the 370 Amerosport in 1988–89) differs from most family express boats due to her somewhat unusual interior layout. Two midcabin floorplans were used in this boat—the first lasted just a year before being replaced in 1989 by a new layout where the midcabin lounge extends right into the salon—something unique in midcabin designs that, according to Chris Craft marketing blurbs, opened up the salon and gave one the impression of being aboard a much larger boat. In reality, the layout was a poor one in that the dinette lounge was too far aft in the salon and the seating arrangement was impractical and generally uncomfortable. So much for the interior, which, by the way, is a tour de force of cheap fabrics and furnishings typical of so many Chris Craft products in the late 1980s and 1990s. The bi-level cockpit, on the other hand, is very spacious with plenty of guest seating, a transom door, a double helm seat and a built-in wet bar. A radar arch and bow pulpit were standard. A good-running boat in a chop, standard 454-cid gas engines will cruise the Chris 360 Express around 18 knots with a top speed of 26–27 knots.

1988 Only

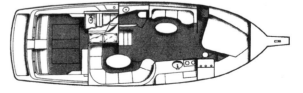

1989–92

See Page 308 for Pricing Information

Chris Craft 380 Continental

Length Overall	39'7"	Fuel	300 gals.
Hull Length	35'5"	Water	77 gals.
Beam	12'6"	Waste	20 gals.
Draft	3'1"	Hull Type	Modified-V
Weight	15,000#	Deadrise Aft	15°
Clearance	10'3"	Production	1993–97

Innovation is great and there's never enough of it, but innovation is not what the 380 Continental was about. This was glitz over practicality—the triumph of Chris Craft's 1990s concept of art over nautical common sense. The styling from the arch forward is contemporary enough, but the semicircular stern makes an otherwise well-proportioned boat seem a little chopped off. Not surprisingly, the circular transom also reduced the 380's usable cockpit space. Belowdecks, there are no bulkheads in the wide-open interior, so floor-to-ceiling track curtains were used to divide up the cabin into separate sleeping quarters. Note that the helm is on the centerline and the helm seat is elevated for improved visibility. A walk-through windshield provides access to the foredeck, and molded steps at the corners and a centerline transom door access the circular swim platform. Anchor handling is interesting: lacking a pulpit, the anchor is retrieved through a bow port. The Continental's extra-wide swim platform has storage lockers and a hot/cold shower. A heavy boat, standard 460-cid gas engines with V-drives will cruise around 16 knots and reach 28 knots wide open.

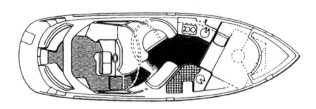

See Page 308 for Pricing Information

Chris Craft 412 Amerosport Express

Length	38'9"	Water	100 gals.
Beam	14'0"	Cockpit	80 sq. ft.
Draft	3'2"	Hull Type	Modified-V
Weight	15,000#	Deadrise Aft	NA
Clearance	9'5"	Designer	R. Avery
Fuel	380 gals.	Production	1987–90

When the Chris Craft 412 Amerosport was introduced back in 1987 she was one of the bigger full-production express cruisers available on the market. Like most Chris Craft models of her era, she was built on a solid fiberglass hull with moderate beam and a shallow keel. Obviously dated by today's Euro-glitz sportboat standards, her bolt-on swim platform and overdone hull graphics seriously detracted from her otherwise conservative appearance. Inside, the downscale furnishings and inexpensive decor of the 412 compared poorly with other boats of her type. Privacy curtains were used to separate the fore and aft sleeping areas from the salon, and a roomy head compartment stands in contrast to a rather compact galley. Outside, the driver's helm position is a bit low, and forward visibility—especially on hard acceleration—is not the best. The cockpit is arranged with facing U-shaped settees with a removable table and seating for eight to ten passengers. Standard 454-cid gas engines will cruise the Chris Craft 412 Amerosport at a steady 17–18 knots and deliver a top speed of about 27 knots. Note that she was called the 400 Express Cruiser in 1990.

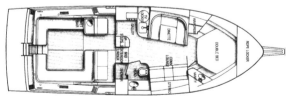

See Page 308 for Pricing Information

Chris Craft 43 Roamer

Length w/Platform	43'6"	Fuel	400 gals.
Beam	14'0"	Water	95 gals.
Draft	3'2"	Waste	35 gals.
Weight	27,000#	Hull Type	Deep-V
Clearance	13'8"	Deadrise Aft	20°
Headroom	6'3"	Production	2003–Current

For those who appreciate simple elegance and above-average build quality, the Chris Craft 43 Roamer embraces those characteristics with an added dose of old-world luxury and sturdy construction. This is a unique yacht; there's no other express quite like the 43 Roamer on the market. Not inexpensive, she rides on a deep-V hull with a relatively wide 14-foot beam. Belowdecks, the Roamer can accommodate two couples overnight in two staterooms, each with a private head. The main cabin has a curved settee across from a huge U-shaped galley, and twin beds in the too-small aft stateroom convert to a double. Throughout, the Roamer's upscale interior is a sophisticated blend of cherry cabinetry, top-quality furnishings, and decorator fabrics. Like most modern express boats, the spacious cockpit is designed for comfortable cruising. Lounge seating is provided for as many as ten adults, and the extended swim platform can accommodate a small dinghy. On the downside, the engine room—accessed from a small cockpit hatch—is a tight fit. Twin 440hp Yanmar diesels will cruise the 43 Roamer at 18 knots and reach a top speed in the neighborhood of 25 knots.

Cobalt 360

Length	36'0"	Fuel	174 gals.
Beam	10'6"	Water	35 gals.
Draft, Up	2'3"	Waste	28 gals.
Draft, Down	3'6"	Hull Type	Deep-V
Weight	13,710#	Deadrise Aft	22°
Clearance	9'6"	Production	2002–Current

Cobalt's flagship model, the 360 offers an impressive blend of sportiness, luxury, and quality. This is a very stylish sportcruiser—so stylish, in fact, that she"d be at home in just about any high-profile Mediterranean marina. Built on a Kevlar-reinforced deep-V hull, the Cobalt's expansive helm/cockpit area is as comfortable as it is innovative. Facing settees in the aft cockpit will seat five, and single sun pads (with storage under) flank the center transom walk-through. Wood and leather accents dress up the Cobalt's tiered dash where there's space to flush-mount a full array of electronic add-ons. Because of her spacious cockpit, the 360 is a day boat first and her belowdecks accommodations are modest. Headroom is limited to just 6 feet, and the small midcabin berth is probably better suited for storage than sleeping. The plush Ultraleather dinette converts to a V-berth, and while the head compartment is quite roomy, the 360's compact galley is not designed for serious meal-prep activities. Cherry interior cabinetry and a cockpit wet bar are standard. A fast ride with 415hp MerCruiser sterndrives, the Cobalt 360 will reach a top speed of close to 50 knots.

Deck Plan

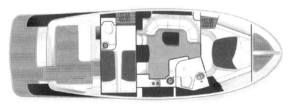

Interior Plan

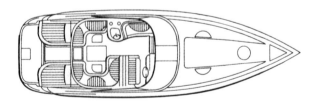

See Page 309 for Pricing Information

See Page 309 for Pricing Information

Cranchi 33 Endurance

Length Overall	34'10"	Fuel	166 gals.
Hull Length	34'1"	Water	40 gals.
Beam	10'2"	Waste	NA
Draft, Down	3'1"	Hull Type	Deep-V
Weight	12,915#	Deadrise Aft	19°
Clearance	10'10"	Production	2003–Current

In a sea of expensive 30-something sportcruisers, the Cranchi 33 Endurance stands apart for her sleek Italian styling and innovative deck layout. Indeed, it's hard to ignore the Cranchi's unique center helm position and offset radar mast, and how many 33-footers have a tender garage built into the transom? The garage has pros and cons, of course—it consumes a lot of deck space (which limits cockpit seating), and while it's a great convenience to have a tender available, it can't exceed 4 feet, 6 inches in length and still fit in the garage. The center helm, however, is refreshingly different, and the sculpted dash is a real eye-catcher. Below, the cherrywood interior provides a traditional contrast to the Cranchi's avant-garde cockpit. The compact midcabin layout is arranged with a convertible U-shaped dinette/V-berth forward, portside galley, and a standup head with shower. Note that instead of the usual express-cruiser radar arch, the Endurance has a sleek mast. A cockpit wet bar, teak cockpit sole, and aft sun pad are standard. On the downside, engine access is difficult and storage space is at a premium. Twin 285hp Volvo sterndrives will cruise the Endurance at 30 knots and deliver a top speed of about 40 knots.

Cranchi 34 Zaffiro

Length Overall	37'7"	Fuel	151 gals.
Hull Length	34'0"	Water	50 gals.
Beam	11'4"	Waste	40 gals.
Draft	3'0"	Hull Type	Deep-V
Weight	14,944#	Deadrise Aft	18°
Clearance	9'1"	Production	1997–Current

A downsized version of the Cranchi Smeraldo 36, the Zaffiro 34 is a high-quality Italian sportboat with elegant cabin accommodations, a good-running deep-V hull, and a first-class deck layout. The subdued decor of the Zaffiro's midcabin interior is a refreshing change from the high-glitz decors of so many sportboats. Unlike most of her competitors, both staterooms are fitted with privacy doors (instead of curtains), and the European appliances and rounded corners give the Zaffiro that distinctive Continental character. (On the downside, the companionway steps are way too steep.) Outside, there's plenty of guest seating with a settee opposite the helm and a big U-shaped cockpit settee with a removable cocktail table. The two-tiered helm provides space for flush-mounting the necessary electronics, and a molded wet bar is abaft the helm seat. Because the side decks are quite narrow, a walk-through windshield provides access to the bow. Additional features include a folding radar arch, adequate dry storage, and good engine access. An impressive performer with relatively small 230hp Volvo diesel sterndrives, the Zaffiro will cruise at 25 knots and reach a top speed of nearly 30 knots.

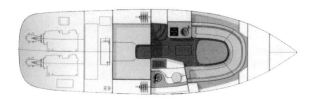

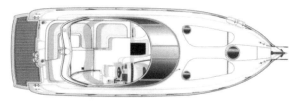

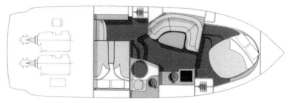

See Page 309 for Pricing Information

See Page 309 for Pricing Information

Cranchi 36/37 Smeraldo

Length Overall	38'8"	Fuel	141 gals.
Hull Length	35'10"	Water	59 gals.
Beam	12'6"	Waste	48 gals.
Draft	2'10"	Hull Type	Deep-V
Weight	16,247#	Deadrise Aft	25°
Clearance	9'2"	Production	1993–Current

The Smeraldo 37 (called the Smeraldo 36 until 1998 when the swim platform was extended) has been a popular model in the Cranchi fleet for many years. She's built on a solid fiberglass hull with moderate beam, and with a steep 25 degrees of transom deadrise her deep-V hull makes for a particularly well-behaved ride in a chop. Her midcabin floorplan is arranged in the conventional manner with private staterooms fore and aft, a convertible portside dinette, a compact galley (a bit small by U.S. standards), and an enclosed head with shower. Aside from the meticulous finish, what sets these accommodations apart from the norm are the stylish European appliances and the rounded bulkhead doors. On deck, a comfortable L-shaped settee is opposite the helm on the bridgedeck, and a U-shaped settee in the cockpit converts into a large sun pad. Hatches in the cockpit sole provide good access to the starboard engine, but getting to the portside motor means moving some furniture. Additional features include a foredeck sun pad, an elegant burlwood dashboard, and excellent storage. Among several engine options, twin 260hp Volvo diesel sterndrives will cruise in the mid 20s and reach about 30 knots wide open.

Cranchi 39 Endurance

Length Overall	40'8"	Fuel	206 gals.
Hull Length	39'3"	Water	64 gals.
Beam	11'5"	Waste	47 gals.
Draft	3'0"	Hull Type	Deep-V
Weight	16,675#	Deadrise Aft	23°
Clearance	10'2"	Production	1997–2003

The Endurance 39 has the distinction of having been one of only a few sportcruisers built on a stepped hull. Cranchi's willingness to break away from the norm results in a boat that's fun to drive with higher speeds than many of her counterparts. Aside from her unique hull design, the most notable feature of the Endurance is her huge cockpit with the large sun pad aft concealing a storage compartment for a tender. With so much of the Cranchi's length given over to the cockpit, it's not surprising that the interior is smaller than other express cruisers in her class. It's also unusually arranged: a dinette is forward rather than the traditional stateroom, and the only sleeping quarters are aft in the private midcabin. All of this adds up to a superb day boat—a design that will appeal to those placing more emphasis on fun in the sun than on extended cruising. Highlights include an exceptional helm layout, anchor/windlass locker with fender storage, excellent handling, and a foredeck sun pad. On the downside, engine room access is difficult and the galley is quite small. A well-built boat offered at a surprisingly affordable price, twin 285hp Volvo diesel sterndrives deliver a top speed of over 35 knots.

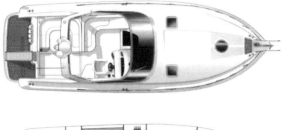

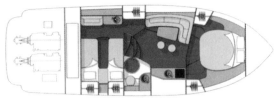

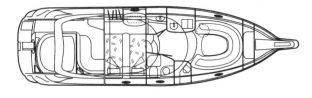

See Page 309 for Pricing Information

See Page 309 for Pricing Information

Cranchi 40/41 Mediterranee

Length Overall	42'5"	Water	106 gals.
Beam	12'6"	Waste	33 gals.
Draft	2'8"	Headroom	6'2"
Weight	18,150#	Hull Type	Deep-V
Clearance	10'0"	Deadrise Aft	19°
Fuel	233 gals.	Production	1993–2002

Marketed as a 40-footer until 1998 when Cranchi added an extended swim platform, the Italian-built 41 Mediterranee proved a popular model for Cranchi following her introduction in 1993. By today's sportboat standards, the Mediterranee's styling is conservative and her narrow 12-foot, 6-inch beam takes a toll on the interior dimensions. Note that there's no midcabin under the cockpit of the 41 Mediterranee; this is a straight-inboard boat and the central location of the engines dictates that the cabin accommodations not extend aft of the companionway. Built on a deep-V hull with prop pockets, the two-stateroom layout is an Italian blend of quality furnishings, high-end hardware, and pastel wall coverings. With her narrow beam and well-forward center of gravity, this is an exceptional rough-water boat. Outside, the helm and companion seat are elevated from the cockpit level for improved visibility. A hatch in the teak cockpit sole provides access to a surprisingly spacious engine compartment—a rarity in any European boat. Additional features include a cockpit wet bar, foredeck sun lounge, and an anchor chute. The Mediterranee will cruise in the mid 20s (about 30 knots top) with a pair of 370hp Volvo diesels.

Cranchi 41 Endurance

Length Overall	42'6"	Fuel	172 gals.
Hull Length	39'1"	Water	50 gals.
Beam	11'5"	Headroom	6'3"
Draft	2'20"	Hull Type	Deep-V
Weight	15,542#	Deadrise Aft	19°
Clearance	12'5"	Production	2004–Current

Among other attributes, the Cranchi 41 Endurance is one of the smallest sportcruisers available with a transom garage for housing a tender or PWC. She's also one of the most affordable boats in her class as well as being one of the fastest. Built on a Kevlar-reinforced stepped hull, the slender beam of the Endurance enhances performance while limiting the space available for cabin accommodations. Additionally, the transom garage pushes the cockpit forward which further reduces interior volume. The result is a terrific day boat with a spacious cockpit and a huge aft sun pad, but whose compact interior lacks the amenities required for extended cruising. Highlighted with leather seating and teak cabinetry, the single-stateroom layout includes a convertible dinette forward and a small galley and head. Topside, the cockpit is arranged with U-shaped seating, wet bar, and an electric grill. Visibility from the superb helm position is excellent, but the Cranchi's side decks are narrow and the engine room is a tight fit. A bow thruster, extended swim platform, foredeck sun pad, and teak-and-holly cabin sole are standard. A fast ride, Volvo 310hp diesel sterndrives will deliver a top speed in excess of 35 knots.

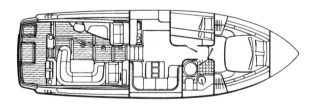

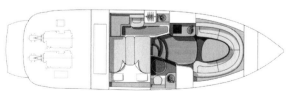

See Page 309 for Pricing Information

See Page 309 for Pricing Information

Cranchi 50 Mediterranee

Length Overall	50'3"	Fuel	352 gals.
Hull Length	49'4"	Water	110 gals.
Beam	14'2"	Waste	45 gals.
Draft	3'5"	Hull Type	Deep-V
Weight	39,859#	Deadrise Aft	19°
Clearance	13'1"	Production	2001–Current

The largest Cranchi ever built, the 50 Mediterranee further enhances the Cranchi reputation for engineering excellence and quality construction. This is a beautifully styled yacht, finely finished and designed with many practical features. Like all Cranchi models, the Mediterranee rides on a solid fiberglass hull with moderate beam and prop pockets to reduce draft requirements. The floorplan includes three staterooms—similar-size competitors generally have only two—with the master suite forward and two guest cabins aft, one with a double and the other with single berths. There are two heads in this layout, both rather small, and a curved leather settee wraps around an adjustable table in the salon. The high-gloss cherry woodwork is meticulously finished. Aft in the cockpit, the sun pad opens to reveal a garage for a tender; when opened, an electric windlass can launch and retrieve the tender on a small ramp. Additional features include a retractable gangway, cockpit galley with grill, an easily accessed engine room, superb helm position, and bow thruster. Twin 480hp Volvo diesels will cruise in the mid 20s (just over 30 knots top), and optional 715hp Volvo diesels will cruise at 30 knots and hit a top speed in excess of 35 knots.

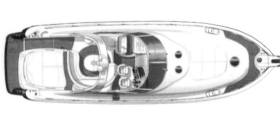

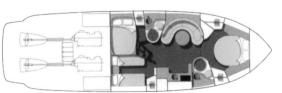

Crownline 270 CR

Length w/Platform	28'8"	Fuel	85 gals.
Hull Length	26'8"	Water	25 gals.
Beam	8'6"	Waste	25 gals.
Draft	34"	Hull Type	Modified-V
Weight	7,400#	Deadrise Aft	18°
Headroom	6'1"	Production	2003–Current

One of the largest trailerable sportcruisers available, the 270 CR offers the proven mix of performance and value typical of late-model Crownline boats. Big trailerable boats are notoriously overstyled in an attempt to conceal their ungainly lines, but not so the 270 CR. Indeed, sleek styling is one of her more notable aspects (although no one is likely to confuse her for a pure-bred European sportboat). Built on a stable modified-V hull, the mid-cabin interior of the Crownline 270 CR includes a convertible V-berth/dinette forward, a compact galley, stand-up head with sink and shower, and a sizable aft cabin. Corian counters and cherry woodwork highlight the decor, and four opening ports provide adequate ventilation. In the cockpit, a wet bar is standard and the stern lounge seat—which lifts electrically for engine access—folds down to form a comfortable sun pad. Additional features include a double helm seat with flip-up bolsters, cockpit wet bar with removable cooler, snap-in cockpit carpet, and extended swim platform. A single 320hp Volvo sterndrive will cruise in the low 20s and reach a top speed of just over 30 knots.

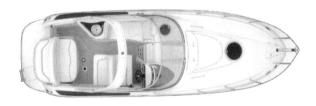

Crownline 290 CR

Length w/Pulpit & Platform	31'2"	Fuel	146 gals.
Hull Length	28'11"	Water	20 gals.
Beam	10'4"	Max Headroom	6'2"
Draft, Down	2'11"	Hull Type	Modified-V
Weight	9,000#	Deadrise Aft	16°
Clearance	8'6"	Production	1999–2004

The affordably priced Crownline 290 CR may not win any beauty awards with her high-freeboard profile, but she has a lot to offer when it comes to cabin and cockpit accommodations. Built on a beamy modified-V hull of solid fiberglass construction, the midcabin floorplan of the 290 CR was originally arranged with a canted forward berth coupled with an L-shaped dinette/lounge across from the galley and a spacious head compartment. The layout was updated in 2001 with a large U-shaped dinette/double berth forward. Privacy curtains separate the sleeping areas from the main cabin, and four opening ports and three deck hatches allow for plenty of cabin ventilation. The cockpit can accommodate as many as six. The seat bottom of the doublewide helm seat flips up to create a leaning post, and a molded cockpit galley/wet bar faces the U-shaped lounge. Additional features include built-in fender storage at the transom, a walk-through windshield, removable rear bench seat, and recessed anchor storage at the bow. From a wide choice of sterndrive engine options, a pair of 5.7-liter MerCruisers will cruise the 290 CR at 23 knots and reach a top speed of 35+ knots.

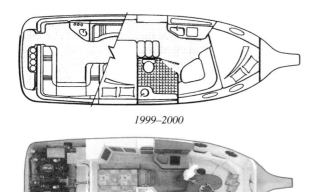

1999–2000

2001–Current

See Page 309 for Pricing Information

Crownline 330 CR

Length w/Pulpit	33'7"	Fuel	225 gals.
Beam	11'7"	Water	51 gals.
Draft, Up	1'5"	Waste	30 gals.
Draft, Down	2'11"	Hull Type	Modified-V
Weight	13,800#	Deadrise Aft	16°
Clearance	9'2"	Production	1996–2000

The Crownline 330 CR is a modern midcabin express from a company best known for its series of bowriders and sportboats. Built on a conventional modified-V hull with moderate beam and transom deadrise, she was yet another entry in the highly competitive family cruiser market dominated by Bayliner, Cruisers and Sea Ray. The interior of the Crownline 330 seems surprisingly open and spacious—a visual reaction to the absence of a forward stateroom bulkhead and the cabin's extraordinary headroom. Curtains separate both sleeping areas from the salon, and the large U-shaped settee and long galley combine with some excellent fit and finish to make this a very comfortable and notably upscale interior. On deck, there's seating for seven in the cockpit along with a built-in wet bar and removable dinette. Additional features include an electrically operated engine hatch, a vented windshield with a centerline walk-through for bow access, and a separate bolt-on stern platform wide enough to handle a PWC. Standard 260hp MerCruiser sterndrives will cruise at 17–18 knots and reach top speeds in excess of 30 knots. Optional 310hp Mercs will cruise at 24–25 knots (about 40 knots top).

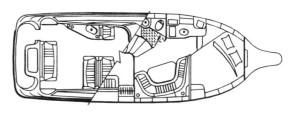

See Page 309 for Pricing Information

Cruisers 2870 Express; 280 Express

Length w/Platform . . . . 31'0"	Fuel . . . . 100 gals.
Hull Length . . . . 28'6"	Water . . . . 25 gals.
Beam . . . . 10'0"	Waste . . . . 20 gals.
Draft, Down . . . . 2'11"	Hull Type . . . . Modified-V
Weight . . . . 10,000#	Deadrise Aft . . . . 16°
Clearance, Arch . . . . 9'8"	Production 1998–Current

The 280 Express (called the 2870 Express in 1998–2003) is a modern midcabin design whose practical layout and good performance have made her a popular model for Cruisers. A fairly heavy boat at 10,000 pounds, she's built on a stable modified-V hull with a wide beam and moderate transom deadrise. Like most midcabin boats her size, the floorplan of the 280 is very open and airy with curtains (rather than bulkheads) separating the fore and aft sleeping areas from the main salon. The dinette converts into a double berth suitable for kids, and while the galley is small, it's nonetheless suitable for basic food-prep activities. The topside layout incorporates a doublewide helm seat, fore- and aft-facing cockpit settees, and a walk-through windshield with molded-in steps for easy foredeck access. Space at the helm for electronic add-ons is limited. Additional features include a removable cockpit table, sport arch, transom door and swim platform. Among several gas and diesel engine choices, a single 375hp MerCruiser will cruise the 2870 Express at 22–23 knots, and twin 225hp Volvo I/Os will cruise in the mid 20s and reach a top speed of 35+ knots.

Cruisers 2870/2970 Rogue

Length w/Pulpit . . . . 28'8"	Fuel . . . . 120 gals.
Hull Length . . . . 26'0"	Water . . . . 30 gals.
Beam . . . . 9'6"	Hull Type . . . . Modified-V
Draft . . . . 3'2"	Deadrise Aft . . . . NA
Weight . . . . 7,800#	Designer . . . . Cruisers
Clearance . . . . 8'8"	Production 1990–95

Introduced in 1990 as the 2870 Holiday, called the 2870 Rogue in 1991–94, and ending production in 1995 at the 2970 Rogue, this generic midcabin cruiser was a relatively popular model for Cruisers thanks to her comfortable layout and an affordable price. Like most boats of her type, the Rogue rides on a conventional modified-V hull with moderate beam and solid fiberglass construction. The floorplan is arranged with a convertible dinette/double berth forward, a configuration that leaves room for a larger galley than a boat this size might otherwise contain. Privacy curtains separate the sleeping areas from the main cabin, and sliding cabin windows and two overhead hatches provide ventilation. Topside, the cockpit can seat eight and includes a wet bar and a fold-down jump seat hidden in the back of the dual helm seat. There's a sun pad for the foredeck, but getting there is difficult since there are practically no side decks to speak of. A radar arch was a popular option, and a transom door and bow pulpit were standard. Among several engine options, twin 245hp Volvo sterndrives will provide a cruising speed of 24 knots and a top speed of 36 knots.

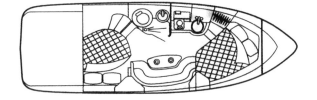

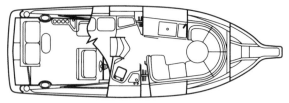

See Page 309 for Pricing Information

See Page 310 for Pricing Information

Cruisers 286/2860/3000 Rogue

Length w/Pulpit . . . . 32'11"	Headroom . . . . 6'1"
Hull Length. . . . . 27'4"	Fuel . . . . 120 gals.
Beam . . . . 10'0"	Water. . . . . 31 gals.
Draft, Down . . . . 3'0"	Hull Type . . . . Deep-V
Weight. . . . . 7,900#	Deadrise Aft . . . . NA
Clearance . . . . NA	Production 1987–89

Introduced in 1987 as the 286 Rogue, Cruisers changed the model designation of this boat twice during the next two years: in 1988 she was called the 2860 Rogue, and in 1989 (the last year of production) she was called the 3000 Rouge. She was a fairly stylish boat in her day with dramatic hull graphics, an integrated swim platform, and an elongated bow pulpit. Built on a solid fiberglass deep-V hull with moderate beam, the Rogue's midcabin floorplan differed from most of her 1980s counterparts in that the forward stateroom can be closed off from the main cabin for privacy. A convertible dinette is opposite the compact galley, and teak veneers are used for bulkheads and cabinets. In the cockpit, a doublewide companion seat and facing settees aft seat as many as six passengers. An unusually wide transom door on the centerline provides easy access to the swim platform. On the downside, the side decks are narrow and cabin headroom is just over 6 feet. Note that the 286 and 2860 models came standard with a radar arch. Among several engine options available during her production years, twin 260hp I/Os will cruise at 23 knots (about 33–34 knots top).

Cruisers 296 Avanti Vee

Length Overall . . . . 28'8"	Fuel . . . . 200/250 gals.
Length WL . . . . 24'11"	Water. . . . . 45 gals.
Beam . . . . 10'8"	Hull Type . . . . Modified-V
Draft. . . . . 2'9"	Deadrise Aft . . . . 17°
Weight. . . . . 9,000#	Designer. . . . . Jim Wynne
Clearance. . . . . 7'5"	Production 1984–87

Introduced in 1984, the 296 Avanti Vee is a beamy family cruiser whose 1980s styling is obviously dated by today's express-boat standards. Like several Cruisers models of her era, she was built on a modified-V, prop-pocket hull with moderate beam and solid fiberglass construction. Her interior is somewhat unusual in that the dinette is placed aft in the salon, beneath the raised helm—almost a midcabin layout but not quite. An offset double berth is fitted into the forward stateroom (with a draw curtain for privacy), and with the dinette converted the Avanti Vee provides berths for four adults. A distinguishing feature of the 296 is her positive foam flotation—a genuine rarity in a boat this size. Visibility from the elevated helm position is excellent, and the cockpit is large enough for several pieces of deck furniture. There's a walk-through in the transom, and the radar arch was standard. Additional features include better-than-average storage, a well-arranged galley, and easy access to the engines. Twin 260hp gas engines provide a cruising speed of 19–20 knots and a top speed of around 30 knots. Note that the Cruisers 291 Sea Devil (1984–85) is the same boat in sportfishing trim.

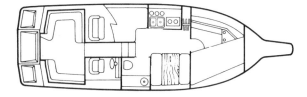

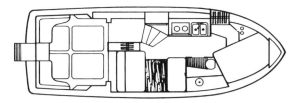

Cruisers 297 Elegante; 2970 Esprit

Length Overall	28'8"	Fuel	200/250 gals.
Length WL	24'11"	Water	45 gals.
Beam	10'8"	Hull Type	Deep-V
Draft	2'9"	Deadrise Aft	17°
Weight	9,000#	Designer	Jim Wynne
Clearance	7'5"	Production	1986–91

The Cruisers 2970 Esprit (called the 297 Elegante in 1986–87) offered her late 1990s buyers an attractive blend of interior comfort and responsive handling in a sturdy, modestly priced package. While she has the very same exterior profile as the Cruisers 296 Avanti Vee (1984–87), the Esprit's midcabin floorplan made her a much more popular boat than the Avanti Vee (which did not employ a midcabin interior). Built on a solid fiberglass hull with moderate beam and prop pockets, the hull is filled with foam flotation—a safety feature seldom found in boats this size. Below, the contemporary decor features teak paneling and good-quality hardware and appliances. Like a lot of small cruisers, both the fore and aft berths have draw curtains rather than solid doors for nighttime privacy. Note that headroom in the mid stateroom is more generous than in other boats of this type. Topside, visibility from the elevated helm is excellent, and the side decks—while narrow—are wide enough to reach the bow in safety. A radar arch, bow pulpit and swim platform were standard. Twin 260/270hp gas engines will cruise the 2970 Esprit around 20 knots with a top speed of 29–30 knots.

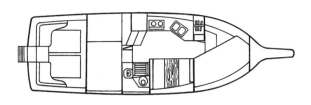

Cruisers 300 Express

Length w/Platform	31'0"	Fuel	150 gals.
Beam	10'6"	Water	30 gals.
Draft, Up	21"	Waste	25 gals.
Draft, Down	36"	Hull Type	Modified-V
Weight	10,600#	Deadrise Aft	18°
Clearance, Arch	9'3"	Production	2005–Current

Modern styling, wide-open cabin accommodations, and a good turn of speed combine to make the Cruisers 300 Express competitive with the better boats in her class. A forward-facing arch is her most distinctive feature, but there's more to this boat than just a pretty face. Aside from her solid construction, the 300 Express boasts two generous sleeping areas below along with a large galley and a head/shower with full standing headroom. Privacy curtains separate the fore and aft berths from the main salon, and a blend of cherry cabinetry and attractive fabrics give the interior of the Cruisers 300 an upscale and very classy appearance. The cockpit is arranged with a crescent-shaped settee opposite the helm, a wet bar with removable cooler, and a comfortable transom seat. Molded steps provide easy access to the walk-through windshield, and fender storage bags snap into the concealed windlass compartment. Note that the radar arch houses cockpit lights and stereo speakers. Standard features include trim tabs, power steering, cockpit carpeting, remote-controlled spotlight, air conditioning, and a deep swim platform. A good performer with Volvo 320hp gas sterndrives, she'll cruise at 30 knots and reach a top speed of close to 40 knots.

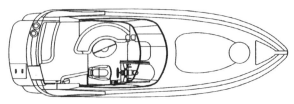

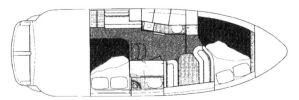

See Page 310 for Pricing Information

40

See Page 310 for Pricing Information

Cruisers 3070 Rogue

Length w/Pulpit . . . . 30'8"	Clearance. . . . . 8'9"
Hull Length. . . . . 28'8"	Fuel. . . . . 170 gals.
Beam.. . . . . 10'6"	Water. . . . . 35 gals.
Draft, Down . . . . 3'0"	Hull Type. . . . . Deep-V
Draft, Up . . . . 2'1"	Deadrise Aft . . . . 20°
Weight. . . . . 9,800#	Production 1990–94

In her day, the Cruisers 3070 Rogue was considered one of the better-styled 30-foot cruisers available on the market. While she's clearly a bit dated by today's express-boat standards, she still holds her own pretty well compared with many of her more recent counterparts. Built on a solid fiberglass, deep-V hull, the interior of the 3070 Rogue is arranged like most midcabin designs with double berths fore and aft, a convertible dinette, a full galley, and a standup head compartment with sink and shower. Privacy curtains separate the berths from the main cabin, and the refrigerator is located above the galley counter—a genuine convenience. Note that the head is quite compact without much elbowroom. Cabin ventilation is excellent thanks to six opening ports and three deck hatches, all with screens. Topside, the 3070's cockpit includes a wet bar, a double helm seat, stern seats, and a walk-through transom door to the swim platform. The side decks are wide enough for secure foredeck access, and a radar arch was a popular option. Standard 230hp I/Os will cruise at 20 knots (32–33 knots top), and optional 300hp motors will cruise at 24 knots and deliver a top speed of 40+ knots.

Cruisers 3075 Express

Length w/Pulpit & Platform . . 33'4"	Fuel. . . . . 150 gals.
Length w/o Pulpit . . . . 32'1"	Water. . . . . 30 gals.
Beam . . . . 10'4"	Headroom . . . . 6'3"
Draft, Down . . . . 2'9"	Hull Type . . . . Modified-V
Weight. . . . . 9,500#	Deadrise Aft . . . . 16°
Clearance. . . . . 9'7"	Production 1997–2003

A good-looking boat with sweeping lines to mask her relatively high freeboard, the 3075 Express combines the modern styling and upscale amenities common to all late-model Cruisers yachts. Like most family cruisers, she comes with a conventional midcabin floorplan with double berths fore and aft, a small galley, and a convertible dinette. The head compartment, conveniently located to port just down from the companionway steps, is quite spacious—always a pleasant surprise in a boat this size. The primary layout for the 3075 Express features a fixed double berth aft, but owners may select an alternate layout that includes an aft settee that converts to a sleeper. Topsides, there's a doublewide seat at the helm, and molded steps next to the helm provide access via the walk-through windshield to the foredeck. A U-shaped settee at the stern converts into a big sun pad. Additional features include a cleverly designed integrated anchor platform, good engine access, and a well-arranged helm with comfortable seating. Among several sterndrive or V-drive engine options, twin 260hp MerCruisers will cruise the 3075 Express at 20 knots and reach a top speed in the low to mid 30s.

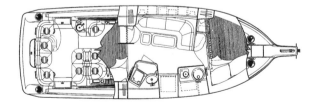

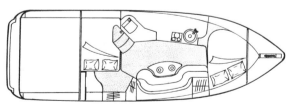

Cruisers 3020/3120 Aria

Length w/Pulpit . . . . 30'8"	Clearance. . . . . 9'4"
Hull Length. . . . . 28'8"	Fuel. . . . . 200 gals.
Beam.. . . . . 10'6"	Water. . . . . 32 gals.
Draft, Down . . . . 3'0"	Hull Type. . . . . Deep-V
Draft, Up . . . . 2'1"	Deadrise Aft . . . . 20°
Weight. . . . . 8,800#	Production 1992–97

Sharing the same fully cored hull as the 3070 Rogue (1990–94), the 3120 Aria—called the 3020 Aria from 1992–94—stands out from other 30-foot express cruisers for her enormous cockpit. Indeed, about two-thirds of her overall hull length is devoted to cockpit space, resulting in a superb day boat with room for a party-size gathering. The entire stern section of the cockpit is lined with seating that folds away and disappears in the inwales. With all of the seat sections deployed, the cockpit becomes a giant sun lounge. A wet bar/galley is located in the cockpit where it's easily accessed by guests and crew. Note that a huge storage bin is located beneath the cockpit floor. Belowdecks, the Aria's compact interior features a convertible dinette/V-berth forward, storage compartments, mini-galley with sink and stove, and an enclosed head with vanity and sit-down shower. A midcabin berth was optional beneath the helm; otherwise that space is used for storage. An anchor roller, dockside water inlet, shore power and trim tabs were standard. Among several engine options, twin 350-cid sterndrives will cruise at 21 knots (35 top), and optional 454-cid engines will cruise at 25 knots (about 40 knots wide open).

Cruisers 3175 Rogue

Length w/Pulpit & Platform . . 32'8"	Clearance w/Arch. . . . . 9'10"
Length w/Platform . . . . 30'8"	Fuel . . . . 163 gals.
Beam . . . . 10'6"	Water. . . . . 32 gals.
Draft, Up . . . . 2'1"	Hull Type . . . . Deep-V
Draft, Down . . . . 3'0"	Deadrise Aft . . . . 20°
Weight. . . . . 9,300#	Production 1995–98

Introduced in 1995, the Cruisers 3175 is a generic midcabin cruiser with twin-sterndrive power and the Euro styling features typical of many late-1990s family express boats. (Note the unique shape of the bow pulpit makes it seem like an extension of the foredeck.) Built on a deep-V hull with balsa coring in the hullsides, the interior of the 3175 is remarkably open for a 31-footer with plenty of natural lighting thanks to three overhead hatches. The floorplan is arranged with a convertible dinette/V-berth forward, a compact galley to port, a roomy head compartment with a separate stall shower, and another double berth aft. A privacy curtain separates the midcabin area from the salon, and cabin headroom is a full 6 feet, 3 inches in the galley. Topsides, visibility from the elevated helm position is excellent. Additional features include a walk-through windshield, foredeck sun pad, cockpit wet bar, dockside water inlet, trim tabs, and wraparound lounge seating in the cockpit. A radar arch was a popular option. Among several engine choices, twin 245hp/5.7-liter Volvo sterndrives will cruise the Cruisers 3175 Rogue at 23 knots and reach a top speed of 38–39 knots.

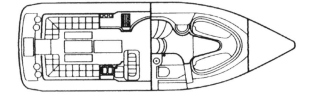

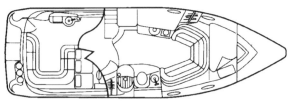

Cruisers 3260/3270 Esprit

Length . . . . 30'10"	Water . . . . 45 gals.
Beam . . . . 10'10"	Hull Type . . . . Modified-V
Draft . . . . 2'10"	Deadrise Aft . . . . 18°
Weight . . . . 10,500#	Designer . . . . Jim Wynne
Clearance . . . . 7'0"	Production, 3160/3260 . . . 1988–90
Fuel . . . . 200/250 gals.	Production, 3170/3270 . . . 1988–94

A pair of look-alikes, the Cruisers 3260 and 3270 Esprit models (note that they were originally called the 3160 and 3170 respectively) appear the same on the outside with the difference being the midcabin layout in the 3270 compared to the dinette arrangement in the 3260. Notably, the popularity of the midcabin floorplan kept the 3270 in production through the 1994 model year whereas the 3260 was dropped from the Cruiser's lineup after just a couple of years. Both were built on a modified-V hull with integrated swim platforms and solid fiberglass construction. Belowdecks, there are berths for six in the midcabin 3270, while the 3260 model sleeps four. With nearly 11 feet of beam, these are fairly roomy boats below with good headroom and ventilation. The cockpits are the same in both, and the U-shaped seating behind the helm on the raised bridgedeck is quite unusual. With the standard 350-cid Crusader gas engines, the Cruisers 3260/3270 Esprit models will cruise at 19–20 knots and reach a top speed of 30 knots. Note that the 3270 uses V-drives, while straight drives are used in the 3260. Also, with 250 gallons of fuel capacity, the 3260 has an additional 50 gallons over her sistership.

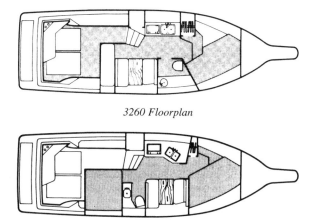

3260 Floorplan

3270 Floorplan

Cruisers 3275 Express; 320 Express

Length w/Platform . . . . 35'9"	Fuel . . . . 200 gals.
Beam . . . . 11'3"	Water . . . . 40 gals.
Draft, Up . . . . 2'0"	Waste . . . . 30 gals.
Draft, Down . . . . 2'11"	Hull Type . . . . Modified-V
Weight . . . . 12,400#	Deadrise Aft . . . . 16°
Clearance, Arch . . . . 11'5"	Production 2002–Current

Given the great number of mid-range express boats to choose from in today's market, it's often difficult to distinguish one from another. So it is with the Cruisers 320 Express (called the 3275 Express in 2002–03); she doesn't set any new standards in comfort or performance and the styling is conservative at best, but there is a good deal of value here for those seeking a well-bred family boat at a reasonable price. Built on a conventional modified-V hull with an integral swim platform, the floorplan of the 320 is arranged with a convertible settee in the aft lounge area, which is very open to the salon—a notable contrast to many midcabin boats this size with cramped, cave-like aft cabins. Curtains separate the fore and aft sleeping areas from the salon, and cabin headroom—about 6 feet, 4 inches—is excellent. Topside, a windshield walk-through provides access to the bow. The anchor is deployed through a chute, and a double sun pad with a molded headrest is fitted on the foredeck. For engine access, the aft cockpit deck swings up on a pair of rams to expose the motors. Among several sterndrive engine options, twin 320hp MerCruiser I/Os will cruise the 320 Express at 20 knots and top out in the mid 30s.

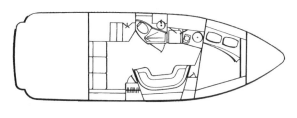

Cruisers 336 Ultra Vee

Length	32'10"	Water	70 gals.
Beam	11'10"	Headroom	6'3"
Draft	2'9"	Hull Type	Modified-V
Weight	11,500#	Deadrise Aft	18°
Clearance	8'6"	Designer	Jim Wynne
Fuel	250/300 gals.	Production	1983–88

With her high-freeboard profile and abundant hull graphics, the 336 Ultra Vee (called the 3360 Esprit in 1988) is definitely showing her age. That said, the appeal of the 336 for today's used-boat buyers lies in her unique interior, comfortable ride, and sturdy construction. Inside, the Ultra Vee's midcabin is actually the master stateroom with partial standing headroom, a privacy door, and direct access to the head—a completely innovative floorplan made possible by the greatly elevated helm seat. A total of eight opening hull ports and three deck hatches provide excellent cabin ventilation, and headroom in the galley area is well over 6 feet. Updates in 1985 included an additional 50 gallons of fuel capacity and the introduction of a more upscale interior decor with less emphasis on teak woodwork. In the cockpit, bench seating is built into the transom and twin removable hatches in the floor access the engine compartment. Visibility from the raised helm seat is about as good as it gets in a boat of this type. Built on a modified-V hull with prop pockets, twin 350hp inboards will cruise at an easy 20 knots and reach a top speed of 28–30 knots.

Cruisers 337/3370 Esprit

Length	32'10"	Water	70 gals.
Beam	11'10"	Headroom	6'3"
Draft	2'9"	Hull Type	Modified-V
Weight	11,500#	Deadrise Aft	18°
Clearance	8'6"	Designer	Jim Wynne
Fuel	300 gals.	Production	1986–94

With her high-freeboard profile and abundant hull graphics, the Cruisers 3370 Esprit (called the 337 Esprit from 1986–87) is definitely showing her age. That said, the Esprit's appeal for today's used-boat buyers lies in her spacious, wide-open interior, comfortable ride, and her sturdy construction. Like many Cruisers models built in the last decade, the 3370 rides on a modified-V hull with prop pockets to reduce the draft and shaft angles. Her midcabin floorplan is more open than most and the aft sleeper-sofa is actually a part of the salon. A bi-fold door separates the forward stateroom from the salon (a curtain is used for the aft berth), and the full galley has enough counter and storage space for serious food-prep efforts. The interior of the 3370 is well appointed with quality fabrics and furnishings although it's obviously dated by today's decor standards. Topside, the raised bridgedeck includes a U-shaped settee aft of the helm seat—a very sociable seating arrangement. A bow pulpit, radar arch and swim platform were standard. A good running boat in a chop, the cruising speed of the 3370 Esprit with twin 454-cid Crusader gas engines is about 21 knots and the top speed is around 30 knots.

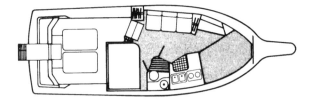

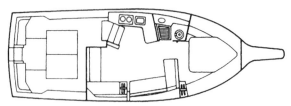

See Page 310 for Pricing Information

See Page 310 for Pricing Information

Cruisers 3375 Esprit

Length w/Platform .... 35'6"	Fuel .... 240 gals.
Beam .... 11'8"	Water .... 50 gals.
Draft .... 3'0"	Waste .... 30 gals.
Weight .... 12,500#	Hull Type .... Modified-V
Clearance .... 9'3"	Deadrise Aft .... 16°
Max Headroom .... 6'4"	Production 1996–2000

Introduced in 1996, the Cruisers 3375 Esprit offered buyers a roomy 33-foot family express with a comfortable layout and a choice of sterndrive or inboard power. The Esprit is not radically different from other boats in her class—the styling is typical of a 1990s-era cruiser, and her traditional midcabin floorplan might best be described as generic. Built on a modified-V hull with balsa coring in the hullsides and bottom, a wide 11-foot, 8-inch beam allows for a spacious interior with a wide-open salon and berths for six. Privacy curtains separate the fore and aft sleeping areas from the main cabin, and while the galley is compact in size, the spacious head features a separate stall shower. Topside, the Esprit's bi-level cockpit seats six and includes a double helm seat, wet bar, and wraparound aft seating which converts into a large sun pad. Additional features include an extended swim platform, radar arch, cockpit shower, trim tabs and a transom door. Twin 260hp MerCruiser I/Os will cruise the 3375 Esprit at 25 knots (about 35 knots top), while a pair of 320hp V-drive gas inboards will cruise in the low 20s and reach just over 30 knots wide open.

Cruisers 3470 Express; 340 Express

Length w/Pulpit & Platform .. 36'6"	Fuel .... 232 gals.
Beam .... 11'8"	Water .... 40 gals.
Draft .... 2'3"	Headroom .... 6'5"
Weight, Gas .... 13,300#	Hull Type .... Modified-V
Weight, Diesel .... 14,300#	Deadrise Aft .... 16°
Clearance, Arch .... 10'0"	Production 2001–Current

Cruisers has been a strong contender in the family express market for years and the company can always be counted on to deliver a good-quality product at a competitive price. There's nothing revolutionary about the 340 Express (called the 3470 Express in 2001–03)—she's a straightforward midcabin cruiser with contemporary styling, modern construction and upscale accommodations. Indeed, the plush interior is unusually spacious for a 34-footer and the layout is both open and inviting. Two floorplans are offered, one with a fixed berth amidships and a dinette with facing seats, and an optional arrangement with a convertible settee in the midcabin and a U-shaped dinette. Privacy curtains separate both sleeping areas from the main cabin, and the head includes a separate stall shower. Additional features include a fully cored hull, cockpit wet bar, transom door, gas-assist engine compartment hatch, foredeck sun pad and a cockpit table. Offered with inboard or sterndrive power, twin 370hp MerCruiser V-drive inboards will cruise the 340 Express in the mid 20s (30+ knots top), and 375hp MerCruiser Bravo III sterndrives will top out in the high 30s.

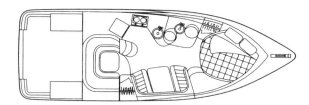

Standard Layout

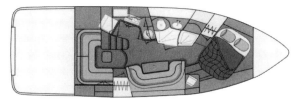

Alternate Layout

See Page 310 for Pricing Information

See Page 310 for Pricing Information

Cruisers 3570/3575 Esprit

Length w/Pulpit & Platform . . 39'3"	Water . . . . 70 gals.
Beam . . . . 13'0"	Headroom . . . . 6'5"
Draft . . . . 3'5"	Hull Type . . . . Modified-V
Weight . . . . 16,000#	Deadrise Aft . . . . 17°
Clearance, Arch . . . . 10'10"	Production, 3570 1995–99
Fuel . . . . 300 gals.	Production, 3575 1996–99

Innovation is an abused term in the marine industry where minor improvements are often touted as major breakthroughs. In the case of the 3570 and 3575 Esprits (same boat, different interiors), Cruisers took a design approach that gave buyers a choice of two dramatically different floorplans in the same express-boat package. The interior of the 3570 Esprit features a very unique amidships master stateroom with a queen-size berth and over 6 feet of headroom that can be closed off from the salon for privacy. A circular dinette/double berth is forward in this floorplan, and while the salon of the 3570 seems a bit compact for a 35-foot boat, the aft-stateroom configuration is innovative indeed. Interesting as this floorplan was, Cruisers introduced an alternate arrangement in 1996—the 3575 model—with a more traditional midcabin floorplan similar to most other express cruisers. Topside, the cockpit seating of the 3570/3575 is equally distinctive with elevated bridgedeck seating forward and L-shaped seating at the transom. Built on a fully cored hull with prop pockets, twin V-drive 320hp MerCruisers will cruise the 3570/3575 Esprit at 18 knots and reach a top speed in the neighborhood of 30 knots.

Cruisers 3672 Express; 370 Express

Length w/Platform . . . . 40'2"	Water . . . . 70 gals.
Beam . . . . 13'0"	Waste . . . . 55 gals.
Draft . . . . 3'5"	Headroom . . . . 6'5"
Weight . . . . 18,000#	Hull Type . . . . Modified-V
Clearance . . . . 12'0"	Deadrise Aft . . . . 16°
Fuel . . . . 300 gals.	Production 2000–Current

With her tall freeboard and sleek appearance, the Cruisers 370 Express (called the 3672 in 2000–02 and the 3772 in 2003) conveys the impression of being a bigger boat than her 36-foot hull length suggests. Built on a cored modified-V hull with prop pockets and an integrated swim platform, she offers a choice of cabin layouts—a rarity in production express boats these days. A very spacious single-stateroom floorplan has an aft sleeper-sofa in the salon, and an optional midcabin floorplan has a small stateroom aft with a full bulkhead and privacy door. What makes these layouts so comfortable is the single-level salon sole; in most other midcabin designs, the settee/aft berth area is a step down from the salon floor. Both interiors are tastefully finished with cherry woodwork and cabinetry, and both are unusually spacious thanks to the 370's wide beam. Additional features include a walk-through windshield (the side decks are very narrow), a stall shower in the head, excellent engine access, and a cockpit wet bar. Twin 370hp V-drive Crusader inboards will cruise at 16 knots (around 28 knots top), and newer models with the 385 8.1L Crusaders will run a couple of knots faster.

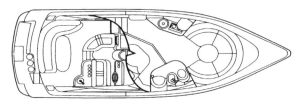

3570 Interior

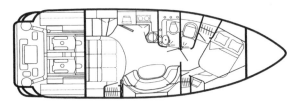

Single-Stateroom Layout

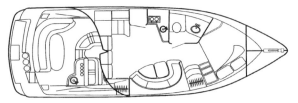

3575 Interior

Twin-Stateroom Floorplan

See Page 310 for Pricing Information See Page 310 for Pricing Information

Cruisers 3670/3675/3775 Esprit

Cruisers 3870 Express

Length w/Pulpit & Platform	39'5"	Water	110 gals.
Length w/Platform	37'3"	Fuel	300 gals.
Beam	13'0"	Hull Type	Modified-V
Draft	2'10"	Deadrise Aft	17°
Weight	17,500#	Production, 3670	1989–93
Clearance	9'7"	Production, 3675/3775	1991–95

The Cruisers 3670 and 3675 are pretty much the same boat on the outside but with different midcabin floorplans and cockpit arrangements. The 3670 came first, followed a couple of years later by the 3675 (renamed the 3775 in 1995). Of the two, the 3670/3775 proved the more popular and production lasted a few years longer than the original 3670. All were built on the same modified-V hull with prop pockets and a relatively steep 17 degrees of deadrise at the transom. Belowdecks, the 3670 has a U-shaped dinette to port and a walkaround double berth forward. The 3675/3775, on the other hand, had two floorplans: the first (diagram not available) was a very open arrangement with no dinette and an offset berth in the forward stateroom, while the later layout (below) brought back a small dinette as well as a centerline double berth. Where the cockpit in the 3670 has a bench seat at the transom, the 3675/3775 has wraparound lounge seating. Both came with a stainless steel arch, a cockpit wet bar, transom door, and a wide swim platform with a hidden boarding ladder and fender racks. Among several V-drive engine options, twin 454-cid gas engines will cruise the Esprit at 19 knots and reach a top speed of 29–30 knots.

Length Overall	43'3"	Fuel	300 gals.
Hull Length	40'8"	Water	75 gals.
Beam	13'6"	Headroom	6'4"
Draft	3'0"	Hull Type	Modified-V
Weight	19,500#	Deadrise Aft	16°
Clearance, Arch	11'2"	Production	1998–2003

The sleek lines of the Cruisers 3870 Express (called the 3870 Esprit in 1998–99 masks one of the more innovative interiors seen in a boat of this type. A scaled-down version of the company's 4270 Esprit (1998–2003), what's notable about the floorplan of the 3870 is her unique amidships stateroom with its standup dressing area, built-in TV, and a private head with shower. The wide-open salon includes a convertible sofa/dinette and a full-service galley with all the amenities. A draw curtain separates the forward island berth from the main cabin, while a bulkhead door insures privacy in the aft stateroom. Notably, the main head contains a separate stall shower. Topside accommodations include an L-shaped lounge opposite the helm, a U-shaped seating area aft, and a built-in wet bar to port. A hatch in the cockpit sole provides access to a rather compact engine compartment, and the deep swim platform is designed to support a personal watercraft. Early models with twin 310hp MerCruiser 7.4-liter gas engines (with V-drives) will cruise at 18 knots (mid-to-high 20s top), and more recent models with the 370hp MerCruiser 8.1-liter motors will top out at around 30 knots.

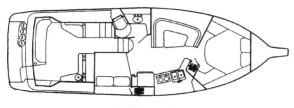

3670 Floorplan

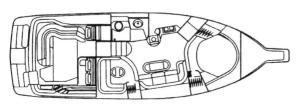

3675/3775 Floorplan (1993–95)

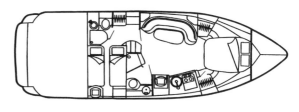

See Page 310 for Pricing Information

See Page 310 for Pricing Information

Cruisers 400 Express

Cruisers 4270 Express

Length w/Platform	43'0"	Fuel	300 gals.
Beam	13'6"	Water	70 gals.
Draft	36"	Waste	50 gals.
Weight, Gas	19,500#	Hull Type	Modified-V
Weight, Diesel	21,000#	Deadrise Aft	16°
Headroom	6'6"	Production	2003–Current

The Cruisers 400 Express (introduced as the 3970 Express in 2003) embodies the conservative styling and spacious accommodations typical of most American sportcruisers together with a choice of floorplans and a roomy cockpit with seating for a small crowd. Built on a modified-V hull with a solid fiberglass bottom, the luxury interior of the 400 Express gets high marks for headroom, storage and finish. In the area aft of the salon, Cruisers offers two different layouts. The standard plan has an aft settee open to the salon, while the optional layout encloses this area behind a bulkhead and door. High-gloss cherry woodwork and decorator furnishings highlight the interior, and both floorplans incorporate fore and aft heads with stall showers. Note the absence of any drawers in the galley, only cabinets. A wet bar with refrigerator, walk-through windshield, double helm seat and U-shaped aft lounge are standard in the bi-level cockpit. Crusader 425hp V-drive gas engines will cruise the 400 Express at 20 knots (29–30 knots top), and Yanmar 370hp V-drive diesels will cruise in the mid 20s with a top speed of just under 30 knots.

Length w/Platform	46'6"	Fuel	400 gals.
Hull Length	41'6"	Water	100 gals.
Beam	14'0"	Waste	50 gals.
Draft	3'6"	Hull Type	Modified-V
Weight	22,000#	Deadrise Aft	16°
Clearance	10'10"	Production	1997–2003

The Cruisers 4270 is a big, full-bodied express with a luxurious two-stateroom interior and cockpit seating for a small crowd. Heavily built on a fully cored hull with a wide beam and prop pockets, the sleek profile of the 4270 is accented by her long foredeck, reverse radar arch, and an extended swim platform. The expansive interior contains a unique midcabin suite with twin single berths (convertible into a queen-size bed) and a private standup head compartment—a notable departure from the cramped midcabin layouts found in most express cruisers. The U-shaped galley in this yacht is huge with wood flooring and plenty of counter and storage space. Topside, the cockpit includes removable wraparound seating, wet bar with refrigerator and icemaker, and a walk-through windshield for easy foredeck access. Additional features include a large helm console with space for flush-mounted electronics, a gas-assist engine room hatch in the cockpit, and a concealed, remote-controlled anchor windlass. A well-finished boat, early models with optional 350hp Cat V-drive diesels will cruise at 24 knots (about 28 knots top), and later models with 420hp V-drive Cats cruise at 28 knots and reach a top speed in the neighborhood of 33–34 knots.

Standard Layout

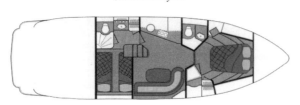

Optional Layout

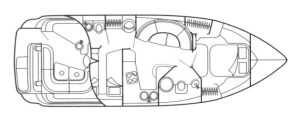

Cruisers 440 Express

Length w/Platform	46'9"	Fuel	400 gals.
Beam	14'0"	Water	95 gals.
Draft	42"	Waste	50 gals.
Weight, Gas	24,300#	Hull Type	Modified-V
Weight, Diesel	25,900#	Deadrise Aft	16°
Headroom	6'7"	Production	2003–Current

The Cruisers 440 Express (called the 4370 Express in 2003) offers upscale buyers the versatility of a big express cruiser with the interior luxury of an aft-cabin motor yacht. With her wide beam, tall freeboard and extended swim platform, the 440 is a big boat for her size. While there are several express-style yachts her size available on the market, only the 440 offers a full-size master stateroom (with private head and shower) aft of the salon. The headroom found throughout the interior is exceptional, and the decor is a lavish blend of posh upholstery, quality wall coverings, and acres of high-gloss cherry cabinetry. The bi-level cockpit is large enough to seat as many as eight guests in comfort. A walk-through windshield offers easy access to the foredeck, and an electric hatch in the aft cockpit sole provides entry to the engine compartment. A cockpit shower, windlass, and radar arch are standard, and a stylish fiberglass hardtop (pictured above) is optional. Several diesel V-drive engine options are available for the Cruisers 440. Among them, a pair of Yanmar 440s will cruise at 25 knots—sedate performance by European sportboat standards, but suitable for the domestic market.

Cruisers 500 Express

Length w/Platform	52'3"	Fuel	500 gals.
Beam	15'6"	Water	150 gals.
Draft	3'8"	Waste	75 gals.
Weight	42,000#	Hull Type	Modified-V
Clearance, Hardtop	13'2"	Deadrise Aft	15°
Headroom	6'6"	Production	2005–Current

A spacious interior and a full array of luxury appointments characterize the Cruisers 500, a modern express yacht whose excellent performance compares well with most of her European counterparts. Built on a modified-V hull with a solid fiberglass bottom, the twin-stateroom floorplan of the 500 offers the comforts of a small motor yacht. In the salon, an opulent Ultraleather sectional with double recliners seats eight for cocktails, and the portside galley (which conceals an optional dishwasher) has a glass-encased liquor cabinet built into the end of the counter. The forward stateroom comes with either a queen- or twin-berth layout, while the full-beam master stateroom enjoys excellent natural lighting thanks to the vertical ports installed on either side of the hull. On deck, the cockpit is dominated by a huge U-shaped lounge whose rear section pulls out from the transom to form a sun pad. Visibility from the helm is excellent, and an extended swim platform can carry a small inflatable. Additional features include cherry interior joinery, walk-through windshield, fender storage, windlass, and salon entertainment center. A fiberglass hardtop is optional. Volvo 675hp V-drive diesels will deliver a top speed in excess of 30 knots.

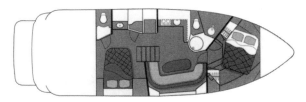

Standard Layout

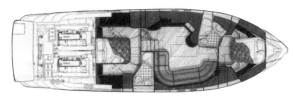

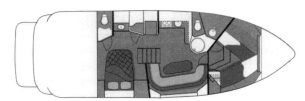

Optional Layout

See Page 311 for Pricing Information

49

See Page 311 for Pricing Information

Cruisers 540 Express

Length	58'0"	Fuel	650 gals.
Beam	16'0"	Water	150 gals.
Draft	3'10"	Waste	100 gals.
Weight	46,000#	Hull Type	Modified-V
Clearance	12'7"	Deadrise Aft	15°
Headroom	6'6"	Production	2001–Current

Once a rarity in the world of full-production boats, 50-something express yachts now constitute a fast-growing segment of the luxury yacht market. The 540 Express (called the 5370 Express in 2001–02, and the 5470 Express in 2003) is the largest express-boat offering yet from Cruisers. The interior is finished entirely in cherrywood with excellent detailing, and Cruisers offers a choice of two- or three-stateroom layouts. Each stateroom has a full head with shower and a washer/dryer can be added in either configuration. (Note that the hardwood dinette table in the salon retracts electrically into the floor when not in use.) Topside, the circular lounge aft in the cockpit converts at the push of a button into a huge sun pad. Visibility from the walkaround helm is excellent and wide side decks provide secure access to the foredeck. Additional features include a fully cored hull, prop pockets, excellent access to the spacious engine room, and an extended swim platform with a transom compartment for an optional davit. Among several engine choices, twin 800hp V-drive Cat diesels will cruise the 540 Express at 28 knots and reach a top speed of in the low-to-mid 30s.

Donzi Z27 Express

Length Overall	29'3"	Fuel	103 gals.
Beam	8'6"	Water	20 gals.
Draft, Drive Up	1'9"	Headroom	6'4"
Draft, Drive Down	3'5"	Hull Type	Deep-V
Weight	6,500#	Deadrise Aft	19°
Clearance	7'0"	Production	1995–2000

The Donzi Z27 Express (called the 275 Medallion in 1995 and the 275 LXC from 1996–98) is an entry-level family cruiser whose narrow beam makes her one of the largest trailerable express boats ever produced. Affordably priced, she's built on a deep-V hull with cored hullsides, a single-piece inner liner, and a solid fiberglass bottom. Because of the limited 8-foot, 6-inch beam (required for trailering), the interior of the Donzi Z27 is more compact than other 27-footers, most of which have wider beams. The floorplan is arranged with a convertible dinette/V-berth forward, a second double berth in the midcabin, a well-equipped galley, and a spacious standup head with hand shower. There's plenty of headroom thanks to her high freeboard and elevated foredeck. In the cockpit, a walk-through windshield with molded steps leads to the bow and an L-shaped lounge aft provides seating for five. Three hatches in the cockpit sole provide good access to the engine compartment. Additional features include windshield vents, anchor locker, and a cockpit wet bar. Among several sterndrive engine choices, a single 7.4-liter I/O will cruise the Donzi Z27 at 21–22 knots and reach a top speed of about 35 knots.

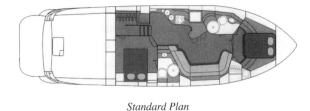

Standard Plan

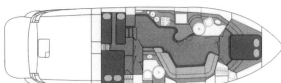

Alternate Plan

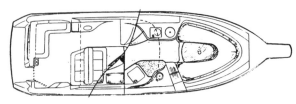

See Page 311 for Pricing Information

50

See Page 312 for Pricing Information

Donzi Z32 Express

Length Overall	33'8"	Fuel	198 gals.
Beam	11'0"	Water	35 gals.
Draft, Drives Up	2'4"	Headroom	6'5"
Draft, Drives Down	3'1"	Hull Type	Deep-V
Weight	11,500#	Deadrise Aft	19°
Clearance	NA	Production	1996–2000

The Donzi Z32 (called the 3250 LXC in 1996–98 and the Z3250 in 1999) is an aggressively designed family cruiser whose principal appeal was an affordable price and impressive sterndrive performance. (Indeed, she'll run circles around her inboard-powered counterparts although sterndrives may not appeal to everyone in a 32-footer.) Built on a deep-V hull with a wide 11-foot beam and a single-piece inner liner, the interior of the Z32 sleeps four with double berths forward and a convertible semicircular dinette. The head is conveniently located just inside the companionway (where it's easily accessible from the cockpit), and a folding door provides privacy in the forward stateroom. Headroom is excellent thanks to the boat's high freeboard and raised cabintop. On deck, a cockpit wet bar is opposite the doublewide helm seat. Unlike most other family cruisers her size, the Z32 has a centerline transom door and facing settees in the cockpit (rather than an offset transom door and a big U-shaped settee). Additional features include wide side decks, an integral swim platform with transom shower, and a windlass. A good performer, 7.4-liter I/Os will cruise at 28 knots and reach over 40 knots wide open.

Donzi 39 ZSC

Length Overall	39'10"	Fuel	302 gals.
Beam	12'2"	Water	40 gals.
Draft, Drives Up	2'3"	Headroom	6'3"
Draft, Drives Down	3'3"	Hull Type	Deep-V
Weight	15,500#	Deadrise Aft	22°
Clearance	8'6"	Production	2001–Current

Largest boat in the Donzi fleet, the 39 ZSC is an expensive, high-powered sportcruiser with the aggressive appearance of a European import. The Donzi nameplate has long been associated with performance, and the 39 combines the company's trademark go-fast engineering with a level of creature comfort never before seen in a Donzi. Built on a stepped-hull deep-V bottom, the layout of the ZSC, with its spacious cockpit and compact interior, marks her as more day boat than family cruiser. Her lush cherrywood interior is completely open and efficiently arranged with a small sleeping berth to port (under the cockpit seat), a rather elegant galley, enclosed head and a long V-berth/dinette forward. The cockpit will seat six adults around a high-low table, and drop-down bolster seats at the helm and a portside wet bar are standard. Aft, the power-lift sun pad provides excellent access to the engine compartment. Note that the bow is reached via a walk-through in the windshield. Overall, this is an extremely well finished boat with above-average attention to detail. A fast ride with 425hp MerCruiser gas sterndrives, the Donzi 39 ZSC will reach a top speed of over 40 knots.

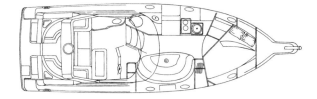

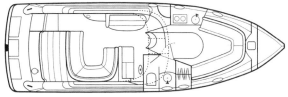

EXPRESS CRUISERS

Doral 270 Prestancia

Length w/Pulpit	27'1"	Clearance	8'8"
Hull Length	25'4"	Fuel	106 gals.
Beam	9'6"	Water	28 gals.
Draft, Down	2'9"	Hull Type	Modified-V
Draft, Up	1'7"	Deadrise Aft	17°
Weight	7,175#	Production	1989–95

Those seeking a comfortable weekend cruiser with conservative lines and better-than-average quality would do well to consider the Canadian-built Doral 270. (Note that she was called the Doral 270 Monticello in 1989–90.) She was built on a fully cored, modified-V hull with generous beam and a relatively modest 17 degrees of deadrise at the transom. Her midcabin interior is arranged like most boats of this size and type with double berths fore and aft, a standup head compartment, convertible dinette and a small galley with plenty of storage. While the original decor is obviously dated by today's art-deco standards, this is a very open and user-friendly layout with good headroom and storage. Topside, an L-shaped lounge across from the helm comes with a built-in wet bar, and a hidden cockpit shower is located near the transom gate. Additional features include a foredeck sun pad, molded pulpit, radar arch, and a wide swim platform. A good performer, twin 205hp V-6 MerCruiser sterndrives will cruise the Doral 270 at a brisk 24 knots and reach a top speed in the neighborhood of 34 knots.

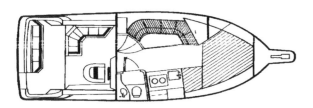

Doral 270 SC

Length	27'1"	Water	30 gals.
Beam	8'6"	Waste	30 gals.
Draft, Up	1'6"	Headroom	6'2"
Draft, Down	2'6"	Hull Type	Deep-V
Weight	7,100#	Deadrise Aft	18°
Fuel	100 gals.	Production	1996–2002

Those seeking a large trailerable family cruiser with plenty of cockpit space will find a lot to like in the Doral 270 SC. This is an excellent choice for day boaters who prefer an expansive cockpit for entertaining and sightseeing at the expense of more limited cabin accommodations. Not everyone will go for this layout of course, but it makes a lot of sense for those who seldom find themselves planning extended cruises to distant ports where the benefits of a spacious interior are most appreciated. The truth is, most folks spend the majority of their time in the cockpit, and it's here that the 270 delivers big-time with more seating and passenger amenities than one would expect in a 27-footer. A swim platform shower and built-in wet bar were standard, and the helm layout is particularly well done. If the midcabin interior is compact, there are still berths for five along with a full galley and a head with shower. On the downside, side decks are practically nonexistent. Built on a fully cored deep-V hull, a single 5.7-liter sterndrive will cruise the Doral 270 at 22 knots (32–33 knots top), and a single 7.4-liter MerCruiser will deliver a cruising speed of 26 knots and reach a top speed of around 36 knots.

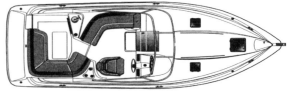

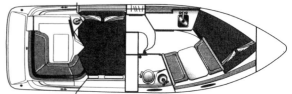

Doral 28 Prestancia

Length w/Platform	32'2"	Fuel	110 gals.
Hull Length	27'9"	Water	30 gals.
Beam	10'1"	Waste	30 gals.
Draft, Down	3'2"	Hull Type	Modified-V
Weight	10,000#	Deadrise Aft	19°
Headroom	6'2"	Production	2003–Current

With so many midsized family cruisers to choose from these days, the Doral 28 Prestancia stands apart for her quality construction and rakish—some might say excessive—styling. Aesthetics aside, there's a lot to like about the Prestancia, and it's fair to say that she's one of the biggest 28-footers around. Indeed, the cabin accommodations are surprisingly expansive for a boat this size with berths for six, a full galley, and a standup head with sink and shower. Privacy curtains separate the fore and aft sleeping areas from the main cabin, and the forward berth has an adjustable backrest for late-night readers. Note that counter space in the galley is limited, which is typical of most small cruisers. Topside, the Prestancia's cockpit is expandable; the aft lounge slides aft at the flip of a switch to increase space. On the downside, it's difficult for two people to share the double helm seat because the steering wheel is centered. A cockpit wet bar and extended swim platform are standard, and a unique mahogany lounge on the foredeck adjusts into a chair. Among several engine choices, twin 225hp MerCruiser Bravo III drives will deliver a top speed of 32–33 knots.

Doral 300 Prestancia

Length w/Pulpit	30'3"	Fuel	136 gals.
Hull Length	28'0"	Water	34 gals.
Beam	10'0"	Headroom	6'3"
Draft	2'11"	Hull Type	Deep-V
Weight	8,275#	Deadrise Aft	18°
Clearance	9'2"	Production	1989–95

The 300 Prestancia was a popular model in the Doral fleet during her extended 6-year production run, and used models continue to enjoy a good deal of popularity in both the Canadian and northern U.S. markets. Built in Quebec on a fully cored, deep-V hull, her 10-foot beam is quite generous considering that this is really a 28-foot boat. While she lacks the modern integrated swim platform seen in her more modern counterparts, the Prestancia's conservative lines benefit from her curved windshield, subdued hull graphics, radar arch, and fully integrated bow pulpit. With no interior bulkheads, the interior is wide open with privacy curtains for both staterooms, full galley, standup head, and a U-shaped dinette that converts into a huge 6-foot, 8-inch double berth. Seating for six is provided in the cockpit (a bench seat is hidden in the transom), and a convenient hot-and-cold shower is recessed into the transom as well. A well-finished boat inside and out, standard 4.3-liter MerCruiser I/Os will cruise the Doral 300 Prestancia at a respectable 18–19 knots (about 30 top, depending on the load), and optional 5.7-liter I/Os will cruise at 24 knots and reach around 40 knots top.

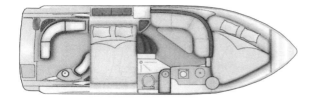

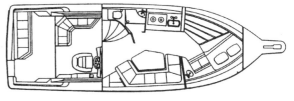

See Page 312 for Pricing Information

See Page 312 for Pricing Information

EXPRESS CRUISERS

Doral 300 SC/SE

Length . . . . 30'2"	Water . . . . 30 gals.
Beam . . . . 10'2"	Headroom . . . . 6'5"
Draft, Up . . . . 1'11"	Hull Type . . . . Deep-V
Draft, Down . . . . 2'9"	Deadrise Aft . . . . 19°
Weight . . . . 8,916#	Production, SC 1996–2001
Fuel . . . . 134 gals.	Production, SE 1996–2001

In a market crowded with 30-foot midcabin cruisers, the Doral 300 SE's oversized cockpit and distinctive styling set her apart from most competitive models her size and type. Indeed, the cockpit dimensions of the 300 SE are extravagant with lounge seating for seven or eight guests and room left over for a built-in wet bar behind the doublewide helm seat. Obviously designed with outdoor entertainment in mind, Doral engineers crafted in the 300 SE one of the most expansive cockpits to be found in a 30-foot express boat. While the belowdecks accommodations are a bit compact, her midcabin floorplan can sleep six although the forward berth is definitely a tight fit for adults. A full inner liner makes cleanup easy, and the flow-through ventilation ports in the midcabin are unique. Note that Doral also offered a sistership to the 300 SE— the 300 SC—with a larger interior and slightly reduced cockpit dimensions. Built on a fully cored hull, twin 5.7-liter MerCruisers I/Os will cruise both models at 23–24 knots and reach a top speed of around 38 knots. With only 134 gallons of fuel, the cruising range is limited.

Doral 31 Intrigue

Length w/Platform . . . . 33'2"	Headroom . . . . 6'2"
Hull Length . . . . 30'6"	Fuel . . . . 166 gals.
Beam . . . . 11'2"	Water . . . . 40 gals.
Draft, Down . . . . 3'7"	Hull Type . . . . Modified-V
Draft, Up . . . . 2'5"	Deadrise Aft . . . . 19°
Weight . . . . 12,500#	Production 2001–Current

Dramatic styling, spacious accommodations, and a good turn of speed characterize the Doral 30 Intrigue (called the 310 SE in 2001–03), a well-built Canadian cruiser priced in the middle range of the 30-foot cruiser market. Built on a fully cored hull with a wide 11-foot, 2-inch beam, the Intrigue's interior layout—with its curved, aft-facing dinette, ample galley and stylish woodwork—offers something different from most boats in her class. The forward berth is more for kids than adults, but the aft stateroom is surprisingly large and includes a cushioned seat in the entryway. Throughout the Intrigue's interior one finds very good workmanship and many quality amenities. Topside, the cockpit can seat up to ten by extending the convertible aft bench out over the swim platform (which adds about 20 square feet to the cockpit area). There's space at the helm for flush-mounting extra electronics, and a windshield walk-through provides easy access to the foredeck. Visibility from the raised helm is excellent. A cockpit wet bar, removable table, and fender racks are standard. Among several engines offered over the years, twin 300hp MerCruisers I/Os will cruise in the high 20s and reach a top speed of about 40 knots.

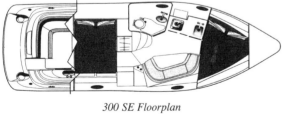

300 SE Floorplan

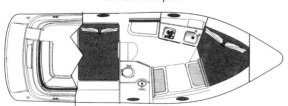

300 SC Floorplan

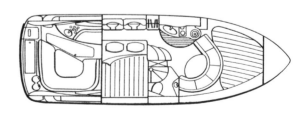

See Page 312 for Pricing Information

54

See Page 312 for Pricing Information

Doral 33 Elegante

Length w/Platform . . . . 37'6"	Fuel . . . . 230 gals.
Hull Length . . . . 33'2"	Water . . . . 44 gals.
Beam . . . . 11'11"	Headroom . . . . 6'4"
Draft, Down . . . . 3'8"	Hull Type . . . . Modified-V
Weight . . . . 15,200#	Deadrise Aft . . . . 18°
Clearance . . . . 9'11"	Production 2001–Current

The Doral Elegante (called the Doral 330 SE in 2001–03) is a heavily styled midcabin cruiser whose bold appearance and innovative interior offer something different in express-boat design. Built on a conventional modified-V hull, a forward-raked arch and fiberglass-capped windshield are her most distinctive features. Belowdecks, there are two tables in the salon; the larger one forward lowers electrically to convert the curved settee into a huge double berth. A privacy door separates the spacious midcabin—with standing headroom at the entrance—from the salon, and the galley is notable for its generous storage. Topside, the Doral's single-level cockpit is a real crowd-pleaser with wraparound seating for a small crowd. Visibility from the double helm seat is very good and a cockpit wet bar is standard. Two criticisms, however: the walk-through windshield steps next to the helm are too narrow, and the transom door is made of plastic rather than fiberglass. Additional features include excellent engine access, a foredeck sun pad, and a transom shower. Offered with several engine options, the Elegante will cruise in the low 20s with twin 320hp MerCruiser I/Os and reach a top speed of 33–34 knots.

Doral 350 Boca Grande

Length w/Pulpit . . . . 35'8"	Fuel . . . . 260 gals.
Hull Length . . . . 33'7"	Water . . . . 80 gals.
Beam . . . . 12'6"	Waste . . . . 45 gals.
Draft . . . . 3'0"	Hull Type . . . . Modified-V
Weight . . . . 13,900#	Deadrise Aft . . . . 16°
Clearance, Arch . . . . 10'0"	Production 1990-92

Obviously dated by today's express-boat standards, the 350 Boca Grande was the largest boat in Doral's fleet during the early 1990s. She was built on a solid fiberglass hull with moderate transom deadrise, and her 12-foot, 6-inch beam is about average for a modern 33-foot boat. The midcabin floorplan of the Boca Grande is arranged with an offset double berth forward and a convertible settee in the step-down amidships stateroom. The U-shaped dinette converts into a double berth for kids, and it's notable that there's a separate stall shower in the head compartment. Headroom is very good, and three hatches in the deck provide plenty of cabin ventilation. Topside, the bi-level cockpit is highlighted by an adjustable doublewide helm seat, a molded wet bar with icemaker, a bench seat at the stern and a walk-through transom door. A swim platform was standard, and the side decks are wide enough for secure bow access. Additional features include a molded bow pulpit, foredeck sun pad, an electro-hydraulic cockpit hatch for engine access, and a radar arch. A well-finished boat, the Boca Grande will cruise at 17–18 knots with standard 340hp MerCruiser V-drive inboards and reach around 28 knots wide open.

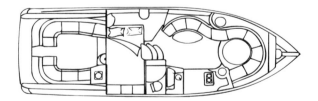

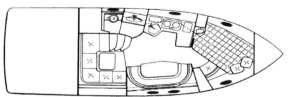

Doral 350 SC

Doral 36 Boca Grande

Length	36'10"	Fuel	210 gals.
Beam	12'0"	Water	32 gals.
Draft, Up	1'8"	Headroom	6'5"
Draft, Down	3'2"	Hull Type	Deep-V
Weight	12,774#	Deadrise Aft	20°
Clearance, Arch	8'5"	Production	1996–99

Length w/Platform	39'3"	Water	50 gals.
Hull Length	36'2"	Waste	37 gals.
Beam	12'6"	Headroom	6'5"
Draft	3'5"	Hull Type	Modified-V
Weight	18,800#	Deadrise Aft	18°
Fuel	258 gals.	Production	1998–Current

A quality-built boat with a modern express-boat profile, the Doral 350 SC combines a spacious midcabin interior with a cockpit large enough to accommodate a small group of passengers. Built on a fully cored deep-V hull, her belowdecks layout is arranged with double berths fore and aft, a large, well-equipped galley, a convertible dinette, and a standup head with shower. The 350 has more storage space than many boats her size, and three overhead deck hatches provide excellent lighting and cabin ventilation. The Doral's spacious bi-level cockpit will seat up to eight guests and comes standard with a molded wet bar and a very stylish helm with a woodgrain steering wheel and instrument panel. Fender racks were built into the transom, and wide side decks provide secure access to the bow. Note that the cockpit lounge complicates lifting the engine room hatch. Additional features include side exhausts, a large engine compartment, radar arch, and a foredeck sun pad. A good open-water performer, standard 7.4-liter MerCruiser sterndrives will cruise the Doral 350 SC at an easy 20 knots and reach a top speed of 35–36 knots.

B old styling is the hallmark of the Doral Boca Grande (called the 360 SE until 2003), an eye-catching French-Canadian design whose forward-facing arch and curvaceous windshield make her a distinctive boat in a sea of look-alike family cruisers. She's constructed on a conventional modified-V hull, fully cored with a wide beam and an integral swim platform. Her midcabin interior features an accordion privacy partition for the forward stateroom (instead of a curtain), an enormous head with a Lexan shower enclosure, and excellent cabin ventilation. Note that the 360's full-size refrigerator is a rarity on a 36-footer. Topside, there's seating for up to eight in the cockpit with its doublewide helm seat, three settees and wet bar. Note that the entire aft cockpit deck rises on hydraulic rams for engine room access. Additional features include a walk-through windshield, fender storage, foredeck sun pad and cockpit wet bar. While a pair of 320hp sterndrives are standard, serious cruisers might opt for the optional 420hp 8.1-liter MerCruiser inboards with V-drives. These engines will cruise the Boca Grande at 22–23 knots and reach a top speed in the low 30s.

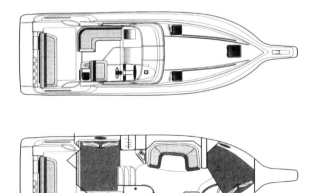

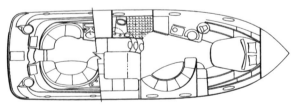

Dyer 29

Length Overall . . . . 28'6"	Water . . . . 24 gals.
Length WL . . . . 26'0"	Fuel . . . . 110 gals.
Beam . . . . 9'5"	Clearance . . . . NA
Draft . . . . 2'6"	Hull Type . . . . Semi-Disp.
Weight . . . . 7,400#	Designer . . . . Nick Potter
Clearance . . . . 6'0"	Production 1955–Current

Designed for cruising, fishing, or as a general utility boat, the durable Dyer 29 is an industry classic. Indeed, there are those who think she's one of the most alluring small boats ever designed. Production of the Dyer 29 began over 40 years ago making her the longest-running fiberglass model in the business. Each of the over 325 sold has been customized to some extent and no two are exactly alike. At 7,400 pounds, the Dyer 29 would be considered a light boat were it not for her narrow beam. She's built on a soft-chine hull with a long, prop-protecting keel and an uncommonly graceful sheer. The ability of the hull to tackle heavy sea conditions is legendary. Those who own these boats tolerate her tight cabin quarters and inconvenient engine box, while delighting in the fingertip control and positive response of this easily driven hull. Among several engine options, a single 250hp diesel will cruise the Dyer 29 efficiently at 19 knots (23–24 knots top). In addition to the popular Trunk Cabin and Bass Boat models, the 29 is available in hardtop and express versions. Note that more recent models locate the engine under the bridgedeck which eliminates the old engine box. Over 350 Dyer 29s have been built to date.

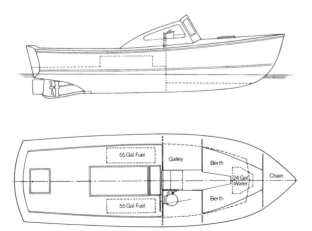

Ellis 36 Express

Length . . . . 35'10"	Fuel . . . . 200 gals.
Beam . . . . 13'2"	Water . . . . 100 gals.
Draft . . . . 3'10"	Waste . . . . NA
Weight . . . . 15,500#	Hull Type . . . . Modified-V
Clearance . . . . NA	Deadrise Aft . . . . 0°
Headroom . . . . 6'3"	Production 1998–Current

Looking for a true Downeast lobster yacht? The primary designer of the Ellis 36 was the late Ralph Ellis who, with partner Ray Bunker, developed the original wooden lobster boats back in the 1950s. Today's Ellis 36 is a refined version of the original Ellis full-keel hull, a beautifully crafted small yacht built with modern materials and loaded with first-class amenities. She comes with a standard soft top or optional hardtop, and buyers can choose a windshield-forward version (pictured above) if increased cockpit space is a priority, or the windshield aft for those who wish to maximize cabin accommodations. The Ellis 36 is not only beautiful, but she's loaded with practical features. In the single-level cockpit, side tables fold out, stern seats are brought forward, and innovative helm/navigation seats adjust to seat a party of eight for dinner. There's a separate stall shower in the head, and the galley is more than adequate for producing a full-scale meal. A bow thruster, swim platform, bow pulpit, and teak dining tables are standard in the Express Cruiser. A seriously expensive ride, a single 440hp Yanmar diesel will cruise the Ellis 36 at 20 knots (23–24 knots top). Note that twin waterjet propulsion is also available.

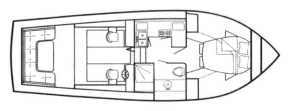

See Page 313 for Pricing Information

See Page 314 for Pricing Information

Fairline 40 Targa

Length Overall	41'6"	Clearance	NA
Beam	12'0"	Headroom	6'4"
Draft, Down	3'2"	Hull	Deep-V
Weight	16,000#	Deadrise Aft	17°
Fuel	197 gals.	Designer	B. Olesinski
Water	79 gals.	Production	2000–Current

The Fairline 40 Targa is a quality European sportcruiser from a company that seldom misses the mark when it comes to building well-styled, good-running boats. Built on a deep-V hull with moderate beam, the Targa's sleek exterior conceals a dinghy garage at the stern—a useful feature seldom found in a boat this size. The cockpit, which is impeccably detailed and finished, has a convenient food-prep unit across from the U-shaped lounge with a barbecue, refrigerator and sink. Belowdecks, the midcabin interior of the 40 Targa is an impressive display of high-gloss woodwork and practical design. Headroom is excellent; there's a separate stall shower in the head, and both staterooms have doors instead of privacy curtains. The engine room, beneath the transom garage, is roomy enough but can only be accessed if the dinghy is removed. Note that the king-size sun pad aft rises hydraulically for access to the tender storage compartment below. A bow thruster is standard—a definite plus—but the side decks are narrow and bow access is difficult. Twin 260hp Volvo diesel sterndrives will cruise the 40 Targa at 27–28 knots and reach a top speed in the low 30s.

Fairline 48 Targa

Length	49'10"	Water	120 gals.
Beam	12'11"	Headroom	6'8"
Draft	3'3"	Hull Type	Deep-V
Weight	24,600#	Deadrise Aft	19°
Clearance	NA	Designer	B. Olesinski
Fuel	360 gals.	Production	1998–2002

A striking yacht, the Fairline 48 Targa is a purebred Mediterranean sportcruiser whose sleek profile (dominated by a fiberglass-framed elliptical windshield) compares well with anything Sea Ray or Sunseeker has produced to date. She's built on a deep-V hull with shallow prop pockets to reduce draft, and her narrow, easily driven hull goes a long way toward explaining her good performance with relatively modest power. Fitting three staterooms in the Targa 48 was a challenge solved by placing side-by-side guest cabins below the helmdeck, each with twin single berths. While the salon is quite spacious and expertly finished, the en suite head attached to the forward stateroom is quite small and the doors to the aft cabins are narrow. On deck, the cockpit is divided into three areas: the command bridge at the front, settee and wet bar in the middle, and a centerline garage for a tender aft with a hydraulically activated door. A teak cockpit sole is standard and the side decks are wide and safe. Considered a benchmark boat in the eyes of many aficionados, twin 430hp Cats—shoehorned into a tight engine room—will cruise the 48 Targa in the mid 20s and reach a top speed of 30+ knots.

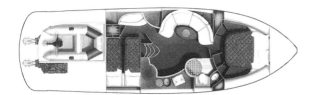

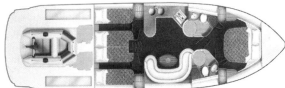

See Page 314 for Pricing Information

See Page 314 for Pricing Information

Fairline 52 Targa

Length Overall	53'3"	Fuel	480 gals.
Beam	14'0"	Water	120 gals.
Draft	3'7"	Hull Type	Deep-V
Weight	35,200#	Deadrise Aft	19°
Clearance	15'10"	Designer	B. Olesinski
Headroom	6'6"	Production	2003–Current

Replacing the very popular 48 Targa in 2003, the 52 Targa is further evidence (if anyone needs it) of Fairline's ability to combine comfort and performance is a modern, state-of-the-art sportcruiser. The Targa is a very impressive yacht—the finish is exemplary, and the accommodations define comfort and luxury. Her standard three-stateroom interior is arranged with the master stateroom forward and two identical guest staterooms aft. A central seating unit forms the back to the galley, and both heads are fitted with separate stall showers. Note that the galley sole is an awkward step down from the salon floor that seems unnecessary considering the Targa's tall headroom. High-gloss cherry cabinetry dominates the interior, and an optional den/office can replace the port guest cabin. Topside, the transom garage is big enough to handle a 12-foot tender, and access to the engine room—under the garage—is very good. Additional features include a superb helm position, foredeck fender lockers, teak cockpit sole, and excellent cabin and cockpit storage. A good-handling yacht, the 52 Targa will cruise in the high 20s with 715hp Volvo diesels and top out at 35 knots.

Fairline 62 Targa

Length Overall	61'11"	Water	145 gals.
Beam	15'7"	Waste	48 gals.
Draft	4'6"	Hull	Deep-V
Weight	46,400#	Deadrise Aft	20°
Clearance	18'2"	Designer	B. Olesinski
Fuel	780 gals.	Production	2004–Current

European sportcruisers are usually defined by their sleek styling, spacious cockpits, and plentiful sunbathing capabilities. Throw in a power hardtop that completely encloses the teak-soled cockpit and a lavish cherrywood interior with a full-beam master stateroom, and one might begin to accurately assess the Fairline Targa 62. A sleek profile only hints at the lavish accommodations and thoughtful amenities found aboard this muscular sportyacht. The retractable hardtop allows the bridgedeck to be transformed at the push of a button from a completely open-air deck to a fully enclosed and air-conditioned salon. Her opulent three-stateroom interior features a full-width salon with a large overhead skylight, utility room with washer and dryer, and a state-of-the-art entertainment center in the main salon. The angled berth in the master stateroom is accessible from three sides, and large windows set into the hullsides brighten the cabin considerably. Additional features include a tender garage, cockpit galley with fridge and barbecue, a huge foredeck sun pad, and teak decks. Cat 1,015hp engines will cruise the Targa 62 at an honest 30 knots—impressive performance for a 60-foot boat.

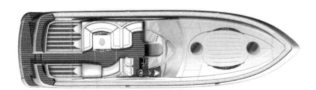

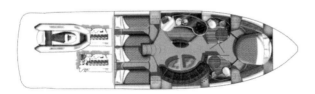

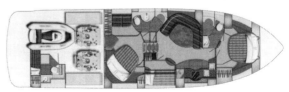

Formula 27 PC

Length Overall . . . . 28'3"	Fuel . . . . 107 gals.
Hull Length . . . . 27'0"	Water . . . . 26 gals.
Beam . . . . 9'7"	Waste . . . . 30 gals.
Draft . . . . 3'1"	Hull Type . . . . Deep-V
Weight . . . . 9,500#	Deadrise Aft . . . . 18°
Clearance . . . . 9'6"	Production 1994–Current

A popular boat since her introduction in 1994, the Formula 27 PC is a proven blend of quality construction, comfortable accommodations and good open-water performance. Built on a solid fiberglass deep-V hull, the 18-degree aft deadrise is a good compromise between stability and performance. Her midcabin floorplan is arranged with a built-in entertainment center facing the dinette in addition to a large head, a stylish pod-type galley, and berths for four. This is one of the more luxurious interiors to be found in a 27-footer with quality hardware and furnishings throughout. Lacking side decks (foredeck access is via a walk-through in the windshield), the full-width cockpit of the 27 PC is very spacious and comes with a doublewide helm seat, tilt wheel, wet bar, and a stowaway aft bench. Note that an electrically activated in-deck hatch provides access to the engine compartment. Additional features include a radar arch, an adjustable cocktail table for the cockpit with filler cushion, and a tilt steering wheel. A single 310hp MerCruiser (available through 1999) will cruise the Formula 27 at 22 knots (34–35 knots top), and twin 310hp MerCruisers will cruise at 25 knots (about 40 knots top).

Formula 28 PC

Length Overall . . . . 30'6"	Fuel . . . . 160 gals.
Hull Length . . . . 28'0"	Water . . . . 39 gals.
Beam . . . . 10'0"	Hull Type . . . . Deep-V
Draft . . . . 2'10"	Deadrise Aft . . . . 24°
Weight . . . . 7,850#	Designer . . . . J. Adams
Clearance . . . . 8'4"	Production 1985–87

M idcabin boats were rapidly gaining in buyer acceptance during the mid 1980s and Formula was one of many manufacturers to incorporate this now-standard floorplan in their evolving line of express cruisers. The 28 PC was considered an upscale boat during her production years, and her rugged construction and stylish hull graphics allowed her to age gracefully well into the 1990s. Belowdecks, the midcabin floorplan is arranged with the forward stateroom separated from the salon by a bi-fold door—a configuration seldom seen in newer boats with their more open layouts. (Note, however, that a section of the upholstered wall separating the salon from the forward stateroom is actually a sliding panel: leave it down for a more open salon.) The aft cabin includes facing settees and game table that convert to a double bed at night. In the cockpit, L-shaped lounge seating is opposite the helm, and the engine compartment (the hatch rises hydraulically) is huge. Additional features include an integral bow pulpit, a sturdy bow rail, swim platform and boarding ladder. A good performer, twin 260hp sterndrives will cruise the Formula 28 PC at 23 knots and reach 35 knots top.

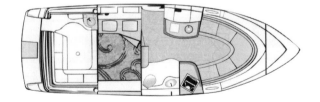

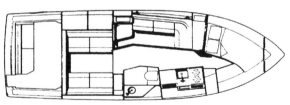

Formula 29 PC

Length Overall . . . . 33'9"	Fuel . . . . 165 gals.
Hull Length . . . . 29'0"	Water . . . . 50 gals.
Beam . . . . 10'7"	Hull Type . . . . Deep-V
Draft . . . . 2'6"	Deadrise Aft . . . . 20°
Weight . . . . 9,700#	Designer . . . . J. Adams
Clearance . . . . 8'9"	Production 1988–92

Introduced in 1988 as a replacement for the aging Formula 28 PC, the Formula 29 PC is basically an enlarged version of her predecessor with additional beam and weight, a little less transom deadrise, and improved styling (note the curved windshield and swept-back radar arch). Built on a solid fiberglass deep-V hull with a relatively wide beam, the interior of the 29 PC is similar to most midcabin floorplans built since the early 1990s with the forward stateroom open to the salon and a convertible dinette for sleeping a couple of kids. The galley has enough counter space for some serious galley work, and privacy curtains separate the fore and aft sleeping areas from the main cabin. Formula used quality fabrics and furnishing in the 29 PC, and while the interior decor is dated by today's standards it has held up very well indeed compared with most boats of her era. In the cockpit, the helm seat swivels to face aft, and the back seat slides into a transom recess providing access to the motors. (The deck rises hydraulically to expose a big engine compartment.) Twin MerCruiser or Volvo 350-cid sterndrives will cruise at 21 knots and reach 33–34 knots top. This is, by the way, an especially good-handling boat.

Formula 31 PC (1993–2004)

Length Overall . . . . 34'0"	Fuel . . . . 180 gals.
Hull Length . . . . 31'0"	Water . . . . 50 gals.
Beam . . . . 11'0"	Waste . . . . 40 gals.
Draft . . . . 3'2"	Hull Type . . . . Modified-V
Weight . . . . 11,730#	Deadrise Aft . . . . 18°
Clearance . . . . 10'0"	Production 1993–2004

A popular model for Formula over the years, the 31 PC enjoys top billing among late-model midcabin cruisers for her quality construction, upscale accommodations, and solid performance. Like all of Formula's PC series, the 31 is built on a modified-V hull that strikes a balance between stability and open-water performance. Belowdecks, the midcabin floorplan is organized in the conventional manner with overnight accommodations for six, a large head compartment, and privacy curtains for both staterooms. Typical of all Formula products, the hardware, fabrics, furnishings, and appliances are all first rate. The cockpit is arranged with a lounge seating opposite the double helm seat, and the U-shaped aft lounge converts into a big sun pad. Additional features include a transom shower, foredeck sun pad, cockpit wet bar, removable cocktail table, and a concealed swim ladder. A gas-assist hatch in the cockpit floor combined with a foldaway transom seat provides relatively easy access to the motors. MerCruiser 320hp engines will cruise the 31 PC at 25 knots and reach a top speed in the high 30s. (Note that an updated Formula 31 PC was introduced in 2005.)

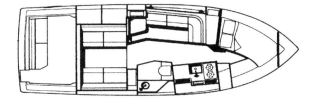

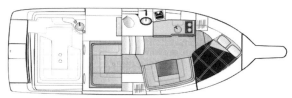

Formula 31 PC (Current)

Length Overall	33'1"	Fuel	180 gals.
Beam	11'0"	Water	50 gals.
Draft, Up	2'6"	Waste	40 gals.
Draft, Down	3'4"	Hull Type	Modified-V
Weight	14,100#	Deadrise Aft	18°
Clearance	10'4"	Production	2005–Current

Introduced in 2005, the Formula 31 PC is an updated version of the company's original 31 PC (previous page) considered by many to be among the best express cruisers in her class. The new model retains the top-of-the-line construction features of her predecessor while adding a sporty forward-facing radar arch, an extended swim platform, and an all-new interior scheme notable for its cherry-finished cabinets and Ultraleather upholstery. The cockpit contains a comfortable U-lounge with tables that can be lowered and converted into a large sun pad. Tables and cushions can be stored along with fenders in the huge transom trunk, and twin foredeck sun pads are reached by way of an opening windshield with molded steps. Belowdecks, the 31's designer interior is as elegant as it is practical. Corian counters are found in the galley and head, a six-person lounge is served by a solid cherry table, and overall fit and finish is the equal of any European sportboat. Major standard features include a windlass, trim tabs, hot and cold transom shower, 15-inch flat-screen TV/DVD, motorized engine hatch, and a premium VacuFlush toilet. Not inexpensive, twin 320hp MerCruiser sterndrives will reach a top speed of 35+ knots.

Formula 31 SC Express

Length	31'4"	Water	45 gals.
Beam	12'0"	Headroom	6'1"
Draft	2'6"	Hull Type	Deep-V
Weight	10,500#	Deadrise Aft	18°
Clearance	8'4"	Designer	J. Adams
Fuel	200 gals.	Production	1981–85

Aside from her distinctive reverse arch, the most striking feature of the Formula 31 SC is her wide beam—wider in fact than just about any other family cruiser her size in the early 1980s. Built on a solid fiberglass deep-V hull, the 31 SC's trunk cabin appearance is clearly dated (modern express designs incorporate a much sleeker foredeck profile). The floorplan—note that this is not a midcabin layout—is arranged with a double berth in the forward stateroom (which has a folding privacy door), convertible dinette to port, and a settee opposite. While this configuration offers plenty of salon seating, it results in a rather small galley and head compartment. Topside, the spacious single-level cockpit is arranged with doublewide helm and companion seats and removable bench seating aft. Note that the large cockpit of the 31 SC lends itself quite well to fishing although there's no transom door. Additional features include wide side decks, teak swim platform, and teak covering boards. A good-handling boat thanks to her deep-V hull, optional 350hp inboards will cruise the Formula 31 SC at 18–19 knots and about 27 knots top. Note that a full sportfishing version was also available.

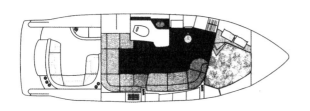

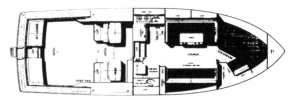

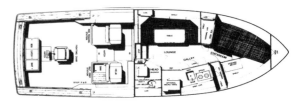

See Page 315 for Pricing Information

See Page 315 for Pricing Information

Formula 34 PC (1991–2002)

Length Overall . . . . 37'0"	Fuel . . . . 222 gals.
Hull Length . . . . 34'0"	Water . . . . 60 gals.
Beam . . . . 12'0"	Headroom . . . . 6'5"
Draft . . . . 2'6"	Hull Type . . . . Deep-V
Weight . . . . 13,500#	Deadrise Aft . . . . 18°
Clearance, Arch . . . . 10'0"	Production 1991–2002

Introduced back in 1991, the 34 PC was a strong-selling boat for Formula during her decade-long production run and used models are nearly always in demand. Like all of Formula's PC (Performance Cruiser) designs, she's built on a constant deadrise deep-V hull with moderate beam and solid fiberglass construction. The midcabin interior will sleep six and comes with an island berth in the forward stateroom and convertible facing settees in the aft cabin. Both staterooms have privacy curtains, and a bi-fold door in the head isolates the shower from the vanity. On deck, a triple-wide companion seat is opposite the helm and the entire aft section of the cockpit can be turned into a giant sunken sun pad. Additional features include well-secured side decks, a molded bow pulpit, transom shower, foredeck sun pad, and a cockpit wet bar. Generally considered a sterndrive model, V-drive inboards were optional (but never all that popular) from 1994–99. A good performer, twin 310hp Volvo or MerCruiser sterndrives will cruise the 34 PC at 23–24 knots and reach a top speed in the mid 30s. Cruising speeds with twin 310hp MerCruiser inboards are a few knots slower.

Formula 34 PC (2004–Current)

Length Overall . . . . 35'7"	Headroom . . . . 6'6"
Hull Length . . . . 34'3"	Fuel . . . . 206 gals.
Beam . . . . 11'6"	Water . . . . 55 gals.
Draft . . . . 3'0"	Hull Type . . . . Deep-V
Weight . . . . 13,916#	Deadrise Aft . . . . 18°
Clearance . . . . 11'4"	Production 2004–Current

Introduced in 2004, the Formula 34 PC replaces Formula's original—and very popular—34 PC built during 1991–2002. The styling is updated and so are the cabin and cockpit accommodations, and the extended swim platform of the new 34 will be appreciated by swimmers and divers. Built on a deep-V hull with slightly less beam than her predecessor, the Formula sleeps six in a midcabin floorplan typical of express boats this size. Privacy curtains separate both sleeping areas from the main cabin, and a luxurious Ultraleather lounge in the salon converts to a double berth for extra guests. This is a very inviting layout with lots of headroom, high-gloss cherry cabinetry and vinyl overheads. The galley is notable for its concealed stove, generous storage, and Corian counter. Cockpit seating includes a double helm seat, a U-shaped settee aft, and a bench seat opposite the helm. A wet bar is standard, and molded steps beside the companionway lead up to the windshield walk-through. Additional features include a reverse radar arch, power engine hatch lift, and transom storage locker. A fast ride, twin 320hp MerCruiser Bravo III sterndrives will cruise the Formula 34 PC in the mid 20s and top out at over 35 knots.

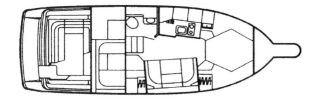

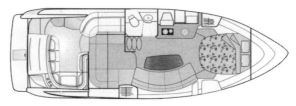

Formula 35 PC

Length Overall	40'0"	Fuel	275 gals.
Hull Length	35'0"	Water	50 gals.
Beam	12'0"	Hull Type	Deep-V
Draft	2'8"	Deadrise Aft	20°
Weight	13,750#	Designer	J. Adams
Clearance	10'2"	Production	1986–89

Largest of the Formula Performance Cruiser (PC) fleet in the late 1980s, the 35 PC is a roomy family express cruiser with a still-attractive profile and a comfortable midcabin interior layout. Construction is solid fiberglass, and her deep-V hull is designed with prop pockets to reduce the draft and shaft angles. Below, the PC's wide-open floorplan includes a superb U-shaped galley area—one of the best we've seen in any express boat this size—and a step-down midcabin with facing settees that convert into a big double bed at night. There's a centerline island berth in the forward stateroom (with a draw curtain for nighttime privacy), and the quality fabrics, hardware, furnishings, and appliances were considered first rate in their day. The cockpit is arranged with a big L-shaped lounge opposite the helm and foldaway bench seating at the transom. Additional features include side-dumping exhausts, a transom door, bow pulpit, radar arch, and swim platform. Accessed via a motorized hatch lift, twin 340hp MerCruiser gas engines (with V-drives) will cruise the Formula 35 PC at 21–22 knots and reach a top speed of around 30 knots.

Formula 36 PC

Length Overall	38'3"	Fuel	300 gals.
Hull Length	36'0"	Water	60 gals.
Beam	13'3"	Hull Type	Deep-V
Draft	2'8"	Deadrise Aft	18°
Weight	17,600#	Designer	J. Adams
Clearance	10'9"	Production	1990–95

A popular model during her 6-year production run, the 36 PC is a contemporary midcabin cruiser whose attractive lines and comfortable accommodations make her a desirable boat on today's used market. She was built on a solid fiberglass deep-V hull with fairly high freeboard and prop pockets to reduce her draft requirements. Inside, the midcabin floorplan is arranged in the conventional manner, having an island bed in the forward stateroom (with a door for privacy) and facing settees in the step-down aft cabin. There's a built-in entertainment center on the aft bulkhead above the midcabin facing the salon—very innovative. In the cockpit, a big L-shaped lounge is opposite the helm, and a hydraulically operated hatch provides outstanding access to the engine compartment. Note that unlike most modern midcabin cruisers of her type and size, the Formula 36 PC has straight inboard power rather than V-drives. Standard 454-cid gas engines will cruise at 17 knots and reach 26–27 knots top. Note that in 1990 (only) Formula offered an Express version of the 36 PC without the midcabin but with a huge engine room and extra storage.

See Page 315 for Pricing Information

See Page 315 for Pricing Information

Formula 37 PC

Length Overall	38'5"	Fuel	236 gals.
Hull Length	37'0"	Water	55 gals.
Beam	11'11"	Waste	57 gals.
Draft	2'6"	Hull Type	Deep-V
Weight	16,500#	Deadrise Aft	18°
Clearance	12'3"	Production	2000–Current

The Formula 37 PC is a top-shelf family express whose aggressive good looks (note the reverse radar arch) and sumptuous interior are designed to appeal to upmarket cruisers willing to pay a little extra for the built-in quality of a Formula product. She's built on a beamy deep-V hull with prop pockets and a relatively modest 18 degrees of deadrise at the transom. The midcabin floorplan of the 37 PC is unusually wide open and spacious thanks to the absence of any interior cabin bulkheads. Headroom is excellent, the decor is quite elegant, and the furnishings and appliances are first rate. Draw curtains rather than doors are used to separate both sleeping areas, however—a privacy issue for some. The cockpit, with its U-shaped lounge (which converts into a big sun pad), wet bar and triple-wide helm seat, can accommodate 10 passengers. Note that the entire transom and rear seat unit can be raised for excellent (and innovative) engine access. Additional features include a walk-through windshield, a huge transom locker, foredeck sun pads and an optional PWC lift. Among several sterndrive and inboard power options, twin 375hp Volvo gas engines (with V-drives) will cruise in the mid 20s and top out at just over 30 knots.

Formula 370 Super Sport

Length	37'0"	Water	43 gals.
Beam	10'6"	Waste	50 gals.
Draft	3'0"	Waste	50 gals.
Weight	14,400#	Hull Type	Deep-V
Clearance	10'0"	Deadrise Aft	21°
Fuel	238 gals.	Production	2001–Current

The Formula 370 Super Sport is a sleek, aggressively styled sport-cruiser with an enviable combination of superior construction, first-rate accommodations and excellent open-water performance. She's basically a Euro-style sportboat with considerably more cockpit space—and less interior volume—than traditional express cruisers. Performance is important in a boat like this, and the 370's narrow beam and high-speed stepped hull deliver the fast ride and luxurious accommodations that few other sportboats can match. Her spacious and well-equipped cockpit provides seating and amenities for a small crowd. A removable cocktail table stores in a transom storage locker, and a cockpit galley comes complete with a sink, cooler and refrigerator. The cabin of the 370, which is quite opulent, has a convertible V-berth/dinette forward, an athwartships mid-berth aft, and a compact galley. Additional features include a walk-through windshield, transom shower, tilt steering, and a flip-up bolster seat at the helm. Like all Formula boats, the fit and finish of the 370 Super Sport is very impressive. A pair of 420hp sterndrives will cruise the 370 SS at 30 knots and reach a top speed of around 45 knots.

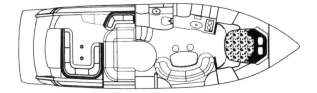

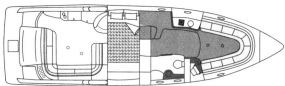

See Page 315 for Pricing Information

See Page 315 for Pricing Information

Formula 40 PC

Length	42'7"	Fuel	250 gals.
Beam	12'8"	Water	55 gals.
Draft	2'11"	Waste	57 gals.
Weight, Gas	18,510#	Hull Type	Deep-V
Weight, Diesel	19,304#	Deadrise Aft	18°
Clearance	11'7"	Production	2003–Current

Most long-time boaters know that Formula's series of family cruisers are built to high standards, which is to say they aren't inexpensive. That's certainly true of the Formula 40 PC, a high-end express designed for those who place a priority on luxury and performance. With her sleek styling, optional hardtop, and extended swim platform, the Formula is as practical as she is handsome. It's her belowdecks accommodations, however, that set the 40 PC apart from much of the competition. Here, a tasteful blend of high-gloss cherry cabinetry, Ultraleather upholstery, and top-quality hardware and furnishings combine to create an impressive display of luxury and comfort. Hidden privacy doors separate the forward stateroom from the main cabin, and the Formula's tall headroom gives the impression of a much larger boat. Topside, an extended swim platform—sturdy enough to carry a jet bike—makes boarding easy. At the helm, a double flip-up seat allows the driver to drive while standing. A walk-through windshield, transom storage locker, and radar arch are standard. A comfortable ride in a chop, twin 420hp Yanmar V-drive diesels will cruise the Formula 40 PC at 22–24 knots.

Formula 400 Super Sport

Length	40'0"	Water	48 gals.
Beam	11'0"	Waste	50 gals.
Draft	3'0"	Headroom	6'1"
Weight	15,500#	Hull Type	Deep-V
Clearance	10'6"	Deadrise Aft	22°
Fuel	250 gals.	Production	1999–Current

The Formula 400 Super Sport is an American-built entry into the high-performance luxury sportboat market dominated in recent years by a handful of pricey European imports. Long and narrow, the 400 is built on Formula's "Fas3Tech" hull bottom—a double-stepped deep-V affair designed to reduce the water's grip on the hull. The result, according to company engineers, is a faster and more stable boat that runs at near-optimal running angles without the need to constantly trim the drives. Beautifully styled, the Super Sport is a superb day boat with plenty of cockpit space and a wide-open interior. With the owner's stateroom aft, the salon is dominated by a rich Ultraleather wraparound lounge forward and four overhead translucent hatches. On deck, the doublewide helm seat folds away for standup driving, and a walk-through windshield opens to a wide stretch of nonskid leading to the bow. Notable features include a recessed anchor storage compartment, a hinged storage locker at the transom, and good engine access. Twin 425hp gas sterndrives will achieve a top speed of close to 45 knots, while Volvo 350hp diesel I/Os top out at close to 40 knots.

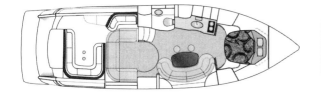

See Page 315 for Pricing Information

See Page 315 for Pricing Information

Formula 41 PC

Length Overall . . . . 43'1"	Fuel, Gas. . . . . 300 gals.
Hull Length. . . . . 41'0"	Fuel, Diesel . . . . 350 gals.
Beam . . . . 13'6"	Water. . . . . 81 gals.
Draft. . . . . 2'9"	Hull Type . . . . Deep-V
Weight. . . . . 18,520#	Deadrise Aft . . . . 18°
Clearance. . . . . 11'0"	Production 1996–2004

Flagship of the Formula fleet for several years, the 41 PC is a well-engineered express cruiser with the precise handling and quality construction typical of Formula products. This is a big boat inside and out, and a long foredeck and shapely profile make her a standout in any marina. The midcabin accommodations of the Formula 41 are impressive indeed with staterooms fore and aft and a long salon with room for a crowd. There's a separate stall shower in the double-entry head, a big galley with plenty of counter space, excellent storage, and a walkaround island berth in the forward stateroom. Outside, the cockpit is arranged with a doublewide seat at the helm and a U-shaped settee aft that converts into a huge sun pad. The lounge seat opposite the helm can be raised hydraulically to expose a big storage compartment below. A walk-through in the windshield provides access to the foredeck, and hydraulic rams lift the entire cockpit sole for engine access. Running on a deep-V hull with prop pockets, 8.2-liter gas engines will cruise at 16–17 knots (around 28 knots wide open), and 450hp Cummins diesels cruise at 24–25 knots (about 30 knots top).

Formula 47/48 Yacht

Length . . . . 51'0"	Fuel . . . . 400 gals.
Beam . . . . 14'0"	Water. . . . . 100 gals.
Draft. . . . . 3'8"	Waste . . . . 75 gals.
Weight. . . . . 35,750#	Hull Type . . . . Deep-V
Clearance. . . . . 14'0"	Deadrise Aft . . . . 18°
Max Headroom . . . . 7'0"	Production 2003–Current

For a company whose name has long been associated with performance, the Formula 48 Yacht (called the 47 Yacht in 2003–04) is much more concerned with luxury than speed. This is Formula's largest and most expensive cruising yacht ever, and she retains the high level of quality that long-time boaters have come to expect in a Formula product. Built on a deep-V hull with prop pockets and moderate beam, the 48's lavish accommodations are both elegant and spacious. Headroom exceeds 7 feet in the salon and varnished cherrywood cabinetry, Ultraleather upholstery, and designer fabrics dominate the interior. The huge L-shaped galley rivals that of a small motor yacht, and the aft stateroom—which can easily double as a den—has its own private head with shower. Across from the salon, a built-in LCD television automatically tilts for the best viewing angle. The expansive cockpit of the Formula 48 provides seating for ten, and the helm layout is as good as it gets in a big express. Unlike most sterndrive-powered European sportcruisers, the Formula is an inboard design that many boaters prefer for maintenance reasons. Twin 660hp Cummins diesels will cruise in the mid 20s and reach 32–33 knots wide open.

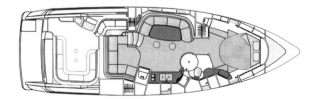

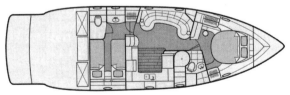

See Page 315 for Pricing Information

See Page 316 for Pricing Information

Fountain 38 Express Cruiser

Length	37'11"	Headroom	6'4"
Beam	10'6"	Fuel	270 gals.
Draft, Up	1'10"	Water	50 gals.
Draft, Down	3'2"	Hull Type	Deep-V
Weight	13,500#	Deadrise Aft	22°
Clearance	9'0"	Production	2002–Current

The Fountain name has long been synonymous with quality and performance, so it's hardly a surprise that the 38 Express Cruiser is one of the fastest, best-handling boats in her class. One look at this sleek speedster and you know she's a Fountain; the dual helm is similar to a Fountain racing boat with the throttles to the left of the wheel for two-person operation. The 38 rides on a slender deep-V hull with twin steps and Fountain's signature notched transom and pad keel. Like all express cruiser designs, the Fountain 38 is designed for entertaining. The cockpit, which seats eight, is arranged with electric drop-down bolster seats at the helm, companion lounge, U-shaped lounge seating aft, and a wet bar with icemaker. Below, the narrow beam of the Fountain results in compact accommodations for a 38-foot boat. The master stateroom is comfortable enough, but the aft stateroom is claustrophobic and the salon dimensions are modest. A motorized engine hatch, high-performance trim tabs, and radar arch are standard. Quality doesn't come cheap, and besides being fast, the 38 Express Cruiser is an expensive boat. Twin 425hp MerCruiser gas sterndrives will reach a top speed in excess of 50 knots.

Fountain 48 Express Cruiser

Length	48'6"	Fuel	457 gals.
Beam	12'0"	Water	80 gals.
Draft, Up	2'8"	Waste	36 gals.
Draft, Down	3'10"	Hull Type	Deep-V
Weight	22,000#	Deadrise Aft	22°
Clearance	10'0"	Production	2003–Current

The Fountain 48 Express cruiser doesn't just raise the performance bar for boats of her type; she sets an entirely new standard. Indeed, speed is what this sleek sportster is all about, something she achieves with extraordinary ease thanks to her lightweight stepped hull. But there's more to the 48 Express Cruiser than simply going fast. While a slender 12-foot beam limits the size of her belowdeck accommodations, her two-stateroom, two-head interior is as opulent as it is comfortable. The expansive forward stateroom has a pedestal queen berth and private en suite head, while the second stateroom, located amidships, also has a queen-size bed. (Note that neither head has a separate stall shower.) Faux granite countertops in the galley and rich cherrywood cabinetry highlight this very well finished interior. In the cockpit, a huge U-shaped settee can seat a small crowd. A raised sun pad aft has tremendous storage underneath, and both chairs at the helm have power seats that drop to form bolsters. Equipped with triple 440 Yanmars and Twin Disk surface drives, the 48 Express Cruiser planes in under five seconds, cruising well over 400 miles at 45 knots with a top speed of about 55 knots.

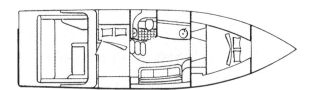

Four Winns 278 Vista

Length	27'2"	Water	38 gals.
Beam	9'4"	Headroom	5'10"
Draft	3'3"	Hull	Modified-V
Weight	6,650#	Deadrise Aft	17°
Clearance w/Arch	8'6"	Designer	Four Winns
Fuel	110 gals.	Production	1994–98

The Four Winns 278 Vista is a maxi-cube pocket cruiser whose stylish appearance has kept her from showing her age since she went out of production in 1998. Like many family boats her size, her modified-V hull (with a keel pad) provides a stable and comfortable ride in a variety of weather conditions. The Vista's accommodations are evenly divided between a roomy and well-arranged cockpit and the full-width cabin with its conventional midcabin floorplan. There are double berths fore and aft and both sleeping areas have a curtain for privacy. Notably, the galley has plenty of storage and counter space. There's a shower in the standup head, and the dinette table converts into a kid-sized berth. Outside, visibility from the double helm seat is excellent. Additional features include a walk-through windshield, space at the helm for flush-mounted electronics, and foldaway bench seating at the transom. Note that oval cabin ports replaced the original sliding cabin windows in 1996, and the cockpit was redesigned in 1998. A single 7.4-liter OMC sterndrive cruises at 22 knots (about 30+ knots top), and a pair of OMC 5.7-liter sterndrives will cruise at 24–25 knots (35+ knots top).

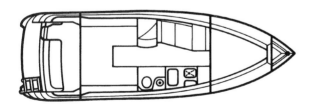

Four Winns 285 Express

Length	28'11"	Water	35 gals.
Beam	10'2"	Fuel	140 gals.
Draft	3'3"	Hull	Modified-V
Weight	9,060#	Deadrise Aft	19°
Clearance	8'6"	Designer	Four Winns
Cockpit	NA	Production	1991–93

A reworked version of Four Winns' earlier 285 Vista (1988–90), the 285 Express is a contemporary family express with what was considered a rakish profile in the early 1990s (note the circular deck hatches and colorful hull graphics) and roomy accommodations. She's built on a straightforward modified-V hull with cored hullsides, a relatively wide beam, and a solid fiberglass bottom. The 285 Express is somewhat unusual in that she was offered with a choice of two midcabin layouts—most production family cruisers this size typically offer just a single floorplan. The standard, more popular, interior has a wraparound lounge/dinette/V-berth forward with seating for six adults. An alternate layout had a separate dinette in the salon and a double berth forward. Outside, the passenger seat opposite the helm rotates to face the cockpit—a convenient feature for socializing. Additional features include foldaway bench seating at the transom, good access to the engines, a molded bow pulpit and a swim ladder with an assist rail. Among several engine options, twin 5.7-liter OMC sterndrives will cruise the 285 Express at 23–24 knots and reach about 38 knots top.

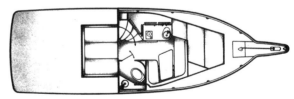

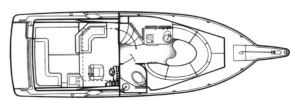

EXPRESS CRUISERS

Four Winns 285 Vista

Length w/Pulpit	28'11"	Water	35 gals.
Hull Length	27'5"	Clearance	NA
Beam	10'0"	Hull Type	Modified-V
Draft	2'9"	Deadrise Aft	19°
Weight	9,670#	Designer	Four Winns
Fuel	150 gals.	Production	1988–90

Introduced in 1988, the 285 Vista was aimed at existing Four Winns owners who were looking to move up from their trailerable models into a full-size midcabin cruiser. Construction is solid fiberglass from the rail down, and the tri-tone hull graphics are typical of Four Winns boats back in the 1980s and early 1990s. The Vista's relatively wide beam results in a spacious and wide-open interior for a 28-footer with berths for six. While the galley area is limited, the headroom is very good (6 feet, 3 inches at the entry), and there's plenty of storage space under the berths and settees. Topside, the cockpit is arranged with an L-shaped lounge to port (that pivots fore and aft) and bench seating aft. Note the distinctive circular foredeck hatches. Standard 200hp OMC sterndrives will cruise the 285 Vista at 22–23 knots (30+ knots top). In 1990, Four Winns introduced the 285 SE model, a less expensive single-engine version with a slightly revised interior layout. Among several single- and twin-screw power choices, a single 340hp 7.4L sterndrive engine will cruise at 19–20 knots (about 30 knots top), and twin 260hp sterndrive engines will run a few knots faster.

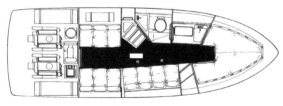

Standard 285 Floorplan

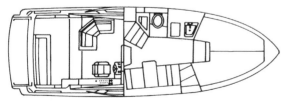

285 SE Floorplan

See Page 316 for Pricing Information

Four Winns 288 Vista

Length w/Platform	30'0"	Water	25 gals.
Beam	9'8"	Waste	25 gals.
Draft, Down	3'3"	Max Headroom	6'3"
Weight	10,380#	Hull Type	Modified-V
Clearance, Arch	9'0"	Deadrise Aft	18°
Fuel	120 gals.	Production	2004–Current

Introduced in 2004, the Four Winns 288 Vista's blend of solid construction, comfortable accommodations, and competitive price makes her a strong contender in the under-30-feet segment of today's express-boat market. Built on a modified-V hull with cored hullsides, the interior of the 288 Vista is a little larger than other boats in her class thanks to a wide 9-foot, 8-inch beam. The layout—which differs little from other midcabin cruisers—sleeps six with double berths fore and aft and a convertible Ultraleather settee in the main cabin. The midcabin area is a tight fit, but the head is large, and the galley has the refrigerator located above the microwave so you don't have to bend down to reach it. For after-hours privacy, curtains separate the sleeping areas from the main cabin. Topside, the cockpit is configured with a U-shaped lounge aft, refreshment center with slide-out cooler, removable table, and an electric engine hatch. Note that the double helm seat has a flip-up bolster for the driver. An extended swim platform, aluminum radar arch, tilt steering wheel, and transom shower are standard. With twin 270hp Volvo sterndrives, the 288 Vista will cruise in the low 20s and reach 30+ knots wide open.

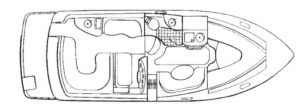

See Page 316 for Pricing Information

70

Four Winns 298 Vista

Length w/Platform . . . . 30'11"	Fuel . . . . 140 gals.
Hull Length . . . . 28'0"	Water . . . . 31 gals.
Beam . . . . 10'6"	Headroom . . . . 6'1"
Draft . . . . 3'3"	Hull Type . . . . Modified-V
Weight . . . . 10,650#	Deadrise Aft . . . . 19°
Clearance, Arch . . . . 9'2"	Production 1999–Current

With her wide beam, generous accommodations and impressive standard equipment list, the 298 Vista has been a popular model in the Four Winns fleet since her 1999 introduction. She's built on a relatively heavy modified-hull with cored hullsides, and her extended swim platform—strong enough to carry a PWC—adds much to her modern appearance. The 298's plush interior is arranged in the conventional manner with double berths fore and aft, a convertible dinette, a well-equipped galley, and a standup head compartment with a VacuFlush toilet. Note that the companionway hatch is backed by a sliding screen door—a useful item indeed. On deck, the seat cushion on the driver's side of the double helm seat flips up to create a leaning post, and molded steps in the console provide access to the foredeck via the walk-through windshield. Standard features include a removable aft seat, cockpit table, tilt wheel and full camper canvass. On the downside, the engine compartment is a tight fit, and the wide beam makes for a hard (and wet) ride in a chop. Twin 270hp Volvo 5.7-liter sterndrives will cruise the 298 Vista at 25 knots and deliver a top speed of around 40 knots.

Four Winns 315/325 Express

Length w/Pulpit . . . . 30'6"	Fuel . . . . 150/180 gals.
Beam . . . . 11'0"	Water . . . . 35 gals.
Draft . . . . 3'4"	Hull . . . . Modified-V
Weight . . . . 10,600#	Deadrise Aft . . . . 19°
Clearance . . . . 9'0"	Production, 315 1988–93
Max Headroom . . . . 6'3"	Production, 325 1991–93

The introduction of the Four Winns 315 Vista in 1988 was a big step for a company whose reputation had previously been made in the trailerable-boat business. She was a conventional midcabin boat with sterndrive power and an abundance of the hull graphics so popular in the late 1980s. A popular model, in 1991 Four Winns brought out the 325 Express that was identical to 315 but with inboard power—another Four Winns first—in a slightly lengthened hull with prop pockets. Both the 315 and 325 were heavily built on a maxi-beam hull with relatively high freeboard, cored hullsides and a solid fiberglass bottom. Both boats shared identical midcabin interiors with double berths fore and aft, a convertible dinette (note that two different dinette configurations are available), a full galley and a compact head. Topside, the cockpits of the 315 and 325 are very similar with bench seating at the stern and an L-shaped lounge opposite the helm. For performance, a pair of 260hp sterndrives will cruise the 315 Express at 23 knots (about 35 knots top), and optional 340hp engines will cruise at 30 knots. The 325 Express with 270hp inboards will cruise at 18 knots and top out in the high 20s. Note the fuel increase in 1991.

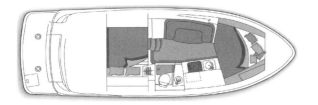

Standard Floorplan

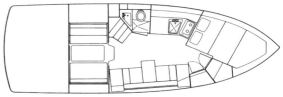

Alternate Floorplan

See Page 316 for Pricing Information

See Page 316 for Pricing Information

Four Winns 328 Vista

Length w/Platform	35'7"	Fuel	220 gals.
Hull Length	33'5"	Water	45 gals.
Beam	11'9"	Waste	30 gals.
Draft	3'2"	Hull Type	Modified-V
Weight	12,600#	Deadrise Aft	19°
Clearance, Arch	9'2"	Production	1999–Current

A stylish design with a graceful sheer and a tall, forward-sloped arch, the Four Winns 328 Vista is an attractively priced entry in the always-crowded midsize family cruiser market. She's built on modified-V hull with cored hullsides and a wide 11-foot, 9-inch beam. The Vista is a big boat inside and out with generous accommodations for a boat this size. Her floorplan is typical of most midcabin cruisers her size with double berths fore and aft, a large U-shaped settee, full galley (with plenty of storage drawers and cabinets), and a fair-size head with shower. Note that a sliding screen door backs the companionway hatch. In the single-level cockpit, the big U-shaped lounge aft converts into a sun pad and a molded entertainment center comes with an icemaker and sink. Molded steps in the console provide easy access to the bow via the walk-through windshield. Standard features include a large transom locker, tilt wheel, six opening ports, and an extended swim platform. Twin 280hp Volvo sterndrive engines will cruise the 328 Vista at 25 knots and reach a top speed of about 35 knots. Note that the Four Winns 348 Vista is an inboard version of this boat.

Four Winns 348 Vista

Length w/Platform	35'7"	Fuel	220 gals.
Hull Length	33'5"	Water	44 gals.
Beam	11'9"	Waste	30 gals.
Draft	3'3"	Hull Type	Modified-V
Clearance, Arch	9'2"	Deadrise Aft	19°
Headroom	6'4"	Production	2001–Current

T he Four Winns 348 Vista (called the 338 Vista when she was introduced in 2001) is an inboard version of the Four Winns 328 Vista. Like her sistership, the 348 is an attractively priced entry in the very crowded midsize family cruiser market. She's built on modified-V hull with cored hullsides and a wide 11-foot, 9-inch beam. The Vista is a big boat inside and out with generous accommodations for a boat this size. Belowdecks, the floorplan is typical of most midcabin cruisers her size with double berths fore and aft, a large U-shaped settee, full galley (with plenty of storage drawers and cabinets), and a fair-size head with shower. Note that a sliding screen door backs the companionway hatch. In the single-level cockpit, the big U-shaped lounge aft converts into a sun pad and a molded entertainment center comes with an icemaker and sink. Molded steps in the console provide easy access to the walk-through windshield. Standard features include a large transom locker, tilt wheel, six opening ports and an extended swim platform. MerCruiser 320hp inboards will cruise n the low 20s and reach (30+ knots top), and 320hp sterndrives cruise in the high 20s (37–38 knots wide open).

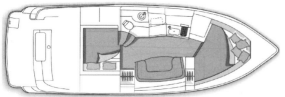

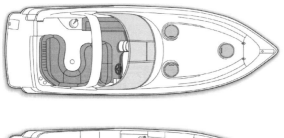

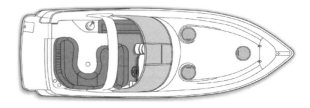

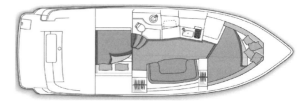

See Page 316 for Pricing Information

72

See Page 316 for Pricing Information

Four Winns 365 Express

Length w/Pulpit	36'0"	Water	98 gals.
Beam	13'2"	Headroom	6'4"
Draft	3'2"	Hull Type	Modified-V
Weight	18,600#	Deadrise Aft	16°
Clearance	10'4"	Designer	Four Winns
Fuel	315 gals.	Production	1991–94

Obviously dated by today's Euro-style cruisers, the Four Winns 365 was considered a stylish boat indeed when she was introduced back in 1991. (She also offered something unique and truly useless among family cruisers of her era—an optional Jacuzzi spa hidden below the island berth in the forward stateroom.) She was built on a conventional modified-V hull with a wide beam and prop pockets to reduce shaft angles and draft. Note the long, sweeping foredeck of the 365—the helm is well aft in this boat, thus reducing cockpit space in favor of an unusually spacious and wide-open interior. Sliding panels separate the forward berth from the salon, and the U-shaped midcabin lounge converts into a big double berth. Notable features include hidden foredeck lockers, a unique foldaway dinette table, excellent access to the engines and generator, a tilt steering wheel, side exhausts, and a unique air induction system designed to lower the risk of cockpit fumes. Crusader 350hp gas inboards (with V-drives) will cruise the Four Winns 365 at a respectable 18–19 knots (about 30 knots top), and optional 300hp Cummins diesels cruise at 20 knots and deliver around 26 knots wide open.

Four Winns 378 Vista

Length w/Platform	41'3"	Fuel	300 gals.
Hull Length	37'9"	Water	66 gals.
Beam	12'9"	Waste	42 gals.
Draft	3'6"	Hull Type	Modified-V
Weight	20,000#	Deadrise Aft	19°
Clearance, Arch	11'6"	Production	2002–Current

Four Winns' largest boat ever, the 378 Vista joins a growing list of midsize family cruisers vying for the attention of the nation's boaters. The Vista is a well-styled boat with her flowing lines and forward-facing arch, and she has one of the larger cockpits to be found in a 37-footer. Rather than the typical midcabin interior, the 378 features an expansive salon with two convertible sofas, one along the aft bulkhead and the other along the starboard side. Privacy curtains separate the fore and aft sleeping areas from the main salon, although an aft-cabin bulkhead with door is optional. The galley offers abundant storage and counter space, enhanced by faux granite countertops and cherry cabinets. Note that air-conditioning and a central vacuum system are standard, as is the flat-screen TV installed above the galley. On deck, a walk-through windshield provides easy access to the foredeck. Cockpit seating includes a U-shaped lounge aft, double helm seat and a portside lounge, and the engine compartment is reached through a deck access panel or the standard power hatch. Twin 420hp MerCruiser gas inboards will cruise the 378 Vista in the low 20s and top out at just over 30 knots.

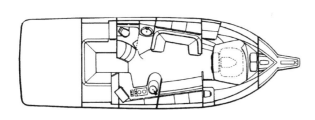

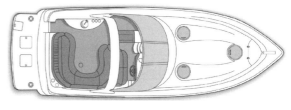

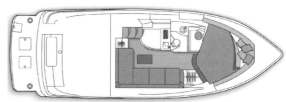

See Page 316 for Pricing Information

73

See Page 316 for Pricing Information

Glastron GS 279 Sport Cruiser

Eastbay 38 Express

Length	27'5"	Fuel	72 gals.
Beam	8'6"	Water	18 gals.
Draft, Down	3'4"	Cockpit Depth	3'0"
Weight	5,375#	Hull Type	Deep-V
Clearance	7'0"	Deadrise Aft	20°
Headroom	6'2"	Production	2002–Current

Length Overall	38'0"	Water	95 gals.
Length WL	34'5"	Clearance	9'3"
Beam	13'2"	Hull Type	Deep-V
Draft	3'4"	Deadrise Aft	18°
Weight	27,201#	Designer	Hunt Assoc.
Fuel	344 gals.	Production	1994–2004

Glastron has long been known for their series of sportboats and runabouts, but their lineup has never included anything as big as the GS 279 Sport Cruiser. With her 8-foot, 6-inch beam, the 279 is one of the larger trailerable midcabin boats on the market. She's also light (only 5,375 pounds) and affordably priced—features sure to appeal to trailer-boat buyers on a budget. Glastron designed this boat with the emphasis on cockpit space in the belief that most weekend boaters prefer to spend their time in the sun rather than below. There's room for nine (according to Glastron) in the single-level cockpit, which includes a doublewide helm/aft-facing seat that converts into a sun pad. A comfortable sun lounge is opposite the helm, and there's a removable bench seat at the transom. Belowdecks, the cabin of the GS 279 is compact but efficiently arranged with a V-berth/dinette forward, a small head with shower, a mini-galley, and a mid-berth aft with sitting headroom. Additional features include a cockpit sink, an integral swim platform, and a walk-through windshield. A good handling boat, a single 315hp Volvo sterndrive engine will cruise the 279 Sport Cruiser at 21 knots (about 35 knots top).

The Eastbay 38 Express is a high-quality cruising yacht for those whose appreciation for traditional design, luxurious accommodations and meticulous craftsmanship outweigh any concern over expense. Built by Grand Banks, the Eastbay rides on a smooth-riding deep-V hull with prop pockets, a relatively wide beam, and Divinycell coring above the waterline. Her traditional teak interior has been available in several single-stateroom configurations over the years, all of which reflect the upscale elegance typical of Eastbay products. Indeed, outstanding fit and finish and tasteful design are evident throughout the interior. Topside, helm visibility from the raised bridgedeck is excellent and there's enough space in the aft cockpit for a couple of light-tackle anglers. Additional features include a teak cockpit sole, good access to the motors (via a hydraulic-assist deck hatch), wide side decks, and a teak swim platform. Cat 300hp diesels will cruise the Eastbay at 20 knots (mid 20s top), and a pair of 375hp Cats will cruise at 23 knots (high 20s top). Note that a hardtop version became available in 2002. Over 130 hulls were delivered during her production run.

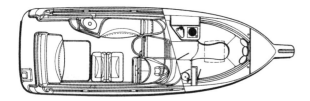

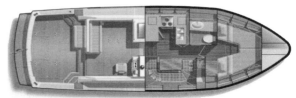

Standard Floorplan

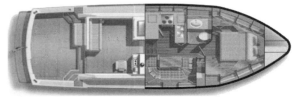

Optional Layout

See Page 316 for Pricing Information

See Page 317 for Pricing Information

Eastbay 43 Express

Eastbay 43 HX

Length	43'0"	Water	110 gals.
Beam	13"2"	Headroom	6'4"
Draft	3'8"	Hull Type	Deep-V
Weight	33,000#	Deadrise Aft	18°
Clearance	16'6"	Designer	Hunt Assoc.
Fuel	450 gals.	Production	2000–04

Length Overall	43'0"	Fuel	450 gals.
Length WL	39'5"	Water	110 gals.
Beam	13'2"	Hull Type	Modified-V
Draft	3'7"	Deadrise Aft	14°
Weight	29,760#	Designer	Grand Banks
Clearance, Mast	14'0"	Production	2004–Current

The 43 Express was yet another addition to the popular Eastbay series of classic Downeast cruisers introduced by Grand Banks back in 1994. These are well-designed yachts with striking lines, excellent finish and impressive performance. The 43 may look traditional on the outside, but she's built on a modern Hunt-designed deep-V hull with moderate beam and prop pockets to reduce draft and shaft angles. The two-stateroom floorplans of the Eastbay 43 Express, with its hand-rubbed teak woodwork and off-white headliner, is an impressive display of genuine nautical elegance. There are over/under bunks in the small guest cabin, and Eastbay offers a choice of either a V-berth or a centerline double bed in the forward stateroom. The helmdeck, three steps up from the cockpit, is huge with plenty of lounge seating and a teak sole. Additional features include wide side decks, a well-arranged engine room, a roomy head compartment, teak swim platform, teak-and-holly cabin sole, and a total of seven opening ports for ventilation. Standard 435hp Cats will cruise the Eastbay 43 Express at 24 knots and deliver a top speed of 27–28 knots. Note that a hardtop model became available in 2002.

A modern display of old-world elegance, the Eastbay 43 HX combines classic Downeast styling with a modern offshore hull capable of extended offshore cruising. The Grand Banks reputation for top-shelf engineering and construction is very much on display in the 43 HX, and even novice boaters will appreciate her beautiful joinery and exemplary fit and finish. From the roomy cockpit, it's three steps up to the semi-enclosed bridgedeck with its wraparound lounge seating and comfortable helm. The standard twin-stateroom interior is arranged with an L-shaped dinette and a single head compartment, while an optional layout has a large single stateroom forward, separate head and shower compartments, and a U-shaped dinette. While there are many 43-footers with more interior volume than the Eastbay, few can match her traditional elegance and none can claim her prestigious Grand Banks heritage. Additional highlights include wide side decks, teak cockpit sole, radar mast, a well-designed engine room, and a teak swim platform. A seriously expensive ride, twin 440hp Yanmar diesels will cruise the Eastbay 43 HX at close to 25 knots (28–29 knots top).

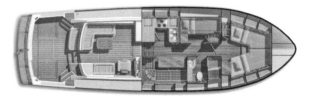

Standard Plan

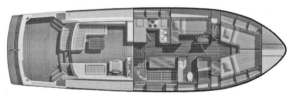

Standard Layout

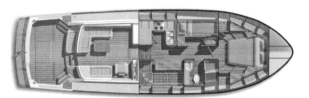

Optional Plan

Alternate Layout

See Page 318 for Pricing Information

See Page 318 for Pricing Information

Eastbay 43 SX

Length Overall	43'0"	Fuel	450 gals.
Length WL	39'5"	Water	110 gals.
Beam	13'2"	Hull Type	Modified-V
Draft	3'7"	Deadrise Aft	14°
Weight	29,760#	Designer	Grand Banks
Clearance, Mast	14'0"	Production	2004–Current

Graceful, luxurious, and expensive, the Eastbay 43 SX combines classic Downeast styling with a modern offshore hull capable of extended offshore cruising. The Grand Banks reputation for top-shelf engineering and construction is very much on display in the 43 SX, and even novice boaters will appreciate her beautiful interior joinery and exemplary fit and finish. Stepping aboard, it's three steps up from the cockpit to the fully enclosed salon with its rich teak woodwork, wraparound windows, and posh accommodations. The standard two-stateroom interior has a large master forward and separate head and shower compartments, while an alternate layout adds a second head compartment aft at the expense of reduced galley and master stateroom dimensions. Helm visibility is excellent in all directions, and storage is very adequate throughout the boat. While there are many 43-footers with more interior volume than the Eastbay, few can match her traditional elegance and none can claim her prestigious Grand Banks heritage. Additional highlights include wide side decks, a teak cockpit sole, and a teak swim platform. Twin 440hp Yanmar diesels will cruise at close to 25 knots (28–29 knots top).

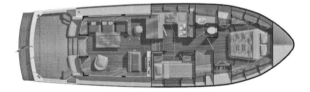

Standard Layout

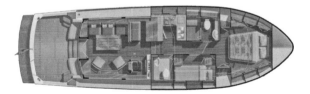

Alternate Layout

See Page 318 for Pricing Information

Eastbay 49 HX

Length Overall	49'0"	Fuel	760 gals.
Length WL	45'0"	Water	175 gals.
Beam	16'0"	Hull Type	Deep-V
Draft	4'4"	Deadrise Aft	18°
Weight	45,000#	Designer	Hunt Assoc.
Clearance	NA	Production	1999–Current

The Eastbay 49 is a top-quality hardtop express whose elegant appearance and meticulous construction represent the ultimate in classic American yachting. A strikingly handsome yacht with a long foredeck and traditional Downeast styling, she's built on a modified deep-V hull with a short keel and prop pockets for reduced draft. If the Eastbay's rich two-stateroom interior—a blend of hand-rubbed teak cabinetry, a teak-and-holly cabin sole, Corian counters and custom hardware—comes up a little short on salon space, her spacious semi-enclosed helm deck (where guests will certainly prefer to congregate) provides comfortable seating for a small crowd. The beautifully finished molded hardtop is an integral part of the design, and access to the engine room is through a hinged section of the cockpits bench seat. Additional features include wide side decks, a power-assisted center windshield panel, transom door and a teak swim platform. A distinctive yacht with a price tag to match, Caterpillar 435hp diesels will cruise the Eastbay 49 at 18 knots (24–25 knots top), and twin 660hp Cat diesels will cruise at 26 knots and reach a top speed of around 30 knots.

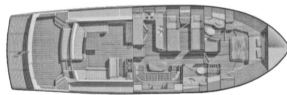

Standard Layout

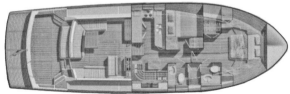

Optional Layout

See Page 318 for Pricing Information

Eastbay 54 SX

Length Overall	53'9"	Fuel	935 gals.
Length WL	49'6"	Water	200 gals.
Beam	16'0"	Hull Type	Deep-V
Draft	4'4"	Deadrise Aft	18°
Weight	56,500#	Designer	Hunt Assoc.
Clearance	16'3"	Production	2003–Current

The Eastbay 54 SX incorporates the exquisite craftsmanship and classic styling for which Grand Banks has always been known. Like most quality yachts, the 54 is expensive and she's built to standards not often found in a production yacht. She rides on a Hunt-designed deep-V hull, and at over 56,000 pounds, the Eastbay is no lightweight. Aside from her handsome lines, perhaps the most striking feature of the Eastbay 54 is her elegant raised salon with its varnished teak cabinetry, gleaming teak-and-holly sole, and huge wrap-around windows. Visibility from the helm is excellent in all directions, and a navigation station opposite the helm is large enough for a full-size chart. The standard galley-down, two-stateroom floorplan of the 54 is notable for its spacious staterooms and huge galley. An optional three-stateroom floorplan relocates the galley in the salon. An office area with desk and washer/dryer combo is standard in either layout. On deck, the aft cockpit features built-in seating, teak decking, and lift-up engine room access. A superb rough-water performer, 800hp Cats will cruise the Eastbay 54 in the low 20s and reach nearly 30 knots wide open.

Hatteras 39 Sport Express

Length	39'0"	Clearance	8'9"
Beam	13'7"	Headroom	6'5"
Draft	4'8"	Hull Type	Modified-V
Weight	30,500#	Deadrise Aft	9°
Fuel	458 gals.	Designer	Hatteras
Water	120 gals.	Production	1995–98

Tiara started the trend toward big, dual-purpose (fish or cruise) express boats with the introduction in 1991 of their 4300 Open. Viking and Bertram soon came out with 43-footers, and Hatteras followed with the 39 Sport Express in 1995. She is unquestionably a handsome boat—among the best in her class when it comes to styling. (The cruising version, with curved bridgedeck seating and a sport arch, is pictured above.) She's built on the same deep-draft hull used for the Hatteras 39 Convertible with moderate beam, a flared bow and cored hullsides. The Sport Express is a big boat on the outside with a party-size bridgedeck and a cockpit large enough to handle a full-size chair. Originally offered with curved seating opposite the helm, later models have more traditional L-shaped lounge seating. Cockpit features include an in-deck fish box, molded tackle center, transom door, and direct access to the engine room. Inside, the single-stateroom floorplan will sleep four to six and comes complete with a stall shower in the head. Twin 435hp Cats will cruise at 23 knots (about 27 knots top), and 465hp Detroit 6-71s will provide a 25-knot cruising speed (28–29 knots wide open).

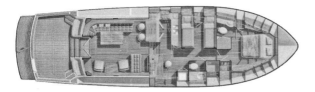

Standard Two-Stateroom Plan

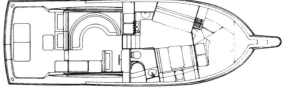

Standard Layout, L-shaped Seating

Optional Three-Stateroom Plan

Curved Bridge Seating

See Page 318 for Pricing Information

See Page 319 for Pricing Information

Hatteras 43 Sport Express

Length	43'2"	Water	154 gals.
Beam	14'3"	Headroom	6'6"
Draft	4'5"	Hull Type	Modified-V
Weight	38,000#	Deadrise Aft	9°
Clearance	9'8"	Designer	Jack Hargrave
Fuel	530 gals.	Production	1996–98

The Hatteras 43 Sport Express was designed to be an open cruiser that anglers would love. She was one of the largest open express boats in existence during the late 1990s and, because she was a Hatteras, one of the most expensive. Notably, she's built on the same hull used in the production of the popular Hatteras 43 Convertible (1991–98), a proven offshore design with moderate beam and an unusually deep keel. The huge bi-level cockpit of the 43 Sport Express came with a complete rigging station, lift-out fish boxes, livewell, transom door, and washdowns. Access to the engine room is beneath the aft-facing bench seat in the cockpit that rises for easy walk-through entry. Two interior layouts were offered with the standard plan including berths for four and a separate stall shower in the head. (An optional cabin layout with an aft head and smaller galley has a convertible settee and dinette that raised the sleeping capacity to six.) Additional features include light oak interior woodwork, a low-profile radar arch, side-dumping exhausts, and a bow pulpit. A good-running boat, twin 535hp 6-92 Detroit diesels will cruise the 43 Sport Express at a fast 27 knots and deliver a top speed of 30+ knots.

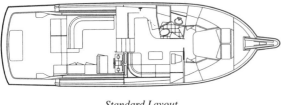

Standard Layout

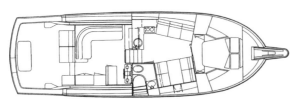

Optional Arrangement

See Page 319 for Pricing Information

Hinckley 36 Picnic Boat

Length Overall	36'5"	Water	30 gals.
Length WL	34'0"	Clearance	11'4"
Beam	10'0"	Hull	Modified-V
Draft	1'6"	Deadrise Aft	15°
Weight	11,500#	Designer	Bruce King
Fuel	166 gals.	Production	1995–Current

A major sales success since her introduction in 1994, the Hinckley 36 Picnic Boat is a waterjet-driven 36-foot weekender with an absolutely elegant profile and stunning performance. The innovative product of one of the world's premier builders, the Picnic Boat's fully cored, vacuum-bagged hull weighs in at an extremely light 11,500 pounds. With the jet-drive, she draws only 18 inches and can be beached or operated in very shallow water. The long open cockpit of the Picnic Boat is an excellent entertainment platform (the centerline engine box can be used as a seat or table), and the semi-enclosed helm allows her to be comfortably used in poor weather conditions. Belowdecks, the varnished mahogany interior contains a V-berth, compact galley, and a big head compartment—upscale (if basic) accommodations for a cruising couple. On the downside, the cabin headroom is less than 6 feet. Note that an optional extended pilot-house version with additional seating became available in 2001. A good performer with a single Yanmar 350hp diesel jet drive, the Picnic Boat will cruise at 20 knots (26–27 knots top). Late models with a 440hp Yanmar diesel will top out at close to 30 knots. Over 300 have been built to date.

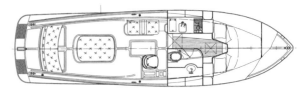

See Page 323 for Pricing Information

Hinckley Talaria 40

Length Overall	40'1"	Fuel	340 gals.
Length WL	37'1"	Water	80 gals.
Beam	12'5"	Hull Type	Modified-V
Draft	2'2"	Deadrise Aft	16°
Weight	26,000#	Designer	Bruce King
Clearance	8'7"	Production	2002–Current

A beautifully styled yacht whose flawless finish is a Hinckley trademark, the Talaria 40 bears a strong resemblance to her hugely successful predecessor, the Hinckley 36 Picnic Boat. Both are essentially day boats with large cockpits and relatively small interiors, and both come with Hinckley's patented JetStick steering and control system incorporating waterjet propulsion and a bow thruster. Narrow of beam, the fully cored, shallow-draft hull of the Talaria 40 is notable for its high-tech composite construction and generous tumblehome at the transom. The pilothouse is arranged with port and starboard helm seats as well as facing L-shaped settees aft of the helm. Additional seating is found in the cockpit, beyond the shelter of the hardtop, and both the cockpit and pilothouse are on a single level. The two aft-facing cockpit settees can be raised electrically for engine access. While the Talaria's interior is small for a 40-footer, the accommodations are nonetheless elegant and certainly adequate for a weekend cruise. An exhilarating boat to drive, the price of ownership is high. Twin 440hp Yanmar diesels matched to Hamilton waterjets will cruise the Talaria 40 at 28 knots and reach a top speed of 32–33 knots.

Hinckley Talaria 42

Length Overall	41'9"	Water	110 gals.
Length WL	38'7"	Clearance	12'6"
Beam	13'8"	Hull	Semi-Disp.
Draft	4'4"	Deadrise Aft	5°
Weight	22,000#	Designer	Spencer Lincoln
Fuel	400 gals.	Production	1990–98

The Hinckley Talaria 42 is an elegant Downeast cruiser for those able to afford the luxury of owning a finely crafted yacht from one of America's preeminent boatbuilders. (Note that she was introduced in 1990 as a 39-footer—two were built, basically the same as the 42 but with a smaller cockpit.) Constructed on a Kevlar-strengthened, semi-displacement hull with a long, prop-protecting keel, the superior craftsmanship of the Talaria is evident in every corner of the boat. Two floorplans were offered: a single-stateroom layout with a spacious salon and the galley down, and a two-stateroom arrangement with the galley in the salon. A lower helm is standard, and the beautiful teak interior woodwork is flawless. (Note that the cabin sole "floats" on rubber bushings to reduce vibration.) Additional features include wide side decks, an underwater exhaust system, teak cockpit sole, radar mast and a big cockpit. Among several engine options, a single 435hp Cat (or 520hp MAN) diesel will cruise at 16–17 knots and reach a top speed of around 22 knots. Of the 17 built, only one Talaria 42 was delivered with twin engines.

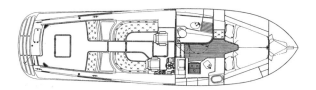

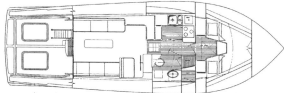

Single-Stateroom Floorplan

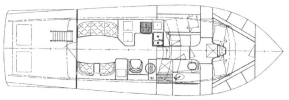

Two-Stateroom Layout

See Page 323 for Pricing Information

See Page 323 for Pricing Information

Hinckley Talaria 44 Express

Length Overall . . . . 44'10"	Water . . . . 100 gals.
Length WL . . . . 41'0"	Max Headroom . . . . 6'6"
Beam . . . . 13'6"	Hull . . . . Modified-V
Draft . . . . 2'3"	Deadrise Aft . . . . 16.5°
Weight . . . . 29,000#	Designer . . . . Bruce King
Fuel . . . . 500 gals.	Production 1999–Current

An enlarged version of Hinckley's successful 36 Picnic Boat, the Talaria 44 is an advanced, twin-waterjet cruising yacht of the highest order. This is a beautifully crafted (and very expensive) boat, easily handled with an excellent ride and remarkable maneuverability. Built on an efficient modified-V hull with moderate beam, her high-tech construction features a Kevlar outer skin, a carbon-fiber inner skin and balsa coring in the hullsides and bottom. The heart of the Talaria is her spacious, semi-enclosed deckhouse with its plush settees, dinette table, stylish helm and visually stunning joinerwork. (The settees can be raised on hydraulic rams for access to the engines.) Below deck, the Talaria can be ordered with one or two staterooms. Neither floorplan can be called roomy, but the legendary Hinckley reputation for craftsmanship is on display in every corner. Notable features include a grain-matched teak interior, aft-facing cockpit seating, wide side decks (but no bow rails), shallow draft, and a JetStick control system for easy docking. Twin 420hp Yanmar diesels, matched to Hamilton waterjets, will cruise the Talaria 44 at 25 knots and reach a top speed of 30+ knots.

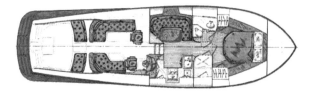

Single-Stateroom Floorplan

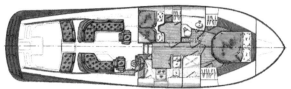

Two-Stateroom Layout

See Page 323 for Pricing Information

Hunt 29 Surfhunter

Length . . . . 29'6"	Water . . . . 31 gals.
Beam . . . . 10'6"	Headroom . . . . 5'8"
Draft . . . . 3'0"	Hull Type . . . . Deep-V
Weight . . . . 7,500#	Deadrise Aft . . . . 22°
Clearance . . . . 5'9"	Designer . . . . Hunt & Assoc.
Fuel . . . . 150 gals.	Production 2004–Current

Traditional styling and outstanding open-water performance are the hallmarks of the Hunt 29 Surfhunter, a well-designed express whose upscale price hints at her quality construction. The Surfhunter is essentially a day boat; her spacious cockpit results in a fairly compact interior more suitable for an occasional overnight stays than extended cruising. Built on a deep-V hull with cored hullsides and a solid fiberglass bottom, the Surfhunter's single-level cockpit features an L-lounge, removable transom seating, and an aft-facing bench seat atop the engine box. Going forward is easy thanks to wide side decks, good nonskid, and high rails. The interior of the Surfhunter includes a good-sized galley and head in addition to a standard V-berth and a classy teak-and-holly sole. While the overall finish is very good, the cabin headroom is a bit low for most. Back in the cockpit, the engine cover lifts to reveal a single Volvo 310hp diesel with jackshaft, a rod connecting the engine to the drive. This excellent propulsion system allows the engine weight to be located forward, thus optimizing the boat's center of gravity for a more comfortable ride. With a cruising speed in the mid 20s (30 knots top), the 29 Surfhunter excels in rough-water conditions.

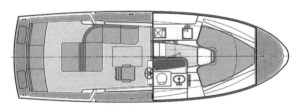

See Page 323 for Pricing Information

Hunt 33 Express

Length . . . . 32'9"	Water . . . . 30 gals.
Beam . . . . 10'10"	Headroom . . . . 6'1"
Draft . . . . 3'0"	Hull Type . . . . Deep-V
Weight . . . . 10,000#	Deadrise Aft . . . . 20°
Clearance . . . . 15'0"	Designer . . . . Hunt & Assoc.
Fuel . . . . 125 gals.	Production 1999–2004

The Hunt 33 is a semicustom diesel cruiser with traditional Downeast styling, elegant appointments, and modern, state-of-the-art construction. Beauty is of course a matter of personal taste, but by any standard the Hunt is a singularly graceful and handsome yacht. Built on a fully cored deep-V hull with moderate beam and a propeller tunnel to reduce draft, the Hunt 33 is available in express, hardtop express, and hardtop sedan (pictured above) versions. The cabin, with its varnished mahogany trim and teak-and-holly sole, is reminiscent of a high-quality sailboat. Headroom is limited, but the accommodations are beautifully finished and the attention to detail is obvious. For access to the engine, the entire bridgedeck rises on hydraulic rams. Additional features include a standard bow thruster, wide side decks, an underwater exhaust system, four opening ports, and a roomy cockpit. Designed for the cruising couple, a 370hp Cummins diesel will cruise the Hunt 33 at an economical 24 knots and reach a top speed of around 30 knots—impressive numbers for a 33-footer with just a single engine. An optional 440hp Yanmar diesel will run a couple of knots faster.

Hunt 36 Harrier

Length . . . . 36'6"	Water . . . . 50 gals.
Beam . . . . 11'0"	Waste . . . . 20 gals.
Draft . . . . 3'0"	Hull Type . . . . Deep-V
Weight . . . . 13,500#	Deadrise Aft . . . . 22°
Clearance . . . . 8'0"	Designer . . . . Hunt & Assoc.
Fuel . . . . 250 gals.	Production 2003–Current

The Hunt 36 Harrier is an impressive blend of classic express-boat styling, superb build quality, and terrific open-water performance. There's a lot to like about this boat, and while she's hardly inexpensive, most would agree that the Harrier ranks among the leaders in the high-end, midsize express market. With her lightweight construction (the hull is fully cored), slender 11-foot beam, and deep-V bottom, the Harrier is designed to take on some seriously rough water. Below, the open cabin layout is simple, yet beautifully appointed, with the galley to port at the base of the companionway steps, an island berth forward, and an enclosed head to starboard. Satin-finished cherry cabinetry, Corian counters, and a rich teak-and-ash floor give the Harrier's interior an upscale and very elegant flavor. Topside, the L-shaped settee on the helmdeck can be extended by lowering the forward passenger seat, and the cockpit can be left open for fishing or set up with extra seating for cruising. For access to the engines, the entire deck rises on a pair of hydraulic rams. A quick performer, the Harrier will cruise at 30 knots with a pair of 370hp Yanmar diesels and reach a top speed of about 35 knots.

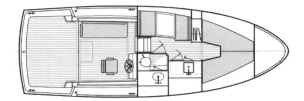

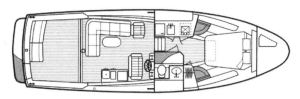

Larson 270 Cabrio

Length w/Pulpit . . . . 26'1"	Water . . . . 18 gals.
Beam . . . . 9'0"	Waste . . . . 18 gals.
Draft . . . . 2'9"	Hull Type . . . . Modified-V
Weight . . . . 6,000#	Deadrise Aft . . . . 18°
Clearance w/Arch . . . . 9'4"	Designer . . . . H. Schoell
Fuel . . . . 85 gals.	Production 1996–2001

Called the 260 Cabrio in 1996, the Larson 270 is a roomy midcabin cruiser whose stepped hull design is worth noting. Unlike most trailerable cruisers with their conventional modified-V hulls, the 270 rides on what Larson calls a Duo DeltaConic hull. Rather than a smooth bottom, the Cabrio has a hull "step" halfway back from the bow, which, by introducing air under the hull, is said to reduce drag and boost the top speed. Like most family cruisers of her type, the length of the Cabrio is about evenly divided between the cabin and cockpit. Below, a comfortable settee wraps around the cabin and doubles as a seat for the convertible dinette. Headroom is just over 6 feet, and a full galley and head with vanity and shower were standard. The 270's bi-level cockpit features a double helm seat, a single companion seat, and an L-shaped aft lounge. Lacking side decks, a walk-through windshield provides access to the bow. A transom door and cockpit shower were standard. Twin 280hp MerCruiser sterndrives will cruise the Larson 270 Cabrio at 20 knots (about 30+ knots top). With just 85 gallons of fuel, the cruising range is a bit limited for a boat of this size.

Larson 270 Mirado; 270 Cabrio

Length . . . . 27'3"	Fuel . . . . 100 gals.
Beam . . . . 9'0"	Water . . . . 20 gals.
Draft . . . . 2'10"	Hull Type . . . . Modified-V
Weight . . . . 7,800#	Deadrise Aft . . . . 18°
Clearance . . . . 9'0"	Designer . . . . H. Schoell
Cockpit . . . . NA	Production 1989–93

This boat has had several names over the years. Introduced in 1989 as the Milano 27, during 1990–91 she was called the 270 Mirado, and for 1992–93 she was known as the 270 Cabrio. A popular model for Larson, she's a straightforward express cruiser with modern sportboat lines and a well-arranged interior. Note the fully integrated swim platform, oval ports, and the sleek Euro-style curved windshield. A sun pad is recessed into the foredeck, and the cockpit—with its curved lounge seating and standard wet bar—offers excellent visibility from the raised helm. Below, the midcabin interior includes a surprisingly large galley with generous storage, a standup head compartment, dinette, and double berths (with privacy curtains) fore and aft. The roomy, bi-level cockpit is arranged with a double helm seat, a built-in wet bar to port, and lounge seating on either side of the centerline transom door. Among several engine options offered over the years, a single 300hp MerCruiser or Volvo sterndrive will cruise the 270 Cabrio at 18–20 knots, and twin 230hp MerCruisers will cruise in the mid 20s. Note the limited fuel capacity.

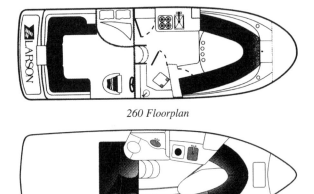

260 Floorplan

270 Floorplan

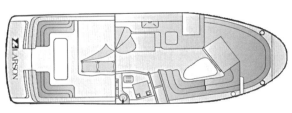

See Page 328 for Pricing Information   82   See Page 328 for Pricing Information

Larson 274 Cabrio

Larson 280/290 Cabrio

Length Overall	28'0"
Beam	8'6"
Draft, Up	2'0"
Draft, Down	2'10"
Weight	6,000#
Clearance, Arch	9'0"
Headroom	6'2"
Fuel	85 gals.
Water	28 gals.
Hull Type	Modified-V
Deadrise Aft	18°
Production	2002–Current

Length w/Pulpit	28'11"
Beam	10'0"
Draft	2'10"
Weight	7,500#
Clearance, Arch	9'4"
Fuel	125 gals.
Water	33 gals.
Waste	33 gals.
Hull Type	Modified-V
Deadrise Aft	18°
Designer	H. Schoell
Production	1994–2001

Introduced in 2002, the Larson 274 Cabrio is one of the biggest trailerable midcabin cruisers on the market. She differs from other boats of her type in that she rides on a notched hull that is said to improve both efficiency and performance. The Cabrio's compact interior offers 6 feet, 2 inches of headroom along with berths for four, full galley, and a head with shower. The galley is highlighted with a faux granite counter, a single-burner electric stove, and under-counter refrigerator. The cabinets are trimmed in bright maple, and the galley sole is covered with an easy-to-clean woodgrain composite. There's a big double in the midcabin where a curtain provides privacy from the main cabin. Topside, the cockpit is arranged with a double helm seat forward, a wet bar, and facing seats aft. Note that the Cabrio's 2-foot swim platform offers plenty of room for carrying an inflatable tender. Additional features include a tilt wheel, radar arch, transom door, CD player, and walk-through windshield. A good performer with a single 250hp Volvo Duoprop sterndrive engine, the 274 Cabrio will cruise in the mid 20s and top out at over 30 knots.

A good-looking boat, the Larson 290 Cabrio (called the 280 Cabrio in 1994–96) is well-appointed express whose roomy accommodations and affordable price struck a good balance between comfort and value. She was built on what Larson calls a Duo DeltaConic hull, which incorporates a notched bottom design said to improve both lift and top-end performance. Below, the Cabrio sleeps six in three double berths. The list of standard equipment included an electric refrigerator, alcohol/electric stove, and an enclosed head with vanity and shower. With a wide 10-foot beam, there's a surprising amount of room below and Formica cabinetry and oak trim present an upscale impression. Above deck, the cockpit is arranged with a removable L-shaped lounge and a double-wide, back-to-back seat at the helm. Additional features include a tilt wheel, reasonably wide side decks, a power-assist engine hatch, and a walk-through transom. Several sterndrive power options were available. Among them, a single 310hp MerCruiser will reach a top speed in excess of 35 knots, and twin 250hp Mercs will top out at 40+ knots.

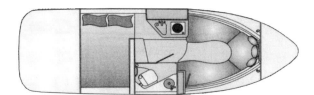

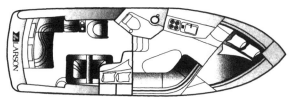

Larson 300/310 Cabrio

Larson 310 Cabrio

Length w/Pulpit	32'6"	Fuel	170 gals.
Hull Length	29'11"	Water	30 gals.
Beam	10'6"	Hull Type	Modified-V
Draft	2'10"	Deadrise Aft	14°
Weight	9,500#	Designer	H. Schoell
Clearance	7'4"	Production	1991–98

Length	31'0"	Headroom	6'3"
Beam	10'6"	Fuel	160 gals.
Draft, Up	1'8"	Water	46 gals.
Draft, Down	2'10"	Hull Type	Modified-V
Weight	10,400#	Deadrise Aft	18°
Clearance, Arch	9'4"	Production	2003–Current

The affordably priced Larson 310 Cabrio (called the 300 Cabrio in 1991–94) was the largest model in the Larson fleet for much of the 1990s. Basically, the Cabrio is a redesign of an earlier Larson model—the Contempra DC-300 (1988–90)—with a streamlined profile and an upgraded cabin layout. Built on a stable DeltaConic hull with a relatively wide beam, the original midcabin interior of the Cabrio has a large island berth area in the bow, two hanging lockers, a double berth aft, and a convertible dinette that might sleep a single (small) adult. In 1994, an all-new floorplan with an angled berth forward opened up the salon considerably, allowing space for a full-size dinette and a slightly enlarged galley. On deck, the Cabrio's cockpit is arranged with a double-wide (reversible) helm seat, a covered wet bar (very slick), and a gas-assist engine access hatch in the sole. A bow pulpit, windshield vents, and a cockpit shower were standard. Among several engine options, twin 205hp 5.0-liter MerCruiser sterndrives will cruise the Larson 310 Cabrio at about 20 knots (about 30+ knots top), and a pair of 235hp 5.7-liter Mercs will deliver a top speed in the high 30s.

Larson's reputation for delivering a lot of boat for the money is on full display in the 310 Cabrio, a roomy midcabin cruiser whose moderate price includes an impressive inventory of standard equipment. Built on a solid fiberglass hull with a notched bottom, the Cabrio's wide-open interior is dominated by a curved lounge that extends from the head compartment all the way around to the galley. A dinette table is to port, and the midcabin is tucked behind the companionway steps, which leaves it open to the salon. Privacy curtains separate the sleeping areas from the main cabin, and the head contains a separate stall shower—a luxury on any 30-foot boat. On deck, the cockpit has a U-shaped settee aft as well as a wet bar, and the driver's side of the double helm seat has a drop-down bolster for standup driving. A large transom locker stores fenders and docklines, etc. There are no side decks on the Cabrio, so a walk-through windshield—with no handrail—provides access to the foredeck. A tilt wheel, radar arch, and transom shower are standard. Among several sterndrive options, twin 280hp Volvo gas engines will cruise in the low 30s and reach a top speed of 40+ knots.

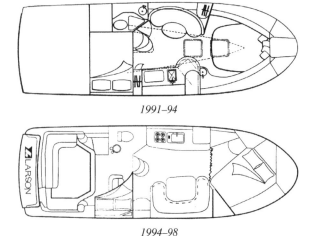

1991–94

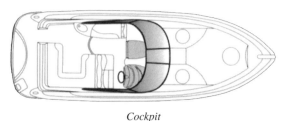

Cockpit

1994–98

Cabin

See Page 328 for Pricing Information

See Page 328 for Pricing Information

Larson 330 Cabrio

Length	32'0"	Headroom	6'3"
Beam	11'6"	Fuel	240 gals.
Draft, Up	2'0"	Water	46 gals.
Draft, Down	2'10"	Hull Type	Modified-V
Weight	11,400#	Deadrise Aft	14°
Clearance, Arch	9'4"	Production	1999–Current

Neither high-tech nor expensive, the Larson 330 Cabrio is an economy-class cruiser with generous cabin accommodations, plenty of storage, and a well-arranged cockpit. Like all recent Cabrio models, the 330 rides on a stepped hull, a bottom design said to reduce drag and improve performance by breaking the water's grip on the hull. The interior of the 330 will sleep six with an angled double berth forward, a large midcabin berth, and a convertible dinette. The galley contains plenty of storage cabinets and counter space, and a roomy head compartment has overhead storage and a large vanity, but no shower stall. Topside, a double helm seat, wet bar, and U-shaped settee are standard in the cockpit. Lacking side decks, a windshield walk-through provides access to the bow. A radar arch and transom door are also standard, and a filler turns the cockpit into a large sun pad. Note that an extended swim platform has been a popular option. On the downside, the engine compartment is a tight fit. A fast ride with twin 300hp MerCruiser sterndrives, the 330 Cabrio will cruise in the mid 20s and reach a top speed of around 40 knots.

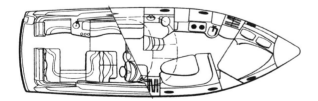

Larson 370 Cabrio

Length	36'11"	Fuel	266 gals.
Beam	13'0"	Water	35 gals.
Draft, Up	2'6"	Waste	35 gals.
Draft, Down	3'4"	Hull Type	Deep-V
Weight	16,800#	Deadrise Aft	22°
Clearance, Arch	9'9"	Production	2004–Current

Larson's largest boat ever, the 370 Cabrio is one of those boats that can be characterized as delivering good value for the money. There's nothing high-tech or cutting-edge about this boat—hull construction is solid fiberglass; fit and finish is adequate considering the price; and the styling is on a par with most the competition. The Cabrio's base price, however, is refreshingly attractive and she comes with enough standard equipment to make her a true turnkey boat. Starting with a well-designed cockpit and including a spacious interior, the Cabrio offers most of the amenities of her higher-priced counterparts with little sacrifice in quality. Her midcabin floorplan is typical of boats her size with berths for six, a spacious galley, and a double-entry head compartment. A solid door separates the master stateroom from the salon, and attractive cherrywood laminates are applied liberally throughout the interior. A wet bar is standard in the cockpit along with wraparound aft seating, carry-on cooler, and a removable cocktail table. Also standard are a genset, radar arch, microwave, VacuFlush toilet, windlass, and air conditioning. Twin 375hp Volvo I/Os will cruise at 25 knots (about 30 knots wide open).

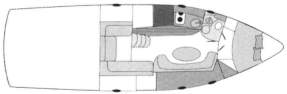

See Page 328 for Pricing Information

85

See Page 328 for Pricing Information

Legacy 28 Express

Length	28'0"	Waste	25 gals.
Beam	9'6"	Headroom	6'0"
Draft	2'2"	Hull Type	Modified-V
Weight	6,500	Deadrise Aft	5°
Fuel	120 gals.	Designer	Bill Langan
Water	30 gals.	Production	1999–Current

The Legacy 28 Express joins the ranks of a handful of premium small cruisers whose traditional styling and top-quality construction set them well apart from the norm. Built on a conventional hard-chine hull with moderate beam, a short keel and a fairly flat stern, the Legacy provides a remarkably smooth ride in a variety of sea conditions. Her upscale interior comes with a V-berth forward, a complete galley, four large opening ports, an enclosed head with shower and an abundance of grain-matched cherry woodwork. Visibility from the helm is excellent and wide side decks make it easy to reach the bow, however the inboard-facing bench seats (as opposed to L-shaped seating) on the bridgedeck are a compromise. Additional features include a full-width transom seat, a quiet underwater exhaust system, and a well-arranged helm console. On the downside, there's no transom door, and the ride can be a little harsh when the seas pick up. Not inexpensive, a single 250hp Yanmar diesel will cruise the Legacy 28 Express in the low 20s (about 25 knots top), while a 300hp Yanmar will cruise at 25 knots and top out at close to 30 knots.

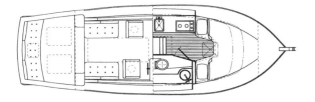

Legacy 34 Express

Length	34'0"	Waste	35 gals.
Beam	12'5"	Headroom	6'5"
Draft	3'6"	Hull Type	Modified-V
Weight	16,500	Deadrise Aft	17°
Fuel	251 gals.	Designer	Mark Ellis
Water	94 gals.	Production	1996–Current

A scaled-down version of the Legacy 40, the Legacy 34 is a high-quality cruiser from Freedom Yachts, builder of Freedom sailboats. She's a very handsome small yacht, which is no big surprise considering that her designer, Mark Ellis, has drawn many Downeast-style yachts over the years, all sharing a classic New England look. The 34 is built on a fully cored hull with a sharp entry and a deep skeg for directional stability and—in the single-screw version—prop and rudder protection. The interior of the Legacy 34 will easily suit the needs of the cruising couple, and the level of fit and finish is superb. Extra-large cabin windows provide all-around visibility, and the varnished mahogany woodwork and teak-and-holly sole add much to the traditional feel of the boat. Notable features include a deck door at the helm, wide side decks, a separate stall shower in the head, and a gas-assist engine room hatch. With a single 440hp Cummins diesel the Legacy will cruise at a comfortable 16–18 knots (20-plus knots top) with a fuel burn of better than 1 nautical mile per gallon. Twin-diesel options ranging from 315 to 440 hp will cruise in the mid-to-high 20s.

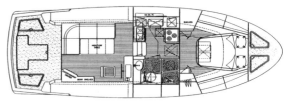

Express Floorplan

Sedan Floorplan

See Page 328 for Pricing Information

See Page 328 for Pricing Information

Luhrs 30 Alura

Length Overall	30'0"	Fuel	196 gals.
Length WL	28'0"	Water	38 gals.
Beam	10'3"	Cockpit	110 sq. ft.
Draft	2'11"	Hull Type	Semi-Disp.
Weight	7,800#	Deadrise Aft	NA
Clearance	NA	Production	1987–90

With her deep cockpit and distinctive Downeast profile, the Alura 30 is a versatile, full-keel fishing boat suitable for diving, day-tripping or weekend cruising. The cockpit measures a spacious 110 square feet in size, and the scooped area at the transom allows for easy access to the water. With her high freeboard and good nonskid, the cockpit is a secure place for kids. A pair of adjustable chairs are forward, and molded-in fish boxes and a baitwell were standard. Helm visibility is very good, and the windshield can be opened for ventilation—a real plus in hot weather. The wide side decks are notable. With 6 feet, 4 inches of headroom, the interior of the Alura 30 is easily capable of comfortable weekend cruises. There are berths for four (including two swing-up bunks), an enclosed head with shower, and a full galley with sink, pressure hot and cold water, alcohol stove and icebox. Additional features include an anchor locker, four opening ports, and a swim platform. Note that the keel was redesigned in 1988 to reduce vibration problems. A single 270hp gas inboard provides an efficient cruising speed of 14–15 knots and a top speed of around 22 knots.

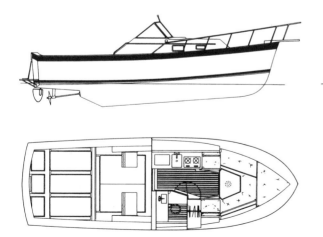

Luhrs 35 Alura

Length	35'5"	Water	55 gals.
Beam	12'2"	Headroom	6'2"
Draft	2'11"	Hull Type	Modified-V
Weight	12,800#	Deadrise Aft	15°
Clearance	NA	Designer	Luhrs
Fuel	260 gals.	Production	1988–89

Enjoying only a brief two-year production run, the Alura 35 is an inexpensive open sportfishing boat with a roomy cockpit and comfortable cruising accommodations. She rides on a conventional modified-V hull with a wide beam and a shallow keel for increased directional stability. In her day, the Alura was considered a lot of boat for the money. There's lots of fishing room in her spacious cockpit, and the midcabin interior sleeps four with a fair degree of privacy. The galley is complete with an electric/alcohol stove, pressure hot and cold water, Corian counters and refrigerator, and the enclosed head includes a sink and shower. A teak-and-holly cabin sole adds a touch of luxury, and cabin headroom is about 6 feet, 4 inches. The 35's large bi-level cockpit is deep and well-suited to the demands of anglers as well as weekend cruisers. A small tackle center is behind the helm seat, a swim platform was standard, and foredeck access is easy thanks to the wide side decks. On the downside, there's no transom door, and fit and finish is less than impressive. Twin 270hp Crusader gas engines will cruise the Alura 35 at around 17 knots with a top speed of 25–26 knots.

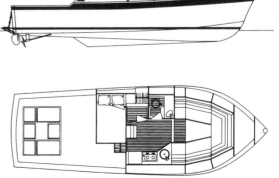

Magnum 40 Sport

Length . . . . 40'0"	Water. . . . . 75 gals.
Beam . . . . 12'3"	Headroom . . . . 6'3"
Draft. . . . . 3'4"	Hull Type . . . . Deep-V
Weight. . . . . 25,500#	Deadrise Aft . . . . 24°
Clearance, Arch. . . . . 8'6"	Designer. . . . . Magnum
Fuel . . . . 400 gals.	Production 1982–96

When the Magnum 40 Sport came out back in 1982 there were few boats like her on the American market. Long and sleek and built to very high production standards, the Sport was originally aimed more to the tastes of the sophisticated European buyer than to the domestic market. She quickly acquired an American following, however, in spite of her upscale price. Indeed, the fact that she enjoyed such a long production run says much about her enduring popularity. To many, the Magnum 40 represented a marriage of race-boat style and 1980s-style luxury. A semicustom boat (about 60 were built), several single- and twin-stateroom floorplans were available over the years with a broad selection of designer fabrics and furnishings. The same is true of the cockpit: the 40 could be configured as a cruising boat with lounge seating and a full-width sun pad, or as a fisherman with a deep uncluttered cockpit. Among a great many engine options (including gas or diesel, inboards or high-performance Arneson outdrives), twin 425hp Cat inboard diesels will cruise the Magnum 40 Sport at 28–30 knots with a top speed of around 35 knots.

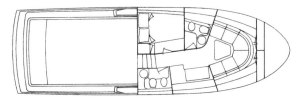

Midships Stateroom

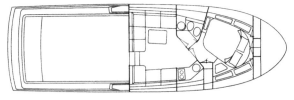

Bow Stateroom

See Page 330 for Pricing Information

Magnum 53 Sport

Length . . . . 52'11"	Water. . . . . 149 gals.
Beam . . . . 15'9"	Headroom . . . . 6'4"
Draft. . . . . 3'0"	Hull Type . . . . Deep-V
Weight. . . . . 54,500#	Deadrise Aft . . . . 24°
Clearance, Arch. . . . . 9'6"	Designer. . . . . Magnum
Fuel . . . . 1,000 gals.	Production 1978–96

Introduced in 1978, the Magnum 53 Sport's sleek Mediterranean styling, exciting performance, and lavish accommodations set the standards for big express yachts long before they became popular in the American market. The 53 Sport is built on a rugged deep-V hull of solid fiberglass or—optionally—lighter, more expensive, Kevlar-reinforced construction. Because she was a semi-production yacht, the Magnum 53 could be highly personalized and each is a little different. A variety of floorplans were available over the years, most with two staterooms, and nearly all were delivered with posh Euro-style furnishings. Thanks to her relatively broad beam, the cockpit of the Magnum 53 is huge with room for a massive sun pad as well as such amenities as a wet bar, lounge seating, and a radar arch. The entire aft section of the cockpit lifts for excellent access to the engine room. Among many engine options, a pair of 1,080hp 12V92 Detroits matched with Arneson surface drives will cruise the Magnum 53 Sport at 35–38 knots (40+ knots top), and twin 1,200 Cats will cruise at 37–40 knots and reach about 45 knots wide open. Note that about 50 of these yachts were built, most of which were delivered to European buyers.

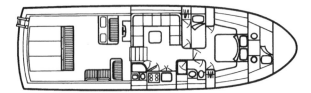

See Page 330 for Pricing Information

Magnum 63 Sport

Length . . . . 63'0"	Fuel . . . . 1,200 gals.
Beam . . . . 17'0"	Water . . . . 250 gals.
Draft, Std. Drives . . . . 6'0"	Hull Type . . . . Deep-V
Draft, Surface Drives . . . . 3'0"	Deadrise Aft . . . . 24°
Weight . . . . 75,000#	Designer . . . . Magnum
Clearance . . . . NA	Production 1984–98

With her imposing appearance and high-performance capabilities, the Magnum 63 commands attention wherever she goes. The styling is by Pininfarina—the design team behind Ferrari—and her rugged deep-V hull is built entirely of hand-laminated Kevlar for strength and lightness. Not inexpensive, the Magnum 63 is a semi-custom yacht and each was personalized to some extent to meet customer desires. Several two-stateroom floorplans (some with crew quarters forward) were offered during her production run, and a wide 17-foot beam provides plenty of interior volume in the salon. The cockpit of the 63 Sport is huge and may be configured with massive amounts of lounge seating as well as a six-person sun pad aft. Notable features include a beautifully crafted Italian dash, a sleek wraparound windshield, reverse arch, excellent engine access, and abundant storage. Standard 1,400hp 16V92 Detroits with Arneson surface drives (recommended) will cruise the Magnum 63 at 38–40 knots (close to 45 knots top), and optional 1,800hp MTUs are capable of reaching a top speed in the neighborhood of 55 knots.

Mainship 30 Pilot

Length w/Pulpit . . . . 33'1"	Weight, Sedan . . . . 11,000#
Hull Length . . . . 30'0"	Headroom . . . . 6'3"
Beam . . . . 10'3"	Fuel . . . . 175 gals.
Draft, Original Hull . . . . 2'11"	Water . . . . 40 gals.
Draft, Series II . . . . 2'3"	Hull Type . . . . Semi-Disp.
Weight, Express . . . . 10,000#	Production 1998–Current

A very popular boat, the Mainship 30 Pilot is a Downeast-style cruiser whose practical layout and affordable price have catapulted this model into the ranks of classic designs. Built on a solid fiberglass, semi-displacement hull with a prop-protecting skeg, the Pilot is suited to a variety of uses. A large cockpit makes her a competent fish or dive platform, and her economical operation and comfortable accommodations appeal to weekend cruisers. Don't look for a lot of glitz in the Pilot—this is a basic boat with modest amenities and average workmanship. The cabin was originally arranged with a V-berth/dinette forward, a good-sized head, and a teak-and-holly cabin sole. In 2003, the updated Series II Pilot includes a new cherry interior and a revised cabin layout with a V-berth that folds in half when not in use. (Note that the Series II also incorporates a shortened keel, propeller tunnel, and a five-blade prop.) Early models with a single 170hp Yanmar diesel will cruise at 14 knots (16–17 knots top), and those with a 230hp Yanmar will cruise at 16 knots (19–20 knots top). Series II models with a 315hp Yanmar will cruise at a steady 18 knots and reach a top speed in the low 20s.

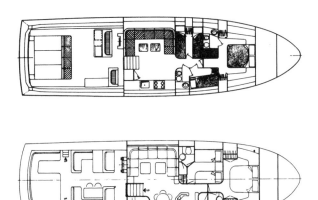

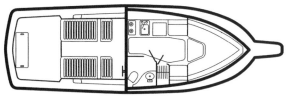

See Page 330 for Pricing Information

See Page 330 for Pricing Information

Mainship 34 Pilot

Length w/Pulpit & Platform	36'1"	Headroom	6'4"
Hull Length	34'0"	Fuel	250 gals.
Beam	12'3"	Water	70 gals.
Draft	3'3"	Hull Type	Semi-Disp.
Weight	15,000#	Deadrise Aft	NA
Clearance	9'0"	Production	1999–Current

The Mainship 34 Pilot is an enlarged version of the hugely popular Mainship 30 Pilot, an efficient Downeast-style cruiser introduced by Mainship in 1998. Where the 30 is essentially a dayboat, the larger interior of the 34 provides the additional volume required for more comfortable cruising. Offered in both Express and Sedan configurations, the Pilot rides on a semi-displacement hull with a sharp entry and a long, prop-protecting keel. The cabin accommodations are arranged with a single stateroom forward with a bi-fold door for privacy. A large U-shaped dinette seats four, and a TV mounted on a swivel platform in the forward cabin can be viewed from the salon as well. In the cockpit, facing bench seats behind the helm and companion seats are designed to double as extra berths. A centerline hatch in the deep cockpit provides excellent access to the engine. Additional features include a standard bow thruster, tilt-away helm, transom door, and wide side decks. On the downside, the head is a little small. A single 350hp Yanmar diesel will cruise the 34 Pilot at 14 knots (burning just 8–10 gph) and reach a top speed of 16–17 knots. Twin 240hp Yanmar diesels will cruise at 18 knots and reach a top speed of just over 20 knots.

Mainship 35 Open; 36 Express

Length Overall	36'5"	Fuel	250 gals.
Length WL	NA	Water	75 gals.
Beam	12'5"	Hull Type	Modified-V
Draft	2'8"	Deadrise Aft	NA
Weight	13,500#	Designer	Mike Peters
Clearance	10'6"	Production	1990–93

The Mainship 36 Express (called the Mainship 35 Open in 1990–91) is an unimpressive express cruiser whose early 1990s styling is completely dated by today's sportboat standards. There's really not much to recommend this boat—the finish is poor, the interior cabinetry and wall coverings are cheap, and the faux-European exterior styling touches are tacky. What the 36 does have, however, is a big cockpit with acres of lounge seating as well as a wide sun lounge. (Note that the portside helm position is a little unusual.) Belowdecks, the midcabin floorplan (upgraded in 1992) is arranged with double berths in both staterooms, a compact galley, and stall shower in the head compartment. The lack of interior bulkheads adds to the impression of space inside the 36, but with only curtains to separate the staterooms from the salon, nighttime privacy is practically nonexistent. A hatch in the cockpit sole provides good access to the engines and V-drives. Additional features include a radar arch, cockpit wet bar, and an integrated swim platform. Twin Crusader 454-cid gas engines will cruise the Mainship 36 Express at 19 knots and reach a top speed in the neighborhood of 27–28 knots.

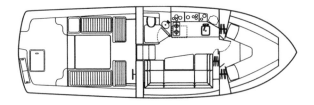

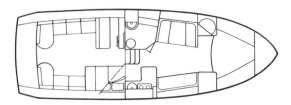

Mainship 39 Express

Length . . . . 39'2"	Water . . . . 80 gals.
Beam . . . . 14'1"	Headroom . . . . 6'3"
Draft . . . . 3'4"	Hull Type . . . . Modified-V
Weight . . . . 15,000#	Deadrise Aft . . . . 12°
Clearance . . . . 8'0"	Designer . . . . Mike Peters
Fuel . . . . 320 gals.	Production 1989–93

The Mainship 39 Express (called the Mainship 39 Open in 1989–91) was considered a rakish design when she was introduced back in 1989 although she's clearly dated by today's sportboat standards. Built on a low-deadrise, modified-V hull, the wide beam of the 39 Express allows for some very spacious accommodations. Indeed, there's seating for a small crowd in the single-level cockpit, which includes a large sun lounge and wraparound bench seating at the transom. (Note that the helm position is to port rather than to starboard as it is in most boats.) Belowdecks, the spacious cabin contains two staterooms, a full-size galley, and a large head with a separate stall shower. If you're looking for upscale furnishings and designer fabrics, forget it—this is a pretty plain-Jane interior, poorly finished with cheap cabinetry and low-cost wall coverings. Additional features include a unique bi-level transom design, twin foredeck sun pads, side exhausts, and a radar arch. Note that the side decks are extremely narrow on this boat and going forward is a dicey proposition while underway. Twin big-block Crusader gas engines will cruise the Mainship 39 at 20 knots and reach a top speed of 28–29 knots.

Marinette 28 Express

Length . . . . 28'0"	Fuel, Twin . . . . 100 gals.
Beam . . . . 11'0"	Water . . . . 35 gals.
Draft . . . . 2'0"	Hull Type . . . . Modified-V
Weight, Single . . . . 5,800#	Deadrise Aft . . . . NA
Weight, Twin . . . . 7,000#	Construction . . . . Aluminum
Fuel, Single . . . . 75 gals.	Production 1969–89

A sturdy and well-regarded boat, the Marinette 28 Express was a notably popular model for many years thanks to her versatile personality and affordable cost. Like all Marinettes, the 28 was constructed entirely of marine grade aluminum, and at just 7,000 pounds for the twin-engine model, she's a relatively light boat for her size. The 28 Express provides accommodations for four below with V-berths forward, a convertible dinette, a small galley area and a standup head with shower. Large cabin windows provide excellent cabin ventilation, and large compartments under the dinette and forward berths provide generous storage. On deck, the helm is weather-protected on three sides and visibility is excellent in all directions. The cockpit, which is nearly 10 feet long, is large enough for a couple of light-tackle anglers and their gear. The side decks are wide, and a swim platform was standard. A good performer, twin small-block 220hp Chrysler gas engines will cruise the Marinette 28 in the low 20s and reach a top speed of 30+ knots. Note that the 28 Fisherman built from 1981–89 is the same boat with a small flybridge.

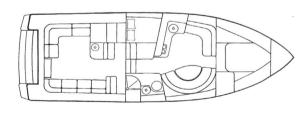

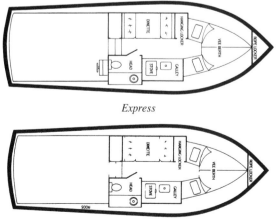

Express

Fisherman

EXPRESS CRUISERS

See Page 330 for Pricing Information

See Page 333 for Pricing Information

Maxum 2700 SE

Length Overall	28'1"	Fuel	89 gals.
Beam	9'5"	Water	30 gals.
Draft, Up	1'10"	Headroom	6'4"
Draft, Down	3'3"	Hull Type	Modified-V
Weight	7,200#	Deadrise Aft	16°
Clearance	7'4"	Production	2001–Current

Spacious accommodations are a strong point of the Maxum 2700 SE (called the 2700 SCR in 2001–02), a beamy, maxi-volume express cruiser with contemporary styling and a lengthy list of standard features. Built on a solid fiberglass modified-V hull, the high freeboard of the 2700 permits a very expansive interior with an impressive 6 feet, 4 inches of headroom in the salon. The midcabin floorplan is arranged in a conventional manner with a convertible V-berth/dinette forward, an efficient galley to port with built-in microwave, an enclosed head with electric toilet and shower, and an athwartships double berth aft with privacy curtain. On deck, a sun lounge is opposite the doublewide helm seat and there's enough cockpit seating for eight adults. A gas-assist hatch in the cockpit sole provides easy access to the engine. Additional features include a wet bar, transom door, freshwater shower, walk-through windshield, four opening ports and stereo/CD player. Among several engine options, a single 320hp MerCruiser sterndrive will cruise the 2700 SE at 20 knots and reach 30+ knots top. Note the limited fuel capacity.

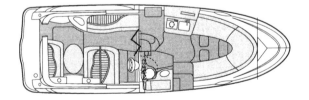

Maxum 2700/2800 SCR; 2900 SE

Length Overall	29'10"	Fuel	102 gals.
Beam	9'9"	Water	30 gals.
Draft, Up	1'10"	Waste	16 gals.
Draft, Down	3'3"	Hull Type	Deep-V
Weight	7,300#	Deadrise Aft	21°
Clearance	9'7"	Production	1993–Current

A good-selling boat over the years, the Maxum 2900 SE (called the 2700 SCR in 1993–96, the 2800 SCR in 1997–2000, and the 2900 SCR in 2001) has been one of the most affordable midsize cruisers available since her introduction in 1993. Hull construction is solid fiberglass, and her deep-V hull delivers a stable and comfortable ride in spite of her high freeboard. The 2900 is a surprisingly big boat on the inside because her full-width cabin eliminates the side decks in order to take maximum advantage of the beam. The floorplan is arranged in the usual way with double berths fore and aft, a convertible dinette, compact galley, and an enclosed head with standing headroom. Privacy curtains separate the sleeping areas from the main cabin. There's seating for six in the cockpit with facing settees aft and a double-wide seat at the helm. Note that the 102-gallon fuel capacity is small for a boat this size. Twin hatches in the cockpit sole provide good access to the engine(s). A single 260hp MerCruiser sterndrive will top out in the mid-to-high 20s. Later models with a 320hp MerCruiser I/O will hit a top speed of 30+ knots, and twin 190hp MerCruisers will reach around 35 knots wide open.

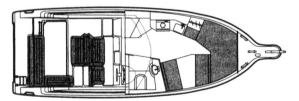

See Page 333 for Pricing Information

See Page 333 for Pricing Information

Maxum 3000 SCR

Length Overall	32'9"	Fuel	150 gals.
Beam	9'11"	Water	40 gals.
Draft, Drives Up	1'10"	Waste	30 gals.
Draft, Drives Down	3'7"	Hull Type	Deep-V
Weight	11,500#	Deadrise Aft	18°
Clearance	9'7"	Production	1997–2001

The Maxum 3000 SCR is a budget-priced family express whose contemporary styling and comfortable interior make her a lot of boat for the money. Like her sisterships in the Maxum fleet, she's built on a solid fiberglass deep-V hull with a molded pulpit and integrated transom. Her midcabin floorplan is arranged in the conventional manner with a convertible U-shaped lounge aft and a double berth in the forward stateroom. Both cabins have foldaway accordion privacy doors—a definite improvement over the privacy curtains so often found in other midcabin designs. By offsetting the forward berth, Maxum designers created a very open interior in the SCR, larger in fact than the actual dimensions might suggest. Storage is plentiful, and three overhead hatches and six opening ports provide excellent lighting and ventilation. A gas-assist hatch in the cockpit sole provides good access to the engine compartment. Additional features include a walk-through windshield, wet bar, and a foredeck sun pad. A little light on fuel for a boat this size, twin 220hp MerCruiser sterndrives will cruise the 3000 SCR in the mid 20s (about 35 knots top), and a single 310hp MerCruiser will cruise in the low 20s (about 30 knots wide open).

Maxum 3100 SE

Length	30'9"	Fuel	150 gals.
Beam	10'6"	Water	35 gals.
Draft, Up	2'1"	Waste	30 gals.
Draft, Down	3'5"	Hull Type	Modified-V
Weight	11,000#	Deadrise Aft	18°
Clearance	12'9"	Production	2002–Current

Maxum has built its reputation by delivering affordable, well-styled boats to an entry-level, budget-minded public. The Maxum 3100 SE (called the 3100 SCR in 2002) fits into this mold nicely—a modern sterndrive cruiser with a midcabin interior and a very competitive price. She's built on a solid fiberglass, modified-V hull with moderate beam and reverse chines to dampen spray. Belowdecks, privacy curtains separate the fore and aft sleeping areas from the main cabin. Between them is an expansive salon with a semicircular lounge/dinette (which converts to a double berth) to starboard, an enclosed head with sink and shower, and a full galley to port with abundant storage. There are six opening ports for ventilation, and the absence of any interior bulkheads makes for a very open floorplan. The cockpit has a doublewide helm seat, an L-shaped lounge opposite, and U-shaped seating aft complemented by a sink and cooler space. An opening windshield provides access to the foredeck with its twin sun pads. A capable performer, twin 260hp MerCruiser sterndrives will cruise the 3100 SE in the mid 20s and reach 33–34 knots top.

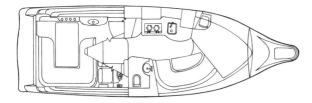

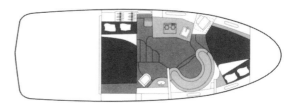

See Page 333 for Pricing Information

See Page 333 for Pricing Information

Maxum 3200 SCR

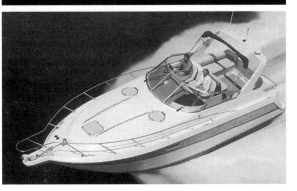

Maxum 3300 SE

Length Overall	34'9"	Fuel	186 gals.
Beam	11'0"	Water	36 gals.
Draft, Up	2'3"	Waste	30 gals.
Draft, Down	3'8"	Hull Type	Modified-V
Weight	10,800#	Deadrise Aft	17°
Clearance	9'6"	Production	1994–98

Length Overall	35'7"	Water	36 gals.
Beam	11'1"	Waste	30 gals.
Draft	3'6"	Headroom	6'6"
Weight	11,500#	Hull Type	Modified-V
Clearance	10'6"	Deadrise Aft	17°
Fuel	179 gals.	Production	1999–Current

Largest boat in the Maxum fleet when she was introduced in 1994, the 3200 SCR is a low-cost sterndrive cruiser with functional deck and cabin layouts and an impressive list of standard features. During her production years, she was among the least expensive boats of her type on the market. Hull construction is solid fiberglass, and the Maxum's 11-foot beam—together with the lack of any side decks—results in an unusually spacious interior for a 32-footer. The midcabin layout is arranged in the usual manner with double berths fore and aft, a convertible dinette, complete galley, and a standup head with sink and shower. A curtain forward and a folding door aft separate the sleeping areas from the salon, and headroom is excellent, even in the small aft cabin. On deck, the cockpit is arranged with facing settees aft and a double-wide seat at the helm (which folds out into a lounge). A windshield walk-through provides access to the foredeck sun pad and bow platform. Note that there's little space around the console for extra electronics. Among several sterndrive engine options, twin 250hp MerCruisers will cruise the Maxum 3200 SCR at 20 knots and reach a top speed of 30+ knots.

A stylish boat with her reverse arch and long foredeck, the Maxum 3300 SE (called the 3300 SCR in 1999–2002) is one of the most affordable family cruisers in her size range. Like her sisterships in the Maxum fleet, she's built on a straightforward modified-V hull with an integral swim platform and bow pulpit. The midcabin interior is arranged with an offset double berth forward, a convertible dinette to starboard and a full galley (with Corian countertops and a hardwood floor) opposite. The head is aft, across from the entryway where it's easily accessed from the cockpit. There are plenty of storage bins and lockers below, and three overhead hatches and three opening ports provide good cabin ventilation. The cockpit of the 3300 is set up a little different than most with facing settees aft, a centerline transom door, and an aft-facing lounge behind the (triple-wide) helm seat. A cockpit entertainment bar is standard, and a walk-through windshield provides access to the foredeck sun pad. Among several sterndrive engine options, twin 320hp MerCruisers will cruise the 3000 SCR in the low-to-mid 20s and reach a top speed of 35+ knots.

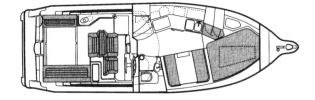

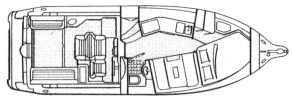

Maxum 3500 Sport Yacht

Length Overall	35'0"	Water	42 gals.
Beam	12'2"	Waste	42 gals.
Draft, Down	3'1"	Headroom	6'4"
Weight	15,870#	Hull Type	Modified-V
Clearance	12'6"	Deadrise Aft	15°
Fuel	240 gals.	Production	2001–Current

Distinctive styling has been the hallmark of Maxum designs ever since the company introduced its first boats in the late 1980s. In a market crowded with midsize family cruisers, the 3500 Sport Yacht (called the 3500 SCR in 2001–02) offers a combination of aggressive good looks, spacious accommodations and a practical cockpit layout, all at a moderate price compared with the upmarket products of Sea Ray, Formula and Cruisers. Built on a beamy modified-V hull, the absence of side decks allows for a particularly expansive interior. The floorplan contains an offset double berth forward with privacy curtain, a semicircular lounge, a midcabin aft with twin bunks (that convert into a double), and a compact galley with built-in microwave. In the cockpit, a U-shaped seating area converts into a sun pad, and visibility from the elevated helm is excellent. A hatch in the bridgedeck sole provides good access to the engine space. A transom shower, walk-through windshield, and wet bar are standard. Early models with twin 310hp MerCruiser V-drive inboards will cruise in the low 20s (close to 30 knots top), and later models with 370hp MerCruisers will cruise in the mid 20s and top out in the mid 30s.

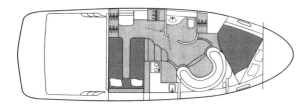

Maxum 3700 SCR

Length Overall	39'3"	Water	65 gals.
Beam	13'0"	Waste	50 gals.
Draft	3'7"	Headroom	6'4"
Weight	20,700#	Hull Type	Modified-V
Clearance	12'11"	Deadrise Aft	15°
Fuel	244 gals.	Production	1998–2001

Patterned after the popular 4100 SCR, the Maxum 3700 SCR is an affordably priced express cruiser whose wide-open interior and sporty appearance will appeal to a cross section of budget-minded family cruisers. She's built on a solid fiberglass modified-V hull with an integrated swim platform and moderate beam, and at just over 20,000 pounds, she's a relatively light boat for her size. The midcabin interior of the 3700 SCR—essentially a scaled-down version of the larger 4100 SCR—is extremely open thanks to the absence of a fixed bulkhead separating the stateroom from the salon. A large and well-equipped galley is to port, and the twin berths in the aft cabin easily convert into a queen bed. Headroom is about 6 feet, 4 inches in the main cabin, and a circular stall shower is located in the head. On deck, the bi-level cockpit of the 3700 SCR comes with a double-wide helm seat, wet bar, transom door, and an aft lounge that converts into a sun pad. Twin 380hphp V-drive MerCruiser inboards will cruise the Maxum 3700 SCR at 18 knots (26–27 knots top), and optional 370hp Cummins diesels will cruise in the mid 20s and top out at close to 30 knots.

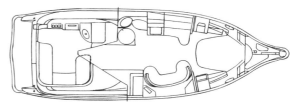

See Page 333 for Pricing Information
See Page 334 for Pricing Information

Maxum 3700 Sport Yacht

Length Overall	37'2"	Fuel	300 gals.
Beam	13'0"	Water	80 gals.
Draft, Up	2'4"	Waste	45 gals.
Draft, Down	3'6"	Hull Type	Modified-V
Weight	17,800#	Deadrise Aft	15°
Clearance	10'8"	Production	2003–Current

In a market always crowded with midsize express boats, the Maxum 3700 is notable for her modern styling and very competitive price. Maxum has excelled at delivering a lot of boat for the money ever since the company was founded in 1987, and the Sport Yacht manages to combine a balanced blend of comfort and performance at a price considerably below much of the competition. Hull construction is solid fiberglass, and a wide 13-foot beam allows for an expansive interior as well as a large cockpit area. The belowdeck layout is similar to many midcabin boats this size with berths for six, a large head with separate shower, and a full galley with Corian counters and plenty of storage. A faux teak-and-holly sole is installed in the galley area, and cherry woodwork is liberally applied throughout the cabin. For privacy, the forward stateroom has a privacy door while the aft stateroom uses a curtain. The cockpit, with its U-shaped lounge aft and double helm seat, will seat as many as eight in comfort. Standard 320hp MerCruiser inboards will cruise the 3700 Sport Yacht at 18 knots and reach a top speed in the mid 20s. Optional 370hp MerCruisers will reach a top speed of around 30 knots.

Maxum 4100 SCR

Length Overall	43'7"	Water	77 gals.
Beam	13'6"	Waste	45 gals.
Draft	3'2"	Hull Type	Modified-V
Weight	18,800#	Deadrise Aft	16°
Clearance	13'4"	Designer	Maxum
Fuel	330 gals.	Production	1996–99

The Maxum 4100 SCR (called the 3900 SCR in 1996) is a well-styled cruiser whose roomy interior and low price appealed to budget-minded buyers. Like all Maxum models, she's constructed on a solid fiberglass hull, and a reverse arch and huge swim platform add considerably to her pleasing profile. The 4100 SCR was one of the larger express boats available in the late 1990s, and it's no surprise that her cockpit accommodations are generous indeed. There's seating for eight with double bench seats forward and facing settees aft, each with a removable table. A wet bar was standard, and a pair of gas-assist hatches in the cockpit sole provide access to the engine compartment. At each corner of the transom are molded steps leading to the side decks—a useful feature. Belowdecks, the midcabin interior of the 4100 SCR is arranged with a convertible U-shaped lounge in the midcabin and an island berth forward. The salon sofa also converts, and folding doors provide privacy for the fore and aft sleeping areas. Note that fit and finish is rather poor. Twin 400hp V-drive gas inboards will cruise at 22 knots (26–27 knots top), and optional 370hp Cummins diesels cruise at 20 knots (about 23 knots top).

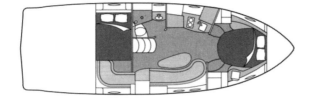

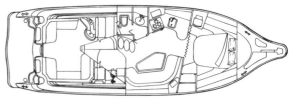

See Page 334 for Pricing Information

See Page 334 for Pricing Information

Maxum 4200 Sport Yacht

Length . . . . 42'8"	Water . . . . 130 gals.
Beam . . . . 14'10"	Waste . . . . 72 gals.
Draft . . . . 3'3"	Headroom . . . . 6'4"
Weight . . . . 22,700#	Hull Type . . . . Modified-V
Clearance, Hardtop . . . . 12'0"	Deadrise Aft . . . . 18°
Fuel . . . . 480 gals.	Production 2002–Current

With her "floating" fiberglass hardtop, the Maxum 4200 Sport Yacht (called the Maxum 4200 SCR in 2002) is a very distinctive yacht indeed. Without the hardtop, the 4200 might easily be confused with a European sportboat; with it, however, the visual impact is striking. Built on a beamy modified-V hull with an integrated swim platform, the two-stateroom, two-head interior of the 4200 is much more spacious than most of her European counterparts. High-gloss cherry cabinetry, teak-and-holly flooring, and Ultraleather upholstery combine to give the salon a rich and fairly elegant ambiance (although the fit and finish is something less than impressive). Privacy doors separate both staterooms from the salon, and the forward head is fitted with a separate stall shower. In the cockpit, the arching side windows and elevated hardtop provide plenty of protection from sun and wind. Molded steps in the transom corners lead up to the side decks, and the aft seating section rises hydraulically for engine access. An affordably priced boat with many standard features, twin 450hp Cummins V-drive diesels will cruise the Maxum 4200 in the low-to-mid 20s and reach 27–28 knots top.

McKinna 60 Express

Length Overall . . . . 60'0"	Water . . . . 270 gals.
Beam . . . . 17'3"	Headroom . . . . 6'8"
Draft . . . . 3'6"	Hull Type . . . . Modified-V
Weight . . . . 51,500#	Deadrise Aft . . . . NA
Clearance . . . . NA	Designer . . . . H. Apollonio
Fuel . . . . 700 gals.	Production 2000–Current

A handsome and well-proportioned yacht, the McKinna 60 Express is notable for her spacious interior and a truly innovative cockpit layout that takes luxury cruising to the next level. The McKinna is a big boat: her 17-foot, 3-inch beam is wider than most yachts of her size, and her standard two-stateroom interior (with nearly 7 feet of headroom) is as opulent as it is comfortable. The master stateroom is aft, and the large galley is fully integrated into the salon with a breakfast bar extending out almost to the center. On deck, the unique cockpit arrangement of the 60 Express is focused on a centerline entertainment console with a wet bar, electric or propane grill, three bar stools and a slide-out countertop. A large sun pad is aft, and a roomy transom garage (which reduces engine room space) can store a pair of PWCs or an inflatable. Additional features include a teak cockpit sole, underwater exhausts, wide side decks, and a bow thruster. Built on a modified-V hull with a shallow keel and prop pockets, the McKinna is a good performer for her size. Optional 800hp Cat diesels will cruise at 25 knots and reach a top speed of 30+ knots.

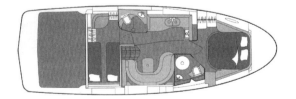

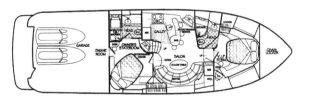

Two-Stateroom Layout

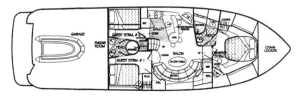

Three-Stateroom Layout

Mediterranean 38 Express

Length w/Pulpit . . . . 41'11"	Fuel . . . . 390 gals.
Hull Length . . . . 38'4"	Water . . . . 107 gals.
Beam . . . . 12'8"	Headroom . . . . 6'4"
Draft . . . . 3'4"	Hull Type . . . . Modified-V
Weight . . . . 21,000#	Deadrise Aft . . . . 18°
Clearance, Arch . . . . 9'6"	Production 1999–Current

The Mediterranean 38 Express is an uncomplicated, economy-class express suitable for both fishing or family cruising. This has been one of the better values in the boating world; whatever the 38 might lack in finish and detailing is more than compensated for by her sturdy construction and a low, factory-direct price. Her standard single-stateroom interior is arranged with an island berth in the private bow stateroom, a large U-shaped convertible settee, and a compact galley abaft the head compartment. Unlike most express boats her size, the Mediterranean has no midcabin berth beneath the helm. (She does, however, have a big engine room—something few midcabin boats can claim.) Topside, an L-shaped lounge is opposite the helm, and the entire helmdeck can be raised electrically for access to the motors. Additional features include a wide transom door, bow pulpit, cockpit wet bar, and an aft-facing cockpit seat. A swim platform is a popular option. A good performer with optional 420hp Yanmar—or 430hp Volvo—diesels, the Mediterranean 38 Express will cruise in the mid 20s and reach a top speed in the neighborhood of 30 knots.

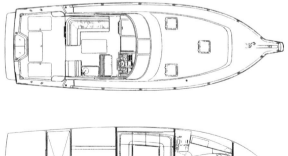

Monterey 265/276 Cruiser

Length w/Pulpit . . . . 29'0"	Fuel . . . . 100 gals.
Hull Length . . . . 26'10"	Water . . . . 32 gals.
Beam . . . . 9'6"	Waste . . . . 21 gals.
Draft, Down . . . . 3'0"	Hull Type . . . . Deep-V
Weight . . . . 6,500#	Deadrise Aft . . . . 20°
Clearance, Arch . . . . 9'2"	Production 1993–99

The Monterey 276 Cruiser (called the 265 Cruiser in 1993–94) is a value-priced weekend cruiser with roomy accommodations, a practical deck plan, and good open-water performance. She's constructed on a solid fiberglass, deep-V hull with an integral swim platform and a relatively wide 9-foot, 6-inch beam. Her midcabin interior is arranged in the usual way with a convertible dinette/U-shaped settee, a compact galley with sink, refrigerator, and stove, an enclosed head with shower, and twin settees in the midcabin that convert into a big double berth. There's near-standing headroom in the main cabin, and a large hanging locker provides plenty of storage. Topside, the Monterey's roomy bi-level cockpit has a double helm seat forward and bench seating at the transom. Additional features include a walk-through windshield (the side decks are quite narrow), foredeck sun pad, cockpit wet bar and sport arch. A single 310hp MerCruiser sterndrive will cruise the Monterey in the mid 20s and reach a top speed of just under 40 knots. Twin 190hp Mercs (or Volvos) will cruise in the high 20s and top out at 40+ knots.

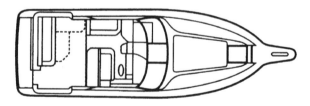

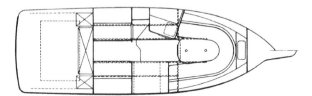

See Page 334 for Pricing Information

See Page 335 for Pricing Information

Monterey 282 Cruiser

Monterey 296 Cruiser

Length w/Platform	30'10"	Fuel	142 gals.
Hull Length	28'9"	Water	38 gals.
Beam	10'0"	Waste	22 gals.
Draft, Down	3'1"	Hull Type	Deep-V
Weight	10,100#	Deadrise Aft	19°
Clearance, Arch	10'6"	Production	2001–Current

Length w/Pulpit	31'6"	Water	44 gals.
Hull Length	28'10"	Waste	21 gals.
Beam	10'0"	Clearance, Arch	9'4"
Draft, Down	3'1"	Hull Type	Deep-V
Weight	8,000#	Deadrise Aft	19°
Fuel	140 gals.	Production	1993–2000

Monterey always packs a lot of features into their sportcruisers, and the Monterey 282 has everything a family needs to enjoy a long weekend afloat. Built on a deep-V hull with a wide 10-foot beam, the 282 is a comfortable boat below and her floorplan—with its booth-style dinette—is quite different from most midsize cruisers. Although the galley is on the small side with little counter space, the big dinette is both functional and very innovative in design. The head is also quite large and comes with a hinged seat over the toilet, which makes changing clothes (or taking a shower) very comfortable. An athwartships double berth is forward, and twin settees in the midcabin convert into a large double berth. (Note that the dinette can also be converted into a berth for a couple of kids.) Topside, the cockpit is arranged with an aft-facing seat behind the double helm, wet bar with storage to port, and a removable rear seat. A transom door opens to a big swim platform where dock lines and fenders can be stored in a transom box. A fast ride with optional 260hp MerCruiser sterndrives, the Monterey 282 will cruise at close to 30 knots and reach a top speed of 40+ knots.

A well-styled cruiser by the standards of her day, the 296 Cruiser was Monterey's first entry into the highly competitive market for 30-foot sterndrive family weekenders. (Called the 286 Cruiser in 1993–94, the cockpit was revised in 1995 when she became the 296 Cruiser.) Hull construction is solid fiberglass, and her deep-V bottom provides a stable, comfortable ride in most weather conditions. The interior of the 296 is arranged in the usual fashion with double berths fore and aft, a convertible dinette, enclosed head and shower, and generous storage. Two bench seats in the midcabin provide seating, and between them is a fold-down table that converts the seats into the roomiest berth in the boat. Originally designed with a single helm chair, a double helm seat (with an aft-facing bench seat) became standard in 1995. Additional features include a walk-through windshield, a wide swim platform with fender racks, good main cabin headroom, a sport arch, and a molded bow platform. Among several sterndrive engine options, twin 250hp Volvos will cruise in the high 20s and reach a top speed in excess of 40 knots. Note that the 140-gallon fuel capacity is pretty slim for a 29-foot boat.

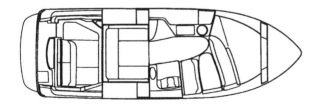

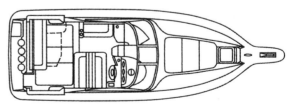

See Page 335 for Pricing Information

See Page 335 for Pricing Information

Monterey 302 Cruiser

Monterey 322 Cruiser

Length w/Pulpit	32'6"	Headroom	6'4"
Hull Length	30'5"	Fuel	150 gals.
Beam	10'6"	Water	45 gals.
Draft, Down	3'1"	Hull Type	Deep-V
Weight	10,770#	Deadrise Aft	19°
Clearance	10'6"	Production	2000–Current

Length w/Pulpit	33'3"	Headroom	6'4"
Hull Length	32'2"	Fuel	200 gals.
Beam	10'10"	Water	45 gals.
Draft, Down	3'4"	Hull Type	Deep-V
Weight	12,800#	Deadrise Aft	18°
Clearance	10'0"	Production	1998–Current

A handsome design, the Monterey 302 is an affordably priced family cruiser with attractive lines and a practical accommodation plan. Like all current Monterey sportboats, she rides on a solid fiberglass deep-V hull with moderate beam and reverse chines to reduce spray. The 302's midcabin interior differs from most others in her class in one important respect: instead of being open to the salon with just a curtain for privacy, the 302's aft stateroom is fully enclosed with a solid bulkhead and cabin door. The salon may seem a little less open, but many will agree that the true privacy this layout affords is worth it. Topside, there's a double-wide companion seat (with a reversible backrest) at the helm, a wet bar, a removable transom bench seat and an extended swim platform (optional). The side decks are narrow, so the bow area is accessed from a walk-through windshield. Additional features include a reverse arch, transom storage locker, tilt steering, foredeck sun pad and a removable cockpit table. A good performer, twin 260hp MerCruiser sterndrives will deliver a cruising speed of 25 knots and a top speed of just under 40 knots.

Like her smaller sisterships in the Monterey fleet, the 322 Cruiser is a well-executed blend of crisp styling, solid construction, and comfortable cabin accommodations. She's a good-looking boat with her reverse arch and wraparound windshield, and she lacks the bloated, tall-freeboard appearance seen in many other express cruisers her size. Built on a deep-V hull with moderate beam, the midcabin floorplan of the Monterey is an attractive mix of Corian counters, a curved earth-tone sofa, and premium fixtures. The midcabin is particularly spacious, and privacy curtains separate both sleeping areas from the salon. Three overhead hatches and five opening ports provide adequate cabin ventilation. In the cockpit, visibility from the elevated helm is excellent; there's seating for six at the U-shaped lounge behind the helm and a wet bar is standard. Note that a walk-through windshield provides access to the bow. Additional features include a foredeck sun pad, a molded pulpit, anchor locker, fender racks at the transom, and a foldaway transom seat. MerCruiser 320hp gas sterndrives will cruise the Monterey 322 in the mid 20s and reach a top speed of about 40 knots.

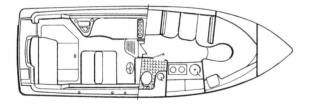

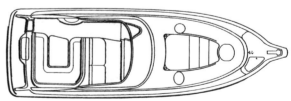

See Page 335 for Pricing Information

100

See Page 335 for Pricing Information

Monterey 350 Sport Yacht

Length Overall	37'0"	Fuel	230 gals.
Beam	11'6"	Water	48 gals.
Draft, Up	2'4"	Waste	38 gals.
Draft, Down	3'6"	Hull Type	Modified-V
Weight	15,500#	Deadrise Aft	17°
Clearance	10'0"	Production	2005–Current

Monterey's largest boat ever, the 350 Sport Yacht combines bold styling and very aggressive performance in a luxurious, reasonably priced package. Many express cruisers in this size range are designed with inboard power, but for flat-out speed it's difficult to match the performance of the Monterey's sterndrive power. Stepping aboard, one of the most striking features of the 350 SY is the massive Euro-style helm with its matte gray finish and Faria gauges. A U-shaped lounge in the aft cockpit offers seating for six and converts to a sun pad with the insertion of a filler, and the standard wet bar comes with a sink and 48-quart cooler. Belowdecks, the layout differs from many other cruisers in her class in that the midcabin is a true stateroom with standing headroom and a solid cherrywood door rather than just a privacy curtain. The salon is carpeted except for the area in front of the galley, which is finished with cherry-and-holly flooring. Engine access is through an electric hatch in the cockpit sole. On the downside, the single helm seat precludes the mate from joining the skipper. A fast ride with optional 420hp Volvo sterndrives, the 350 Sport Yacht will reach a top speed in excess of 40 knots.

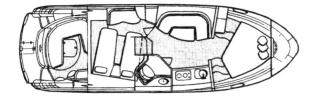

Packet Craft 360 Express

Length Overall	41'8"	Fuel	300 gals.
Hull Length	38'7"	Water	75 gals.
Beam	12'0"	Waste	30 gals.
Draft	2'8"	Hull Type	Modified-V
Weight	18,000#	Deadrise Aft	14°
Headroom	6'4"	Production	2002–Current

The Packet Craft 360 is the first powerboat from sailboat manufacturer Island Packet Yachts. This is a company with a reputation for high-quality engineering and construction, and the Packet Craft represents a distinctive blend of classic beauty and traditional cruising elegance. Built on a modified-V hull, deep prop pockets allow the engines to lie almost flat beneath the cockpit sole. The 12-foot beam of the 360 Express—slender compared with many of today's mega-beam designs—makes for an easily driven and notably efficient hull. The bridgedeck (which lifts on hydraulic rams for access to the engines) is arranged with an L-shaped settee opposite the helm, and opening forward and side windows provide plenty of ventilation on hot days. Additional guest seating is found in the cockpit, and wide side decks make foredeck access safe and secure. Belowdecks, a teak-and-holly cabin sole and varnished teak woodwork highlight the 360's elegant single-stateroom interior. A beautifully finished yacht, additional features include an integral swim platform and bow pulpit, eight opening ports, a transom door, and side-dumping exhausts. Twin 370hp Yanmar diesels will cruise the Packet Craft in the mid 20s and reach a top speed of nearly 30 knots.

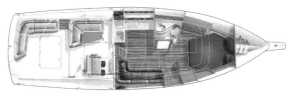

See Page 335 for Pricing Information

101

See Page 341 for Pricing Information

Pearson True North 33

Length	36'2	Fuel	200 gals.
Beam	12'4"	Water	80 gals.
Draft	3'4"	Waste	25 gals.
Weight	12,500#	Hull Type	Modified-V
Clearance, Mast	11'7"	Deadrise Aft	16°
Headroom	6'3"	Production	2004–Current

The Pearson True North 33 is a scaled-down version of the True North 38 Pearson introduced in 2002. Possessing the same Downeast styling as her sibling, the plumb bow, sharply raked transom, and low-profile pilothouse of the True North distinguish her from just about anything else on the water. The tapered hull carries the beam well forward, and the rudder and prop are fully protected by an integral skeg. Note that the transom incorporates a pair of wide "clamshell" doors, which make it possible to lift a dinghy into the cockpit for storage—a feature experienced cruisers are sure to appreciate. The layout of the True North 33 has the galley and dinette on the pilothouse level, which is open to the cockpit, a design that affords the helmsman excellent all-around visibility. (The forward dinette seat can be converted at the touch of a button into a forward-facing bench seat.) Sleeping accommodations and a full-sized head with shower are below, and the level of finish found throughout the interior is impressive in every respect. A relatively light boat for her size, she'll cruise at 20 knots with a single 440hp Yanmar diesel.

Pearson True North 38

Length	38'6"	Fuel	220 gals.
Beam	13'6"	Water	100 gals.
Draft	3'6"	Waste	35 gals.
Weight	15,000#	Hull Type	Modified-V
Clearance	15'5"	Deadrise Aft	12°
Headroom	6'3"	Production	2002–Current

The Pearson True North 38 is one of those rare cases where beauty and practicality seem to merge in perfect harmony. Innovation is an overused term in the yachting industry, but it certainly applies to the True North. Her Downeast styling is unique, and the twin doors built into the 38's reverse transom can open wide enough to haul a dinghy into the cockpit for storage. A life raft, bikes, or kayak can lie atop the hardtop, and extra-wide side decks provide seating space along both sides of the cockpit. Built on high-tech hull with a deep forefoot and skeg-mounted rudder, the deck plan of the True North 38 includes a sliding seat arrangement at the dinette that expands seating from four to six people while also converting to a double berth at night. A "sleeping loft" for young children is located above the V-berths, and the galley is positioned aft in the semi-enclosed pilothouse where it's convenient to the cockpit. (Note that the pilothouse can be fully enclosed with an optional bulkhead and door.) A bow thruster is standard. A single 440hp Yanmar diesel will cruise the True North 38 at 20 knots and reach a top speed of 25–26 knots.

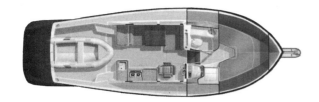

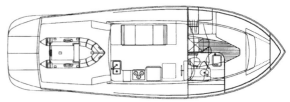

Phoenix 27 Weekender

Length Overall . . . . 27'3"	Fuel, Std. . . . . 200 gals.
Length WL . . . . 23'6"	Fuel, Opt. . . . . 250 gals.
Beam . . . . 9'10"	Water. . . . . 24 gals.
Draft. . . . . 1'10"	Hull Type . . . . Deep-V
Weight. . . . . 7,200#	Deadrise Aft . . . . 20°
Clearance. . . . . 6'9"	Production 1979–94

A popular model for many years, the Phoenix 27 Weekender is a straightforward offshore express without a lot of frills. Construction is solid fiberglass, and a full-length inner liner is bonded to the hull for added strength. As with other Jim Wynne designs, the Phoenix 27 has propeller pockets recessed into her deep-V hull for reduced shaft angles. Since over half of the boat's length is devoted to the single-level cockpit, the interior is necessarily compact with V-berths, a complete galley with refrigerator and storage, and standup head with shower. The engines are located under raised engine boxes that can easily double as bait-watching seats. The cockpit is spacious for a 27-footer with about 100 square feet of fishing space. In addition to the standard Weekender model, the 27 was offered in a "Fishbuster" version (1979–89) with the galley located forward and to port in the cockpit. Standard 270hp gas engines will cruise the Phoenix 27 at 22–23 knots (about 30 knots top), and optional 200hp Volvo diesels will cruise around 25 knots and top out in the high 20s. With a pair of 250hp Yamaha outboards, the 27 Weekender will hit a top speed of 40 knots.

Phoenix Blackhawk 909

Length w/Pulpit . . . . 32'5"	Fuel. . . . . 140 gals.
Hull Length. . . . . 30'1"	Water. . . . . 40 gals.
Beam . . . . 10'0"	Hull Type . . . . Deep-V
Hull Draft . . . . 1'10"	Deadrise Aft . . . . 21°
Weight. . . . . 9,150#	Designer. . . . . Jim Wynne
Clearance. . . . . 8'0"	Production 1985–87

Phoenix had a reputation for building good fishing boats, so it was something of a surprise when they introduced the Euro-style Blackhawk 909 express cruiser back in 1985. Built on a solid fiberglass hull with prop pockets, the 909 was a sterndrive boat (also a first for any Phoenix model) until 1986 when inboards became available. A molded full-length inner liner—used to create the interior—added a good deal of rigidity and strength to the hull. Belowdeck, a U-shaped lounge/dinette at the bow seats five and converts into a large double berth at night. Another couple can sleep in the small midcabin tucked beneath the bridgedeck. While the absence of interior bulkheads makes the interior seem very open, the lack of natural cabin lighting and ventilation is apparent. Additional features include a unique sliding transom door, curved windshield, good headroom below, and an integral swim platform and bow pulpit. Twin 270hp gas inboards cruise the Blackhawk 909 at a respectable 22 knots and reach a top speed in the neighborhood of 30 knots. Twin 200hp Volvo diesels were optional. Note the limited fuel capacity.

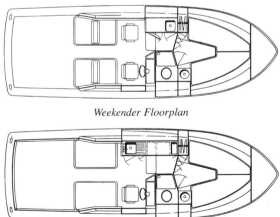

Weekender Floorplan

Fishbuster Floorplan

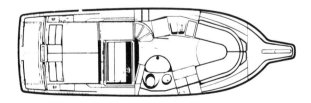

Pro-Line 33 Express

Length	33'0"	Water	48 gals.
Beam	12'6"	Cockpit	115 sq. ft.
Draft	3'5"	Max Headroom	6'3"
Weight	14,500#	Hull Type	Deep-V
Clearance	7'8"	Deadrise Aft	19°
Fuel	300 gals.	Production	1999–2004

The 33 Express (called the 3310 Sportfish in 1999) is a rugged inboard-powered canyon runner—the very first inboard design from Pro-Line—whose upmarket price tag comes as a surprise considering the company's reputation for producing affordable, budget-friendly boats. Heavily built on a deep-V hull with cored hullsides and a molded inner liner, the 33 is obviously meant for fishing although her passenger-friendly bridgedeck and comfortable interior work well for occasional family cruising. An impressive list of standard fishing amenities includes both transom and in-deck fish boxes, a 35-gallon livewell, bait-prep center, fresh- and saltwater washdowns, bolster cushions, and a transom door. Belowdecks, the interior of the 33 Express is arranged with a convertible dinette/V-berth forward, a full galley and enclosed head to port, and a cleverly shaped pedestal dining table lowers to create a huge berth. Like several other high-end express fishermen, the entire bridgedeck rises hydraulically for access to the engines. Twin 350hp Cat (or Yanmar) diesels will cruise the Pro-Line 33 Express in the high 20s and reach a top speed in the mid 30s.

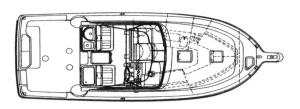

Pursuit 2670 Denali

Length w/Pulpit	29'10"	Water	18 gals.
Hull Length	26'5"	Waste	13 gals.
Beam	9'3"	Hull Type	Deep-V
Draft	3'0"	Deadrise Aft	21°
Weight	5,400#	Max HP (2665)	400
Fuel	150 gals.	Production	2003–Current

More pleasure boat than hard-core fisherman, the Pursuit 2670 will appeal to experienced boaters who have an eye for quality and long-term value. Unlike conventional express cruisers with their glitzy styling, cluttered cockpits, and overstuffed interiors, the Denali offers beautiful styling, a spacious, wide-open cockpit, and a simple interior with V-berths and a concealed head. This is an ideal boat for dayboaters who enjoy fishing, swimming, and cruising with friends and family. Her deep-V hull can run any inlet with confidence, and the Denali's meticulous finish is as good as it gets in a small production boat. The centerpiece of the 2670 is the aft-facing bench seat in the center of the cockpit, which pulls out and converts into a full-length sun pad. The centerline helm position—unusual in any boat—is notable for its exceptional visibility and intelligent dash layout. For anglers, a 12-gallon livewell, in-sole fish box with pumpout, tackle lockers, cockpit sink, and cabin rod storage are all standard. The 2670 Denali will reach a top speed of 45 knots with a pair of Yamaha 225 outboards. (Note that the 2665 Denali is the same boat with sterndrive power.)

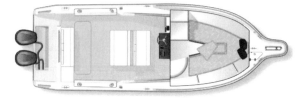

2670 Floorplan

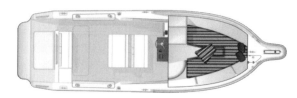

2665 Floorplan

See Page 343 for Pricing Information   See Page 344 for Pricing Information

Pursuit 2860/2865 Denali

Length w/Pulpit . . . . 32'10"	Fuel . . . . 148 gals.
Hull Length. . . . . 28'0"	Water. . . . . 30 gals.
Beam . . . . 9'6"	Waste . . . . 20 gals.
Draft, Down . . . . 3'0"	Hull Type . . . . Deep-V
Weight. . . . . 7,600#	Deadrise Aft . . . . 21°
Clearance, Windshield . . . . . . 8'0"	Production 1997–2004

The Pursuit 2860 is an upmarket sterndrive pleasure boat whose practical layout will appeal to anglers and daycruisers alike. Only a few 28-footers can claim the built-in versatility of the Denali—this is a boat equally well adapted to fishing, swimming, or leisurely weekend cruising. Built on a seaworthy deep-V hull with moderate beam and an integrated swim platform, the focal point of the Denali is her spacious bridgedeck with its posh L-shaped lounge seating, wet bar, and well-designed helm. The aft cockpit is large enough for several anglers and their gear, and the transom contains a freshwater sink, insulated fish box/cooler, and raw-water washdown. Belowdecks, the Denali's well-appointed cuddy cabin contains berths for two with a teak-and-holly sole, removable table, galley with sink, refrigerator and stove, and an enclosed head with shower. Updated in 2002, the revised 2865 Denali featured a pair of aft-facing seats in the cockpit, a restyled transom, and a new curved windshield. Built-in tackle drawers, a bow pulpit, dash glove box, and an electric helm seat were all standard. Among several single engine options, a Volvo 375hp gas I/O will reach a top speed of 35+ knots.

Regal 260 Valenti; 272 Commodore

Length w/Pulpit . . . . 28'6"	Fuel . . . . 105 gals.
Hull Length. . . . . 26'7"	Water. . . . . 27 gals.
Beam . . . . 9'2"	Waste . . . . 17 gals.
Draft. 3'6"	Hull Type . . . . Deep-V
Weight. . . . . 6,200#	Deadrise Aft . . . . 21°
Clearance, Arch. . . . . 6'9"	Production 1991–96

The 272 Commodore (called the Valenti 260 in 1991–92) was a popular family cruiser in the 1990s with traditional lines and a surprisingly spacious interior. Like most boats of her type and length, the 272 has a lot of unattractive freeboard—a necessity for standing cabin headroom. Featuring a molded bow pulpit and an integrated swim platform in addition to a curved windshield, the 272 was constructed on a fully cored, deep-V hull with a wide 9-foot, 2-inch beam. Her midcabin interior—slightly revised and updated in 1995—is arranged with a semicircular dinette/double berth forward, a standup head with vanity, and a spacious queen-size berth aft. Privacy curtains separate both sleeping areas from the main cabin, and the decor is a blend of quality furnishings and off-white cabinetry. On deck, the cockpit is arranged with a triple-wide helm seat forward and bench seating aft. A large, electrically operated hatch in the cockpit sole provides good access to the engine compartment. Among several sterndrive engine options, twin 180hp Volvos will cruise the 272 Commodore at 22 knots (high 30s top), while a single 300hp MerCruiser will cruise at 20 knots and top out around 35 knots.

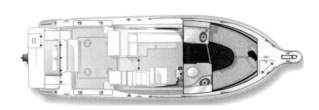

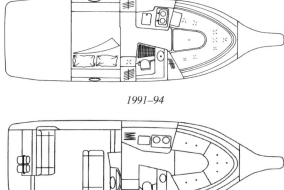

1991–94

1995–97

See Page 344 for Pricing Information

105

See Page 345 for Pricing Information

Regal 2660/2765 Commodore

Length . . . . 29'10"	Water. . . . . 28 gals.
Beam . . . . 8'6"	Waste . . . . 28 gals.
Draft, Down . . . . 2'9"	Headroom . . . . 6'1"
Weight. . . . . 6,100#	Hull Type . . . . Deep-V
Clearance. . . . . 7'2"	Deadrise Aft . . . . 21°
Fuel . . . . 76 gals.	Production 1999–Current

Regal's largest trailerable cruiser, the 2765 Commodore (called the 2660 Commodore from 1999–2001) has all the amenities a cruising family will need for comfortable overnight outings. Several manufacturers produce similar models, but the 2765's notched hull sets her apart from the others. (Notched hulls—originally designed for high-performance racing boats—are said to be more efficient than conventional V bottoms and able to attain higher top speeds.) The midcabin floorplan will comfortably sleep four adults, and while it can't be described as spacious, the cabin includes a compact head compartment, good ventilation, and a complete galley. On deck, the cockpit is arranged with a removable rear bench seat, a sun lounge opposite the helm (with a reversible backrest), swivel helm seat and a refreshment center with a removable cooler. Lacking side decks, molded steps next to the helm lead to an opening windshield. Note the large bolt-on swim platform. A single 310hp MerCruiser stern-drive will cruise the Regal 2765 at 20 knots (35–36 knots top), and twin 220hp MerCruisers I/Os will cruise in the low-to-mid 20s and reach a top speed in excess of knots.

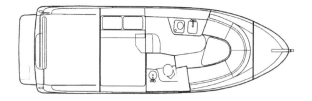

Regal 265/270/276 Commodore

Length w/Pulpit . . . . 29'6"	Fuel . . . . 110 gals.
Hull Length. . . . . 26'10"	Water. . . . . 35 gals.
Beam . . . . 9'6"	Hull Type . . . . Deep-V
Draft. 2'8"	Deadrise Aft . . . . 19°
Weight. . . . . 6,500#	Designer . . . . Regal
Clearance. . . . . 9'8"	Production 1990–93

Regal introduced this wide-body model in 1990 as the 265 Commodore—a well-finished family cruiser with a maxi-volume interior and berths for six. (Note that she was called the 270 Commodore in 1991–92 and the 276 Commodore in 1993.) Built on a beamy deep-V hull, her 9-foot, 6-inch beam is very wide for a 27-foot boat. Belowdecks, the Commodore's unusual floorplan leaves a lot to be desired. A double berth in the forepeak is reached by climbing over the semicircular sofa/dinette, and the effect of this arrangement is to make the main cabin seem very small indeed. A privacy door provides separates the aft cabin (and its standup dressing area) from the salon, while curtains isolate the forward berth, which, by the way, is only large enough for a couple of kids. Note that the head compartment is a tight fit. Topside, a back-to-back companion seat is opposite the helm, and engine access is via hatches in the cockpit sole. Additional features include a molded bow pulpit, foredeck sun pad, transom door, and bench seating at the transom. A single 330hp MerCruiser sterndrive will cruise at 19–20 knots (30+ knots top), and twin 180hp I/Os will top out in the high 30s.

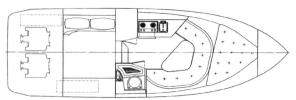

See Page 345 for Pricing Information

See Page 345 for Pricing Information

Regal 2760/2860 Commodore

Length Overall . . . . 30'7"	Water . . . . 27 gals.
Beam . . . . 9'11"	Waste . . . . 17 gals.
Draft . . . . 3'3"	Headroom . . . . 6'4"
Weight . . . . 7,800#	Hull Type . . . . Deep-V
Clearance . . . . 8'10"	Deadrise Aft . . . . 21°
Fuel . . . . 110 gals.	Production 1998–Current

The Regal 2870 (called the 2760 from 1998–2001) is a well-built express with innovative cockpit seating and a space-efficient interior. She's unlike other boats of her type and size in that she rides on a stepped hull, a race-bred design said to improve performance by ventilating the bottom. Like most modern express cruisers, the Commodore incorporates a midcabin floorplan with berths for six. The fore and aft sleeping areas, each with a double berth, are separated from the main cabin by a privacy curtains. (Note that the elbow room in the aft cabin is at a premium.) In a departure from the norm, the refrigerator is under the forward berth, which frees up some storage space beneath the galley counter. Topside, the cockpit is arranged with a double-wide seat at the helm, an L-shaped settee opposite, and a bench seat at the transom. A walk-through windshield provides access to the big foredeck sun pad. Additional features include a molded bow pulpit, radar arch, cockpit wet bar, tilt wheel, and a transom door. Among several engine options, twin 220hp MerCruisers I/Os will cruise at 22–23 knots and reach a top speed in the mid-to-high 30s.

Regal 277XL/280/290/300 Commodore

Length, 277XL/280 . . . . . . 27'1"	Fuel . . . . 140 gals.
Length, 290/300 . . . . 32'5"	Water . . . . 35 gals.
Beam . . . . 10'0"	Hull Type . . . . Modified-V
Draft . . . . 3'2"	Deadrise Aft . . . . 16°
Weight . . . . 8,200#	Designer . . . . Regal
Clearance . . . . 9'3"	Production 1982–94

Introduced in 1982 as the Regal 277XL, this model went through more model upgrades and name changes than just about any other boat in the business. After five years of production as the 277XL, Regal redesigned the deckhouse and added a curved windshield in 1988 and reintroduced her as the 280 Commodore. In 1990, a new integral swim platform was added—a major styling improvement—and she became the 290 Commodore. In 1993 she was marketed as the 300 Commodore—basically the same boat as the 290, but with a new name to more accurately reflect her longer length with the swim platform. Aside from cosmetic and decor updates, the midcabin interior layout remained unchanged until 1994 (the last year of production) when a new midcabin floorplan was introduced for the 300 Commodore. Built on a solid fiberglass hull with moderate beam, several single and twin sterndrive power options were offered over the years. Among them, a pair of 5.0-liter 4-cylinder MerCruisers will cruise at 18 knots (about 30 knots top), and the more popular 5.7-liter engines (Volvo or MerCruiser) will cruise around 23 knots (37–38 knots top).

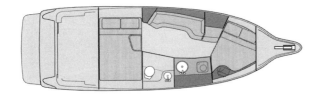

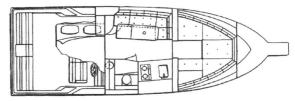

277XL/280 Commodore

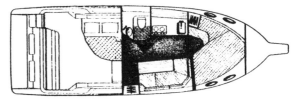

290/300 Commodore

See Page 345 for Pricing Information

See Page 345 for Pricing Information

Regal 292/2960/3060 Commodore

Length w/Ext. Platform . . . . . 31'10"	Waste . . . . 30 gals.
Hull Length . . . . 28'9"	Clearance, Arch . . . . 10'9"
Beam . . . . 11'2"	Headroom . . . . 6'3"
Weight . . . . 9,500#	Hull Type . . . . Deep-V
Fuel . . . . 150 gals.	Deadrise Aft . . . . 18°
Water . . . . 35 gals.	Production 1995–2003

The Regal 3060 Commodore (called the 292 Commodore in 1995–99 and the 2960 Commodore in 2000–2001) is an upmarket sterndrive cruiser with an attractive blend of crisp styling and comfortable accommodations. She was built on a solid fiberglass hull with a relatively wide beam, a sharp entry, and innovative trim tab pods beneath the swim platform. In the European fashion, she was one of a growing number of 1990s sportboat designs with no bow pulpit. Her plush, full-beam interior (there are no side decks) includes double berths fore and aft and a convertible dinette in the salon— berths for four adults and two kids. There are privacy curtains for both staterooms, and the rich furnishings and Corian countertops lend a touch of luxury seen only in better-quality boats. The cockpit has a U-shaped lounge aft that converts into a sun pad, a transom door, and a wet bar. Additional features include a walk-through windshield, a stylish radar arch, and—after 2002—an optional extended swim platform. Among several engine choices, twin 260hp MerCruiser I/Os will cruise at 22 knots and top out in the high 30s, and twin 280hp Volvo gas engines will cruise at 24 knots (about 40 knots top). Note that an all-new 3060 Commodore was introduced in 2004.

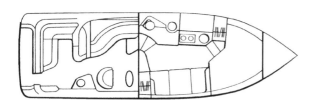

Regal 3060 Commodore

Length . . . . 30'10"	Fuel . . . . 151 gals.
Beam . . . . 10'6"	Water . . . . 35 gals.
Draft, Up . . . . 1'8"	Waste . . . . NA
Draft, Down . . . . 3'2"	Hull Type . . . . Modified-V
Weight . . . . 10,500#	Deadrise Aft . . . . 18°
Headroom . . . . 6'2"	Production 2004–Current

Aggressive styling is the hallmark of the Regal 3060 Commodore, a sporty midcabin express from a company with a long history of building good-quality family cruisers. Built on a modified-V hull with an extended swim platform, the sleek profile of the 3060 is accented by her rakish cat-eye cabin windows and sharply angled radar arch. The helm area keeps things sociable by positioning a circular lounge adjacent to the driver's seat. A foldaway bench seat in the cockpit provides additional seating, and there's a light switch inside the transom door for boarding at night. Belowdecks, the Regal 3060 has the distinction of being the only express cruiser in her class with a forward windshield, a design innovation that bathes the forward part of the cabin in an avalanche of natural lighting. The well-appointed interior compares well with other midcabin boats her size with berths for four, removable dinette table, full galley, and a good-sized head with sink and shower. Additional features include a companionway screen, swivel helm seat, cockpit wet bar with cooler, trim tabs, and hot/cold transom shower. Twin 260hp MerCruisers I/Os will cruise the Regal 3060 at 25 knots and reach a top speed in the low-to-mid 40s.

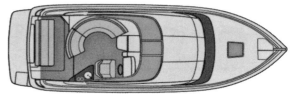

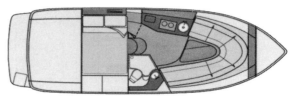

Regal 320 Commodore

Length	31'10"	Fuel	178 gals.
Beam	11'2"	Water	50 gals.
Draft, Up	1'8"	Hull Type	Deep-V
Draft, Down	2'11"	Deadrise Aft	19°
Weight	11,000#	Designer	Regal
Clearance	9'4"	Production	1988–92

A stylish boat by the standards of her day, the graceful profile of the Regal 320 Commodore still draws compliments from boaters today—a testament to her enduring popularity on the used market. She was built on a solid fiberglass, deep-V hull, and her 11-foot, 2-inch beam is modest compared with many of today's mega-beam cruisers. Belowdecks, the 320's midcabin floorplan is arranged in the conventional manner with double berths fore and aft and a convertible U-shaped dinette in the cabin. Privacy curtains separate the primary sleeping areas from the salon, and a deep storage bin is located beneath the midcabin berth. A full galley, lots of storage, an enclosed head/shower, and good headroom round out this comfortable interior. The cockpit—with seating for seven—came with a wet bar with ice maker, a centerline transom gate, a swim platform with fender storage, and a transom shower. Unlike a lot of sportboats, the 320 has side decks (although they are rather narrow). A foredeck sun pad and tilt steering wheel were standard. Twin 260hp sterndrives will cruise around 22 knots (about 35 knots top), and optional 340hp gas engines will cruise at 25 knots and reach a top speed of around 40 knots.

Regal Ventura 9.8; 322/3260 Commodore

Hull Length	32'0"	Water	50 gals.
Beam	11'2"	Waste	30 gals.
Draft	3'2"	Headroom	6'4"
Weight	11,800#	Hull Type	Deep-V
Clearance w/Arch	10'1"	Deadrise Aft	19°
Fuel	172 gals.	Production	1993–2004

The Regal 3260 Commodore (called the Ventura 9.8 in 1993–94 and the 322 Commodore from 1995–99) was a notably popular model for Regal. (Indeed, it's a rare event when a major manufacturer keeps a boat in production for a full decade.) Built on a deep-V hull with cored hullsides, the deluxe interior of the 322/3260 Commodore is a blend of high-end furnishings and quality components. The floorplan is arranged with an angled double berth forward, a posh Ultraleather sofa/dinette in the salon, and handsome U-shaped aft cabin seating that converts into a queen-size bed. (Note that in the inboard version a queen bed is permanent.) On deck, the cockpit is set up with a double-wide helm seat forward, wraparound guest seating aft, a built-in wet bar, and a transom door. An electric engine hatch provides access to the motors. Additional features include a radar arch, walk-through windshield, foredeck sun pad, and large transom lockers. A fast boat with 300hp MerCruiser sterndrives, the Regal 322/3260 will cruise at 25 knots and top out in the low 40s. With 300hp V-drive inboards, the cruising speed is around 22 knots with a top speed in the mid 30s. Note that engine access for inboard models is a tight fit.

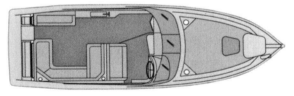

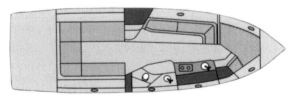

See Page 346 for Pricing Information

109

See Page 346 for Pricing Information

Regal 3560 Commodore

Length w/Ext. Platform	38'0"	Fuel	276 gals.
Hull Length	34'8"	Water	67 gals.
Beam	12'2"	Waste	30 gals.
Draft	3'0"	Hull Type	Deep-V
Weight	15,200#	Deadrise Aft	19°
Clearance, Arch	11'2"	Production	2003–Current

In a market crowded with midsize family cruisers, the Regal 3560 Commodore ranks near the top of her class in luxury, performance, and cost. Built on a conventional modified-V hull, the strong point of this yacht is her spacious interior with its high-gloss cherry cabinetry, Corian counters, and leather upholstery. A solid wood pocket door insures privacy in the forward stateroom, and the salon flows seamlessly into the midcabin, creating a large area for entertaining. The starboard settee folds out to become a double berth, and the refrigerator is positioned above the galley counter so you don't have to bend down every time you want a cold one. An elegant cherry-and-holly floor is standard, as is a flat-screen 15-inch TV/DVD in the main cabin. Abovedeck, the cockpit is arranged with a horseshoe lounge opposite the helm and a foldaway seat aft. Note that the single helm seat precludes the mate from joining the skipper. Offered with inboard or sterndrive power, Volvo 420hp Duoprop sterndrives will cruise at a fast 28–30 knots (40+ knots top), and 420hp MerCruiser inboards will cruise in the mid 20s and reach a top speed of close to 35 knots.

Regal 360 Commodore

Length	36'1"	Fuel	280 gals.
Beam	13'1"	Water	125 gals.
Draft	2'10"	Waste	65 gals.
Weight	17,000#	Hull Type	Modified-V
Clearance	9'7"	Deadrise Aft	17°
Headroom	6'8"	Production	1985–90

Introduced in 1985, the Regal 360 Commodore was the largest boat in the Regal fleet during her production years and one of the more popular big express cruisers of her era. By combining a streamlined design with a spacious interior, designer Jim Ginter sought to make the Commodore sophisticated enough to suggest performance, yet functional enough for extended cruising. Built on a solid fiberglass hull with prop pockets and a relatively wide beam, the midcabin interior of the Regal 360 sleeps six with double berths fore and aft and a convertible salon dinette that sleeps two more. The forward stateroom is a bit unusual in that the berth is oriented diagonally, a design that frees up additional space in the salon. A big semicircular sofa dominates the salon, and the head is divided into two sections with the sink/vanity forward and the stand-up shower compartment with toilet aft. A highlight of the 360 Commodore is her wide-open cockpit with its U-shaped lounge seating, double-wide helm and passenger seats, and full wet bar. A bow pulpit, teak swim platform, transom door, and foredeck sun pad were standard. MerCruiser 340hp gas inboards will cruise the Regal 360 at 20 knots and reach a top speed of around 28 knots.

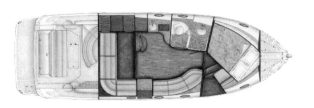

Regal 3860 Commodore

Length w/Platform	40'1"	Water	75 gals.
Beam	13'0"	Waste	40 gals.
Draft	3'3"	Headroom	6'6"
Weight	19,000#	Hull Type	Modified-V
Clearance, Arch	11'9"	Deadrise Aft	18°
Fuel	277 gals.	Production	2002–Current

A scaled-down version of the company's 4260 Commodore, the Regal 3860 Commodore may lack the cutting-edge sex appeal of a Pershing or Sea Ray, but she has a number of other attributes that make her a strong contender in the luxury cruiser market. Built on a modified-V hull with a solid fiberglass bottom, her two-stateroom interior differs from other mid-range express cruisers in that a second head compartment is tucked into the aft stateroom—a convenience seldom found in a boat this size. Both staterooms come with sliding privacy doors (rather than curtains), and a hardwood floor in the galley accents the high-gloss cherry cabinetry in the salon. In the cockpit, a semicircular settee offers plenty of guest seating. A wet bar is standard, and a walk-through windshield provides bow access. Note that the entire rear deck of the cockpit lifts hydraulically to permit walk-in access to the engine compartment from the swim platform. Additional features include a foredeck sun pad, an anchor washdown, and a power windshield vent. Standard 420hp V-drive gas engines will cruise at 18 knots (30+ knots top), and optional 370hp Cummins diesels will cruise at 22 knots and reach a top speed of 30 knots.

Regal 380/400/402 Commodore

Length w/Pulpit	42'0"	Fuel	265 gals.
Hull Length	39'5"	Water	125 gals.
Beam	13'1"	Waste	65 gals.
Draft	3'0"	Hull Type	Modified-V
Weight	16,000#	Deadrise Aft	17°
Clearance	9'5"	Production	1991–99

Regal is one of those manufacturers prone to renaming the same boat every so often just to keep it fresh in the minds of dealers and customers. Such is the case with this popular family cruiser: called the 380 Commodore in 1991–92, she was re-branded as the 400 Commodore in 1993–94, and in 1995—with a new interior and redesigned cockpit—she became the 402 Commodore. Always a popular model, she rides on a modified-V hull with a solid fiberglass bottom and prop pockets to reduce draft. Belowdecks, the floorplans of all three models feature privacy doors for both staterooms, a full galley, and a separate stall shower in the head. The 402 Commodore has an offset double berth in the forward stateroom as well as a leather salon sofa, while the aft galley location in the 380 and 400 models makes it easily accessed from the cockpit. Note the standing headroom in the aft cabin—a rare luxury in a boat this size. Additional features include an electric engine compartment hatch, side exhausts, and a roomy cockpit with seating for eight. Standard 310hp MerCruiser gas engines will cruise at 18–19 knots (27–28 knots top), and optional Cummins 330hp diesels cruise at 26 knots (about 30 knots top).

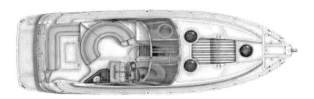

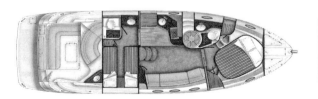

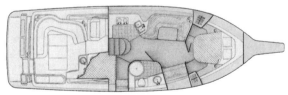

380/400 Layout

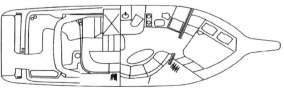

402 Layout

Regal 4160/4260 Commodore

Length w/Platform	44'4"	Fuel	328 gals.
Hull Length	40'10"	Water	101 gals.
Beam	14'0"	Waste	48 gals.
Draft	2'11"	Hull Type	Deep-V
Weight	20,375#	Deadrise Aft	20°
Clearance, Arch	10'7"	Production	2000–Current

Flagship of today's Regal fleet, the 4260 Commodore (called the 4160 during her first two years of production) is a high-style luxury sportyacht with a spacious, well-arranged interior and a particularly innovative cockpit layout. She rides on a beamy deep-V hull with propeller pockets, and her aggressive profile owes much to a gracefully integrated bow pulpit and a unique fore-and-aft arch design. Boarding from one of two transom gates, one is struck by the cockpit configuration—the aft section is small, but the elevated bridgedeck is huge with a large U-shaped settee and table opposite the helm. This is a very social layout since most of the guest seating is centered near the double-wide helm rather than aft as it is on most express cruisers. The Regal's plush two-stateroom interior is notable in that both cabins have pocket doors for privacy (rather than curtains) and each has its own head. Additional features include a walk-through windshield, cockpit wet bar, a power-assist windshield vent, foredeck sun pad, and a large transom storage locker. A good performer with optional 450hp Cummins (or 480hp Volvo) diesels, the Regal 4260 will cruise at 28 knots and reach a top speed of just over 30 knots.

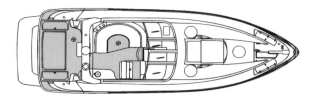

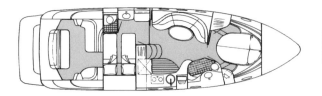

Rinker 270 Fiesta Vee

Length w/Platform	27'10"	Fuel	100 gals.
Hull Length	27'10"	Water	33 gals.
Beam	9'1"	Waste	27 gals.
Draft, Up	1'10"	Hull Type	Modified-V
Draft, Down	3'0"	Deadrise Aft	18°
Weight	7,350#	Production	1999–Current

Bargain hunters looking for a big 27-foot family cruiser with a midcabin layout and a low price will want to check out Rinker's 270 Fiesta Vee. Indeed, this is a boat that offers a lot of bang for the buck, and as long as one isn't too obsessed with fine detailing the Fiesta Vee should satisfy the demands of most entry-level buyers. Built on a solid fiberglass modified-V hull, the 270 is not trailerable like many 27-footers thanks to her generous 9-foot, 1-inch beam. The interior is arranged like most midcabin cruisers her size with a convertible dinette/V-berth forward, complete galley, enclosed head with shower, and a double berth aft with a curtain for privacy. The single-level cockpit—updated in 2002 with a wet bar and double helm seat—has lounge seating aft and a transom door. Standard features include a walk-through windshield, electric engine hatch (which is actually part of the rear seat) windshield wiper, and transom shower. Among many sterndrive engine choices, a single 320hp MerCruiser 6.2L will cruise the 270 Fiesta Vee in the low 20s and top out at 35+ knots. With just 100 gallons of fuel capacity, don't plan any long trips.

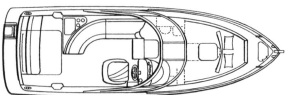

1999–2001

2002–Current

Rinker 280 Fiesta Vee

Length w/Pulpit . . . . 30'2"	Fuel . . . . 120 gals.
Beam . . . . 10'0"	Water . . . . 33 gals.
Draft, Up . . . . 1'10"	Waste . . . . 27 gals.
Draft, Down . . . . 3'0"	Hull Type . . . . Deep-V
Weight . . . . 8,680#	Deadrise Aft . . . . 20°
Clearance, Arch . . . . 8'11"	Production 1993–99

Like all Rinker models, the 280 Fiesta Vee is a budget-priced, no-glitz package with a lot of standard features that other manufacturers consider as extra-cost options. Hull construction is solid fiberglass, and her 10-foot beam is about average for an express cruiser her size. She's a good-looking boat with her integral swim platform and curved windshield, and despite the low price, the overall fit and finish is surprisingly good. The 280's midcabin floorplan is typical of family cruisers her size with double berths fore and aft, convertible dinette, and a compact galley. Privacy curtains separate the sleeping areas from the salon. Headroom is excellent throughout, and there are plenty of storage bins and lockers. On deck, the cockpit is arranged with a big L-shaped settee opposite the helm and bench seating at the transom. Note that the side decks are narrow and foredeck access is no easy matter, especially underway. The fuel capacity is pretty light as well. Twin 180hp 4.3-liter sterndrives will cruise the Rinker 280 around 20 knots (about 30 knots top), and optional 235hp 5.7-liter Mercs will cruise in the mid 20s and reach 35+ knots wide open. Note the limited fuel capacity.

Rinker 290/300 Fiesta Vee

Length w/Platform . . . . 31'6"	Fuel . . . . 150 gals.
Beam . . . . 10'6"	Water . . . . 33 gals.
Draft, Up . . . . 1'10"	Waste . . . . 47 gals.
Draft, Down . . . . 3'0"	Hull Type . . . . Modified-V
Weight . . . . 11,100#	Deadrise Aft . . . . 18°
Headroom . . . . 6'4"	Production 2003–Current

The Rinker 300 Fiesta Vee (called the 290 Fiesta Vee in 2003–04) is an entry-level family cruiser whose low price and impressive inventory of standard equipment makes her one of the better values in a boat of this type. For a so-called "price boat," the 300 manages to deliver most of the features found in more expensive boats. While the materials and finish may not compare with a Sea Ray or Regal, the Fiesta Vee is a capable entertainment platform with a comfortable cabin layout and plenty of cockpit seating. Built on a solid fiberglass hull, the interior is arranged in the typical fashion with a forward V-berth (which is a little narrow), a double midcabin berth, and a convertible dinette. The TV/VCR is positioned for easy viewing from the dinette, and cherry laminate cabinetry and a faux granite counter accents the compact galley. Topside, an L-lounge opposite the helm and a bench seat at the transom will seat several passengers in comfort. An electric hatch provides good access to the engine compartment. A radar arch, extended swim platform, windlass and tilt steering wheel are all standard. Twin 260hp MerCruiser I/Os will cruise the Rinker 290/300 in the mid 20s and reach a top speed of over 35 knots.

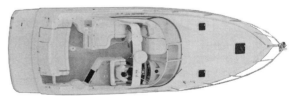

Rinker 300 Fiesta Vee

Length w/Pulpit	33'11"	Water	34 gals.
Beam	10'6"	Waste	25 gals.
Draft, Up	1'8"	Clearance, Arch	9'8"
Draft, Down	2'10"	Hull Type	Modified-V
Weight	10,000#	Deadrise Aft	18°
Fuel	140 gals.	Production	1990–97

A good-selling model for Rinker during the 1990s, the 300 Fiesta Vee owed her popularity to a very affordable price, a comfortable interior, and surprisingly good performance. Hull construction is solid fiberglass, and the Fiesta Vee's generous 10-foot, 6-inch beam results in spacious cabin accommodations well-suited to the needs of a small family. Her midcabin floorplan is arranged in the normal manner with double berths fore and aft, a convertible dinette in the salon, fully equipped galley, and a very spacious head compartment. Storage—including the aircraft-style overhead lockers—is excellent. Note that the midcabin, with its removable table, is a separate seating area during the day, while a privacy curtain separates it from the main salon at night. With its integrated swim platform and bow pulpit, the 300 Fiesta Vee looks like a larger boat. Lounge seating in the cockpit can easily accommodate six adults, however narrow side decks makes a trip to the foredeck a bit of a challenge. Note, too, that the fit and finish is unimpressive. Among several engine choices, twin 260hp 5.7-liter MerCruiser sterndrives will cruise the Rinker 300 in the low 20s while delivering a top speed in excess of 35 knots.

Rinker 310/312/320 Fiesta Vee

Length w/Platform	33'4"	Water	51 gals.
Beam	11'4"	Waste	45 gals.
Draft, Down	3'0"	Headroom	6'5"
Weight	12,360#	Hull Type	Modified-V
Clearance	9'6"	Deadrise Aft	18°
Fuel	165 gals.	Production	2000–Current

One of the most affordable boats in her class, the Rinker 320 Fiesta Vee (called the 310 Fiesta Vee in 2000–02 and the 312 Fiesta Vee in 2003–04) is a roomy family cruiser that might best be described as a lot of boat for the money. Rinker has a reputation for building solid, well-equipped boats at prices much lower than the competition, and the 320 will appeal to entry-level buyers suffering sticker-shock from their last visit to a Sea Ray dealer. Built on a beamy modified-V hull with relatively high freeboard, the Fiesta Vee is an notably spacious boat inside with excellent headroom and plenty of storage. The midcabin floorplan will sleep six, and while the decor is a little plain compared with some of her more upscale counterparts, the accommodations are arranged in a practical and very utilitarian manner. In the cockpit, a comfortable U-shaped settee is opposite the helm with a mini-galley and transom seating is aft. Additional features include a radar arch, transom door, swim platform, fender storage, and an electric engine access hatch. A good performer, twin 260hp 5.0-liter sterndrive engines will cruise the Fiesta Vee at 20 knots and reach a top speed of 35+ knots.

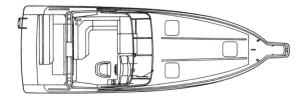

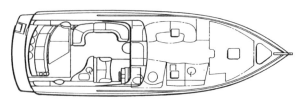

Rinker 330/340/342 Fiesta Vee

Length w/Platform . . . . 37'0"	Water . . . . 51 gals.
Beam . . . . 12'0"	Waste . . . . 45 gals.
Draft, Down . . . . 2'11"	Headroom . . . . 6'5"
Weight . . . . 14,280#	Hull Type . . . . Modified-V
Clearance . . . . 9'8"	Deadrise Aft . . . . 18°
Fuel . . . . 200/235 gals.	Production 1998–Current

The Rinker 342 Fiesta Vee (called the 330 Fiesta Vee in 1998–99, and the 340 in 2000–2001) is a midsize family cruiser whose chief attractions are a spacious interior and a very affordable price. Built on a beamy semi-V hull, the Fiesta Vee's original midcabin floorplan was arranged a little different from the norm in that the galley refrigerator is forward, under the double berth. On the downside, sitting headroom in both the fore and aft berths was very low in early models. Significantly, Rinker updated the boat for 2000 (when she became the 340 Fiesta Vee) with a lowered floor in the salon and new, taller, foredeck tooling that increased cabin headroom and overall living space. An all-new floorplan was introduced in 2002—along with an extended swim platform and additional fuel—when she became the 342 Fiesta Vee. The cockpit, with seating for six to eight, includes a full wet bar with sink and refrigerator. Additional features include a walk-through windshield, electric engine hatch, extended swim platform, and transom shower. Among several sterndrive options, twin 280hp Volvo gas sterndrives will cruise the Fiesta Vee in the low-to-mid 20s and reach a top speed of around 35 knots.

Rinker 360 Fiesta Vee

EXPRESS CRUISERS

Length . . . . 39'4"	Fuel . . . . 235 gals.
Beam . . . . 12'3"	Water . . . . 51 gals.
Draft, Up . . . . 2'0"	Waste . . . . 45 gals.
Draft, Down . . . . 3'0"	Hull Type . . . . Modified-V
Weight . . . . 18,200#	Deadrise Aft . . . . 18°
Clearance, Arch . . . . 13'0"	Production 2005–Current

The Rinker 360 Fiesta Vee offers buyers what marketing people call a lot of boat for the money. Indeed, with her crisp styling, brisk performance and comfortable accommodations, the 360 easily holds her own against many of the more expensive boats in her class. Built on a solid fiberglass hull with relatively modest beam, the interior of the Rinker 360 differs from the typical midcabin boat in that the forward stateroom is separated from the salon by a solid wood bulkhead door rather than just a curtain. (This is no small feature for those who value privacy when cruising with family or friends.) The salon galley is large enough for serious meal-preparation activities, and the midcabin—partially obstructed by the companionway steps—is unusually spacious. The head compartment is also quite large and includes a separate shower enclosure. On deck, the cockpit has a full wet bar with sink, icemaker, refrigerator, and built-in blender. A flip-up helm seat allows for stand-up driving, and molded steps access the walk-through windshield. Note that the entire aft deck can be raised on hydraulic rams to reach the engines. A good performer, twin 375hp MerCruiser sterndrives deliver a top speed of just over 40 knots.

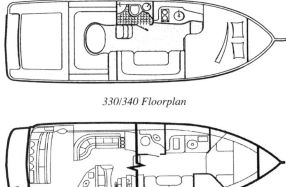

330/340 Floorplan

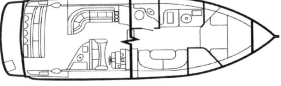

342 Floorplan

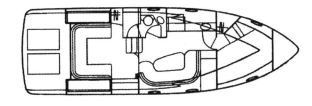

See Page 346 for Pricing Information

See Page 346 for Pricing Information

Rinker 410 Fiesta Vee

Length w/Platform	43'6"	Fuel	300 gals.
Beam	13'10"	Water	100 gals.
Draft	3'2"	Waste	88 gals.
Weight	23,500#	Hull Type	Modified-V
Clearance	12'10"	Deadrise Aft	18°
Headroom	7'0"	Production	2004–Current

Rinker's largest boat ever, the 410 Fiesta Vee (called the 390 Fiesta Vee in 2004) is a roomy midcabin cruiser whose affordable price includes an impressive array of standard features. Built on a beamy modified-V hull with a solid fiberglass bottom, the highlight of the 410 is her spacious interior with its 7-foot headroom, full-size sofa, and massive amounts of storage space. Privacy doors separate the fore and aft staterooms from the main salon, and both staterooms come with individual climate controls as well as a built-in TVs. (Note that the aft stateroom has a separate berth for one child.) In the alcove just off the head is a full-size washer/dryer combination, while the galley features not just the expected microwave, but a real oven. Topside, the cockpit comes with a double helm seat, wet bar with refrigerator, icemaker and blender, six-speaker CD changer, and a U-shaped aft lounge that converts into a big sun pad. Additional features include cherry interior cabinetry, salon entertainment center, transom storage locker, folding radar arch, and a gas grill that slides into a base of the extended swim platform. Twin V-drive 420hp gas engines will cruise at 22–23 knots (about 30 knots top), and 370hp Cummins diesels will cruise at 25–26 knots (also 30 knots top).

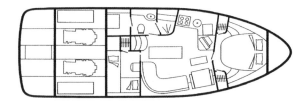

Riviera 3000 Offshore

Length w/Platform	34'9"	Fuel	164 gals.
Hull Length	30'10"	Water	61 gals.
Beam	11'4"	Hull Type	Modified-V
Weight	12,141	Deadrise Aft	18°
Draft	2'11"	Designer	Riviera
Headroom	6'2"	Production	2000–03

Introduced into the U.S. market in 2000, the conservative styling of the Riviera 3000 Offshore lacks the sex appeal of most American and European sportboats. Hidden beneath her plain-Jane exterior, however, is something seldom found in a 30-foot express—standard inboard diesel power. Built on a solid fiberglass hull with a moderate 11-foot, 4-inch beam, the most noted downside of the Riviera 3000 is her compact interior. Although nicely finished and including a full galley as well as a convertible dinette and standup head compartment, these are tight accommodations for a 30-footer with virtually no counter space in the galley and very modest storage. The Offshore's bi-level cockpit, on the other hand, is particularly spacious. The entire bridgedeck rises on hydraulic rams for access to the motors, and the aft cockpit is large enough for two or more anglers and their gear. Standard features include excellent nonskid surfaces, generator, windlass, wide side decks, swim platform, and fiberglass fuel tanks—a real plus in the eyes of many. Volvo 260hp diesels will cruise the Riviera 3000 in the mid-to-high 20s and top out at over 30 knots. Note the small fuel capacity.

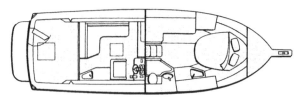

Riviera 4000 Offshore

Rivolta 38 Jet Coupe

Length Overall	44'7"	Water	119 gals.
Hull Length	41'0"	Headroom	6'4"
Beam	14'4"	Hull Type	Modified-V
Draft	3'11"	Deadrise Aft	15°
Weight	25,353#	Designer	Riviera
Fuel	394 gals.	Production	1998–2003

Length	38'4"	Fuel	290 gals.
Beam	12'4"	Water	137 gals.
Draft	1'6"	Waste	40 gals.
Weight	17,867#	Hull Type	Modified-V
Clearance	10'0"	Deadrise Aft	14°
Headroom	6'2"	Production	2002–Current

Riviera's first-ever express when she was introduced in 1998, the 4000 Offshore is a competitively priced family cruiser with conservative lines (note the absence of an integrated swim platform) and a well-arranged interior. She's constructed on a solid fiberglass semi-V hull with a wide 14-foot, 4-inch beam and a shallow keel for directional stability. Below, the oak-finished interior provides a sleeping capacity for four people, including a large forward cabin with an island berth. The salon dinette converts to double berth, and the Riviera's large head compartment includes a separate shower stall. A mirror-backed cocktail cabinet separates the dining area from the forward stateroom. On deck, the cockpit has a double helm seat, a second dinette with a molded-in freezer and sink, and a hydraulic midship hatch for engine room access. (Note that the Riviera has a spacious engine room—something that wouldn't be possible with a conventional midcabin interior.) Additional features include a cockpit transom door, radar arch, swim platform, and a bow pulpit. Among several engine options, a pair of 450hp Cummins (or 435hp Cat) diesels will cruise the 4000 Offshore in the mid 20s and reach a top speed of close to 30 knots.

Free of propellers, shafts and rudders, the jet-powered Rivolta 38 is an ideal shallow-water cruiser whose timeless appearance will likely attract a crowd wherever she goes. Waterjet power makes a lot of sense for boaters who often find themselves in skinny water, and with a draft of just 18 inches the Rivolta will be difficult boat to run aground. Aside from her beautiful styling, the focal point of this semicustom yacht is her partially enclosed helm area with its glove-leather seating, rooftop vents, wet bar, and opening side windows. Belowdecks, the compact interior of the Rivolta 38 sleeps four in a practical layout that includes a private forward stateroom, athwartship midcabin berth, and an opulent U-shaped galley in the main cabin area. One of the more appealing aspects of the Rivolta is her large cockpit—partially shaded by the extended hardtop—which is perfect for entertaining or fishing. Additional highlights include cherry interior cabinetry, underwater exhausts, swim platform, and an easily accessed engine compartment. Because a jet boat handles differently from a traditional inboard boat, some time is required to adjust to the joystick controls. Twin Yanmar 350hp diesels will cruise in the mid 20s and reach a top speed of over 30 knots.

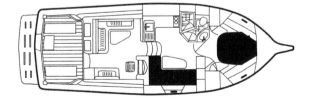

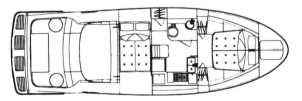

Sabreline 36 Express

Length w/Pulpit	40'1"	Fuel	300 gals.
Hull Length	36'0"	Water	100 gals.
Beam	12'6"	Headroom	6'5"
Draft	3'4"	Hull Type	Modified-V
Weight	18,500#	Deadrise Aft	14°/18°
Clearance, Mast	12'0"	Production	1996–2003

Traditional styling, comfortable accommodations, and quality construction are the hallmarks of the Sabreline 36 Express, a Downeast classic that will turn heads in any marina. Built on a fully cored hull with moderate beam, the bottom was redesigned in 2000 (the MKII version) by increasing the transom deadrise from 14 to 18 degrees and eliminating the skeg of the earlier model. While the Sabreline's bi-level cockpit is roomy enough for some light-tackle fishing—and the bridgedeck has adequate seating for family and friends—it's the elegant interior that captures the hearts of purists. Here, a blend of varnished hardwood cabinetry, solid panel doors, and a teak-and-holly sole create a warm and completely inviting living area. Notable features of the Sabreline 36 include wide side decks, a transom door, side exhausts, radar mast, and a well-arranged engine room. On the downside, there's no shower stall in the head. Early hull models with 300hp Cat diesels will cruise at 20 knots (around 24 knots top), and later MKII versions with 315hp Yanmars will cruise in the mid 20s (around 28 knots top), and optional 370hp Yanmars will cruise in the mid 20s and top out at 30+ knots.

Sabreline 38 Express

Length	36'8"	Fuel	350 gals.
Beam	13'8"	Water	100 gals.
Draft	3'4"	Headroom	30 gals.
Weight	21,500#	Hull Type	Modified-V
Clearance, Mast	13'5"	Deadrise Aft	16°
Headroom	6'5"	Production	2005–Current

The Sabreline 38 Express combines classic Downeast styling and lively performance in a hardtop cruising yacht of exceptional beauty. Built on vacuum-bagged hull with a wide 13-foot, 8-inch beam and prop pockets, the focal point of the 38 Express is her semi-enclosed pilothouse with its swivel helm and companion seats, folding teak table, and full wet bar with refrigerator and icemaker. Stepping below, the handcrafted cherry interior of the 38 Express offers all the conveniences and amenities sophisticated cruisers demand, from a recessed entertainment center with flat-screen TV and DVD player to a beautiful inlaid dinette table crafted in cherry and bird's-eye maple. A sliding door separates the master stateroom from the salon, and the compact but functional galley is positioned close to the companionway steps where it's convenient to the helm deck. The hardtop has a pair of screened hatches for ventilation and the side windows slide open. The wide side decks of the Sabreline are notable in that they permit excellent access to the foredeck area—a safety feature often overlooked in modern yachts. Yanmar 440hp diesels will cruise the Sabreline 38 at 25–26 knots and reach a top speed of just over 30 knots.

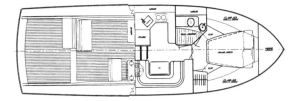

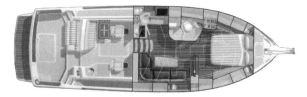

See Page 347 for Pricing Information

See Page 347 for Pricing Information

Sabreline 42 Express

Length . . . . 42'3"	Water . . . . 160 gals.
Beam . . . . 14'4"	Waste . . . . 60 gals.
Draft . . . . 3'9"	Headroom . . . . 6'6"
Weight . . . . 29,000#	Hull Type . . . . Modified-V
Clearance, Mast . . . . 13'3"	Deadrise Aft . . . . 16°
Fuel . . . . 450 gals.	Production 2004–Current

Introduced in 2004, the Sabreline 42 Express embodies the graceful styling, luxurious accommodations, and high-quality construction common to all Sabreline yachts. The 42 is a particularly handsome yacht, and her low-profile cabintop conceals a considerable amount of living space below. Built on a modified-V hull with a wide beam and prop pockets, the focal point of the 42 Express is her semi-enclosed pilothouse with its swivel helm and companion seats, folding teak table, and full wet bar. Belowdecks, the traditional two-stateroom interior is highlighted with varnished cherrywood cabinetry, leather upholstery, and a beautiful teak-and-holly sole. The master stateroom can be fitted with a pedestal berth or V-berths. The guest stateroom contains a double berth, and both cabins share a large head with a circular shower stall. On the downside, the galley is small for a 42-foot yacht. A transom door, radar mast, and bow pulpit are standard. Note that the hull of the Sabreline 42 is built with vacuum-bagged PVC foam core making it light and extremely strong. Twin 420hp Yanmar diesels cruise in the low 20s (26–27 knots top), and 465hp Yanmars will cruise in the mid 20s and reach a top speed of around 30 knots.

San Juan 38

Length Overall . . . . 40'7"	Fuel . . . . 300 gals.
Beam . . . . 12'2"	Water . . . . 80 gals.
Draft . . . . 2'2"	Hull Type . . . . Modified-V
Weight . . . . 15,800#	Deadrise Aft . . . . 14°
Clearance . . . . 9'11"	Designer . . . . Greg Marshall
Headroom . . . . 6'1"	Production 2000–Current

The San Juan 38 is a Downeast-inspired runabout with an impressive blend of beautiful styling, state-of-the-art hull construction, and luxurious accommodations. Her sophisticated, foam-cored hull is vacuum-bagged, and the use of Kevlar in the construction process greatly increases strength and impact resistance. The heart of the San Juan 38 is her semi-enclosed pilothouse with its 360-degree visibility, convertible dinette, and elegant teak helm station. Port and starboard sun pads, extending aft into the cockpit, lift to provide excellent service access to the engines. Belowdeck, the San Juan's traditional two-stateroom interior is richly appointed with varnished teak cabinetry, faux granite counters, and a teak-and-holly sole. The layout has a V-berth forward and a queen berth amidships, abaft the companionway stairs. The arched doorways are notable, as are the quality fabrics and hardware. Additional features include a transom seat, bow thruster, custom drop curtain, wet bar, and teak exterior trim. A lightweight boat for her size, Yanmar 350hp diesel inboards will cruise the San Juan 38 in the mid 20s and reach a top speed of close to 30 knots.

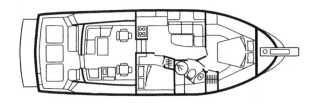

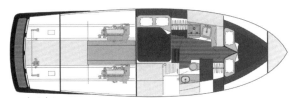

Sea Ray 270 Amberjack

Length w/Pulpit	29'3"	Fuel	200 gals.
Hull Length	27'7"	Water	28 gals.
Beam	10'0"	Cockpit	NA
Draft, Down	2'8"	Hull Type	Deep-V
Drive, Up	1'3"	Deadrise Aft	22°
Weight	7,000#	Production	1986–90

A good-selling boat for Sea Ray during her late 1980s production years, the 270 Amberjack is a roomy express fisherman with an unusually large cockpit to go with her basic cabin accommodations. Construction is solid fiberglass, and her 10-foot beam is wide for a 27-footer. The single-level cockpit is arranged with a fore-and-aft companion seat opposite the helm and foldaway bench seating at the transom. There's a storage bin between the two seats, and additional storage is located under the gunwales. Inside, the cabin is fitted with V-berths, an enclosed standup head compartment with shower, and a compact galley area. Because of her generous cockpit dimensions, the interior of the Amberjack is smaller than many other express boats her size—a design decision anglers will appreciate. A single hatch at the transom provides good access to the engines. Additional features include a small transom door, swim platform with ladder, teak bow pulpit, and teak covering boards. Among several engine choices, a pair of 260hp MerCruiser sterndrives will cruise the Sea Ray 270 Amberjack in the low 20s and reach a top speed of over 30 knots.

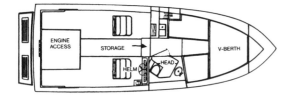

Sea Ray 270 Sundancer (1982–88)

Length w/Pulpit	29'2"	Water	28 gals.
Hull Length	27'7"	Headroom	6'2"
Beam	10'0"	Hull Type	Deep-V
Draft	2'8"	Deadrise Aft	22°
Weight	6,700#	Designer	Sea Ray
Fuel	120 gals.	Production	1982–88

An extremely popular boat with family-size accommodations and a comfortable ride, the 270 Sundancer enjoyed a long and successful production run for Sea Ray during the mid-to-late 1980s. She was built on a solid fiberglass deep-V hull, and a wide 10-foot beam provides plenty of room belowdecks for a comfortable interior. Aside from the normal fabric and decor updates, the 270's midcabin floorplan layout remained essentially unchanged over the years. With a complete galley and enclosed standup head, there are berths for six including a V-berth forward, a double berth aft, and a convertible dinette in the main cabin. In 1987, the original mica interior woodwork gave way to teak, and a radar arch became standard. The cockpit is arranged with an elevated double-wide helm seat, in-deck storage, transom door, and bench seating at the transom. A teak bow pulpit and swim platform with ladder were standard. Several sterndrive engine options were offered during her production years. Among them, a pair of 260hp MerCruisers will cruise the 270 Sundancer in the low 20s and reach a top speed of close to 35 knots.

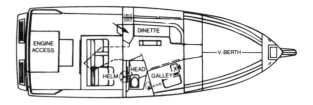

Sea Ray 270 Sundancer (1992–93)

Length w/Pulpit . . . . 28'6"	Clearance. . . . . 7'0"
Hull Length. . . . . 26'9"	Fuel . . . . 99 gals.
Beam . . . . 8'6"	Water. . . . . 24 gals.
Draft, Up . . . . 1'8"	Hull Type . . . . Deep-V
Draft, Down . . . . 3'0"	Deadrise Aft . . . . 20°
Weight. . . . . 5,600#	Production 1992–93

Second in a series of 270 Sundancers from Sea Ray, this particular model evolved from the original 250 Sundancer introduced back in 1988. Unlike the original 270 Sundancer (previous page), this 270 Sundancer is trailerable thanks to her 8-foot, 6-inch beam. (It's worth noting that most 27-foot boats are not trailerable since it takes a heavy-duty truck to tow a load this size.) A good-looking boat with a still-stylish profile, the 270 Sundancer is built on a solid fiberglass hull with a molded bow pulpit and an integrated swim platform. Belowdecks, the conventional midcabin floorplan is arranged with V-berths forward, a removable dinette table, an efficient galley area, and a standup head with shower. The double berth in the aft cabin is big enough for two adults and may be curtained off for privacy. Cockpit accommodations include a three-person transom settee facing another two-seater behind the helm. A single 330hp 7.4-liter MerCruiser sterndrive will cruise the Sea Ray 270 Sundancer at 20 knots (around 32–33 knots top), and optional 190hp 4.3-liter sterndrives cruise in the low-to-mid 20s and top out in the neighborhood of 35 knots.

Sea Ray 270 Sundancer (1994–97)

Length w/Pulpit . . . . 29'11"	Fuel . . . . 100 gals.
Hull Length. . . . . 27'4"	Water. . . . . 24 gals.
Beam . . . . 8'6"	Hull Type . . . . Deep-V
Draft, Up . . . . 1'11"	Deadrise Aft. . . . . 19.5°
Draft, Down . . . . 3'0"	Designer. . . . . Sea Ray
Weight. . . . . 6,400#	Production 1994–97

A good-selling boat, the 270 Sundancer (note that there were two earlier versions of the 270 Sundancer) is built on the same solid fiberglass hull used for her immediate predecessor, but with a revised deck profile and an updated cockpit layout. With a relatively narrow (for a 27-footer) 8-foot, 6-inch beam, this is a trailerable boat, but only with a 3/4-ton truck. The companionway is on the centerline in this model, and the old bi-fold companionway door of the previous model was replaced with a sliding acrylic door that's easier to operate. Below, the Sundancer's midcabin floorplan features a convertible dinette/V-berth forward, a complete galley with generous counter space, and a standup head with sink and shower. The mid-stateroom includes a double bunk, sliding windows, and a privacy curtain. On deck, a double helm seat with an aft-facing seat, refreshment center, and foldaway rear seat were standard. A single 330hp 7.4-liter MerCruiser sterndrive will cruise the Sundancer in the low 20s and reach a top speed of about 35 knots. Out of production in 1998, she was briefly reintroduced into the Sea Ray fleet for 1999 as the 270 Sundancer "Special Edition."

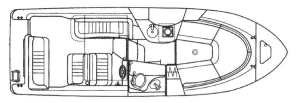

Sea Ray 270 Sundancer (1998–2001)

Sea Ray 270 Weekender

Length w/Platform	29'10"	Fuel	100 gals.
Hull Length	27'8"	Water	28 gals.
Beam	9'2"	Waste	28 gals.
Draft, Up	1'11"	Hull Type	Deep-V
Draft, Down	3'5"	Deadrise Aft	21°
Weight	7,500#	Production	1998–2001

Length w/Pulpit	28'6"	Clearance	6'10"
Hull Length	26'9"	Fuel	100 gals.
Beam	8'6"	Water	24 gals.
Draft, Up	1'8"	Hull Type	Deep-V
Draft, Down	3'0"	Deadrise Aft	20°
Weight	5,600#	Production	1992–93

There have been several 270 Sundancer models in the Sea Ray fleet going back to the early 1980s. Unlike her predecessors, however, this most recent version of the 270 Sundancer is not trailerable—a notable difference that results in a roomier (and heavier) boat. Built on a deep-V hull with a wide 9-foot, 2-inch beam, the 270 Sundancer is a well-styled cruiser with clean lines and simple hull graphics. With her wider beam, the interior is spacious for a 27-footer with comfortable accommodations for as many as six. There's a V-berth forward, a double berth in the mid-stateroom, a full galley (but not much counter space), and a standup head with sink and shower. In the cockpit, a portside settee is opposite the helm and a cooler is located under the aft-facing jump seat. Note that the foredeck steps are molded into the cabin door—a useful feature that opens up space at the helm. Additional features include a transom storage bin, cockpit shower, an extended swim platform, and a gas-assist engine hatch. A single 310hp MerCruiser sterndrive will cruise the 270 Sundancer at 20 knots (about 32–33 knots top), and twin 190hp Mercs will top out in the mid-to-high 30s.

The Sea Ray 270 Weekender, a well-styled boat that still looks pretty good today, is a trailerable family dayboat with a spacious cockpit and a compact interior with accommodations for two. A 27-foot cruiser is a lot of boat to tow, and the Weekender is one of just a handful of boats her size narrow enough to be legally trailerable without a permit. From a distance, she looks quite similar to her sistership of the early 1990s, the Sea Ray 270 Sundancer. But where the Sundancer has a midcabin layout with berths for four, the Weekender has a much smaller interior with a convertible dinette/V-berth forward, a mini-galley, and a standup head with shower. The Weekender's single-level cockpit, however, is very spacious with plenty of room for fishing or entertaining. In a word, the Weekender will appeal to those placing a premium on outdoor fun rather than cabin space. Standard features include a transom door, an integral swim platform, transom shower, a foldaway bench seat at the transom, and a bow pulpit. Built on a solid fiberglass deep-V hull, a single 300hp MerCruiser sterndrive engine will cruise the Sea Ray 270 Weekender at 20 knots and reach a top speed of 30+ knots.

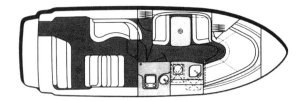

Sea Ray 270/290 Sundancer (1990–93)

Sea Ray 280 Sundancer (1989–91)

Length w/Pulpit	30'6"	Water	24 gals.
Hull Length	28'7"	Clearance	NA
Beam	9'0"	Hull Type	Deep-V
Draft	3'1"	Deadrise Aft	20°
Weight	5,800#	Designer	Sea Ray
Fuel	100 gals.	Production	1990–93

The Sea Ray 290 Sundancer (called the 270 Sundancer in 1990–91) combined sporty performance and comfortable accommodations in an affordable, well-styled package. She's built on a solid fiberglass deep-V hull, and her integral swim platform, curved windshield and molded pulpit combine to give her the sleek profile common to all recent Sea Ray sportboats. (Note that her 9-foot beam is quite modest for a boat this size.) The original midcabin floorplan is arranged in the conventional manner with double berths fore and aft, a full galley, and a standup head with shower. Draw curtains are used for privacy in the staterooms, and storage space is at a premium (as it is in just about all family boats this size). In 1993, Sea Ray introduced an alternate floorplan with a U-shaped dinette to starboard and the galley and head to port. The cockpit came standard with a radar arch, foldaway stern seating, refreshment center and a transom door. Visibility from the raised double-wide helm seat is very good. A single 300hp MerCruiser sterndrive will cruise the Sea Ray 270/290 Sundancer at 20 knots and reach a top speed of about 35 knots.

Length w/Pulpit	31'11"	Fuel	120 gals.
Hull Length	28'0"	Water	35 gals.
Beam	10'6"	Hull Type	Deep-V
Draft	2'8"	Deadrise Aft	20°
Weight	8,000#	Designer	J. Michelak
Clearance	9'0"	Production	1989–91

The Sea Ray 280 Sundancer was introduced in 1989 as a replacement for the very popular Sea Ray 270 Sundancer (1982–88). A good-looking cruiser with her curved windshield and integrated swim platform, the 280 rides on a solid fiberglass deep-V hull with a flared bow and relatively wide 10-foot, 6-inch beam. Below, the Sundancer's wide-open cabin layout delivers comfortable overnight accommodations for as many as six adults. The floorplan is arranged in the conventional manner with V-berths forward and a wide double berth in the good-sized midcabin. Curtains are used for privacy in both staterooms, and the dinette converts into a double berth for extra overnight guests. Topside, visibility from the elevated double helm seat is excellent, and bench seating in the cockpit will accommodate several guests. A pair of hatches in the cockpit sole provide good access to the engines. Additional features include a molded bow pulpit, radar arch, cockpit bolsters, cockpit refreshment center, and a transom door. Twin 260hp MerCruiser sterndrives will cruise the 280 Sundancer in the mid 20s and reach a top speed of about 35 knots.

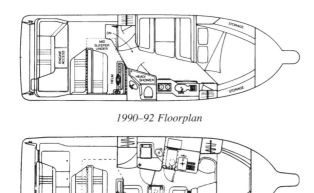

1990–92 Floorplan

1993 Floorplan

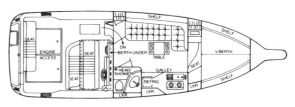

See Page 348 for Pricing Information

See Page 348 for Pricing Information

Sea Ray 280 Sundancer (2001–Current)

Sea Ray 290 Amberjack

Hull Length	31'1"	Water	28 gals.
Beam	9'5"	Waste	28 gals.
Draft	2'10"	Hull Type	Deep-V
Weight	8,000#	Deadrise Aft	21°
Clearance	7'0"	Designer	Sea Ray
Fuel	100 gals.	Production	2001–Current

Length w/Platform	31'4"	Fuel	230 gals.
Hull Length	29'0"	Water	30 gals.
Beam	10'6"	Waste	28 gals.
Draft, Up	2'5"	Hull Type	Deep-V
Draft, Down	2'10"	Deadrise Aft	21°
Weight	11,300#	Production	1998–Current

Those looking for a small midcabin family cruiser will find a lot to like in the Sea Ray 280 Sundancer. The styling is crisp—a Sea Ray trademark these days—and the interior makes the most out of available space with berths for four adults (and two kids), decent headroom, a full galley, and a V-berth that converts into a second dinette. Built on a deep-V hull with a moderate beam and an integrated swim platform, the Sundancer's curved radar arch is an appealing design touch that's showing up on a good many express boats these days. The single-level cockpit is arranged with a sun pad opposite the helm, an aft-facing bench seat, wet bar, and a retractable rear bench seat that folds up into the transom when it's necessary to get into the engine compartment. A large storage locker is built into the transom, and molded steps at the helm provide easy access to the walk-through windshield. On the downside, the midcabin and head dimensions are fairly small, and the engine compartment hatch is heavy. Powered with twin 260hp MerCruiser sterndrives, the 280 Sundancer will cruise in the mid-to-high 20s and reach a top speed in the neighborhood of 40 knots.

Sea Ray, with their on-again, off-again series of Amberjacks, has made halting efforts over the years to market fishing boats to veteran anglers. The 290 Amberjack isn't a serious fishing machine by any means; she is, however, a capable family cruiser/fisherman with the emphasis on comfortable accommodations. Built on a deep-V hull with a relatively wide beam, the Amberjack's fishing amenities are comprised of molded bait-prep station (with livewell) behind the helm, cockpit rod storage, and an optional aluminum arch with rocket launchers. The 290's interior is plush for a fishing boat with a convertible dinette, head with shower, and a well-equipped galley with a built-in microwave. Note that the mid-berth is very shallow and suitable for only a single adult. Additional features include a removable aft bench seat, power vent windshield, transom door and swim platform, and freshwater washdown. Among many engine choices, twin 260hp MerCruiser sterndrives will cruise the Amberjack in the low 20s (about 35 knots top), and 300hp sterndrives will cruise in the mid 20s (40+ knots wide open). With 300hp V-drive inboards, she'll cruise in the low 20s and top out around 30 knots.

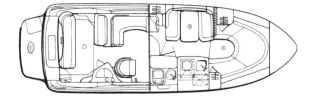

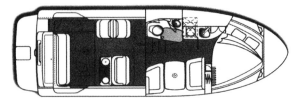

Sea Ray 290 Sundancer (1994–97)

Length w/Pulpit . . . . 32'1"	Clearance. . . . . 8'0"
Hull Length. . . . . 29'4"	Fuel . . . . 130 gals.
Beam . . . . 9'8"	Water. . . . . 24 gals.
Draft, Up . . . . 2'0"	Hull Type . . . . Deep-V
Draft, Down . . . . 3'9"	Deadrise Aft. . . . . 20.5°
Weight. . . . . 8,500#	Production 1994–97

Sea Ray nearly always gets it right when it comes to their series of family cruisers, and the introduction of the 290 Sundancer in 1994 is a good illustration of why this company dominates the market for upmarket express boats. Loaded with amenities, this versatile weekender is a 1990s blend of crisp styling, comfortable accommodations and good performance. She rides on a solid fiberglass hull with a sharp entry and a moderate 9-foot, 8-inch beam. Two floorplans were offered in the 290, one with a U-shaped dinette and the other with a conventional dinette with facing seats. Both staterooms are fitted with double beds and privacy curtains, and storage space—with two large hanging lockers—is notable. On deck, the 290's cockpit is arranged with an elevated triple-wide helm seat, and a U-shaped lounge aft converts into a sun pad. There's a protected chart flat at the helm (very nice), and the faux-burlwood instrument panel is well laid out. On the downside, the engine compartment is a tight fit. A single 300hp MerCruiser sterndrive will cruise the 290 Sundancer at 20 knots (30+ knots top), and a pair of 190hp sterndrives will cruise in the mid 20s and reach a top speed of about 35 knots.

Sea Ray 290 Sundancer (1998–2001)

Length . . . . 29'8"	Fuel. . . . . 130 gals.
Beam . . . . 10'2"	Water. . . . . 28 gals.
Draft, Up . . . . 2'3"	Headroom . . . . 6'0"
Draft, Down . . . . 3'1"	Hull Type . . . . Deep-V
Weight. . . . . 10,500#	Deadrise Aft . . . . 21°
Clearance. . . . . 8'8"	Production 1998–2001

A handsome boat with sculptured lines and first-rate accommodations, the Sea Ray 290 Sundancer (note that an earlier 290 Sundancer was built in 1994–97) offers just about everything one could desire in a quality midsize family cruiser. Sea Ray always builds a solid boat, and at over 10,000 pounds, the Sundancer is no lightweight. The interior was originally offered in two configurations: Plan A has a convertible dinette forward, and Plan B has a double berth forward with the dinette table in front of the starboardside settee. In 1999 a new cabin layout replaced the original floorplans. Topside, the cockpit includes a portside sun lounge and a removable aft bench seat in addition to a very stylish helm console. Standard features include a cockpit shower and wet bar, excellent storage, a drop-down helm seat, and a transom door. Note that the side decks are narrow and the engine room is a tight fit. Among several engine options, a single 310hp MerCruiser sterndrive will cruise the 290 Sundancer at 18–19 knots (about 25 knots top), and twin 260hp MerCruisers will cruise in the low 20s and reach a top speed of around 35 knots.

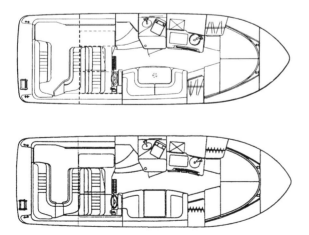

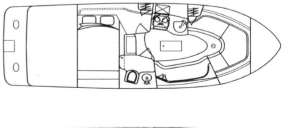

Sea Ray 300 Express

Sea Ray 300 Sundancer (1985–89)

Length w/Pulpit	30'11"	Fuel	130 gals.
Hull Length	29'7"	Water	40 gals.
Beam	11'6"	Headroom	6'2"
Draft	2'5"	Hull Type	Deep-V
Weight	10,000#	Deadrise Aft	23°
Clearance	NA	Production	1978–81

In her day, the Sea Ray 300 Express was one of the larger family cruisers of her type available from a production manufacturer. No one would confuse her with a modern express cruiser and, while her appearance is dated, Sea Ray sold a lot of these boats and they are fairly common on the used market. Construction was solid fiberglass, and her deep-V hull provides a good ride in a chop. The cabin, with its old-fashioned veneer paneling and carpeted overhead, is best described as dated by today's standards. With the dinette converted, there are berths for four below, and sliding cabin windows provide some much-needed ventilation. (Note that a bi-fold door provides privacy for the stateroom.) In the cockpit, there are storage cabinets beneath the double helm seats, while a pair of aft-facing lounge seats will accommodate a couple of guests. The cockpit is large enough for fishing, and visibility from the helm is very good. Additional features include a vented windshield, cushioned foredeck seats, underwater exhausts, good engine access, and a teak bow pulpit and swim platform. Among several engine options, twin 250hp gas inboards will cruise the 300 Express at 16–18 knots and top out in the mid 20s.

Length w/Pulpit	31'4"	Clearance	NA
Hull Length	29'8"	Fuel	140 gals.
Beam	11'0"	Water	40 gals.
Draft, Down	2'11"	Hull Type	Deep-V
Draft, UP	1'6"	Deadrise Aft	21°
Weight	9,800#	Production	1985–89

The Sea Ray 300 Sundancer of the early 1980s—the first of several 300 Sundancer models that followed in later years—is a mid-cabin family cruiser with sterndrive power and comfortable cockpit and cabin accommodations. This was a good-selling boat for Sea Ray, and while she's obviously dated by today's styling standards, she remains a good selection for used-boat buyers looking for a well built express. She rides on a solid fiberglass hull, and her 11-foot beam results in a spacious interior with berths for four adults and two kids. The floorplan is arranged with double berths fore and aft, and privacy curtains separate the staterooms from the main cabin. A shower is fitted in the standup head, two hanging lockers offer adequate storage, and the interior is finished with a good deal of teak trim. The Sundancer's cockpit is dominated by an elevated double helm seat, which contains a flip-down, aft-facing jump seat in addition to a built-in refreshment center. There are storage pockets under the gunnels, and a transom door was standard. Additional features include a radar arch, teak bow pulpit, and a swim platform. The Sundancer will cruise in the mid 20s with twin 260hp sterndrives and reach a top speed of 35+ knots.

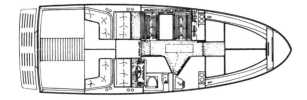

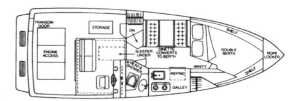

Sea Ray 300 Sundancer (1992–93)

Length w/Pulpit	31'11"	Fuel	120 gals.
Hull Length	29'9"	Water	35 gals.
Beam	10'6"	Hull Type	Deep-V
Draft	2'8"	Deadrise Aft	21°
Weight	8,300#	Designer	Sea Ray
Clearance	8'8"	Production	1992–93

A stylish boat when she was introduced in 1992, the Sea Ray 300 Sundancer combined a contemporary profile and comfortable accommodations in an affordable package aimed at the entry-level family cruiser market. Like most Sea Ray cruisers of her era, the 300 rides on a solid fiberglass deep-V hull with an integrated transom and a wide 10-foot, 6-inch beam. Two floorplans were available in this boat, both featuring a large midcabin aft and a V-berth forward. The galley is large enough to include plenty of storage as well as a cutting board, and the decor is an old-fashioned blend of carpet and mica. Topside, visibility from the elevated triple-wide helm is excellent. Guest seating is provided for six in the cockpit, and the bench seat at the transom folds away for access to the engine compartment. Additional features include an integral bow pulpit, sliding cabin windows, transom door, and cockpit refreshment center. A radar arch was a popular option. Among several engine choices, twin 230hp MerCruiser V-drive inboards will cruise at 19–20 knots (about 30 knots top), and the same motors with sterndrives will cruise in the low 20s and top out at close to 35 knots. Note the limited fuel capacity.

Sea Ray 300 Sundancer (1994–97)

Length w/Pulpit	33'1"	Fuel	200 gals.
Hull Length	30'6"	Water	35 gals.
Beam	10'6"	Waste	28 gals.
Draft	2'11"	Hull Type	Deep-V
Weight	10,200#	Deadrise Aft	21°
Clearance	8'8"	Production	1994–97

With her oval portlights, low-profile arch, and sculptured lines, this third version of Sea Ray's 300 Sundancer series was one of the best-looking sportboats in the market during the late 1990s. She's built on the same easy-riding deep-V hull used in the production of the previous 300 Sundancer model (1992–93), but with a restyled profile, an updated interior, additional (and badly needed) fuel capacity, and a revised cockpit layout. Accommodations for six are provided below in two different floorplan configurations, both with a standup head with shower, full galley, two hanging lockers, and a convertible dinette. On deck, visibility from the triple helm seat is very good, and a protected chart flat is built into the dash. A filler converts the U-shaped cockpit seating aft of the helm into a large sun pad. Additional features include a walk-through transom, molded bow pulpit, radar arch, and good engine access. The 300 Sundancer was available with a choice of inboard or sterndrive power. A very popular model for Sea Ray, twin 250hp MerCruiser V-drive inboards will cruise at 19–20 knots (about 30 knots top), and the less-popular sterndrive versions of the same engines will cruise in the low 20s and top out at close to 35 knots.

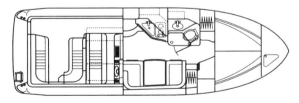

Dinette with Facing Seats

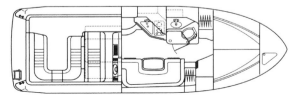

Circular Dinette

Sea Ray 300 Sundancer (2002–Current)

Length w/Platform	33'4"	Headroom	6'6"
Beam	10'5"	Fuel	170 gals.
Draft, Up	2'0"	Water	35 gals.
Draft, Down	3'4"	Hull Type	Deep-V
Weight	12,000#	Deadrise Aft	21°
Clearance	10'7"	Production	2002–Current

Lots of manufacturers build 30-foot midcabin express cruisers, but few have been at it as long as Sea Ray and fewer still do it better. This is the fourth in a series of 300 Sundancer models Sea Ray has produced since 1985, and an extended 30-inch swim platform makes this the longest of the pack. Like her predecessors, this Sundancer rides on a deep-V hull with moderate beam and a solid fiberglass bottom. Buyers can pick from two interior floorplans. The standard layout has a dinette that converts into a berth, while the optional configuration features a curved sofa bed with a matching table. Both plans include an enclosed head and shower, a double berth forward, and of course a mid-berth aft. Privacy curtains separate the sleeping areas from the main cabin, which is highlighted by three overhead hatches and attractive burlwood cabinetry. The cockpit comes with a wet bar and a removable table in addition to a fore-and-aft facing bench seats, and the entire cockpit sole rises on hydraulic rams to reveal the engine compartment. The stylish tiered helm is particularly well arranged. Twin 260hp MerCruiser sterndrive gas engines will cruise the 300 Sundancer at 20 knots and reach a top speed of around 35 knots.

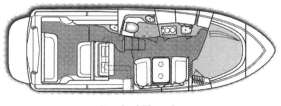

Standard Floorplan

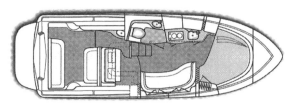

Optional Floorplan

Sea Ray 300 Weekender (1975–81)

Length w/Pulpit	30'11"	Fuel	130 gals.
Hull Length	29'7"	Water	40 gals.
Beam	11'6"	Headroom	5'5"
Draft	2'5"	Hull Type	Deep-V
Weight	9,500#	Deadrise Aft	23°
Clearance	NA	Production	1975–81

Considering the overwhelming presence of Sea Ray in today's market, it's interesting to note that the 300 Weekender was one of Sea Ray's largest models back in the late 1970s. Obviously dated by today's express-boat standards, the Weekender was a very popular boat in her day thanks to her clean styling, a practical interior, lots of cockpit space, and an attractive new-boat price. Indeed, the styling of the 300 Weekender is still her most enduring quality although her flush foredeck makes for modest headroom belowdeck. The cabin accommodations are basic with V-berths forward, a convertible dinette, a compact galley area and a too-small head compartment. Lots of wall carpeting, inexpensive veneers, etc.—not much to get excited about, but still adequate for those on a budget. The roomy cockpit lacks the built-in lounges and wet bar seen in more modern boats so you can actually do some fishing in the Weekender without difficulty. Additional features include a solid fiberglass deep-V hull, a teak bow pulpit and cabin rails, swim platform, underwater exhausts and sliding cabin windows. Among several engine options, a pair of 228hp MerCruiser inboards will cruise at 16–18 knots.

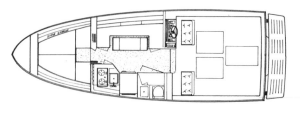

See Page 348 for Pricing Information

See Page 348 for Pricing Information

Sea Ray 300 Weekender (1985–89)

Length w/Pulpit	31'4"	Fuel	200 gals.
Hull Length	29'8"	Water	40 gals.
Beam	11'0"	Headroom	6'3"
Draft	2'5"	Hull Type	Deep-V
Weight	9,500	Deadrise Aft	21°
Clearance	NA	Production	1985–89

The Sea Ray 300 Weekender of the early 1980s is a straightforward express cruiser with inboard power, a flush cockpit, and practical cabin accommodations. While the Weekender is somewhat dated by today's styling standards, she remains a good selection for used-boat buyers looking for a reliable and well-built express. She rides on a solid fiberglass deep-V hull, and a wide 11-foot beam results in a rather spacious interior with berths for two adults and two kids. Unlike her sistership, the Sea Ray 300 Sundancer (1985–89), the Weekender does not have a mid-berth aft. In other respects, however, the floorplans of the two boats are identical. A double berth is located in the forward stateroom, which has a sliding curtain for privacy. A convertible dinette is to port, and the standup head compartment contains a sink and shower. Because there's no midcabin, the Weekender's cockpit is flush—a feature that provides for a more open cockpit. Double-wide helm and companion seats are forward, and a removable lounge seat at the transom seats three. There are storage pockets under the gunnels, and a transom door was standard. Additional features include a radar arch, teak bow pulpit, and a swim platform. A pair of 260hp inboards will cruise the Weekender at 24 knots and reach a top speed of 30+ knots.

Sea Ray 300 Weekender (1991–95)

Length w/Pulpit	31'11"	Fuel	200 gals.
Hull Length	29'9"	Water	28 gals.
Beam	10'6"	Hull Type	Deep-V
Draft	2'8"	Deadrise Aft	21°
Weight	7,800#	Designer	Sea Ray
Clearance	NA	Production	1991–95

Attractive sportboat styling, a big, single-level cockpit, and cabin accommodations for two characterize the Sea Ray 300 Weekender (called the 280 Weekender in 1991), a popular daycruiser from the early 1990s. Aside from her solid construction, the Weekender's main draw is her large cockpit with its side-panel storage, a portside cooler, drink holders, and transom door. A removable bench seat at the stern was a popular option, and twin hatches in the aft cockpit floor provide good access to the engines. Below, the Weekender's interior is arranged with a convertible dinette/V-berth forward, a small galley, and a standup head with sink and shower—comfortable accommodations for two adults. Built on a deep-V hull with a generous 10-foot, 6-inch beam and an integrated swim platform, the 300 Weekender came with a choice of inboard or sterndrive power. Among several engine options, twin 250hp MerCruiser inboards (with V-drives) will cruise in the mid 20s (30+ knots top), and the 250hp MerCruiser sterndrives will top out at close to 40 knots. Note that inboard models have prop pockets and side exhausts.

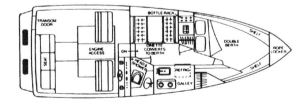

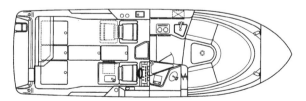

See Page 348 for Pricing Information

See Page 348 for Pricing Information

Sea Ray 310 Amberjack

Sea Ray 310 Sundancer (1982–83)

Length . . . . 31'2"	Fuel . . . . 296 gals.
Beam . . . . 11'5"	Water . . . . 40 gals.
Draft . . . . 3'1"	Hull Type . . . . Modified-V
Weight . . . . 10,500#	Deadrise Aft . . . . 18°
Cockpit . . . . 57 sq. ft.	Designer . . . . Sea Ray
Clearance . . . . NA	Production 1992–94

Length w/Platform . . . . 32'4"	Fuel . . . . 175 gals.
Hull Length . . . . 30'6"	Water . . . . 52 gals.
Beam . . . . 11'11"	Headroom . . . . 6'2"
Draft . . . . 2'5"	Hull Type . . . . Deep-V
Weight . . . . 10,000#	Deadrise Aft . . . . 21°
Clearance . . . . NA	Production 1982–83

Sportboat enthusiasts will find much to like in the Sea Ray 310 Amberjack, a versatile, good-looking dayboat with the aggressive low-profile appearance of a small Bertram or Blackfin. She's built on a modified-V hull with cored hullsides, a wide beam, prop pockets, and a relatively steep 18 degrees of transom deadrise. The Amberjack's original design emphasis was in the large and well-organized fishing cockpit. The cockpit can be fitted with in-deck fish boxes, rod holders, and a transom livewell. While cabin space is at a premium, the Amberjack manages to include a convertible dinette/V-berth forward as well as a standup head with shower and a small galley area. Topside, the side decks are wide enough for safe access to the bow, and motor boxes make it easy to get at the engines for routine service. Note that in 1994 Sea Ray engineers replaced the dinette opposite the helm with an elevated lounge area. Additional features include side-dumping exhausts, a removable cockpit table, cabin rod racks, cockpit lights, and a bow pulpit. A good performer with twin 310hp MerCruiser gas engines, she'll cruise in the low-to-mid 20s and reach a top speed of just over 30 knots.

The first in a series of 31-foot Sundancer models Sea Ray has built over the years, the 310 Sundancer is a wide-beam family cruiser with a roomy midcabin interior and a very spacious cockpit. Notably, she was one of the larger boats in the Sea Ray fleet during her production years. Built on a solid fiberglass hull, the interior of the 310 was among the largest to be found in a boat this size during the early 1980s. Originally arranged with a bulkhead separating the forward stateroom from the salon, the interior was completely revised in 1983 when Sea Ray eliminated the cabin bulkhead and introduced a more open (and even more spacious) layout. There are sleeping accommodations for six with either configuration—four adults and two kids—along with an enclosed, standup head and a full galley. The cockpit seating is a little unusual: a double-wide passenger seat with fold-down aft-facing jump seats resides in the center of the cockpit, just behind the helm. Note the absence of a transom door. Among several engine choices, twin 350hp gas inboards will cruise the Sea Ray 310 Sundancer around 20 knots with a top speed in the neighborhood of 30 knots.

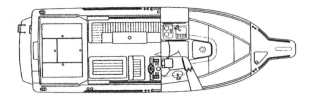

Floorplan Not Available

Length w/Platform	33'10"	Fuel	200 gals.
Hull Length	31'6"	Water	35 gals.
Beam	11'2"	Waste	28 gals.
Draft, Up	1'11"	Hull Type	Deep-V
Draft, Down	3'7"	Deadrise Aft	23°
Weight	12,000#	Production	1998–2002

Length w/Pulpit	35'4"	Fuel	200 gals.
Hull Length	32'10"	Water	40 gals.
Beam	11'5"	Hull Type	Deep-V
Draft, Inboard	2'3"	Deadrise Aft	21°
Draft, I/Os	3'0"	Designer	Sea Ray
Weight	10,000#	Production	1990–95

With her striking profile and comfortable interior, the Sea Ray 310 Sundancer was designed for upscale cruisers willing to pay top dollar for a quality midsize express. This is a well-crafted boat, better finished than previous Sea Ray models and incorporating high-grade hardware, appliances, and furnishings. When the 310 was introduced in 1998, she came with an unusual floorplan that required those using the forward kidney-shaped berth to climb over the circular dinette seat. Sea Ray dumped that plan in 1999, replacing it with a more conventional layout with an angled double berth forward and a conventional dinette with facing seats. In both configurations, a roomy midcabin offers true seclusion thanks to a real door instead of a curtain. The Sundancer's large cockpit has everything for relaxing and entertaining including a triple helm seat (with a flip-up seat for the driver), U-shaped aft seating, and a refreshment center with wet bar and cooler. For engine access, the entire bridgedeck rises electrically at the push of a button. Among several engine choices, twin 260hp MerCruiser V-drive inboards will cruise the 310 Sundancer at 18 knots (26–27 knots top), and 260hp MerCruiser sterndrives will top out in the mid 30s.

Introduced as the 310 Express Cruiser in 1990–91, the Sea Ray 330 Express was a good-selling boat in the early 1990s thanks to her crisp styling and a very roomy interior. Like most Sea Rays of her era, she was built on a solid fiberglass hull with an integrated swim platform and a generous 11-foot, 5-inch beam. (Note that inboard models incorporated prop pockets and side-dumping exhausts.) While she eschews the midcabin floorplan popular in most express boats, the wide-open salon of the 310/330 EC is unusually spacious for a boat this size. The salon is dominated by a huge wraparound sofa (which converts into a sleeper by night), and a privacy curtain separates the stateroom from the main cabin. Because the interior is so large, the cockpit of the 310/330 is on the small side. The companion and double helm seats hold three adults, while an aft-facing bench seat has room for two more. A foldaway transom seat and radar arch were popular options. Among several sterndrive and inboard engine choices, twin 300hp MerCruiser sterndrives will cruise in the mid 20s and reach a top speed of over 30 knots. Note that oval ports replaced the original sliding cabin windows in 1994.

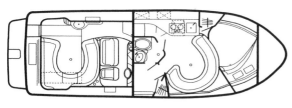

1998 Floorplan

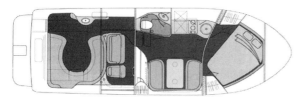

1999–2002

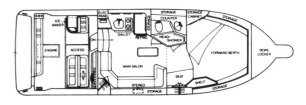

Sea Ray 310/330 Sundancer (1990–94)

Sea Ray 320 Sundancer

Length w/Pulpit	35'4"	Fuel	180 gals.
Hull Length	32'10"	Water	40 gals.
Beam	11'5"	Waste	28 gals.
Draft, Inboards	2'3"	Hull Type	Deep-V
Draft, I/Os	3'0"	Deadrise Aft	21°
Weight	10,000#	Production	1990–94

Length w/Platform	35'6"	Fuel	200 gals.
Beam	11'5"	Water	40 gals.
Draft	2'9"	Waste	28 gals.
Weight	13,200#	Hull Type	Deep-V
Clearance	10'2"	Deadrise Aft	21°
Headroom	6'3"	Production	2003–Current

An extremely popular model, the Sea Ray 330 Sundancer (called the 310 Sundancer in 1990 when she was introduced) was the first of two 330 Sundancer models developed by Sea Ray during the 1990s. The sales success of this durable cruiser derived from a combination of features, most notably her graceful appearance and a surprisingly roomy interior. Like all Sundancer models, the 330 came with a midcabin floorplan with berths for six, a fully equipped galley, and a spacious salon with a large U-shaped dinette. Storage is generous for a boat this size, and privacy curtains separate the sleeping area from the main cabin. The cockpit, with seating for eight, is arranged with a triple-wide helm seat, aft-facing bench seating, a small entertainment center, and lounge seating at the transom. A transom door and cockpit bolsters were standard, and engine access is relatively easy. Built on a good-running deep-V hull (with more transom deadrise than the later 330 Sundancer model), twin 330hp V-drive inboards will cruise the 310/330 Sundancer in the low 20s and reach a top speed of close to 30 knots. Those equipped with 300hp MerCruiser sterndrives will top out at over 30 knots.

Sea Ray has been setting the standards for express cruisers for over 20 years, so it's hardly a surprise that the 320 Sundancer delivers just the right blend of style, comfort and performance. Sea Ray's dedication to quality is everywhere to see, from the elegant burlwood dash, to her near-flawless gelcoat and quality hardware. Below, the 320's interior is brightly lit and completely open. High-gloss cherry paneling and mirrored accents highlight a decor rich in luxury and sophistication. The salon settee converts to a double, an island berth is forward, and the stateroom aft of the companionway steps doubles as a secondary conversation area. Curtains separate both sleeping areas from the main salon, and faux granite counters and Formica cabinets are found in the galley. The Sundancer's cockpit layout is arranged with U-shaped seating aft for four, a stylish dual helm seat with flip-up bolster, and a full wet bar. On the downside, the side decks are quite narrow, and engine access is a little difficult. A quality sportcruiser at the high end of the price spectrum, the 320 Sundancer will cruise in the mid 20s with a pair of 320hp MerCruiser sterndrives and reach a top speed of about 30 knots.

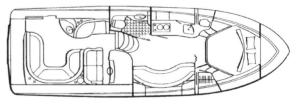

Sea Ray 330 Sundancer (1995–99)

Length w/Pulpit	35'10"	Fuel	225 gals.
Hull Length	33'6"	Water	40 gals.
Beam	11'5"	Waste	28 gals.
Draft, Inboards	2'1"	Hull Type	Modified-V
Draft, I/Os	3'0"	Deadrise Aft	17°
Weight	11,200#	Production	1995–99

An updated version of Sea Ray's earlier 310/330 Sundancer (1990–94), the Sea Ray 330 is a more stylish boat than her predecessor with a softer profile, increased fuel capacity, and a redesigned hull bottom. The styling is low and lean—a company trademark in recent years—and it's notable that the hull of the 330 incorporates less transom deadrise than most other Sea Ray hulls. Belowdecks, the interior follows the standard Sundancer formula with a midcabin berth aft, full galley, convertible dinette, standup head with shower, and a double berth forward. Privacy curtains separate the sleeping areas from the main cabin, and three hanging lockers provide plenty of storage. In the cockpit, a four-person bench seat across the transom faces a smaller, aft-facing one behind the helmsman, and the gap can be filled to produce a large sun pad. Additional features include a transom door, cockpit wet bar, good engine access, transom storage locker, and wide side decks. Available with sterndrive or inboard power, twin 330hp MerCruiser sterndrives will cruise the 330 Sundancer in the high 20s and reach a top speed of 35+ knots, and twin 310hp V-drive inboards will cruise in the mid 20s and top out in the low 30s.

Sea Ray 330 Express; 340 Amberjack

Length w/Platform & Pulpit	38'0"	Water	50 gals.
Hull Length	33'6"	Waste	28 gals.
Beam	13'5"	Headroom	6'4"
Draft	3'0"	Hull Type	Deep-V
Weight	16,500#	Deadrise Aft	19.5°
Fuel	275 gals.	Production	1997–2003

A versatile boat capable of serious fishing activities as well as comfortable family cruising, the Sea Ray 340 Amberjack (called the 330 Express Cruiser in 1997–2001) is one of the roomiest boats in her class thanks to a super-wide 13-foot, 5-inch beam. Indeed, this is a big 33-footer with a wide-open cockpit and a very spacious interior. Built on a fully cored deep-V hull with prop pockets, the original Express Cruiser floorplan was arranged with a V-berth in the forward stateroom and a sofa in the salon. In 2001—when she became the 340 Amberjack—the interior was redesigned to include an angled double berth forward and a full-size dinette in the salon, In both layouts, the stateroom is separated from the salon by two sliding doors. Cockpit amenities include an in-deck livewell and fish box, a foldaway bench seat at the transom, and a clever dual-purpose bait-prep station/wet bar behind the helm seat. The entire bridgedeck can be raised electrically for engine access. Additional features include a centerline windshield vent, radar arch, wide side decks, and rod storage in the cabin sole. Twin 370hp MerCruiser inboards will cruise at 20 knots and top out at close to 30 knots.

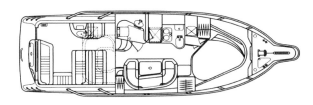

Express Cruiser Floorplan (1997–2000)

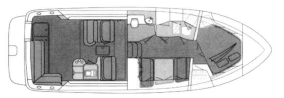

Amberjack Layout (2001–03)

See Page 349 for Pricing Information

See Page 349 for Pricing Information

Sea Ray 340 Express Cruiser

Length w/Platform . . . . 35'11"	Fuel . . . . 204/250 gals.
Hull Length. . . . . 33'7"	Water. . . . . 52 gals.
Beam . . . . 11'11"	Headroom . . . . 6'4"
Draft. . . . . 2'5"	Hull Type . . . . Deep-V
Weight. . . . . 12,100#	Deadrise Aft . . . . 21°
Clearance . . . . NA	Production 1984–89

The 340 Express Cruiser proved one of Sea Ray's most popular models during the 1980s. A big boat by the standards of her day, the 340's sleek styling (obviously dated by today's sportboat standards) and spacious interior were her chief attributes. Built on a solid fiberglass hull with prop pockets and a wide 12-foot beam, three floorplans were offered during her production years, all with the forward stateroom open to the main cabin. The original layout was arranged with the dinette to starboard and a small galley and settee to port. In 1986 Sea Ray came out with a more functional interior featuring a big U-shaped galley as well as a reconfigured dinette. Finally, in 1998 the island berth in the bow stateroom was replaced with a full-width bed and (optional) built-in entertainment center. Topside, the 340's single-level cockpit included double-wide helm and companion seats and a removable bench seat at the transom. Large hatches in the cockpit floor provide good access to the engines. A radar arch, transom door, side exhausts, and swim platform were standard. Among several engine options, 340hp MerCruiser gas inboards will cruise the 340 Express in the low 20s and reach 30+ knots wide open. Note that the fuel capacity was increased in 1987.

Sea Ray 340 Sundancer (1984–89)

Length w/Platform . . . . 35'11"	Fuel . . . . 172 gals.
Hull Length. . . . . 33'7"	Water. . . . . 52 gals.
Beam . . . . 11'11"	Headroom . . . . 6'4"
Draft. . . . . 2'5"	Hull Type . . . . Deep-V
Weight. . . . . 12,500#	Deadrise Aft . . . . 21°
Clearance . . . . NA	Production 1984–89

Sea Ray got it right back in 1984 with the introduction of the 340 Sundancer, a roomy midcabin cruiser with sleeping space for three couples and a smooth-riding deep-V hull. The Sundancer was considered a big boat in her day, and her blend of big-boat accommodations and an affordable price struck a responsive chord with the boating public. Three floorplans were offered during her production years, all with a private aft cabin and a forward stateroom open to the main cabin. The original layout was arranged with the dinette to starboard and a small galley and settee to port. In 1986 Sea Ray came out with a more functional interior featuring a big U-shaped galley as well as an enlarged dinette. Finally, in 1998 the island berth in the bow stateroom was replaced with a full-width bed and (optional) built-in entertainment center. In the cockpit, elevated helm and companion seats are to starboard, and a removable bench seat at the transom holds four adults. Removable hatches in the aft cockpit sole provide good access to the motors. Standard 340hp MerCruiser V-drive gas inboards will cruise the Sundancer in the low 20s and and reach about 30 knots top. Note the small 172-gallon fuel capacity.

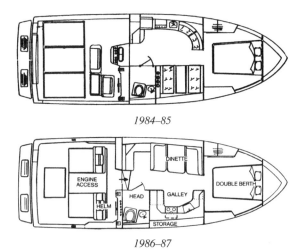

1984–85

1986–87

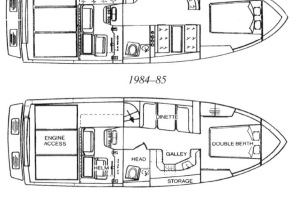

1984–85

1986–87

See Page 349 for Pricing Information

See Page 349 for Pricing Information

Sea Ray 340 Sundancer (1999–2002)

Length w/Platform	33'6"	Water	40 gals.
Beam	11'5"	Waste	28 gals.
Draft	2'5"	Headroom	6'3"
Weight	13,000#	Hull Type	Modified-V
Clearance	NA	Deadrise Aft	17°
Fuel	225 gals.	Production	1999–2002

A popular boat for Sea Ray, the 340 Sundancer (note that an earlier 340 Sundancer was produced from 1984–89) is a good example of why Sea Ray continues to lead the market for midcabin express boats. Attractively styled and built to high standards, the 340 is a superb entertainment platform with a wide-open interior and a cockpit large enough to accommodate a small crowd. Two floorplans were available, both with the forward stateroom open to the main cabin and a mid-stateroom disguised as a sunken conversation area by day. Privacy curtains separate the sleeping areas from the salon, and a hidden TV/VCR pulls out and swivels so it can be viewed from anywhere in the boat. Rich cherry woodwork and posh furnishings highlight the Sundancer's interior, but storage is hard to come by. Topside, an adjustable helm seat overlooks a tiered dash configuration, and facing bench seats, a cockpit table, and wet bar make the cockpit a comfortable place for guests. On the downside, the engine compartment is a tight fit and the side decks are narrow. Twin 320hp MerCruiser V-drive inboards will cruise the 340 Sundancer at 20 knots and reach a top speed of around 30 knots.

Sea Ray 340 Sundancer (Current)

Length	37'6"	Fuel	225 gals.
Beam	12'0"	Water	45 gals.
Draft, Up	2'3"	Waste	28 gals.
Draft, Down	3'1"	Hull Type	Deep-V
Draft, Inboards	2'8"	Deadrise Aft	21°
Weight	14,600#	Production	2003–Current

Introduced in 2003, the Sea Ray 340 Sundancer replaced the previous 340 Sundancer (1999–2002), a popular model in the builder's line for several years. Wider in the beam than her predecessor, with a newly designed cockpit and a deep-V hull, the sleek styling of the 340 Sundancer conceals an interior that seems remarkably spacious for a 34-foot boat. The cabin is well-lit with seven ports and overhead hatches, and the upscale decor is accented with rich cherry cabinetry and earth-tone fabrics and upholstery. The layout is typical of most Sundancer interiors with a pedestal berth forward and convertible settees in the salon and midcabin area. Corian counters and quality hardware are found in the galley, and privacy curtains separate the sleeping areas from the main cabin. Semicircular lounge seating is aft in the cockpit, and an electric hatch lifts to reveal a rather compact engine compartment. The helm is notable for its excellent design and good visibility. A premium express finished to very high standards, MerCruiser 370hp V-drive inboards will cruise the Sea Ray 340 Sundancer at 24–25 knots and reach a top speed in the low 30s.

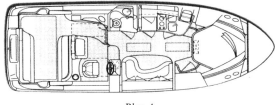

Plan A

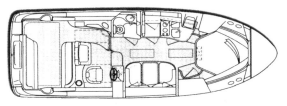

Plan B

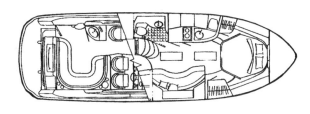

See Page 349 for Pricing Information

See Page 349 for Pricing Information

Sea Ray 350/370 Exp. Cruiser (1990–95)

Length w/Pulpit	36'10"	Water	70 gals.
Hull Length	36'10"	Waste	20 gals.
Beam	12'4"	Hull Type	Deep-V
Draft	2'5"	Deadrise Aft	21°
Weight	13,100#	Designer	Sea Ray
Fuel	250 gals.	Production	1990–95

Like many Sea Ray models, the 370 Express Cruiser (called the 350 Express Cruiser in 1990–92) has aged well over the years. She was a stylish boat when she came out in 1990, and she remains a handsome yacht even by today's high-glitz standards. Built on a deep-V hull with prop pockets and a wide 12-foot, 4-inch beam, the interior of the Express Cruiser differs from Sea Ray's Sundancer models in that there is no mid-stateroom below the helm. The wide-open salon is dominated by a huge semicircular sofa that converts to a sleeper for two. Forward, through a privacy curtain, the stateroom has an angled double bed as well as a mirrored vanity. The head contains a separate stall shower, and an optional TV/VCR swivels out for easy viewing from anywhere in the cabin. Topside, the spacious single-level cockpit has a double helm seat forward, an aft-facing double cockpit seat, wet bar, and a bench seat at the transom. Additional features include side exhausts, an integral bow pulpit and swim platform, and a transom door. Standard 310hp MerCruiser inboards will cruise at 20 knots and reach a top speed of 28–29 knots. Note that in 1994 the original sliding cabin windows were replaced with oval portlights.

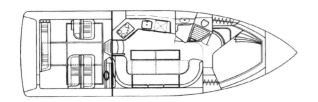

Sea Ray 350/370 Sundancer (1990–94)

Length w/Platform	39'5"	Fuel	250 gals.
Hull Length	36'10"	Water	70 gals.
Beam	12'4"	Hull Type	Deep-V
Draft	2'5"	Deadrise Aft	21°
Weight	13,500#	Designer	Sea Ray
Clearance	NA	Production	1990–94

Like many Sea Ray models, the 350 Sundancer (called the 370 Sundancer in 1992–94) has aged well over the years. She was a stylish boat when she was introduced in 1990, and she remains a handsome yacht even by today's sportboat standards. Built on a deep-V hull with a wide 12-foot, 4-inch beam, the Sundancer's interior is fairly conventional with a midcabin area aft and a stateroom forward. The salon is dominated by a huge semicircular sofa that converts to a sleeper for two, and while a curtain is used for mid-stateroom privacy, a door separates the forward stateroom from the main cabin. The head contains a separate stall shower, and an optional TV/VCR swivels out for easy viewing from anywhere in the cabin. Topside, the Sundancer's cockpit is arranged with a double helm seat, an aft-facing bench seat, an aft bench seat, and a wet bar with sink and cooler. An integral bow pulpit, radar arch, and a transom door were standard. Twin 310hp MerCruiser V-drive inboards will cruise at 20 knots and reach a top speed of 28–29 knots. Note that in 1994 Sea Ray added U-shaped seating in the cockpit and replaced the original sliding cabin windows with oval portlights.

1990–93

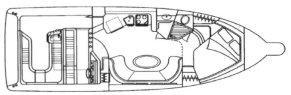

1994

Sea Ray 360 Express Cruiser

Length	36'6"	Fuel	300 gals.
Beam	13'11"	Water	100 gals.
Draft	2'7"	Hull Type	Deep-V
Weight	17,900#	Deadrise Aft	NA
Clearance	9'7"	Designer	Sea Ray
Cockpit	NA	Production	1979–83

An innovative and unusual design, the Sea Ray 360 Express Cruiser is distinguished by her unique T-shaped hardtop and spoiler section. Supported by the windshield, the forward end of the top provides wind protection while underway. To get all-weather protection, the slots in the T-top can be closed with clear snap-in vinyl inserts or Plexiglas panels. She was equally innovative below, where angled bulkheads give the staterooms and head compartment unusual shapes—a notable departure from the rigid, squared-off interiors found in most boats of the early 1980s. The interior is very spacious thanks to an extra-wide 13-foot, 11-inch beam. The highlight of the floorplan is a huge galley with acres of counter space and tons of storage. On deck, the cockpit is huge with double helm and companion seats and a full-width bench seat at the transom. (Note the absence of a transom door.) A teak pulpit and swim platform were standard, and three in-deck cockpit hatches provide good access to the motors. Built on a solid fiberglass hull with propeller pockets, twin 330hp gas inboards will cruise the 360 Express Cruiser around 17 knots and deliver a top speed in the mid 20s.

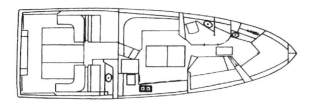

Sea Ray 360 Sundancer

Length w/Platform	39'0"	Fuel	250 gals.
Beam	12'6"	Water	55 gals.
Draft	3'1"	Waste	35 gals.
Weight	18,500#	Hull Type	Deep-V
Clearance	11'4"	Deadrise Aft	21°
Headroom	6'7"	Production	2002–Current

Knowledgeable cruisers will be hard-pressed to find a more capable midsized express than the Sea Ray 360 Sundancer. Gracefully styled and impressively finished, the 360 delivers a careful balance of performance and comfort, albeit at a rather upscale price. Built on a deep-V hull with moderate beam, the Sundancer's midcabin interior gets high marks for its quality furnishings and fixtures. This is a comfortable layout with plenty of storage, a built-in entertainment center, a plush Ultraleather lounge, and excellent headroom. A two-part pocket door provides privacy for the forward stateroom, and both the salon sofa and midcabin lounge convert easily into double berths. At the helm, a bucket seat with a flip-up bolster allows for standup driving and there's space in the tiered, burled dash for electronics. Engine access is excellent; the entire cockpit floor rises on hydraulic rams to completely expose the motors and V-drives. Additional features include an extended swim platform, an underwater exhaust system, a transom storage locker, and a cockpit wet bar. MerCruiser 8.1-liter 370hp V-drive gas engines will cruise the 360 Sundancer at 18 knots and reach a top speed of 30+ knots.

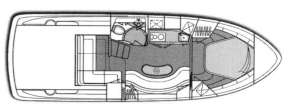

EXPRESS CRUISERS

Sea Ray 370 Express Cruiser

Sea Ray 370 Sundancer (1995–99)

Length w/Platform	41'4"	Fuel	350 gals.
Hull Length	37'0"	Water	70 gals.
Beam	14'2"	Waste	28 gals.
Draft	3'3"	Hull Type	Deep-V
Weight	18,000#	Deadrise Aft	19.5°
Clearance	10'8"	Production	1997–2000

The 370 Express Cruiser was an effort by Sea Ray to develop a serious tournament-level fishing boat. In that regard, she followed the approach Tiara so successfully pioneered with their 3600 and 3700 Open models—a top-quality express with a big, well-designed cockpit and a lavish, family-friendly interior. Not inexpensive, the Sea Ray 370 is a big boat thanks to her wide 14-foot, 2-inch beam. The cockpit offers lots of space for fishing, and there's plenty of room for a fighting chair or for storing loose gear such as coolers. A bait-prep center with sink is positioned for easy access, and a pair of lift-out fish boxes were standard. The 370's machinery space is reached via a centerline hatch, and for complete access the bridge sole can be raised at the push of a button. Below, the plush interior will sleep four with a double berth in the private bow stateroom, and a lounge to starboard that pulls out into a double berth. Additional features include rod storage beneath the cabin sole, a fold-up transom seat, prop pockets, and a fully cored hull. Optional 340hp Caterpillar diesels will cruise the 370 Express Cruiser in the mid 20s and deliver a top speed of around 30 knots.

Length w/Pulpit	40'1"	Water	70 gals.
Hull Length	37'6"	Waste	28 gals.
Beam	12'7"	Clearance	11'2"
Draft	2'8"	Hull Type	Deep-V
Weight	17,000#	Deadrise Aft	20°
Fuel	275 gals.	Production	1995–99

For years, Sea Ray has dominated the market for midcabin cruisers with their state-of-the-art styling and innovative features. The introduction in 1995 of the 370 Sundancer was yet another in the company's evolving series of Sundancer models, each a little nicer than the last, and each a little more expensive. Built on a fully cored hull, the Sundancer's interior seems unusually spacious, perhaps because the aft stateroom—with its U-shaped settee and removable table—is wide open to the main cabin. A sliding privacy door closes off the forward stateroom by night, and the salon sofa converts to a double bed for extra guests. This is, in fact, a very well-executed layout, and the built-in breakfast bar, faux granite countertops, and sculptured overhead panels are worthy of note. Topside, the 370's cockpit can easily handle a crowd, and a wet bar with sink, cooler, trash bin, and cutting board were standard. Additional features include an underwater exhaust system, an distinctive two-tier swim platform, good engine access, and very secure side decks. Twin V-drive 310hp gas inboards will cruise the 370 Sundancer at 18 knots (about 30 knots top), and 300hp Cummins diesels will cruise in the low 20s.

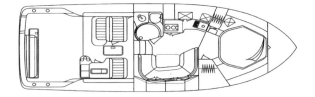

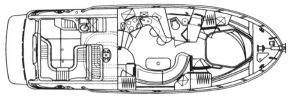

Sea Ray 380 Sundancer

Length w/Platform	42'0"	Fuel	275 gals.
Hull Length	38'0"	Water	70 gals.
Beam	13'0"	Waste	42 gals.
Draft	2'8"	Hull Type	Deep-V
Weight	20,000#	Deadrise Aft	19.5°
Clearance	10'6"	Production	1999–2003

Great styling has long been a Sea Ray trademark, and while few American sportboats are as glamorous as their European counterparts, the quality found in late-model Sundancers is second to none. Built on a fully cored deep-V hull with a wide beam, few imports can match the spacious interior of the 380 Sundancer with her superb galley (including a full-size refrigerator), excellent storage, and wide-open floorplan. The layout is typical of most Sundancers with double berths fore and aft and a sofa in the salon that converts to a double berth for extra guests. The midcabin stateroom serves as a conversation area during the day, then electrically converts into a bed at night. A door separates the forward stateroom from the main cabin, while a curtain provides privacy for the midcabin. On deck, the spacious cockpit provides wraparound seating for six to seven and comes with a wet bar, fender storage, and a removable table that converts into a sun pad. An electric hatch provides access to a rather compact engine compartment. Standard 370hp V-drive inboards will cruise at 18 knots (mid 20s top), and optional 340hp Cat diesels will cruise in the mid 20s (about 30 knots top).

Sea Ray 390 Express Cruiser

Length	39'0"	Water	100 gals.
Beam	13'11"	Headroom	6'4"
Draft	2'4"	Hull Type	Deep-V
Weight	16,400#	Deadrise Aft	19°
Clearance	NA	Designer	Sea Ray
Fuel	300 gals.	Production	1984–91

The 390 Express Cruiser turned out to be one of the most popular boats ever built by Sea Ray. First of the big production express boats when she came out in 1984, her sleek lines and European styling—tame by today's design standards—made a lasting impression on the mid-1980s sportboat market. Below, her expansive two-stateroom interior is arranged with a queen berth forward and a combined galley-and-breakfast bar facing the curved settee in the salon. The guest stateroom is unique: it's separated from the salon by a retractable mirrored bulkhead. Slide it away, convert the bunk berths into a sofa, and the area actually becomes a part of the main cabin. The 390's interior was updated twice over the years, changing from the original woodgrain mica to teak in 1986, and to a white-mica/teak-trim decor in 1988. Topside, the single-level cockpit is huge with seating for as many as eight passengers. Twin 340hp inboard MerCruisers will cruise the 390 Express Cruiser at 17–18 knots (mid-to-high 20s top), and optional 375hp Cats will cruise in the mid 20s and reach a top speed of close to 30 knots. Note that the sliding cabin windows are prone to leaking.

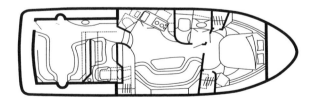

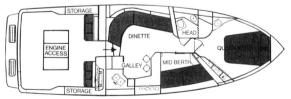

See Page 350 for Pricing Information

See Page 350 for Pricing Information

Sea Ray 390 Sundancer

Length w/Platform . . . . 41'0"	Fuel . . . . 275 gals.
Beam . . . . 13'2"	Water . . . . 70 gals.
Draft . . . . 3'4"	Waste . . . . 42 gals.
Weight . . . . 19,300#	Hull Type . . . . Deep-V
Clearance . . . . 13'3"	Deadrise Aft . . . . 19°
Headroom . . . . 6'5"	Production 2004–Current

Among several big express cruisers available in today's market, the Sea Ray 390 Sundancer is notable for her sleek styling and distinctive fiberglass hardtop. Sea Ray has been building good-quality family cruisers since the 1980s, but it's only been in the last few years that the company has become a recognized leader in sportboat styling and design. Built on a deep-V hull with prop pockets and a solid fiberglass bottom, the lavish interior of the 390 Sundancer is a blend of high-gloss cherrywood cabinetry, Ultraleather upholstery, and vinyl wall coverings. A flat-screen TV is built in above the galley countertop, and by splitting the head into two compartments— toilet to port and shower to starboard—the salon dimensions are those of a slightly larger boat. For privacy, a sliding door separates the master stateroom from the salon. The 390's cockpit is similar to other Sundancer layouts with a U-shaped seating area aft, flip-up helm seat, and Corian-topped wet bar with sink and faucet. The entire cockpit sole can be raised on hydraulic rams for access to the engines. With standard 370hp V-drive gas engines, the 390 Sundancer will cruise in the low 20s and reach a top speed of close to 30 knots.

Sea Ray 400 Express Cruiser

Length w/Pulpit . . . . 43'0"	Fuel . . . . 300 gals.
Hull Length . . . . 40'4"	Water . . . . 100 gals.
Beam . . . . 13'0"	Waste . . . . 30 gals.
Draft . . . . 3'3"	Hull Type . . . . Deep-V
Weight . . . . 18,000#	Deadrise Aft . . . . 19°
Clearance . . . . NA	Production 1992–99

With her classic sportcruiser styling, huge cockpit, and luxurious interior, the Sea Ray 400 Express Cruiser was considered a state-of-the-art boat when she was introduced back in 1992. This was the long-awaited replacement model for the 390 Express Cruiser (1984–91), and while she has less beam than her predecessor, she was a big step up in luxury and appearance. Built on a deep-V hull with a solid fiberglass bottom, the two-stateroom interior of the 400 Express offers overnight accommodations for six. The master stateroom includes a pedestal island berth as well as a TV/VCR and a privacy door, and a circular pocket door closes off the starboard sitting room, converting it into a private stateroom with a full-size bed and convertible upper bunk. A separate shower stall is found in the head, and the large galley includes a breakfast bar and generous storage. On deck, double helm and companion seats are forward in the cockpit, while U-shaped seating aft converts into a sun pad. An extended swim platform was a popular option in later models. Twin 340hp Mercury inboards will cruise at 18 knots (mid 20s top), and optional Cat 340hp diesels cruise in the mid 20s and reach a top speed of 28–29 knots.

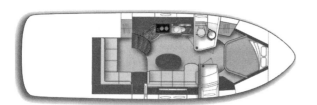

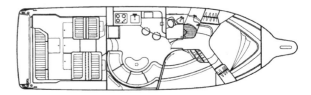

Original Cockpit Seating

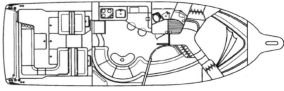

U-Shaped Cockpit Seating

See Page 350 for Pricing Information

See Page 350 for Pricing Information

Sea Ray 400 Sundancer

Length w/Platform	44'4"	Fuel	330 gals.
Hull Length	41'6"	Water	100 gals.
Beam	13'8"	Waste	28 gals.
Draft	3'4"	Hull Type	Deep-V
Weight	22,500#	Deadrise Aft	19°
Clearance	10'0"	Production	1997–99

Long on styling and loaded with cruising amenities, the Sea Ray 400 Sundancer combines the key elements of an American sportcruiser including a large, comfortable cockpit and a spacious, well-appointed interior. She's built on a deep-V hull with a solid fiberglass bottom, moderate beam, and prop pockets to reduce the shaft angles of her V-drive engines. The midcabin floorplan of the 400 Sundancer is arranged in the conventional manner with the owner's stateroom forward, an open galley in the main cabin, and a midcabin stateroom/lounge with a privacy door. Note that there's a second head adjoining the midcabin—a very desirable feature indeed. The forward head has a stall shower, and the level of fit and finish throughout is second to none. Topside, the huge U-shaped cockpit lounge will seat a small crowd, and the entire aft section of the cockpit sole rises electrically without moving the aft seat for engine access. Foldaway boarding steps, a radar arch, and a transom storage locker were standard. An extended swim platform was a popular option in later models. Twin 340hp V-drive inboards will cruise at 18 knots (mid 20s top), and optional Cat 340hp diesels cruise in the mid 20s (close to 30 knots top).

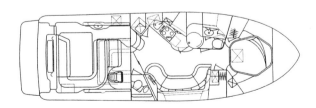

Sea Ray 410 Express Cruiser

Length w/Platform	45'6"	Fuel	335 gals.
Hull Length	41'6"	Water	100 gals.
Beam	13'10"	Waste	42 gals.
Draft	3'4"	Hull Type	Deep-V
Weight	21,000#	Deadrise Aft	19°
Clearance	9'6"	Production	1999–2003

The 410 Express Cruiser exhibits the aesthetically pleasing lines of all modern Sea Ray boats, and it's likely she'll remain a handsome yacht for many years to come regardless of future sportboat trends. Built on a fully cored hull with a wide beam, the 410's two-stateroom floorplan provides luxurious accommodations for six. The forward stateroom has a full-size pedestal bed as well as private head access, and a circular pocket door closes off the starboard sitting room, converting it into a private stateroom with twin bunks. The galley is huge with generous counter space and plenty of storage. High-gloss cherry woodwork, faux granite countertops, and decorator fabrics highlight the interior. Topside, the 410 Express Cruiser provides a large cockpit area as well as wide walkways to the foredeck. The forward cockpit sole lifts electrically for easy engine access, and the helm seat has a flip-up bolster so the captain can drive standing up. Additional features include a cockpit wet bar, foredeck sun pad, an excellent helm layout, transom storage locker, and side exhausts. Among several engine options, 420hp Cat diesels will cruise the 410 in the mid 20s and reach a top speed of close to 30 knots.

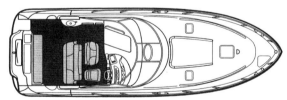

Deck Layout

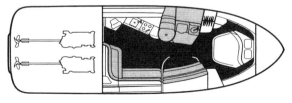

Interior Floorplan

See Page 350 for Pricing Information

See Page 350 for Pricing Information

Sea Ray 410 Sundancer

Length w/Platform	45'6"	Fuel	335 gals.
Hull Length	41'6"	Water	100 gals.
Beam	13'10"	Waste	42 gals.
Draft	3'2"	Hull Type	Deep-V
Weight	21,000#	Deadrise Aft	19°
Clearance	9'6"	Production	2000–03

Sea Ray introduced the 410 Sundancer in 2000 as the replacement boat for the company's popular 400 Sundancer built in 1997–99. Great styling has long been a Sea Ray trademark, and while few American sportboats are as glamorous as their European counterparts, the finish found in late-model Sundancers is second to none. Built on a fully cored hull with a wide beam, the interior features a large bow stateroom with a full-size pedestal bed, TV/VCR, and private access to the forward head. The mid-stateroom, which is open to the salon, has an electrically convertible sleeper/sofa, and the well-organized galley includes plenty of storage and counter space. Both staterooms have doors rather than privacy curtains, and there are two heads in this layout, one for each stateroom. Topside, the cockpit has U-shaped seating with a sun pad, table, and a full wet bar. For engine access, the entire aft section of the cockpit sole can be raised at the flip of a switch. A modest performer with standard 370hp V-drive MerCruisers (16 knots cruise/mid 20s top), optional Cat 340hp V-drive diesels cruise the 410 Sundancer in the mid 20s and reach a top speed of 28–29 knots.

Sea Ray 420 Sundancer

Length Overall	45'0"	Fuel	335 gals.
Beam	14'0"	Water	100 gals.
Draft	3'6"	Waste	42 gals.
Weight	22,500	Hull Type	Deep-V
Clearance	11'3"	Deadrise Aft	19°
Headroom	6'6"	Production	2003–Current

The bold styling of the Sea Ray 420 Sundancer comes about as close as any U.S. builder to emulating the graceful lines of a purebred European sportcruiser. Available with an optional hardtop, the Sundancer rides on a deep-V hull with prop pockets and a wide 14-foot beam. As it is with any yacht of this type, the cockpit is the focal point of the 420 Sundancer. Here, a big U-lounge aft and a double companion seat forward can seat as many as eight adults. A flip-up bolster seat is standard at the helm, and the entire cockpit sole can be raised at the push of a button for engine access. Below, the Sundancer's lavish midcabin interior is an impressive display of lacquered cherry woodwork, leather sofas, and deep-pile carpeting. Privacy doors (not curtains) separate the staterooms from the main salon, and the large galley area features generous storage and plenty of counter space. Topside, wide side decks provide secure access to the foredeck. A good performer with Cummins 450hp V-drive diesels, the 420 Sundancer will cruise in the mid 20s and top out around 30 knots. Note the small fuel capacity.

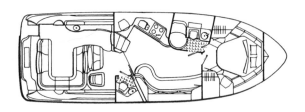

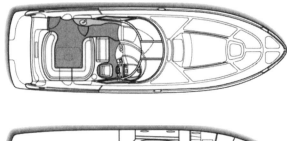

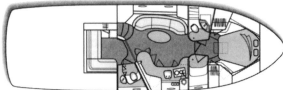

See Page 350 for Pricing Information

See Page 350 for Pricing Information

Sea Ray 420/440 Sundancer

Length w/Pulpit	47'1"	Fuel	400 gals.
Hull Length	44'0"	Water	100 gals.
Beam	13'11"	Waste	28 gals.
Draft	3'3"	Hull Type	Deep-V
Weight	20,000#	Deadrise Aft	19°
Clearance	NA	Production	1989–95

Introduced in late 1989 as the 420 Sundancer, Sea Ray made some hull changes and reintroduced this boat in 1992 as the 440 Sundancer. She's built on a solid fiberglass bottom with cored hullsides and a wide 13-foot, 11-inch beam. (Note that the 440's hull has prop pockets while the original 420 hull did not.) A high-style boat in her day, the Sundancer's wide-open interior is a blend of curved bulkheads, white Formica cabinetry, and light oak woodwork. Offering complete privacy for two couples, a sliding pocket door closes off the roomy mid-stateroom at night. The salon sofa converts to a double bed for extra guests, and the aft cabin has a vanity and sink as well as a concealed portable head. Topside, the cockpit is arranged with a triple companion seat at the helm, wet bar, and U-shaped lounge seating aft. Additional features include a bow pulpit, radar arch, and side-dumping exhausts. Twin 330hp MerCruiser V-drive gas inboards will cruise at 17–18 knots (low-to-mid 20s top), and 300hp Cat (or Cummins) diesels will cruise at 20 knots and reach a top speed in the mid 20s. Optional 425hp Cats will top out in the high 20s. In 1994 the original sliding cabin windows were replaced with oval ports.

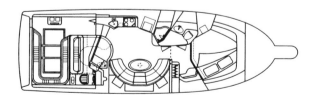

Sea Ray 450 Sundancer

Length w/Pulpit	48'1"	Water	100 gals.
Hull Length	45'6"	Waste	60 gals.
Beam	13'11"	Clearance	12'0"
Draft	3'7"	Hull Type	Deep-V
Weight	23,500#	Deadrise Aft	20°
Fuel	400 gals.	Production	1995–99

The Sea Ray 450 Sundancer was one of the largest sportcruisers available when she was introduced in 1995. Her bold styling has held up well over the years, and with a wide 14-foot beam, the interior of the Sundancer provides comfortable accommodations in very elegant surroundings. Like most late-model Sea Ray yachts, the 450 rides on a fully cored hull with prop pockets and a steep 20 degrees of transom deadrise. Sea Ray offered two floorplans for the 450 during her 5-year production run, both with private staterooms fore and aft, two full heads, and a convertible salon sofa. Faux granite countertops highlight the galley, and high-gloss oak cabinetry is applied throughout the interior. In the cockpit, a circular aft-facing seat, U-shaped seating and cocktail tables convert into a huge sun pad. A wet bar and transom door were standard, and a gas-assist hatch in the cockpit sole provides good access to the engine compartment. Additional features include a reverse sport arch, transom storage locker, underwater exhaust system, and an extended swim platform. A good-running boat, twin 340hp V-drive Cat diesels will cruise the 450 Sundancer in the low 20s, and 420hp Cats will cruise in the mid 20s and top out at 30+ knots.

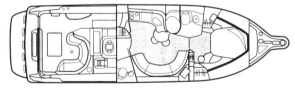

1995–97

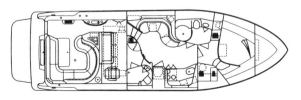

1998–99

Sea Ray 460 Express Cruiser

Sea Ray 460 Sundancer

Length	45'6"	Water	150 gals.
Beam	14'11"	Cockpit	NA
Draft	3'2"	Headroom	6'3"
Weight	27,500#	Hull Type	Modified-V
Clearance	9'9"	Deadrise Aft	17°
Fuel	420 gals.	Production	1985–89

Length w/Pulpit & Platform	51'4"	Fuel	400 gals.
Hull Length	45'6"	Water	100 gals.
Beam	14'8"	Headroom	6'6"
Draft	3'7"	Hull Type	Modified-V
Weight	28,000#	Deadrise Aft	15°
Clearance	11'2"	Production	1999–2003

When she was introduced in 1985, the Sea Ray 460 Express Cruiser reigned supreme as the largest full-production sport-yacht on the market. With her aggressive, low-profile appearance and reverse arch, her appeal was such that the 460 became a very good-selling model for Sea Ray. She rides on a solid fiberglass hull with prop pockets and a wide 14-foot, 11-inch beam. Originally, the 460 came with a two-stateroom interior (Plan A) with two heads—a lay-out designed for extended cruising with family or guests. In 1988 a new single-stateroom floorplan with a single head (Plan B) resulted in a much larger salon with two conversation areas (as well as a wet bar and built-in entertainment center) and a huge bow stateroom. Outside, the big bi-level cockpit is arranged with double helm and companion seats forward and a foldaway bench seat at the transom. Large hatches in the bridgedeck floor provide good access to the engines. Additional features include wide side decks, teak covering boards, transom door, swim platform, and side-dumping exhausts. Twin 375hp Cat diesels will cruise the 460 Express at 20 knots (mid 20s top), and optional 550hp 6V92 Detroit cruise in the mid 20s and reach a top speed of around 30 knots.

One of the largest domestic express yachts when she was intro-duced in 1999, the Sea Ray 460 Sundancer is a balanced blend of modern sportboat styling, luxurious accommodations, and top-quality construction. While her styling isn't as glamorous as her European counterparts, a wide beam and an expansive two-state-room, two-head floorplan provide the 460 with cabin dimensions that European imports—with their relatively narrow beams—can only envy. Sea Ray interiors are among the best in the business, and the accommodations of the 460 are impressive in every respect. In addi-tion to its own head, the mid-stateroom has complete privacy behind two sliding doors in addition to a standard washer/dryer combo. (Note that the settees in both the salon and mid-stateroom convert to double berth at the touch of a button.) In the cockpit, the facing aft settees convert electrically into a huge sun pad, and a gas-assist hatch provides access to the engine room. Additional features include underwater exhausts, foredeck sun pad, and an extended swim plat-form. Twin 430hp V-drive Volvo (or Cummins) diesels will cruise the 460 Sundancer in the low 20s and reach a top speed of 27–28 knots.

Plan A

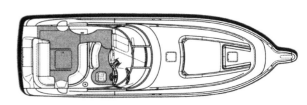

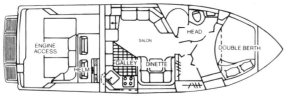

Plan B

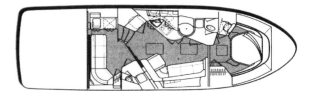

See Page 350 for Pricing Information

144

See Page 350 for Pricing Information

Sea Ray 480/500 Sundancer

Length w/Platform......... 55'8"	Water............... 150 gals.
Hull Length.............. 50'1"	Waste .... 68 gals.
Beam .... 15'0"	Clearance .... NA
Draft.................... 4'0"	Hull Type........... Modified-V
Weight............... 34,500#	Deadrise Aft .... 17°
Fuel............... 500 gals.	Production 1990–2000

A good-selling yacht, the 500 Sundancer (called the 480 Sundancer in 1990–91) was one of the largest sportcruisers on the market during her 1990s production years. With her long foredeck and sleek profile, the 500 combined luxury and extravagance in what was once a state-of-the-art package. Her sheer size is impressive enough, but it's the expansive, high-style interior that caused first-time viewers to catch their breath. Here, laid out on a single level and presenting a panorama of curved bulkheads and designer furnishings, the Sundancer's accommodations rival those of a small motor yacht. There are two private staterooms, two heads (each with a stall shower), a plush U-shaped sofa aft, and a wide-open salon with excellent headroom throughout. The cockpit—with its triple companion seat, full wet bar, and circular lounge seating—can seat a small crowd. Additional features include a reverse sport arch, wide side decks, and a huge engine room. Early models with 485hp 6-71 V-drive diesels will cruise the Sundancer in the low 20s (about 25 knots top), and later models with 735hp 8V92s will cruise at nearly 30 knots. Note that oval ports replaced the leak-prone sliding cabin windows in 1994.

Sea Ray 500 Sundancer

Length .... 53'4"	Fuel................. 560 gals.
Beam .... 15'3"	Water................ 150 gals.
Draft.................... 4'2"	Waste .... 68 gals.
Weight............... 38,500#	Hull Type .... Deep-V
Clearance............... 14'0"	Deadrise Aft .... 19°
Max Headroom .... 6'8"	Production 2003–Current

While the Sea Ray 500 Sundancer may lack the flat-out sex appeal of the best European yachts, it's safe to say that she takes a back seat to few other yachts of her type when it comes to engineering and construction. Built on a deep-V hull with prop pockets to reduce the shaft angle, the Sundancer's innovative cockpit layout is notable. Arranged with a unique rotating lounge, the cockpit forms a single entertaining area rather than the divided space found in other express yachts. Another major change is found below; instead of the ubiquitous midcabin floorplan, both of the Sundancer's staterooms are forward. While there's a foldout bed option aft, this area is now part of the main salon making it even grander than before with posh Ultraleather sofas, 6-foot, 8-inch headroom, and built-in 22-inch flat-screen TV/DVD. There are two heads in this layout, and the galley includes plenty of storage as well as a hardwood floor. An extended swim platform, cherry interior cabinetry, and a hardtop are standard. An extremely well-finished yacht, 640hp Cummins V-drive diesels will cruise the Sea Ray 500 Sundancer at 26–28 knots and reach a top speed of over 30 knots.

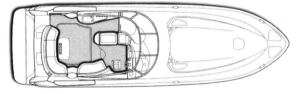

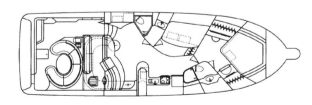

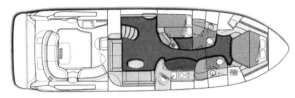

Sea Ray 510 Sundancer

Length w/Platform . . . . 53'6"	Fuel . . . . 600 gals.
Hull Length . . . . 50'6"	Water . . . . 150 gals.
Beam . . . . 15'8"	Headroom . . . . 6'8"
Draft . . . . 4'3"	Hull Type . . . . Modified-V
Weight . . . . 38,500#	Deadrise Aft . . . . 18°
Clearance . . . . 12'3"	Production 2000–03

The Sea Ray 510 Sundancer is a top-quality American sportyacht with a distinctive profile (note the integrated radar arch/hardtop) and a lavish two-stateroom interior. Unlike her narrow-beam European counterparts (Sunseeker, Cranchi, Pershing, etc.) with their compact interiors, the Sundancer rides on wide-beam hull with a wide-open interior positively loaded with luxury features. Indeed, the accommodations of the 510 Sundancer are as impressive as they are spacious—a lavish display of exquisite woodwork, quality hardware, and plush furnishings well suited to the mega-volume interior demands of the American market. The standard two-stateroom, two-head layout is ideal for extended cruising with guests, and the cockpit—with its wraparound helm console, retractable sun pad and stylish hardtop—offers plenty of seating in spite of the limited space. Notable features include a hideaway bar in the galley, separate stall showers in both heads, an underwater exhaust system, good engine access and a washer/dryer. Twin 660hp V-drive Cats cruise at 25 knots (about 30 knots top), and 770hp Cats will cruise in the high 20s and top out in the low 30s.

Sea Ray 540 Sundancer

Length w/Platform . . . . 57'8"	Fuel . . . . 600 gals.
Hull Length . . . . 54'11"	Water . . . . 150 gals.
Beam . . . . 15'11"	Waste . . . . 68 gals.
Draft . . . . 3'11"	Hull Type . . . . Modified-V
Weight . . . . 39,000#	Deadrise Aft . . . . 17°
Clearance, Arch . . . . 11'3"	Production 1998–2001

Introduced in 1998, the Sea Ray 540 Sundancer is a mega-volume sportcruiser whose muscular good looks and luxurious accommodations can still turn heads. This boat offers a seemingly endless list of high-tech features, and her extravagant interior is a study in comfort, beginning with the huge Ultraleather sofa that converts electrically into a slide-out bed. The Sundancer carries most of her beam forward, which creates plenty of living space below. The master stateroom is amidships and has a queen bed as well as a private head compartment. Forward, the guest stateroom has a full-size berth and space for a washer/dryer combo. The galley is open in the salon, and storage cabinets are abundant throughout the boat, all finished in high-gloss cherry woodwork. In the cockpit, two immense L-shaped settees, which can accommodate a small crowd, convert at the push of a button into a massive sun pad. Additional features include a foredeck sun pad, a superb helm console, and a hydraulic high-low swim platform to facilitate the launch of a tender. Twin 640hp Cat diesels will cruise in the mid 20s (30+ knots top), and 745hp 8V-92s will cruise in the high 20s and reach a top speed of 32–33 knots.

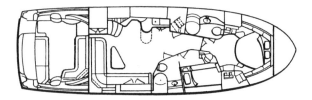

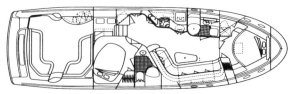

See Page 351 for Pricing Information

See Page 351 for Pricing Information

Sea Ray 550 Sundancer

Length w/Platform	57'8"	Fuel	600 gals.
Beam	15'11"	Water	150 gals.
Draft	4'0"	Waste	68 gals.
Weight	39,000#	Hull Type	Modified-V
Clearance	NA	Deadrise Aft	17°
Headroom	6'5"	Production	2002–04

The Sea Ray 550 Sundancer is basically an updated version of the company's earlier 540 Sundancer (1998–2001) with a revised interior, a restyled hardtop, and an overhead skylight to add some natural lighting to the salon. Built on a modified-V hull with a solid fiberglass bottom, the 550's luxurious two-stateroom layout is highlighted by its beautiful high-gloss cherry woodwork, a long, curved Ultraleather sofa to port (which converts electrically into a slide-out bed), and a curved galley to starboard with a built-in 42-inch plasma TV and a Lexan wine rack. Both staterooms include double berths, and the small refrigerator at the base of the companionway steps can be replaced by a washer/dryer combo. In the spacious cockpit, the two L-shaped settees convert at the push of a button into a massive sun pad. Additional features (among many) include a foredeck sun pad, a superb helm console, and a standard bow thruster. Note that the engine room is a tight fit. Twin 640hp Cat inboard diesels will cruise the Sea Ray 550 Sundancer in the mid 20s (about 30 knots top), and a pair of 765hp MANs will cruise at 28 knots and reach a top speed in the neighborhood of 32–33 knots.

Sea Ray 580 Super Sun Sport

Length w/Platform	60'10"	Water	200 gals.
Hull Length	58'11"	Waste	68 gals.
Beam	15'9"	Headroom	6'5"
Draft	4'1"	Hull Type	Modified-V
Weight	48,000#	Deadrise Aft	17°
Fuel	700 gals.	Production	1997–2002

An innovative design when she came out in 1997, the Sea Ray 580 Super Sun Sport has the sleek appearance of a purebred European sportcruiser. She's a sexy boat with her rakish profile and molded hardtop, and the transom—with its PWC garage and flanking walkways—is a real eye-catcher. The 580 is built on a fully cored hull with prop pockets and a relatively wide 15-foot, 9-inch beam. Belowdecks, the opulent salon is dominated by a full-length Ultraleather sofa that converts into a double bed at the touch of a button. The master stateroom, with its private head and queen-size bed, is aft, while the guest stateroom is forward. Both heads have separate stall showers, and the home-style galley features acres of counter space and very generous storage. Cockpit highlights include a big U-shaped lounge aft of the helm, full wet bar, hidden foldout boarding steps in the coaming, and a sun lounge atop the PWC compartment. Note that there are two entrances to the engine compartment, one via a cockpit deck hatch and the other by lifting the floor of the garage. Among several diesel engine options, twin 776hp Cats (or 735hp Detroits) will cruise in the high 20s and top out in the low 30s.

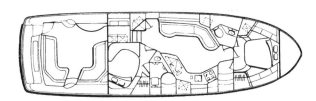

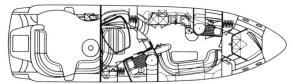

Standard Floorplan

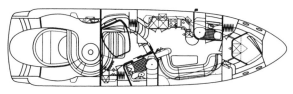

Alternate Floorplan

See Page 351 for Pricing Information

See Page 351 for Pricing Information

Sea Ray 630 Sun Sport; 630 Sundancer

Sealine S37 Sports Cruiser

Length w/Platform	64'6"	Fuel, Sundancer	1,061 gals.
Beam	15'9"	Water	200 gals.
Draft	5'0"	Waste	70 gals.
Weight, Sun Sport	54,500#	Hull Type	Deep-V
Weight, Sundancer	64,000#	Deadrise Aft	19°
Fuel, Super Sport	800 gals.	Production	1991–2001

Length	37'1"	Fuel	237 gals.
Beam	12'2"	Water	29 gals.
Draft, Up	2'5"	Headroom	6'1"
Draft, Down	3'1"	Hull Type	Modified-V
Weight	15,000#	Deadrise Aft	18°
Clearance	12'6"	Production	1996–2003

The 630 Super Sun Sport and her sistership, the 630 Sundancer, are a pair of visually impressive yachts (note the long foredeck) with the accommodations of a small motor yacht. While they look alike on the outside, the Sundancer uses Arneson surface drives to reduce draft and drag—an installation that results in a much higher top speed. Both are built on fully cored, deep-V hulls with moderate beam (the Sun Sport has prop pockets) and an integrated transom. Sharing similar floorplans, the massive salon is dominated by sculptured overhead panels and a long contoured leather sofa. The master stateroom is all the way forward, and a day head is in the salon. Note the crew quarters in the Sun Sport hidden beneath the transom and accessed via the cockpit sun pad. Additional features include a reverse arch, two transom doors, circular lounge seating in the cockpit, and a well-arranged engine room with push-button access. An excellent performer with 1,075hp 12V92 diesels, the Sun Sport will cruise at 30 knots (32–33 knots top). The Sundancer, available during 1995–99, can reach a top speed of nearly 45 knots with 1,300hp surface-drive Cats.

The Sealine S37 Sports Cruiser is a full-bodied family express with conservative lines and generous interior accommodations. Built the old-fashioned way on a solid fiberglass hull, the Sports Cruiser's deep-V hull insures a smooth and comfortable ride in a chop. Clearly, she lacks the sleek, sweptback profile of a Sea Ray or Sunseeker, but the seven-berth layout of the Sealine S37 and her separate head and shower compartments make a lot of sense in a family cruiser. In this boat, it's possible to take a shower without tying up the head at the same time. Further, both compartments can be accessed from the salon as well as the forward stateroom—very unusual. There's a standup dressing area in the midcabin, and four angled aluminum-framed doors close off the salon from the staterooms and head areas. On deck, the bi-level cockpit has a big semicircular settee/sun lounge aft of the helm, a wet bar to port, and a transom door that opens to a small swim platform with a teak sole. Note that the side decks are quite narrow and engine access, via a gas-assist hatch in the cockpit floor, is tight. Optional Volvo 250hp diesels will cruise the Sealine S37 in the mid 20s and reach a top speed of over 30 knots.

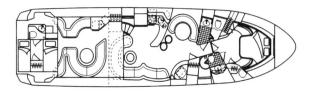

Sun Sport Floorplan

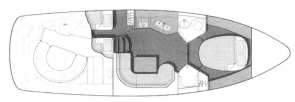

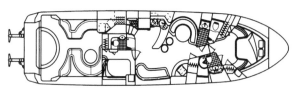

Sundancer Floorplan

See Page 351 for Pricing Information

See Page 351 for Pricing Information

Sealine C39 Coupe

Length . . . . 39'3"	Headroom . . . . 6'4"
Beam . . . . 12'3"	Fuel . . . . 276 gals.
Draft, Up . . . . 2'1"	Water . . . . 96 gals.
Draft, Down . . . . 3'4"	Hull Type . . . . Modified-V
Weight . . . . 18,700#	Deadrise Aft . . . . 18°
Clearance, Arch . . . . 13'10"	Production 2003–Current

Sealine launched the C39 Coupe in 2003 with three different drive systems: sterndrives, Arneson surface-drive diesels, and a closed-tunnel drive system called Trimax that, like the Arneson, uses surface drive propellers. Beyond the propulsion choices, the C39 is a very distinctive boat in her own right. Unlike the usual open-backed hardtop sportcruisers from Sunseeker and Sea Ray, etc., the fully enclosed C39 provides complete protection from the elements. The tall, rounded house is unique; it creates a spacious salon area with excellent headroom and superb visibility from the raised two-seat helm position. A compact-but-complete galley is located opposite the convertible dinette, and power side windows and a big overhead sunroof provide plenty of ventilation. Below, the living quarters consist of two staterooms and two heads, both with a stylish washbasin, but neither of which has a separate shower stall. The cockpit, which can be extended 25 inches at the push of a button, includes a separate life raft compartment. Arneson or Trimax surface drives will both reach a top speed of close to 35 knots with a pair of 310hp Volvo diesels.

Sealine S41 Sports Yacht

Length . . . . 42'3"	Fuel . . . . 306 gals.
Beam . . . . 13'4"	Water . . . . 84 gals.
Draft . . . . 3'7"	Waste . . . . 34 gals.
Weight . . . . 21,500#	Hull Type . . . . Modified-V
Clearance, Mast . . . . 14'2"	Deadrise Aft . . . . 18°
Headroom . . . . 6'2"	Production 2000–03

In many ways, the Sealine S41 is quite unlike any other European sportboat on the market. It's not just the partial hardtop with its sliding roof panel that sets her apart—what Sealine calls a Solar Protection System; the real surprise is found below where the S41's two-stateroom floorplan delivers a motor yacht–size aft cabin with full standing headroom, a walkaround queen berth and a private head. By any standard, this is an impressive layout for an express cruiser, one made possible by locating the engines aft and using sterndrive power rather than inboards. On deck, the bi-level cockpit is very spacious with plenty of seating, a dedicated life raft locker, wet bar and sun pad. An overhead storage bin in the hardtop stores the cockpit table and the two-part enclosure. Note that there have been some reports that the hardtop, which has no forward supports, may flex at higher speeds. Additional features include a teak cockpit sole, an electric sunroof, twin bolster seats at the helm and a surprisingly large galley. The engine room is a tight fit. Twin 300hp Volvo diesel I/Os will cruise the Sealine S41 in the mid 20s (about 30 knots top). Note that the Sealine S43 Sports Yacht is the same boat with inboard power.

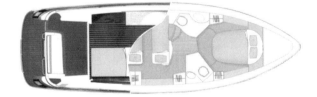

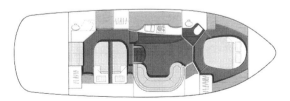

Sealine S48 Sports Yacht

Length . . . . 48'7"	Fuel . . . . 534 gals.
Beam . . . . 13'4"	Water . . . . 156 gals.
Draft . . . . 3'8"	Hull Type . . . . Deep-V
Weight . . . . 35,000#	Deadrise Aft . . . . 19°
Clearance, Hardtop . . . . 14'5"	Designer . . . . Sealine
Headroom . . . . 6'6"	Production 2002–Current

Even if the styling of the Sealine S48 seems a little overdone, few will disagree that this is one of the most innovative sportyachts on the market. Foremost among her unique features, an ingenious sliding transom section allows for the easy float-on/float-off launch and recovery of a dinghy or PWC. The spacious cockpit is notable for its seating for ten around two cocktail tables, and the Sealine's hardtop houses a bimini extension to completely shade the aft cockpit. Note the cockpit side door, a thoughtful feature that greatly simplifies foredeck access. Below, the S48's stylish interior consists of two private staterooms, each with a queen-size berth and en suite head. At first glance, the aft cabin seems the most inviting place to bunk until the lack of storage space is noticed. The large galley area would embarrass many 60-footers, and two overhead hatches provide plenty of lighting and fresh air into the salon. Note that the S48 was the first Sealine to offer a computer-controlled joystick steering system fed with inputs from both engines and thrusters. Volvo 480hp diesel inboards will top out at just over 30 knots, and optional 635hp Cummins diesels will reach a top speed of about 35 knots.

Shamrock 270 Mackinaw

Length w/Pulpit . . . . 30'6"	Fuel . . . . 156 gals.
Hull Length . . . . 28'10"	Water . . . . 20 gals.
Beam . . . . 9'3"	Headroom . . . . 6'4"
Draft . . . . 2'5"	Hull Type . . . . Modified-V
Clearance . . . . 8'2"	Deadrise Aft . . . . 14°
Weight . . . . 7,525#	Production 2000–Current

Shamrock's 270 Mackinaw is a single-engine inboard cruiser with a season-stretching hardtop and a large cockpit. This is a boat ideally suited for northern anglers and cruisers alike, and she's in a class by herself since there are no other production inboard boats of her type on the market. Unlike smaller Shamrock models, the 270 forgoes their famous "Keel Drive" for a more conventional modified-V hull bottom with a prop pocket to reduce the draft and shaft angle. With only 27 feet to work with, the Mackinaw's interior is practical but necessarily confining. The cabin contains a small galley as well as a dinette with a removable table and a fully equipped helm station to starboard. A V-berth below sleeps two comfortably, but the enclosed head is very small with only sitting headroom. The cockpit has aft-facing bench seating, and standard features include a transom door, an in-deck fish box, transom livewell, opening cabin windows and a bow pulpit. A swim platform is a popular option. Heavily built and well finished, the 270 Mackinaw will cruise at 18 knots with a standard 320hp gas engine and reach a top speed of around 30 knots. Close to 100 have been built to date.

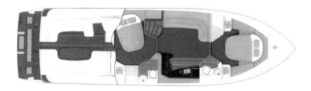

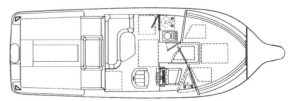

Silverton 271 Express

Length w/Pulpit	29'9"	Fuel	109 gals.
Hull Length	27'10"	Water	30 gals.
Beam	8'6"	Clearance	NA
Draft, Up	1'8"	Hull Type	Modified-V
Draft, Down	3'1"	Deadrise Aft	14°
Weight	7,643#	Production	1995–97

The Silverton 271 is a contemporary family cruiser with accommodations for four and the versatility of being trailerable. (Trailerable, yes, but with an over-the-road weight approaching 9,000 pounds including trailer, it'll take a 1-ton tow vehicle to do the job.) Built on a solid fiberglass hull with moderate transom deadrise, the 271 Express is a big boat on the inside thanks to her very high freeboard. The midcabin floorplan is arranged in the normal manner with double berths fore and aft, a full galley, removable dinette, and an enclosed head with shower. The high freeboard of the 271 permits plenty of cabin headroom, but there's no denying the fact that her high profile gives her a top-heavy appearance. A wraparound settee is opposite the helm, and the integrated swim platform has a hot and cold shower, swim ladder, and a handy storage locker. Lacking side decks, a walk-through windshield provides access to the foredeck. A single 250hp 5.7-liter MerCruiser sterndrive will cruise the Silverton 271 at a rather sluggish 15 knots (about 25 knots top), and an optional 300hp 7.4-liter engine delivers a more respectable 18–19 knots at cruise and close to 30 knots wide open.

Silverton 30X Express

Length	30'8"	Water	37 gals.
Beam	10'10"	Headroom	6'2"
Draft	3'0"	Hull Type	Modified-V
Weight	9,100#	Designer	M. Peters
Clearance	8'5"	Deadrise Aft	NA
Fuel	185 gals.	Production	1988–89

The 30X Express was second in a series of sportboat designs introduced by Silverton in the late 1980s, beginning with the original 34X model in 1987. In spite of her shorter length, the addition of an integral swim platform made the 30X a better-looking boat than her predecessor. Unlike most modern express cruiser designs, the 30X does not have a midcabin interior with sterndrive power. Instead, the 30X has a single-stateroom floorplan, which allows for a real engine room and the installation of straight-inboard power. The main cabin features a full-length convertible lounge, hanging locker, and a large U-shaped dinette. Three overhead hatches provide plenty of natural light, and the forward double berth is flanked by shelving and a vanity. Topside, a companion seat to port and bench seating along the transom will seat five or six guests. Additional features include four opening ports, a radar arch, a molded bow pulpit, and transom door. With standard 270hp gas engines, the 30X will cruise in the low 20s and reach a top speed of 30 knots. Perhaps because she lacked a midcabin interior, the 30X didn't last very long in the market and production lasted only two years.

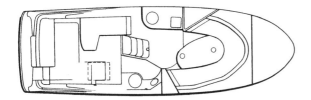

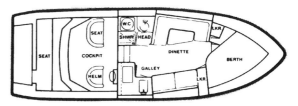

Silverton 31 Gulfstream

Length . . . . 31'0"	Water. . . . . 40 gals.
Beam . . . . 11'11"	Cockpit . . . . 115 sq. ft.
Draft. . . . . 2'11"	Hull Type . . . . Modified-V
Weight. . . . . 9,500#	Deadrise Aft . . . . NA
Clearance . . . . NA	Designer . . . . Bob Rioux
Fuel . . . . 250 gals.	Production 1979–86

When the Silverton 31 Gulfstream was introduced in 1979, she represented a dramatic break from Silverton's past market reliance on flybridge convertibles and family cruisers. Built on a solid fiberglass hull with a relatively wide beam, the 31 Gulfstream was designed to appeal to entry-level buyers seeking an inexpensive dayboat with plenty of cockpit space and basic cabin accommodations. Indeed, she's a conservative design when measured against today's Euro-style sportboats and her styling reflects her late-1970s roots. Belowdecks, there are berths for four adults along with a standup head, a U-shaped dinette, and a compact galley. The Gulfstream was never offered with a radar arch or a curved windshield, but she does have a surprisingly large cockpit capable of accommodating a number of guests without being crowded. Twin 270hp Crusaders were standard (18–19 knots cruise/28 knots top) with big-block 350hp gas engines (around 24 knots cruise/32–33 knots top) offered as an option. Interestingly, V-drives were used through the 1982 model year, and in 1983 she was redesigned with straight inboards.

Silverton 310 Express

Length . . . . 32'0"	Water. . . . . 54 gals.
Beam . . . . 11'6"	Waste . . . . 35 gals.
Draft. . . . . 2'2"	Hull Type . . . . Modified-V
Weight. . . . . 9,202#	Deadrise Aft . . . . 14°
Clearance. . . . . 10'5"	Designer. . . . . Silverton
Fuel . . . . 150 gals.	Production 1994–2000

A good-looking boat with her colorful hull graphics and still-modern profile, the Silverton 310 Express is a low-priced mid-cabin cruiser with a big interior and good overall performance. Like all Silverton boats, the 310's hull is solid fiberglass, and her 11-foot, 6-inch beam is reasonably wide for a 30-footer. Going below, the entryway steps are suspended by aluminum weldments, and the open design makes the aft cabin—tucked below the cockpit—seem unusually spacious. There are berths for six, and the opening ports and deck hatches provide excellent cabin ventilation. The cockpit is arranged with three seating areas (including a double-wide helm seat that tilts up for use as a bolster), and the cockpit table can be converted into a sun pad. Additional features include a walk-through windshield, privacy curtains for both staterooms, a foldaway transom seat, cockpit wet bar, and fender racks built into the swim platform. Standard 250hp 5.7-liter MerCruiser sterndrives will cruise the 310 Express at 19–20 knots (35 knots top), and optional 300hp 7.4-liter engines will deliver a 25-knot cruising speed and a top speed of around 36–37 knots.

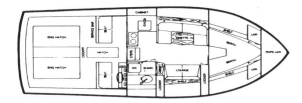

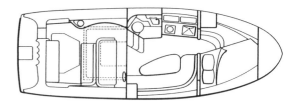

See Page 352 for Pricing Information

See Page 352 for Pricing Information

Silverton 34 Express (1987–89)

Length	34'6"	Water	40 gals.
Beam	12'7"	Cockpit	62 sq. ft.
Draft	3'8"	Hull Type	Modified-V
Weight	11,000#	Deadrise Aft	17°
Clearance	12'7"	Designer	M. Peters
Fuel	250 gals.	Production	1987–89

With her bolt-on swim platform and squared-off windshield, the Silverton 34 Express may be dated by today's sportboat standards, but she was a good-selling boat in her day thanks to a roomy interior and cockpit and a very attractive price. Built on a solid fiberglass hull with moderate beam and a shallow keel, the 34 Express evenly divides her hull length between the cockpit and interior. Her midcabin floorplan is arranged with an L-shaped settee to port in the salon and double berths fore and aft. The aft cabin has a door for privacy—a rare luxury—while the forward stateroom has only a curtain. Note that there's a stall shower in the head compartment. On deck, the cockpit has built-in bench seating aft as well as a transom door, and visibility from the raised bridgedeck is excellent. Hinged hatches in the cockpit sole provide good access to the engines. A bow pulpit, radar arch, transom door, and swim platform were standard. On the downside, the side decks are very narrow and difficult to negotiate. Twin 350hp Crusader V-drive gas engines will cruise the Silverton 34 Express at a respectable 20 knots and reach a top speed in the neighborhood of 30 knots.

Silverton 34 Express (1990–94)

Length	34'3"	Water	47 gals.
Beam	12'8"	Cockpit	62 sq. ft.
Draft	3'1"	Hull Type	Modified-V
Weight	16,500#	Deadrise Aft	17°
Clearance	9'3"	Designer	M. Peters
Fuel	254 gals.	Production	1990–94

The Silverton 34 Express is an updated version of the company's original 34-foot Express (1987–89) with a streamlined profile and a new interior. The cabin windows of the earlier 34 are eliminated in this newer version; cabin ventilation and natural lighting now come from six small deck hatches just forward of the windshield. Built on the same modified-V hull as her predecessor, the graceful profile of the 34 Express might still be considered contemporary were it not for the absence of a curved windshield. Belowdecks, the interior is a tasteful blend of earth-tone fabrics and off-white furnishings. Privacy curtains separate both sleeping areas from the main salon, and the head contains a separate stall shower. There's a lot of counter space in the galley—always a pleasant surprise. An L-shaped sun lounge is opposite the helm on the bridgedeck, and the aft cockpit came with a wet bar, transom door, and a bench seat at the stern. Additional features include a hydraulically operated engine access hatch, foredeck sun pad, radar arch, fender storage racks, and a bow pulpit. Twin 300hp gas engines (with V-drives) will cruise the Silverton 34 Express at 20 knots and deliver a top speed of 27–28 knots.

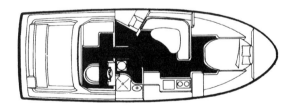

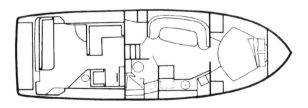

See Page 352 for Pricing Information

See Page 352 for Pricing Information

Silverton 360 Express

Silverton 38 Express

Length	36'1"	Waste	40 gals.
Beam	12'11"	Clearance	9'10"
Draft	2'6"	Hull Type	Modified-V
Weight	16,032#	Deadrise Aft	12°
Fuel	286 gals.	Designer	Silverton
Water	100 gals.	Production	1995–2000

Length	37'7"	Water	110 gals.
Beam	13'11"	Cockpit	NA
Draft	3'7"	Hull Type	Modified-V
Weight	21,000#	Deadrise Aft	17°
Clearance	9'9"	Designer	M. Peters
Fuel	300 gals.	Production	1990–94

Introduced in 1995, the Silverton 360 Express combined the elements of style, comfort, and performance in a contemporary sportboat package offered at a very affordable price. She was built on a solid fiberglass, low-deadrise hull with a wide beam and prop pockets to reduce draft. The midcabin floorplan of the 360 Express is arranged with double berths fore and aft, a full galley, and a circular salon dinette. There are privacy doors for both staterooms—a convenience seldom found in midcabin cruisers these days—and the interior is tastefully finished with cherrywood joinery and earth-tone fabrics. There's comfortable seating in the cockpit for six, and the transom has a built-in storage and a hot-and-cold water shower. Lacking side decks, a walk-through windshield provides access to the foredeck. Note the sporty air intake vents in the hullsides. Additional features include a radar arch, swim platform, transom door, cockpit wet bar, and a foredeck sun pad. Twin 320hp Crusader gas inboards (with V-drives) will cruise the Silverton 360 Express at 18–19 knots and reach a top speed in the high 20s. (Note that she was called the Silverton 361 Express in 1995–96.)

The Silverton 38 Express is a boat that may have turned a few heads in the 1990s, but whose overall styling just hasn't held up very well over the years. She was built on the same hull used for the Silverton 37 Convertible, a proven design with a wide beam and relatively high freeboard. The midcabin floorplan is arranged with double berths in both staterooms, and a unique, though essentially useless, Plexiglas window-wall separates the forward stateroom from the salon. The decor is comprised of mostly inexpensive furnishings and earth-tone wall coverings and upholstery. A cluster of six overhead skylights provide the only outside lighting, although the liberal use of mirrors makes the interior seem quite open and spacious. Sold with a long list of standard equipment, the 38 Express has a spacious bi-level cockpit with enough fore and aft seating to accommodate a small crowd. A wet bar and icemaker were standard, and a transom door opens to the integral swim platform. Twin 355hp Crusader gas engines (with V-drives) will cruise the Silverton 38 Express at 20 knots and deliver a top speed in the high 20s. Note that 425hp Cats were optional.

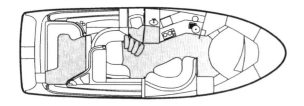

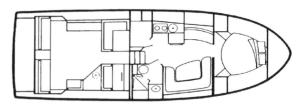

Sunseeker 44 Camargue

Length	44'0"	Water	80 gals.
Beam	13'6"	Headroom	6'4"
Draft	3'5"	Hull Type	Deep-V
Weight	29,000#	Deadrise Aft	20°
Clearance	9'10"	Designer	Don Shead
Fuel	265 gals.	Production	1998–2002

One of Sunseeker's more popular models during her production years, the Camargue 44 is a well-equipped sportcruiser with a large cockpit and a very inviting interior. Like all Sunseekers, the Camargue rides on a smooth-riding deep-V hull with propeller tunnels, and the standard of fit and finish is very good for a production yacht. The Camargue's spacious cockpit is fitted with a full-size sun-lounge as well as a wet bar and seating for eight around a folding dining table. Below, the luxurious midcabin interior is dominated by a stunning array of high-gloss cherry woodwork, top-quality appliances, and rich designer furnishings. With a master stateroom forward and a twin-berth aft, both with en suite facilities, the greatest amount of space has been saved for the salon amidships. Additional features include wide, secure side decks, an extended swim platform, foredeck fender storage, a drop-down helm seat, teak cockpit sole, bow thruster, and an underwater exhaust system. Note that the anchor windlass is stored inside the rode locker. A solid performer with twin 420hp Caterpillar diesels, the Camargue 44 will cruise in the mid 20s and reach a top speed in excess of 30 knots.

Sunseeker 47 Camargue

Length	46'9"	Water	100 gals.
Beam	13'5"	Headroom	6'5"
Draft	3'3"	Hull Type	Deep-V
Weight	30,644#	Deadrise Aft	23°
Clearance	9'4"	Designer	Don Shead
Fuel	365 gals.	Production	1996–99

Introduced at the 1996 London Boat Show, the Sunseeker 47 Camargue is a sleek English-built sportcruiser with a huge cockpit, a lush cherrywood interior, and aggressive 1990s styling. Sunseeker has long been recognized for their exemplary production standards and the 47 is a case in point: the exterior glasswork and overall fit and finish are impressive. Like all Sunseeker sportboats, the 47 rides on a slender deep-V hull with prop pockets, a proven offshore design with excellent seakeeping qualities and a good turn of speed. The Camargue's opulent midcabin interior contains two heads, a large galley with hidden appliances, and an array of lacquered woodwork and rich upholstery. On deck, the extensive single-level cockpit is a spacious entertainment center with plenty of lounge seating, a wet bar and a foldaway table. The sun pad sits atop a transom garage for an inflatable dinghy. Additional features include a teak swim platform, hidden swim ladder, radar arch, and a stunning wraparound windshield. A good performer with 435hp inboard Cats, the Camargue will cruise at 25–26 knots (about 30 knots top), and optional 625hp Detroits will cruise at 30 knots (34–35 knots top).

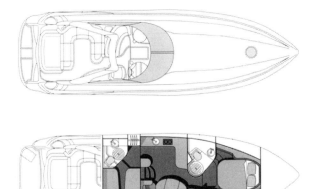

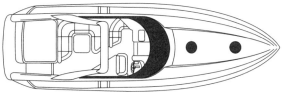

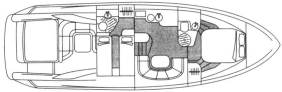

See Page 355 for Pricing Information

155

See Page 355 for Pricing Information

Sunseeker 50 Camargue

Length . . . . 52'11"	Water . . . . 112 gals.
Beam . . . . 14'7"	Headroom . . . . 6'3"
Draft . . . . 4'7"	Hull Type . . . . Deep-V
Weight . . . . 41,400#	Deadrise Aft . . . . 22.5°
Clearance . . . . 12'6"	Designer . . . . Don Shead
Fuel . . . . 528 gals.	Production 2001–Current

The Sunseeker 50 Camargue has been one of the more popular sportcruisers on the international market for several years thanks to her excellent build quality, aggressive styling, and luxurious cabin accommodations. Like any good Med-style cruiser, the focal point of the Camargue is her large cockpit with its wraparound lounge seating, full wet bar, and large aft sun pad. A transom garage beneath the sun pad is designed to store a hard-bottomed tender or two-person PWC, and a hatch in the teak cockpit sole provides access to the engine compartment. Below, the Camargue's elegant two-stateroom interior is accented with high-gloss cherry cabinetry, recessed lighting, and rich designer fabrics. The open salon offers generous seating, a folding dining table, entertainment center, and a well-equipped galley. Hardwood doors separate the fore and aft staterooms from the salon, and both staterooms are fitted with private en suite heads with stall showers. A hardtop is a popular option. Twin 660hp inboard Cats—straight inboards, not V-drives—will cruise the 50 Camargue in the mid 20s and reach a top speed of about 30 knots.

Sunseeker 51 Camargue

Length . . . . 49'0"	Water . . . . 130 gals.
Beam . . . . 14'5"	Headroom . . . . 6'2"
Draft . . . . 3'8"	Hull Type . . . . Deep-V
Weight . . . . 42,460#	Deadrise Aft . . . . 23°
Clearance . . . . 12'9"	Designer . . . . Don Shead
Fuel . . . . 465 gals.	Production 1994–98

Introduced into the U.S. market in 1994, the Sunseeker 51 Camargue helped define the Sunseeker reputation in this country for sophisticated styling, meticulous workmanship, and exciting sportboat performance. Indeed, the Camargue was considered a very high-tech yacht in the mid 1990s with the sleek styling and luxury features American buyers found so attractive in European sportboats. Built on a deep-V hull with moderate beam and prop pockets, two floorplans were offered during her 5-year production run. The original interior has a single stateroom and a full head aft of the salon, while an updated arrangement has two staterooms aft with the second head in the salon. Either of these interiors is a lavish display of rich cherry woodwork and deluxe furnishings. On deck, the Camargue's elegant cockpit has seating for eight with generous storage and a huge sun lounge aft. Beneath the aft sun lounge is a garage for a tender or jet bike (with an electric winch for launch and recovery). On the downside, the engine room—accessed from under the on-deck dinette—is a seriously tight fit. Twin 600hp Cat (or 625hp 6V92 Detroit) diesels with V-drives will cruise the Sunseeker 51 Camargue in the mid 20s and reach 30+ knots wide open.

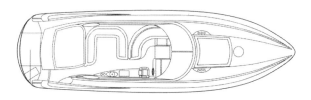

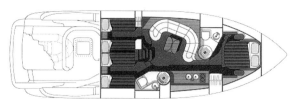

Three-Stateroom Interior

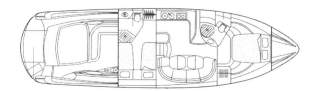

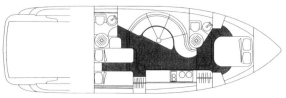

Two-Stateroom Interior

See Page 355 for Pricing Information

See Page 355 for Pricing Information

Sunseeker 53 Portofino

Length	55'9"	Fuel	528 gals.
Beam	15'1"	Water	106 gals.
Draft	4'0"	Waste	24 gals.
Weight	42,500#	Hull Type	Deep-V
Clearance	14'5"	Deadrise Aft	19°
Headroom	6'4"	Production	2004–Current

A luxurious sportyacht, the 53 Portofino incorporates the dramatic styling and spirited performance buyers have come to expect in a Sunseeker product. This is as good as it gets in a modern express cruising yacht, and for those who can afford the price the Portofino opens the door to luxury on a grand scale. With not one, but two twin-berth guest cabins as well as a spacious main salon and good-sized galley, the beautiful high-gloss cherry interior of the 53 Portofino is perfect for casual entertaining and weekend getaways. Each cabin has a flat-screen TV as standard, and both head compartments are fitted with separate shower stalls. The cockpit includes a slick foldaway table, a large U-shaped lounge and sunbathing area, and double helm and companion seats forward. The rear sun pad lifts at the push of a button to reveal a tender and storage garage, and a ladder from a hatch under the cockpit table provides access to a fairly compact engine compartment. Additional features include a cockpit wet bar, radar arch, foredeck sun pad, anchor windlass, and teak bathing platform. Built on a deep-V hull with prop pockets to reduce draft, 715hp Cat (or Volvo) diesels will cruise the Sunseeker 53 at 27–28 knots and reach a top speed of 30+ knots.

Sunseeker 55 Camargue

Length	55'0"	Water	150 gals.
Beam	14'7"	Headroom	6'3"
Draft	4'1"	Hull Type	Deep-V
Weight	39,970#	Deadrise Aft	23°
Clearance	11'2"	Designer	Don Shead
Fuel	753 gals.	Production	1994–96

A popular model, the Camargue 55 helped define the Sunseeker reputation in this country for sleek styling, luxurious accommodations, and exciting open-water performance. The Camargue was an impressive yacht when she came out in 1994 with deck and cabin accommodations that could only be described as opulent. The spacious cockpit, which consumes about half of the boat's length, provides seating for three at the helm along with a mid-cockpit dinette and a huge aft sun lounge. Beneath the sun lounge is a garage for a tender or jet bike with an electric winch for launch and recovery. Belowdecks, the Camargue's three-stateroom interior was updated in 1995 when a curved galley and dinette replaced the original U-shaped galley and dinette. In both configurations, the blend of high-gloss cherry woodwork, expensive galley appliances, and plush furnishings can only be described as lush. Additional features include a teak cockpit sole, bow storage locker, radar arch, and a hot/cold transom shower. On the downside, the engine room is a tight fit. Among several diesel options, twin 760hp 8V92 Detroits will cruise the 55 Camargue in the high 20s and reach 30+ knots top.

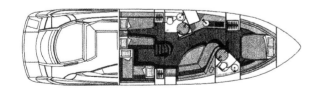

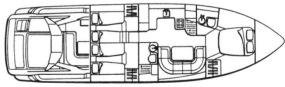

1994 Interior

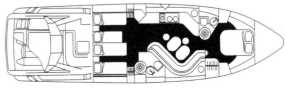

1995–96 Interior

See Page 355 for Pricing Information

See Page 355 for Pricing Information

Sunseeker 56 Predator

Length	60'2"	Water	172 gals.
Beam	15'1"	Headroom	6'5"
Draft	4'5"	Hull Type	Deep-V
Weight	52,030#	Deadrise Aft	19°
Clearance	12'9"	Designer	Don Shead
Fuel	621 gals.	Production	2000–04

In terms of luxury, quality, and flat-out performance, the Sunseeker 56 Predator set the standards for big sportyachts during her 2000–2004 production years. The Predator boasted an array of sophisticated features including a hydraulic swim platform for launching and retrieving a tender as well as an optional hardtop with retractable sunroof. Her expansive, wide-open cockpit is still among the class leaders for comfort and amenities, and the Predator is one of the few European sportboats whose engine room offers decent service access. Belowdecks, an elegant two-stateroom interior includes a full-width owner's stateroom aft and a large guest cabin forward. There are two heads in this layout, and while most would view the aft cabin as the master suite, it doesn't have a private head; there's a salon entrance. A washer/dryer is located in the galley, and the salon is dominated by a full-length leather settee and plenty of high-gloss cherry cabinetry. Additional features include a teak cockpit sole, wide side decks, cockpit engine room access, and a telescopic passerelle. An excellent performer with 660hp Cat V-drive diesels, the 56 Predator will cruise in the mid-to-high 20s and reach a top speed of 32–33 knots.

Sunseeker 58/60 Predator

Length	57'11"	Water	170 gals.
Beam	15'1"	Headroom	6'8"
Draft	4'5"	Hull Type	Deep-V
Weight	48,400#	Deadrise Aft	22.5°
Clearance	10'8"	Designer	Don Shead
Fuel	753 gals.	Production	1997–2002

Ever since the first of Sunseeker's Predator models was launched back in 1995, these elegant yachts have set the standard for quality and performance in the 50-foot-plus luxury sportcruiser market. Long and slender, the sleek styling of the Predator 60 (called the Predator 58 in 1997–98) has aged very little since she went out of production in 2002. Below, her lush accommodations are arranged with a sweeping settee opposite the galley and a bar set along the port side. Forward is the master stateroom with its en suite bathroom, and twin guest cabins aft share an equally generous head compartment. The cockpit, which seats six at a U-shaped lounge behind the helm, is dominated by an oval sun pad that sits atop a dinghy/PWC garage with a built-in launch-and-retrieval winch. Additional features include a cockpit wet bar, wide side decks, foredeck sun pad, a teak cockpit sole, and stunning wraparound stainless-steel windshield. Note that a hardtop with sunroof was a popular option. Running on a deep-V hull with prop pockets, twin 800hp V-drive MANs (or 760hp Detroits) will cruise at 26–28 knots and top out in the mid 30s.

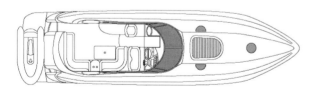

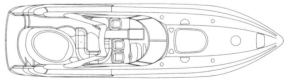

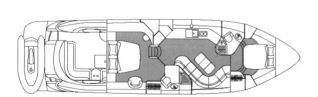

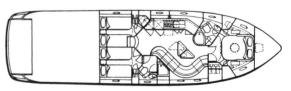

See Page 355 for Pricing Information

See Page 355 for Pricing Information

Sunseeker 60 Renegade

Sunseeker 61 Predator

Length Overall	62'6"	Fuel	940 gals.
Hull Length	56'1"	Water	153 gals.
Beam	15'11"	Hull Type	Deep-V
Draft	3'3"	Deadrise Aft	20°
Weight	50,795#	Designer	Don Shead
Clearance	12'3"	Production	1991–95

Length	64'0"	Water	165 gals.
Beam	15'1"	Headroom	6'6"
Draft	4'5"	Hull Type	Deep-V
Weight	57,320#	Deadrise Aft	19°
Clearance	16'1"	Designer	Don Shead
Fuel	779 gals.	Production	2002–Current

Impressive from a distance and enormous up close, the Renegade 60 stands apart from other high-performance express yachts thanks to her exotic waterjet propulsion, an Italian-made water-drive system that pumps some 32,000 gallons of water per minute at full throttle. The result is a top speed of just over 45 knots—a good deal faster than a conventional prop-driven boat this size can reach. (Surface drives, however, will attain these higher speeds as well, although they're a lot noisier.) Jet drives make boat handling a strange sensation, and this is certainly not a yacht in which to make your first attempt at backing into a tight berth. Like all Sunseeker models, the 60 Renegade is finished to extremely high production-boat standards. Notable features include an elegant three-stateroom interior with two full heads, a beautifully engineered cockpit with a huge mid-cockpit settee/dinette and a garage under the aft sun lounge with a retractable hoist to lower the dinghy into the water. A completely impressive yacht with an exciting blend of luxury and performance, the 60 Renegade's complicated drive system—and the associated maintenance requirements—will limit her appeal among conventional U.S. boat buyers.

The 61 Predator is a good example of why Sunseeker continues to set the standards for high-end European sportcruisers. Aside from her aggressive styling and dazzling performance, the 61 employs the latest innovations in construction and design. Most 61s have been delivered with an optional hardtop (with retractable sunroof), and the Predator's hydraulic swim platform makes launching and retrieving a tender from the aft garage simple and easy. Below, the exceptional interior finish is enhanced by high-gloss cherrywood paneling, plush leather seating, and hidden galley appliances. A fully equipped en suite master stateroom is forward, and the twin aft staterooms share a day head to starboard in the salon. The spacious cockpit of the 61 Predator has seating for eight as well as a barbecue, full wet bar, and aft sun pad. A hatch in the teak sole provides access to a fairly tight engine room, and wide side decks lead to the foredeck where a large sun lounge is positioned just forward of the windshield. A fast ride with 1,050hp V-drive MANs, the 61 Predator can reach a top speed of over 35 knots. Note the generous fuel capacity.

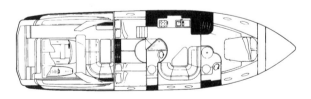

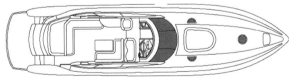

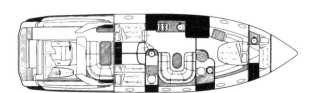

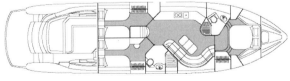

See Page 355 for Pricing Information

See Page 355 for Pricing Information

Sunseeker 63 Predator

Length Overall	63'0"	Fuel	798 gals.
Beam	15'6"	Water	185 gals.
Draft	4'1"	Hull Type	Deep-V
Weight	48,400#	Deadrise Aft	21°
Clearance	14'5"	Designer	Don Shead
Headroom	6'3"	Production	1995–99

For the deep-pocket buyer looking to make the ultimate fashion statement, the Sunseeker Predator 63 was about as good as it got in the late 1990s in the luxury sportcruiser market. At 63 feet overall, she was among the largest production yachts of her type available. Built on a deep-V hull with cored hullsides and prop pockets, the Predator's state-of-the-art construction and extraordinary craftsmanship typify the level of commitment Sunseeker has been putting into its boats for nearly three decades. The enormous cockpit comes with a huge U-shaped settee with removable high-low table abaft the helm, and a massive sun lounge at the transom conceals a garage capable of storing—and electrically launching—a 13-foot jet boat. The 63 also features a unique power-driven convertible hardtop for that extra degree of cruising comfort. Belowdecks, the palatial interior sleeps six in three lush staterooms. The galley is to starboard in the full-width salon, and the lacquered woodwork, sumptuous upholstery, and quality hardware make this one of the most sensuous interiors to be found in any production yacht. Twin 1100hp MAN diesels (jammed into a tight engine room) will cruise the 63 at a fast 32 knots with a top speed of 37–38 knots.

Sunseeker 75 Predator

Length Overall	74'2"	Water	225 gals.
Beam	17'10"	Headroom	6'5"
Draft	4'7"	Hull Type	Deep-V
Weight	74,100#	Deadrise Aft	20°
Clearance	16'8"	Designer	Don Shead
Fuel	1,321 gals.	Production	1999–Current

Standing next to a Predator 75 is to appreciate firsthand the sheer size and bulk of this beautifully proportioned yacht. Bold and aggressive, the Predator is among the larger express boats available and the gold standard in quality and design. Built on a beamy, fully cored deep-V hull with propeller tunnels, the Predator's layout is dominated by her fully enclosed helmdeck with five pedestal chairs at the helm, opening side windows, twin sunroofs and massive stainless-and-glass sliding doors that open to the cockpit. There are three staterooms and three heads on the lower level, and the ultra-luxurious salon—with its facing settees, high-gloss joinerwork, full-length galley, and lush furnishings—is quite overwhelming. A huge sun pad sits atop the transom garage aft and an optional hydraulic swim platform facilitates launching and retrieving a PWC. Additional features (among many) include a teak cockpit sole, a circular foredeck sun pad and compact crew quarters aft, under the cockpit. A superb performer for a yacht this size, twin 1200hp MAN diesels will cruise the Predator 75 at a fast 28 knots and reach a top speed of around 32 knots. Note that triple diesels with surface drives are available.

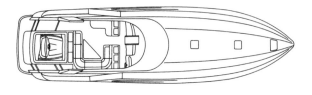

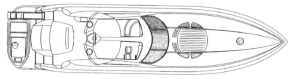

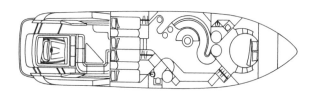

Sunseeker 80 Predator

Length Overall	81'6"	Water	274 gals.
Beam	19'5"	Headroom	6'6"
Draft	4'11"	Hull Type	Deep-V
Weight	100,100#	Deadrise Aft	20°
Clearance	13'2"	Designer	Don Shead
Fuel	1,584 gals.	Production	1997–2002

Among the largest production sportboats in the world, the Predator 80 is a magnificent blend of sleek styling, lush accommodations, and high-speed performance. She's built on a deep-V hull with a unique bottom configuration designed to ensure a clean flow of water to the central prop. While the interior can be customized to meet an owner's requirements, the standard floorplan includes three owner and guest staterooms and a small two-bunk crew cabin. Like all Sunseekers, the Predator's polished cherrywood interior is simply lavish, although the passageways and cabin doors are quite narrow. A pair of sliding glass doors separate the enclosed deckhouse (or day salon) from the aft deck, and the transom opens to reveal a huge garage for storing a personal watercraft or an inflatable. A few of her more notable features include a hydraulically operated sunroof, bow and stern thrusters, teak decks, cockpit and foredeck sun pads, and good access to the engines via port and starboard deck hatches in the cockpit. Triple 1,200hp MAN diesels linked to Arneson surface drives will cruise the Predator 80 at a fast 35 knots and reach a top speed of just over 40 knots.

Thompson 3100 Santa Cruz

Length w/Pulpit	33'0"	Water	42 gals.
Hull Length	31'9"	Clearance	8'2"
Beam	11'4"	Hull Type	Modified-V
Draft	2'7"	Deadrise Aft	18°
Weight	11,200#	Designer	Thompson
Fuel	208 gals.	Production	1991–98

The Thompson 3100 Santa Cruz (note that she was called the 310 Santa Cruz when she was introduced in 1991) is an affordably priced midcabin family express with contemporary lines, a very roomy interior, and twin sterndrive power. She's constructed on a solid fiberglass hull with a wide beam and a relatively steep 18 degrees of deadrise at the transom. The interior of the Santa Cruz, with its wide beam and excellent headroom, is big for a 31-footer because the cabin bulkhead is set well aft into what might be considered the cockpit area in other boats her size. There are double berths fore and aft (each with a privacy curtain) as well as a complete galley, an enclosed head with a sit-down shower, and a convertible dinette. Outside, the flush cockpit has a double-wide seat at the helm and bench seating for three at the transom. Since there's no windshield walk-through, passengers must use the narrow walkarounds to reach the bow. A good performer in a chop, twin 250hp 5.7-liter Volvo sterndrives will cruise the Thompson 3100 in the mid 20s and reach a top speed of 35 knots. Note that an all-new Thompson 3100 model was introduced in 1999.

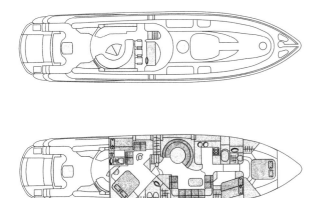

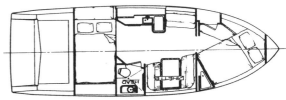

See Page 355 for Pricing Information

161

See Page 356 for Pricing Information

Tiara 2700 Continental

Length	27'6"	Clearance	7'0"
Beam	9'10"	Cockpit Length	11'0"
Hull Draft	2'8"	Hull Type	Deep-V
Weight	7,400#	Deadrise Aft	20°
Fuel	137 gals.	Designer	L. Slikkers
Water	24 gals.	Production	1982–86

The 2700 Continental was one of the first express cruisers ever built by Tiara, a company whose reputation was made with its series of high-quality saltwater fishing boats. The hull construction of the 2700 is solid fiberglass, and her deep-V bottom and relatively wide beam provide a stable and comfortable ride in a chop. Although clearly dated by today's high-glitz sportboat standards, the 2700 retains a certain elegance seldom seen in today's boats. Belowdecks, the upscale interior is arranged with a V-berth/dinette forward and a double berth in the midcabin—comfortable accommodations for four adults. As usual, the quality furnishings and materials found in the 2700 reflect Tiara's emphasis on workmanship and finish. The cockpit is quite large for a 27-footer with bench seating aft and a raised helm position with a double helm seat. Additional features included a beautifully crafted aluminum windshield, wide side decks, a teak swim platform, and good access to the engines. A very capable performer, twin 260hp MerCruiser sterndrives will cruise the Tiara 2700 Continental at 24–25 knots and deliver a top speed of 36+ knots.

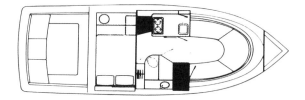

Tiara 2700 Open

Length w/Pulpit	29'5"	Fuel	240 gals.
Hull Length	27'0"	Water	20 gals.
Beam	10'0"	Hull Type	Deep-V
Draft	2'0"	Deadrise Aft	22°
Weight	7,500#	Designer	L. Slikkers
Clearance	7'0"	Production	1988–93

The Tiara 2700 Open is essentially the same boat as the Pursuit 2700 (1983–93) without the Pursuit's tackle centers and fishing amenities. She's built on a deep-V hull with moderate beam, balsa-cored hullsides, and a steep 22 degrees of deadrise at the transom—a good offshore design with proven handling characteristics. The popularity of this boat has much to do with her built-in versatility. As a fisherman, her spacious single-level cockpit is completely uncluttered and large enough for a mounted chair. As a family cruiser, the 2700 Open offers the advantages of inboard power (most of her competitors have outboards or I/Os) and a proven offshore hull to go with her upscale interior. The cabin is arranged with a convertible V-berth/dinette forward, a compact galley with an electric stove, and a standup head with sink and shower. As it is in all Tiara products, the finish is exemplary for a production boat. Additional features include engine boxes, wide side decks, bow pulpit and swim platform. Crusader 270hp gas engines will cruise the Tiara 2700 Open around 23 knots and reach a top speed in the neighborhood of 30 knots.

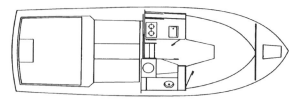

Tiara 2900 Coronet

Length w/Pulpit . . . . 31'7"	Fuel . . . . 200 gals.
Hull Length . . . . 28'2"	Water . . . . 30 gals.
Beam . . . . 11'4"	Waste . . . . 20 gals.
Draft . . . . 2'8"	Hull Type . . . . Modified-V
Weight . . . . 10,000#	Deadrise Aft . . . . 19°
Clearance . . . . NA	Production 1997–Current

The Tiara 2900 Coronet is an attractively priced sportcruiser with a great deal of versatility, unique styling and a huge cockpit. She's constructed on a modified-V hull with a wide beam and a substantial 19 degrees of transom deadrise, and while the Coronet may be the smallest boat in the current Tiara fleet, she retains the superb fit and finish found in all Tiara models. By design, the Coronet's emphasis is on open-air enjoyment and her large single-level cockpit will seat as many as eight in comfort. The engines are under the two seat boxes, and the entire forward section of the deck can be electrically raised for access to the motors. Aside from the generous seating arrangements, the cockpit is equipped with a wet bar aft of the helm seat as well as coaming bolsters and a centerline transom door. The high windshield is notable, not just for its sturdy construction, but for the reverse-angled spray guard along the top. Belowdecks, the compact interior provides berths for two with an enclosed head, mini-galley, and a teak-and-holly cabin sole. The Coronet will cruise at 21–22 knots with a pair of 320hp gas inboards and reach a top speed of about 31 knots.

Tiara 2900 Open

Length w/Pulpit . . . . 30'9"	Fuel . . . . 200 gals.
Hull Length . . . . 28'9"	Water . . . . 30 gals.
Beam . . . . 11'4"	Waste . . . . 20 gals.
Draft . . . . 2'8"	Hull Type . . . . Modified-V
Weight . . . . 10,700#	Deadrise Aft . . . . 19°
Clearance . . . . 7'8"	Production 1993–Current

With her conservative styling and quality construction, the Tiara 2900 Open has long appealed to those seeking a dual-purpose express capable of serious fishing pursuits as well as comfortable family cruising. She's built on a proven modified-V hull with cored hullsides and a relatively wide beam, and anyone who's spent much time aboard the 2900 Open will attest to her excellent finish and rugged construction. The interior is simple and efficient. An angled double berth forward and a convertible dinette will sleep four, and the galley comes with an electric stove, Corian counters and a refrigerator. While the cabin is very comfortable for a 29-footer, it's the large, unobstructed cockpit that draws the attention of serious anglers. A transom door and coaming bolsters are standard, and the nonskid is about as good as it gets in a fishing boat. Note that the entire bridgedeck of the 2900 rises electrically to reveal the engine compartment (although it's a tight fit getting down there). Twin 320hp 5.7-liter gas inboards will cruise the 2900 Open at 20 knots and reach a top speed of 30+ knots. Note that the interior was slightly revised in 1997. A popular boat, resale values have been very good for this model.

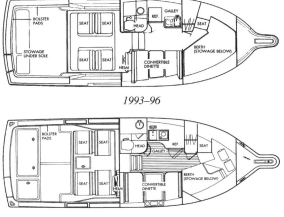

1993–96

1997–Current

See Page 356 for Pricing Information

See Page 356 for Pricing Information

Tiara 3100 Open (1979–91)

Length w/Pulpit	33'9"	Fuel	196 gals.
Hull Length	31'3"	Water	36 gals.
Beam	12'0"	Headroom	6'2"
Draft	2'9"	Hull Type	Modified-V
Weight	10,500#	Deadrise Aft	14°
Clearance, Arch	7'6"	Production	1979–91

The Tiara 3100 Open is one of those boats whose enduring popularity has made her a classic design in every sense of the word. (Indeed, she remained basically unchanged from her 1979 introduction until she was replaced in the Tiara fleet in 1992 with an all-new 3100 Open model.) Aside from her quality construction and sporty profile, the appeal of the 3100 has much to do with her large fishing cockpit and comfortable, teak-trimmed interior. Lots of builders talk about versatility in a particular model, but few boats can really walk the walk. The 3100 does: install some outriggers, fish box and a baitwell, and she's a serious tournament-level fishing machine. If you're into cruising, a radar arch, swim platform and extra cockpit seating will turn the 3100 into an extremely capable family cruiser with the guts to handle most open-water conditions (although she can be a wet headsea ride in a chop). Notable features include wide side decks, bow pulpit, good engine access, and excellent nonskid. Standard 350hp gas inboards will cruise in the low 20s and reach a top speed of 32–33 knots. Note that Tiara continued to produce this boat well into the 1990s as the Pursuit 3100 Express Fisherman.

Tiara 3100 Open (1992–2004)

Length w/Pulpit	33'10"	Fuel	246 gals.
Hull Length	31'6"	Water	38 gals.
Beam	12'0"	Waste	20 gals.
Draft	3'0"	Hull Type	Deep-V
Weight	12,300#	Deadrise Aft	18°
Clearance, Arch	8'7"	Production	1992–2004

Introduced in 1992, the latest Tiara 3100 Open is a complete update of the original Tiara 3100 Open built from 1979–91. Her reworked hull features a sharper entry, additional transom deadrise (18 degrees vs. the 14-degree deadrise of the original 3100), greater bow flare for a drier ride, and prop pockets to reduce shaft angles. Significantly, the 3100 Open also has a new bi-level cockpit layout that allows for the installation of optional Volvo, Cat, or Cummins diesels in an enlarged engine compartment. Tiara has always been a conservative builder and it's no surprise that the new 3100 looks a lot like the original— basically a no-glitz express with quality construction, systems, and hardware. The slightly enlarged interior of the new 3100 has a little more headroom than her predecessor, and there's also a bigger U-shaped dinette. Additional updates included increased fuel, a tilt-away helm console, recessed trim tabs, and an in-deck fish box and livewell in the cockpit. Note that a transom door became standard in 1994. Early models with 350hp gas engines will cruise at 20–21 knots (about 30 knots top), and later models with optional 330 Cummins diesels will cruise efficiently in the mid 20s (30+ knots wide open).

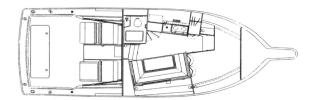

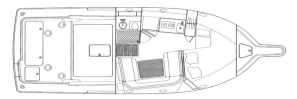

See Page 356 for Pricing Information

See Page 356 for Pricing Information

Tiara 3200 Open

Length w/Pulpit	35'1"	Fuel	256 gals.
Hull Length	32'7"	Water	38 gals.
Beam	13'0"	Waste	20 gals.
Draft	3'0"	Hull Type	Modified-V
Weight	12,500#	Deadrise Aft	18°
Clearance	NA	Production	2004–Current

The Tiara 3200 Open was filling some big shoes when she replaced the popular 3100 Open in the Tiara fleet for 2004. Gracefully styled and boasting some impressive performance figures with standard gas power, the 3200 is designed to satisfy the needs of both anglers and cruisers. Her bi-level deck layout is arranged with L-shaped lounge seating to port on the helmdeck, and an aft-facing seat (or optional bait-prep station or wet bar) is positioned abaft the helm seat. A livewell can be added in place of the standard fold-down transom seat in the cockpit. Below, the well-crafted interior of the 3200—big for a 32-footer—is a traditional blend of solid teak cabinetry, Ultraleather seating, and hardwood flooring. A privacy curtain separates the forward berth from the salon at night, and the settee converts to a double lower berth and single upper berth. The entire helmdeck of the 3200 rises on a pair of rams for access to the engine room. Additional features include a bow pulpit, wide side decks, in-deck fish boxes, swim platform, and prop pockets. A hardtop is a popular option. Crusader 385hp gas engines will cruise the 3200 Open at 22 knots (about 30 knots top), and 310hp Volvo diesels cruise at 25 knots with a top speed of 28–29 knots.

Tiara 3300 Open

Length w/Pulpit	35'8"	Fuel	295 gals.
Hull Length	32'10"	Water	46 gals.
Beam	12'6"	Waste	20 gals.
Draft	2'3"	Hull Type	Modified-V
Weight	13,500#	Deadrise Aft	14°
Clearance	8'8"	Production	1988–97

Tiara's 3300 Open is a versatile family cruiser whose muscular profile, quality construction and dependable inboard power make her an attractive alternative to most of the Euro-style stern-drive cruisers her size. She's built on a rugged modified-V hull with cored hullsides, generous beam, and a shallow keel for directional stability. Unlike the Tiara 3100 Open, the 3300 was not designed as a dedicated fisherman. Instead, she's more at home in the family cruiser role where her plush interior and sportboat profile are most appreciated. Her interior accommodations include berths for six in a cabin of unusual elegance and luxury. A private forward stateroom—rare in a 33-footer—holds a double berth, and the starboard lounge converts to upper and lower berths. In spite of her generous interior dimensions, the 3300 still manages to provide a roomy cockpit with a transom door, cockpit bolsters, and cockpit washdowns as standard equipment. Engine access is very good. A stiff ride in a chop, twin 350hp inboard gas engines will cruise the 3300 Open at 22 knots (30+ knots top), and optional 300hp GM 8.2 diesels will cruise in the mid 20s.

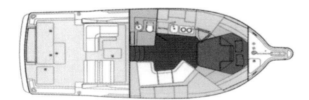

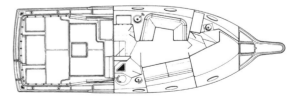

Tiara 3500 Express

Length w/Pulpit	38'10"	Clearance w/Arch.	9'10"
Hull Length	35'8"	Fuel	354 gals.
Beam	13'9"	Water	124 gals.
Draft	2'10"	Hull Type	Modified-V
Weight, Gas	18,600#	Deadrise Aft	18°
Weight, Diesel	21,500#	Production	1995–2003

A scaled-down version of Tiara's popular 4000 Open, the 3500 Express is a high-style family cruiser with impressive accommodations and an upscale price tag. She's heavily built on a beamy modified-V hull with a shallow keel and prop pockets to reduce the draft. The interior is huge for a 35-footer thanks to her super-wide beam. The big lounge next to the cockpit steps can be converted into a private stateroom at night, and both sleeping areas have folding privacy doors instead of curtains. A removable pedestal seat allows the dinette to seat five, and a nighttime lighting system activates when you step on the top companionway step. All in all, this is easily one of the nicest interiors we've seen in any midsize express. Additional features include a teak cabin sole, a huge storage trunk built into the transom, single-level cockpit seating for eight, and an optional 4-foot swim platform for stowing an inflatable or PWC. Optional 370hp V-drive Cummins diesels will cruise the Tiara 3500 at 24 knots (27–28 knots top), and 420hp Cummins (or 435hp Cat) diesels cruise in the mid 20s and reach a top speed of around 30 knots. Standard big-block gas engines will cruise around 18 knots.

Tiara 3500 Open

Length w/Pulpit & Platform	40'8"	Fuel	360 gals.
Hull Length	35'6"	Water	70 gals.
Beam	13'3"	Waste	30 gals.
Draft	3'3"	Hull Type	Modified-V
Weight	14,000#	Deadrise Aft	18°
Clearance	8'8"	Production	1998–2004

Few domestic builders can match Tiara's reputation for engineering and quality, and fewer still exceed the company when it comes to timeless design. The 3500 Open is a case in point: hardly revolutionary in concept, she's a beautifully crafted express cruiser whose classic styling will still look good a decade from now. She's built on a beamy modified-V hull with a well-flared bow and prop pockets to reduce draft and shaft angles. Primarily a cruising boat, the large cockpit of the 3500 Open provides an excellent platform for anglers as well. A transom door, wet bar, and in-deck fish box are standard, and the entire bridgedeck rises on hydraulic rams for access to the motors. Belowdecks, the spacious single-stateroom interior of the 3500 Open can only be described as lush, with handcrafted teak joinery, leather upholstery, and a full teak-and-holly cabin sole. Additional features include an L-shaped lounge opposite the helm, aft-facing cockpit seats, an electric windshield vent, an integral swim platform, and a bow pulpit. Standard big-block gas inboards will provide a cruising speed of 18 knots (29–30 knots top), and optional 370hp Cummins diesels will cruise at 25–26 knots and reach a top speed of around 30 knots.

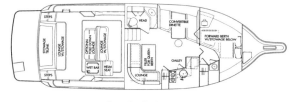

Standard Floorplan

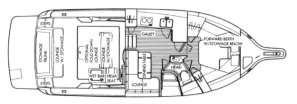

Optional Layout

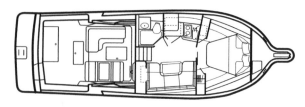

See Page 356 for Pricing Information

See Page 356 for Pricing Information

Tiara 3600 Open (1985–96)

Tiara 3600 Open (Current)

Length w/Pulpit	36'8"	Fuel	396 gals.
Beam	13'9"	Water	85 gals.
Draft	2'11"	Headroom	6'3"
Weight	16,500#	Hull Type	Modified-V
Clearance	9'7"	Deadrise Aft	14°
Headroom	6'2"	Production	1985–96

Length	36'5"	Fuel	400 gals.
Beam	13'3"	Water	70 gals.
Draft	3'5"	Waste	30 gals.
Weight	15,850#	Hull Type	Modified-V
Clearance	9'10"	Deadrise Aft	18°
Headroom	6'6"	Production	2005–Current

A very popular boat for Tiara with a long production run, the 3600 Open is a handsome express fisherman/family cruiser with a big cockpit, upscale cabin accommodations, and surprisingly agile performance. The 3600 is truly a versatile boat; outriggers and a tackle center will turn her into a serious fishing machine, while a radar arch, wet bar and extra cockpit seating will make the 3600 into a very comfortable cruiser. Built on a beamy modified-V hull, the 3600 is a notably stable fishing platform but a wet ride when the seas pick up. The original interior slept four with an island berth forward and a separate stall shower in the head. An alternate layout introduced in 1989 sleeps six with a convertible settee opposite the dinette and the head aft (without the stall shower). Either way, the upscale interior is a blend of grain-matched teak joinery and quality hardware and furnishings—just what you expect in a Tiara product. The cockpit is large enough for a mounted chair, and the entire bridgedeck lifts on hydraulic rams for engine access. Standard 350hp gas engines will cruise at 20 knots (about 28 knots top), and optional 375hp Cats will cruise efficiently in the mid 20s.

The Tiara 3600 Open (note that Tiara built an earlier 3600 Open from 1985–96) is designed to satisfy both anglers and cruisers with a functional, 70-square-foot cockpit and a comfortable, well-appointed cabin. Like most late-model Tiaras, the 3600 rides on a modified deep-V hull with a sharp entry, solid fiberglass bottom, and a relatively broad beam. Experienced anglers will appreciate the Tiara's professional-grade cockpit with its aft-facing seats, overbuilt transom door, in-deck fish boxes, and fold-down transom seat. The helmdeck has a portside lounge (with insulated cooler) along with a wet bar and tilt-away dash. Belowdecks, the posh interior is a blend of solid-wood floors, flawless teak joinery, Ultraleather upholstery, and brushed stainless-steel hardware. The U-shaped dinette converts into a double berth, and the backrest flips up to create a Pullman berth. Note that a sliding door provides real privacy in the master stateroom. Additional features include fresh- and raw-water washdowns, excellent nonskid, reasonably wide side decks, and padded cockpit bolsters. On the downside, engine access is tight even with the helmdeck fully raised. Cummins 380hp diesels will cruise the 3600 Open at 28 knots and top out at 32–33 knots.

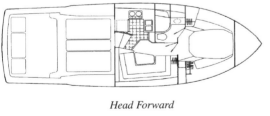

Head Forward

Head Aft

Tiara 3600 Sovran

Length w/Pulpit . . . . 41'8"	Fuel . . . . 326 gals.
Hull Length . . . . 36'4"	Water . . . . 105 gals.
Beam . . . . 13'0"	Waste . . . . 40 gals.
Draft . . . . 3'8"	Hull Type . . . . Modified-V
Weight . . . . 18,000#	Deadrise Aft . . . . 19°
Clearance . . . . NA	Production 2004–Current

A dedicated cruising yacht from a builder with a reputation for quality, the conservative profile of the Tiara 3600 Sovran masks a yacht of enviable comfort and sophistication. While the Sovran may lack the all-out sex appeal of other high-end sportyachts, few would disagree that she's a very handsome and sophisticated design. Below, the interior of the Sovran is a traditional blend of teak cabinetry, Corian counters, and plush leather upholstery. The head is conveniently positioned adjacent to the entryway, and the bulkhead between the master stateroom and the salon has both a door and a panel that slides open. In the salon, the dinette and portside settee convert to berths. (Note that a teak-and-holly cabin sole is a must-have option.) The bi-level cockpit of the Sovran is arranged with a plush L-lounge opposite the helm, aft-facing seats, foldaway rear seat, and a full wet bar. An electrically operated transom locker stows the fenders, and the entire helmdeck can raised at the push of a button for access to the engines. The hardtop and extended swim platform—large enough for a dinghy—are standard. Standard 385hp V-drive Crusader gas engines will cruise in the low 20s and reach 30 knots top.

Tiara 3700 Open

Length w/Pulpit . . . . 39'8"	Fuel . . . . 411 gals.
Hull Length . . . . 37'1"	Water . . . . 98 gals.
Beam . . . . 14'2"	Waste . . . . 40 gals.
Draft . . . . 3'9"	Hull Type . . . . Modified-V
Weight . . . . 21,800#	Deadrise Aft . . . . 18°
Clearance . . . . 10'4"	Production 1995–2000

Introduced in 1995 to replace the original Tiara 3600 Open (1985–96), the Tiara 3700 Open retained the classic profile and versatile layout of her predecessor, and for good reason. Like her predecessor, the 3700 is a true dual-purpose boat with the comfortable accommodations demanded by family cruisers and the cockpit dimensions of a serious sportfishing machine. She has more beam and deadrise than the 3600, and she's a measurably better rough-water performer. The luxurious teak interior of the 3700 Open is arranged with a private stateroom forward, a huge U-shaped dinette, a double-entry head, and a surprisingly roomy galley. As it is in all Tiara boats, the joinerwork, appliances, fabrics, and hardware are first-rate throughout. In the cockpit, an L-shaped lounge is opposite the helm, and the big 72-square-foot cockpit has a transom door and coaming bolsters. Note that the entire bridgedeck can be raised electrically for access to the engines. A bow pulpit was standard, and a radar arch, cockpit shower and foldaway rear cockpit seat were popular options. Among several diesel engine choices, twin 435hp Cat 3208s will cruise the 3700 Open in the mid 20s and reach a top speed of just over 30 knots.

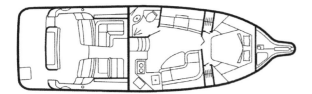

See Page 357 for Pricing Information

See Page 357 for Pricing Information

Tiara 3800 Open

Length w/Pulpit . . . . 40'9"	Fuel . . . . 411 gals.
Hull Length . . . . 38'4"	Water . . . . 110 gals.
Beam . . . . 14'2"	Waste . . . . 40 gals.
Draft . . . . 3'6"	Hull Type . . . . Modified-V
Weight . . . . 22,500#	Deadrise Aft . . . . 18°
Clearance . . . . 9'7"	Production 2000–Current

Tiara is one of the country's premier builders of dual-purpose express boats with hard-core fishing capabilities and beautifully crafted interiors. Like all of Tiara's Open models, the 3800 can be ordered as a tournament-ready fishing machine or equipped with the cruising amenities of a comfortable family express. Her elegant single-stateroom interior is dominated by a huge U-shaped settee to starboard, opposite the galley. There's a separate stall shower in the head, and the beautiful teak-and-holly cabin sole gives the interior of the 3800 a traditional feel found in few other boats. (Note that an alternate floorplan introduced in 2003 has a smaller head but adds a portside settee.) The cockpit, with about 70 square feet of space, can be ordered with an aft-facing jump seat or a complete tackle center. The entire helmdeck lifts mechanically for easy access to the large engine room. Additional features include a hideaway TV in the salon, a cockpit wet bar, a fold-down transom seat, transom door and shower, side exhausts and wide side decks. Note that prop pockets are used to reduce the shaft angles and draft. Cummins 480hp diesels will cruise the Tiara 3800 at 25–26 knots (about 30 knots top).

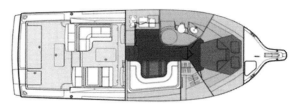

Standard (Port Galley)

Optional (Starboard Galley)

See Page 357 for Pricing Information

Tiara 4000 Express

Length w/Pulpit . . . . 43'6"	Fuel . . . . 444 gals.
Hull Length . . . . 40'6"	Water . . . . 160 gals.
Beam . . . . 14'6"	Waste . . . . 57 gals.
Draft . . . . 4'0"	Hull Type . . . . Modified-V
Weight . . . . 26,500#	Deadrise Aft . . . . 18°
Clearance . . . . 10'2"	Production 1994–2003

An innovative boat when she was introduced in 1994, the 4000 Express was the first midcabin design ever built by Tiara. With her sleek profile, lush interior and wide-open cockpit, the 4000 became a popular model during her production years in spite of a very upmarket price. The interior of the Tiara 4000 is very spacious indeed for a 40-footer. A huge 11-foot salon lounge will seat a small crowd around the extendible table, and the open galley includes a separate freezer and tremendous storage. The two staterooms simply define luxury, and the midcabin has a full 7 feet of headroom and a small head hidden beneath a cushioned seat. (Note that an alternate floorplan introduced in 1994 has an enlarged salon but no aft cabin.) Twin transom doors lead down to the extended swim platform, and built into the transom is a large, hydraulically opened trunk for storing bikes or dive equipment. Note that a pair of hydraulic rams lifts the entire center section of the cockpit sole for access to the engines. Additional features include radar arch, foredeck sun pad, electric helm seat and a cockpit wet bar. Twin 450hp Cummins (or 435hp Cat) diesels will cruise the Tiara 4000 at 23–24 knots with a top speed of about 27 knots.

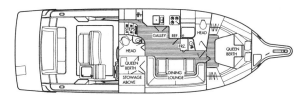

Standard Floorplan

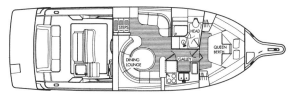

Optional Layout

See Page 357 for Pricing Information

Tiara 4100 Open

Length w/Pulpit	43'6"	Fuel	524 gals.
Hull Length	41'3"	Water	130 gals.
Beam	14'8"	Waste	50 gals.
Draft	3'6"	Hull Type	Modified-V
Weight	27,500#	Deadrise Aft	17.5°
Clearance	10'4"	Production	1996–2002

Tiara has built a solid reputation over the years for its series of conservatively designed, high-quality cruisers and express boats. Among the more impressive is the 4100 Open, a dual-purpose model capable of appealing to the upscale family cruiser as well as serious anglers looking for a sturdy fishing platform. The 4100 is built on a beamy modified-V hull with a shallow keel and prop pockets to reduce draft. Unlike some express cruisers her size, the 4100 is not a midcabin design, which allows her to have a full-size engine room (under the bridgedeck) with straight shafts rather than V-drives. Her spacious, light ash interior has a comfortable owner's stateroom forward, a large galley area, and a stall shower in the oversized head. A curved companion seat is opposite the helm, and the cockpit—three steps down from the bridgedeck—comes with a transom door, in-deck fish box, and direct engine room access. Additional features include side exhausts, cockpit wet bar, and wide side decks. Among several diesel engine options offered over the years, twin 435hp Cat diesels will cruise the Tiara 4100 Open at 22 knots and reach a top speed of 26–27 knots.

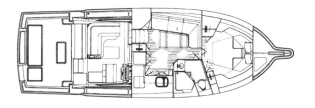

Tiara 4200 Open

Length w/Pulpit	44'10"	Fuel	520 gals.
Hull Length	42'6"	Water	130 gals.
Beam	14'11"	Waste	50 gals.
Draft	4'2"	Hull Type	Modified-V
Weight	28,000#	Deadrise Aft	17.5°
Clearance	12'4"	Production	2003–Current

A quality cruising yacht capable of serious fishing pursuits, the sophisticated engineering and exemplary finish of the Tiara 4200 Open set this versatile boat apart from most of the competition. She's a good-looking express with her rakish windshield and slightly reversed transom, and a wide 14-foot, 11-inch beam gives the 4200 plenty of cockpit and cabin space. Built on a modified-V hull with prop pockets and a shallow keel, two interior floorplans are available. Plan A (the original layout) has a portside lounge/dinette with the galley and head opposite, while Plan B adds a starboard lounge with curtain or solid enclosure, creating a second stateroom. In both layouts, Tiara's satin-finished teak joinery and traditional teak-and-holly sole offer a pleasant contrast to the high-gloss cherry interiors found in so many of today's yachts. Topside, the cockpit is arranged with a companion lounge opposite the helm and an aft-facing lounge (with engine room entry under) in the cockpit. A fold-down rear seat and wet bar are standard, and a livewell and bait-prep station are optional. Note that the engine room is a little tight. Cummins 660hp diesels will cruise the 4200 Open in the mid 20s and reach a top speed of 32–33 knots.

Plan A

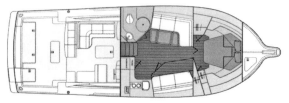

Plan B

Tiara 4300 Open

Length w/Pulpit	46'7"	Cockpit	167 sq. ft.
Hull Length	43'2"	Fuel	525 gals.
Beam	15'2"	Water	150 gals.
Draft	4'0"	Hull Type	Modified-V
Weight	29,500#	Deadrise Aft	16°
Clearance	10'4"	Production	1991–2002

Conservatively styled (note the absence of an integrated swim platform) and elegantly appointed, the Tiara 4300 Open was one of the largest production sportboats available when she was introduced in 1991. Built on a beamy modified-V hull, the Open has enough built-in luxury to satisfy family cruisers and a cockpit large enough to meet the demands of hard-core anglers. The belowdeck accommodations are plush with light ash woodwork, leather upholstery, a teak-and-holly cabin sole, a hydraulically operated dinette, and a spacious master stateroom with a walkaround island bed and built-in TV. Topside, the huge bi-level cockpit—reinforced for a mounted chair—comes with in-deck storage compartments, cockpit steps, and a transom door with gate. Additional features include a superb helm console with room for flush-mounting an array of electronics, wide side decks, excellent engine room access, and a hideaway bench seat at the transom. Note that in 1999 the cockpit was slightly redesigned with more comfortable seating. A quick boat with 550hp 6V92s, she'll cruise around 27 knots and reach 31–32 knots wide open. Later models with 660hp Cats will cruise at 26–27 knots.

Tiara 4400 Sovran

Length w/Platform & Pulpit	50'4"	Fuel	526 gals.
Hull Length	43'8"	Water	150 gals.
Beam	14'6"	Waste	50 gals.
Draft	4'5"	Hull Type	Modified-V
Weight	33,150#	Deadrise Aft	17°
Clearance	11'4"	Production	2003–Current

Lots of manufacturers build quality, high-end sportcruisers, but only a few reach the standards of engineering and finish consistently attained by Tiara. In the 4400 Sovran, Tiara has delivered a yacht of remarkable luxury and design sophistication. Not inexpensive, the Sovran's handsome styling is highlighted by her fully integrated hardtop, graceful sheer, and slightly reversed transom. Focusing on comfort and function, the posh, two-stateroom interior of the Sovran offers a luxurious blend of satin-finished teak woodwork, Corian counters, and Ultraleather seating. The large salon settee seats five and is served by a bird's-eye maple table. Each stateroom has an en suite head, and a washer/dryer combo is concealed in the aft stateroom. Topside, an impressive Stidd helm seat can be raised or lowered electrically. An L-lounge is opposite the helm, and fore- and aft-facing seats and a pair of hydraulically operated high/low tables are found in the cockpit. The Sovran's extended swim platform is large enough to accommodate a dinghy or PWC. On the downside, the engine room is a tight fit. Cummins 660hp diesels will cruise at 28 knots and reach a top speed of 32–33 knots.

Standard

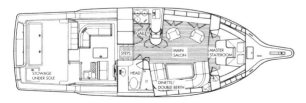

Optional

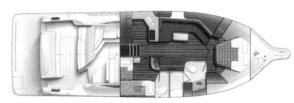

See Page 357 for Pricing Information

171

See Page 357 for Pricing Information

Tiara 5000 Express

Tiara 5000 Open

Length w/Platform & Pulpit	55'0"	Fuel	700 gals.
Hull Length	50'9"	Water	200 gals.
Beam	15'11"	Waste	80 gals.
Draft	5'1"	Hull Type	Modified-V
Weight	38,600#	Deadrise Aft	17°
Clearance	12'1"	Production	1999–2003

Length w/Pulpit	53'0"	Cockpit	93 sq. ft.
Hull Length	50'1"	Fuel	650 gals.
Beam	15'9"	Water	200 gals.
Draft	5'1"	Hull Type	Modified-V
Weight	43,500#	Deadrise Aft	17°
Clearance	11'6"	Production	2002–03

Flagship of the Tiara fleet when she was introduced in 1999, the 5000 Express is a distinctly American sportcruiser from a company whose reputation for quality is recognized throughout the industry. The 5000 may lack the sleek styling and high-performance persona of her European counterparts, but her cockpit is larger and the cabin more spacious than any sportboat import of her day. Built on a fully cored hull with prop pockets and a shallow keel, the posh interior of the 5000 Express is a blend of teak cabinetry, solid-wood floors, vinyl overheads, and Ultraleather upholstery. Two floorplans were available: Plan A is a two-stateroom layout with a huge salon and the galley aft, while Plan B features three private staterooms with the galley forward in the salon. In the cockpit, electric tables rise for dining and lower for use as a cushion-covered sun pad. A 100-square-foot storage trunk is built into the transom, and the swim platform is designed to carry a dinghy or PWC. An extended fiberglass hardtop was a popular option. Twin 800hp Cat diesels will cruise the 5000 Express at a respectable 25–26 knots and deliver a top speed of just over 30 knots.

A true dual-purpose design, the Tiara 5000 Open can be fitted out as a tournament-level fishing machine or a feature-laden family cruiser. Lots of boats promise that kind of user flexibility, but few manufacturers have been more successful in this realm than Tiara. Built on a smooth-riding, modified-V hull with a shallow keel, prop pockets, and a solid fiberglass bottom, the spacious cockpit of the 500 Open is arranged with plenty of lounge seating on the bridgedeck and a transom door and aft-facing bench seat on the lower level. Anglers can choose a full tackle center with freezer, and cruisers can add a factory hardtop, foldaway transom seat, and swim platform. Belowdecks, the two-stateroom, two-head interior is a lavish display of solid teak (or cherry) woodwork, hardwood floors, and rich designer fabrics. This is a very traditional and elegant interior—a little confining—but finished to a very high standard. Additional features include space for a washer/dryer, cockpit engine room access, wet bar, a power center windshield section, and a central vacuum system. A premium boat, 800hp Cats will cruise the 500 Open at 26–27 knots and reach a top speed of 30+ knots.

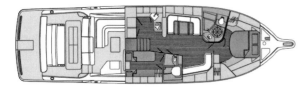

Plan A

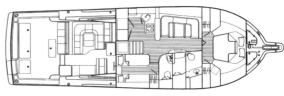

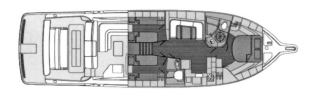

Plan B

See Page 357 for Pricing Information

See Page 357 for Pricing Information

Tiara 5200 Sovran Salon

Length w/Platform & Pulpit	58'3"	Fuel	700 gals.
Hull Length	50'9"	Water	200 gals.
Beam	15'11"	Waste	80 gals.
Draft	5'1"	Hull Type	Modified-V
Weight	49,000#	Deadrise Aft	17°
Clearance	12'1"	Production	2003–Current

Flagship of today's Tiara fleet, the 5200 Sovran is a distinctly American sportcruiser from a company whose reputation for quality is recognized throughout the industry. The 5200 may lack the sleek styling and high-performance persona of her European counterparts, but her completely enclosed command bridge/helm—with its dual reclining seats, built-in wet bar, and concealed 22-inch flat-panel TV—creates additional living space not found on any of the imports. Built on a fully cored hull with prop pockets and a shallow keel, the posh interior of the Sovran is a blend of teak cabinetry, solid-wood floors, vinyl overheads, and Ultraleather upholstery. Two floorplans are available: Plan A is a two-stateroom layout with a huge salon and the galley aft, while Plan B features three private staterooms with the galley forward in the salon. In the cockpit, electric tables rise for dining and lower for use as a cushion-covered sun pad. A 100-square-foot storage trunk is built into the transom, and the swim platform is designed to carry a dinghy or PWC. Note the electric sunroof in the hardtop. Twin 800hp Cat diesels will cruise the 5000 Express at a respectable 25–26 knots and deliver a top speed of just over 30 knots.

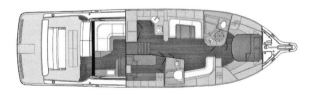

Plan A

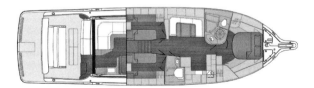

Plan A

See Page 357 for Pricing Information

173

Trojan 8.6 Meter Mid-Cabin

Length	28'8"	Fuel	140 gals.
Beam	10'6"	Cockpit	NA
Draft	2'2"	Hull Type	Modified-V
Weight	9,500#	Deadrise Aft	14°
Clearance	8'7"	Designer	H. Schoell
Water	40 gals.	Production	1987–90

The 8.6 Meter Mid-Cabin was the smallest of Trojan's series of Euro-style express boats the company introduced throughout the 1980s. With her bold hull graphics and streamlined profile, the 8.6 was a high-style boat in her day. Built on low-deadrise hull, her mid-cabin interior is arranged in the conventional manner with berths for six. The main cabin has a convertible dinette and a full galley, and both fore and aft sleeping areas are fitted with double berths. While the dark decor of the 8.6 is dated by today's high-glitz standards, the floorplan makes good use of the boat's wide beam. On deck, the single-level cockpit is set up with a triple-wide elevated helm seat, removable bench seating at the transom, and a centerline transom gate. Twin hatches in the cockpit sole provide good access to the engines, and visibility from the helm is excellent in all directions. A fiberglass radar arch was a popular option. Note that the side decks are narrow. Additional features include plenty of cabin storage, a swim platform, and a bow pulpit. Standard 260hp sterndrives will cruise the Trojan 8.6 Mid-Cabin Express at 25 knots and reach a top speed in the mid 30s.

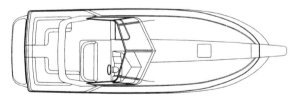

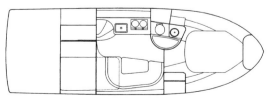

See Page 359 for Pricing Information

Trojan 10 Meter Express

Length	33'0"	Fuel	242 gals.
Beam	13'0"	Headroom	6'4"
Draft	2'0"	Hull Type	Modified-V
Weight	11,250#	Deadrise Aft	9°
Clearance	9'4"	Designer	H. Schoell
Water	40 gals.	Production	1981–89

First of Trojan's popular Euro-style International series, the 10 Meter Express was something of a breakthrough design when she was introduced in 1981. Boldly styled and featuring all-new modular construction, the "experts" had a field day with this boat, calling her too wide and too glitzy for the conservative American market. Nevertheless, she quickly captured the public's imagination and soon became a marketing success. Hull construction is solid fiberglass, and she rides on a beamy DeltaConic hull with moderate transom deadrise. Below, the original, somewhat gaudy interior was toned down in later years, but her Mediterranean styling, curved bulkheads, and distinctive decor were soon copied by other manufacturers. Notable features include electrically operated sliding doors to the head and forward cabin, a big bi-level cockpit with an offset companionway, teak covering boards, side-dumping exhausts, and a curved cockpit windshield. Engine access is good compared with other express boats this size. Standard 350hp gas engines cruise the Trojan 10 Meter at 19–20 knots with a top speed of around 28 knots.

Trojan 10 Meter Mid-Cabin Express

Length	33'0"	Fuel	250 gals.
Beam	13'0"	Headroom	6'4"
Draft	2'0"	Hull Type	Modified-V
Weight	12,500#	Deadrise Aft	9°
Clearance	9'4"	Designer	H. Schoell
Water	55 gals.	Production	1986–92

A well-styled boat by the standards of her day, the wide 13-foot beam of the Trojan 10 Meter Mid-Cabin made her one of the biggest 33-foot express boats in the business. (Indeed, even today it's rare to find a boat this size with quite so much beam.) Built on a stable, low-deadrise hull, the spacious midcabin interior includes an L-shaped dinette in the main salon and a convertible U-shaped settee in the mid stateroom. A solid door provides privacy for the bow stateroom, while a curtain separates the midcabin from the salon. Notably, a stall shower is found in the head compartment—always a plus for serious cruisers. Topside, the Trojan's huge bi-level cockpit is arranged with a double helm and companion seat (on storage boxes) on the bridgedeck, and bench seating at the transom. A radar arch, swim platform and bow pulpit were standard. Removable hatches in the forward cockpit sole provide good access to the engines. Updates in 1989 included a bolt-on swim platform and white powder-coated deck rails—very appealing. With the standard 350hp gas engines, the 10 Meter Mid-Cabin will cruise at 17–18 knots and reach a top speed in the mid 20s.

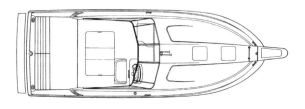

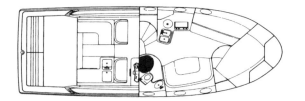

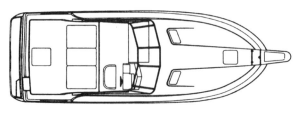

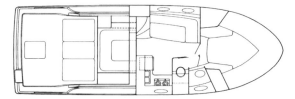

Trojan 10.8 Meter Express

Length w/Pulpit . . . . 39'4"	Water . . . . 91 gals.
Hull Length . . . . 35'5"	Fuel . . . . 280 gals.
Beam . . . . 13'2"	Hull Type . . . . Deep-V
Draft . . . . 3'7"	Deadrise Aft . . . . 20°
Weight . . . . 19,572#	Designer . . . . Trojan
Clearance . . . . 11'0"	Production 1991–92

A good-looking boat with plenty of eye appeal, the 10.8 Meter Express was introduced in 1991 by Trojan just before the company declared bankruptcy. (For the record, Trojan's assets—including the name—were quickly acquired by Miramar Marine, owner of Hatteras, Wellcraft, Carver, etc., and this boat was reintroduced in 1993 as the "new" Trojan 370 Express.) The 10.8 Meter was constructed on a solid fiberglass deep-V hull with a relatively wide beam for her length. Note that unlike other Trojan express cruisers, the 10.8 Meter did not employ a DeltaConic hull bottom. The midcabin floorplan is very spacious for a 35-footer with double berths fore and aft, a good-size galley, full dinette, and a separate stall shower in the head. A draw curtain provides privacy aft while the forward stateroom has a door—a definite plus. Outside, there's plenty of room for a crowd in the bi-level cockpit, and the entire deck aft of the helm can be hydraulically raised for access to the engines and V-drives. Among several engine options, big-block 502-cid gas inboards will cruise the 10.8 Meter Express at 18 knots and reach a top speed of about 28 knots.

Trojan 350/360 Express

Length w/Pulpit & Platform . . 37'8"	Water . . . . 60 gals.
Beam . . . . 12'0"	Waste . . . . 30 gals.
Draft . . . . 2'10"	Headroom . . . . 6'5"
Weight . . . . 16,500#	Hull Type . . . . Modified-V
Clearance . . . . 9'8"	Deadrise Aft . . . . 16.5°
Fuel . . . . 220 gals.	Production, 360 1995–2002

The Trojan 360 Express (called the 350 Express in 1995–98) is a traditional midcabin express whose contemporary styling and affordable price made her a fairly popular boat in the late 1990s. She was built on a solid fiberglass hull with moderate beam, and propeller pockets are used to reduce the shaft angles. The cockpit and floorplan of the 350/360 remained essentially unchanged during her production years. The midcabin interior is arranged in the conventional manner with double berths in both staterooms and a convertible dinette in the main cabin. A sliding door provides privacy for the forward stateroom—a curtain is used for midcabin privacy—and headroom is a full 6 feet, 5 inches. (Note that the floorplan was slightly rearranged in 1999 when an L-shaped settee replaced the original U-shaped dinette.) Topside, a bi-level cockpit has a triple-wide helm seat forward together with a built-in wet bar and wraparound lounge seating aft. A bow pulpit, radar arch, and swim platform were standard. Among several engine options, twin 320hp V-drive gas inboards will cruise the Trojan 360 at a leisurely 15–16 knots and deliver a top speed in the mid-to-high 20s.

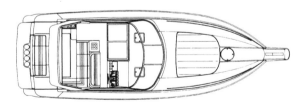

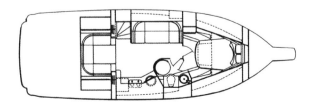

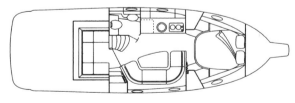

350 Interior

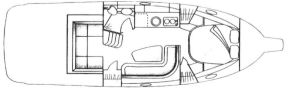

360 Layout

See Page 359 for Pricing Information

See Page 359 for Pricing Information

Trojan 11 Meter Express (1983–89)

Length	37'6"	Water	100 gals.
Beam	14'0"	Headroom	6'3"
Draft	3'3"	Hull Type	Modified-V
Weight	16,800#	Deadrise Aft	14°
Clearance	9'4"	Designer	H. Schoell
Fuel	350 gals.	Production	1983–89

Obviously dated by today's crop of high-style family sportboats, the Trojan 11 Meter Express was considered a radical design when she was introduced back in 1983. With her dramatic hull graphics (toned down in later years) and super-wide 14-foot beam, the 11 Meter is a very big 37-footer. Like all of Trojan's early express boats, she rides on a stable DeltaConic hull, and it's notable that the entire hull—including the bottom—is cored. Belowdecks, the interior is a blend of curved bulkheads, indirect lighting, and off-white laminates—what Trojan marketing gurus called a Euro-style decor. This interior, however, may not appeal to everyone. For one thing, there's no mid stateroom (a standard feature in most modern sportboats), and the L-shaped galley extends far into the salon, which interrupts the flow of traffic. On deck, the bi-level cockpit is arranged with L-shaped lounge seating forward and bench seating aft. A bow pulpit, radar arch and swim platform were standard. Twin 350hp gas engines will cruise at 18 knots (26–27 knots top). Optional 375hp Cat diesels will cruise at 24 knots, and 485hp 6-71s will cruise at 28–29 knots and reach a top speed in the low 30s.

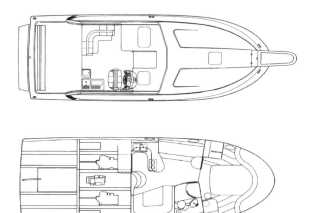

Trojan 11 Meter Express (1990–92)

Length w/Pulpit	39'0"	Water	100 gals.
Beam	14'0"	Headroom	6'4"
Draft	3'3"	Hull Type	Modified-V
Weight	16,800#	Deadrise Aft	14°
Clearance	9'4"	Designer	H. Schoell
Fuel	350 gals.	Production	1990–92

While the Trojan 11 Meter Express retains the same DeltaConic hull of Trojan's original 11 Meter Express (1983–89), she added such new features as powder-coated railings and deck fittings, an integral swim platform, and a completely new single-stateroom floorplan. Indeed, the interior of the 11 Meter is far more open and spacious than her predecessor. There is no forward stateroom as such; instead, a huge sofa extends from the starboardside galley all the way around the forepeak to the portside head compartment. The backrest can be swung up to form a single bunk, and the dinette table converts the bow area into a double berth. A private stateroom is to port with a full-size double berth as well as private head access. This is an unusual layout, but for all of its features, it's still not as spacious as a conventional midcabin floorplan with double berths fore and aft. On deck, the bi-level cockpit is arranged with L-shaped lounge seating forward and bench seating aft. Twin 360hp gas engines will cruise at 18 knots and top out in the high 20s. Optional 425hp Cats will cruise at 24 knots, and 485hp 6-71TIs will cruise at nearly 30 knots.

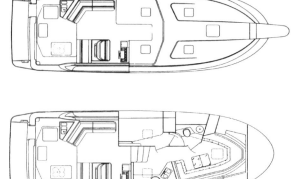

See Page 359 for Pricing Information

See Page 359 for Pricing Information

Trojan 370/390/400 Express

Trojan 12 Meter Express

Length w/Pulpit & Platform	41'2"	Fuel	280 gals.
Hull Length	35'5"	Water	91 gals.
Beam	13'6"	Waste	52 gals.
Draft	3'7"	Hull Type	Modified-V
Weight	19,500#	Deadrise Aft	17°
Clearance	12'0"	Production	1993–2002

Length	39'9"	Fuel	325 gals.
Beam	14'3"	Headroom	6'4"
Draft	3'8"	Hull Type	Modified-V
Weight	18,000#	Deadrise Aft	12°
Clearance	NA	Designer	H. Schoell
Water	95 gals.	Production	1989–92

The history of this model is a bit difficult to follow. She was introduced by Trojan in 1993 as the 370 Express—basically a reworked version of the company's earlier 10.8 Meter Mid-Cabin model (1991–92). In 1995 she became the Trojan 390 when a new extended swim platform increased her length, and in 1998—for no apparent reason—she became the Trojan 400 Express. Through all of the name changes, the cockpit and interior remained basically unchanged. Curved companionway steps lead into a comfortable salon with cherrywood cabinetry and 6 feet, 4 inches of headroom. A bi-fold door separates the forward stateroom from the salon, while a curtain provides privacy in the midcabin. In the head, the toilet is hidden under a seat in the shower to conserve space. Topside, the 440's cockpit has a triple helm seat to starboard as well as a large L-shaped lounge aft. Note that the entire aft deck can be raised on hydraulic rams for access to a very roomy engine compartment. Additional standard features included a radar arch, bow pulpit, and a foredeck sun pad. Among several engine options, twin 320hp V-drive gas inboards will cruise at 18 knots (26–27 knots top), and optional 330hp Cummins diesels will cruise in the mid 20s.

One of the best-looking express cruisers of her era, the Trojan 12 Meter Express set the standards for many of today's sportboat designs when she was introduced back in 1989. She rides on a fully cored, DeltaConic hull with prop pockets, and with over 14 feet of beam, the 12 Meter is a big 40-footer. Belowdecks, the salon is open and spacious and can easily be transformed into separate sleeping areas. An accordion-style privacy curtain hidden in a small bulkhead door converts the portside settee into a unique stateroom, and the U-shaped dinette (also convertible into a double berth) serves as the social center of the boat. The master stateroom is completely private with its own head access. On deck, the cockpit is arranged with lounge seating fore and aft, a very high-style helm console, and a hydraulically operated, in-deck storage well for an inflatable. The powder-coated all-white deck hardware and bow rails are especially attractive. Additional features include wide side decks, a bow pulpit and a swim platform with molded boarding steps. Optional 485hp 6-71 diesels will cruise the 12 Meter Express at 26–27 knots and reach a top speed of around 30 knots.

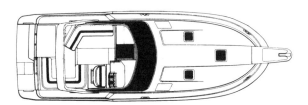

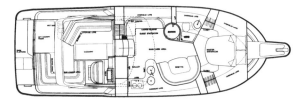

See Page 359 for Pricing Information

See Page 359 for Pricing Information

Trojan 13 Meter Express

Length	43'0"	Fuel	510 gals.
Beam	16'3"	Headroom	6'4"
Draft	3'2"	Hull Type	Modified-V
Weight	24,000#	Deadrise Aft	12°
Clearance	10'1"	Designer	H. Schoell
Water	175 gals.	Production	1984–90

The most compelling feature of the Trojan 13 Meter Express is her massive beam—the cockpit and cabin proportions in this boat are truly immense. (Indeed, the 13 Meter is so wide that she'll be a tight fit in many 45-foot slips.) She's built on a fully cored, low-deadrise hull with broad chine flats and side-dumping exhausts. Belowdecks, her spacious two-stateroom floorplan is a blend of designer fabrics, curved bulkheads, and white Formica counters—a high-style decor in the 1980s, but definitely dated by today's earth-tone standards. The forward stateroom in the 13 Meter is huge and came with an air-operated compartment door. There are over/under berths in the guest stateroom, and the dinette table in the salon can be electrically raised and lowered. Visibility from the double helm seat is surprisingly good, and there's room in the enormous cockpit to entertain a small army. A center vent in the windshield is electrically operated, and large hatches in the bridgedeck provide access to the big engine room. (Note the absence of a cockpit transom door.) A bow pulpit, swim platform, and radar arch were standard. Optional 735hp 8V92 diesels will provide an honest 30-knot cruising speed and a top speed of 32+ knots.

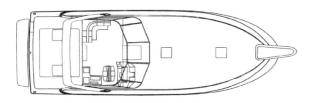

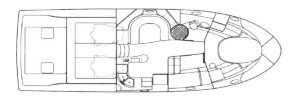

See Page 359 for Pricing Information

Trojan 440 Express

Length	44'7"	Water	104 gals.
Beam	15'0"	Waste	88 gals.
Draft	4'0"	Headroom	6'5"
Weight	30,000#	Hull Type	Modified-V
Clearance	10'11"	Deadrise Aft	16.5°
Fuel	432 gals.	Production	1995–2002

The Trojan 440 Express was a leading-edge design when she was introduced in 1995 as well as being one of the larger express boats of her day. Built on a modified-V hull with a wide beam, the 440 is a spacious boat both inside and out. There were two very similar floorplans offered during her production years. Originally designed with two staterooms, in 1998 the sprawling Ultraleather sofa was shortened to make room for a tiny third stateroom to starboard. The decor is an appealing mix of cherry cabinetry and off-white wall coverings, and a full-size refrigerator is included in the galley. Topside, the spacious cockpit is dominated by a wraparound lounge aft (convertible into a huge sun pad) along with a wet bar, transom door and refrigerator. The sporty burlwood helm is large enough for flush-mounting several pieces of electronics. A hydraulic drive-on swim platform for PWCs—or a regular extended swim platform for swimmers—were optional. Additional features include a hidden anchor windlass, radar arch, an air-conditioning outlet at the helm, and a gas-assisted engine access hatch in the cockpit sole. A modest performer, 450hp Cummins diesels with V-drives will cruise the Trojan 440 at 22 knots (25–26 knots top).

1995–97

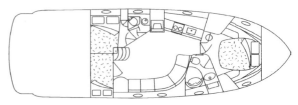

1998–2002

See Page 360 for Pricing Information

Viking V40 Express

Length Overall	39'11"	Clearance	10'3"
Beam	12'6"	Headroom	6'4"
Draft	3'0"	Hull Type	Deep-V
Weight	16,800#	Deadrise Aft	21°
Fuel	209 gals.	Designer	B. Olesinski
Water	88 gals.	Production	1995–99

The Viking V40 Express (originally called the Viking V39 Express) is a purebred Mediterranean performance cruiser with the sleek styling and upscale accommodations European buyers expect in a contemporary sportboat design. Built in England where she was marketed as the Princess V40, her midcabin interior is arranged around a comfortable salon with a big U-shaped lounge opposite a large and well-equipped galley. Privacy doors separate both fore and aft staterooms from the main cabin, and the aft cabin comes with twin single berths that convert into a double, a small settee, and a hidden washbasin. Note that the head compartment includes a separate stall shower. Topside, the open spaces of the V40 are divided between an elevated bridgedeck with an L-shaped settee, and the aft cockpit with U-shaped lounge seating that expands into a sun lounge. Additional features include wide side decks, a cockpit wet bar, foredeck sun pad, and a reverse radar arch. Note that the engine room is a very tight fit. An excellent performer, twin 420hp V-drive Cat (or 430hp Volvo) diesels will cruise the Viking V40 Express at 28 knots with a top speed of 32–33 knots.

Viking V50 Express

Length Overall	51'0"	Clearance	11'5"
Beam	14'1"	Headroom	6'3"
Draft	3'6"	Hull Type	Deep-V
Weight	35,840#	Deadrise Aft	21°
Fuel	490 gals.	Designer	B. Olesinski
Water	105 gals.	Production	1999–Current

A well-styled yacht, the Viking V50 is a finely crafted, Med-style express yacht with more interior volume and elbow room than most other European sportboats her size. Like her sisterships in the Viking Sport Cruisers fleet, she rides on a solid fiberglass deep-V hull with a relatively wide beam and shallow prop pockets to reduce draft. Her elegant cherrywood interior includes two double cabins with en suite heads, a concealed galley, and a plush U-shaped dinette in the salon. Both heads contain stall showers, and privacy doors—not curtains—separate both staterooms from the main cabin. Contoured seating topside provides seating for six in the cockpit, and a three-person sun pad aft rises at the touch of a button to reveal a tender garage below. Note that a machinery space behind the engine room houses the generator, batteries and steering gear. Additional features include a teak cockpit sole, a drop-down double helm seat, wet bar with refrigerator, radar arch, windshield washers, and a well-arranged engine room with good access to the motors. Twin 610hp Volvo diesel inboards will cruise the Viking V50 Express at 28 knots and reach a top speed of 32–33 knots.

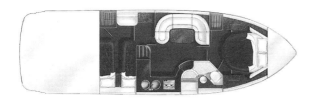

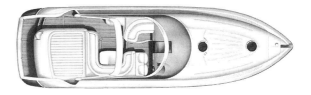

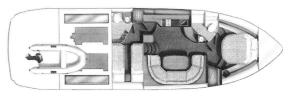

See Page 361 for Pricing Information

179

See Page 362 for Pricing Information

EXPRESS CRUISERS

Viking V55 Express

Length Overall	55'0"	Water	107 gals.
Beam	14'4"	Headroom	6'3"
Draft	3'6"	Hull Type	Deep-V
Weight	32,032#	Deadrise Aft	21°
Clearance	11'1"	Designer	B. Olesinski
Fuel	540 gals.	Production	1995–2002

While the demand for luxury express cruisers is limited by the number of buyers who can afford such toys, there's little doubt that this is one of the most dynamic segments of the marine marketplace. The Viking V55 Express (called the Viking V52 until 1997 when the swim platform was extended) was one of the original Viking Sport Cruisers imported by Viking from UK-based Marine Products, Ltd. Still a handsome yacht a decade after her introduction, the V55 is a modern Mediterranean sportboat with an enormous cockpit and an innovative three-stateroom interior layout. While the cabin accommodations are well arranged (note the identical midcabin staterooms), more than half of the hull length is devoted to cockpit space including a huge sun pad atop a PWC garage with its own hydraulic lift system. The straight-drive engines are located below the cockpit sole where a centerline hatch provides access to the engine room. A bow thruster was standard. Built on a slender deep-V hull with prop pockets, the V55 Express is a good performer with either 610hp MAN diesels (30 knots cruise/34–35 knots top) or optional 800hp MANs (32-knots cruise/36 knots top).

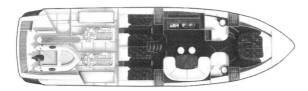

V52 Floorplan

V55 Floorplan

Viking V58 Express

Length	58'11"	Fuel	660 gals.
Beam	15'5"	Water	125 gals.
Draft	3'6"	Waste	54 gals.
Weight	44,800#	Hull Type	Deep-V
Clearance	16'6"	Deadrise Aft	19°
Headroom	6'5"	Production	2003–Current

An impressive yacht with powerful lines and unsurpassed luxury, the Viking V58 is a sophisticated blend of modern engineering and state-of-the-art construction. Sleek and sporty topsides with molded spray rails and a deep-V bottom define the hull, and high-gloss cherry joinery highlights the spacious interior. While many sportcruisers are available with optional hardtops, the V58's folding sunroof offers the advantage of making the roof disappear and letting the sun shine in. The cockpit layout is centered around a huge U-shaped lounge for seating or dining. A double helm converts to a leaning post for rough-water passages, and a plush upholstered aft sun pad rises at the push of a button to reveal a large bay for a tender or PWC. The belowdecks accommodations allows six adults to sleep in three staterooms. The amidships master has a double berth and en suite head, as does the forepeak VIP cabin. A large part of the salon is laid with a parquet-style floor. Additional features include a spacious engine room, teak cockpit sole, hidden galley appliances, and cockpit grill. An excellent performer with 860hp MANs, the V58 will cruise at an honest 30 knots and top out at close to 35 knots.

See Page 362 for Pricing Information

180

See Page 362 for Pricing Information

Viking V65 Express

Length Overall . . . . 65'2"	Water . . . . 180 gals.
Beam . . . . 16'11"	Headroom . . . . 6'6"
Draft . . . . 4'5"	Hull Type . . . . Deep-V
Weight . . . . 64,752#	Deadrise Aft . . . . 21°
Clearance . . . . 14'3"	Designer . . . . B. Olesinski
Fuel . . . . 960 gals.	Production 2000–Current

A beautifully styled yacht with a striking profile, the Viking V65 is an exciting, state-of-the-art luxury express that delivers excellent performance and truly impressive accommodations. The hardtop gives the V65 the best of both worlds, the security of a weather-protected helm and—with the sunroof retracted—the enjoyment of an open express design. Built on a relatively narrow deep-V hull with propeller tunnels, the three-stateroom interior is highlighted by lacquered cherry woodwork and an elegant designer decor. The master stateroom is amidships, and all three heads are fitted with stall showers. On deck, the cockpit contains a complete wet bar, an electric grill and plenty of seating. At the stern, beneath huge sun pads, are a pair of storage garages, one for a small tender and the other for a PWC. Additional features include a teak cockpit sole, a foredeck sun pad, bow thruster and wide side decks. On the downside, the engine room is a tight fit. An outstanding performer, optional 1,300hp MANs will cruise the Viking V65 Express at a fast 32 knots and reach a top speed of 37–38 knots. Compared with competitive models, this is a boat that leaves little to complain about.

Wellcraft 2700/2800 Martinique

Length w/Pulpit . . . . 28'4"	Clearance . . . . 7'5"
Hull Length . . . . 26'6"	Fuel . . . . 100 gals.
Beam . . . . 9'6"	Water . . . . 28 gals.
Draft, Up . . . . 2'0"	Hull Type . . . . Modified-V
Draft, Down . . . . 3'6"	Deadrise Aft . . . . 17°
Weight . . . . 6,600#	Production 1994–99

The Wellcraft 2800 Martinique (called the 2700 Martinique in 1994–96) is a fairly typical midcabin cruiser whose principal assets are a roomy interior and—during her production years—a very affordable price. Built on a solid fiberglass, modified-V hull with a wide 9-foot, 6-inch beam, the Martinique sleeps six below, two in the angled forward berth, two in the midcabin, and two more in the convertible dinette. The accommodations are basic—the cabinetry and carpeting are obviously inexpensive and the no-frills decor is unimpressive. Storage is adequate, however, and the galley has more counter space than most cruisers her size. On deck, visibility from the elevated helm is excellent. Cockpit seating includes a triple-wide helm seat and an aft-facing companion seat forward, and an L-shaped bench seat aft. A transom door, bow pulpit, and transom shower were standard. Lacking side decks, access to the foredeck is via a walk-through in the windshield. Note that a radar arch was a popular option. A comfortable ride in a chop, a single 310hp sterndrive engine will cruise the Martinique at 21 knots (30+ knots top), and twin 190hp engines will top out in the mid-to-high 30s.

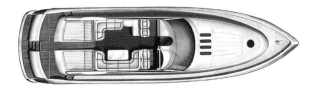

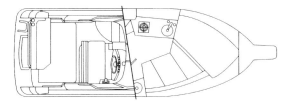

Wellcraft 2800 Martinique

Length	27'10"	Fuel	100 gals.
Beam	9'6"	Water	28 gals.
Draft, Up	2'0"	Headroom	6'2"
Draft, Down	3'6"	Hull Type	Deep-V
Weight	6,600#	Deadrise Aft	20°
Clearance w/Arch	8'6"	Production	2001–02

The Wellcraft 2800 Martinique offers all of the necessary features required in an affordably priced, sub-30-foot family cruiser. This is a crowded segment of the market with entries from many manufacturers, all incorporating a standard midcabin floorplan with berths for six, an enclosed head, compact galley and standing headroom in the main cabin. What sets the Martinique apart from many of her competitors is her clean styling—she's a good-looking boat in spite of her high freeboard. Built on a deep-V hull with an integrated transom, the cockpit is fitted with a double-wide helm (with storage under) and U-shaped lounge seating aft, which converts into a sun pad with the optional cocktail table. A tilt wheel was standard, and a walk-through windshield provides access to the bow. The entry light switch at the transom door is a convenient touch, and an electric engine hatch makes it easy to get to the motor. A transom shower was also standard. Among several single and twin-engine options, a pair of 210hp sterndrive engines will cruise the 2800 Martinique in the mid 20s and reach a top speed of about 40 knots. Note that production lasted only two years.

Wellcraft 2800 Monte Carlo

Length	27'7"	Fuel	115 gals.
Beam	9'11"	Water	28 gals.
Draft, Up	1'9"	Hull Type	Modified-V
Draft, Down	2'9"	Deadrise Aft	16°
Weight	7,200#	Designer	Wellcraft
Clearance	NA	Production	1986–89

Obviously dated by today's sportboat standards, an affordable price, bold hull graphics, and spacious accommodations made the 2800 Monte Carlo one of the more popular models in the Wellcraft fleet a few years back. Hull construction is solid fiberglass, and she rides on a conventional modified-V hull with a relatively wide 9-foot, 11-inch beam. Below, the Monte Carlo sleeps six—two in the forward V-berth, two in the midcabin, and two kids on the converted dinette. The absence of any cabin bulkheads—privacy curtains separate the fore and aft sleeping areas from the main cabin—results in a wide-open interior with plenty of elbow space. Note that the aft cabin has near-standing headroom, which is quite unusual in a midcabin boat this size. On deck, the single-level cockpit is arranged with a double-wide helm seat (with a fold-down aft jump seat) and removable bench seating at the transom. Additional features include a swim platform, good engine access, trim tabs, and a bow pulpit. A radar arch was a popular option. Twin 260hp MerCruiser sterndrives will cruise the 2800 Monte Carlo at an easy 25 knots and deliver a top speed in the neighborhood of 35 knots.

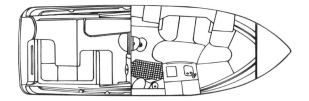

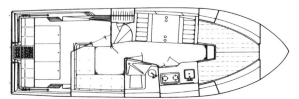

See Page 363 for Pricing Information

See Page 363 for Pricing Information

Wellcraft 287 Prima

Length w/Pulpit	28'7"	Fuel	100 gals.
Hull Length	26'1"	Water	20 gals.
Beam	9'8"	Headroom	6'1"
Draft	3'0"	Hull Type	Modified-V
Weight	7,900#	Deadrise Aft	18°
Clearance	7'0"	Production	1990–93

The Wellcraft 287 Prima is a maxi-cube family cruiser with a high-freeboard profile (note the elevated foredeck) and good all-around performance characteristics. Sharing her hull with Wellcraft's 2600 Coastal fishing boat, she's constructed on a solid fiberglass, modified-V hull with moderate beam and a steep 18 degrees of transom deadrise. Belowdecks, the Prima's full-width midcabin floorplan will sleep five with privacy curtains separating the fore and aft sleeping areas from the rest of the cabin. There's a flexible shower in the head compartment, and the absence of interior bulkheads results in a wide-open layout. Note, however, that headroom is only 6 feet in the main cabin. The cockpit is arranged with a double helm seat forward and bench seating aft. Engine access is via removable hatches in the cockpit sole. Additional features include a walk-through windshield, an integral swim platform, foredeck sun pad, bow pulpit, and oval ports in the hullsides. Twin 155hp MerCruiser V-6 sterndrives will cruise at 21–22 knots (about 30 knots top), and a single Volvo 330hp Duoprop will cruise at an efficient 25 knots and top out in the mid-to-high 30s.

Wellcraft 2900 Express

Length	28'8"	Water	28 gals.
Beam	10'8"	Cockpit	NA
Draft	2'6"	Hull Type	Modified-V
Weight	9,000#	Deadrise Aft	16°
Clearance	7'4"	Designer	B. Collier
Fuel	120 gals.	Production	1981–87

A spacious, single-level cockpit, practical cabin accommodations, and a low price made the Wellcraft 2900 Express (called the 288 Suncruiser in 1981–82) a fairly popular model for Wellcraft in the 1980s. She rides on a solid fiberglass, modified-V hull with a relatively wide 10-foot, 8-inch beam. While sterndrives were available in the 2900, most were sold with straight inboards with the engines located under the forward cockpit sole. Inboards are great—they're certainly more dependable than sterndrives—but in order to have inboards in a midsize express, you have to give up the midcabin interior so common in most family cruisers. There are berths for four in the 2900 with a V-berth forward and a convertible dinette in the main cabin. The no-frills interior is roomy, but the fabrics and furnishings were cheap and these are not what one would describe as luxury accommodations. (In 1995 the floorplan was updated to include an angled double berth forward.) A teak bow pulpit and swim platform were standard. Twin 230hp MerCruiser gas engines will cruise the 2900 Express at an economical 19–20 knots and top out in the high 20s. Note the very limited fuel capacity.

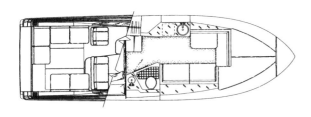

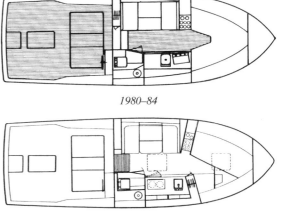

1980–84

1985–87

Wellcraft 3000 Martinique

Length w/Pulpit . . . . 32'4"	Fuel . . . . 160 gals.
Beam . . . . 10'6"	Water . . . . 41 gals.
Draft, Drives Up . . . . 2'3"	Headroom . . . . 6'3"
Draft, Drives Down . . . . 3'1"	Hull Type . . . . Modified-V
Weight . . . . 11,000#	Deadrise Aft . . . . 16°
Clearance . . . . 8'7"	Production 1998–2003

The affordably priced Wellcraft 3000 Martinique is a contemporary family cruiser with comfortable cabin accommodations and a good turn of speed. She's built on a solid fiberglass modified-V hull, and her generous 10-foot, 6-inch beam results in a spacious interior. Like most express cruisers in this size range, the Martinique has a midcabin floorplan that will accommodate four adults and two kids. Privacy curtains separate the sleeping areas from the main salon, and galley storage is increased by locating the refrigerator under the forward dinette seat. In the cockpit, the driver's side of the double-wide helm flips up to form a bolster for standup driving. Lacking side decks, molded steps and a walk-through windshield provide access to the bow. The cockpit also comes with a portside sink/refrigerator while a removable table converts the U-shaped lounge into a dinette. An electrically operated hatch in the sole lifts up to reveal a spacious engine compartment. On the downside, the swim platform is quite narrow. A good performer with twin 250hp or 300hp I/Os, the 3000 Martinique will cruise in the mid 20s and hit a top speed in excess of 40 knots.

Wellcraft 3000 Monaco

Length w/Pulpit . . . . 30'2"	Clearance . . . . 7'6"
Hull Length . . . . 28'2"	Fuel . . . . 120 gals.
Beam . . . . 10'8"	Water . . . . 31 gals.
Draft, Drive Up . . . . 1'11"	Hull Type . . . . Modified-V
Draft, Drive Down . . . . 3'0"	Deadrise Aft . . . . 16°
Weight . . . . 9,800#	Production 1989–92

Considered by some to be a stylish boat when she was introduced in 1989, it's fair to say that the Wellcraft 3000 Monaco is seriously dated by today's sportboat standards. (Indeed, the Monaco wasn't much to look at to begin with, and the so-so finish and inexpensive cabin furnishings make her even less appealing.) Built on a solid fiberglass hull with a relatively wide beam, the Monaco's interior sleeps six—two in the (very) small mid-berth, two in the forward double berth, and two kids on the converted dinette. With no bulkheads, the interior is quite spacious although the absence of natural lighting is notable. The Monaco's galley gets high marks for its generous counter space and storage cabinets—a rarity in most express cruisers. Curtains separate the sleeping areas from the main cabin, and the aft cabin is arranged with facing settees. Topside, the bi-level cockpit includes an L-shaped settee opposite the helm and removable bench seating aft. Lacking side decks, a molded centerline step provides access to the Monaco's walk-through windshield. Among several sterndrive options, twin 240hp Volvo gas engines will cruise the 3000 Monaco in the low-to-mid 20s and reach a top speed of about 35 knots.

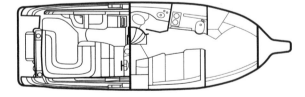

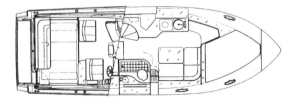

See Page 363 for Pricing Information   See Page 364 for Pricing Information

Wellcraft 3100 Express

Length . . . . 31'3"	Water . . . . 28 gals.
Beam . . . . 11'6"	Headroom . . . . 6'4"
Draft . . . . 2'11"	Hull Type . . . . Deep-V
Weight . . . . 10,200#	Deadrise Aft . . . . 19°
Clearance . . . . 8'1"	Designer . . . . Wellcraft
Fuel . . . . 160 gals.	Production 1979–85

The Wellcraft 3100 Express (called the 310 Suncruiser in 1979–82) is a typical 1980s-style express whose roomy accommodations, low price, and dependable inboard power made her a popular model for Wellcraft. Built on a solid fiberglass, deep-V hull, the large cockpit and spacious interior of the 3100 are made possible by her generous 11-foot, 6-inch beam. Although she lacks the midcabin berth found in most express cruisers, there are berths for six below when the dinette is converted and the settee's hinged backrest is lifted to create twin pipe berths. Both the galley and dinette are on the small side, and a privacy curtain separates the stateroom from the main cabin. The 3100's uncomplicated decor is plain compared with today's high-glitz interiors, and the finish leaves a lot to be desired. Topside, double helm and companion seats are forward in the cockpit and a bench seat is provided at the transom. Removable hatches in the cockpit sole access the engines and V-drives, which, incidentally, are quite close together due to the outboard fuel tanks. Twin 260hp inboard gas engines will cruise the 3100 Express at 18–19 knots and reach a top speed in the mid-to-high 20s.

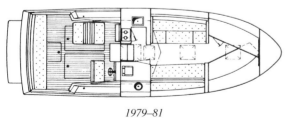

1979–81

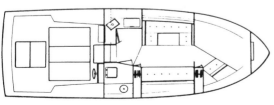

1982–85

See Page 364 for Pricing Information

Wellcraft 3200 Martinique

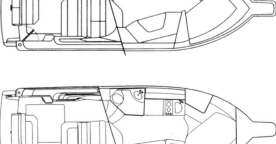

Length w/Pulpit . . . . 34'5"	Fuel . . . . 162 gals.
Hull Length . . . . 32'0"	Water . . . . 43 gals.
Beam . . . . 11'2"	Hull Type . . . . Modified-V
Draft . . . . 3'1"	Deadrise Aft . . . . 16°
Weight . . . . 10,300#	Designer . . . . Wellcraft
Clearance . . . . 8'0"	Production 1994–2000

The 3200 Martinique is a maxi-volume family cruiser with an attractive profile (in spite of her sloping foredeck) and a conventional midcabin floorplan. She's built on a solid fiberglass modified-V hull with moderate beam and transom deadrise. The interior of the Martinique will sleep six and includes a roomy galley (with good storage and counter space), a standup head with shower, and a low-overhead aft cabin with a dinette that converts into a big double bed. Draw curtains are used for privacy in the fore and aft sleeping areas, and translucent deck hatches and decent-sized cabin windows combine to provide a good deal of natural lighting below. Outside, the Martinique's bi-level cockpit features a triple-wide helm seat, an aft-facing bench seat, a walk-through windshield, and an L-shaped lounge seating aft. A transom door and shower were standard. Twin Volvo 310hp sterndrives will cruise the 3200 Martinique at 25 knots (about 36 knots top), and a pair of inboard 320hp V-drive MerCruisers will cruise at 23 knots and reach a top speed of 33–34 knots. Note that the cockpit was updated in 1998 with U-shaped seating.

Wellcraft 3200 St. Tropez

Wellcraft 33 St. Tropez

Length	31'8"	Water	40 gals.
Beam	11'8"	Cockpit	NA
Draft	2'10"	Hull Type	Modified-V
Weight	10,300#	Deadrise Aft	16°
Clearance	8'5"	Designer	B. Collier
Fuel	180 gals.	Production	1985–93

Length w/Pulpit	33'7"	Fuel	180 gals.
Hull Length	31'5"	Water	40 gals.
Beam	11'8"	Hull Type	Modified-V
Draft	3'1"	Deadrise Aft	16°
Weight	11,200#	Designer	B. Collier
Clearance, Arch	9'0"	Production	1990–92

The 3200 St. Tropez was among the first American-built cruisers to sport the then-new "Euro" look that was fast becoming a trend in 1980s sportboat design. Some 1,700 of these inboard cruisers were built making the St. Tropez the most successful Wellcraft cruiser ever. Below, the mauve-colored fabrics, gray carpeting, and brushed aluminum trim was a clear departure from the traditional teak-trimmed interiors of other family cruisers. There are berths for six—a notable accomplishment since there is no aft cabin. The St. Tropez's single-level cockpit is arranged with a double helm seat forward, a companion seat opposite, and removable bench seating aft. This is, incidentally, a very uncluttered cockpit with room for some light-tackle fishing. There were several cosmetic updates over the years, but the most signification modification came in 1988 with the addition of a new swim platform and transom door. On the downside, the engine room is a tight fit, and the interior decor is way dated by today's standards. Standard 260hp V-drive gas engines will cruise the 3200 St. Tropez at 20–21 knots (about 28 knots top), and optional 340hp MerCruisers will cruise in the mid 20s and reach a top speed of over 30 knots.

Not to be confused with the original—and hugely popular—3200 St. Tropez, the 33 St. Tropez lasted only three years in production before being retired from the Wellcraft fleet in 1992. She was built on a solid fiberglass hull with moderate beam and a substantial 16 degrees of transom deadrise—the same proven hull used in the production of the first St. Tropez. There were two interior layouts used in the 33. The first, which was identical to the original 3200 St. Tropez, had an island double berth forward and berths for six. In 1991 the layout was revised to include a longer salon settee and an angled double berth forward. While both configurations are similar to the original St. Tropez interior, the elevated cabintop of the 33 adds some much-needed cabin headroom as well as additional exterior freeboard. On deck, the single-level cockpit is arranged with a double helm seat, transom door, and L-shaped bench seating aft. Lacking side decks, a walk-through windshield provides access to the bow. Twin 260hp inboard gas engines (with V-drives) will cruise the 33 St. Tropez at a respectable 20 knots and reach a top speed of just under 30 knots.

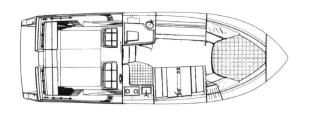

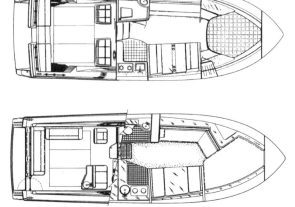

See Page 364 for Pricing Information

See Page 364 for Pricing Information

Wellcraft 3300 Martinique

Length	33'2"	Water	40 gals.
Beam	11'7"	Waste	35 gals.
Draft	2'11"	Headroom	6'3"
Weight	11,000#	Hull Type	Deep-V
Clearance, Arch	9'0"	Deadrise Aft	22°
Fuel	226 gals.	Production	2001–03

In production for only a few years before Wellcraft turned their attention to fishing boats only, the 3300 Martinique was the company's economy-class entry in the highly competitive midsize sport-boat market. The Martinique's inboard power is notable—most other express boats this size come with sterndrive power. Notable, too, is her deep-V hull, which delivers an exceptional rough-water ride. The interior follows the standard midcabin approach seen in most of today's family cruisers with berths for six, a capable galley area (with lots of counter space), decent storage, and a compact head with sink and shower. Privacy curtains separate the fore and aft sleeping areas from the main cabin, and two overhead hatches and four opening ports provide adequate cabin ventilation. The cockpit is arranged with a sun lounge opposite the helm, a U-shaped settee aft, wet bar, and transom door. Service access to the engines is very good, and a walk-through windshield provides access to the bow. On the downside, the so-so finish is unimpressive. Among several engine options, twin 310hp V-drive MerCruisers will cruise the 3300 Martinique at 20 knots and reach a top speed of close to 30 knots.

Wellcraft 3400 Gran Sport

Length w/Pulpit	35'5"	Fuel	270 gals.
Length	33'7"	Water	75 gals.
Beam	12'6"	Hull Type	Modified-V
Draft	3'0"	Deadrise Aft	16°
Weight	13,400#	Designer	B. Collier
Clearance	9'4"	Production	1984–92

A popular model for many years, the Wellcraft 3400 Gran Sport (called the 3400 Express in 1984) owed her success to a balanced blend of aggressive styling, a spacious midcabin interior, and a very affordable price. Built on a solid fiberglass hull with generous beam, perhaps the chief attraction of the Gran Sport is her wide-open floorplan—a feature made possible by the absence of any structural cabin bulkheads. The interior (updated in 1986) will sleep six: two in the bow stateroom, two on the converted dinette, and two more when the U-shaped settee in the midcabin is converted into a double berth. In 1988 a bolt-on swim platform was added, and in 1990 the Gran Sport was again updated on the outside with new hull graphics and a stylish white-on-white helm console. Additional features include a bow pulpit, transom door, a well-arranged engine compartment, and wide side decks. Note that a cockpit wet bar and a radar arch were popular options. A good-running boat with plenty of cockpit seating, standard 340hp gas engines will cruise the Wellcraft 3400 Gran Sport in the low 20s and reach a top speed of around 30 knots.

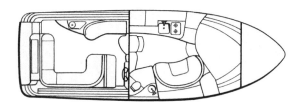

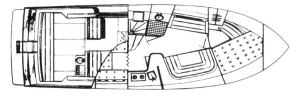

1984–85

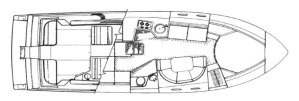

1986–92

See Page 364 for Pricing Information

See Page 364 for Pricing Information

Wellcraft 3500 Corsair; 3600 St. Tropez

Length w/Pulpit	38'7"	Water	76 gals.
Hull Length	33'10"	Clearance, Arch	9'9"
Beam	12'6"	Hull Type	Modified-V
Draft	2'9"	Deadrise Aft	16°
Weight	14,400#	Designer	Wellcraft
Fuel	270 gals.	Production	1992–93

Lasting only two years in production, this entry-level family cruiser was introduced in 1992 as the 3500 Corsair and renamed the 3600 St. Tropez the following year. She was a rakish boat by the standards of her day with an integrated swim platform, a tall arch, and a wraparound windshield. By eliminating the side decks, Wellcraft engineers were able to able to create a wide-open and expansive interior with plenty of elbow space. Where many other express boats this size have midcabin floorplans, the Corsair/St. Tropez has a conventional layout with a single stateroom and berths for six. There's a separate stall shower in the head, and the starboard settee converts into upper and lower bunks. Note that a solid door provides privacy in the stateroom—a rare luxury in a modern family express. Topside, cockpit seating includes a triple helm seat, aft-facing bench seating, and another bench seat at the transom. Lacking side decks, a windshield walk-through provides access to the bow. Twin 400hp (502-cid) MerCruiser gas inboards (with V-drives and side exhausts) will cruise at about 20 knots and reach a top speed in the neighborhood of 30 knots.

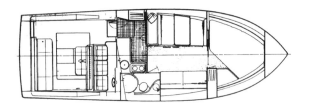

Wellcraft 3600 Martinique

Length w/Pulpit	38'0"	Fuel	264 gals.
Hull Length	35'6"	Water	47 gals.
Beam	12'6"	Headroom	6'2"
Draft	3'0"	Hull Type	Modified-V
Weight	15,000#	Deadrise Aft	16°
Clearance, Arch	9'10"	Production	1994–2000

The 3600 Martinique is basically an updated version of the Wellcraft 3500 Corsair/3600 St. Tropez (1992–93) with a new floorplan and a redesigned cockpit. She's built on a conventional modified-V hull with a solid fiberglass bottom, an integral swim platform, and prop pockets to reduce the shaft angle. Inside, the Martinique was built without bulkheads to create a more open and spacious cabin. Her midcabin floorplan sleeps six—two forward, two on the converted dinette, and two more when the midcabin lounge is converted. While the L-shaped galley counter extends into the salon, it doesn't restrict traffic. (Note that the galley floor is covered with a vinyl nonskid.) On deck, the cockpit is configured with a triple-wide helm seat, an aft-facing bench seat, and L-shaped lounge seating aft. (Note that in 1999 the cockpit seating was redesigned.) Lacking side decks, a windshield walk-through provides access to the bow. Additional features include a transom door, radar arch, bow pulpit, and a well-arranged engine room. Among several engine options, twin 310hp MerCruiser gas inboards (with V-drives and side exhausts) will cruise the Martinique at 18–19 knots and top out in the high 20s.

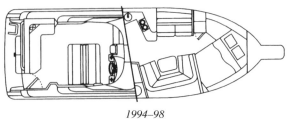

1994–98

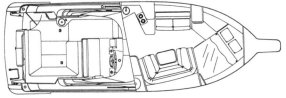

1999–2000

Wellcraft 37 Corsica

Length . . . . 36'11"	Water . . . . 100 gals.
Beam . . . . 13'6"	Headroom . . . . 6'3"
Draft . . . . 3'1"	Hull Type . . . . Modified-V
Weight . . . . 16,800#	Deadrise Aft . . . . 16°
Clearance . . . . 9'9"	Designer . . . . B. Collier
Fuel . . . . 300 gals.	Production 1990-91

Lasting only two years in production, the Wellcraft 37 Corsica is an unremarkable midcabin cruiser whose spacious interior and low price were designed to appeal to entry-level buyers on a budget. Built on a solid fiberglass hull with generous beam, the Corsica's original midcabin layout was judged too confining so Wellcraft engineers devised an all-new floorplan after the first 15 boats had been built. The small dinette found in the original layout was replaced by a wet bar and a serving counter—an unusual design since dinettes are almost taken for granted in modern sportboats—and storage space was greatly improved. Outside, the cockpit is arranged with excellent seating accommodations including a double-wide helm seat, an L-shaped settee to port, and bench seating at the transom. A wet bar and walk-through transom door were standard. Additional features include wide side decks, plenty of cabin headroom, a bow pulpit, and a radar arch. An average performer even with big-block 502-cid V-drive gas engines, the Wellcraft 37 Corsica will cruise at 20 knots and reach a top speed of just under 30 knots.

Wellcraft 3700 Martinique

Length . . . . 36'11"	Water . . . . 57 gals.
Beam . . . . 13'0"	Waste . . . . 35 gals.
Draft . . . . 3'4"	Headroom . . . . 6'3"
Weight . . . . 16,400#	Hull Type . . . . Deep-V
Clearance . . . . 9'5"	Deadrise Aft . . . . 22°
Fuel . . . . 288 gals.	Production 2001–03

Good styling, a spacious interior, and a very affordable price made the Wellcraft 3700 Martinique a serious competitor in the big family cruiser market of the early 2000s. Built on a good-running deep-V hull with a wide beam, the Martinique sleeps six below in a midcabin floorplan that seems surprisingly open and comfortable. In a departure from so many midcabin interiors, a solid door—instead of a curtain—separates the bow stateroom from the main cabin. The galley may be a little compact, but there are more storage lockers and compartments in the Martinique than in most other boats her size. Laminated cherry woodwork is used throughout the interior, and a pair of deck hatches provide a small amount of natural lighting. Outside, the single-level cockpit can accommodate a small crowd with a sun lounge opposite the double helm seat and wraparound lounge seating aft. Additional features include a cockpit wet bar, a walk-through windshield, an electrically activated engine room hatch, transom door, and transom shower. Twin 380hp MerCruiser gas engines (with V-drives) will cruise the 3700 Martinique at 20 knots and reach a top speed of just under 30 knots.

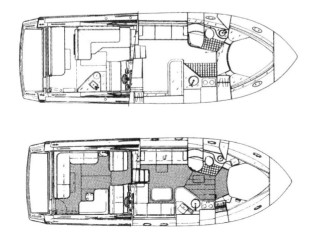

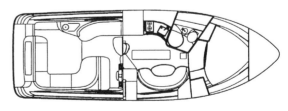

See Page 364 for Pricing Information
See Page 364 for Pricing Information

Wellcraft 38 Excalibur

Length	37'11"	Fuel	240 gals.
Beam	10'8"	Water	60 gals.
Draft, Drive Up	2'3"	Headroom	6'0"
Draft, Drive Down	3'2"	Hull Type	Deep-V
Weight	13,200#	Deadrise Aft	21°
Clearance	7'5"	Production	1996–2002

The 38 Excalibur is one of several current and past Wellcraft models manufactured in Australia by Riviera Marine. She was built on a solid fiberglass, deep-V hull with a rounded keel and a narrow, performance-enhancing beam. With her long foredeck and sleek profile, the 38 Excalibur is considered by many to be one of the better-looking express boats of recent years. Experienced boaters will be impressed with the Excalibur's level of fit and finish—the tooling and gelcoat work is excellent. The interior is arranged with the master stateroom forward (with a curtain for privacy), a comfortable Ultrasuede sofa, full galley and head, and an aft bunk suitable for a couple of kids. On deck, cockpit seating is comprised of a two-person helm with a bucket seat opposite and an L-shaped aft lounge. A wet bar (with refrigerator) is standard as is a transom door and shower. Engine access, under the aft cockpit seat, is very good, but the Excalibur's side decks are narrow. Note that the helm seat can be adjusted electrically. A good performer with MerCruiser 385hp gas sterndrives, she'll cruise at 30–32 knots and reach a top speed of over 40 knots.

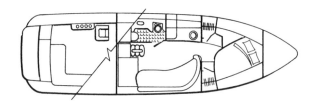

Wellcraft 43 Portofino

Length w/Pulpit	45'7"	Fuel, Gas	300 gals.
Hull Length	42'10"	Fuel, Diesel	436 gals.
Beam	14'6"	Water	82 gals.
Draft	3'0"	Hull Type	Modified-V
Weight	20,000#	Deadrise Aft	14°
Clearance	10'3"	Production	1987–97

A good-selling boat during her decade-long production years, the 43 Portofino was one of the largest production express cruisers on the market when she came out in the late 1980s. With her bold Euro-style appearance and spacious accommodations, the Portofino conveyed an aura of comfort and luxury seldom seen in earlier express boats. She was constructed on a low-deadrise hull with a wide 14-foot, 6-inch beam, and prop pockets were used to move the engines as far aft as possible. Originally offered with a single-stateroom interior, in 1990 a two-stateroom floorplan proved more practical for cruising with friends. Either way, the head contains a separate stall shower and the sofa converts to a double berth. On deck, the Portifino's huge bi-level cockpit provides seating for a dozen guests. Note that hull graphics were reduced and the helm console upgraded in 1990. Engine access is excellent—the hatch in the bridgedeck reveals a ladder that leads down between the engines. With standard 340hp gas engines, the 43 Portofino has a barely respectable cruising speed of 16 knots and a top speed of about 25 knots. Optional 375hp Cat diesels will cruise at 20–22 knots and top out in the mid 20s.

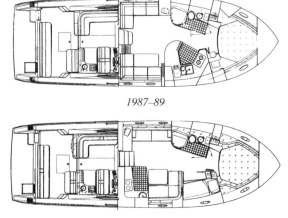

1987–89

1990–97

See Page 364 for Pricing Information
190
See Page 364 for Pricing Information

Wellcraft 45 Excalibur

Length	44'6"	Water	70 gals.
Beam	11'8"	Headroom	6'5"
Draft	3'3"	Hull Type	Deep-V
Weight	14,600#	Deadrise Aft	21°
Clearance	8'6"	Designer	Riviera Marine
Fuel	274 gals.	Production	1995–2001

Built for Wellcraft by Australian-based Riviera Marine, the 45 Excalibur strikes a balance between a purebred sportboat and a traditional family-style express cruiser. The Excalibur is constructed on a solid fiberglass deep-V hull, and while her narrow beam restricts interior volume, the payoff is a more efficient and easily driven hull capable of higher speeds than most other express designs with greater beam. The cockpit is arranged with an elevated helm position, a full wet bar to port, and a U-shaped lounge/sun pad aft. Under the sun pad is a large storage well, and the entire aft section of the cockpit floor rises electrically for access to the engines. Belowdecks, the salon of the Excalibur's midcabin interior is dominated by a richly upholstered four-person settee opposite the portside galley. Both sleeping areas are separated from the salon with privacy doors. Additional features include a separate stall shower in the head, cockpit boarding steps, anchor windlass locker, radar arch, transom door, and a concealed swim ladder. Big-block 415hp gas sterndrive engines will cruise the Wellcraft 45 Excalibur at 28 knots and reach a top speed in the low 40s.

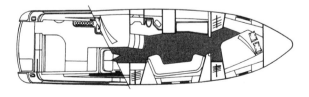

See Page 365 for Pricing Information   191

Flybridge Cruisers

Design Assets
Roomy cabin accommodations, moderate fishability, good bridge visibility

Design Limitations
Small cockpit, narrow sidedecks

Price Leaders
Bayliner, Carver, Mainship, Silverton, Navigator

Quality Leaders
Azimut, Eastbay, Sea Ray, Cruisers

Albin 35 Convertible

Length w/Pulpit . . . . 36'11"	Fuel . . . . 370 gals
Hull Length. . . . . 34'11"	Water. . . . . 160 gals.
Beam . . . . 12'4"	Cockpit. . . . . 80 sq. ft.
Draft. 3'0"	Hull Type . . . . Modified-V
Weight. . . . . 18,000#	Deadrise Aft . . . . 13°
Clearance. . . . . 12'0"	Production 1995–Current

A handsome boat with a distinctive Downeast profile, the Albin 35 Convertible is a moderately priced family cruiser/weekend fisherman with comfortable accommodations and a cockpit that's large enough to meet the needs of weekend anglers. She's built on a fully cored hull with moderate beam, a well-flared bow, and a shallow keel for stability and tracking. Buyers have a choice of interior layouts: the standard version has a single-stateroom floorplan with the galley down, and the second moves the galley up and adds a second stateroom. Either way, the interior of the Albin 35 is bright and cheery, and wraparound cabin windows provide plenty of natural lighting. A lower helm is optional, and the flybridge can be configured with the helm aft for fishing or forward for cruising. Additional features include wide side decks, transom door, integral bow pulpit, six opening cabin ports, sliding salon windows, and a separate stall shower in both floorplans. Among several single- and twin-engine options, a pair of 300hp Cat (or GM) diesels will cruise the Albin 35 Convertible at an economical 21–22 knots, and a single 420hp Cat will cruise in the neighborhood of 17–18 knots.

Bayliner 288 Classic Cruiser

Length w/Pulpit . . . . 30'7"	Fuel. . . . . 113 gals.
Beam . . . . 10'0"	Water. . . . . 34 gals.
Draft, Up . . . . 1'8"	Waste . . . . 26 gals.
Draft, Down . . . . 3'2"	Hull Type . . . . Modified-V
Weight. . . . . 8,090#	Deadrise Aft . . . . 17°
Clearance. . . . . 10'3"	Production 1996–Current

Called the 2858 Ciera Command Bridge from 1996–2002, the popular Bayliner 288 Classic Cruiser has the distinction of being one of the smaller flybridge cruisers built in recent years. The reason there are so few under-30-foot flybridge boats on the market is easily understood: the added weight of two or three adults on the flybridge of any small boat increases rolling and detracts from overall stability. With her wide beam and small bridge, however, the 288 Classic offsets this problem to a large extent. For a 28-footer, the accommodations are impressive. The layout includes a private mid-cabin berth below the raised salon settee, a V-berth forward, an enclosed head and shower aft, and a full galley in the salon. A lower helm is standard, and large cabin windows and excellent headroom add considerably to the sense of space. Like all Bayliners, the detailing and joinerwork leave a lot to be desired but the low price will certainly appeal to budget-minded boaters. Note that the fuel tank is small and the side decks are narrow. A single 310hp MerCruiser sterndrive engine provides a cruising speed of around 22 knots and a top speed of 32–33 knots.

Single-Stateroom Layout

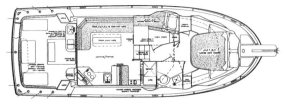

Two-Stateroom Floorplan

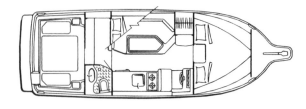

See Page 294 for Pricing Information

See Page 296 for Pricing Information

Bayliner 2950/2958 Command Bridge

Length	28'8"	Fuel	121 gals.
Beam	10'6"	Water	29 gals.
Draft, Drives Up	2'0"	Waste	13 gals.
Draft, Drives Down	3'6"	Hull Type	Deep-V
Weight	8,750#	Deadrise Aft	20°
Clearance	11'8"	Production	1988–90

When she was introduced back in 1988, the Bayliner 2958 Command Bridge was considered a rather stylish—if basic—flybridge cruiser with a very attractive price tag. Construction is solid fiberglass, and at just under 9,000 pounds, she's a relatively light boat for her size. For a 29-footer, the salon is unusually spacious. A large U-shaped dinette will seat four in comfort, and wraparound cabin windows provide plenty of natural lighting. There are two "staterooms" in this floorplan: a midcabin berth with sitting headroom is located below the dinette, and the forward V-berth area can be separated from the galley with a privacy curtain. Visibility from the lower helm, with its double seat, is very good. While the cockpit is extremely small, the lounge seating on the flybridge will accommodate several guests. A hatch in the cockpit provides access to the engine compartment where working space is at a premium. Additional features include a radar arch, swim platform, sliding cabin windows, and a bow pulpit. Twin 230hp sterndrive engines (standard) give the 2985 Command Bridge a cruising speed of 19 knots and a top speed of around 29 knots.

Bayliner 3258 Ciera Command Bridge

Length w/Platform	35'2"	Fuel	180 gals.
Hull Length	32'11"	Water	52 gals.
Beam	11'0"	Clearance	11'7"
Draft, Drives Up	2'0"	Hull Type	Modified-V
Draft, Drives Down	3'3"	Deadrise Aft	17°
Weight	10,230#	Production	1995–2000

With her rakish lines and aggressive profile, the Bayliner 3258 Ciera was an attractive choice for budget-minded buyers in the late 1990s looking for a spacious flybridge sedan at an affordable price. Like all Bayliner models of her era, she was built on a lightweight, solid fiberglass hull with moderate beam and transom deadrise. The cabin window treatment is very Euro-style—easily her most distinctive feature—and the small cockpit virtually guarantees an exceptionally roomy interior layout. The 3258's salon is split into two distinct areas. The forward section is a step up from the salon sole with a small settee opposite the helm. In the aft section of the salon, a U-shaped dinette faces the in-line galley with its generous counter space. The entrance to the aft cabin is forward, beneath the windshield, and the head (which has a separate stall shower) is under the lower helm console. Given the expansive interior dimensions, it's no surprise that the cockpit of the 3258 is small. Note too that the side decks are practically nonexistent. A radar arch, bow pulpit, and a transom door were standard. Twin 250hp MerCruiser I/Os will cruise at 20–22 knots (around 28 knots top), and optional 310hp Mercs will cruise at a brisk 25 knots and reach a top speed of around 35 knots.

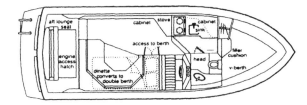

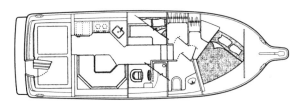

FLYBRIDGE CRUISERS

Bayliner 3270/3288 Motor Yacht

Length Overall	32'1"	Fuel	200 gals.
Length WL	28'10"	Water	65/89 gals.
Beam	11'6"	Waste	23 gals.
Draft	2'11"	Hull Type	Modified-V
Weight	12,500#	Deadrise Aft	6°
Clearance	13'10"	Production	1981–95

A popular model for many years and the all-time best-selling boat in her class, the Bayliner 3288 Motor Yacht was introduced back in 1981 as the 3270 Explorer. She became the Bayliner 3270 Motor Yacht in 1985, and evolved into the 3288 Motor Yacht in 1989. First marketed (in an era of escalating fuel prices) as an efficient family cruiser, the original flybridge was updated and a radar arch became standard in 1985. The midcabin floorplan of the 3270/3288 remained essentially unchanged over the years aside from minor cosmetic updates. A lower helm was standard, the salon is quite spacious with big wraparound cabin windows, and the private aft cabin extends beneath the elevated dinette in the salon. The cockpit is fitted with teak handrails, and the side decks are wide enough for easy access to the bow. The 3288's lightweight hull results in an extremely fuel-efficient package. The engine compartment, accessed via two cockpit hatches, is a tight fit. Several gas and diesel engines were offered over the years. Early models with 110hp Hino diesels will cruise at 12 knots, and later models with 150hp turbo Hinos will cruise at 16–17 knots. A pair of 5.7-liter gas inboards will cruise at 17–18 knots. Over 3,000 were sold during her 14-year production run.

Bayliner 3388 Motor Yacht

Length	32'11"	Water	90 gals.
Beam	11'6"	Waste	30 gals.
Draft	2'8"	Headroom	6'4"
Weight	15,500#	Hull Type	Modified-V
Clearance	13'6"	Deadrise Aft	6°
Fuel	200 gals.	Production	1996–2000

The Bayliner 3388 Motor Yacht was one of the most affordable twin-diesel family cruisers available during her production years. She's basically an updated version of the popular Bayliner 3288 MY (1981–95) with a fresh profile and several hull refinements. The midcabin interior of the 3388 is similar to her predecessor with the galley down and amidships guest cabin located beneath the elevated dinette. A lower helm is standard, and there's a separate stall shower in the head compartment. An accordion door provides privacy for the forward stateroom. If there's a downside to the 3388, it has to be the unusual salon arrangement. The staircase leading down to the midcabin, just inside the salon door, causes the dinette to be moved so far forward that it's hard to get between it and the lower helm chair. The salon, in other words, is far less spacious than one expects in a 33-footer. Additional features include a low-profile arch, prop pockets, a midcabin vanity and sink, swim platform, and a bow pulpit. Standard 260hp gas inboards will cruise the Bayliner 3388 at 16 knots and reach a top speed of around 25 knots. Note that the cabin and bridge are a single mold, which, according to Bayliner, reduces problems with window leakage.

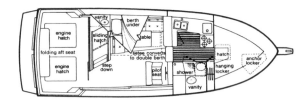

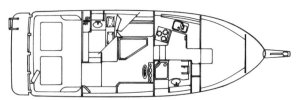

See Page 297 for Pricing Information

See Page 297 for Pricing Information

FLYBRIDGE CRUISERS

Bayliner 3488 Avanti Command Bridge

Length Overall . . . . 36'7"	Fuel . . . . 180 gals.
Hull Length . . . . 34'4"	Water . . . . 52 gals.
Beam . . . . 11'0"	Waste . . . . 52 gals.
Draft . . . . 3'5"	Hull Type . . . . Modified-V
Weight . . . . 12,549#	Deadrise Aft . . . . 17°
Clearance, Arch . . . . 11'7"	Production 1996–99

Produced for several years in the late 1990s, the Bayliner 3488 Avanti Command Bridge is a handsome and very spacious flybridge cruiser whose affordable price made her an appealing choice for many budget-minded buyers. Bayliner's production-line manufacturing process has always allowed the company to deliver a lot of boat for the money, and this was particularly true of the 3488—a design that undercut the competition by thousands of dollars. Built on a solid fiberglass modified-V hull, the Avanti's midcabin interior is arranged with two staterooms, one forward and the other tucked below the elevated settee opposite the lower helm. There's a separate stall shower in the head (a convenience not always found in a 34-footer), and the L-shaped galley in the salon provides plenty of counter space and storage. The Avanti's cockpit is large enough for a couple of deck chairs, and the flybridge has the helm forward with wraparound guest seating. Additional features include a molded bow pulpit, radar arch, and a swim platform. Standard 310hp MerCruiser gas inboards (with V-drives) will cruise the 3488 Avanti at 18 knots and reach a top speed of close to 30 knots.

Bayliner 3488 Command Bridge

Length . . . . 35'0"	Water . . . . 92 gals.
Beam . . . . 11'8"	Waste . . . . 30 gals.
Draft . . . . 3'2"	Headroom . . . . 6'4"
Weight . . . . 17,000#	Hull Type . . . . Modified-V
Clearance, Arch . . . . 13'6"	Deadrise . . . . 7.5°
Fuel . . . . 224 gals.	Production 2001–02

The 3488 Command Bridge was the first boat built using Bayliner's modular production system, a process of assembling pre-built modules—the engine room, forward stateroom, and salon modules, etc.—into the hull. This construction process reduced production costs and, according to the Bayliner, provided a more precise fit with improved structural integrity. Built on a solid fiberglass hull with very modest deadrise and an integral swim platform, the 3488's conservative styling and practical midcabin floorplan make for an altogether pleasant and practical family cruiser. Both staterooms are fitted with double berths; a lower helm is optional; and a spacious galley with plenty of counter and storage space is to starboard in the salon. On deck, a flybridge overhang shades the small cockpit from the sun. Molded steps lead up to the flybridge, which is large for a 34-footer. Additional features include a stall shower in the head, a teak-and-holly galley sole, and a transom door. Standard 260hp MerCruiser gas inboards will cruise at 14 knots (about 20 knots top), and optional 250hp Cummins diesels will cruise at 18 knots and reach a top speed of 22–23 knots.

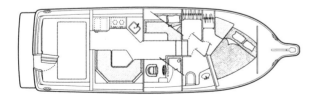

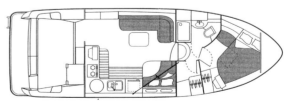

See Page 297 for Pricing Information

See Page 297 for Pricing Information

Bayliner 3688 Motor Yacht

Length	36'1"	Water	96 gals.
Beam	12'2"	Cockpit	NA
Draft	2'11"	Hull Type	Modified-V
Weight	13,700#	Deadrise Aft	14°
Clearance	13'10"	Designer	Bayliner
Fuel	250 gals.	Production	1992–94

Built on a conventional modified-V hull with a moderate beam and prop pockets to reduce draft, the Bayliner 3688 Motor Yacht (some might call this a Flybridge Sedan) is an entry-level family cruiser with a rakish profile and a somewhat innovative midcabin floorplan. In an unusual design configuration, a portside staircase located just inside the salon door leads down to the midcabin, where there's partial standing headroom and a built-in vanity. The downside of this arrangement is that the space devoted to the staircase consumes a fair amount of salon space. Consequently, this seems like small salon for a 36-footer with little room to move around between the raised dinette and lower helm. Privacy for the forward stateroom is limited to a sliding curtain, and the absence of a stall shower in the head is notable. Additional features include an integral swim platform with built-in shower and transom door, port and starboard cockpit steps (to access the side decks), and a comfortably large flybridge with seating for six. Twin 200hp U.S. Marine diesels (with V-drives) will cruise at 15 knots (at an efficient 1 mpg) and reach a top speed of around 17–18 knots. Optional 250hp diesels will cruise a couple of knots faster.

Bayliner 3788 Motor Yacht (1996–99)

Length	38'6"	Waste	30 gals.
Beam	13'4"	Headroom	6'5"
Draft	2'11"	Clearance, Arch	14'0"
Weight	20,000#	Hull Type	Modified-V
Fuel	250 gals.	Deadrise Aft	10°
Water	100 gals.	Production	1996–99

Aside from her modern, contemporary lines and long list of standard equipment, the most notable feature about the Bayliner 3788 Motor Yacht was her extremely affordable price. Indeed, she was one of the least expensive family cruisers of her size and type available during her production years. She was constructed on a lightweight, solid fiberglass hull with low transom deadrise and a wide beam. Her two-stateroom, galley-up floorplan is efficiently arranged with a queen berth in the forward stateroom and a double berth in the small second cabin that extends below the standard lower helm. A bathtub is fitted in the head compartment, and the engine room (accessed via two gas-assist salon hatches) provides good service access to the motors. Outside, the cockpit is small but the side decks are wide and safe. On the downside, the flybridge ladder is quite steep. Standard 7.4-liter gas inboards will cruise at 19 knots (about 30 knots top), and twin 250hp Cummins diesels cruise the 3788 MY at 19–20 knots with a top speed of about 24 knots. Because of her shallow deadrise and wide beam, the 3788 can be a hard ride when the seas pick up. Note that a newer Bayliner 3788 came out in 2001.

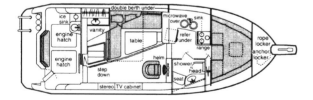

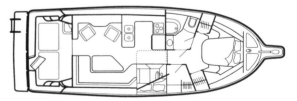

Bayliner 3788 Motor Yacht (2001–02)

Length	39'4"	Waste	36 gals.
Beam	13'7"	Headroom	6'5"
Draft	3'4"	Clearance w/Arch	14'1"
Weight	22,274#	Hull Type	Modified-V
Fuel	300 gals.	Deadrise Aft	10°
Water	125 gals.	Production	2001–02

The Bayliner 3788 Motor Yacht is an updated version of the original 3788 Motor Yacht (1996–99) with a fresh appearance and a new two-stateroom interior. Built on a conventional modified-V hull with a relatively flat 10 degrees of transom deadrise, the 3788 is a good-looking boat with more than a hint of European styling. Large cabin windows make the salon seem open and spacious, and the dinette (or optional lower helm station) is elevated to provide headroom for the mid-stateroom beneath. The galley is up, and the master stateroom has a walkaround center berth. Hatches in the salon sole provide access to the engine compartment. Topside, the flybridge accommodates five adults, and a long overhang shades the cockpit. Molded steps (instead of a ladder) make reaching the flybridge easy and safe. Additional features include a swim platform, transom door, opening side windows, foredeck sun pad and a tub/shower in the head. Standard 310hp MerCruiser gas inboards will cruise at 17–18 knots. Optional 330hp Cummins diesels will cruise the 3788 at 20 knots and reach a top speed of around 25 knots. Note that a revised version of this boat was introduced in 2003 as the Meridian 381 Sedan.

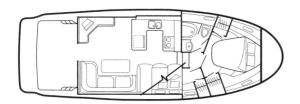

Bayliner 3870/3888 Motor Yacht

Length	38'2"	Fuel	304 gals.
Beam	13'5"	Water	80 gals.
Draft	3'2"	Hull Type	Modified-V
Weight	17,500#	Deadrise Aft	6°
Clearance	14'10"	Designer	Bayliner
Cockpit	NA	Production	1983–94

A good-selling boat for Bayliner during her decade-long production run, the 3888 Motor Yacht (called the 3780 MY from 1983–89) has long been recognized as a good value for those seeking a comfortable diesel cruiser at an affordable price. Built on a low-deadrise modified-V hull, the key feature of the 3870/3888 was her innovative midcabin floorplan with a double berth that extends under the salon sole. A lower helm was standard in the salon, and there's a surprisingly large master stateroom forward. Note that there are two heads in this layout, one with a tub/shower stall. On deck, the cockpit is large enough for a couple of deck chairs, and there's seating for three on the flybridge. Early models were powered with twin 135hp Mitsubishi 6-cylinder diesels, but these engines were dropped in 1986 in favor of U.S. Marine 175hp diesels—an update that boosted the cruising speed from 14 to 16 knots. Later models with twin 210hp Hino diesels cruise at 17–18 knots. Fuel consumption at cruising speed is about a mile per gallon, which makes the 3888 MY an extremely fuel-efficient boat. About a thousand were built during her production years, a truly remarkable figure for a boat this size.

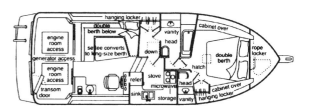

FLYBRIDGE CRUISERS

FLYBRIDGE CRUISERS

Length w/Pulpit	46'3"	Water	100 gals.
Hull Length	39'0"	Waste	36 gals.
Beam	14'1"	Clearance	14'10"
Draft	3'3"	Hull Type	Modified-V
Weight	21,000#	Deadrise Aft	10°
Fuel	298 gals.	Production	1995–2002

A stylish boat in her day with a rakish bridge and canted windows, the Bayliner 3988 is a value-priced family cruiser with roomy accommodations and a long list of standard equipment. She's built on a shallow-deadrise modified-V hull with moderate beam and prop pockets to reduce shaft angles. Inside, the two-stateroom, two-head floorplan is arranged with an island bed forward and a double berth in the small second stateroom that extends below the elevated dinette in the salon. The master head is fitted with a bathtub that provides sitting headroom only since it's located beneath the lower helm station. Large salon windows make the interior seem spacious and completely wide open. Additional features include a stylish integral swim platform with shower and transom door, port and starboard cockpit steps, wide side decks, and a comfortable flybridge with seating for six. Most 3988s were delivered with twin Hino or Cummins diesels ranging from 200 to 330 horsepower. Among them, twin 250hp Cummins diesels will cruise at 20 knots (about 24 knots top), and later models with the 330hp Cummins engines cruise at 24 knots and reach 27–28 knots top.

Length	43'1"	Water	100 gals.
Beam	14'3"	Waste	46 gals.
Draft	3'0"	Hull Type	Modified-V
Weight	19,000#	Deadrise Aft	14°
Clearance	13'6"	Designer	Bayliner
Fuel	300 gals.	Production	1991–94

With her Euro-style profile and rakish appearance, the Bayliner 4388 Mid-Cabin MY combined the big-boat accommodations most cruising families expect in a boat this size with a surprisingly affordable price. She was built on a solid fiberglass modified-V hull with a relatively wide beam, shallow keel, and an integrated swim platform. Her two-stateroom interior is arranged with the U-shaped galley forward of the salon which results in an expansive and very comfortable layout. The owner's stateroom is forward, and a small mid-stateroom (with partial standing headroom) extends under the galley. Note the common shower stall between the two head compartments. While the interior accommodations are generous, the cockpit is quite small with only enough space for a couple of deck chairs. Additional features include a spacious flybridge, good access to the engines, and a standard lower helm station. Twin 250hp Hino diesels (with V-drives) cruise the Bayliner 4388 at a respectable (and efficient) 19 knots and deliver a top speed of 24–25 knots. Optional 310hp diesels will run a couple of knots faster. The small 300-gallon fuel capacity of the 4388 limits her cruising range.

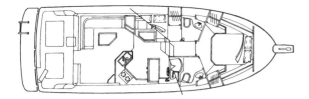

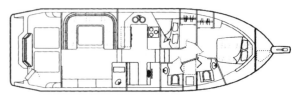

Bertram 30 Flybridge Cruiser

Length	30'7"	Water	61 gals.
Beam	11'4"	Cockpit	101 sq. ft.
Draft	3'0"	Hull Type	Deep-V
Weight	16,500#	Deadrise Aft	18.5°
Clearance	8'5"	Designer	D. Napier
Fuel	220 gals.	Production	1984–85

Bertram rarely misfires when it comes to new model introductions, so it's notable when one of their designs fails to catch on with the public. Such was the case with the mid-1980s Bertram 30 Flybridge Cruiser, the boat Bertram designed as a replacement for the classic Bertram 31. (For the record, no boat will ever equal the popularity of the Bertram 31—a true industry classic if there ever was one.) She's exactly the same length as the Bertram 31 but with slightly smaller cockpit dimensions, less transom deadrise (18.5° vs. 23°), improved trolling stability and a notably drier ride. The improvements carried into the interior as well where the Bertram 30's stylish oak-paneled accommodations provide luxuries undreamed of in the old Bertram 31. Note that the engine boxes in the cockpit provide convenient seating. Lasting only two years in production, the Bertram 30 Flybridge Cruiser proved too expensive for the market and she was unceremoniously withdrawn from the Bertram lineup in 1985. With standard MerCruiser 340hp gas engines, she'll cruise at 22 knots and reach a top speed of about 30 knots. Note that the equally short-lived Bertram 30 Express Cruiser (1984–85) is the same boat without the flybridge.

Blue Seas 31

Length Overall	30'8"	Fuel	200 gals.
Length WL	29'2"	Water	80 gals.
Beam	11'6"	Cockpit	NA
Draft	3'0"	Hull Type	Semi-Disp.
Weight	11,000#	Designer	R. Lowell
Clearance	9'2"	Production	1988–91

The Blue Seas 31 was one of the last designs introduced by Hinterhoeller Yachts, the Canadian builder best known for their high-quality series of Nonsuch sailboats. The Blue Seas was introduced at the 1988 Toronto boat show by the original builder, the Blue Seas Boat Co. of Clinton, Ontario. Production under the Hinterhoeller nameplate commenced in late 1989 and continued until Hinterhoeller shut down in 1991. A lobster-boat design with a Downeast heritage, the Blue Seas was built on a single-piece hull with three watertight compartments, a nearly plumb bow, rounded bilges, and a full-length keel. Inside, a privacy door separates the salon from the lower level galley and stateroom—very unusual. Originally offered with a shortened deckhouse and larger cockpit, the "long house" version became standard in later models. Her roomy cockpit provides plenty of space for deck chairs or light-tackle fishing. The single 210hp Cummins diesel engine will cruise economically at 14 knots and reach a top speed of around 17–18 knots. Offered with or without a flybridge, the Blue Seas 31 is well constructed and very easy on the eye.

FLYBRIDGE CRUISERS

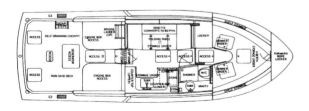

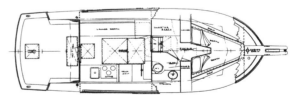

Two Staterooms, Galley Up

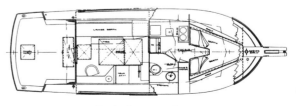

Single-Stateroom Layout

See Page 298 for Pricing Information

See Page 301 for Pricing Information

Californian 35 Convertible

Length	34'11"	Water	75 gals.
Beam	12'4"	Headroom	6'4"
Draft	3'2"	Hull Type	Modified-V
Weight	18,000#	Deadrise Aft	15°
Clearance	10'8"	Designer	J. Marshall
Fuel	300 gals.	Production	1985–87

Still a good-looking small cruiser in spite of her age, the 35 Convertible was introduced during the time of Wellcraft's ownership of Californian Yachts in the mid-1980s. A sporty profile and a unique window treatment give the 35 a distinctive look and she's an easy boat to spot in a crowd. Built on the same hull used for the Californian 35 MY with a flared bow and shallow keel, the 12-foot, 4-inch beam is relatively wide for a 35-footer. Equally at home as a family cruiser or weekend fisherman, the interior of the Californian 35 is quite open and airy (thanks in part to her wraparound salon windows) and the grain-matched teak cabinetry is impressively finished. Berths for four are provided, and a separate stall shower is fitted in the head compartment. On deck, the relatively small cockpit can support some light-tackle fishing although the step along the cabin bulkhead prevents the installation of a tackle center. Molded cockpit steps lead to wide side decks making foredeck access easy and secure. Gas engines were standard, but 210hp Cat diesels proved a popular option. At a 16-knot cruising speed, the Cats burn just 15 gph—better than a mile per gallon.

Californian 38 Convertible

Length	37'8"	Water	100 gals.
Beam	13'3"	Cockpit	NA
Draft	3'6"	Hull Type	Modified-V
Weight	25,000#	Deadrise Aft	15°
Clearance	14'6"	Designer	J. Marshall
Fuel	400 gals.	Production	1984–87

Designed for family fishing or weekend cruising, the Californian 38 Convertible never achieved the widespread popularity of more dedicated convertible fishing boats from Bertram, Viking and Hatteras in the late 1980s. Wellcraft built her on a solid fiberglass modified-V hull with a shallow keel—the same hull used in the production of the Californian 38 Motor Yacht. Her standard two-stateroom interior was arranged with a big L-shaped galley in the salon opposite a built-in settee. Both staterooms are fitted with double berths, and there's a stall shower in the single head compartment. On deck, the cockpit is large enough for the occasional fishing venture, but there are no in-deck storage bins and the step along the salon door prevents the installation of a molded tackle center. Like all Californian models, the side decks of the 38 Convertible are notably wide with molded steps in the cockpit for easy access. Additional features include a bow pulpit, wraparound cabin windows, and a well-arranged flybridge with bench seating forward of the helm. Twin 210hp Caterpillar diesels will cruise the Californian 38 around 15 knots (18–19 knots top), and the larger 300hp Cats will cruise at 21 knots and deliver a top speed of 24–25 knots.

FLYBRIDGE CRUISERS

Californian 39 SL

Length . . . . 39'0"	Fuel . . . . 250 gals.
Beam . . . . 15'0"	Water . . . . 100 gals.
Draft . . . . 4'4"	Cockpit . . . . 60 sq. ft.
Weight . . . . 27,500#	Hull Type . . . . Modified-V
Clearance . . . . NA	Deadrise Aft . . . . NA
Headroom . . . . 6'5"	Production 1999–Current

The Californian nameplate was revived in 1999 with the introduction of the Californian 39 SL, the first of an all-new series of Californian yachts built by the same owners who developed the original Californian designs back in the early 1970s. The 39 SL is a twin-stateroom cruising yacht distinguished by her conservative styling and very affordable price. Built the old-fashioned way on a solid fiberglass hull, the unusual interior of the 39 SL is certainly her most notable feature. Stepping into the bi-level salon, the location of the dinette—centered on the pilothouse level, next to the helm—is completely unique. The galley, to starboard in the salon, extends forward into the pilothouse where the raised floor reduces the counter's height, making it awkward to use. There are two double staterooms and two full heads on the lower level, and if the interior of the 39 SL is a little plain, visibility from the lower helm is excellent. A stairway leads from the small cockpit to the bridge, which is large enough to accommodate a dinghy and davit. A radar arch, transom door, and generator are standard. Volvo 318hp diesels will cruise the Californian 39 SL at 20 knots and reach 23–24 knots wide open.

Camano 28/31

Length w/Pulpit . . . . 31'0"	Fuel . . . . 100/133 gals.
Hull Length . . . . 28'0"	Water . . . . 77 gals.
Beam . . . . 10'6"	Headroom . . . . 6'3"
Draft . . . . 3'3"	Hull Type . . . . Modified-V
Weight . . . . 10,000#	Deadrise Aft . . . . 8°
Aft Deck . . . . 40 sq. ft.	Production 1990–Current

For those who enjoy a little character in their boats we present the Camano 31 (originally called the Camano 28), a salty little sedan cruiser from British Columbia with a distinctive profile and an efficient cabin layout. She's built on a lightweight flat-bottom hull with a wide beam, cored hullsides, and an unusually wide prop-protecting keel. (Indeed, the keel cavity is big enough to contain the engine, which keeps the weight down low for added stability.) The Camano's no-nonsense interior is well-finished, and her trolley-style foredeck windows are almost unique in the boating world. With the galley down, the salon is big for a 28-footer and visibility from the lower helm is excellent in all directions. The cockpit, on the other hand, is small with just enough room for a couple of folding deck chairs. With her wide beam, the Camano is able to carry a relatively large flybridge without difficulty—a feat few 28-footers can claim. A single 150hp Volvo diesel will cruise the Camano 28 at 12 knots (16–17 knots top), and more recent models with 200hp Volvo run a couple of knots faster. Note that a bow thruster is standard and the fuel was increased to 133 gallons in 2003. A popular, well-finished boat, she's also very expensive.

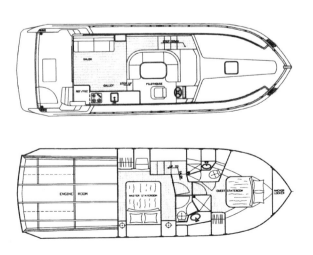

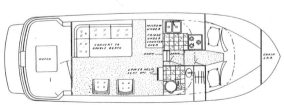

See Page 302 for Pricing Information

203

See Page 302 for Pricing Information

Cape Dory 28 Flybridge

Length Overall . . . . 27'11"	Fuel . . . . 120 gals.
Length WL . . . . 25'11"	Water . . . . 45 gals.
Beam . . . . 9'11"	Cockpit . . . . 56 sq. ft.
Draft . . . . 2'11"	Hull Type . . . . Semi-Disp.
Weight . . . . 8,000#	Designer . . . . Cape Dory
Clearance . . . . 11'2"	Production 1985–95

Introduced in 1985 and lasting a decade in production, the Cape Dory 28 is a graceful Downeast-style cruiser whose lobster-boat heritage can be seen in her salty, workboat profile. She was available in several configurations over the years—the Flybridge model pictured above proved very popular as did the Open—and a number were produced for commercial applications. The 28 was built on an easy-riding semi-displacement hull with a moderate beam, rounded bilges, and a fully protected prop. The Flybridge and Open models both have a single-stateroom floorplan with a V-berth forward, a compact galley, and an enclosed, standup head compartment. Note that in 1990 several upgrades were made including a reengineered and retooled flybridge. Additional features include wide side decks, good service access to the engine, and sliding cabin windows in the Flybridge model. Most Cape Dory 28s were fitted with the optional 200hp Volvo diesel (about 14 knots cruise/17 knots top) rather than the once-standard single gas engine. A very popular boat, over 220 Cape Dory 28s (mostly flybridge models) were built during her production years.

Cape Dory 33 Flybridge

Length . . . . 32'10"	Water . . . . 100 gals.
Beam . . . . 12'2"	Cockpit . . . . 65 sq. ft.
Draft . . . . 2'11"	Headroom . . . . 6'4"
Weight . . . . 13,500#	Hull Type . . . . Modified-V
Clearance . . . . 12'8"	Deadrise Aft . . . . 15°
Fuel . . . . 260 gals.	Production 1988–94

With the mid-1980s sailboat market in the doldrums, several builders best known for their line of sailboats began producing powerboats as a means of pure survival. Cape Dory was among them, and the 33 Flybridge became a fairly popular model for the company thanks to her quality construction, good performance, and—perhaps most importantly—her salty Downeast appearance. Built on a modified-V hull with a wide beam and cored hullsides, the full-length keel of the 33 provides protection to the prop and rudder. Her teak interior includes a single stateroom forward with the galley down and a separate stall shower in the head. Wraparound cabin windows make for an open and airy salon, and visibility from the lower helm is excellent. The cockpit is large enough for light-tackle fishing activities, and the flybridge has guest seating aft of the helm. Note that the level of fit and finish is quite high. The Cape Dory 33 was offered with several single- or twin-engine options, gas or diesel, during her production years. Among them, a pair of 200hp Volvos will cruise at 17 knots and reach 21 knots top. Note that an updated version of the Cape Dory 33 is marketed as the Robinhood 33 Poweryacht.

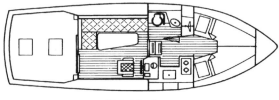

Flybridge Layout

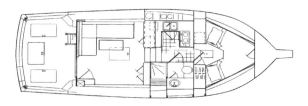

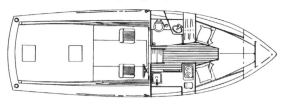

Open Fisherman Layout

See Page 303 for Pricing Information

See Page 303 for Pricing Information

Carver 27/630/300 Santego

Length Overall	31'2"	Headroom	6'1"
Hull Length	27'3"	Fuel	100 gals.
Beam	10'0"	Water	41 gals.
Draft	2'8"	Hull Type	Modified-V
Weight	8,400#	Deadrise Aft	8°
Clearance	9'2"	Production	1988–93

One of Carver's most popular models following her 1988 introduction, the 27 Santego (called the 630 Santego during 1991–92 and the 300 Santego in 1993) was a low-cost, entry-level family cruiser whose spacious interior remains her most compelling feature. Flybridge boats this size can become quite tender when more than a couple of people gather on the bridge, but this problem is mitigated to some extent in the Santego because the salon sole sits low in the hull, effectively reducing the boat's center of gravity. Built on a solid fiberglass hull, the Santego's full-width interior includes an amidship stateroom with a double berth, a forward V-berth, and a dinette/lounge that converts into a double berth. A compact galley is opposite the head in the main cabin, and privacy curtains separate the fore and aft sleeping areas at night. In the small cockpit, bench seating is built into the transom, and lounge seating on the flybridge will seat a couple of guests. Note that a hatch in the cockpit sole provides good access to the engines. A hard ride in a chop, twin 205hp stern-drives (among several engine choices) will cruise the 27 Santego at 19–20 knots and reach a top speed of just over 30 knots.

Carver 28 Mariner/Voyager

Length	28'0"	Fuel	150 gals.
Beam	11'1"	Water	51 gals.
Draft	2'10"	Waste	20 gals.
Weight	10,300#	Hull Type	Modified-V
Clearance	9'11"	Deadrise Aft	10°
Headroom	6'3"	Production	1983–90

One of Carver's most popular models during her production years, the Carver 28 is what a lot of brokers mean when they talk about a "lot of boat for the money." She was offered in Voyager or Mariner configurations, the difference being the choice of interior floorplans. The Mariner layout has the galley and head forward, whereas in the Voyager they're located aft, just inside the salon door. Notably, the Voyager had a lower helm and the Mariner didn't. Both models have plenty of seating (for a 28-footer) in the salon, the head compartments are surprisingly large, and the cockpit is roomy enough to handle a couple of deck chairs or light-tackle anglers. The flybridge on this boat is huge with seating for six and a table that converts into a full-width sun pad. (Underway, the weight of just a few people on the bridge will make her very tender—guaranteed!) Additional features include a bow pulpit, transom door, reasonably wide side decks, and a swim platform. If there's a downside to the Carver 28, it has to be her uneven fit and finish. She's also a harsh ride in a chop. Standard 220hp gas engines (with V-drives) will cruise the Carver 28 at 18 knots and reach 26–27 knots wide open.

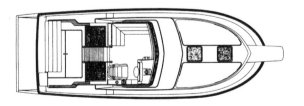

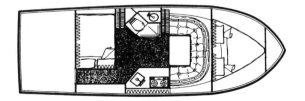

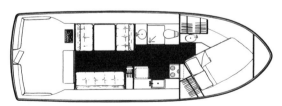

Mariner

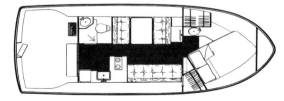

Voyager

See Page 303 for Pricing Information

See Page 303 for Pricing Information

FLYBRIDGE CRUISERS

Carver 280 Sedan

Length w/Pulpit . . . . 29'11"	Fuel . . . . 112 gals.
Hull Length . . . . 27'9"	Water . . . . 45 gals.
Beam . . . . 9'6"	Waste . . . . 20 gals.
Draft . . . . 2'4"	Hull Type . . . . Modified-V
Weight . . . . 9,778#	Deadrise Aft . . . . 15°
Clearance . . . . 8'0"	Production 1991–98

Although she was best known as the 280 Sedan, this model was originally introduced in 1991 as the Carver 26 Command Bridge, a good-looking small inland cruiser with clean-cut lines and a sporty profile. (She became the 280 Sedan in 1993 when Carver began including swim platforms in their length measurements, and in 1998 Carver called her the 280 Voyager.) Now out of production, the 280 was one of the smallest flybridge cruisers then (or since) available on the market. She's a beamy boat for her length and the house is placed well forward on the deck in order to maximize interior space. The cabin is bright and well arranged with wraparound windows, good headroom throughout, and plenty of seating. A lower helm was a popular option. Fortunately, Carver designers left some room in the floorplan for a fair-size cockpit that has enough room for a couple of deck chairs. Topside, the compact flybridge will seat two passengers aft of the helm. A relatively heavy boat for her size, single or twin sterndrives engine options were offered. Twin MerCruiser (or Volvo) V-6 sterndrives will cruise the Carver 280 Sedan/Voyager at a respectable 18–20 knots and reach 30+ wide open.

Carver 2866 Santa Cruz

Length . . . . 28'4"	Fuel . . . . 160 gals.
Beam . . . . 10'4"	Water . . . . 30 gals.
Draft . . . . 3'5"	Hull Type . . . . Modified-V
Weight . . . . 7,630#	Deadrise Aft . . . . 11°
Clearance . . . . 9'6"	Designer . . . . Carver
Cockpit . . . . 70 sq. ft.	Production 1976–82

Introduced in 1976, the Carver 2866 Santa Cruz was a low-cost coastal and inland fisherman with a small, efficiently arranged interior and a fairly spacious cockpit. Popular with light-tackle anglers, she was constructed on a solid fiberglass hull with moderate beam and a relatively flat 11 degrees of transom deadrise. The Santa Cruz was a relatively good-selling model for Carver and she remained pretty much unchanged during her production years with only minor cosmetic updates. Her single-level floorplan is set three steps down from the cockpit level and includes a V-berth forward, a convertible dinette to port, a complete galley, and a standup head with shower. Needless to say, the interior decor, with its inexpensive fabrics and cheap carpeting, is completed dated, and none of Carver's 1970s–1980s products were ever noted for their fine finish. Most 2866s were sold with a lower helm station. The engines are accessed below the cockpit, and the small flybridge has seating for two guests. Several inboard and sterndrive engine options were offered over the years. Among them, twin 230hp gas engines will cruise the 2866 Santa Cruz at 16–17 knots and attain a top speed of around 22 knots.

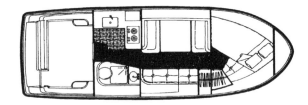

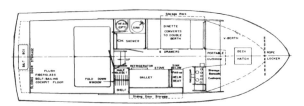

See Page 303 for Pricing Information

See Page 303 for Pricing Information

FLYBRIDGE CRUISERS

Carver 28 Sedan

Length Overall	30'6"	Fuel	150 gals.
Length w/Platform	30'6"	Water	51 gals.
Beam	11'10"	Hull Type	Modified-V
Draft	2'11"	Deadrise Aft	16°
Weight	12,500#	Designer	Carver
Clearance	9'1"	Production	1991–93

The Carver 28 Sedan—called the 300 Sedan in her final year of production—is one of the largest 28-foot flybridge boats built by any manufacturer in recent years. She was constructed on a solid fiberglass modified-V hull, and her wide 11-foot, 10-inch beam provides the added stability necessary in a small flybridge boat. Designed for coastal and inland waters, two floorplans were offered, one with a lower helm and a small head compartment and the other (less popular) with a large head forward but no lower helm. Berths are provided for up to six in either layout, and a solid door (rather than just a curtain) provides stateroom privacy. The generous interior accommodations of the Carver 28 result in a very small cockpit. The flybridge, however, is huge for a 28-footer with guest seating that converts into a sun lounge. Hatches in the cockpit sole provide access to the engines, and the V-drives are reached through the salon sole. Additional features include a bow pulpit, swim platform, transom door, and a handheld cockpit shower. Among several engine options, twin Crusader 260hp gas engines will cruise the Carver 28 Sedan at 17 knots and reach 26–27 knots top.

Carver 30/634/340 Santego

Length Overall	33'7"	Fuel	150 gals.
Length w/Platform	30'0"	Water	48 gals.
Beam	11'0"	Hull Type	Deep-V
Draft	3'1"	Deadrise Aft	19°
Weight	11,150#	Designer	Carver
Clearance	14'10"	Production	1988–94

The Carver 340 Santego (called the Carver 30 Santego in 1988–90 and the 634 Santego in 1991–92) was a popular model for Carver thanks primarily to a very expansive interior. She may not have been the best-looking boat in the marina, but when it came to accommodations the Santego stood head and shoulders above most of the competition. Her full-width salon—the Santego has no side decks—is huge for a boat this size with facing settees and excellent headroom. The entire floorplan is laid out on a single level that adds greatly to the impression of size and space. With her private stateroom and twin convertible dinettes, there are berths for six in the Santego. Topside, the flybridge is equally large for a 30-footer with seating for a small crowd. Note that a walk-through bridge (for improved foredeck access) was introduced in 1991. There's room in the cockpit for a couple of deck chairs, and hatches in the sole provide good access to the motors. On the downside, the Santego's bolt-on swim platform looks cheap. Available with several inboard or sterndrive engine options, twin 7.4-liter V-drive inboards will cruise at 22–23 knots (about 32 knots top). Sterndrive 5.7-liter engines will run a couple of knots slower.

FLYBRIDGE CRUISERS

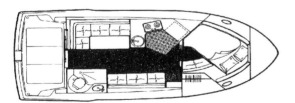

Lower Helm Floorplan

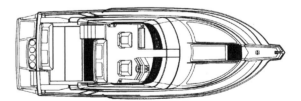

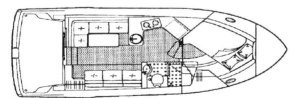

No Lower Helm

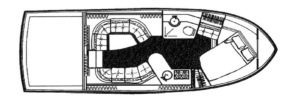

See Page 303 for Pricing Information

See Page 303 for Pricing Information

Carver 310 Santego

Carver 32 Convertible

Length w/Platform & Pulpit	33'5"	Fuel	130/164 gals.
Hull Length	31'3"	Water	66 gals.
Beam	11'0"	Waste	30 gals.
Draft	2'9"	Headroom	6'4"
Weight	12,500#	Hull Type	Modified-V
Clearance	9'10"	Production	1994–98

Length	32'0"	Fuel	220 gals.
Beam	11'7"	Water	84 gals.
Draft	2'10"	Waste	20 gals.
Weight	12,600#	Hull Type	Modified-V
Clearance	11'6"	Deadrise Aft	10°
Cockpit	56 sq. ft.	Production	1984–93

Entry-level buyers seeking a maxi-volume family cruiser with the amenities of a small apartment will find much to like in the 310 Santego. Introduced in 1994, she was built on a beamy modified-V hull with an integral swim platform, a bow pulpit, and relatively high freeboard. Note the absence of side decks; the Santego's full-width cabin is extended to the hullsides resulting in a notably spacious and wide-open interior. Stepping below from the small cockpit, the floorplan is arranged on a single level with the owner's stateroom forward and lounge seating on both sides of the salon. The starboard dinette converts to a double berth, and the portside lounge converts to an upper and lower bunk and includes a privacy curtain. Additional features include a doublewide helm seat with guest seating forward, good engine access, cockpit shower, transom door, and swim platform with storage lockers. Available with V-drive inboard or sterndrive power, twin 4.3-liter Volvo I/Os will cruise the 310 Santego at 18 knots (about 30 knots top), and 5.7-liter inboards cruise at 22 knots and reach 30 knots top. Note that the fuel capacity was increased in 1997 to 164 gallons.

Introduced in 1984, the 32 Convertible became one of Carver's best-selling boats in the 1980s thanks to an affordable price and a very innovative floorplan. Like most Carvers of her era, the 32 was built on a solid fiberglass hull with a wide beam, relatively high freeboard, and very little transom deadrise. Her conservative profile masks what was once considered a very unusual cabin layout. Where most convertibles have the engine room under the salon floor, in the 32 the engines are farther aft, under the cockpit sole. This allowed Carver designers to insert a rather spacious midcabin under the dinette, accessed from the galley, with a double berth and a large hanging locker. With that, the Carver 32 is an honest two-stateroom boat—rare in any 32-footer. There's a full-size refrigerator in the galley, and a stall shower is included in the head. Two lift-out hatches in the cockpit sole provide good service access to the engines. Additional features include a transom door, swim platform, flybridge seating for five, and a bow pulpit. A hard ride in a chop, Crusader 270hp V-drive gas engines will cruise the Carver 32 Convertible at 17 knots and reach a top speed of 26–27 knots. Note that she was called the 330 Convertible in 1993.

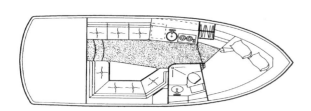

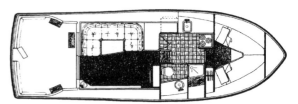

See Page 303 for Pricing Information

See Page 303 for Pricing Information

Carver 320 Voyager

Length w/Platform & Pulpit . . 35'0"	Fuel . . . . 188 gals.
Length w/Platform . . . . 32'2"	Water . . . . 56 gals.
Beam . . . . 11'10"	Waste . . . . 20 gals.
Draft . . . . 2'11"	Hull Type . . . . Modified-V
Weight . . . . 15,200#	Deadrise Aft . . . . 16°
Clearance . . . . 13'4"	Production 1994–99

Introduced in 1994, the Carver 320 Voyager was marketed as an inexpensive, entry-level family cruiser with a stylish profile and generous cabin accommodations. She was built on a solid fiberglass hull with a wide beam and a moderate 16 degrees of deadrise at the transom. The Voyager, which is a very roomy boat below, was originally offered with or without a lower helm; without the helm, there was room for a stall shower in the head. Either way, the stateroom has an offset double berth (and a privacy door), and the dinette and salon sofa convert into double berths. In 1996, Carver introduced a completely new two-stateroom floorplan with the head and galley aft in the salon and a mini-cabin beneath the elevated dinette. Outside, the integral swim platform features a built-in fender rack and a hideaway boarding ladder. Access to the engines and V-drives is via hatches in the cockpit sole. The oversize flybridge of the 320 Voyager has the helm forward and guest seating for five. The side decks are narrow and foredeck access is heel-to-toe. Standard 350-cid Crusader gas engines will cruise at 17 knots and deliver a top speed of 27–28 knots.

Carver 32/330 Mariner

Length Overall . . . . 35'5"	Fuel . . . . 192 gals.
Hull Length . . . . 32'3"	Water . . . . 92 gals.
Beam . . . . 12'4"	Hull Type . . . . Modified-V
Draft . . . . 2'9"	Deadrise Aft . . . . 6°
Weight . . . . 12,000#	Designer . . . . R. MacNeill
Clearance . . . . 10'10"	Production 1985–96

The Carver 32 Mariner (called the 330 Mariner from 1994–96) was introduced in 1985 as a downsized version of the larger 36 Mariner, a very popular model for Carver. While it's true that the 32 Mariner has drawn a lot of abuse over the years for her ungainly appearance, over 650 of these boats were sold during a decade-long production run, which says a lot about Carver's ability to please the public. The great appeal of the 32 Mariner is the enormous single-level, step-down interior that successfully uses every possible square inch of space available in the hull. The result is a truly social boat with an apartment-size salon featuring facing settees. (Natural lighting is poor, however, because the cabin windows are so tiny.) A ladder in the salon provides convenient inside access to the flybridge, which is another huge entertainment center in itself. Additional features include a centerline transom door, bow pulpit, swim platform, and a foredeck sun pad. Standard 270hp gas engines (with V-drives) are located beneath the cockpit. A thirsty and decidedly hard-riding boat in a chop, the Carver 32 Mariner burns around 20 gph at a modest cruising speed of 16 knots. The top speed is around 25–26 knots.

FLYBRIDGE CRUISERS

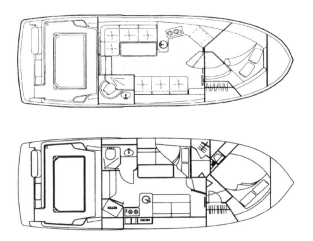

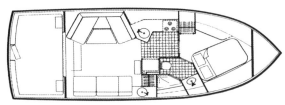

See Page 304 for Pricing Information

See Page 304 for Pricing Information

Carver 33 Mariner

Length	32'6"	Water	75 gals.
Beam	12'0"	Cockpit	NA
Draft	2'6"	Hull Type	Modified-V
Weight	11,620#	Deadrise Aft	NA
Clearance	NA	Designer	Carver
Fuel	145 gals.	Production	1975–84

Beginning with her introduction in 1975, the 33 Mariner was one of Carver's more popular models for nearly a decade. Known primarily for her oversized interior and boxy appearance, the original 33 Mariner was built with a plywood superstructure (1975–76), while later models are all fiberglass in construction. Stepping down into the wide-open cabin, one is immediately impressed with the spacious dimensions of the combined salon and galley area. Designed for family cruising, the Mariner has a separate stall shower in her double-entry head compartment, facing salon settees, and a unique bulkhead ladder in the salon for indoor access to the flybridge. (A cockpit ladder is available as well, but the interior passage is a more convenient and quicker route.) The Mariner's flybridge is huge for a boat this size with an L-shaped lounge that converts into an outdoor double berth when the weather is right. Note that the 33's side decks are practically nonexistent. On the downside, the Mariner was an inexpensive boat and fit and finish left a lot to be desired. Several V-drive engine options were offered over the years, and most provide cruising speeds from 17–20 knots and top speeds to around 27 knots.

Carver 33 Super Sport

Length w/Platform	37'3"	Fuel	311 gals.
Beam	13'1"	Water	78 gals.
Draft	3'1"	Waste	37 gals.
Weight	21,753#	Hull Type	Modified-V
Clearance	14'8"	Deadrise Aft	11.5°
Headroom	6'6"	Production	2005–Current

Carver introduced the 33 Super Sport in 2005 in an effort to recapture some of the entry-level boaters the company forfeited in previous years with their move into the big-boat market. This is the smallest model in the current Carver fleet, and while she's not exactly inexpensive, the 33 does offer the features many are looking for in a small flybridge cruiser. Chief among her attributes is a spacious and exceedingly comfortable interior. The large, full-beam salon maximizes interior volume, and a convertible dinette, nicely equipped galley (with upright refrigerator and Corian counter), and a separate stall shower in the head make this a very livable boat for the cruising family. In the cockpit, molded sidedeck steps and molded bridge steps make getting around the Super Sport easy. A transom door opens to an extended swim platform deep enough to carry a dinghy. Additional features include a large engine room (reached via a hatch in the salon sole), generous cabin storage, radar arch, and good helm visibility both fore and aft. On the downside, the Super Sport's modified-V hull isn't too fond of a chop. Crusader 320hp gas engines will cruise at 18 knots (26–28 knots top.)

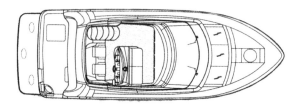

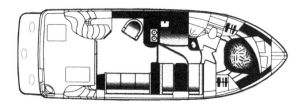

Carver 33 Voyager

Length	32'9"	Fuel	200 gals.
Beam	12'0"	Cockpit	45 sq. ft.
Draft	2'3"	Hull Type	Modified-V
Weight	13,000#	Deadrise Aft	NA
Clearance	11'9"	Designer	Carver
Water	70 gals.	Production	1977–81

The Carver 33 Voyage packed a lot of living space into her 33-foot by 12-foot fiberglass hull—berths for six, a full galley, an enclosed head, and upper and lower steering stations. When all this is shoehorned into a 33-foot boat, some concessions are unavoidable. In the Voyager's case there are two: since the forward cabin has been stretched as much as possible, there is no room for a chain locker in the forepeak; and with the deckhouse carried well aft, there's not much space for a cockpit. On balance, however, the Voyager succeeded in delivering family-sized accommodations at a very affordable price. The lower helm was standard; the galley included a full-size refrigerator; and a separate shower stall is fitted into the head compartment. While the cockpit is indeed small, it's still large enough for a couple of deck chairs. The side decks are wide enough for safe bow access, and the helm is forward on the flybridge with guest seating for three. Several engine choices were offered in the Carver 33 Voyager over the years, all with V-drives. The cruising speed with the popular 270hp Crusader gas engines is 16–17 knots, and the top speed is around 24 knots.

Carver 350 Voyager

Length w/Pulpit & Platform	39'0"	Fuel	280 gals.
Hull Length	33'10"	Water	100 gals.
Beam	13'3"	Headroom	6'5"
Draft	2'7"	Hull Type	Modified-V
Weight	17,000#	Deadrise Aft	11°
Clearance	11'0"	Production	1992–94

The Carver 350 Voyager (called the 34 Voyager when she was introduced in 1992) was the forerunner of the popular 370/374 Voyager built from 1993 through 2002. Built on a solid fiberglass modified-V hull with a wide beam, the 350 will appeal to those who appreciate the versatility of a raised pilothouse layout—even a small one. With both galley and dinette on the main level, the Voyager still manages to include two private staterooms forward and a comfortable salon in a rather expansive and well-arranged floorplan. This is a big interior for a 34-footer with good visibility from the lower helm and large wraparound windows in the salon. Another attraction of the 350 is her spacious flybridge with seating for several guests. The cockpit, on the other hand, is quite small with room for just a couple of deck chairs. Additional features include a spacious flybridge with seating for six (including a sun lounge), transom door, a stall shower in the head, an optional lower helm, and a handy pass-through from the galley to the bridge. Standard 300hp Crusader gas engines will cruise at 18–19 knots (about 28 knots top), and optional 225hp Volvo diesels will cruise at 20 knots and reach a top speed of around 23 knots.

With Optional Lower Helm

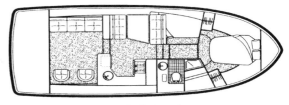

Standard Floorplan

Carver 34/638/380 Santego

Length w/Platform & Pulpit	41'8"	Fuel	216 gals.
Length w/Platform	38'5"	Water	90 gals.
Beam	13'2"	Waste	37 gals.
Draft	3'4"	Hull Type	Deep-V
Weight	19,300#	Deadrise Aft	19°
Clearance	14'8"	Production	1989–2002

Introduced as the 34 Santego in 1989, Carver's marketing gurus confused everyone by calling her the 638 Santego in 1992 before finally settling on the 380 Santego designation in 1993. This was a popular boat in the Carver fleet for many years thanks to her spacious condo-style interior and a very competitive pricing structure. The Santego's expansive salon—with facing wraparound settees and twin dinettes—create the kind of party-time accommodations seldom encountered in a boat this size. A pair of full-height sliding glass cockpit doors provides an abundance of exterior lighting, and the wide-open expanse of a single-level floorplan has to be seen. There's seating for a crowd on the huge flybridge where concealed steps in the windshield fold out to provide a walkway to the foredeck. Hatches in the cockpit sole provide good access to the motors and V-drives, and there's built-in lounge seating in the small cockpit. On the downside, Carver never replaced the Santego's bolt-on swim platform with a more stylish integral platform. A surprisingly good-riding boat in a chop, standard 7.4-liter gas engines will cruise at 18 knots and reach 26–27 knots top.

Carver 350 Mariner

Length w/Platform	36'7"	Water	75 gals.
Beam	12'9"	Waste	20 gals.
Draft	3'1"	Headroom	6'3"
Weight	18,800#	Hull Type	Modified-V
Clearance, Arch	14'2"	Deadrise Aft	NA
Fuel	246 gals.	Production	1997–2003

Introduced in 1997, the Carver 350 Mariner is aimed at first-time buyers whose desire for interior volume overwhelms any concerns they might have for aesthetics. Indeed, the Mariner is a truly unattractive boat with a full-bodied profile that might best be described as bloated. That said, the Mariner is notable for her expansive single-level interior as well as her roomy flybridge with its lounge seating for several guests. Instead of conventional side decks, wide walkways sweep up from the deck to the bridge, a design that makes it easy to get around the boat. Below, the Mariner's full-beam salon, accessed through a double sliding door or directly from the bridge via a hatch and ladder, is remarkable for its size and comfort. A sofa and convertible dinette will seat eight, and the full galley offers all the comforts of home. The master stateroom has an angled double berth and direct access to the head, which has a separate shower stall. The engine compartment, which is under the cockpit sole, is a tight fit. Note that the foredeck bench seat converts into a sun pad. No racehorse, twin 320hp V-drive gas engines will cruise at 14–15 knots and reach a top speed of around 20 knots.

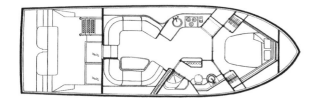

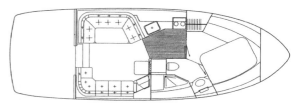

Carver 36 Mariner (1984–88)

Length Overall	35'7"	Fuel	274 gals.
Length WL	31'4"	Water	103 gals.
Beam	12'6"	Hull Type	Modified-V
Draft	3'2"	Deadrise Aft	8°
Weight	19,500#	Designer	R. MacNeill
Clearance	13'6"	Production	1984–88

The cavernous interior of the Carver 36 Mariner comes as a surprise to most first-time observers. Her profile may be a little hard on the eye, but the spacious belowdecks accommodations and huge flybridge of the 36 Mariner have seldom been matched in other boats her size. An outstanding design from the standpoint of space engineering, the Mariner was a very successful model for Carver in spite of her Clorox-bottle appearance. She was built on the same "dual mode" hull originally used for the Carver 36 Aft Cabin—a cross between a conventional modified-V planing hull and a slower semi-displacement design said to provide efficient performance at both low and high speeds. Inside, her wide-open cabin is arranged on a single level, a couple of steps down from the cockpit. Using the full width of the boat's hull, the Mariner's vast interior can handle the demands of a very large family. Note that the side decks actually lead around the command bridge. Additional features include a foredeck sun pad, a salon ladder leading up to the bridge (very convenient), and a fairly roomy cockpit with a transom door. Performance is not terribly impressive: 15–16 knots at cruise and around 25 knots at the top with standard 350hp Crusader V-drive gas engines.

Carver 360 Sport Sedan

Length w/Platform	37'8"	Fuel	280 gals.
Beam	13'2"	Water	75 gals.
Draft	2'7"	Waste	25 gals.
Weight	24,746#	Hull Type	Modified-V
Clearance, Arch	14'6"	Deadrise Aft	14°
Max Headroom	6'5"	Production	2003–Current

The mission of the Carver 360 Sport Sedan is to pack as much living space as possible into a compact yacht. In that regard, she achieves her purpose, albeit at the expense of aesthetics. Sporting a full-size cockpit and a huge swim platform, the 360 Sport Sedan is a versatile cruising yacht whose expansive two-stateroom interior is her most appealing feature. The main cabin is arranged with a unique raised dinette/lounge forward with Ultraleather seating, and all bulkheads, counters, drawers and furniture are high-gloss cherrywood. A curved staircase below the dinette leads down to the aft guest stateroom with convertible twin berths, and the forward stateroom with an island berth. The hardwood floor in the galley area is a nice touch, and the tiered windows admit plenty of natural lighting into the salon. Getting around the Sport Sedan is easy: in each forward corner of the cockpit, a five-step stairway leads to the raised side decks while an additional staircase takes you to the bridge. Topside, the helm is on the centerline flanked by companion seats. Among a wide range of engine options, twin 320hp gas inboards will cruise at 18 knots and top in the low 20s. Note that the engine room is a tight fit.

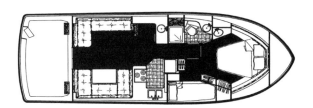

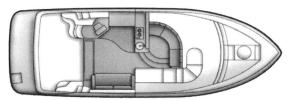

Main Deck Plan

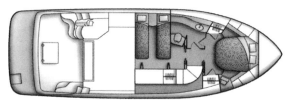

Lower-Level Plan

See Page 304 for Pricing Information

See Page 304 for Pricing Information

FLYBRIDGE CRUISERS

Carver 38 Santego

Length Overall	37'6"	Water	92 gals.
Length WL	32'7"	Fuel	265 gals.
Beam	14'0"	Hull Type	Modified-V
Draft	3'5"	Deadrise Aft	12°
Weight	19,000#	Designer	R. MacNeill
Clearance	14'3"	Production	1988–90

Big brother to the 380 Santego and featuring an almost-identical floorplan, the Carver 38 Santego was one of the early sedan bridge designs that have since become so popular with entry-level buyers. (Note that a later 380 Santego model was built from 1993 to 2002.) Like most Carvers of her era, she was constructed on a moderate-deadrise hull with balsa coring in the hullsides and a solid fiberglass bottom. The Santego is a great boat for entertaining and she has one of the most user-friendly bridge layouts imaginable. Guest seating surrounds the elevated helm console, and a cutout forward reveals a set of molded steps leading to the foredeck—a real necessity since there are no side decks. Below, the Santego's single-level interior uses the full width of the hull to create a cavernous main salon. A two-stateroom floorplan was introduced in 1990 as an alternative to the original single-stateroom layout. The cockpit is roomy enough, but the bolt-on swim platform looks like a cheap afterthought. For power, the Santego uses 454-cid gas engines (with V-drives) located beneath the cockpit sole. Cruising speed is a lackluster 14–15 knots, and the top speed is around 24 knots.

Carver 410 Sport Sedan

Length w/Platform	46'4"	Fuel	400 gals.
Hull Length	41'0"	Water	95 gals.
Beam	13'11"	Waste	75 gals.
Draft	2'8"	Hull Type	Modified-V
Weight	31,625#	Deadrise Aft	NA
Clearance, Arch	19'2"	Production	2002–03

The 410 Sport Sedan is a lot of boat for the money if you like expansive accommodations. The interior is larger than most 40-foot sedans (especially in the salon), and while the styling may have its detractors, the 410 manages to deliver the features most cruisers are looking for at an affordable price. Built on a modified-V hull with generous beam and cored hullsides, the wide-open spaces in the Sport Sedan's salon are the result of raising the side decks to near-flybridge level. A curved settee is to starboard in the salon, the galley is just opposite, and an aft-facing dinette is forward. (A lower helm was optional.) There are two staterooms and two heads on the lower level, and a hatch in the salon sole provides access to the engine room. In the cockpit, molded steps to port lead around the house to the bow while starboardside steps lead up to the flybridge with its wet bar, circular lounge, and three helm chairs. Additional features include an integral swim platform, transom door, radar arch, and an entertainment center. Volvo 375hp gas engines will cruise at 15 knots, and optional 370hp Volvo diesels cruise at 18 knots (24–25 knots top). Note the short 2-year production run.

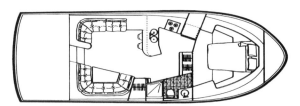

Standard Single-Stateroom Floorplan

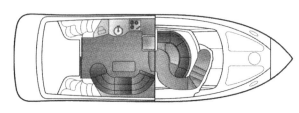

Optional Two-Stateroom Floorplan (1990 Only)

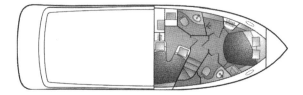

See Page 304 for Pricing Information

See Page 305 for Pricing Information

Carver 42 Cockpit MY

Length	42'0"	Water	170 gals.
Beam	15'0"	Headroom	6'5"
Draft	3'6"	Hull Type	Modified-V
Weight	23,150#	Deadrise Aft	12°
Clearance	16'6"	Designer	R. MacNeill
Fuel	400 gals.	Production	1986–88

Despite the name, the Carver 42 Cockpit Motor Yacht is actually a flybridge sedan with a rather aggressive profile (note the rakish cabin windows and reverse arch) and generous interior accommodations. Following by a year the successful introduction of Carver's 42 Motor Yacht—and using the same moderate-deadrise hull—the 42 Cockpit MY turned out to be a market disappointment, and she was withdrawn from production in 1988. (There's a limited market out there for 42-foot sedans, as buyers in this size range tend to favor the privacy of an aft-cabin layout.) Two floorplans were offered in the 42 CMY: a single-stateroom arrangement with a dinette, and the more popular two-stateroom layout without a dinette. The interior woodwork is teak, and the stylish hardware and fixtures in the galley and heads were quite impressive by 1980s standards. The cockpit is spacious enough for some light-tackle fishing, and the flybridge has a raised command console with an overhead electronics box built into the radar arch. Standard 454-cid gas engines cruise at a sluggish 13–14 knots cruise (about 23 knots top), and optional Cat 375hp diesels will cruise easily at 20 knots, reaching 23–24 knots wide open.

Chris Craft 292 Sunbridge

Length	28'11"	Water	25 gals.
Beam	10'9"	Cockpit	NA
Draft	2'3"	Hull Type	Modified-V
Weight	7,800#	Deadrise Aft	NA
Clearance	9'4"	Designer	Chris Craft
Fuel	125 gals.	Production	1986–89

Introduced as a replacement for the aging 28 Catalina—and built on the 28 Catalina's hull—the Chris Craft 292 Sunbridge is a versatile family boat with a still-attractive profile and an unusually spacious cockpit for a 29-foot cruiser. (Note that the deckhouse is set well forward on the deck to allow space aft for the large cockpit.) The hull is solid fiberglass, and a wide beam results in a fairly roomy interior. The single-level floorplan is almost the same as the older 28 Catalina with berths for six and good headroom throughout. The (very) small galley will handle most basic food-prep necessities, and the standup head compartment is equipped with a shower. Topside, the flybridge has seating for the helmsman and up to four guests. Lift-out hatches in the cockpit sole provide good access to the engine compartment. Topside, the flybridge is arranged with the helm forward and seating for four. An efficient performer with a pair of 220hp Crusader gas engines, the Chris Craft 292 Sunbridge will cruise easily at 19 knots at just 17 gph—excellent economy indeed. The top speed is about 28–29 knots depending upon the load.

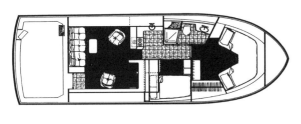

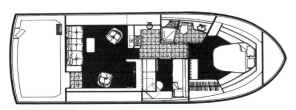

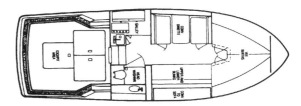

See Page 305 for Pricing Information

See Page 307 for Pricing Information

Chris Craft 320 Amerosport Sedan

Length . . . . 31'11"	Fuel . . . . 200 gals.
Beam . . . . 11'11"	Water . . . . 50 gals.
Draft . . . . 2'8"	Hull Type . . . . Modified-V
Weight . . . . 12,000#	Deadrise Aft . . . . NA
Clearance . . . . 10'9"	Designer . . . . S. Leonard
Cockpit . . . . NA	Production 1987–90

An inexpensive but rather distinctive boat with a rakish profile and aggressive styling, the 320 Amerosport (note that she was called the 322 Catalina when she was introduced in 1990) had a moderately successful four-year production run before Chris Craft dropped her from the lineup in 1991. She was built on a conventional modified-V hull with solid fiberglass construction and a relatively wide beam. Inside, the Amerosport's midcabin floorplan is arranged with a second "stateroom" tucked below the elevated salon dinette. A lower helm was optional, and the wide beam and 360-degree cabin windows make for a spacious and wide-open interior. The original teak woodwork was updated in 1990 to light oak. Outside, the cockpit comes with built-in bench seating at the transom, and the flybridge has the helm forward with guest seating aft. Note the bolt-on reverse swim platform—it makes the boat look cheap. Additional features include fairly wide side decks, a walk-through transom gate, and a separate stall shower in the head. With a pair of 270hp gas engines the Amerosport Sedan will cruise about 19 knots and reach 26 knots top.

Chris Craft 333 Sedan

Length . . . . 33'0"	Headroom . . . . 6'3"
Beam . . . . 12'1"	Cockpit . . . . NA
Draft . . . . 2'9"	Hull Type . . . . Deep-V
Weight . . . . 13,000#	Deadrise Aft . . . . 18°
Fuel . . . . 250 gals.	Designer . . . . Chris Craft
Water . . . . 50 gals.	Production 1981–87

Sharing the same good-running deep-V hull used in the production of the 332 Express, the Chris Craft 333 Sedan is a traditional flybridge cruiser with a distinctive profile and an unusually open cabin layout. Construction is solid fiberglass, and a relatively wide beam creates a roomy interior with berths for six and good headroom throughout. The floorplan of the Chris 333 is arranged with the galley and dinette forward, a few steps down from the salon. A lower helm was standard, and a double berth is found in the single stateroom. While the cockpit isn't large enough for a fighting chair and includes no livewell or fish box, it's still big enough for a couple of light-tackle anglers. Topside, the small flybridge will seat three on a single bench seat. In 1984, the deckhouse profile was redesigned for a more modern appearance, and in 1986—the last year of production—a revised flybridge relocated the helm farther aft and added bench seating forward of the console. A good rough-water performer, standard 350hp Crusader gas engines will cruise the Chris 333 Sedan comfortably at 20 knots and deliver a top speed in the neighborhood of 30 knots.

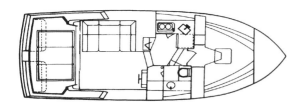

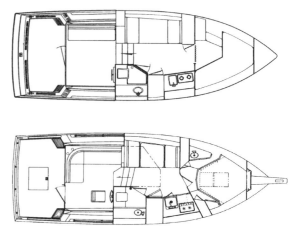

Chris Craft 421 Continental

Length . . . . 43'3"	Water . . . . 108 gals.
Beam . . . . 13'6"	Headroom . . . . 6'4"
Draft . . . . 3'2"	Hull Type . . . . Modified-V
Weight . . . . 18,700#	Deadrise Aft . . . . 17°
Clearance . . . . 13'11"	designer . . . . Chris Craft
Fuel . . . . 350 gals.	Production 1993–94

A very unusual design with her sloped-foredeck profile and semi-circular cockpit, the Chris 421 Continental was a budget-priced family cruiser for those who appreciated the Chris Craft approach to unorthodox (some might say ridiculous) styling. She was built on a solid fiberglass, modified-V hull with moderate beam and prop pockets to reduce her shaft angles and draft requirements. The two-stateroom floorplan is arranged on a single level with excellent headroom and plenty of overhead lighting to compensate for the absence of cabin windows. The oversize galley may occasionally be useful, but it eats up cabin space that might otherwise be used for additional seating. If the interior is a little small for a 42-footer, the cockpit dimensions are relatively spacious, although the oval transom design still consumes a lot of cockpit space. The engine compartment (beneath the cockpit sole) is a tight fit. Additional features include a spacious flybridge, molded foredeck seating, and a big swim platform. Lasting only two years in production (thankfully), standard 300hp V-drive gas inboards will cruise the Chris 421 around 14–15 knots, and optional 320hp Volvo diesels cruise around 21 knots.

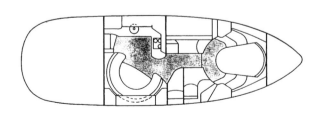

Cruisers 288/298 Villa Vee; 2980 Esprit

Length Overall . . . . 28'8"	Fuel . . . . 150/180 gals.
Length WL . . . . 24'11"	Water . . . . 45 gals.
Beam . . . . 10'8"	Hull Type . . . . Modified-V
Draft . . . . 2'9"	Deadrise Aft . . . . 17°
Weight . . . . 9,500#	Designer . . . . Jim Wynne
Clearance . . . . 9'5"	Production 1978–90

Introduced in 1978 as the 288 Villa Vee, called the 298 Villa Vee from 1984–87 and the 2980 Esprit from 1988 through 1990, this small flybridge cruiser was a remarkably popular boat for Cruisers through more than a decade of production. She was built on a solid fiberglass hull with moderate beam and prop pockets to reduce the shaft angles. Several single-stateroom interiors were offered during her production years, all with the galley down and a dinette in the salon. A lower helm was a popular option since many of these boats were sold in northern, cold-weather climates. While the cabin accommodations might best be described as compact, the cockpit is quite spacious for a boat of this type with built-in stern seating and wrap-around handrails. The side decks are narrow so bow access must be undertaken with care. Topside, a swivel helm seat and L-shaped settee will seat up to four persons. Note that a bow pulpit, teak interior woodwork and a swim platform were standard. Among many engine options offered in the Villa Vee, twin 230hp gas engines will cruise at 18 knots (25 knots top), and 260hp engines will cruise at 20 knots and reach 28–29 knots top.

Original Floorplan

Mid-1980s Floorplan

See Page 308 for Pricing Information

See Page 310 for Pricing Information

FLYBRIDGE CRUISERS

FLYBRIDGE CRUISERS

Length	32'10"	Water	70 gals.
Beam	11'10"	Headroom	6'4"
Draft	2'10"	Hull Type	Modified-V
Weight	13,000#	Deadrise Aft	18°
Clearance	11'6"	Designer	Jim Wynne
Fuel	300 gals.	Production	1985–94

Length w/Extended Platform	39'3"	Headroom	6'6"
Length without Platform	37'4"	Fuel	300 gals.
Beam	13'0"	Water	70 gals.
Draft	3'5"	Hull Type	Modified-V
Weight	18,200#	Deadrise Aft	16°
Clearance	13'7"	Production	1996–99

The Cruisers 3380 Esprit (called the 338 Chateau Vee in 1985–87) was a popular model for Cruisers and remained in production for nearly a decade before being retired in 1994. She was built on a solid fiberglass, modified-V hull with prop pockets, and her rakish profile was enhanced by some bold hull graphics and a flybridge that extended aft over the cockpit. The Esprit's midcabin, galley-down interior is arranged with double berths in both staterooms, and the head compartment features a separate stall shower. The U-shaped settee in the salon converts to sleep two adults, and a lower helm station was a popular option. There's a full-size refrigerator in the galley, but not much counter space. Topside, the cockpit comes with built-in bench seating at the corners, and the oversized flybridge has the helm forward with a wraparound seating aft. Additional features include a molded bow pulpit, sliding cabin windows, teak interior trimwork, cockpit engine access, and a swim platform. A good open-water performer with a comfortable ride, the 3380 Esprit will cruise at 20 knots and reach a top speed of around 30 knots with a pair of 340hp Crusader gas engines.

A distinctively styled flybridge cruiser with a very rakish profile, perhaps the most notable design feature of the Cruisers 3580/3585 (same boat, different floorplans) is the molded-in flybridge steps that replace the traditional ladder in the cockpit. This was, back in the mid-1990s, an innovative design in a boat of this type, and while these steps eat up some valuable cockpit space, there's no disputing the fact that they make bridge access a whole lot more civilized. Built on a conventional modified-V hull with cored hullsides and prop pockets to reduce shaft angles, the original 3580 interior has the galley down with an optional lower helm (with poor outside visibility), while the newer 3585 floorplan introduced in 1998 has an elevated lower helm as standard with the galley forward in the salon. Both floorplans are arranged with a small midcabin that extends under the salon. Note that the side decks are quite narrow and the engine compartment, beneath the cockpit sole, is a tight fit. An optional extended swim platform is wide enough for a personal watercraft. Standard 7.4-liter V-drive gas inboards will cruise the Cruisers 3580/3585 at 18 knots and reach 26–27 knots wide open.

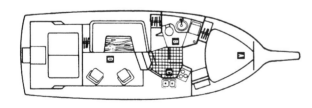

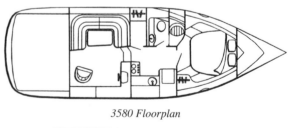

3580 Floorplan

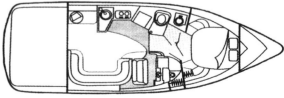

3585 Floorplan

See Page 310 for Pricing Information

See Page 310 for Pricing Information

Cruisers 4280/4285 Express Bridge

Length . . . . 42'0"	Water . . . . 160 gals.
Beam . . . . 14'6"	Hull Type . . . . Modified-V
Draft . . . . 3'6"	Deadrise Aft . . . . 16°
Weight . . . . 27,000#	Designer . . . . Jim Wynne
Clearance . . . . 13'3"	Production, 4280 1988–94
Fuel . . . . 400 gals.	Production, 4285 1990–95

For those who enjoy their socializing on a grand scale, the Cruisers 4280/4285 Express Bridge is loaded with features not usually expected in a midsize cruising yacht. Both the 4280 and 4285 look identical on the outside with their high-freeboard hulls and prominent arches, but they're entirely different boats on the inside. The 4280 has a two-stateroom layout with two heads and a small galley, while the 4285 has a more expansive single-stateroom interior with a large galley and wide-open salon. (Note that Cruisers updated the original 4280 layout in 1992.) Both of these floorplans are laid out on a single level which makes them appear unusually spacious indeed. Topside, there's seating for a small crowd on the massive flybridge, the hands-down social focus of the boat. Molded steps on both sides of the cockpit lead up to the bridge as well as leading directly out to the foredeck. The modified-V hull of the 4280/4285 is fully cored with prop pockets for reduced shaft angles. A real party barge, standard 350hp gas engines provide a sluggish 13 knots at cruise (about 20 knots top), and optional 375hp Cats or 400hp Detroit 6V53s will cruise at 20–21 knots with a top speed of around 24 knots.

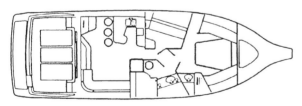

4280 Floorplan

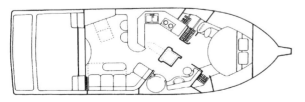

4285 Floorplan

See Page 311 for Pricing Information

Eastbay 40/43 Flybridge

Length . . . . 43'0"	Water . . . . 110 gals.
Beam . . . . 13'4"	Headroom . . . . 6'6"
Draft . . . . 3'8"	Hull Type . . . . Deep-V
Weight . . . . 33,000#	Deadrise Aft . . . . 18°
Clearance . . . . 16'6"	Production, 40 1996–97
Fuel . . . . 450 gals.	Production, 43 1998–2004

The Eastbay 43 Flybridge is an extended-cockpit version of the original Eastbay 40 Sedan of which 20 were built from 1996–97. She's a handsome Downeast-style cruiser whose upscale interior and excellent performance are a departure from the traditional go-slow Grand Banks product of old. The Eastbay's deep-V hull employs prop pockets to reduce shaft angles, a feature that also allows for relatively shallow-water running. The standard two-stateroom, galley-up floorplan has a single head with a stall shower, and an alternate two-stateroom floorplan has the galley down and two smaller heads. Typical of any Grand Banks product, the Eastbay's traditional full teak interior is meticulously crafted throughout. Note that the newer 43 with its enlarged cockpit is a better-looking and more balanced boat than the original Eastbay 40 with the added advantage of additional fuel capacity. Standard features include wide walkaround decks, a teak cockpit sole, radar mast, transom door and shower, and a well-arranged flybridge. Not inexpensive, twin 300hp Cat diesels will cruise at 18–20 knots (about 22 knots top), and optional 375hp Cats will cruise at 22–24 knots and deliver a top speed in the high 20s.

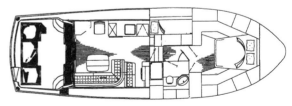

Standard Floorplan

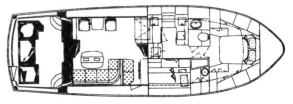

Optional Layout

See Page 318 for Pricing Information

FLYBRIDGE CRUISERS

Hatteras 36 Sedan Cruiser

Length . . . . 36'6"	Water. . . . . 115 gals.
Beam . . . . 13'7"	Cockpit . . . . NA
Draft. 3'9"	Hull Type. . . . . Modified-V
Weight. . . . . 25,500#	Deadrise Aft . . . . 18°
Clearance. . . . . 12'6"	Designer. . . . . Jim Wynne
Fuel . . . . 355 gals.	Production 1986–87

Not remembered as a particularly successful model (production lasted only two years), the Hatteras 36 Sedan is basically the same boat as the Hatteras 36 Convertible (1983–87) but with a larger interior and smaller cockpit dimensions. Hull construction is solid fiberglass, and the hull is designed with moderate beam, a shallow keel, and prop pockets. Two mid-galley interior layouts were available in the 36 Sedan: a dinette floorplan with a single stateroom, and a two-stateroom arrangement without the dinette. Either way, the head compartment is very large and includes a separate stall shower. The interior is finished with traditional teak woodwork throughout, and it's notable that a lower helm option was never offered. While the salon is quite roomy for a 36-footer, the cockpit is too small for any serious fishing activities. Additional features include a big flybridge, good engine access, and fairly wide side decks. An unexciting performer with standard 350hp Crusader gas engines, the Hatteras 36 Sedan will cruise at 14 knots and reach a top speed in the neighborhood of 23 knots. Diesels were optional and faster.

Hi-Star 44 Convertible

Length . . . . 43'9"	Water. . . . . 250 gals.
Beam . . . . 15'2"	Cockpit . . . . 65 sq. ft.
Draft. 3'6"	Hull Type. . . . . Modified-V
Weight. . . . . 33,000#	Deadrise Aft . . . . 16°
Clearance . . . . NA	Designer . . . . C. Chang
Fuel . . . . 500 gals.	Production 1986–92

The Hi-Star 44 is a generic Asian-built flybridge sedan whose conservative styling masks an unusually spacious interior. While Hi-Star never became one of the big-name Taiwan imports, their boats were notable for excellent engineering and above-average construction features. With her extended deckhouse and small cockpit, the 44 makes no pretense of being a fishing boat. Instead, the emphasis is on interior volume, and it's no exaggeration to say that her two-stateroom floorplan is among the largest to be found in any boat her size. The galley is forward in the salon, opposite the standard lower helm, and the master stateroom is huge. Like most Asian boats, the interior of the Hi-Star is solid teak, which—by today's decor standards, at least—is a little boring. A roomy and well-arranged engine room is accessed by lifting the steps forward of the galley. As previously noted, the small cockpit is better suited to the demands of cruisers rather than anglers. (The factory tackle center is small, poorly designed, and best suited for storage.) Topside, the large flybridge is arranged with bench seating forward of the helm. A good performer, 375hp Cats will cruise at 18 knots cruise and top out in the low 20s.

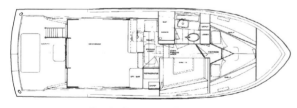

Single-Stateroom Floorplan

Twin-Stateroom Floorplan

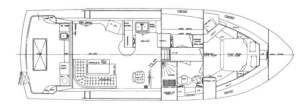

See Page 319 for Pricing Information

See Page 322 for Pricing Information

Hi-Star 48 Convertible

Length . . . . 47'9"	Water . . . . 250 gals.
Beam . . . . 15'2"	Cockpit . . . . 108 sq. ft.
Draft . . . . 3'8"	Hull Type . . . . Modified-V
Weight . . . . 37,000#	Deadrise Aft . . . . 16°
Clearance . . . . 13'6"	Designer . . . . Chas. Chang
Fuel . . . . 500 gals.	Production 1986–92

Taiwan builders have never been successful in building a convertible sportfishing boat that met with the approval of serious anglers. Indeed, most convertible designs from Asian yards have been more oriented to the cruising market with only a passing nod to fishability. Such a boat is the Hi-Star 48, a well-built flybridge cruiser whose roomy interior, quality construction, and efficient hull are her most notable design characteristics. Her expansive two-stateroom floorplan is arranged with the galley and salon on a single level and separated by a stylish, drum-shaped serving counter. A lower helm was standard, and wraparound cabin windows provide plenty of natural lighting. Forward, a centerline double berth is located in the very large master stateroom, and over/under bunks are fitted in the guest cabin. Note that a double-entry stall shower serves both heads—an innovative and space-saving feature. The superb teak interior joinerwork and well-designed engine room are impressive. Note also the wide side decks. With standard 375hp Cat diesels, the Hi-Star 48 will cruise at 18 knots and reach a top speed of around 22 knots—good performance indeed for relatively small engines.

Hinckley Talaria 44 Flybridge

Length Overall . . . . 44'10"	Water . . . . 100 gals.
Length WL . . . . 41'0"	Max Headroom . . . . 6'6"
Beam . . . . 13'6"	Hull . . . . Modified-V
Draft . . . . 2'3"	Deadrise Aft . . . . 16.5°
Weight . . . . 29,000#	Designer . . . . Bruce King
Fuel . . . . 500 gals.	Production 2003–Current

The Talaria 44 Flybridge is yet another display of Hinckley's commitment to boatbuilding excellence. This is a stunningly beautiful yacht whose blend of sensuous styling and jet-powered propulsion is as distinctive as it is unique. The heart of the 44 Flybridge is her elegant, enclosed pilothouse with its varnished cherry woodwork, teak-and-holly floor, and leather helm seat. Curved glass windows enclose the aft end of the pilothouse, and visibility from the lower helm is excellent is all directions. While Hinckley allows for several interior variations, the standard floorplan is arranged with the galley down, a split head, and two double staterooms. (Note that the shower compartment in this layout does not offer private access from the master stateroom.) The Hinckley's spacious cockpit includes built-in seating for several guests as well as a centerline transom door and six-step bridge ladder. What really sets the 44 apart, however, is her idiot-proof JetStick control system. In a word, handling is a dream—something that must be experienced to fully appreciate. Twin 440hp Yanmar diesels matched with Hamilton jet drives will cruise the Talaria 44 in the mid 20s and reach a top speed of over 30 knots.

FLYBRIDGE CRUISERS

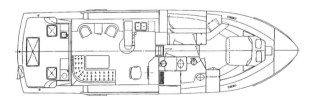

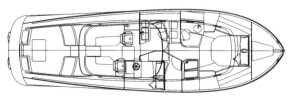

See Page 322 for Pricing Information

See Page 323 for Pricing Information

Island Gypsy 40 Motor Cruiser

Length Overall . . . . 40'0"	Fuel . . . . 400 gals.
Length WL . . . . 35'3"	Water . . . . 200 gals.
Beam . . . . 14'3"	Headroom . . . . 6'4"
Draft . . . . 3'6"	Hull Type . . . . Semi-Disp.
Weight . . . . 33,500#	Designer . . . . H. Halvorsen
Clearance . . . . 13'3"	Production 1986–94

A versatile boat with a conservative trawler-style appearance, the Island Gypsy 40 Motor Cruiser is built on a semi-displacement hull with a wide beam, hard chines, and a full-length prop-protecting keel. Her cockpit is on the same level as the salon resulting in a wide-open and completely practical sedan-style floorplan—the ideal cruising layout in the eyes of many. There are two staterooms forward and the head has a separate stall showerl. The L-shaped galley configuration is unusual in a boat this size—it does chop the salon up a bit, but the added counter space is a blessing. Burmese teak is liberally applied throughout the interior, and the decks and rails are teak as well. Topside, the flybridge is arranged with the helm aft and lounge seating (including a table) forward of the console. Note that the cockpit is shaded by a flybridge extension. Additional features include a sliding deck access door in the salon, a well-arranged engine room, and a swim platform. Twin 135hp Lehman diesels were standard in the Motor Cruiser (8 knots at cruise/11 knots top), and twin 210hp Cummins (12 knots cruise/15 top) or 375hp Cats (19 knots cruise/22 knots top) were offered as options.

Island Gypsy 44 Motor Cruiser

Length Overall . . . . 44'3"	Fuel . . . . 720 gals.
Length WL . . . . 38'9"	Water . . . . 320 gals.
Beam . . . . 15'4"	Headroom . . . . 6'5"
Draft . . . . 4'3"	Hull Type . . . . Semi-Disp.
Weight . . . . 38,500#	Deadrise Aft . . . . NA
Clearance . . . . 13'7"	Production 1983–96

With her rakish profile and roomy three-stateroom interior, the Island Gypsy 44 Motor Cruiser is a good-looking and practical flybridge sedan with just a hint of her trawler heritage. The 44 was built in China on a wide-beam semi-displacement hull with hard aft chines and a full-length prop-protecting keel. Notably, only a few sedan-style boats in this size range have three staterooms. The owner's stateroom is amidships in this layout (where the ride is better), and the L-shaped galley is forward in the salon, opposite the lower helm. All of the interior woodwork is Burmese teak, and the outside decks and rails are teak as well. Topside, the helm console is aft on the bridge with guest seating forward. The extended flybridge shades the cockpit, and a fold-down stairwell in the bridge coaming makes foredeck access easy. A variety of engines were offered over the years. Among them, twin 250hp Cummins diesels will cruise at 12 knots (15 knots top), and popular 375hp Cats will cruise at 15 knots (21 knots top). Note that the 44 Motor Cruiser was briefly reintroduced in 2001 after having been out of production for several years.

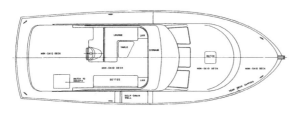

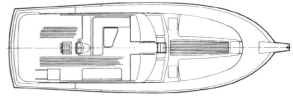

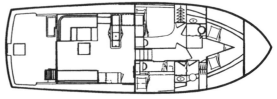

FLYBRIDGE CRUISERS

Islander 34 Convertible

Length	33'9"	Water	54 gals.
Beam	13'0"	Headroom	6'3"
Draft	3'4"	Hull Type	Deep-V
Weight	21,000#	Deadrise Aft	19°
Clearance	15'10"	designer	Hunt Assoc.
Fuel	300 gals.	Production	1993–2002

The Islander 34 Convertible (built by well-known sailboat manufacturer Catalina Yachts) began life in 1989 as the Pearson 34, a good-running deep-V design aimed at the family cruiser market. Catalina obtained the tooling to this model in 1993 when Pearson went out of business and introduced her as the Islander 34—a completely reengineered boat with a revised interior favored by many for its utility and space utilization. With 6 feet, 4 inches of headroom and a light, airy salon, the Islander's two-stateroom floorplan is arranged with a midcabin berth tucked under the elevated dinette—an innovative and seldom-seen configuration capable of sleeping eight people. The forward stateroom has an island berth, and the head compartment is very spacious. On the downside, the galley is compact with little counter space. While not large, the Islander's cockpit is big enough for a couple of light-tackle anglers. Additional features include a spacious engine room, a large flybridge with bench seating forward of the helm, bow pulpit, and a transom door. Twin 250hp Cummins diesels will cruise the Islander at 18 knots (22–23 knots top), and 315hp Cummins will cruise at 20 knots and deliver a top speed in the mid 20s.

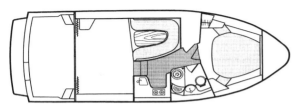

View A: Floorplan Showing Dinette

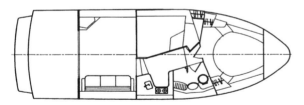

View B: Showing Midship Stateroom

See Page 325 for Pricing Information

Jefferson 37 Convertible

Length Overall	36'10"	Fuel	350 gals.
Length WL	32'6"	Water	120 gals.
Beam	14'5"	Headroom	6'3"
Draft	3'0"	Hull Type	Modified-V
Weight	25,000#	Deadrise Aft	NA
Clearance	15'7"	Production	1988–94

The Jefferson 37 Convertible is an Asian-built family sedan whose conservative profile and all-teak interior appealed to entry-level buyers on a budget. Like most Jefferson models of her era, she was built on a low-deadrise, solid fiberglass hull with a shallow keel and an unusually wide 14-foot, 5-inch beam. With so much beam, the Jefferson 37 is a roomy boat inside and it's hard to feel cramped below in spite of the dark interior woodwork (teak paneling, cabinetry, bulkheads, and teak parquet flooring). Two floorplans were available: a two-stateroom layout with the galley up, and a galley-down arrangement with a single stateroom and a wide-open salon. Both layouts have a double berth in the master stateroom as well as a standard lower helm station. Because the 37 was never conceived as a serious fishing boat, the cockpit is on the small side. Additional features include a stall shower in the double-entry head compartment, a spacious engine room, transom door, radar arch, bow pulpit, and wide side decks. Twin 250hp Cummins diesels will cruise the Jefferson 37 at 16–17 knots (20+ knots top), and 300hp Cummins diesels will cruise at 19–20 knots and top out in the low 20s.

Two-Stateroom Plan

Single-Stateroom Plan

See Page 325 for Pricing Information

FLYBRIDGE CRUISERS

Legacy 40 Sedan

Length Overall	39'4"	Water	120 gals.
Length WL	36'0"	Waste	40 gals.
Beam	13'7"	Hull Type	Modified-V
Draft	3'8"	Deadrise Aft	17°
Weight	22,000#	Designer	Mark Ellis
Fuel	410 gals.	Production	1995–Current

A handsome Downeast-style cruiser, the 40 Sedan introduced in 1995 was Legacy's first entry into the powerboat market. She's built on an easily-driven fully cored hull with a sharp entry, plenty of transom deadrise, and a deep skeg (which protects the prop and rudder in the single-screw version). Not inexpensive, the finely crafted interior of the Legacy 40 is a blend of mahogany woodwork and trim with top-quality fixtures. Her standard galley-down floorplan (which can be altered to fit the requirements of buyers) includes two comfortable staterooms, each with a double berth. While the salon dimensions are modest compared with some 40-foot sedans, the large windows and lovely teak-and-holly cabin sole create a very comfortable and traditional environment indeed. Additional features include a roomy cockpit, wide side decks, radar mast, and a deck access door at the lower helm. Among several engine options available over the years, a single 420hp Cat diesel will cruise an early-model Legacy 40 at 17–18 knots, and later models with twin 370hp Cummins will cruise at 22–23 knots. Note that a single-stateroom Express model is also available.

Luhrs 3400 Motor Yacht

Length	34'0"	Water	60 gals.
Beam	12'6"	Cockpit	NA
Draft	3'2"	Hull Type	Modified-V
Weight	13,500#	Deadrise Aft	15°
Clearance	22'0"	Designer	J. Fielding
Fuel	300 gals.	Production	1990–92

From a company whose name is generally associated with affordable, well-designed fishing boats, the introduction of the Luhrs 3400 Motor Yacht in 1990 was something of a surprise. She was an affordably priced boat with a long list of standard equipment, and the ride delivered by her low-deadrise, modified-V hull is comfortable as long as the seas stay relatively calm. Luhrs engineers gave the 3400 MY a surprisingly spacious interior by keeping the cockpit small. The expansive, single-stateroom floorplan is arranged with a mid-level galley and dinette forward of the salon with a serving counter separating the salon from the dinette area. The head has an interesting twist—the sink and toilet are to port and the shower is across the hallway. Because the interior is so large, the cockpit is way too small for any serious fishing activities. The flybridge, however, is huge for a 34-footer and includes a convenient walk-through to the foredeck (which compensates for the boat's somewhat narrow side decks). Standard 454-cid Crusader gas engines will cruise the Luhrs 3400 MY at 19–20 knots and reach about 28 knots wide open. Twin 300hp Cummins diesels were optional.

Flybridge Interior

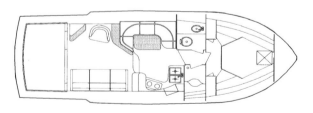

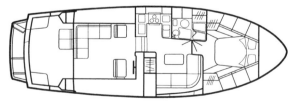

Express Interior

See Page 328 for Pricing Information

See Page 329 for Pricing Information

Luhrs 3420 Motor Yacht

Length	34'0"	Water	60 gals.
Beam	12'6"	Cockpit	50 sq. ft.
Draft	3'2"	Hull Type	Modified-V
Weight	13,500#	Deadrise Aft	15°
Clearance	22'0"	Designer	Luhrs
Fuel	300 gals.	Production	1991–93

Closely resembling the earlier Luhrs 3400 Motor Yacht (1990–92), the Luhrs 3420 Motor Yacht has a larger cockpit, a smaller salon, and a revised flybridge layout without the foredeck walk-through. (No, we don't know why Luhrs called this boat a motor yacht: she looks like a flybridge convertible to us.) Hull construction is solid fiberglass—the same tried-and-true design first used for the Luhrs 340. Inside, the single-stateroom floorplan is arranged with the mid-level galley open to the salon. Note that the head is divided with the sink and toilet to port and the shower across the hallway. The interior is attractively finished with colorful fabrics and accented with a modest amount of teak trim. Outside, the cockpit is small—useful for entertaining and cruising, but not suitable for any serious fishing pursuits. Guest seating is provided forward of the helm console on the flybridge, and the aluminum arch was standard. Additional features include a built-in entertainment center, oak parquet galley sole, fish box, washdown, cockpit bridge overhang, and a swim platform with molded baitwell. Twin 340hp gas engines will cruise the Luhrs 3420 MY at 19–20 knots and reach a top speed of around 28 knots.

Mainship 30 Sedan

Length Overall	30'0"	Water	40 gals.
Beam	10'3"	Headroom	6'2"
Draft	2'3"	Hull Type	Semi-Disp.
Weight	9,300#	Deadrise Aft	NA
Clearance	11'2"	Designer	Mainship
Fuel	150 gals.	Production	1981–83

Introduced in 1981 as a downsized version of the original Mainship 34 Motor Cruiser, the Mainship 30 Sedan incorporated many of the virtues of her larger sistership— in particular, a low price and economical operation—in a smaller, less-expensive package. She's built on a solid fiberglass semi-displacement hull with a deep forefoot, rounded bilges and a shallow keel—an easily driven hull capable of excellent economy at her 6-knot hull speed. With her roomy cockpit, it's hardly surprising that the interior of the Mainship 30 is fairly small. The compact salon came with a high-low table and a sofa that converts to a double berth, and a large head opposite the galley has a separate stall shower. (Note that early models had a foldaway "Pullman" berth that stowed inside a starboard wall locker.) The Mainship's cockpit is quite large with room for several deck chairs, and the flybridge seats three with the helm to port. Additional features include a lower helm, a big engine room, and wide side decks. A single 124hp Volvo diesel will cruise the Mainship 30 Sedan efficiently at 8–10 knots and deliver a top speed of about 14 knots.

FLYBRIDGE CRUISERS

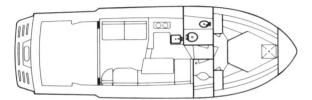

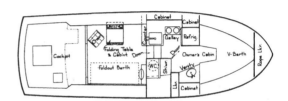

See Page 329 for Pricing Information

See Page 330 for Pricing Information

Mainship 31 Sedan Bridge

Length Overall............33'3"	Fuel.................200 gals.
Hull Length...............31'3"	Water.................50 gals.
Beam..................11'10"	Hull Type...........Modified-V
Draft.....................2'10"	Deadrise Aft..............13°
Weight...............16,000#	Designer..........Mike Peters
Clearance...............14'4"	Production............1994–99

While the chief attraction of the 31 Sedan Bridge may have been her attractive styling and affordable price, those who step below will be immediately impressed with the spacious interior packed into this small cruiser. Like all sedan-bridge designs, the sunken floorplan is made possible by locating the engines aft, under the cockpit, rather than placing them beneath the salon sole. The result is a wide-open interior arranged more or less on a single level from the salon forward. There are two staterooms in this layout—no small achievement in a 31-foot boat. The galley is opposite the dinette in the main salon, and a double-entry head offers private access to the forward stateroom. Outside, molded steps lead up to the flybridge with its wraparound guest seating and portside helm position. With very narrow side decks, a walk-through in the bridge coaming provides direct access to the foredeck. The cockpit comes with a transom door, and the entire cockpit sole lifts up to get at the engines. Additional features include a swim platform, molded cockpit seating, hidden swim ladder, and a bow pulpit. Twin 340hp V-drive gas engines will cruise the Mainship 31 Sedan Bridge at 19–20 knots and reach a top speed of about 30 knots.

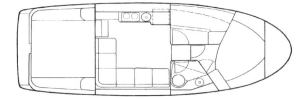

Mainship 34 II

Length.................34'0"	Water.................50 gals.
Beam..................11'11"	Headroom...............6'3"
Draft....................2'10"	Cockpit..............78 sq. ft.
Weight...............14,000#	Hull Type...........Semi-Disp.
Clearance...............13'6"	Designer............Cherubini
WaterFuel............220 gals.	Production............1980–82

Introduced in 1980 as a sistership to the hugely popular Mainship 34 Motor Cruiser (1978–82), the Mainship 34 II is an inexpensive and economical cruiser whose large cockpit would, it was hoped, make her an appealing choice for budget-minded anglers. She rides on the same seakindly, semi-displacement hull as the Motor Cruiser with a full keel and well-protected running gear. Belowdecks, the single-stateroom floorplan of the Mainship II is smaller than the Motor Cruiser, especially in the salon where the dimensions are quite compact. A lower helm was standard, and the head—opposite the galley on the lower level—includes a separate stall shower. The pass-through window from the galley to the salon is a nice touch. A sliding glass door opens to the Mainship's large 70-square-foot cockpit, and a steep ladder leads up to the flybridge, which seats two. Additional features include a roomy engine compartment, wide side decks, a foredeck mast, and teak interior trim. Never a big seller, a single turbocharged 160hp Perkins diesel was standard in the Mainship 34 II. She'll cruise easily around 11 knots (burning just 6 gph) and reach a top speed of 14 knots.

See Page 330 for Pricing Information
See Page 330 for Pricing Information

Mainship 34 III

Length Overall . . . . 34'0"	Fuel . . . . 190 gals.
Length WL . . . . NA	Water . . . . 40 gals.
Beam . . . . 11'11"	Cockpit . . . . NA
Draft . . . . 2'10"	Hull Type . . . . Semi-Disp.
Weight . . . . 14,000#	Designer . . . . Cherubini
Clearance . . . . 13'6"	Production 1983–88

The Mainship 34 III is a refined and more stylish version of the original Mainship 34 (1978–82). In the 34 III, the salon was slightly lengthened and the extended hardtop of the original Mainship 34 was eliminated in favor of a more open cockpit. Designed for fuel-efficient cruising, she rides on a solid fiberglass hull with rounded bilges and a long keel for directional stability. (Note that the keel is deep enough to protect the prop and running gear.) The single-stateroom interior of the 34 III is quite similar to the original Mainship 34, except that light oak woodwork is used rather than teak, and the salon windows are larger. A lower helm was standard in the roomy salon, the galley includes all the necessary food-prep necessities, and a separate stall shower is included in the head. The cockpit is large enough for some light-tackle fishing, and the flybridge seats four around the helm. The Mainship 34 III was powered with a single diesel engine (usually a 165hp or 200hp Perkins) capable of cruising at 7 knots at 2 gph, or 13–14 knots at only 6–7 gph. The fuel efficiency of this coastal cruiser is truly impressive, and used models remain popular in today's market.

Mainship 35 Convertible

Length . . . . 34'11"	Water . . . . 80 gals.
Beam . . . . 12'8"	Cockpit . . . . 80 sq. ft.
Draft . . . . 2'10"	Hull Type . . . . Modified-V
Weight . . . . 16,000#	Deadrise Aft . . . . 12°
Clearance . . . . 15'0"	Designer . . . . Mike Peters
Fuel . . . . 250 gals.	Production 1988–94

The Mainship 35 Convertible (called the Mainship Mediterranean 35 Cockpit from 1988–91) is an inexpensive family sedan with one of the largest interior layouts in her class. The rakish profile of the Mainship 35 speaks for itself—European, streamlined, and very distinctive by the standards of her day. Built on a solid fiberglass hull with a shallow transom deadrise, the Mainship 35 was a fairly popular model during her production years. The original single-stateroom floorplan was replaced with a two-stateroom dinette layout in 1992 when the boat was restyled. Further updates for 1992 included white windshield frames (replacing the earlier black frames), a bigger flybridge with additional seating, and new interior colors. There are few 35-foot boats with two staterooms and a dinette, and the Mainship even manages a roomy salon—very impressive. The cockpit is small with a transom door, engine compartment hatches, and molded-in bridge steps. Note the single-piece Euro-style bow rails and step-down window styling. Standard 320hp Crusader gas engines will cruise the Mainship 35 at 17–18 knots with a top speed of around 28 knots.

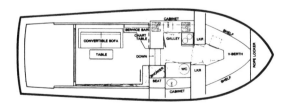

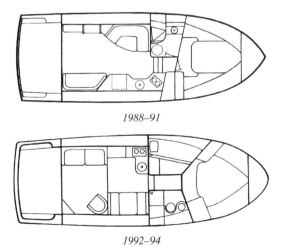

1988–91

1992–94

See Page 330 for Pricing Information

See Page 330 for Pricing Information

Mainship 35 Open Bridge

Length	36'0"	Water	85 gals.
Beam	12'5"	Headroom	6'3"
Draft	2'8"	Hull Type	Modified-V
Weight	13,500#	Deadrise Aft	12°
Clearance	10'0"	Designer	Mike Peters
Fuel	250 gals.	Production	1990–92

While a huge interior is obviously the theme of this boat, the bloated, egg-shaped profile of the Mainship 35 Open Bridge (called the 36 Sedan Bridge in 1992) leaves a lot to be desired from the standpoint of eye appeal. Appearances aside, however, the full-beam interior of the 35 Open is ideally suited to entertaining a small crowd. Built on a low-deadrise, modified-V hull, the single-level interior—with nearly 7 feet of headroom—seems cavernous. The salon can comfortably seat a party of eight for cocktails, and the galley came with a full-size refrigerator and microwave. Note that a separate stall shower is found in the head compartment. On the downside, the cabin windows are very small and the absence of outside natural lighting is notable. Topside, molded steps lead from the small cockpit to the flybridge where a semicircular lounge can seat several guests. Additional features include a centerline walk-through from the bridge to the foredeck, radar arch, cherry interior joinery, and an integrated swim platform. Standard 320hp gas engines will cruise the Mainship 35 Open at a respectable 17–18 knots and deliver a top speed of around 28 knots.

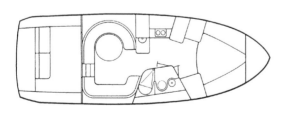

Mainship 36 Sedan

Length	36'2"	Water	100 gals.
Beam	13'0"	Headroom	6'5"
Draft	3'0"	Hull Type	Semi-Disp.
Weight	20,000#	Deadrise Aft	NA
Clearance	11'3"	Designer	Mainship
Fuel	240 gals.	Production	1986–88

Sharing the same efficient, semi-displacement hull as the Mainship 36 Double Cabin, the Mainship 36 Sedan (called the 36 Nantucket Sedan in 1987) has the interior volume of a much larger boat. Indeed, the wide-open salon is unusually generous for a 36-footer due to the fact that the cabin bulkhead is located well aft, vastly increasing the interior dimensions at the expense of cockpit space. A comfortable cruising boat, the profile of the 36 Sedan is on the boxy side and it's doubtful anyone will refer to her as sexy. Two very similar floorplans were offered, each with a deckhouse galley and two private staterooms. A dinette is forward in the salon, and the head includes a separate stall shower. As previously mentioned, the cockpit is too small for much entertaining, however the flybridge is very large with L-shaped lounge seating aft of the helm for several guests. A modest performer with standard 270hp gas engines, she'll cruise at 15 knots and reach a top speed in the low 20s. Note that trim tabs were never available for the 36 Sedan, perhaps because of her semi-displacement hull design. About fifty were built during her three-year production run.

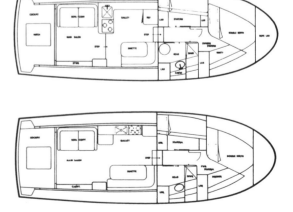

See Page 330 for Pricing Information

See Page 330 for Pricing Information

Mainship 40 Motor Cruiser

Length . . . . 40'0"	Water. . . . . 100 gals.
Beam . . . . 14'0"	Headroom . . . . 6'4"
Draft. 3'4"	Hull Type . . . . Modified-V
Weight. . . . . 23,500#	Deadrise Aft . . . . NA
Clearance. . . . . 17'6"	Designer . . . . Cherubini
Fuel . . . . 320 gals.	Production 1980–84

Following in the wake of the highly successful Mainship 34, the Mainship 40 Motor Cruiser continued the classic, trawler-style profile of her predecessor while retaining the dependability and economy of diesel power. She wasn't a popular model for Mainship (only 20 were sold), but there's a lot to like about this boat for the cruising couple. Indeed, because she has only a single stateroom below, the full-beam salon is unusually wide open and spacious. The pilothouse, on the salon level, is separated from it by a bulkhead with an open doorway to port. The galley is forward in the salon, and a second head is located just inside the sliding cockpit door. The forward stateroom is very roomy and includes an angled double berth in addition to a built-in dresser and private head (with a shower stall). The salon sofa can be converted to a double berth for occasional guests, but otherwise the Mainship 40 is a two-sleeper. Topside, the extended flybridge is huge for a 40-footer with enough deck area to entertain a small crowd. Note the raised bulwarks around the walkways. Twin 165hp Perkins diesels will cruise the Mainship 40 at 10–11 knots (around 15 knots top) burning only 1 gph.

Mainship 40 Sedan Bridge

Length . . . . 40'7"	Water. . . . . 93 gals.
Beam . . . . 13'6"	Headroom . . . . 6'4"
Draft. 3'5"	Hull Type . . . . Modified-V
Weight. . . . . 20,000#	Deadrise Aft . . . . 18°
Clearance. . . . . 17'0"	Designer . . . . Mainship
Fuel . . . . 310 gals.	Production 1993–99

Introduced in 1993, the Mainship 40 Sedan Bridge is an inexpensive family boat whose spacious interior and large flybridge make her an excellent choice for day cruising and entertaining. She was built on a solid fiberglass, modified-V hull with moderate beam, and her low-profile appearance is the result of locating the engines under the cockpit sole. The single-level interior of the 40 Sedan Bridge—a step down from the cockpit level—is arranged with two staterooms forward and a spacious, full-beam salon with lounge seating for eight. A big U-shaped galley is forward in the salon, and a walkaround double berth is found in the master stateroom. This is an expansive floorplan for a 40-footer, however the furnishings are mostly inexpensive and the finish is less than impressive. The cockpit has built-in bench seating, a transom door, and twin hatches in the sole for engine access. Topside, the flybridge has an island helm console with wraparound lounge seating. Lacking side decks, the foredeck is reached via a door in the forward flybridge coaming. Standard 320hp V-drive gas engines will cruise the Mainship 40 at a sedate 16 knots and deliver a top speed in the mid 20s.

FLYBRIDGE CRUISERS

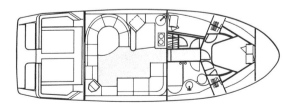

See Page 330 for Pricing Information   See Page 330 for Pricing Information

Mainship 41 Convertible

Length	40'11"	Water	130 gals.
Beam	14'5"	Cockpit	75 sq. ft.
Draft	3'6"	Hull Type	Modified-V
Weight	22,000#	Deadrise Aft	12°
Clearance	11'4"	Designer	Mike Peters
Fuel	375 gals.	Production	1989–92

The Mainship 41 Convertible (originally called the 41 Cockpit Motor Yacht) came out in 1989 when Mainship was marketing an entirely new series of low-cost, Med-style cruising boats for entry-level buyers. Built on a solid fiberglass hull with a wide beam, one of the chief attractions of the 41 Convertible was her spacious interior. Indeed, the salon is unusually expansive for a boat this size with room for entertaining a large group of friends. The original two-stateroom floorplan has the galley forward on the salon level, and in 1991 a revised layout has the galley and dinette forward, a step down from the salon. Either way, the guest stateroom is a tight fit, and the inexpensive furnishings and cheap wall coverings leave a lot to be desired. (Note that small windows restrict natural lighting in the salon.) While the interior of the Mainship 41 is spacious, the cockpit—with its fold-down transom door and molded seating—is small. The flybridge, on the other hand, is huge with plenty of lounge seating. Standard 320hp gas engines cruise the 41 Convertible at 15–16 knots and deliver a top speed in the low 20s. Optional 375hp Cat diesels will cruise at 20+ knots (about 25 knots top).

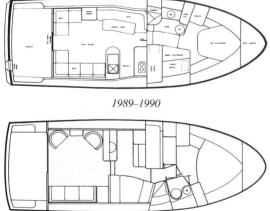

1989–1990

1991–92

See Page 330 for Pricing Information

Marinette 29 Sedan

Length	29'6"	Fuel, Twin	100 gals.
Beam	11'0"	Water	35 gals.
Draft	2'0"	Hull Type	Modified-V
Weight, Single	6,000#	Deadrise Aft	NA
Weight, Twin	7,100#	Construction	Aluminum
Fuel, Single	75 gals.	Production	1985–89

A spacious 29-footer with berths for six and a good turn of speed, the Marinette 29 Sedan proved popular with budget-minded buyers looking for an inexpensive, easily maintained cruising boat. She was built on a low-deadrise hull with a wide 11-foot beam, and lightweight aluminum construction made the 29 an economical boat to operate. The interior consists of a small salon on the cockpit level with a lower helm to starboard and a convertible settee to port. Forward, the lower level has a V-berth in the forepeak, a convertible dinette to port, a full galley opposite, and an enclosed, standup head compartment aft. While the accommodations are simple and basic in nature, teak cabin accents, good headroom, and large cabin windows give the interior a nautical and very open appearance. Visibility from the lower helm is very good, and hatches in the salon sole provide access to a well-arranged engine room. Although the cockpit is modest in size, it's still large enough for a few folding deck chairs. Topside, the small flybridge has bench seating for three. Twin 220hp Chrysler gas engines will cruise efficiently at around 20 knots and reach a top speed of close to 30 knots. (Note the limited fuel capacity.)

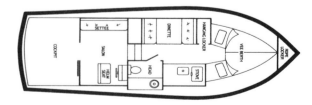

See Page 333 for Pricing Information

Marinette 32 Sedan

McKinna 47 Sedan

Marinette 32 Sedan	
Length . . . . 32'6"	Water . . . . 35 gals.
Beam . . . . 12'0"	Headroom . . . . 6'4"
Draft . . . . 2'0"	Hull Type . . . . Modified-V
Weight . . . . 10,500#	Construction . . . . Aluminum
Clearance . . . . 9'2"	Designer . . . . Marinette
Fuel . . . . 150 gals.	Production 1976–90

McKinna 47 Sedan	
Length Overall . . . . 50'0"	Water . . . . 200 gals.
Beam . . . . 15'0"	Headroom . . . . 6'4"
Draft . . . . 3'10"	Hull Type . . . . Modified-V
Weight . . . . 29,700#	Deadrise Aft . . . . 18°
Clearance . . . . 19'6"	Designer . . . . H. Apollonio
Fuel . . . . 700 gals.	Production 1999–2001

An exceedingly popular boat, over 1,800 Marinette 32s of one type or another were built during her long production run—a highly successful design indeed. Construction is welded marine-grade aluminum, and her conservative 1970s-era styling stands in contrast to her lively performance and practical accommodations. A relatively wide 12-foot beam results in a good deal of living space below and the large cabin windows add to the spacious effect. The 32 Sedan is a practical family cruiser with a roomy single-stateroom interior, a small cockpit, and a well-arranged flybridge with guest seating aft of the helm. A portside lower helm came standard and the interiors were usually finished off with teak paneling and woodwork. Additional features include wide side decks, foredeck seating, and a roomy engine room. On the downside, the 35-gallon freshwater capacity is a bit modest and so is the fuel capacity. Several versions of the Marinette 32 were offered over the years including the popular 32 Express and a 32 Fisherman. At only 10,500 pounds, it's no surprise that her performance is brisk. With a pair of 220hp Chrysler gas engines, she'll cruise at 20 knots and reach a top speed of 28–30 knots.

The McKinna 47 is a Taiwan-built sedan whose conservative profile masks a surprisingly space-efficient interior. She rides on a conventional modified-V hull with a well-flared bow, a shallow keel for stability, and a relatively wide 15-foot beam. Her spacious galley-up floorplan is arranged with two staterooms, both with queen-size berths and built-in vanities, and two heads that share a common shower stall. An L-shaped sofa dominates the salon where the large, wraparound cabin windows provide excellent natural lighting and outside visibility. A lower helm is optional and the interior is finished out in handcrafted maple woodwork. While the McKinna is clearly designed with cruising in mind, her large cockpit—partially shaded by the bridge overhang—is suitable for a couple of light-tackle anglers. Topside, the flybridge is huge with the helm forward and seating for eight. Additional features include wide side decks, a transom door, a teak cockpit sole and freshwater washdowns fore and aft. Standard 330hp Cummins diesels will cruise at 18 knots (about 22 knots top), and optional 370hp Cummins will cruise at 21 knots (24–25 knots wide open).

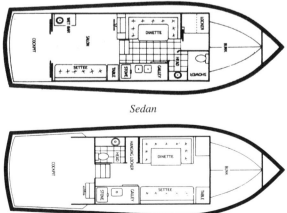

Sedan

Express

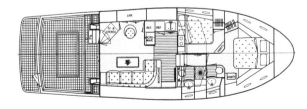

See Page 333 for Pricing Information

See Page 334 for Pricing Information

Length	35'3"	Fuel	224 gals.
Beam	11'8"	Water	92 gals.
Draft	3'2"	Waste	30 gals.
Weight	17,000#	Hull Type	Modified-V
Clearance	13'6"	Deadrise Aft	7.5°
Headroom	6'5"	Production	2003–04

Length	35'10"	Fuel	250 gals.
Beam	12'6"	Water	90 gals.
Draft	4'0"	Waste	35 gals.
Weight	18,254#	Hull Type	Modified-V
Clearance	14'1"	Deadrise Aft	11°
Headroom	6'5"	Production	2005–Current

FLYBRIDGE CRUISERS

The Meridian 341 is one of the lowest-cost boats of her type on the market. This is Meridian's entry-level offering, and there's a lot to like about her from the standpoint of features and value. In fact, the 341 isn't really a "new" model; she was called the Bayliner 3488 Command Bridge when she was introduced in 2001, becoming the Meridian 341 in 2003 when Bayliner went out of the big-boat business and Meridian Yachts was formed. Sharing the same hull, cabin accommodations, and flybridge layout as her predecessor, the 341 is a simple and very practical boat. Her two-stateroom interior is highlighted with cherry woodwork, cedar-lined hanging lockers, and leather upholstery. The head is fitted with a separate stall shower, and wraparound cabin windows provide plenty of natural lighting. In the cockpit, molded steps make bridge access very easy. Additional features include a transom door, radar arch, excellent cabin headroom, and an extended flybridge. Note the narrow side decks. Twin 320hp MerCruiser inboards will cruise the Meridian 341 at 20 knots and reach a top speed of 28–29 knots. Note that an all new 341 Sedan was introduced in 2005.

Introduced in 2005, the Meridian 341 Sedan is not an updated version of the company's original 341 Sedan built in 2003–04. This is a completely different boat with greater beam than her predecessor, more dramatic styling, and a revised two-stateroom interior. Built on a low-deadrise hull with a solid fiberglass bottom, the 341's tiered cabin windows create the impression of great space in the salon. The galley is forward, on the same level as the salon, and the well-appointed decor is an attractive blend of leather seating, vinyl wall coverings, and cherry cabinetry. A head with a stall shower is to starboard, accessed from either the master stateroom or the passageway. If the interior of the 341 Sedan seems unusually spacious for a 34-footer, the cockpit is tiny and the side decks are practically nonexistent. A molded staircase leads up to the extended flybridge with its wet bar and guest seating. Additional features include a transom door, radar arch, fore and aft freshwater washdowns, VacuFlush toilet, and stern and bow thrusters. A lower helm is optional. A modest performer with 320hp gas inboards, she'll cruise at 18 knots and reach 26–27 knots wide open.

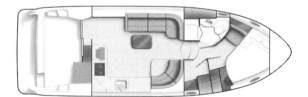

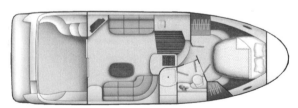

See Page 334 for Pricing Information

See Page 334 for Pricing Information

Meridian 381 Sedan

Length	38'6"	Fuel	300 gals.
Beam	13'7"	Water	125 gals.
Draft	3'4"	Waste	37 gals.
Weight	22,275#	Hull Type	Modified-V
Clearance	14'1"	Deadrise Aft	10°
Headroom	6'4"	Production	2003–Current

The Meridian 381 Sedan is a slightly revised version of the Bayliner 3788 Motor Yacht, which was introduced in 2001. (She became the Meridian 381 in 2003 when Bayliner went out of the big-boat business and Meridian Yachts was formed.) With her modern styling and expansive interior, the affordable price of the 381 makes her an appealing yacht for entry-level buyers on a budget. Built on a low-deadrise hull with a wide beam and shallow keel, the two-stateroom, galley-up interior of the 381 is highlighted with solid-cherry woodwork, faux leather upholstery, and earth-tone fabrics. For a 38-footer, the salon seems exceptionally open and inviting with facing settees aft and a full-size dinette forward. Below, an island berth is located in the master stateroom, while the guest stateroom is partially tucked under the salon floor. In the cockpit, molded steps provide easy access to the flybridge. (Note that the extended flybridge shades most of the cockpit.) A radar arch, transom door, and teak-and-holly galley floor are standard. Twin 320hp MerCruiser gas inboards will cruise the 381 Sedan at 15–16 knots and top out in the mid 20s.

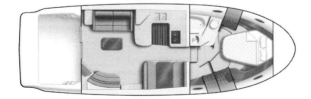

Meridian 411 Sedan

Length	46'0"	Fuel	400 gals.
Beam	14'2"	Water	150 gals.
Draft	3'9"	Waste	55 gals.
Weight	25,000#	Hull Type	Modified-V
Clearance	15'0"	Deadrise Aft	7°
Headroom	6'7"	Production	2003–Current

Introduced in 2003, the Meridian 411 is a competitively priced sedan cruiser whose crisp styling and comfortable accommodations are her most impressive features. Like other Meridian models, the 411 rides on a solid fiberglass hull with generous beam and a relatively flat bottom. Her two-stateroom interior compares favorably with other boats of her type and size, and while the overall finish may lack the polish of a more expensive yacht, the layout is practical and well organized. The expansive salon is arranged with the galley and dinette forward, a step up from the aft salon with its facing settees and entertainment center. The dinette converts to a double berth in the usual fashion, and a hatch in the salon floor provides access to a very well-arranged engine room. Topside, there's seating for eight and a built-in wet bar on the large flybridge. Additional features include an extended swim platform, cherry interior cabinetry, radar arch, and reasonably wide side decks. Note that a lower helm station is optional. Twin 370hp Cummins diesels will cruise the Meridian 411 Sedan in the low 20s and reach a top speed of 26–28 knots.

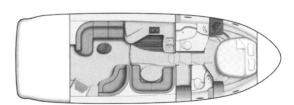

See Page 334 for Pricing Information

See Page 334 for Pricing Information

Midnight Lace 40 Express

Length Overall . . . . 40'3"	Fuel . . . . 430 gals.
Length WL . . . . 35'4"	Water . . . . 100 gals.
Beam . . . . 13'6"	Hull Type . . . . Modified-V
Draft . . . . 3'8"	Deadrise Aft . . . . 14°
Weight . . . . 19,690#	designer . . . . Tom Fexas
Clearance . . . . 16'0"	Production 1991–94

A very distinctive yacht, the Midnight Lace 40 combines the rakish styling and efficient performance common to nearly all yachts designed over the years by Tom Fexas. She was built on a lightweight, fully cored hull with a relatively fine entry and slender 13-foot, 6-inch beam. The original two-stateroom floorplan of the Midnight Lace 40 has the galley to starboard in the salon and facing L-shaped settees. A new arrangement introduced in 1992 offered a much-enlarged galley to port and a full-length L-shaped settee opposite. Topside, the cockpit is raised two steps up from the salon level, and while not intended for any serious fishing, it's large enough to satisfy a couple of weekend anglers and came with a standard transom door. Additional features include excellent engine room access under the cockpit, side exhausts, a unique foredeck cockpit, a varnished teak transom, and a stylish helm console with room to flush-mount most electronics. A good performer with superb seakeeping characteristics, she'll cruise efficiently in the low 20s with a pair of 300hp Cummins diesels while reaching a top speed of 26–27 knots.

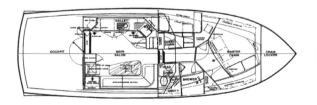

Midnight Lace 44 Express

Length . . . . 44'0"	Water . . . . 130 gals.
Beam . . . . 11'0"	Headroom . . . . 6'4"
Draft . . . . 2'10"	Hull Type . . . . Modified-V
Weight . . . . 15,900#	Deadrise Aft . . . . 8°
Clearance . . . . 16'0"	Designer . . . . Tom Fexas
Fuel . . . . 250 gals.	Production 1978–89

The Midnight Lace 44 is the boat that put Tom Fexas on the map. The prototype was introduced at the Ft. Lauderdale Boat Show in 1978 and it nearly stole the show. Based on the elegant commuter-style boats of the 1920s, the Midnight Lace 44 was a state-of-the-art blend of lightweight cored construction and an efficient "penetrating" hull form with a narrow beam, a well-flared bow, and tightly rounded bilges. The Midnight Lace 44s were built in Hong Kong and came with a choice of single- or twin-stateroom floorplans, both with a full-width salon. While the interior volume is small for a 44-foot boat, comfort and luxury are high and the teak cabinetry is rich. Originally offered as an express, a flybridge became available in 1979 (although most 44s were sold without it). Note the unique forward cockpit accessed from the forward stateroom, and the beautiful brightwork of the house. A remarkably classy and efficient boat, standard 220hp GM 8.2 diesels (driven through V-drives) will cruise the Midnight Lace 44 at 21 knots burning only 14 gph! Top speed is around 25 knots. Larger 260hp GM 8.2s were optional.

See Page 334 for Pricing Information

See Page 334 for Pricing Information

Midnight Lace 52 Express

Length Overall	52'6"	Fuel	480 gals.
Length WL	47'6"	Water	230 gals.
Beam	13'0"	Hull Type	Modified-V
Draft	3'0"	Deadrise Aft	8°
Weight	19,850#	Designer	Tom Fexas
Clearance	20'0"	Production	1982–89

Based upon the popular Midnight Lace 44, the Midnight Lace 52 has the same low-profile, commuter-style lines but with a slightly wider beam and a more contemporary interior. The hull and superstructure are fully cored and—at just under 20,000 pounds—she's a notably lightweight boat for her size. The easily driven, narrow-beam hull of the 52 features a well-flared bow, reverse transom, and rounded bilges. Although the interior dimensions are not large for a boat this size, the accommodations are very comfortable and finished with solid teak cabinetry and paneling. The floorplan is arranged with the owner's stateroom forward, at the end of the S-shaped passageway, with a small guest cabin to starboard. The engines (with V-drives) are located well aft, below the cockpit. The helm position is elevated, and the classy foredeck cockpit of the original Midnight Lace 44 remains in the 52. The flybridge was a popular option, and all but two (of the 16 built) were so equipped. Twin 260hp 8.2 diesels cruise the Midnight Lace 52 efficiently at 20 knots (burning just 20 gph) and reach a top speed of 24 knots.

Mikelson 42 Sedan

Length Overall	41'9"	Fuel	400 gals.
Beam	13'0"	Water	200 gals.
Draft	3'0"	Waste	35 gals.
Weight	24,000#	Hull Type	Modified-V
Clearance	10'4"	Deadrise Aft	NA
Headroom	6'4"	Production	1986–93

The Mikelson 42 is the boat that put Mikelson in the sportfish business back in 1986. Designed by Tom Fexas, she's a notably handsome flybridge sedan whose profile is accented by a long foredeck and large cabin windows. She rides on a fully cored hull with rounded chines and a shallow keel—a hull specifically designed, according to Fexas, for maximum efficiency in the 20-knot range. While several floorplans were offered during her production years, most Mikelson 42s were delivered with a two-stateroom, galley-up layout with a single head. A lower helm was standard, and the interior is completely finished with handcrafted teak cabinetry. The cockpit, partially shaded by a bridge overhang, is large enough for two or three anglers to work without being crowded. For a 42-footer, the Mikelson's flybridge is very large. Additional features include a radar arch, wide side decks, transom door, teak cockpit sole, and teak-and-holly floors throughout the interior. Among several engine options, twin 260hp GM 8.2L diesels will cruise the Mikelson 42 at an efficient 16–18 knots and achieve a top speed of around 20 knots. Note that this boat was also marketed in the U.S. as the Ultimate 42 as well as the Fexas 42.

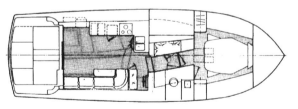

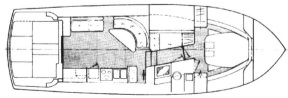

Navigator 3300 Flybridge Sedan

Length Overall . . . . 33'6"	Fuel . . . . 250 gals.
Beam . . . . 11'11"	Water . . . . 70 gals.
Draft . . . . 2'10"	Waste . . . . 30 gals.
Weight . . . . 16,000#	Hull Type . . . . Modified-V
Headroom . . . . 6'4"	Deadrise Aft . . . . 12°
Cockpit . . . . 50 sq. ft.	Production 1993–95

The Navigator 3300 was introduced in 1993 as an affordable fly-bridge sedan with a two-stateroom interior (rare in a boat this size) and excellent cruising economy. Built on a modified-V hull with plenty of beam and an integrated swim platform, the 3300 was aimed at budget-minded family cruisers more interested in spacious interior accommodations than a large cockpit. To their credit, Navigator engineers were able to pack a fair amount of living space into the 3300 and, while the detailing and fit-and-finish are less than impressive, the fact that this 33-foot cruiser has two staterooms as well as a reasonably sized salon and a separate stall shower in the head is notable. Admittedly, the guest stateroom is small and storage is limited, but the forward stateroom is quite spacious and there's seating for four in the salon even with the portside galley and optional lower helm. Additional features include a radar arch, transom door, large cabin windows and a bow pulpit. A good performer with twin 200hp Volvo diesels, the Navigator 3300 will cruise at 20–22 knots and reach a top speed of about 26 knots. Note that the Navigator 3600 Flybridge Sedan is the same boat with a larger cockpit.

Navigator 336 Flybridge Express

Length Overall . . . . 33'6"	Fuel . . . . 190 gals.
Beam . . . . 11'11"	Water . . . . 60 gals.
Draft . . . . 2'10"	Hull Type . . . . Modified-V
Weight . . . . 16,000#	Deadrise Aft . . . . 12°
Clearance . . . . NA	Designer . . . . J. Marshall
Headroom . . . . 6'4"	Production 1990–92

Introduced in 1989, the 336 was the first boat produced by Navigator Yachts. She bears a strong resemblance to Carver's Santego series of express bridge boats popularized in the late 1980s, a cross between a convertible sedan and express cruiser with a spacious single-level interior and V-drive inboard power. Built on a solid fiberglass hull with a relatively wide beam and a full bow, the interior of the 336 was available in a pair of single-stateroom floorplan configurations and both included a separate stall shower in the head. Like all express bridge models, the engines are aft—beneath the cockpit sole rather than under the salon. This allows the interior to be set low in the hull, which, in turn, reduces the boat's overall profile. While the Navigator's accommodations are spacious and well arranged, the absence of larger cabin windows makes for a somewhat claustrophobic interior. Notable features include a fully integrated swim platform, molded flybridge steps, transom door and a bow pulpit. Twin 300hp V-drive gas engines will cruise the Navigator 336 at 20 knots and reach a top speed in the neighborhood of 30 knots.

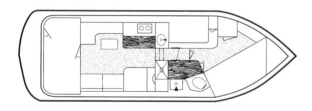

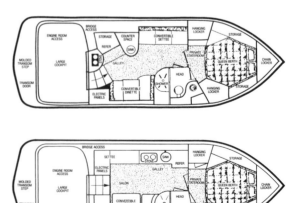

Navigator 42 Classic

Length Overall	42'0"	Fuel	400 gals.
Beam	15'0"	Water	130 gals.
Draft	4'4"	Waste	40 gals.
Weight	30,000#	Hull Type	Modified-V
Clearance	NA	Deadrise Aft	15°
Headroom	6'6"	Production	1995–2001

A very innovative boat in her day, the Navigator 42 Classic ranks among the smaller pilothouse designs to be found in the U.S. market. She rides on the same solid fiberglass modified-V hull used in the production of several other Navigator models (up to 56 feet), and her 15-foot beam—wide for a 42-footer—makes for a very spacious interior. Where most raised pilothouse designs access the staterooms from a companionway near the helm, the two staterooms of the Navigator 42 are reached via a hallway a few steps down from the salon. Both heads are fitted with stall showers; neither head, however, can be reached without first entering one of the staterooms—a minor inconvenience. The pilothouse, two steps up from the salon, is huge—as large as the salon—with the galley to port and the dinette opposite. Visibility from the helm is very good. While the cockpit of the 42 is small, a molded stairway (rather than a ladder) leads up to the flybridge. Additional features include a shaded cockpit, transom door, radar arch, and wide side decks. An affordably priced boat, twin 318hp Volvo diesels will cruise the Navigator 42 Classic at 20 knots and reach a top speed in the neighborhood of 25 knots.

Navigator 4300 Flybridge Sedan

Length Overall	43'3"	Fuel	400/600 gals.
Beam	14'11"	Water	200 gals.
Draft	4'3"	Cockpit	60 sq. ft.
Weight	30,000#	Hull Type	Modified-V
Clearance	NA	Deadrise Aft	15°
Headroom	6'6"	Production	1990–94

The Navigator 4300 has the distinction of being one of the better-looking flybridge boats built in recent years. This is one of Navigator's earliest models; introduced in 1990, she was priced very competitively compared with other boats of her type and size. Like subsequent boats in the Navigator fleet, the 4300 rides on a solid fiberglass modified-V hull with plenty of beam and an integrated swim platform. With her small cockpit, few anglers will find the 4300 to be a serious fishing platform. As a family cruiser, however, she's in her element. At least two floorplans were offered during her production run, both two-stateroom, galley-up affairs with differing galley configurations. Both layouts included a double berth in each cabin, and each head came with a separate stall shower compartment. While the cabin accommodations are spacious for a boat this size, the look and feel of the interior is fairly Spartan. Note that a lower helm station was optional. Additional features include a radar arch, bow pulpit, transom door and reasonably wide side decks. Among several diesel engine options, twin 330hp Volvos will cruise the Navigator 4300 at a respectable 21–22 knots and reach a top speed of around 26 knots.

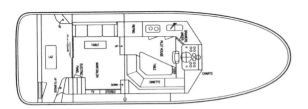

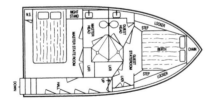

Ocean Alexander 42 Sedan

Length	42'0"	Water	150 gals.
Beam	14'4"	Headroom	6'4"
Draft	3'2"	Hull Type	Modified-V
Weight	23,000#	Deadrise Aft	NA
Clearance	11'6"	Designer	Ed Monk, Jr.
Fuel	500 gals.	Production	1987–94

One of Alexander's most popular models (about 140 were sold during her 7-year production run), the 42 Sedan is a well-proportioned family cruiser with a sensible layout and a fairly conservative profile. Like most Ocean Alexander designs, the 42 was built on an easy-riding modified-V hull with a shallow keel and cored hullsides. An appealing feature of the 42 Sedan is her large cockpit, which provides a good deal of open-air entertaining space for family and guests. Her interior is quite innovative in that a second (guest) stateroom with twin beds is fitted below the elevated galley. Visibility from the lower helm is very good, and most 42 Sedans were delivered with a full teak interior. Additional features include a transom door and swim platform, a well-arranged bridge with the helm forward (revised in 1990 with seating in front of the helm), reasonably wide side decks, and excellent interior joinerwork. A modest performer, standard 250hp Cummins will cruise the Alexander 42 Sedan at 14 knots (17–18 knots top), and 375hp Cats (the most popular choice) will cruise at 20–21 knots and reach a top speed of about 25 knots. Note that the Alexander 46 Sedan is the same boat with an extended salon.

Ocean Alexander 422 Sport Sedan

Length	42'0"	Water	150 gals.
Beam	14'4"	Headroom	6'4"
Draft	3'3"	Hull Type	Modified-V
Weight	33,100#	Deadrise Aft	NA
Fuel	500 gals.	Designer	Ed Monk, Jr.
Clearance	NA	Production	1994–2001

Introduced in 1994 as a replacement for Alexander's very successful 42 Sedan, the 422 Sport Sedan (called the 420 Sport Sedan in 1994–95) has a more rakish profile than her predecessor together with a reworked hull design with propeller tunnels to reduce draft and shaft angles. From the large cockpit, a pair of sliding glass doors open to the single-level salon where an L-shaped settee is to port and a raised galley forward, opposite the lower helm. Two staterooms and a single head are forward, but in the standard floorplan there is no direct entry to the head from the owner's stateroom—an unusual arrangement in a boat this size. Note the step-down storage room (with an engine room access door) behind the head compartment. One of the more attractive features of the 422 Sport Sedan—or any Ocean Alexander yacht for that matter—is the handcrafted interior teak joinerwork. From the cockpit, molded steps at the corners lead to the wide side decks and a transom door opens to the swim platform. Among several engine options, twin 375 Cat diesels deliver a cruising speed of 22 knots and a top speed of about 26 knots. More recent models with twin 420hp Cats deliver about the same speeds.

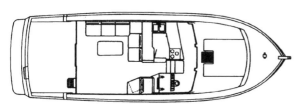

Main Deck

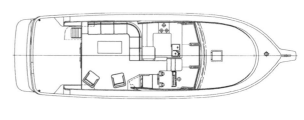

Lower Deck

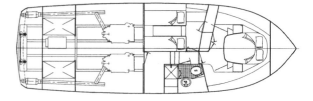

See Page 337 for Pricing Information

See Page 337 for Pricing Information

Pearson 34 Convertible

Length	33'9"	Water	70 gals.
Beam	13'0"	Headroom	6'4"
Draft	3'4"	Hull Type	Deep-V
Weight	19,000#	Deadrise Aft	19°
Clearance	NA	Designer	Hunt & Assoc.
Fuel	310 gals.	Production	1989–91

Pearson introduced the 34 Convertible in the late 1980s when the company was trying to break into the rapidly growing powerboat market. (Unfortunately, those efforts came too late and Pearson shut down a couple of years later.) A well-styled boat with attractive lines and a wide beam, her single-stateroom interior is arranged with the galley and dinette down resulting in a very spacious and comfortable salon. The decor is a tasteful blend of quality furnishings and well-matched teak joinery, and large cabin windows admit plenty of natural lighting. Considering her large interior, it's no surprise that the cockpit of the Pearson 34 is small compared with similar boats her size. The flybridge, however, is quite large for a 34-footer with bench seating forward of the helm. Additional features include a spacious engine room, transom door, bow pulpit, and a swim platform. A good headsea boat, standard 320hp Cat diesels will cruise the Pearson 34 Convertible at a steady 23 knots and reach a top speed in the high 20s. Note that the molds of the Pearson 34 Convertible were later used in the production of the Islander 34 from sailboat builder Catalina Yachts.

President 35 Sedan

Length	34'5"	Fuel	250 gals.
Beam	12'10"	Water	100 gals.
Draft	3'1"	Hull Type	Modified-V
Weight	18,700#	Deadrise Aft	NA
Clearance	11'7"	Designer	President
Cockpit	NA	Production	1987–92

The President 35 Sedan is a sturdy Taiwan import whose contemporary styling, full teak interior and affordable price offered buyers a good deal of value in a small flybridge boat. Built on a solid fiberglass hull with a relatively wide beam, the 35 can serve equally well as a light-tackle fisherman or weekend family cruiser. Buyers could chose either a single- or twin-stateroom interior, both of which came with a roomy head compartment and wraparound salon windows. A lower helm was optional, and hatches in the salon sole provide easy access to the engine room. (Note that the generator is installed beneath the cockpit sole—not the ideal location because of the risk of saltwater corrosion, but certainly quieter than if it were in the engine room.) The President's cockpit is on the small side for a 35-foot convertible although there's sufficient room for a couple of anglers and their gear. The side decks are quite wide, and visibility from the flybridge helm position is excellent in all directions. A transom door, swim platform, and bow pulpit were standard. Among several engine options, a pair of 225hp Lehman diesels will cruise the 35 Sedan at 15 knots and reach a top speed of around 18 knots.

FLYBRIDGE CRUISERS

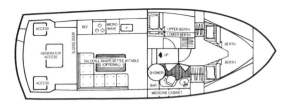

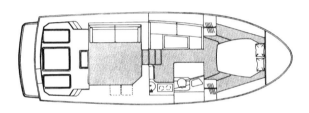

See Page 341 for Pricing Information

239

See Page 343 for Pricing Information

President 37 Sedan

Length	36'6"	Fuel	300 gals.
Beam	12'10"	Water	100 gals.
Draft	3'2"	Waste	40 gals.
Weight	20,400#	Hull Type	Modified-V
Clearance	11'6"	Deadrise Aft	NA
Headroom	6'3"	Production	1986–91

Introduced in the mid-1980s, the President 37 Sedan became popular with entry-level buyers thanks to her spacious interior and a very attractive price. Hull construction is solid fiberglass, and a shallow keel provides a good deal of directional stability. Several single- and twin-stateroom floorplans were available during her production years, all with a single head compartment as well as a spacious salon. Nearly all of these boats were delivered with a full teak interior, although later models offered light oak cabinetry as an option. Large cabin windows provide plenty of natural lighting in the salon, and hatches in the salon sole can be removed for access to the engine room. (Note that the generator is installed beneath the cockpit sole—not the ideal location because of the risk of saltwater corrosion, but certainly quieter than if it were in the engine room.) Above, the flybridge is arranged with guest seating forward of the helm. A bow pulpit, swim platform, and transom door were standard and a lower helm station was optional. Twin 275hp Lehmans provide a 16-knot cruising speed (about 20 knots top), and optional 300hp Cummins diesels will cruise at 21 knots (24–25 knots top).

Regal 3880 Commodore

Length Overall	40'1"	Water	80 gals.
Beam	13'0"	Waste	40 gals.
Draft	3'3"	Headroom	6'5"
Weight	19,300#	Hull Type	Modified-V
Clearance, Arch	16'9"	Deadrise Aft	18°
Fuel	252 gals.	Production	2001–Current

Regal's first-ever flybridge yacht, the 3880 Commodore (called the 3780 when she was introduced in 2001) is a notable departure from the company's 30-year history of producing family runabouts and express cruisers. In the mid-1990s, the rakish styling of the Commodore would have been striking; today it's pretty much the norm for mid-range flybridge sedans. The high side decks of the 3880 may not add much to her appearance, but they allow for a full-beam salon with the kind of living space seen only in a larger boat. The galley is down, opposite the small guest stateroom that extends under the salon. Hatches in the salon sole lift to reveal deep storage bins, and a bar counter divides the salon from the galley. Topside, the Commodore's flybridge is very spacious for a boat this size with seating for six and a double sun pad aft. Additional features include cockpit access to the engine room, a pair of foredeck sun pads, molded flybridge steps, a foldout cockpit seat, transom shower and overhead cockpit storage in the flybridge overhang. Twin 420hp V-drive gas engines will cruise at 20 knots (about 28 knots top), and optional 370hp Cummins diesels will also cruise at 22–23 knots and top out at 30 knots.

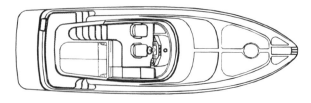

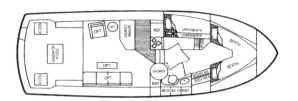

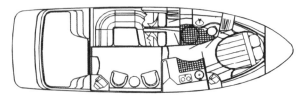

See Page 343 for Pricing Information

See Page 346 for Pricing Information

Roughwater 37

Length Overall . . . . 39'5"	Fuel, Twin . . . . 300 gals.
Length WL . . . . 33'0"	Water . . . . 100 gals.
Beam . . . . 11'7"	Headroom . . . . 6'4"
Draft . . . . 4'0"	Hull Type . . . . Semi-Disp.
Weight . . . . 16,000#	Designer . . . . Ed Monk, Jr.
Fuel, Single . . . . 230 gals.	Production 1981–88

There are several good reasons why the Roughwater 37 has endured so well over the years. Salty styling and functional interior are perhaps her most visible assets, and the Roughwater's slender, easily driven hull offers better speed and economy that most modern semi-displacement designs. The 37 was Roughwater's first all-fiberglass model, and her traditional, single-stateroom interior is ideal for the cruising couple. The main salon, separated from the pilothouse by a two-part hatch, contains a large convertible dinette, which is elevated to allow diners a good outside view. The large galley is flanked by two hanging lockers—just part of the enormous storage space available in this boat. A teak door closes off the stateroom for privacy, and ventilation and lighting in the salon are excellent. In the cockpit, storage boxes are conveniently located on both sides of the pilothouse door. The side decks are very wide, and a two-person bench seat is positioned on the flybridge. Engine room access is via hatches in the pilothouse floor. A single 200hp Perkins diesel will cruise the Roughwater 37 at 8–10 knots, and twin 215hp Detroit diesels will cruise at 14–16 knots.

Sea Ray 300 Sedan Bridge (1976–81)

Length Overall . . . . 30'11"	Water . . . . 40 gals.
Hull Length . . . . 29'7"	Headroom . . . . 6'2"
Beam . . . . 11'6"	Hull Type . . . . Deep-V
Draft . . . . 2'5"	Deadrise Aft . . . . 23°
Weight . . . . 11,300#	Designer . . . . Sea Ray
Fuel . . . . 130 gals.	Production 1976–81

A rakish boat in her day, the Sea Ray 300 Sedan Bridge combined a distinctive profile and family-size accommodations in an affordable package aimed at the family cruiser market. Built on a solid fiberglass hull, a wide 11-foot, 6-inch beam makes the Sedan Bridge a spacious boat below. The galley and dinette are down in this layout, and a lower helm was standard in the compact salon. There's a good deal of inexpensive teak trim and carpeted wall coverings throughout the interior, all of which render the decor completely dated by modern standards. While the cockpit is large enough for some light-tackle fishing, this is definitely not a fishing boat. Notable features include a teak bow pulpit, swim platform, underwater exhausts, cushioned foredeck seating, and a large engine room. On the downside, the fuel capacity is only 130 gallons. Among several engine options, twin 330hp gas inboards will cruise the Sedan Bridge at 18–19 knots and top out in the high 20s. Twin 250hp gas inboards cruise at 16–18 knots (around 25 knots top). Note that the Sea Ray 300 Express (1978–81) is essentially the same boat without the flybridge and salon bulkhead.

FLYBRIDGE CRUISERS

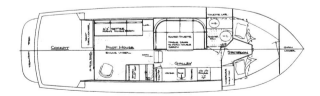

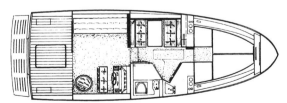

See Page 347 for Pricing Information

See Page 348 for Pricing Information

FLYBRIDGE CRUISERS

Length	29'1"	Water	40 gals.
Beam	11'0"	Cockpit	60 sq. ft.
Draft	2'5"	Hull Type	Deep-V
Weight	10,500#	Deadrise Aft	21°
Clearance	NA	Designer	Sea Ray
Fuel	140 gals.	Production	1985–87

Length	29'10"	Water	60 gals.
Beam	12'0"	Cockpit	40 sq. ft.
Draft	2'6"	Hull Type	Modified-V
Weight	11,500#	Deadrise Aft	18°
Clearance	NA	Designer	Sea Ray
Fuel	200 gals.	Production	1988–89

Introduced in 1985, the Sea Ray 300 Sedan Bridge is a wide-beam flybridge cruiser whose blend of spacious accommodations, contemporary lines, and affordable price appealed to entry-level buyers looking for a lot of boat for the money. Designed primarily for the family market, she features an wide-open and very efficient floorplan with a full galley, a head with shower, and berths for as many as six. An angled double bed is fitted in the forward stateroom (rather than V-berths), and both the dinette and salon sofa convert to into double berths. A lower helm was a popular option in the Sedan Bridge, although visibility is less than ideal. Three lift-out hatches in the cockpit floor provide good access to the engine compartment, and a transom door and swim platform were standard. Topside, the flybridge is arranged cruising-style with the helm forward and guest seating aft. Note that side-dumping exhausts keep noxious fumes out of the cockpit. On the downside, the side decks are quite narrow on this boat. Twin 260hp MerCruiser inboard gas engines (with V-drives) will cruise the 300 Sedan Bridge around 20 knots and top out in the high 20s.

Not remembered for her spectacular styling, the Sea Ray 300 Sedan Bridge (called the 305 Sedan Bridge when she was introduced in 1988) is long on interior accommodations but way short on sex appeal. (Indeed, her ungainly styling probably had something to do with her unusually brief two-year production run.) Built on a solid fiberglass hull with propeller pockets and a wide 12-foot beam, the interior accommodations are very spacious for a boat this size. With a midcabin stateroom tucked beneath the dinette, the 300 Sedan Bridge can boast two private staterooms in addition to a roomy salon with a full-size galley. The athwartships double-berth arrangement in the forward stateroom is innovative in its use of space, and the concealed galley is particularly appealing. The head is located aft in the salon, just inside the companionway door, where access from the outside is most convenient. While the cockpit is very small, the extended flybridge is exceptionally large for a boat this size. Standard 260hp MerCruiser gas engines (with V-drives) will cruise the Sea Ray 300 Sedan Bridge in the low 20s and develop a top speed of around 28–29 knots.

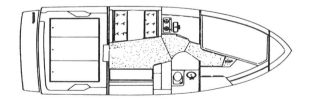

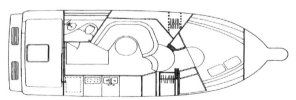

See Page 348 for Pricing Information

See Page 348 for Pricing Information

Sea Ray 310 Sport Bridge

Length w/Pulpit . . . . 33'8"	Cockpit . . . . 57 sq. ft.
Hull Length . . . . 31'2"	Fuel . . . . 296 gals.
Beam . . . . 11'5"	Water . . . . 40 gals.
Draft . . . . 3'1"	Hull Type . . . . Modified-V
Weight . . . . 11,500#	Deadrise Aft . . . . 18°
Clearance . . . . 9'6"	Production 1992–93

A handsome boat with rakish styling and a low-profile appearance, the 310 Sport Bridge is basically a Sea Ray 310 Amberjack with a flybridge and semi-enclosed lower helm. She's built on a solid fiberglass hull with a wide beam, side-dumping exhausts, and prop pockets to reduce shaft angles. With no salon bulkhead, the lower helm is open to the huge cockpit, which consumes well over half of the boat's length. While the 310's layout is basic, the accommodations are certainly up to the demands of hard-core anglers or cruising enthusiasts. A bulkhead separates the cabin from the optional lower helm, and a dinette is to port under the flybridge. While cabin space is at a premium, the 310 manages to include overnight berths for two plus a standup head with shower, small galley, and a removable table. Topside, the compact flybridge has seating for two. Additional features include hinged motor boxes, wide side decks, and a swim platform. Note that storage space is hard to come by on this boat. Twin 310hp MerCruisers will cruise at 23 knots (30–31 knots top), and optional 300hp Cummins diesels will cruise in the high 20s and reach 30+ knots wide open.

Sea Ray 340 Sedan Bridge

Length . . . . 33'7"	Water . . . . 80 gals.
Beam . . . . 11'11"	Headroom . . . . 6'3"
Draft . . . . 2'6"	Hull Type . . . . Deep-V
Weight . . . . 11,400#	Deadrise Aft . . . . 21°
Clearance . . . . NA	Designer . . . . Sea Ray
Fuel . . . . 204 gals.	Production 1983–87

A relatively popular model during her production years, the Sea Ray 340 Sedan Bridge is a roomy flybridge sedan whose rakish styling attracted a good many entry-level buyers. Clearly dated by today's Euro-style standards, the Sedan Bridge succeeded in her objective of providing comfortable accommodations and good handling in an affordable and well-engineered package. Built on the same deep-V hull used in the production of the 340 Express Cruiser, the single-stateroom interior of the Sedan Bridge is arranged with the galley and dinette down from the salon. A lower helm was a popular option, and a separate stall shower is found in the head. With the salon settee and dinette converted, there are overnight accommodations for six adults. The galley, opposite the dinette on the lower level, is very spacious and so is the stateroom. On deck, the cockpit is too small for any serious fishing, and the flybridge, with the helm forward and bench seating aft, is small as well. A transom door, cockpit steps, and swim platform were standard. Twin 350hp gas engines (with V-drives) will cruise the Sea Ray 340 Sedan Bridge at 20 knots with a top speed of around 30 knots.

FLYBRIDGE CRUISERS

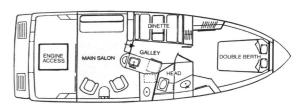

See Page 348 for Pricing Information

See Page 349 for Pricing Information

Sea Ray 340 Sport Fisherman

Sea Ray 340/345 Sedan Bridge

Length	33'7"	Water	52 gals.
Beam	11'11"	Headroom	6'4"
Draft	2'5"	Hull Type	Deep-V
Weight	10,600#	Deadrise Aft	21°
Clearance	NA	Designer	Sea Ray
Fuel	250 gals.	Production	1984–87

The Sea Ray 340 Sport Fisherman can best be described as a 340 Express Cruiser with a flybridge. Same hull, same power, same interior, etc.; the flybridge addition transformed her into a sportfisherman, at least in the eyes of Sea Ray's marketing gurus. In fact, the 340 is a competent light-tackle fishing boat although no one will ever confuse her offshore capabilities with a Bertram or Blackfin. Built on a solid fiberglass deep-V hull with moderate beam and prop pockets, the single-stateroom floorplan of the 340 SF is arranged with berths for four, a large galley, head with shower, and adequate storage. On deck, the partially enclosed helm is well-protected from the weather, and there's plenty of room in the cockpit for a couple of anglers. Unlike a dedicated sportfisherman, however, the cockpit of the 340 SF lacks any fishing amenities—no fish box, bait-prep center, tackle drawers, livewell, etc. Hatches under the helm and companion seats provide good access to the engines. Topside, the flybridge is very small. A transom door and side exhausts were standard. A good-running boat, standard 340hp gas engines will cruise the Sea Ray 340 at 20 knots and reach about 30 knots wide open.

Length	33'9"	Water	100 gals.
Beam	12'6"	Cockpit	44 sq. ft.
Draft	3'9"	Hull Type	Modified-V
Weight	16,500#	Deadrise Aft	NA
Clearance	NA	Designer	Sea Ray
Fuel	250 gals.	Production	1988–89

Lasting only two years in production, Sea Ray introduced this model in 1989 as the 345 Sedan Bridge and—for some marketing-related reason—called her the 340 Sedan Bridge the following year. Clearly, this was not one of Sea Ray's better-looking boats. While the interior is big for a 34-foot sedan, the extended flybridge, unusually tall arch, and small cockpit give the 340/345 Sedan Bridge an ungainly, decidedly unattractive appearance. She was built on a solid fiberglass hull with prop pockets and a wide 12-foot, 6-inch beam. Below, the two-stateroom floorplan will sleep six and includes a private midcabin with partial standing headroom under the dinette. Note that the galley is aft in the salon—an unusual layout in a sedan-style boat, but certainly convenient to those in the cockpit. As previously stated, the cockpit is very small, but its oversized flybridge includes lounge seating aft of the helm. A transom door, swim platform, and bow pulpit were standard. On the downside, the side decks are seriously narrow. Twin 340hp MerCruiser gas engines will cruise the Sea Ray 340/345 Sedan Bridge at 20 knots and deliver a top speed of close to 30 knots.

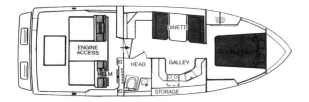

See Page 349 for Pricing Information

See Page 349 for Pricing Information

Sea Ray 350 Express Bridge

Length . . . . 35'4"	Water. . . . . 60 gals.
Beam . . . . 11'5"	Headroom . . . . 6'5"
Draft. . . . . 3'1"	Hull Type . . . . Deep-V
Weight . . . . 11,500#	Deadrise Aft . . . . 18°
Clearance . . . . NA	Designer. . . . . Sea Ray
Fuel. . . . . 200 gals.	Production 1992–94

There's no disguising the fact that the Sea Ray 350 Express Bridge delivers more in the way of accommodations than most any other boat her size on the market. Unlike most flybridge boats with the engine room under the salon, the engines are aft in the Sedan Bridge, under the cockpit. By lowering the salon floor and eliminating the side decks, the single-level interior of the Sedan Bridge seems vast indeed with room to entertain a small crowd. Facing semicircular settees dominate the salon, which is wide open to the large galley to port. The dinette converts into a sleeping area for four by night, and a privacy door separates the forward stateroom from the main cabin. (Note that there is no stall shower in the head.) The cockpit has a bench seat at the transom, and large hatches in the floor provide good access to the engines. Molded steps lead to the spacious flybridge where a door next to the helm opens to another set of steps leading out to the foredeck. A radar arch, transom door, and bow pulpit were standard. Among several engine options, twin 310hp V-drive inboards will cruise in the low 20s (30+ knots wide open), and twin 300hp sterndrives top out around 35 knots.

Sea Ray 355T Sedan

Length . . . . 36'3"	Water. . . . . 100 gals.
Beam . . . . 12'6"	Cockpit. . . . . 36 sq. ft.
Draft. . . . . 2'11"	Hull Type. . . . . Modified-V
Weight . . . . 13,000#	Deadrise Aft . . . . 9°
Clearance. . . . . 10'3"	Designer. . . . . Sea Ray
Fuel. . . . . 300 gals.	Production 1982–83

The Sea Ray 355T is a distinctively styled sedan cruiser with a spacious interior including what is arguably the largest master stateroom to be found in a boat under 40 feet. She was built on a solid fiberglass hull with prop pockets, side exhausts, and a shallow keel for directional stability. Rather than providing the usual two-stateroom interior in a boat this size, Sea Ray opted for a single-stateroom arrangement, which allowed for a very open main cabin. As noted, the master stateroom is enormous with a walkaround island berth, lots of dressing space, and a large hanging locker. A serving counter separates the step-down galley from the salon, and a starboardside lower helm was a popular option. Carpeted overheads, cheap teak-and-mica interior woodwork, and inexpensive furnishings add up to an unimpressive decor package. Topside, the cockpit is tiny, but the flybridge is large for a boat this size with built-in lounge seating aft of the helm. Twin 135hp Perkins diesels will cruise the 355T at an economical 10–12 knots and reach a top speed of about 16 knots. A total of 69 of these boats were built during her production run.

FLYBRIDGE CRUISERS

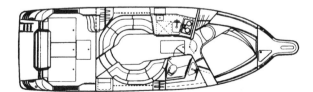

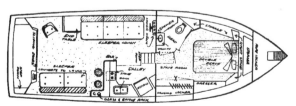

Sea Ray 360 Sedan SF

Length w/Pulpit . . . . 38'2"	Fuel . . . . 400 gals.
Hull Length. . . . . 36'6"	Water . . . . 100 gals.
Beam . . . . 13'11"	Hull Type . . . . Deep-V
Draft . . . . 2'7"	Deadrise Aft . . . . 19°
Weight . . . . 18,400#	Designer . . . . Sea Ray
Clearance . . . . NA	Production 1980–82

Largest model in the Sea Ray fleet back in the early 1980s, the Sea Ray 360 Sedan was marketed as a sportfisherman although it's doubtful that many anglers would find her small cockpit suitable for any serious fishing pursuits. She rides on a solid fiberglass hull with prop pockets and a very wide 13-foot, 11-inch beam. Below, the two-stateroom interior is arranged with an angled bed in the forward cabin and over/under single bunks in the guest stateroom. The head is fitted with a separate stall shower, and the salon is surprisingly spacious for a 36-footer with a recessed bar, high-low coffee table, convertible sofa, and a serving counter overlooking the galley. (Note that the galley includes a full-size, upright refrigerator/freezer.) As mentioned previously, the cockpit is on the small side and the absence of a transom door is notable. Topside, the flybridge is designed with bench seating forward of the helm. Additional features include side-dumping exhausts, swim platform, bow pulpit, and relatively wide side decks. Twin 330hp gas inboards will cruise the 360 Sedan at 17–18 knots and deliver a top speed in the mid 20s. Optional 320hp Cat diesels provide a cruising speed of around 20 knots (23–24 knots top).

Sea Ray 370 Sedan Bridge

Length w/Platform . . . . 40'10"	Water . . . . 70 gals.
Hull Length . . . . 36'10"	Waste . . . . 20 gals.
Beam . . . . 12'4"	Hull Type . . . . Deep-V
Draft . . . . 2'7"	Deadrise Aft . . . . 21°
Weight . . . . 14,600#	Designer . . . . Sea Ray
Fuel . . . . 250 gals.	Production 1991–97

With her long foredeck and relatively small cockpit, the 370 Sedan Bridge is a maxi-volume family cruiser with conservative lines and a very spacious interior. She's built on solid fiberglass deep-V with prop pockets, moderate beam, and side-dumping exhausts. Below, the two-stateroom floorplan of the 370 features an expansive salon with a full-length settee, removable dinette table, breakfast bar, and large wraparound cabin windows. An angled double berth resides in the bow stateroom, and the portside guest cabin has another double berth extending below the salon sole. Oak trim and earth-tone wall coverings highlight the interior, and the double-entry head has a separate stall shower. Topside, the cockpit includes a transom door and optional bench seating, while the flybridge is arranged with L-shaped lounge seating aft of the helm. On the downside, the side decks are rather narrow. Additional features include a radar arch, swim platform, tilt steering wheel, and a bow pulpit. A lower helm station was optional. Standard 310hp MerCruiser gas inboards will cruise the 370 Sedan Bridge at a 18 knots and deliver a top speed in the mid-to-high 20s.

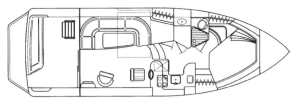

See Page 349 for Pricing Information

See Page 349 for Pricing Information

Sea Ray 400 Sedan Bridge

Length w/Platform	44'0"	Fuel	350 gals.
Hull Length	41'6"	Water	120 gals.
Beam	14'3"	Waste	28 gals.
Draft	3'4"	Hull Type	Deep-V
Weight	22,000#	Deadrise Aft	18.5°
Clearance	NA	Production	1996–2003

The resemblance between the Sea Ray 400 Sedan Bridge and several imported sportyachts of the mid-1990s was more than just skin deep. Aside from her aggressive styling, the interior configurations of the Sedan Bridge are right out of a European design book. Sea Ray offered a choice of two spacious floorplans, both with a pedestal island bed in the forward stateroom. Plan A includes three staterooms on the lower level with the galley in the salon and a portside dinette, while Plan B is a two-stateroom affair with the galley down and a lower helm to port. A wide 14-foot, 3-inch beam provides lot of elbow room below, and high-gloss cabinetry and vinyl overheads highlight the interior. The cockpit is arranged with a built-in transom seat, molded-in flybridge steps, and transom door, and the bridge came with a U-shaped settee or an aft-facing sun lounge. On the downside, the engine room is a tight fit. Built on a fully cored hull with prop pockets and underwater exhausts, twin 370hp MerCruiser inboards will cruise the Sea Ray 400 Sedan Bridge at 20 knots (high 20s top), and optional 340hp Cat diesels cruise at 22 knots (about 25+ knots top).

Sea Ray 440 Express Bridge

Length w/Pulpit	47'1"	Fuel	400 gals.
Hull Length	44'0"	Water	100 gals.
Beam	13'11"	Waste	60 gals.
Draft	3'3"	Hull Type	Modified-V
Weight	28,000#	Deadrise Aft	19°
Clearance	NA	Production	1993–98

A great entertainment platform, the Sea Ray 440 Express Bridge has one of the more expansive interior layouts of any similar boat in her class. Like all of the so-called express bridge designs with their space-saving V-drive power systems and low deckhouse profiles, the 440's sunken salon utilizes the entire width of the hull to create a huge, wide-open floorplan laid out on a single level. With the engines under the cockpit, there's even room for an innovative mid-cabin stateroom beneath the molded cockpit bridge steps—something not seen in other express bridge models. Built on a fully cored hull with moderate beam and prop pockets to reduce the shaft angles, the 440's huge, party-time flybridge is arranged with the wraparound helm console/settee on the centerline and additional bench seating forward. A pass-through in the bridge coaming provides access to the foredeck with its built-in bench seating. The cockpit features a full bench seat at the transom as well as dual transom doors and a gas-assist hatch for engine access. Optional 340hp Cat diesels will cruise the 440 Express Bridge at 20 knots and deliver a top speed of 23–24 knots.

FLYBRIDGE CRUISERS

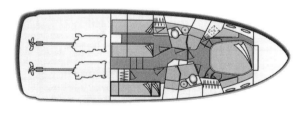

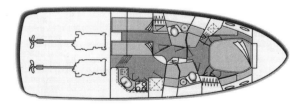

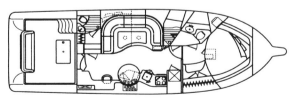

See Page 350 for Pricing Information

See Page 350 for Pricing Information

Sea Ray 450 Express Bridge

Length w/Pulpit & Platform	51'4"	Fuel	400 gals.
Hull Length	45'6"	Water	100 gals.
Beam	14'8"	Headroom	6'8"
Draft	3'5"	Hull Type	Modified-V
Weight	29,500#	Deadrise Aft	15°
Clearance	14'0"	Production	1998–2004

Sea Ray moved the innovation bar up a notch when they introduced the 450 Sedan Bridge in 1998. It wasn't just her sleek styling that drew attention; the real innovation is below where Sea Ray designers were able to incorporate a unique floorplan whose raised salon dinette conceals two staterooms below. The aft stateroom, which is accessed via a private entryway next to the salon door, includes a full-length bed with a hanging locker and built-in washer/dryer. Guests in the amidships stateroom have direct access to one of two heads, and the forward stateroom is fitted with a pedestal bed as well as a full entertainment center. High-gloss cherry cabinetry, faux granite countertops, and vinyl overheads highlight this upscale interior. Topside, the party-time flybridge has an L-shaped centerline helm with a wet bar and seating for a small crowd. A door in the forward bridge coaming provides quick access to the foredeck. Underwater exhausts, a radar arch, and a foldaway cockpit seat were standard, and an extended swim platform is a popular option. Twin 420hp V-drive Cats (or 430hp Cummins) diesels will cruise the Express Bridge at 20 knots and top out in the mid 20s.

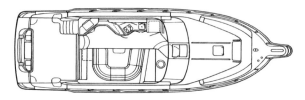

Main Deck

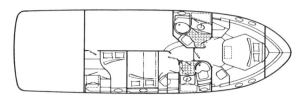

Lower Level

Silverton 29 Sportcruiser

Length	29'2"	Water	40 gals.
Beam	10'10"	Cockpit	50 sq. ft.
Draft	1'7"	Hull Type	Modified-V
Weight	7,800#	Deadrise Aft	NA
Clearance	8'2"	Designer	M. Peters
Fuel	150 gals.	Production	1985–87

A fairly plain design by today's high-glitz sportboat standards, the Silverton 29 Sportcruiser is a surprisingly spacious boat with a very unusual two-stateroom interior and a huge (for a 29-footer) flybridge. Hull construction is solid fiberglass, and—with the engines located under the cockpit sole—prop pockets (and not V-drives) are used to reduce the shaft angles. If her conservative lines are dated, the Sportcruiser's single-level, full-beam floorplan was still a relatively new concept back in the mid-1980s. What really separates her from other boats, however, is the layout. There's a second stateroom aft of the dinette with an athwartships bed, night stand, and a sliding privacy door. This completely unusual arrangement results in a tight salon, however, with very little elbow space. Topside, the flybridge is among the largest to be found in a boat this size with seating for five. Twin hatches in the cockpit provide good engine access, and a bow pulpit was standard. With such narrow side decks, one has to be extremely careful in attempting to get to the foredeck—a very serious issue. Twin 195hp Crusader (V6) gas engines will cruise the Silverton 29 Sportcruiser at 17–18 knots with a top speed in the mid 20s.

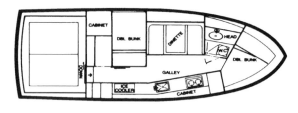

See Page 350 for Pricing Information

See Page 352 for Pricing Information

Silverton 31 Convertible (1976–87)

Length . . . . 31'0"	Water . . . . 40 gals.
Beam . . . . 11'11"	Cockpit . . . . 82 sq. ft.
Draft . . . . 2'11"	Hull Type . . . . Modified-V
Weight . . . . 11,400#	Deadrise Aft . . . . NA
Clearance . . . . 10'8"	Designer . . . . Silverton
Fuel . . . . 220 gals.	Production 1976–87

A popular boat for many years, the appeal of the Silverton 31 Convertible (production ran for over a decade) had much to do with her roomy accommodations, attractive design, and affordable price tag. Compared with other convertibles and family sedans her size, the Silverton 31 gets high marks for a spacious salon—a rare luxury in a boat this small—with room to comfortably seat several guests without being cramped. The single-stateroom interior of the Silverton 31 (updated in 1983) is arranged with V-bunks forward and the galley down. A lower helm was optional, and the salon sofa converts into a double berth for guests. Her large cockpit provides a good platform for swimming and casual fishing activities, and the small flybridge will seat three around a centerline helm. The Silverton 31 received a styling update in 1983 when the deckhouse was redesigned with a more modern profile. A new light oak interior was added in 1985 replacing the original teak woodwork. Among several engine options, a pair of 220hp V-drive gas inboards will cruise the Silverton 31 Convertible around 17–18 knots and deliver a top speed of about 27 knots.

Silverton 31 Convertible (1991–95)

Length . . . . 31'2"	Fuel . . . . 250 gals.
Beam . . . . 11'8"	Water . . . . 84 gals.
Draft . . . . 3'0"	Hull Type . . . . Modified-V
Weight . . . . 11,000#	Deadrise Aft . . . . NA
Clearance . . . . 11'9"	Designer . . . . Silverton
Cockpit . . . . 48 sq. ft.	Production 1991–95

The Silverton 31 has the distinction of being one of the roomier sedans of her size as well as having been one of the least expensive—critical components for any entry-level family boat. Hull construction is solid fiberglass and, with an 11-foot, 8-inch beam, this is a fairly wide 31-footer. Originally offered with a midcabin interior (with a claustrophobic "stateroom" off the galley extending under the salon), in 1992 Silverton offered the option of a single-stateroom "convertible" interior with a larger galley, but without the midcabin's elevated dinette. The salon, incidentally, is very spacious for a boat this size with good headroom and wraparound cabin windows. Both floorplans have an island double berth in the private forward stateroom as well as a separate stall shower in the head. With such generous interior accommodations, it comes as no surprise to find the cockpit of the Silverton 31 is quite small. A transom door was standard, and molded steps at the corners lead to the 31's notably wide side decks. Bench seating on the flybridge will seat as many as five guests. Standard 235hp gas engines will cruise at a respectable 18–19 knots and deliver a top speed in the mid 20s.

1976–82

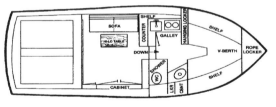

1983–87

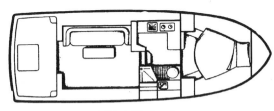

Mid-Cabin Interior

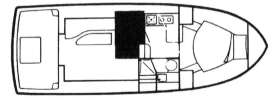

Single-Stateroom Interior

Silverton 312 Sedan Cruiser

Length Overall . . . . 32'0"	Fuel . . . . 160 gals.
Hull Length . . . . 28'0"	Water . . . . 54 gals.
Beam . . . . 11'6"	Waste . . . . 28 gals.
Draft . . . . 2'8"	Hull Type . . . . Modified-V
Weight . . . . 9,937#	Deadrise Aft . . . . 14°
Clearance . . . . 12'3"	Production 1994–99

The 312 Sedan is a budget-priced family cruiser notable for her low price and her unusual sterndrive power. (Indeed, sterndrive-powered convertibles in this size range are practically nonexistent.) Hull construction is solid fiberglass, and the rakish lines and low profile of the 312 give her a rather sporty personality. (Interestingly, the flybridge wasn't an add-on, but part of the deck mold, a cost-effective construction technique that also eliminates the possibility of leaks.) Belowdecks, the 312 sleeps six—no small feat for a 30-footer: two in the forward stateroom, two in a curtained-off open area opposite the head with upper/lower bunks, and two more when the salon dinette is converted into a double berth. A sliding glass door opens to the cockpit where a transom door is standard and a series of molded steps to port lead up to a large flybridge. Fender racks are built into the swim platform, and L-shaped lounge seating on the bridge will seat four. Among several engine options, twin 235hp 5.7-liter MerCruisers will cruise the Silverton 312 at 20 knots and reach a top speed of 30+ knots. Note that V-drive gas inboard engines were optional.

Silverton 330 Sport Bridge

Length Overall . . . . 35'4"	Water . . . . 104 gals.
Beam . . . . 12'4"	Waste . . . . 30 gals.
Draft . . . . 2'11"	Headroom . . . . 6'5"
Weight . . . . 15,685#	Hull Type . . . . Modified-V
Clearance . . . . 11'0"	Deadrise Aft . . . . 16°
Fuel . . . . 214 gals.	Production 1999–Current

Silverton has proven very adept in recent years at marketing afford-ably priced family yachts with mega-volume interiors and innovative design features. The 330 Sport Bridge follows in that tradition, and she's been a popular model for Silverton since her 1999 introduction. Built on a solid fiberglass hull with a wide beam, the single-state-room floorplan of the 330 is laid out on a single level a few steps down from the cockpit. These are expansive accommodations indeed for a 33-foot boat with excellent headroom, attractive furnishings, and a full-beam salon. (Note that the floorplan was rearranged in 2001.) On deck, a stairway in the cockpit leads to an oversized flybridge with a wet bar and seating for six to seven adults, and molded steps on either side of the bridge lead down to the foredeck area. Engine access is via a gas-assist hatch in the cockpit, and a transom door and swim platform are standard. Additional features include opening salon windows, a flybridge sun pad, side exhausts, anchor locker and bow pulpit. Twin V-drive 300hp gas inboards will cruise the 330 Sport Bridge at 18 knots (25–26 knots top), and 385hp engines will cruise at 20 knots and reach a top speed of around 30 knots.

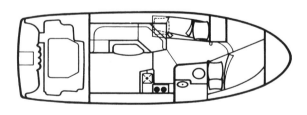

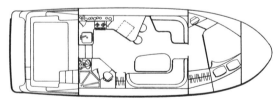

1999–2000

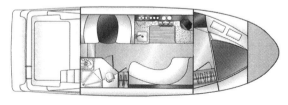

2001–Current

See Page 352 for Pricing Information

See Page 352 for Pricing Information

FLYBRIDGE CRUISERS

Length	34'0"	Water	40 gals.
Beam	12'6"	Cockpit	70 sq. ft.
Draft	3'1"	Hull Type	Modified-V
Weight	12,500#	Deadrise Aft	15°
Clearance	11'6"	Designer	J. Fielding
Fuel	220 gals.	Production	1978–83

Length	34'0"	Water	40 gals.
Beam	12'6"	Cockpit	70 sq. ft.
Draft	3'1"	Hull Type	Modified-V
Weight	12,500#	Deadrise Aft	15°
Clearance	13'3"	Designer	J. Fielding
Fuel	250 gals.	Production	1984–88

First of a series of 34-foot sedans offered by Silverton over the years, the 34 Convertible was a comparatively inexpensive boat when she was introduced in 1978. She was marketed to entry-level buyers looking for a versatile family cruiser with the ability to do a little light-tackle fishing. The 34 rides on a solid fiberglass hull with a well-flared bow and moderate beam—a proven hull design used for several succeeding Silverton models. The low-profile appearance of the Silverton 34 is the result of locating the engines under the cockpit—rather than under the salon sole—where V-drives deliver the power. This permits the salon floor to be lowered, which, in turn, reduces the boat's profile. Her single-stateroom interior will sleep six with both the dinette and salon sofa converted. The galley and dinette are down, a lower helm was standard, and large cabin windows provide plenty of outside natural lighting. A pair of hatches in the cockpit provide good access to the engines, and a bench seat on the small flybridge seats three. A popular boat for Silverton, twin 270hp Crusader gas engines will cruise the Silverton 34 at 18 knots and deliver a top speed of 26–27 knots.

Introduced in 1984, the Silverton 34 Convertible is a restyled and updated version of Silverton's original 34 Convertible (previous entry) built from 1978 to 1983. She was, like her predecessor, a popular model thanks to a low price and a comfortable interior. Built on a solid fiberglass hull, the rakish styling of the 34 has held up well over the years. A pair of single-stateroom, galley-down floorplans were offered—one with a double berth forward and the other with V-berths. There are berths for six with the dinette and salon sofa converted, and a lower helm was a popular option. Large wraparound cabin windows admit plenty of natural lighting, which adds to the perception of space in the salon. Although the 34 was an inexpensive boat with low-cost furnishings and a so-so finish, there's much to admire in her efficient use of space and impressive list of standard equipment. The cockpit is large enough for occasional fishing adventures, and there's seating for four on the flybridge. Additional features include a well-arranged engine room under the salon, wide side decks, bow pulpit, and teak interior trim. Twin 270hp inboard gas engines will cruise at 18–19 knots and top out in the high 20s.

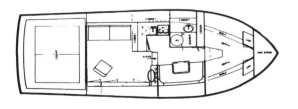

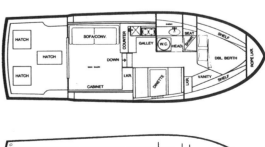

See Page 352 for Pricing Information

See Page 352 for Pricing Information

Silverton 34 Convertible (1989–90)

Length . . . . 34'6"	Water. . . . . 40 gals.
Beam . . . . 12'7"	Cockpit . . . . 56 sq. ft.
Draft. 3'2"	Hull Type . . . . Modified-V
Weight. . . . . 13,500#	Deadrise Aft . . . . 17°
Clearance. . . . . 13'5"	Designer . . . . M. Peters
Fuel . . . . 300 gals.	Production 1989–90

Introduced in 1989 as a replacement for Silverton's previous 34 Convertible (1984–88), this new, more rakish Silverton 34 lasted only two years in production before being replaced herself with an updated model in 1991. She was built on a better-riding hull than her predecessor with additional fuel capacity and an improved bottom design for better headsea performance. Like all Silverton boats, hull construction is solid fiberglass. With her extended deckhouse and small cockpit, it's clear she was designed with family cruising in mind rather than fishing. The interior of the 34 will sleep six in three separate areas—the salon sofa and dinette convert to sleep two each, and an island berth is located in the private stateroom forward. While the salon dimensions aren't overly generous, large wraparound cabin windows and excellent headroom add to the impression of space. (Note that a lower helm was a popular option.) If the cockpit seems small, the flybridge—with the helm forward—is big for a 34-footer. Standard 350hp Crusader inboard gas engines will cruise the Silverton 34 Convertible at 19–20 knots and reach a top speed in the high 20s.

Silverton 34 Convertible (1991–95)

Length . . . . 34'6"	Water. . . . . 40 gals.
Beam . . . . 12'10"	Waste . . . . 28 gals.
Draft. . . . . 2'11"	Cockpit . . . . 56 sq. ft.
Weight. . . . . 13,500#	Hull Type . . . . Modified-V
Clearance. . . . . 13'5"	Deadrise Aft . . . . 17°
Fuel . . . . 300 gals.	Production 1991–95

A restyled version of the company's previous 34-foot convertible (1989–90), the Silverton 34 Convertible offers an impressive combination of low cost, contemporary styling, and comfortable accommodations. She was built on a solid fiberglass hull with a reworked bottom and slightly more beam than her predecessor. Both single- and twin-stateroom floorplans were offered in this boat, both with an island berth in the forward stateroom, and both with the galley down from the salon level. The single-stateroom floorplan has a full-size dinette opposite the galley. In the two-stateroom version, a small cabin with upper/lower berths is available for guests, and the dinette is relocated to the salon. Either way, the salon dimensions are somewhat modest although the wraparound cabin windows, light oak cabinetry and pastel fabrics add to the impression of space. Additional features include a stall shower in the head, wide side decks, side-dumping exhausts, a swim platform, and a bow pulpit. Note that in 1995 the flybridge was restyled. A good-selling boat, standard 350hp Crusader gas inboards will cruise the Silverton 34 at 18 knots and reach a top speed in the high 20s.

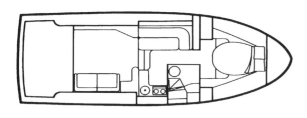

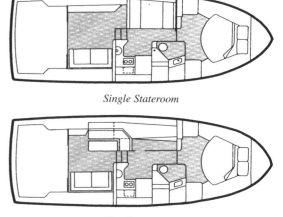

Single Stateroom

Two Staterooms

See Page 352 for Pricing Information

See Page 352 for Pricing Information

Silverton 34 Convertible (Current)

Length	37'7"	Fuel	286 gals.
Beam	13'10"	Water	94 gals.
Draft	3'3"	Waste	37 gals.
Weight	17,440#	Hull Type	Modified-V
Clearance	12'7"	Deadrise Aft	12°
Headroom	6'6"	Production	2004–Current

Silverton has offered a 34-foot convertible in their lineup ever since the late 1970s. This is the latest version, a stylish flybridge cruiser that might best be described as a lot of boat for the money. With nearly 14 feet of beam, this 34 is a more spacious boat than any of her predecessors. The extra volume is especially noticed in the salon where Silverton designers have been able to find room for a dinette in addition to an entertainment center aft and starboardside sofa. The large galley includes an upright refrigerator as well as Corian counters and generous storage. Forward, an angled double berth is found in the master stateroom, while the small guest stateroom is fitted with over/under single berths. To save space, the head is split with the shower stall to starboard. The Silverton's interior is tastefully appointed with cherry cabinetry, vinyl overheads, and earth-tone fabrics. A transom door and in-deck fish box are standard in the small cockpit, and molded access steps lead up to the flybridge. (Note that bridge overhang shades the forward part of the cockpit from the sun.) A modest performer with a pair 330hp gas inboards, the Silverton 34 will cruise at 16 knots and top out at just over 20 knots.

Silverton 34 Sedan

Length	34'0"	Water	40 gals.
Beam	12'6"	Cockpit	100 sq. ft.
Draft	3'1"	Hull Type	Modified-V
Weight	12,500#	Deadrise Aft	15°
Clearance	11'6"	Designer	Silverton
Fuel	220 gals.	Production	1977–80

The Silverton 34 Sedan was conceived as a stylish (for the late 1970s, at least) family cruiser with big-boat accommodations and an affordable price tag. She rides on a solid fiberglass hull with moderate beam, a fairly flat sheer, and considerable flare at the bow. With her engines located under the cockpit sole (rather than beneath the salon), the salon floor sits low in the hull which reduces the profile of the 34. Belowdecks, the interior is arranged on a single level—no steps leading down to the forward stateroom—which creates the impression of a large and very open cabin. The inside helm was a standard feature, and the visibility is quite good considering the lowered salon level. Both the galley and head are located aft, just inside the salon door, where they're within easy reach of those outside. The cockpit measures a full 100 square feet—large for a boat of this type with enough room for two anglers and their gear. Hatches in the cockpit sole provide good access to the motors and V-drive units. Chrysler 250hp gas engines were standard, with 270hp Crusaders offered as options. Cruising speeds for both are 17–18 knots with top speeds are in the mid 20s.

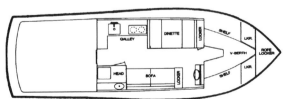

FLYBRIDGE CRUISERS

See Page 352 for Pricing Information

See Page 353 for Pricing Information

Silverton 351 Sedan

Silverton 362 Sedan

Length	38'10"	Water	94 gals.
Beam	13'0"	Waste	37 gals.
Draft	2'5"	Headroom	6'6"
Weight	16,094#	Hull Type	Modified-V
Clearance	12'0"	Deadrise Aft	12°
Fuel	300 gals.	Production	1997–2001

Length	36'1"	Water	100 gals.
Beam	12'11"	Waste	40 gals.
Draft	3'0"	Hull Type	Modified-V
Weight	15,058#	Deadrise Aft	17°
Clearance	13'0"	Designer	Silverton
Fuel	300 gals.	Production	1994–98

With the introduction of the 351 Sedan in 1997, Silverton engineers introduced a dramatically different approach to the design of the modern family cruiser. All manufacturers recognize the appeal of a roomy interior, but Silverton made it happen with the introduction of their "SideWalk" concept, a series of molded steps on the starboard side of the boat leading from the foredeck up to the flybridge and then down again to the cockpit. The result of this clever design is a spacious full-width salon with the floor space of a much larger boat. Built on a modified-V hull with side exhausts and prop pockets, the engines are located aft, beneath the cockpit rather than under the salon, which allows the cabin floor to sit low in the hull. Lacking side decks, the interior is huge and the apartment-sized galley will be a real crowd-pleaser, but with only a single stateroom these expansive living areas come as no great surprise. A pair of glass sliding doors open to a spacious cockpit, and the flybridge is arranged with a walkaround centerline helm and lounge seating forward. No racehorse, a pair of V-drive 320hp gas engines will cruise at 14–15 knots and reach a top speed in the mid 20s. (Note that she was called the Silverton 35 Convertible in 2001.)

A good-looking boat with an attractive deckhouse profile, the Silverton 362 is an affordably priced family cruiser with a lot of living space packed into her 36-foot hull. She's built on a solid fiberglass hull with a wide beam and a relatively steep 17 degrees of transom deadrise. The two-stateroom floorplan is arranged with a mid-level galley and an island berth in the forward stateroom. The guest stateroom (which extends beneath the salon settee) has two single berths that convert into a queen berth with a filler. Note the split head/shower compartments, a great idea that allows someone to take a shower without tying up the head. With her spacious interior dimensions, it's no surprise that the 362's cockpit is on the small side. Two hatches in the sole provide easy access to the engines, and molded steps lead up to the oversize flybridge with its wraparound lounge seating. Additional features include side-dumping exhausts, radar arch, transom door, and foldaway bench seating at the transom. On the downside, the uneven finish reflects her low price. Twin 320hp V-drive Crusader gas inboards will cruise the 362 Sedan at 18 knots and deliver a top speed in the high 20s.

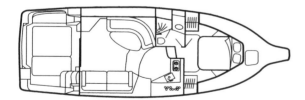

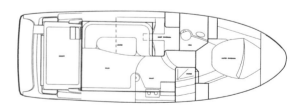

See Page 353 for Pricing Information
See Page 353 for Pricing Information

Length	37'0"	Water	100 gals.
Beam	14'0"	Cockpit	75 sq. ft.
Draft	3'7"	Hull Type	Modified-V
Weight	20,000#	Deadrise Aft	14°
Clearance	12'6"	Designer	Bob Rioux
Fuel	300 gals.	Production	1980–89

Length w/Pulpit	41'3"	Fuel	375 gals.
Hull Length	37'4"	Water	100 gals.
Beam	13'11"	Waste	40 gals.
Draft	3'7"	Hull Type	Modified-V
Weight	21,852#	Deadrise Aft	17°
Clearance	18'2"	Production	1990–2001

Clean lines, a roomy interior, and an attractive price made the Silverton 37 Convertible one of the most popular boats in her class during the 1980s. Unlike many other convertibles this size, the Silverton 37 came with a single-stateroom floorplan with a full-size dinette in place of a second stateroom. The salon is completely open to the galley in this layout, and wraparound cabin windows admit plenty of natural lighting. There's a stall shower in the head, and light oak paneling is applied throughout the interior. (Teak woodwork is found in pre-1985 models.) While the decor is obviously dated, this is a space-efficient layout that can easily be upgraded with new fabrics and furnishings. The cockpit is large enough for a couple of anglers, and the flybridge is arranged with guest seating forward of the helm. Twin 200hp Perkins diesels were standard in early models, but the majority of Silverton 37s were powered with twin 350hp Crusader gas engines. The cruising speed is 18–19 knots with a top speed in the high 20s. Note that Silverton replaced the original V-drive engine installations with straight-drive inboards in 1981—a significant modification.

With her rakish appearance, affordable price, and spacious interior, the 37 Convertible was a highly successful boat for Silverton during the 1990s. (Note that an earlier Silverton 37 Convertible was produced from 1980–89.) Built on a solid fiberglass, modified-V hull with a wide beam and prop pockets to reduce draft, Silverton offered this model with "convertible" and "midcabin" interiors. (Note that the original floorplans were updated in 1993.) The convertible layout contains a single private stateroom forward with the galley and dinette down, while the midcabin features a small guest stateroom with over/under berths opposite the galley. A separate stall shower is found in the double-entry head, and the decor is a tasteful blend of teak or light oak trim and inexpensive fabrics. While the 37 is more family cruiser than fishboat, the cockpit is roomy enough for a couple of light-tackle anglers and features an in-deck fish box and a transom door. Additional features include wide side decks, wraparound lounge seating on the bridge, bow pulpit, a well-arranged engine room, and side-dumping exhausts. No racehorse, standard 320hp gas engines will cruise the Silverton 37 at 15–16 knots with a top speed in the mid 20s.

FLYBRIDGE CRUISERS

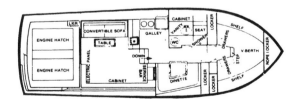

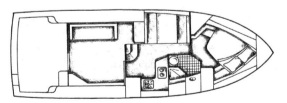

Convertible Interior, 1993–2001

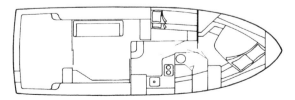

Mi-Cabin Interior, 1993–2001

See Page 353 for Pricing Information

See Page 353 for Pricing Information

Silverton 38 Convertible

Length w/Pulpit	41'3"	Fuel	360 gals.
Beam	14'0"	Water	100 gals.
Draft	3'7"	Waste	40 gals.
Weight	22,852#	Hull Type	Modified-V
Clearance	16'8"	Deadrise Aft	17°
Headroom	6'8"	Production	2003–Current

Modern styling, comfortable accommodations, and competitive pricing are the hallmarks of the Silverton 38 Convertible, a versatile midsize cruiser with fishboat capabilities. At under 25,000 pounds, the 38 is a very weight-efficient boat in spite of her wide beam. The interior, highlighted by plush Ultraleather upholstery and cherry cabinetry, gets high marks for its tasteful decor, large cabin windows, and excellent headroom. There are two staterooms below, and while the pedestal berth in the master stateroom is a bit high, it conceals a washer/dryer unit under the bed. The guest stateroom, which extends under the salon sole, comes with a full-size hanging locker and twin single berths, and the single head is split with the shower to port and the sink and toilet to starboard. The galley, three steps down from the salon, includes plenty of storage as well as a hardwood floor. Outside, the cockpit has two fish boxes in the sole and a storage box in the transom. (A bait-prep center is optional.) A staircase ascends to the bridge, and a cockpit hatch provides access to the engine room. Standard 385hp gas inboards will cruise the Silverton 38 at 18 knots and top out in the mid 20s.

Silverton 38 Sport Bridge

Length	39'9"	Fuel	372 gals.
Beam	14'4"	Water	110 gals.
Draft	2'11"	Waste	40 gals.
Weight	26,900#	Hull Type	Modified-V
Clearance	14'11"	Deadrise Aft	12°
Headroom	6'6"	Production	2005–Current

Silverton has proven adept in recent years at marketing affordably priced family yachts with maxi-volume interiors and innovative features. The 38 Sport Bridge follows in the footsteps of the company's popular 330 Sport Bridge introduced back in 1999. Built on a solid fiberglass hull with a wide beam, the spacious, full-beam interior of the 38 Sport Bridge is made possible by raising the side decks from bow to bridge on both sides of the boat. The result is a wide-open interior whose dimensions resemble those of a much larger boat. The salon is comfortable and brightly lit with windows all around and more headroom than most boats her size. The dinette is a step up from the salon floor to make room for the midcabin below, and the split head is separated with the toilet to starboard and the shower to port. Molded steps in the cockpit lead up to the 38's large flybridge with its generous lounge seating, wet bar, and forward helm position. A hatch in the cockpit sole reveals a removable storage bin, and there's additional storage in the transom for fenders and miscellaneous gear. An extended swim platform and radar arch are standard. Note that the engine room is a tight fit. Expect a cruising speed in the low 20s with 425hp gas engines, and 24–25 knots with optional 355hp Cummins diesels.

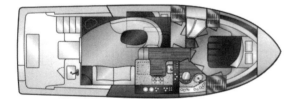

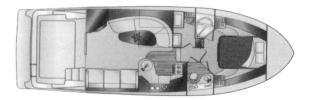

See Page 353 for Pricing Information

See Page 353 for Pricing Information

Silverton 40 Convertible

Length . . . . 40'0"	Water . . . . 100 gals.
Beam . . . . 14'0"	Cockpit . . . . 79 sq. ft.
Draft . . . . 3'0"	Hull Type . . . . Modified-V
Weight . . . . 23,000#	Deadrise Aft . . . . 14°
Clearance . . . . 13'6"	Designer . . . . Bob Rioux
Fuel . . . . 300 gals.	Production 1985–90

A conservatively styled boat with a distinctive profile (note the stepped sheer), the Silverton 40 Convertible was one of the lowest-priced sedan cruisers available in her class during the late 1980s. She was clearly designed to appeal to the weekend cruiser market and came equipped with just about everything required for immediate use. During the first few years of production, her two-stateroom floorplan was arranged with the galley and dinette forward in the salon—a layout that required the galley sole to be sunken in order to have any headroom. In 1989, the interior was redesigned with the galley and dinette down in the conventional manner. Both floorplans include a separate stall shower in the head. Note that a lower helm was never offered. Topside, the cockpit is large enough for a couple of anglers, and the wide side decks make for easy foredeck access. Additional features include a well-arranged engine room, bow pulpit, and a swim platform. No racehorse with the standard 350hp Crusader gas engines, the Silverton 40 Convertible will cruise at 15–16 knots and reach a top speed in the neighborhood of 25 knots. Note that Cat diesels were optional.

Silverton 41 Convertible

Length w/Pulpit . . . . 46'3"	Fuel . . . . 516 gals.
Hull Length . . . . 41'3"	Water . . . . 200 gals.
Beam . . . . 14'10"	Waste . . . . 40 gals.
Draft . . . . 3'7"	Hull Type . . . . Modified-V
Weight . . . . 27,000#	Deadrise Aft . . . . 17°
Clearance . . . . 15'5"	Production 1991–99

The Silverton 41 Convertible is a moderately priced sedan cruiser with a clean-cut profile, a roomy interior, and a good turn of speed with standard big-block gas engines. With her long foredeck, step-down sheer, and rakish bridge, the 41 has the look of a serious fishing boat (although Silvertons have never been noted for building tournament-level boats). The cockpit is large enough for a fighting chair, and there's a large fish box below the sole. Belowdeck, the two-stateroom interior of the Silverton 41 is arranged with the galley and dinette forward, three steps down from the salon. An island berth is located in the forward (master) stateroom, and the guest stateroom is fitted with over/under berths. Buyers could choose from either oak or cherry interior woodwork—neither or which is notable for its joinery. A transom door was standard in the cockpit, and the spacious flybridge is arranged with bench seating forward of the helm. A good-selling boat, standard 385hp gas engines will cruise the Silverton 41 at 19–20 knots (about 28 knots top), and optional 425hp Cat diesels will cruise at 24–25 knots and reach a top speed in the high 20s.

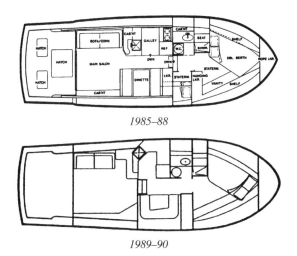

1985–88

1989–90

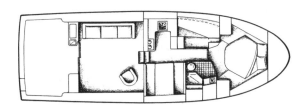

Silverton 410 Sport Bridge

Length Overall	46'3"	Fuel	450 gals.
Beam	14'3"	Water	200 gals.
Draft	3'10"	Waste	40 gals.
Weight	28,495#	Hull Type	Modified-V
Clearance	15'4"	Deadrise Aft	16°
Headroom	6'6"	Production	2001–04

The apartment-size interior of the Silverton 410 Sport Bridge will appeal to those looking for as much living space as possible in a 40-foot boat. Indeed, the innovative interior of this boat is compelling, but traditionalists will find little to like in her slab-sided profile and top-heavy appearance. Built on a modified-V hull with a solid fiberglass bottom, the 410 uses Silverton's signature "SideWalk" design, which elevates the side decks to create a truly cavernous interior. Pushing the superstructure out to the sides of the boat to produce a huge salon gives Silverton the flexibility to create an unusual raised galley and dinette in the middle of the boat, and still leaves room for a spacious twin-cabin, twin-head layout forward. While the cockpit is on the small side, there's plenty of guest seating (and a wet bar) on the large flybridge. The descending walkways on both sides of the bridge provide safe and secure foredeck access. A transom door, radar arch and bow pulpit were standard. Twin 425hp gas inboards will cruise the Silverton 410 Sport Bridge at a modest 15 knots and reach a top speed in the low-to-mid 20s. Optional 420hp Cat diesels will cruise at 20 knots and reach 24–25 knots wide open.

Silverton 42 Convertible

Length Overall	44'1"	Fuel	524 gals.
Beam	14'10"	Water	200 gals.
Draft	3'7"	Waste	60 gals.
Weight	26,300#	Hull Type	Modified-V
Clearance	16'8"	Deadrise Aft	17°
Headroom	6'6"	Production	2000–Current

The Silverton 42 Convertible is an affordable flybridge sedan whose spacious interior and large cockpit make her a good choice for family cruisers who like to do a little fishing. A distinctive design with a rakish hardtop and aggressive styling, she's built on the same proven hull used in the production of the earlier Silverton 41 Convertible. The two-stateroom interior of the Silverton 42 is a tasteful blend of cherry woodwork and earth-tone fabrics. An island double berth is located in the master stateroom, and the guest stateroom—also with a double berth—is tucked under the dinette. Note that the separate shower compartment is to port, opposite the head. On deck, the cockpit has an engine room access door as well as a transom door and built-in tackle center. Molded steps ascend to the flybridge with its centerline helm and bench seating forward. Additional features include very wide side decks, power cabin windows (optional), an overhead rod locker in the salon, and a bow pulpit. Note that the molded hardtop is also optional. A capable performer with twin 430hp Cummins diesels, the Silverton 42 Convertible will cruise at 20 knots and reach a top speed in the mid 20s.

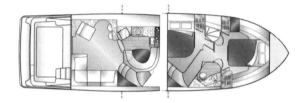

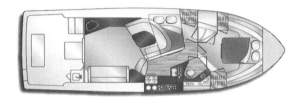

See Page 354 for Pricing Information

258

See Page 354 for Pricing Information

Silverton 48 Convertible

Length w/Pulpit	51'6"	Fuel	775 gals.
Beam	16'3"	Water	200 gals.
Draft	4'0"	Waste	80 gals.
Weight	46,980#	Hull Type	Modified-V
Clearance	17'6"	Deadrise Aft	12.5°
Headroom	6'6"	Production	2004–Current

Introduced in 2004, the Silverton 48 Convertible gets high marks for her modern styling, luxurious accommodations, and very competitive price. This is the biggest convertible ever built by Silverton, and unlike most other convertibles her size, the 48 is more cruising boat that hard-core fisherman. Built on a modified-V hull with a solid fiberglass bottom and prop pockets, the Silverton's comfortable three-stateroom interior is an attractive blend of high-gloss cherry cabinetry, deep-pile carpeting, and quality furnishings. A washer/dryer is standard below, and the master stateroom is fitted with a walkaround queen berth and flat-screen TV that folds down from the overhead. The forward cabin has a queen berth and private access to the second head, while the third stateroom has upper/lower berths. Note that a hatch in the galley sole reveals a huge storage compartment. The cockpit of the Silverton 48 may be on the small side, but the flybridge is among the largest to be found on a 48-footer. A hardtop, salon entertainment center, and central vacuum system are standard. MTU 825hp diesels will cruise the Silverton 48 in the high 20s and reach a top speed of 30+ knots.

Stamas 32 Continental

Length	32'3"	Water	55 gals.
Beam	12'0"	Headroom	6'3"
Draft	2'9"	Cockpit	90 sq. ft.
Weight	12,000#	Hull Type	Modified-V
Clearance	11'6"	Deadrise Aft	NA
Fuel	200 gals.	Production	1982–87

The 32 Continental was an attempt by Stamas to deliver a "Euro-style" cruiser with plush interior accommodations—attributes never previously been associated with the Stamas brand. (Indeed, the company has always been known for its solid, workmanlike products; one seldom associates Stamas with luxury accommodations.) Built on a solid fiberglass hull with moderate beam and a well-flared bow, the Continental was available with or without a flybridge. The flybridge model pictured above combines a comfortable interior with a large cockpit stretching from the lower helm to the transom. Wide side decks make access to the bow easy and safe, and there's seating for three on the flybridge. Below, the floorplan is arranged with a single stateroom forward (with a privacy door), and both the portside dinette and starboard settee convert to form double berths. Engine access is very good as is visibility from the lower helm, and the flush cockpit is large enough for several deck chairs. A good-riding boat, twin 330hp gas engines will cruise the Stamas 32 Continental at 22–23 knots and reach a top speed in the neighborhood of 30–32 knots.

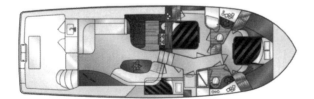

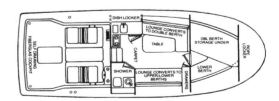

See Page 354 for Pricing Information

See Page 355 for Pricing Information

Stamas 32 Sport Sedan

Length	32'3"	Water	55 gals.
Beam	12'0"	Headroom	6'3"
Draft	2'9"	Cockpit	70 sq. ft.
Weight	13,300#	Hull Type	Modified-V
Clearance	11'6"	Deadrise Aft	NA
Fuel	200 gals.	Production	1974–87

Introduced back in the early 1970s, the Stamas 32 Sport Sedan remained in the Stamas lineup for a good many years thanks to her attractive lines and a reputation for dependable operation. She's obviously dated by today's Euro-style standards, however the solid construction and comfortable layout of the 32 Sport Sedan still has much to offer those seeking a used family cruiser. The 32 rides on a solid fiberglass modified-V hull with moderate beam and relatively low freeboard. Several galley-down floorplans were offered over the years, all with a standard lower helm and a single stateroom forward. A sliding glass door opens to a cockpit large enough for some light-tackle fishing, and wide side decks make access to the bow easy and safe. There's seating for three on the flybridge, and a vented front windshield provides a good deal of cabin ventilation. Additional features include plenty of storage compartments, a well-flared bow, and good access around the motors. Several engine options were offered over the years. Among the most popular, a pair of 260hp gas inboards will cruise the 32 Sport Sedan at 18 knots (about 27 knots top), and larger 330hp gas engines will cruise in the low 20s and reach a top speed of 30+ knots.

Tollycraft 30 Sedan

Length	29'11"	Fuel	200 gals.
Beam	11'9"	Cockpit	NA
Draft	2'6"	Hull Type	Modified-V
Weight	13,500#	Deadrise Aft	NA
Clearance	11'8"	Designer	Ed Monk
Water	58 gals.	Production	1977–84

The Tollycraft 30 Sedan may be a little short on sex appeal (certainly by today's standards, at least), but she's long on interior volume and practicality. The house and flybridge are exceptionally large for a 30-footer and, at 13,500 pounds, she's a heavy boat for her size. By building on a wide-beam hull and extending the salon bulkhead well into the cockpit, Tollycraft designers were able to create a spacious and very open interior with berths for five. A lower helm was standard, and a pass-through window separates the galley from the dinette. Storage space is impressive and includes a full wardrobe locker opposite the head as well as underseat storage in the salon. Note that the interior decor was updated from simulated teak mica to real teak in 1982. As with all Tollycraft designs, the side decks are wide, and extra-large cabin windows provide plenty of natural lighting as well as good lower-helm visibility in all directions. With her big interior, the cockpit dimensions are very compact. Most Tollycraft 30 Sedans were built with twin 270hp Crusader gas engines. The cruising speed is 23–24 knots and the top speed is about 30 knots.

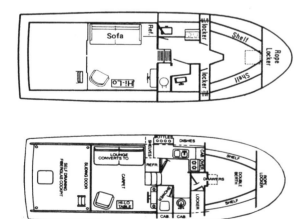

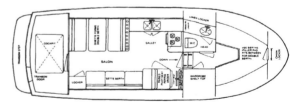

See Page 355 for Pricing Information

See Page 357 for Pricing Information

Tollycraft 30 Sport Cruiser

Length	30'6"	Fuel	150/198 gals.
Beam	11'6"	Cockpit	45 sq. ft.
Draft	2'7"	Hull Type	Modified-V
Weight	11,500#	Deadrise Aft	10°
Clearance	11'8"	Designer	Ed Monk
Water	42 gals.	Production	1985–92

A good-looking small boat with a low, very rakish profile, the Tollycraft 30 is an appealing combination of good styling, quality construction, and a space-efficient interior. The accommodations are impressive for a 30-footer and include a full-size dinette, a surprisingly roomy galley, and a standup head with shower. A two-piece door provides privacy for the forward stateroom, and a lower helm was standard in the salon. On deck, there's room in the cockpit for a couple of light-tackle anglers, and a hatch in the cockpit sole provides good access to the engines and V-drives. The flybridge—one of the largest to be found on any 30-footer—has a settee, a centerline helm position, and bench seating for four. On the downside, the side decks are very narrow, and cabin storage space is at a premium. Additional features include a transom door, swim platform, teak interior woodwork, and a bow pulpit. Built on Tollycraft's efficient Quadra-Lift hull, standard 260hp MerCruiser gas engines cruise the 30 Sport Cruiser at 22–23 knots and reach a top speed in the high 20s. (Note that the fuel capacity was increased in 1988 from 150 to 198 gallons.)

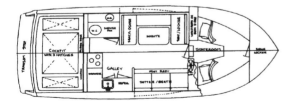

Tollycraft 34 Sport Sedan

Length	34'0"	Water	77/116 gals.
Beam	12'6"	Cockpit	72 sq. ft.
Draft	2'10"	Hull Type	Modified-V
Weight	17,000#	Deadrise Aft	13°
Clearance	13'11"	Designer	Ed Monk
Fuel	200/296 gals.	Production	1987–93

A popular boat during her production years, the Tollycraft 34 Sport Sedan is a well-styled sedan cruiser with an impressive blend of quality construction, comfortable accommodations, and good open-water performance. Built on a solid fiberglass hull with a relatively wide beam, the 34 Sport Sedan features a surprisingly open (and well-appointed) floorplan with two full staterooms—no small achievement in a 34-foot boat. A lower helm was standard, and the traditional teak interior of the Sport Sedan is one of her more appealing attributes. An insulated fish box is built into the cockpit sole, and molded steps at the corners provide easy access to the side decks. Two flybridge designs were offered: a helm-aft arrangement with guest seating forward for East Coast buyers, and a helm-forward layout with guest seating aft for the Pacific market. Additional features include a bow pulpit, swim platform, and a radar arch. Among several engine options (including diesels), twin 340hp Mercury gas engines will cruise the Tollycraft 34 at 20 knots and reach a top speed in the high 20s. Note that fuel and water capacities were increased beginning with the 1988 models.

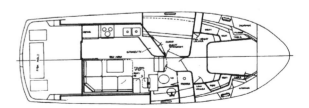

See Page 357 for Pricing Information

See Page 357 for Pricing Information

Tollycraft 40 Sport Sedan

Length	40'2"	Water	140 gals.
Beam	14'8"	Cockpit	101 sq. ft.
Draft	3'0"	Hull Type	Modified-V
Weight	26,000#	Deadrise Aft	10°
Clearance	12'4"	Designer	Ed Monk
Fuel	500 gals.	Production	1987–95

An excellent sea boat, the 40 Sport Sedan is the only dedicated sportfishing design ever offered by Tollycraft. Introduced in 1987, she rides on the proven low-deadrise hull design used in several previous Tollycraft models. Originally offered with the galley in the salon and two staterooms forward, a revised interior in 1989 expanded the main deck area by moving the galley farther forward and separating it from the salon with a snack bar. Finally, in 1995—the final year of production—Tollycraft introduced an all-new, galley-down floorplan with a more open salon and a slightly smaller bow stateroom. In each of these floorplans, a lower helm was optional, and the interior was tastefully decorated with teak woodwork, designer fabrics, and quality hardware and furnishings. Topside, a transom door was standard in the large cockpit, and wide side decks make foredeck access easy and secure. The flybridge—available with the helm forward or aft—seats up to six in comfort. Note that a radar arch was a popular option. Caterpillar 375hp diesels will cruise the Tollycraft 40 at 23 knots (26–27 knots top), and 485hp Detroit 6-71s will cruise in the mid 20s and reach 30 knots wide open.

1987–88

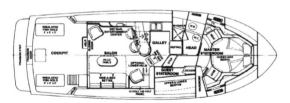

1989–1994

Trojan 32 Sedan

Length	32'0"	Fuel	120/220 gals.
Beam	13'0"	Cockpit	60 sq. ft.
Draft	2'6"	Hull Type	Modified-V
Weight	12,000#	Deadrise Aft	8°
Clearance	12'6"	Designer	Trojan
Water	40 gals.	Production	1973–92

There were more Trojan 32s built (over 2,700 in all) than any other production fiberglass boat over 30 feet in the business. Her appeal was a straightforward combination of an affordable price, contemporary design, and roomy cabin accommodations. Several versions of the Trojan 32 were offered over the years including Hardtop and Express models, a Flybridge Express (with an open lower helm), and the very popular Flybridge Sedan pictured above. All were built on a low-deadrise modified-V hull with a relatively wide beam and solid fiberglass construction. Surprisingly, the basic interior and exterior design of the Sedan remained largely unchanged during her long production run. A lower helm was standard, and wraparound cabin windows give the interior a bright and wide-open appearance. A stable and good-running boat, cruising speed with 250hp Chrysler engines is approximately 18–19 knots and the top speed is around 25 knots. Add 1–2 knots for more recent models equipped with the 270hp Crusaders. Note that the decks of early models were made of teak, and the once-optional 220-gallon fuel capacity became standard in 1984.

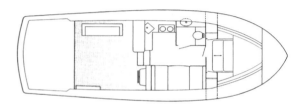

See Page 358 for Pricing Information

See Page 359 for Pricing Information

FLYBRIDGE CRUISERS

Trojan 10 Meter Sedan

Length	33'0"	Fuel	242 gals.
Beam	13'0"	Cockpit	60 sq. ft.
Draft	2'0"	Hull Type	Modified-V
Weight	14,250#	Deadrise Aft	9°
Clearance	12'2"	Designer	H. Schoell
Water	40/55 gals.	Production	1982–89

A high-style boat in the 1980s with a handsome profile and colorful hull graphics, the Trojan 10 Meter is a wide-beam sedan cruiser with a lot of living space packed into her 33-foot length. Hull construction is solid fiberglass, and she's built on an easy-riding DeltaConic hull with moderate transom deadrise and wide chine flats. The original floorplan of the 10 Meter Sedan was a disappointment—an offset companionway (very unusual in a convertible) all but isolated the salon from the lower-level dinette and galley. A revised floorplan introduced in 1984 had a more open layout with an island berth forward and a serving counter overlooking the galley. On deck, the cockpit is large enough for a couple of light-tackle anglers although it was obviously not designed for serious fishing. The flybridge is arranged in the conventional manner with bench seating forward of the helm. Note that a lower helm was standard in pre-1987 models. With twin 350hp Crusader gas engines, the cruising speed of the Trojan 10 Meter Sedan is around 18 knots and she'll hit a top speed in the mid-to-high 20s.

Trojan 10.8 Meter Sedan

Length	35'4"	Water	55 gals.
Beam	13'0"	Cockpit	87 sq. ft.
Draft	2'4"	Hull Type	Modified-V
Weight	15,000#	Deadrise Aft	9°
Clearance	12'2"	Designer	H. Schoell
Fuel	325 gals.	Production	1986–92

The 10.8 Meter Sedan is a stretched version of Trojan's earlier 10 Meter Sedan model. The deck plans and interior layouts are essentially the same in both boats, the difference being the larger cockpit and additional fuel capacity of the 10.8 Meter. Although not specifically designed as a sportfishing boat, a transom door and tackle center were standard in the 10.8, and the enlarged cockpit has enough room for some serious fishing pursuits. The original single-stateroom floorplan of the 10.8 Sedan was updated in 1989 to include a stall shower in the head—a modification that took some elbow space out of the bow stateroom. Note that a two-stateroom floorplan became available in 1989 as well. In all of these layouts, the salon is a wide-open and spacious affair thanks to the boat's wide beam. The engine room, however, is a tight fit. Topside, the flybridge—whose overhang shades the forward part of the cockpit—is arranged in the conventional manner with guest seating forward of the helm. Narrow side decks require care when accessing the foredeck. Standard 350hp gas engines will cruise the 10.8 Meter Sedan at 17–18 knots and reach a top speed in the mid 20s.

FLYBRIDGE CRUISERS

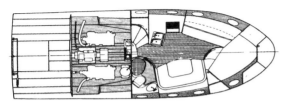

1982–83

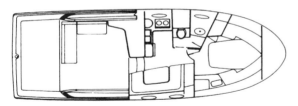

1984–89

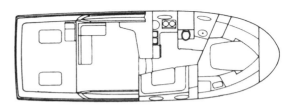

Single-Stateroom Interior

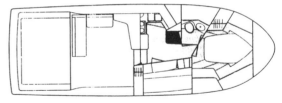

Twin-Stateroom Interior

See Page 359 for Pricing Information

See Page 359 for Pricing Information

Trojan 36 Convertible

Length	36'0"	Fuel	250/350 gals.
Beam	13'0"	Cockpit	75 sq. ft.
Draft	2'11"	Hull Type	Modified-V
Weight	16,000#	Deadrise Aft	9°
Clearance	13'0"	Designer	Trojan
Water	80 gals.	Production	1972–89

One of the most popular production boats ever designed, the Trojan 36 Convertible was an affordable blend of traditional styling, comfortable accommodations, and good all-around performance. She was built on an easy-riding fiberglass hull with moderate beam, nearly flat aftersections, and a shallow keel for directional stability. Single- and twin-stateroom floorplans were available in the Trojan 36 during her long production run with the two-stateroom layout being the more popular. All were arranged with the galley forward, a step down from the salon, and a lower helm was a popular option. For most years, teak trim and wall coverings were used throughout the interior, and large cabin windows admit plenty of natural lighting. On deck, the cockpit is big enough for some light-tackle fishing, and the tournament-style flybridge provides seating for up to five. A teak cockpit sole was standard through 1976—a potential source of problems that bears close examination. A variety of gas and diesel engine options were offered over the years. Among the most popular, twin 350hp Crusaders gas inboards will cruise the 36 Convertible at 19 knots and deliver a top speed in the mid-to-high 20s.

Trojan 11 Meter Sedan

Length	37'6"	Fuel	350 gals.
Beam	14'0"	Headroom	6'5"
Draft	3'5"	Hull Type	Modified-V
Weight	18,000#	Deadrise Aft	14°
Clearance	12'6"	Designer	H. Schoell
Water	100 gals.	Production	1985–88

Aside from her rakish profile and colorful hull graphics, the most notable feature of the Trojan 11 Meter Sedan is her unusually wide beam. Indeed, it's fair to say that she has more interior volume than just about any other boat in her class. Built on a fully cored, modified-V hull with wide chine flats and side exhausts, the 11 Meter Sedan was marketed by Trojan as a Euro-style convertible for the American market. Her single-stateroom floorplan includes a spacious and wide-open salon with a serving counter overlooking the galley. A lower helm was optional, and an island berth is located in the private stateroom. An unusually spacious dinette converts for overnight guests, and the head includes a stall shower. While the cockpit has enough room for some light-tackle fishing, the bridge ladder interferes with traffic flow. Topside, the flybridge is arranged in the conventional manner with bench seating in front of the helm. With standard 350hp Crusader gas engines, the Trojan 11 Meter Sedan will cruise at 18 knots and reach a top speed in the high 20s. Optional 375hp Cat diesels will cruise at 22–23 knots and reach 26–27 knots top.

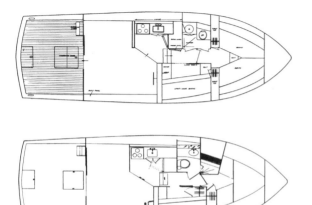

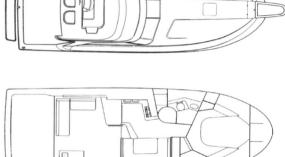

See Page 359 for Pricing Information

See Page 359 for Pricing Information

Trojan 12 Meter Convertible

Length	39'9"	Fuel	400 gals.
Beam	14'3"	Cockpit	110 sq. ft.
Draft	3'6"	Hull Type	Modified-V
Weight	19,000#	Deadrise Aft	12°
Clearance	12'6"	Designer	H. Schoell
Water	100 gals.	Production	1986–92

Originally conceived as a sportfishing boat (a market that Trojan never successfully tapped), the 12 Meter Convertible was a little too glitzy for most anglers in spite of her big-boat accommodations and generous cockpit dimensions. Indeed, with over 14 feet of beam, the 12 Meter is a very roomy boat inside—a fact not lost on weekend cruisers seeking a mega-volume interior. Built on a fully cored DeltaConic hull with wide chine flats and moderate transom deadrise, the 12 Meter's standard two-stateroom floorplan is arranged with the galley down and an island berth in the master stateroom. In 1990, Trojan updated the layout by adding a convertible dinette in the salon. On deck, the cockpit is set up with two in-deck fish boxes, fresh- and saltwater washdowns, a transom door, and molded tackle center. Note that the flybridge is rather small compared with other boats this size. Additional features include a bow pulpit, a full front windshield, and reasonably wide side decks. Standard 350hp gas engines will cruise at 15 knots (24 knots top). Optional 375hp Cat diesels cruise at 22 knots (25–26 top), and 485hp Detroit 6-71s cruise at a fast 26 knots (about 30 knots wide open).

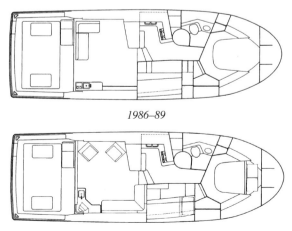

1986–89

1990–92

Uniflite 28 Mega

Length	28'2"	Water	50 gals.
Beam	10'10"	Headroom	6'3"
Draft	2'10"	Hull Type	Modified-V
Weight	10,500#	Deadrise Aft	NA
Clearance	10'0"	Designer	Uniflite
Fuel	140 gals.	Production	1977–84

The Uniflite 28 Mega is an old 1970s sedan cruiser whose enduring popularity with entry-level cruisers had much to do with her affordable price and spacious interior. With her wide 11-foot beam, the Mega delivers a big salon complete with a convertible L-shaped dinette with a facing settee. Most were sold with a portside lower helm, and large wraparound cabin windows admit plenty of natural lighting, which makes the interior seem even larger. The galley in the 28 Mega is two steps down from the salon level, opposite the small head (with shower). Outside, the cockpit area is on the small side but large enough for a couple of folding deck chairs. Access to the engines and V-drives is via removable hatches in the cockpit sole. Seating for five is provided on the bridge, although a prudent helmsman is unlikely to want that much weight topside in a boat this size except in very calm water. Additional features include cockpit railings, teak interior trim, sliding cabin windows, and a swim platform. Like many Uniflites of her era, gelcoat blisters are a common problem. Twin 220hp Crusaders cruise the 28 Mega at 20 knots and top out in the mid-to-high 20s.

FLYBRIDGE CRUISERS

See Page 359 for Pricing Information

See Page 360 for Pricing Information

Uniflite 32 Sport Sedan

Length	31'8"	Water	75 gals.
Beam	11'11"	Cockpit	NA
Draft	2'8"	Hull Type	Modified-V
Weight	15,000#	Deadrise Aft	15°
Clearance	11'0"	Designer	Uniflite
Fuel	200 gals.	Production	1975–84

A solid, well-built boat with a good turn of speed, the Uniflite 32 Sport Sedan was clearly designed with family cruising in mind. She was built on a solid fiberglass hull with a relatively wide beam and moderate transom deadrise. Like all Uniflites, the styling was conservative even by 1975 standards (when she was introduced), and today she looks like a museum piece when compared with her more modern counterparts. Nonetheless, the accommodations are quite expansive for a 32-footer. Uniflite offered a pair of floorplans during her production years; the original layout has the galley aft in the salon, and the more recent floorplan has the galley forward and a portside lower helm. The cockpit of the 32 Sport Sedan is quite spacious with enough room for some light-tackle fishing activities. Topside, the flybridge is arranged with the helm forward and lounge seating aft. Throughout, construction was on the heavy side and the finish is quite good. Powered with twin 270hp Crusaders with V-drives, the Uniflite 32 will cruise at 18–20 knots and top out in the high 20s. Trim tabs are required to keep her running angles down at planing speeds as her tendency is to otherwise run bow-high.

Uniflite 34 Sport Sedan

Length	34'2"	Fuel	200 gals.
Beam	11'11"	Cockpit	75 sq. ft.
Draft	2'9"	Hull	Modified-V
Weight	17,000#	Deadrise Aft	15°
Clearance	11'11"	Designer	Uniflite
Water	100 gals.	Production	1974–84

The Uniflite 34 was introduced in 1974 with two model configurations: a Tournament Fisherman model with the helm aft on the bridge (pictured above) and extra fuel capacity (300 gallons); and the Sport Sedan model with the helm console forward on the bridge. She was built on a solid fiberglass modified-V hull with average beam, a well-flared bow, and moderate deadrise at the transom. Inside, the single-stateroom floorplan features a stall shower in the head, a roomy galley area with good counter space, and berths for six when the dinette and salon settee are converted. Teak paneling and cabinetry are used throughout the interior, and an inside helm was a popular option. The cockpit dimensions are generous for a 34-footer, but the flybridge is small by modern standards. In a notable update, the original sliding glass salon doors were replaced in 1977 with a single hinged door. Additional features include flybridge guest seating, relatively wide side decks, and sliding glass cabin windows. With the 454-cid Crusader gas engines, the Uniflite 34 Sedan will cruise around 20 knots and reach 29–30 knots at full throttle.

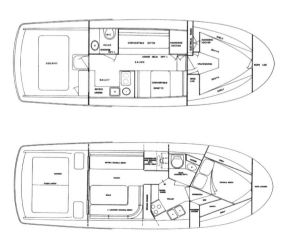

See Page 360 for Pricing Information

266

See Page 360 for Pricing Information

Uniflite 36 Sport Sedan

Length . . . . 36'0"	Fuel, Opt. . . . . 300 gals.
Beam . . . . 12'4"	Water . . . . 100 gals.
Draft . . . . 3'4"	Hull Type . . . . Modified-V
Weight . . . . 20,000#	Deadrise Aft . . . . 11°
Cockpit . . . . 80 sq. ft.	Designer . . . . A. Nordtvedt
Fuel, Std. . . . . 216 gals.	Production 1970–84

The Uniflite 36 Sport Sedan is a traditional sedan-style design with a smart profile and a rugged personality. Built on the same solid fiberglass hull as the 36 Double Cabin (a modified-V with single chines and 11 degrees of deadrise at the transom), she was offered with two basic interior layouts during her production years. The two-stateroom version has an in-line galley to port in the salon, and in the single-stateroom arrangement the galley replaces the guest stateroom on the lower level resulting in a considerably enlarged salon. Outside, the cockpit is large enough for serious fishing, and the side decks are wide enough for secure passage forward. The flybridge is large for a 36-foot boat with the helm console set all the way forward in the West Coast fashion. Additional features include a bow pulpit, plenty of cabin storage compartments, an all-glass salon bulkhead and door, and stainless steel cockpit railings. A popular model during her production years, standard Crusader 454-cid gas engines will cruise the Uniflite 36 Sport Sedan around 19 knots and reach a top speed of 28–29 knots. Optional 210hp Caterpillar diesels cruise at 16 knots and reach a top speed of about 18–19 knots.

Uniflite 37 Coastal Cruiser

Length Overall . . . . 37'9"	Water . . . . 160 gals.
Length WL . . . . 33'9"	Fuel . . . . 300 gals.
Beam . . . . 12'9"	Cockpit . . . . 58 sq. ft.
Draft . . . . 3'10"	Hull Type . . . . Semi-Disp.
Weight . . . . 21,000#	Designer . . . . Uniflite
Clearance . . . . 12'0"	Production 1979–84

The 37 Coastal Cruiser was Uniflite's response to the need for fuel-efficient family cruisers in the late 1970s and early 1980s. Designed to appeal to the trawler market, her efficient semi-displacement hull design allows for a planing-speed performance while still delivering comfortable and economical operation at lower speeds. Below, the all-teak interior features a spacious salon with large wrap-around cabin windows for plenty of natural lighting. A service bar separates the salon area from the mid-level galley. The second "stateroom" is actually a lounge in the passageway with a privacy curtain (the backrest swings up to create over/under berths at night). The large double-entry head is fitted with a shower stall. Outside, a bridge overhang affords some weather protection for the cockpit, and the huge flybridge has seating for eight. Notably, the exhaust ports are underwater. Additional features include a bow pulpit, swim platform, and a portside lower helm station. Standard power was a single 192hp Volvo diesel (11 knots cruise), but most Coastal Cruisers were sold with twin 124hp Volvos for a cruising speed of 14 knots and a top speed of about 17 knots.

FLYBRIDGE CRUISERS

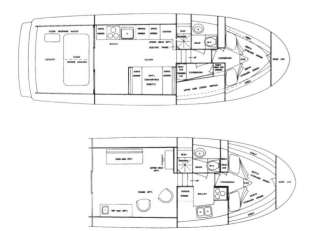

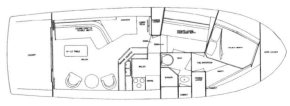

See Page 360 for Pricing Information

See Page 360 for Pricing Information

Uniflite 38 Convertible

Viking 38 Flybridge

Length	38'0"	Fuel, Gas	300 gals.
Beam	13'11"	Water	100 gals.
Draft	3'8"	Cockpit	92 sq. ft.
Weight	24,000#	Hull Type	Modified-V
Clearance	12'8"	Designer	Uniflite
Fuel, Diesel	400 gals.	Production	1977–84

Length Overall	40'2"	Clearance	12'5"
Beam	12'8"	Headroom	6'2"
Draft	3'7"	Hull Type	Deep-V
Weight	21,280#	Deadrise Aft	19°
Fuel	230 gals.	Designer	B. Olesinski
Water	121 gals.	Production	1995–97

FLYBRIDGE CRUISERS

A sturdy and well-engineered boat, the Uniflite 38 Convertible was designed to meet the demands of serious fishing as well as comfortable family cruising. Heavily built, she was available with two basic floorplans: a single-stateroom, galley-down arrangement, and the standard two-stateroom, galley-up plan—the latter being somewhat notable for the small galley wedged into the forward corner of the salon. Both layouts had the convenience of a double-entry head, stall shower, and large staterooms. The 38's salon is spacious for a boat of this size. The portside lower helm station was an option, and most were so equipped. As a sportfisherman, the 38 has a large and uncluttered cockpit with a molded-in fish box and relatively wide side decks. While the 400-gallon fuel capacity is more than adequate in the diesel-powered models, those with gas engines carry only 300 gallons—definitely on the light side. Additional features include a bow pulpit, swim platform, wraparound salon windows, and a well-arranged engine room. Optional 310hp J&T 6-71Ns will cruise the Uniflite 38 at a steady 18 knots and reach 22–23 knots at full throttle. Note that in 1985 Chris Craft reintroduced this boat as the 382 Commander.

One of the early Princess models to be marketed in the U.S. under the Viking nameplate, the 38 Flybridge is a well finished UK-built import with all of the attributes expected in a European sportcruiser of her era. She rides on a solid fiberglass, deep-V hull with moderate beam, prop pockets to reduce the shaft angles, and a fully integrated swim platform. Her contemporary two-stateroom, galley-down interior is arranged with an elevated lower helm (with twin helm seats) forward of a relatively small salon with a convertible U-shaped lounge opposite a settee. The spacious owner's suite is situated in the bow with direct access to the en suite head compartment. The second cabin is fitted with twin berths and offers good headroom thanks to its position below the helm station. There's plenty of seating space in the cockpit (mostly shaded by a flybridge overhang), and molded steps at the corners lead up to wide side decks. Access to the flybridge is via a single-piece molded stairway against the forward bulkhead of the cockpit. Among several diesel engine options, a pair of 350hp Cats will cruise the 38 Sport Cruiser at 24–25 knots and deliver a top speed in the neighborhood of 30 knots.

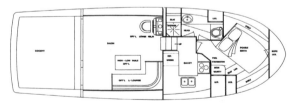

Single Stateroom, Galley Down

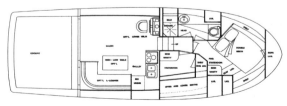

Two Staterooms, Galley Up

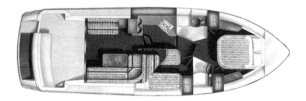

Viking 40 Flybridge

Length Overall	40'8"	Clearance	11'9"
Beam	13'3"	Headroom	6'3"
Draft	3'1"	Hull Type	Deep-V
Weight	25,760#	Deadrise Aft	19°
Fuel	318 gals.	Designer	B. Olesinski
Water	128 gals.	Production	2000–02

Introduced in England as the Princess 40 in 1998, the 40 Flybridge made her debut in this country in 2000 when she became the smallest of Viking's growing fleet of British-built sportcruisers. She's constructed on a good-running deep-V hull with prop pockets and an extended swim platform capable of carrying a personal watercraft. The contemporary two-stateroom interior of the Viking 40, with its high-gloss cherry woodwork and designer fabrics, is arranged with a step-down galley and a notably well-arranged lower helm position. A separate stall shower is found in the owner's head, and the guest cabin is tucked beneath the helm station above. In the cockpit, a large in-sole hatch provides easy access to a rather tight engine room. (Note that an expanded lazarette abaft the engine room houses the generator.) Molded steps ascend from the cockpit to the flybridge where a U-shaped settee and an aft sun lounge were standard. Additional features include a radar mast, transom door, wide side decks, a cockpit shower, and sliding, stainless-steel-framed salon doors. Twin 370hp Volvo (or 350hp Cat) diesels will cruise the Viking 40 at 25 knots and reach a top speed of about 30 knots.

Wellcraft 2900 Sport Bridge

Length	28'8"	Water	45 gals.
Beam	10'8"	Headroom	6'3"
Draft	2'6"	Hull Type	Modified-V
Weight	9,200#	Deadrise Aft	16°
Clearance	NA	Designer	B. Collier
Fuel	200 gals.	Production	1983–86

The Wellcraft 2900 Sport Bridge was introduced in 1983 as a low-cost alternative to more expensive small flybridge fishboats from Bertram, Phoenix and Blackfin. Built on a medium-deadrise hull, a wide 10-foot, 8-inch beam gives the Sport Bridge plenty of cockpit room for fishing or relaxing in a couple of deck chairs. The interior is arranged with a V-berth forward, a compact galley and head compartment to port, and a convertible dinette to starboard—a very efficient layout that will suit the needs of weekend cruisers or a couple of overnight anglers. Engines are accessed via hatches in the raised forward cockpit sole, and bench seating on the flybridge will accommodate three. On the downside, the finish of the Sport Bridge was less than impressive, and the plywood cabin bulkhead requires plenty of maintenance to keep it looking good. (Note also the narrow side decks.) Standard features included rod holders, a teak bow pulpit, and a swim platform. Among several engine options, the 2900 Sport Bridge will cruise economically at 18–20 knots with optional Crusader 270hp (or Volvo 260hp) inboard gas engines and top out in the high 20s.

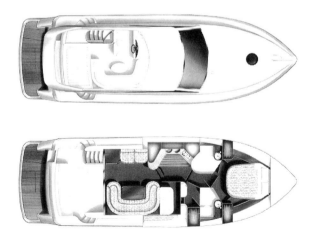

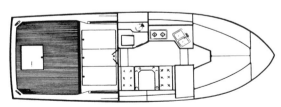

See Page 361 for Pricing Information

See Page 363 for Pricing Information

Wellcraft 310 Sedan

Length	31'3"	Water	50 gals.
Beam	11'6"	Headroom	6'3"
Draft	2'11"	Hull Type	Deep-V
Weight	11,200#	Deadrise Aft	19°
Clearance	11'0"	Designer	R. Cole
Fuel	200 gals.	Production	1981–83

The Wellcraft 310 Sedan was introduced in 1981 as an inexpensive sedan cruiser suitable for light-tackle fishing or weekend cruising. With her raised foredeck and bold graphics, the 310 reflects the conservative styling trends of the early 1980s without being excessive. Unlike most Wellcraft designs, she rides on a deep-V hull, which makes her surprisingly capable in rough water. Belowdecks, big cabin windows and a wide beam make the galley-down floorplan seem unusually wide open and spacious. This is definitely not a luxury interior—the furnishings are basically no-frills in nature and the workmanship is average at best. While the 310's cockpit is too small for any serious fishing, it's still adequate for a couple of light-tackle anglers and their gear. Topside, the helm is forward on the bridge with bench seating aft. A hatch in the salon sole provides access to a fairly spacious engine room. Note that the side decks are quite narrow. A salon wet bar and teak bow pulpit were standard. A variety of gas or diesel engine options were available in the 310 Sedan. Among them, a pair of 235hp MerCruisers (with V-drives) will cruise at 18 knots and reach 24–25 knots top.

Wellcraft 3200 Sedan Bridge

Length	32'0"	Water	80 gals.
Beam	11'6"	Cockpit	70 sq. ft.
Draft	3'0"	Hull Type	Modified-V
Weight	14,200#	Deadrise Aft	14°
Clearance	NA	Designer	B. Collier
Fuel	290 gals.	Production	1985–86

Sharing the same hull as the well-regarded 3200 Coastal fishboat, the Wellcraft 3200 Sedan Bridge is basically the same boat as the Coastal with the addition of a flybridge and an enclosed salon. (Notably, she enjoyed only a short production run before being phased out of the Wellcraft lineup for 1987.) Inside, the galley-down floorplan is arranged with V-berths forward and a full-size dinette opposite the galley and head compartment. With 360-degree wraparound cabin windows, the salon seems particularly open and bright. A lower helm was a popular option, and the interior is completely finished with teak paneling and trim. With some 70 square feet of space, the cockpit is large enough for a couple of light-tackle anglers and their gear. A transom door and in-deck storage were standard, and there's space for a tackle center against the salon bulkhead. Topside, the flybridge is big for a 32-footer with guest seating forward of the helm. Additional features include wide side decks, a bow pulpit, and swim platform. Twin 350hp gas engines will cruise the 3200 Sedan Bridge at a respectable 18–19 knots and top out in the high 20s.

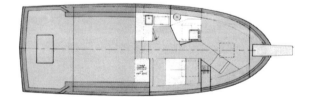

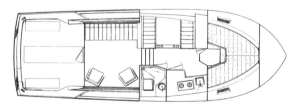

Wellcraft 34 Triumph

Length w/Pulpit . . . . 36'9"	Fuel . . . . 256 gals.
Length on Deck . . . . 34'0"	Water . . . . 60 gals.
Beam . . . . 12'6"	Cockpit . . . . 60 sq. ft.
Draft . . . . 3'0"	Hull Type . . . . Modified-V
Weight . . . . 15,700#	Deadrise Aft . . . . 14°
Clearance . . . . 9'9"	Production 1990–93

When she was introduced in 1990, this maxi-volume family cruiser was presented to the public as the Triumph 34 Bridgedeck Sedan, the product of an all-new boatbuilding company closely associated with the Wellcraft factory. The Triumph operation (they had only two 34-foot models: the Bridgedeck pictured above and the midcabin Americus express) lasted just over a year before being absorbed into the Wellcraft fleet in 1991. The Triumph's low-profile appearance is the result of locating the engines aft, thereby lowering the salon sole and creating a wide-open single-level floorplan. Notable features include a unique pass-through from the galley to the flybridge (very convenient) and a hidden privacy curtain for use when the portside salon settee is converted into a double berth at night. Outside, both the cockpit and flybridge provide plenty of guest seating. Additional features include a bow pulpit, molded foredeck seating, and a swim platform. No racehorse, Crusader 300hp gas engines (with V-drives and side exhausts) will cruise the 34 Triumph at a sedate 15–16 knots and reach a top speed of 26 knots.

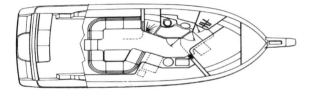

See Page 364 for Pricing Information   271

Runabouts
(Cuddys and Bowriders)

Design Assets

Large cockpit, sporty styling, fun to drive

Design Limitations

Limited range, modest (if any) cabin features

Price Leaders

Rinker, Crownline, Monterey

Quality Leaders

Cobalt, Regal, Sea Ray, Four Winns, Formula

Chaparral 280 SSi

Length w/Platform	29'6"	Fuel	143 gals.
Hull Length	27'6"	Water	30 gals.
Beam	9'3"	Waste	9.5 gals.
Draft	2'11"	Hull Type	Deep-V
Weight	6,800#	Deadrise Aft	22°
Clearance	5'10"	Production	1999–Current

The Chaparral 280 SSi has remained one of the most popular big bowriders around since her introduction in 1999 thanks to an enviable blend of smart styling, first-rate construction and excellent performance. Built on a deep-V hull, the 280's versatile cockpit layout—with its comfortable seating and luxury appointments—is one of her most compelling features. The galley is fitted with a sink, pressure water and refrigerator, and the enclosed head compartment comes complete with a sink, storage bin and opening port for ventilation. A walk-through transom provides easy access to the swim platform, and the helm is thoughtfully designed with additional electronics in mind. Forward, the bow seating area is arranged with hinged seat storage, gunwale drink holders and a spacious in-floor ski locker. Flush-mount bi-fold doors separate the cockpit from the bow to reduce the effects of wind while driving at higher speeds. Recessed trim tabs are standard, and a radar arch and extended swim platform have been popular options. A good performer, twin 300hp Volvo sterndrive engines will cruise the 280 SSi at 30 knots and reach a top speed in excess of 50 knots.

Chaparral 285 SSi

Length w/Platform	29'6"	Fuel	143 gals.
Hull Length	27'6"	Water	30 gals.
Beam	9'3"	Waste	9.5 gals.
Draft	2'11"	Hull Type	Deep-V
Weight	7,200#	Deadrise Aft	22°
Clearance	5'10"	Production	1999–Current

Big day boats with spacious cockpits and modest cabins have become increasing popular in recent years with owners who place a greater emphasis on open-air fun than interior comforts. (Indeed, in most boats of this type the interiors see little use.) Built on a soft-riding deep-V hull, the 285 SSi (called the 2835 SS in 1999) is a well-built sportboat whose combination of solid performance and quality construction have made her a very popular model for Chaparral. The large, divided cockpit is fitted with a U-shaped lounge opposite the helm, fore and aft facing lounges, a removable cocktail table that converts the lounges into a sun pad, wet bar with sink, and a walk-through transom. An electric lift mechanism raises the aft section of the U-shaped lounge and makes access to the engine compartment easy. Cabin amenities include a dinette/double berth, mini-galley, four opening ports, and a private head compartment with a pull-up shower and vacuum-flush toilet. Additional features include an eye-catching burlwood dash panel and side exhausts. A good performer, twin 300hp Volvo sterndrive engines will cruise the 285 SSi at 30 knots and reach a top speed in excess of 50 knots. Note that an optional radar arch became available in 2003.

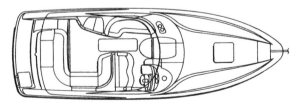

RUNABOUTS

Chaparral 32 Laser

Length	32'2"	Water	34 gals.
Beam	10'8"	Max Headroom	6'3"
Draft, Down	3'6"	Hull Type	Modified-V
Weight	10,500#	Deadrise Aft	12°
Clearance, Arch	8'9"	Designer	Chaparral
Fuel	218 gals.	Production	1988–91

The first wide-beam cruiser Chaparral ever built (all of their previous models had been trailerable), the Laser 32 is a high-performance midcabin express whose high-freeboard sportboat profile concealed a surprisingly spacious interior. (Note the absence of a bow pulpit—a design touch growing in popularity in the late-1980s.) Heavily constructed on a fully cored hull with a modest 12 degrees of transom deadrise, the Laser is quick to accelerate but a hard ride in a chop. The interior is arranged with double berths fore and aft (each sleeping area has a privacy curtain) and a well-appointed salon with a convertible dinette and facing settee. The galley is compact and so is the midcabin, but the head is big and there's seating for six in the salon. Topside, an L-shaped lounge is across from the helm and additional guest seating is provided at the transom. Additional features included two overhead deck hatches, a wraparound windshield (rare in a 1980s boat), and a cockpit wet bar. A quick ride with fast acceleration, twin 260hp sterndrives will cruise the Laser 32 in the high 20s and reach a top speed in excess of 40 knots.

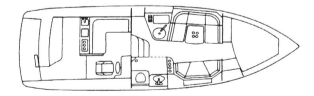

Chris Craft 28 Corsair

Length	28'0"	Headroom	4'0"
Beam	10'0"	Fuel	150 gals.
Draft, Up	1'11"	Water	35 gals.
Draft, Down	3'6"	Hull Type	Deep-V
Weight	7,500#	Deadrise Aft	20°
Clearance	5'5"	Production	2003–Current

With her retro styling and curved aft tumblehome, the 28 Corsair conveys the classic Chris Craft look of yesteryear. First and foremost, the Corsair is a high-quality runabout with a level of finish seldom seen in production boats. And secondly, the Corsair's premium price gives new meaning to the term "sticker shock." Clearly, this is a boat for very affluent boaters willing to drop a bundle for a sexy, drop-dead gorgeous runabout. Built on a deep-V hull with a well-flared bow, the amenities aboard the 28 Corsair are many. The cockpit is notable, not just for its plush Ultraleather seating and custom entertainment center, but for its simplicity and comfort as well. The old-world dashboard is a nostalgic throwback to the 1950s, and an electric engine hatch provides easy access to the engine compartment. The Corsair's curved foredeck conceals a useful cuddy cabin with a V-berth and portable head. The gelcoat is flawless, and the stainless-steel windshield is a work of art. Additional features include a pressure water system, cockpit cooler storage, transom shower, and flip-up bucket seats. Twin 280hp Volvo sterndrives will cruise in the mid 20s, and optional 240hp Yanmar diesels will cruise at a fast 35 knots.

See Page 306 for Pricing Information

See Page 307 for Pricing Information

Chris Craft 28 Launch

Length . . . . 28'0"	Headroom . . . . 4'0"
Beam . . . . 10'0"	Fuel . . . . 150 gals.
Draft, Up . . . . 1'11"	Water . . . . 35 gals.
Draft, Down . . . . 3'6"	Hull Type . . . . Deep-V
Weight . . . . 7,500#	Deadrise Aft . . . . 20°
Clearance . . . . 5'5"	Production 2003–Current

With her retro styling and curved aft tumblehome, the 28 Launch conveys the classic Chris Craft look of yesteryear. First and foremost, the Launch is a high-quality bowrider with a level of finish seldom seen in production boats. And secondly, her premium price will cause even experienced owners to pause. Clearly, this is a boat for very affluent boaters willing to drop a bundle for a sexy, drop-dead gorgeous runabout. Built on a deep-V hull with a well-flared bow, the amenities aboard the 28 Launch are many. The cockpit is notable, not just for its plush Ultraleather seating and custom entertainment center, but for its simplicity and comfort as well. The old-world dashboard is a nostalgic throwback to the 1950s, and an electric engine hatch provides easy access to the engine compartment. The gelcoat is flawless, and the stainless-steel windshield is a work of art. Additional features include a pressure water system, cockpit cooler storage, transom shower, and flip-up bucket seats. Twin 280hp Volvo sterndrives will cruise the 28 Launch in the mid 20s, and optional 240hp Yanmar diesels will cruise at a fast 35 knots.

Cobalt 272

Length . . . . 27'3"	Fuel . . . . 97 gals.
Beam . . . . 8'6"	Water . . . . 10 gals.
Draft, Up . . . . 1'11"	Hull Type . . . . Deep-V
Draft, Down . . . . 3'0"	Deadrise Aft . . . . 20°
Weight . . . . 4,930#	Designer . . . . Peter Granata
Clearance . . . . 5'10"	Production 1993–2000

A good-looking 1990s design, the Cobalt 272 is a finely crafted bowrider whose lush amenities, deep cockpit and beautiful styling make her a standout in any marina. She's heavily built on a Kevlar-reinforced solid fiberglass deep-V hull, and an 8-foot, 6-inch beam makes her trailerable in all states and provinces. Even today, the Cobalt 272 is one of the larger bowriders around and her upscale price placed her in the luxury-cruiser category. The helm and windshield of the 272 are well forward resulting in a large and very comfortable cockpit. Amenities include a sun pad, a stylish wet bar with sink and cabinet, a rear bench seat with storage behind, and a second bench seat that folds away into the gunwale. There's a big ski locker with a gas-assist hatch in the cockpit sole, and the unique electric hideaway swim platform is a particularly innovative concept. A marine head is located inside the portside console—the door can be pulled closed for privacy and there's even a light and vents. Engine access is excellent. A variety of single sterndrive engine options were available. Among them, a 300hp Volvo will cruise the Cobalt 272 at 24–25 knots and deliver a top speed of close to 40 knots.

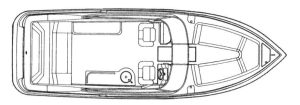

Cobalt 282

Length	28'8"	Max Headroom	4'10"
Beam	9'0"	Fuel	90 gals.
Draft, Up	2'0"	Water	18 gals.
Draft, Down	2'9"	Hull Type	Deep-V
Weight, Single	6,750#	Deadrise Aft	22°
Clearance	5'7"	Production	2002–Current

With a length of nearly 29 feet, the Cobalt 282 is at the top end of the bowrider class. So who buys these big bowriders? People who need more space for friends and family, and people who don't want their boating activities limited to lakes and bays. Built on a deep-V hull with a 9-foot beam, the 282 can handle an offshore chop with ease while still being trailerable for those with a permit and a heavy-duty tow vehicle. (Note the unusual retro-style tail fins—very unique indeed.) Families with young children will appreciate the 282's deep cockpit and forward seating area. Standard storage is plentiful, and bow doors reduce high-rpm windblast. Aside from the posh cockpit seating and convenient center transom walk-through, the 282 is loaded with the kind of quality features expected in any Cobalt product. The radar arch doubles as a wakeboard tower; the flip-up helm seat makes standup driving easy; a head/storage compartment is built into the portside console; and fit and finish is nearly flawless. Note that an air compressor (for inflatable water toys) and cockpit wet bar are standard. Expect a top speed of 40+ knots with a single 375hp MerCruiser Bravo III sterndrive.

Cobalt 292

Length	28'10"	Fuel	130 gals.
Beam	9'6"	Water	31 gals.
Draft, Up	2'2"	Hull Type	Deep-V
Draft, Down	3'0"	Deadrise Aft	20°
Weight, Twins	7,600#	Designer	Cobalt
Clearance	5'8"	Production	1999–2002

One of the larger bowriders on the market during her production years, the Cobalt 292 is among the most luxurious boats in her class with a level of finish that many other production manufacturers might well envy. She's built on the proven hull of Cobalt's popular 293 Cuddy, a deep-V affair with a relatively wide 9-foot, 6-inch beam and a fully integrated transom. Beautifully styled, the deep cockpit of the 292 is arranged with wraparound lounge seating for seven, a molded galley opposite with a sink, storage drawers and refrigerator, in-deck storage, and a walk-through transom door to the swim platform. Hidden within the portside console, the head compartment offers a toilet and over 4 feet of headroom. Like all Cobalt models, the wood dash console is a work of art. Additional features include port and starboard helm seats with flip-up bolsters, a hydraulic engine compartment hatch, leather tilt wheel, anchor locker and a cockpit ice chest. A comfortable and very quiet ride, twin 280hp Volvo sterndrives (among several engine choices) will cruise the Cobalt 292 at 27–28 knots and reach a top speed in the neighborhood of 42 knots.

RUNABOUTS

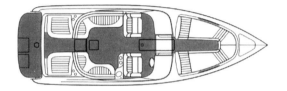

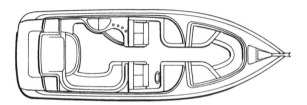

Cobalt 293

Length . . . . 28'10"	Fuel . . . . 111 gals.
Beam . . . . 9'6"	Water . . . . 30 gals.
Draft, Up . . . . 2'2"	Hull Type . . . . Deep-V
Draft, Down . . . . 2'10"	Deadrise Aft . . . . 20°
Weight . . . . 6,950#	Designer . . . . Cobalt
Clearance . . . . 6'2"	Production 1997–Current

Day boats in the 30-foot range have become increasingly popular with weekend boaters more interested in an afternoon on the water with friends than extended family cruising. Among these new-breed designs, the Cobalt 293's rugged construction, graceful styling, and meticulous workmanship set her well apart from the competition. Not inexpensive, the 293 provides every comfort and convenience one could ask for in a modern day boat. The beautifully contoured cockpit comes with a wet bar with refrigeration, removable cockpit table, an extended swim platform, and a rosewood dash that—with its leather-covered steering wheel—can only be described as elegant. In a clever design, the entire transom and rear seat folds away for access to the engine compartment. There's an enclosed head in the cabin along with a V-berth/dinette and a small galley. What makes the Cobalt so special, of course, is the extraordinary fit and finish. A single 7.4-liter sterndrive will cruise the 293 at 22 knots (35–36 knots top), and twin 5.7-liter I/Os will cruise at 30 knots and reach a top speed of around 45 knots.

Cobalt 343

Length w/Platform . . . . 37'2"	Fuel . . . . 200 gals.
Hull Length . . . . 35'4"	Water . . . . 10 gals.
Beam . . . . 9'8"	Waste . . . . NA
Draft . . . . 37"	Hull Type . . . . Deep-V
Weight . . . . 10,200#	Deadrise Aft . . . . 24.5°
Clearance, Top . . . . 8'2"	Production 2004–Current

With her sleek profile, luxurious amenities, and high-performance stepped hull, the Cobalt 343 delivers a full blast of power and raw sex appeal. This is the kind of boat that puts the excitement back into boating—a fast, user-friendly cruiser that attracts a crowd just about everywhere she goes. Built on a slender deep-V hull with a full-length keel pad, the 343 has a cockpit capable of seating six passengers in extreme comfort. The electric center-line captain's seat, with its wraparound dash and excellent visibility, is one of the more notable features of this boat. Molded steps on either side of the cockpit provide easy access to the foredeck, and the cabin door slides on polished stainless runners. Inside, the cabin is as elegant as it is simple. An Ultraleather settee and enclosed head are standard, and while the headroom is modest, the accommodations are plush. An impressive array of standard equipment includes an air compressor, 10-disc CD changer, through-prop exhaust, power motor box and an extended swim platform. A fast ride with twin 425hp MerCruiser engines, the Cobalt 343 will cruise in the high 30s and reach a top speed of 50+ knots.

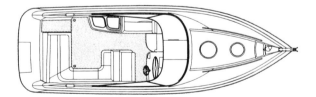

RUNABOUTS

Crownline 270 Bowrider

Length w/Platform	28'3"	Headroom	NA
Hull Length	26'1"	Fuel	88 gals.
Beam	8'6"	Water	12 gals.
Draft, Down	3'0"	Hull Type	Deep-V
Weight	5,500#	Deadrise Aft	23°
Clearance	5'8"	Production	2003–Current

Introduced in 2003, the Crownline 270 is one of the largest trailerable bowriders on the market. Indeed, at over 28 feet in length and weighing in at close to 6,000 pounds, you'll need a heavy-duty tow vehicle to get this full-size package on the road. Built on a solid fiberglass hull, the deep cockpit of the Crownline 270 is arranged with a wraparound rear bench seat with a removable center section for access to the extended swim platform. Twin flip-up bucket seats are forward, and an enclosed head compartment (with sink, exhaust fan, and opening port) is built into the passenger-side console. The 270's helm console is notable for its large storage compartment and well-designed dash with recessed Faria gauges. Like most boats of this type, a wet bar, beverage holders, courtesy lights, and in-floor ski storage are standard in the cockpit. In the bow, an optional upholstered inset converts the seating into a large sun pad. Additional features include twin transom storage compartments, three coolers, pressure water, and a tilt wheel. A quick ride with a single 320hp MerCruiser Bravo III, the Crownline 270 will reach a top speed of close to 45 knots.

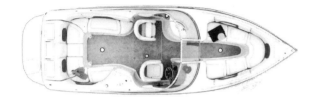

Crownline 275 CCR

Length w/Platform	28'8"	Headroom	5'6"
Beam	8'6"	Fuel	80 gals.
Draft, Up	24"	Water	15 gals.
Draft, Down	39"	Hull Type	Modified-V
Weight	6,700#	Deadrise Aft	18°
Clearance	5'6"	Production	2005–Current

Big cuddy cruisers are popular with owners of heavy-duty tow vehicles, and trailerable models in this category seldom exceed 27 feet in length. Crownline's sporty 275 CCR is aimed at precisely this market—she's as big as you're likely to find in a late-model trailerable boat, she's easy on the eye, and she's priced right. Built on a notched-bottom hull with a keel pad, the 275 is quick to accelerate and fun to drive. The drawing power of this boat has everything to do with Crownline's ability to deliver a lot of boat for the money. The rear seat in the cockpit converts to a big sun lounge, and the helm is fitted with premium Faria gauges, tilt steering, and a Sony stereo system. Cabin accommodations are big for a trailerable boat. A small galley and convertible dinette are standard, and the enclosed head comes with a sink and shower. Performance is also a step up from the norm, although the CCR's stepped hull handles a little differently from the standard V-bottom runabout. Flip-up helm seats, an anchor pulpit, three opening cabin ports, a woodgrain dash, and an electric head are standard. Twin 375hp MerCruiser I/Os will cruise at 30 knots and reach a top speed of 40-45 knots.

RUNABOUTS

See Page 309 for Pricing Information

See Page 309 for Pricing Information

Crownline 288 Bowrider

Length	28'8"	Headroom	4'2"
Beam	9'8"	Fuel	129 gals.
Draft, Up	1'9"	Water	20 gals.
Draft, Down	3'2"	Hull Type	Deep-V
Weight	8,000#	Deadrise Aft	24°
Clearance	6'2"	Production	2001–04

The Crownline 288 is among the new breed of jumbo bowriders that have come into fashion in recent years. With her wide beam and substantial 8,000-pound displacement, she's big enough to accommodate a small crowd and tough enough to handle an offshore chop. Like any good bowrider, the 288 is all about versatility and passenger comfort. A wet bar, pressure water, and an enclosed head compartment (with opening port) were standard, and a unique side-wall entry gate with a foldaway step is located to starboard in the cockpit, just forward of the aft bench seat. Also notable is the mini-cabin concealed within the driver-side console. Accessed from the bow seating area, this small compartment houses a cushioned berth with portlight suitable for catching a quick nap. At the helm, a flip-up bolster seat allows for standup driving. Additional features include an extended swim platform, woodgrain dash, in-floor ski/wakeboard locker, windshield vents, tilt wheel, and drink holders. Among several sterndrive engine options, twin 280hp Volvos will cruise the Crownline 288 in the low-to-mid 30s and reach a top speed in excess of 40 knots.

Formula 280 Bowrider

Length	28'0"	Fuel	120 gals.
Beam	9'2"	Water	20 gals.
Draft	3'0"	Waste	2.6 gals.
Weight, Single	6,100#	Hull Type	Deep-V
Weight, Twins	7,300#	Deadrise Aft	21°
Headroom	5'2"	Production	1998–Current

It's all about fun with the Formula 280 Bowrider, a well-built boat big enough for the ocean but small enough to trailer to local lakes and rivers. (Note, however, that because of her wide 9-foot, 2-inch beam, a permit is required for trailering.) Built on a deep-V hull, the 280 is distinguished for her attractive styling, roominess, and easy handling. She's not the least expensive big bowrider on the market, but the quality is there, and it's no secret that Formulas are built to last. Seating includes a flip-up double helm seat, double companion lounge, and a big U-shaped settee in the cockpit that converts to a sun lounge. Storage for fenders or dive tanks is located under the passenger seat, and a deluxe cockpit galley with sink and storage is standard. The 280's tiered helm position, with its Dino wheel and Kiekhaefer controls, is almost ideal, while the enclosed head includes a sink and opening port. Forward, filler cushions can turn the deep bow section into a huge sun pad. Additional features include a power engine hatch lift, stainless steel props, transom storage locker, and an extended swim platform. Offered with single or twin I/Os, twin 260hp MerCruisers will deliver a top speed in the neighborhood of 45 knots.

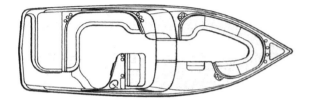

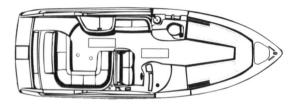

See Page 309 for Pricing Information

See Page 315 for Pricing Information

Formula 280 Sun Sport

Length	28'0"	Fuel	120 gals.
Beam	9'2"	Water	20 gals.
Draft	3'0"	Headroom	5'2"
Weight, Single	6,300#	Hull Type	Deep-V
Weight, Twins	7,300#	Deadrise Aft	21°
Clearance	5'8"	Production	1994–Current

The Formula 280 Sun Sport is a deluxe day cruiser for those who want a boat that's long on cockpit space, handling qualities and workmanship. By any standard, the 280 is a handsome boat and her wraparound windshield and colorful hull graphics only add to her sportboat appeal. With seating for eight, the cockpit is definitely the star attraction of the Sun Sport. Aside from the big U-shaped lounge aft (which converts into a massive sun pad), there's a doublewide seat at the helm and a settee opposite. The on-deck galley makes a lot of sense on a boat like this, and there are many cockpit storage areas including fender storage under the settee. Lacking side decks, a walk-through windshield provides foredeck access, and the engine compartment (under the sun pad) is reached via a motorized hatch lift. Belowdecks, the V-shaped dinette converts into a double berth, and an enclosed head comes with a portable toilet. Among several single or twin sterndrive options, a single 310hp MerCruiser Bravo III engine will cruise the 280 Sun Sport at 21–22 knots (about 37 knots top), and twin 320hp MerCruisers will cruise at 28 knots and reach a top speed in the high 40s.

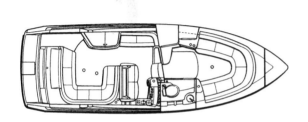

Formula 330 Sun Sport

Length	33'0"	Water	20 gals.
Beam	10'2"	Waste	26 gals.
Draft	2'11"	Headroom	5'7"
Weight	9,700#	Hull Type	Deep-V
Clearance	6'0"	Deadrise Aft	20°
Fuel	160 gals.	Production	1996–Current

With her sleek lines and beautifully designed cockpit, the Formula 330 Sun Sport will appeal to those seeking a high-style family sportboat with the emphasis on open-air entertainment. She's well constructed on a deep-V hull with generous beam (for a sportboat), and the subtle-but-colorful hull graphics do much to accent her low-slung appearance. The spacious cockpit of the Formula 330 is really what this boat is all about. Not surprisingly, it comes at the expense of a rather compact, but comfortable, interior. In spite of the limited cabin volume, the accommodations are very practical below with a U-shaped Ultraleather settee/dinette forward, an enclosed head compartment, and an entertainment center—accommodations well suited for her day boat mission. The cockpit table at the transom converts into a wide sun lounge, and a molded on-deck galley conceals a sink, a 54-quart cooler, and an optional alcohol stove. Additional features include a ski locker, dive-tank racks, a walk-through windshield and guest seating opposite the helm. A good performer with 320hp MerCruiser sterndrives, the Formula 330 SS will cruise at 28 knots and top out in the mid 40s.

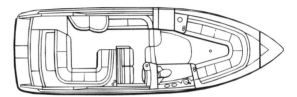

See Page 315 for Pricing Information

See Page 315 for Pricing Information

Four Winns 280 Horizon

Length w/Platform . . . . 27'9"	Fuel . . . . 130 gals.
Beam . . . . 9'4"	Water . . . . 12 gals.
Draft, Up . . . . 1'6"	Waste . . . . 12 gals.
Draft, Down . . . . 3'1"	Hull Type . . . . Modified-V
Weight . . . . 7,140#	Deadrise Aft . . . . 21°
Clearance . . . . 5'0"	Production 2000–Current

At nearly 28 feet in length, the 280 Horizon is the largest bowrider Four Winns has ever built. Big bowriders have become increasingly popular in recent years, and the Horizon, with her wide 9-foot, 4-inch beam, is bigger than most. Built on a modified-V hull, the 280 has the size and weight to handle an ocean chop while still offering the stability so important in any family runabout. Key to the popularity of this boat is her large cockpit with its wraparound seating to starboard and refreshment center (with standard refrigerator, sink, and trash bin) to port. A side settee is opposite the helm, where a flip-up double seat provides plenty of legroom for standup driving. A stylish burlwood dash displays a complete set of Faria gauges as well as a depthfinder, however there's little space for any extra electronics. An enclosed head compartment is built into the portside console, while the starboard console contains a large storage locker. Note that the 280's engine compartment is a tight fit. Additional features include a power engine hatch, transom shower, tilt steering wheel, and an extended secondary swim platform. A fast ride with twin 315hp Volvo I/Os, the Horizon will hit a top speed of around 50 knots.

Four Winns 285 Sundowner

Length w/Platform . . . . 27'9"	Max Headroom . . . . 4'7"
Beam . . . . 9'4"	Fuel . . . . 130 gals.
Draft, Up . . . . 1'6"	Water . . . . 12 gals.
Draft, Down . . . . 3'1"	Hull Type . . . . Modified-V
Weight . . . . 6,380#	Deadrise Aft . . . . 21°
Clearance . . . . 5'0"	Production 2000–Current

The Four Winns 285 Sundowner is a well-appointed day boat whose spacious cockpit can seat as many as eight guests in comfort. Four Winns has a reputation for building a good-quality product, and the Sundowner will easily satisfy the demands of active families more interested in practicality than glitz. Built on what Four Winns calls a "Stable-Vee" hull with a keel pad to increase speed, the Sundowner's deck plan is a model of efficiency. A wraparound lounge aft converts to a sun pad, and a portside mini-galley includes a refrigerator, sink with pressure water, and a trash bin. At the helm, a double flip-up seat provides plenty of legroom for standup driving. Note that the dash area, with its Plexiglas-covered chart flat, is tinted to reduce glare. Going below, the Sundowner's small cuddy is arranged with an enclosed head (with VacuFlush toilet) to port, a microwave cabinet opposite, and a convertible V-berth forward. On the downside, the engine compartment is a tight fit. Standard features include a power engine hatch, secondary extended swim platform, walk-through windshield, and tilt wheel. Among many engine choices, twin 270hp Volvo I/Os will deliver a top speed in excess of 50 knots.

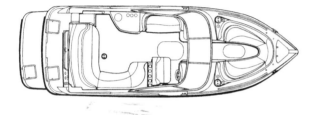

RUNABOUTS

Hinckley Talaria 29C

Length Overall	29'2"	Fuel	100 gals.
Length WL	26'8"	Water	20 gals.
Beam	9'1"	Hull	Modified-V
Draft	1'6"	Deadrise Aft	18°
Weight	7,500#	Designer	Bruce King
Clearance	5'3"	Production	2002–Current

A showcase of design and craftsmanship, the Talaria 29C is the first center console ever built by Hinckley. This is proof that a center console can be a day boat as well as a fishboat, and her water-jet propulsion and shallow 18-inch draft allows the 29C to reach coves and inlets out of reach to a conventional inboard boat. With a price tag high enough to bring even wealthy buyers to their knees, the 29C is a very opulent small boat. Her structure is cored composite with an outer skin of Kevlar-reinforced fiberglass. Vinylester resin is used throughout to virtually eliminate the possibility of osmotic blistering. With comfortable seating for eight, the 29C has a transom settee in addition to a settee in the bow. The engine box doubles as an aft-facing passenger seat as well as the helm seat, and a roomy head compartment is fitted inside the console. The varnished teak helm station is a genuine work of art. Note that the console is positioned well aft, which produces a great ride in a chop. Additional features include a power-lift engine box, joystick steering, teak trim, teak swim platform, cockpit sink, and bow thruster. A relatively light boat, a single Yanmar 440hp diesel will cruise in the high 20s and top out at over 30 knots.

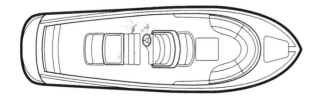

Hinckley Talaria 29R

Length Overall	29'2"	Fuel	100 gals.
Length WL	26'8"	Water	20 gals.
Beam	9'1"	Hull	Modified-V
Draft	1'6"	Deadrise Aft	18°
Weight	7,500#	Designer	Bruce King
Clearance	5'6"	Production	2003–Current

The Hinckley Talaria 29R is an expensive, jet-driven runabout whose beautiful Downeast profile and meticulous finish are guaranteed to stop traffic everywhere she goes. Some have called the 29R a roadster, and it's easy to see why. The hull shape is graceful; the mahogany trim accents add the right touches of elegance; and the cockpit—with its teak helm console, Nardi steering wheel, and posh seating—is reminiscent of an old-time sports car. Built on a cored, Kevlar-reinforced hull, the cockpit of the 29R provides seating for ten with plenty of legroom and storage. The engine box, which doubles as an aft-facing passenger seat, conceals a sink with pressure water and cooler, while the high-end helm and companion chairs both have flip-up bolsters. At the stern is a full-width lounge with storage under. Forward, the cuddy is fitted with a V-berth and a VacuFlush head. Additional features include an electrically lifted engine box, joystick steering, teak swim platform, and bow thruster. Note the absence of a bow rail. A relatively light boat for her size, a single Yanmar 440hp diesel will cruise in the high 20s and top out at over 30 knots. Did we say expensive?

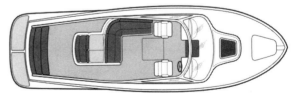

Monterey 298 Sport Cruiser

Length w/Platform . . . . 31'10"	Fuel . . . . 142 gals.
Hull Length. . . . . 29'7"	Water. . . . . 15 gals.
Beam . . . . 9'6"	Waste . . . . 18 gals.
Draft, Up . . . . 1'9"	Hull Type . . . . Deep-V
Draft, Down . . . . 3'1"	Deadrise Aft . . . . 22°
Weight. . . . . 8,500#	Production 2003–Current

To many, the Monterey 298 Sport Cruiser is one of the best-looking sportboats on the market. She's a closed-bow version of the company's popular 298 SS bowrider with surprisingly complete cabin accommodations to go with her exhilarating performance. Built on a deep-V hull, the focal point of the 298 is her large cockpit with its aft bench seat that folds down to increase the size of the existing sun pad. A contoured lounge is opposite the helm, and a forward-raked radar arch and flashy hull colors add to her sex appeal. Below, the 298 offers 5 feet, 5 inches of headroom in the main cabin, and incorporates a compact midcabin aft that stretches beneath the cockpit floor. Amenities include a full galley with cherrywood cabinets, a convertible dinette forward, and a fully enclosed head with shower. The extended swim platform comes with a recessed boarding ladder, and a flip-up seat at the helm permits standup driving. Additional features include a walk-through windshield, transom shower, cockpit wet bar, and good engine access. Twin 280hp Volvo gas sterndrives will cruise in the low 30s and reach a top speed of 45 knots.

Monterey 298 Super Sport

Length w/Platform . . . . 31'10"	Fuel . . . . 142 gals.
Hull Length. . . . . 29'7"	Water. . . . . 15 gals.
Beam . . . . 9'6"	Waste . . . . 18 gals.
Draft, Up . . . . 1'9"	Hull Type . . . . Deep-V
Draft, Down . . . . 3'1"	Deadrise Aft . . . . 22°
Weight. . . . . 8,000#	Production 2001–Current

From the comfortable bow seating to her well-planned cockpit, the Monterey 298 SS is one very spacious boat. In fact, she's one of the largest bowriders ever produced by a major U.S. manufacturer. Built on a deep-V hull with a wide 9-foot, 6-inch beam, the focal point of the 298 is her large cockpit with its aft bench seat that folds down to increase the size of the existing sun pad. A contoured lounge is opposite the helm, abutting a small console with wet bar and sink, and the doublewide helm seat has a flip-up bolster for standup driving. An unusual feature of the 298 SS is the double berth concealed within the portside console. An enclosed head is in the opposite console, and both of these compartments are fitted with an opening port for ventilation. There's plenty of storage under the back-to-back helm seats, and the sun pad lifts up to reveal the engine compartment. Standard features include an extended swim platform, docking lights, pull-up cleats, transom shower, fender storage, and VacuFlush toilet. An excellent open-water performer, twin 280hp Volvo gas sterndrives will cruise in the low 30s and reach a top speed of 45 knots.

Floorplan Not Available

Floorplan Not Available

Regal Ventura 8.3 SC & SE

Hull Length	27'6"	Water	24 gals.
Beam	9'1"	Waste	12 gals.
Draft, Down	2'10"	Headroom	4'8"
Weight	5,600#	Hull Type	Deep-V
Clearance	5'6"	Deadrise Aft	21°
Fuel	101 gals.	Production	1992–97

Sharing identical hulls and cockpit layouts, the Regal Ventura 8.3 SC and SE are a pair of well-designed sportboats whose classic styling has aged well over the years. The SC, which is the cuddy version, came out first in 1992, while the open-bow SE followed in 1994. Built on a deep-V hull, the Ventura's 9-foot, 1-inch beam makes her trailerable, but only with a permit since she exceeds the legal 8-foot, 6-inch maximum width. The enduring popularity of these boats has much to do with their spacious cockpits. Horseshoe-shaped seating in the back runs from immediately aft of the driver's seat all the way around to the portside wet bar, offering room for six to stretch out in comfort. A flip-up helm seat allows for standup driving, and the off-white dash reduces glare on the gauges. The SC's cuddy includes a convertible dinette/double berth forward and a tiny toilet compartment, while the SE has seating for four in the bow. The Ventura's huge engine compartment, with its electrically raised seat/hatch assembly, offers truly outstanding service access. A single 300hp Volvo gas sterndrive will cruise the Ventura 8.3 SC and SE models in the high 20s and max out at 40+ knots.

Regal 2800/2900 LSR

Length	29'2"	Fuel	97 gals.
Beam	9'1"	Water	24 gals.
Draft, Up	1'10"	Waste	12 gals.
Draft, Down	2'10"	Hull Type	Deep-V
Weight	5,900#	Deadrise Aft	24°
Clearance	6'6"	Production	1999–2004

Introduced in 1999, the Regal 2800 LSR (called the 2900 LSR in 2002–04) combines the comforts of a spacious cockpit with the excellent performance of Regal's then-new FasTrac stepped hull bottom. It's only been in recent years that bowriders this large have made their appearance, and their appeal ranges from daycruisers who simply want more seating capacity to enthusiasts who want the offshore capability only a bigger boat can offer. Either way, the LSR remains an impressive blend of comfort and performance. Key to her appeal is a spacious, user-friendly cockpit. Wraparound seating in the back runs from immediately aft of the driver's seat all the way around to the portside wet bar, offering room for six people to stretch out in comfort. A head compartment is located in the port console, and an electric hatch provides good service access to the engine compartment. An extended swim platform was a popular option. Among several engine options, a single 310hp Volvo sterndrive will cruise the 2800/2900 LSR at 30 knots and reach a top speed in excess of 40 knots.

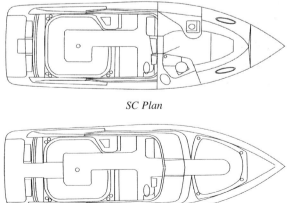

SC Plan

SE Plan

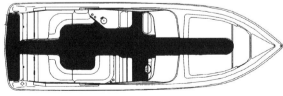

RUNABOUTS

See Page 345 for Pricing Information

See Page 346 for Pricing Information

Regal 3350 Sport Cruiser

Length	34'8"	Max Headroom	5'2"
Beam	11'4"	Fuel	186 gals.
Draft, Up	1'8"	Water	30 gals.
Draft, Down	2'11"	Hull Type	Deep-V
Weight	11,100#	Deadrise Aft	19°
Clearance	7'0"	Production	2005–Current

Sportboats are supposed to be about performance and fun, but many fall short of expectations. Packaged in a bubble of high-octane marketing hype, some so-called sportboats are really nothing more than warmed-over runabouts. Not so with the Regal 3350: this is a well-conceived performance cruiser designed from the bottom up for spirited boating. Built on a deep-V hull with a board beam, the vast cockpit of the 3350 offers more seating than just about any boat in her class. Both the helm and companion seats are doublewide with flip-up bolsters, and the huge U-shaped aft lounge—which converts into a giant sun pad—is bisected by a centerline transom door. (A pair of cockpit tables can be stored in a designated compartment.) While the cockpit is obviously the social center of the 3350, the interior is still large enough to offer a luxurious retreat for after-hours relaxing. Lounge seating wraps around the cabin with the bow section serving as a dinette or roomy double berth. Leather upholstery and a cherry-and-holly sole are standard, however the head is small and headroom is modest. A fast ride with 320hp Volvo sterndrives, expect a top speed in excess of 40 knots. Note the limited 186-gallon fuel capacity.

Rinker 272 Captiva Bowrider

Length	27'0"	Max Headroom	2'10"
Beam	9'0"	Fuel	100 gals.
Draft, Up	1'9"	Water	10 gals.
Draft, Down	3'0"	Hull Type	Deep-V
Weight	5,400#	Deadrise Aft	21°
Clearance	5'7"	Production	1999–2002

Introduced in 1999, the Rinker 272 Captiva Bowrider is notable for her low cost and good open-water performance. Rinker has always delivered a lot of boat for the money, and the Captiva's stepped, deep-V hull allows her to handle an offshore chop better than most big bowriders. Hull construction is solid fiberglass, and her 9-foot beam permits a fairly roomy deck plan with seating for as many as ten. The cockpit configuration differs from the traditional U-shaped aft seating; instead, the Captiva's layout has a curved seat/lounge opposite the helm, and an L-lounge aft, across from an angled single seat and the cockpit galley. Aside from her modest price, this unusual layout may be the high point of the boat since it permits easy movement throughout the cockpit. There's plenty of storage in this boat, and the enclosed head under the passenger-side console is surprisingly large. Additional features include a cockpit refrigerator, in-floor ski storage, tilt steering, and transom shower. A very good performer with a single 320hp MerCruiser Bravo III sterndrive, the Captiva can reach a top speed of nearly 40 knots. Note the very small fuel capacity.

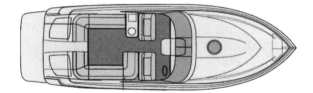

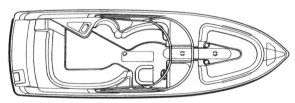

RUNABOUTS

Rinker 272 Captiva Cuddy

Length	27'0"	Max Headroom	4'2"
Beam	9'0"	Fuel	100 gals.
Draft, Up	1'9"	Water	10 gals.
Draft, Down	3'0"	Hull Type	Deep-V
Weight	5,400#	Deadrise Aft	21°
Clearance	5'7"	Production	1999–2002

The Rinker 272 Captiva combines sturdy construction and good performance in one of the most affordable sportboat packages on the market. Rinker has always built boats for budget-conscious buyers, and the Captiva will appeal to entry-level families moving up from runabouts or ski boats. Note that she rides on a stepped hull, a bottom design that breaks the water's grip on the hull, which—when properly configured—can increase a boat's top speed. An excellent dayboat suitable for occasional overnighting, the compact cabin of the Captiva contains a V-berth, an enclosed head, and a hanging locker. The galley (which includes a sink, stove and refrigerator) is located in the cockpit where it's easily accessed by passengers. An L-shaped lounge provides plenty of cockpit seating, and a removable dinette table stores in the cabin. Additional features include a tilt wheel, walk-through windshield, anchor locker, transom shower, and an electric engine hatch. A quick ride with a single 310hp MerCruiser Bravo III sterndrive, the Captiva will reach a top speed of close to 40 knots. With only 100 gallons of fuel capacity, don't plan on going too far from the gas dock.

Rinker 282 Captiva Bowrider

Length	29'0"	Max Headroom	3'10"
Beam	9'0"	Fuel	100 gals.
Draft, Up	1'9"	Water	10 gals.
Draft, Down	3'0"	Hull Type	Deep-V
Weight	6,040#	Deadrise Aft	21°
Clearance	5'8"	Production	2003–Current

The Rinker 282 Captiva Bowrider is based on the earlier 272 Bowrider (1999–2002) with the extra length used to incorporate a unique aft-facing bench seat into the transom. Like her predecessor, the 282 is notable for her low cost and good open-water performance. Rinker has always delivered a lot of boat for the money, and the Captiva's stepped, deep-V hull allows her to handle an offshore chop better than most big bowriders. Hull construction is solid fiberglass, and her 9-foot beam permits a fairly roomy deck plan with seating for as many as ten. Aside from her aforementioned transom seat, the high point of the Captiva 282 is her wide-open cockpit with its bucket seats forward, galley cabinet, and L-seating aft. There's plenty of storage in this boat, and the enclosed head under the passenger-side console is surprisingly large. Additional features include a cockpit refrigerator, trim tabs, in-floor ski storage, tilt steering, and transom shower. A very good performer with a single 320hp MerCruiser Bravo III sterndrive, the Captiva will cruise in the mid 20s and reach a top speed of just under 40 knots. Note the limited fuel capacity.

Floorplan Not Available

Rinker 282 Captiva Cuddy

Length	29'0"	Max Headroom	5'0"
Beam	9'0"	Fuel	100 gals.
Draft, Up	1'9"	Water	10 gals.
Draft, Down	3'0"	Hull Type	Deep-V
Weight	6,240#	Deadrise Aft	21°
Clearance	5'8"	Production	2003–Current

The Rinker 282 Captiva Cuddy is based on the earlier 272 Cuddy (1999–2002) with the extra length used to incorporate a unique aft-facing bench seat into the transom. Like her predecessor, the 282 is notable for her low cost and good open-water performance. Rinker has always delivered a lot of boat for the money, and the Captiva's stepped, deep-V hull allows her to handle an offshore chop better than most big runabouts. Hull construction is solid fiberglass, and her 9-foot beam permits a fairly roomy deck plan with comfortable seating for eight. Aside from a super-competitive price, the high points of the Captiva Cuddy are her practical deck plan and impressive list of standard equipment. The rear-facing transom seat will be a hit with swimmers, and the cockpit seating is configured so that all passengers can face forward. Below, the compact cuddy has a V-berth, hanging locker, and an enclosed head with opening port. A transom shower, cockpit galley, and extended swim platform are standard. An optional 375hp MerCruiser Bravo III sterndrive will deliver a top speed of over 40 knots. Note the Captiva's very small fuel capacity.

Sea Ray 270 Sundeck

Length	26'6"	Max Headroom	4'0"
Beam	8'10"	Fuel	85 gals.
Draft, Up	1'8"	Water	24 gals.
Draft, Down	3'0"	Hull Type	Modified-V
Weight	5,800#	Deadrise Aft	21°
Clearance	6'4"	Production	2002–Current

One of the bigger deckboats on the market, the Sea Ray 270 Sundeck might easily be confused with a full-blown sportboat were it not for her broad bow area with its lounge seating and walk-through boarding gate. The 270 differs from other deckboats in that she includes a berth under the starboard helm console. (It's open to question whether sleeping quarters make much sense in a dayboat of this type, but the area is certainly useful for storing gear and carry-ons.) The passenger-side console houses a lockable head with sink and opening port, and a well-positioned cockpit galley includes a second sink as well as an insulated cooler and faucet with pullout sprayer. An L-shaped settee spans the transom and port side of the cockpit, and the rear section rises to reveal the engine compartment. An extended swim platform is standard. Technically, a permit is required to tow the Sea Ray 270 since her 8-foot, 10-inch beam exceeds the legal 8-foot, 6-inch width restriction; realistically, however, the chances of getting stopped are pretty slim. Among several sterndrive engine options, a single 375hp MerCruiser Bravo III will hit a top speed of over 40 knots. Note the modest fuel capacity.

Floorplan Not Available

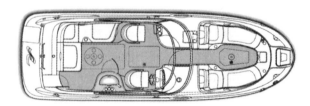

See Page 346 for Pricing Information

See Page 348 for Pricing Information

RUNABOUTS

Sea Ray 280 Bowrider

Length	27'6"	Fuel	127 gals.
Beam	9'6"	Water	24 gals.
Draft, Up	2'2"	Waste (Opt.)	28 gals.
Draft, Down	3'5"	Hull Type	Deep-V
Weight	6,400#	Deadrise Aft	21°
Clearance	NA	Production	1996–2001

A popular model, the Sea Ray 280 Bowrider remains one of the biggest open-bow runabouts produced in recent years. (Indeed, she was the biggest production bowrider you could buy when she was introduced in 1996.) Built on a beamy deep-V hull and weighing in at a hefty 6,400 pounds, the 280 has the size and bulk to handle an offshore chop in relative comfort. The deck plan is arranged with a U-shaped lounge/sun pad forward (with a removable table) and a second wraparound lounge aft. A wet bar with cooler and trash receptacle is located behind the helm, and the rear seat can be raised at the push of a button to expose the engine compartment. A lockable head compartment with sink and shower is concealed below the passenger-side console, and a tilt wheel and flip-up bolster seat are standard at the helm. Additional features include a stereo system, in-floor ski locker, dockside power, and transom shower. Among several engine choices (both single and twin), a pair of 350hp 5.7-liter MerCruiser sterndrives will cruise the 280 Bow Rider at a brisk 35 knots and reach a top speed of around 50 knots.

Sea Ray 280 Sun Sport

Length	27'6"	Fuel	127 gals.
Beam	9'6"	Water	24 gals.
Draft, Up	2'2"	Waste	20 gals.
Draft, Down	3'5"	Hull Type	Deep-V
Weight	8,200#	Deadrise Aft	21°
Clearance	NA	Production	1996–2001

The Sea Ray 280 Sun Sport offers the versatility and performance one expects in a modern sportboat together with a healthy dose of old-fashioned sex appeal. The popularity of the Sun Sport derives from her ability to do several things well. A functional cabins makes the 280 a good overnighter, and her wide 9-foot, 6-inch beam provides the cockpit space required to entertain as many as six guests in comfort. The helm position is particularly well-arranged and includes a burlwood console and a flip-up bolster that's essential on a high-speed sportboat. A wet bar with cooler, glass rack, and trash receptacle is just behind the helm seat, and the aft seating area lifts at the touch of a button to reveal the engines. The 280's big cockpit still leaves enough space below for an expansive U-shaped dinette (with a removable table) as well as an enclosed head with a premium VacuFlush toilet and pullout shower. An extended swim platform and transom shower were standard, and a radar arch was a popular option. Not inexpensive, twin 260hp MerCruiser sterndrives (among many power options) will reach a top speed of around 45 knots.

RUNABOUTS

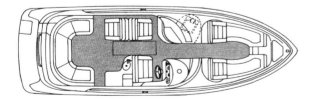

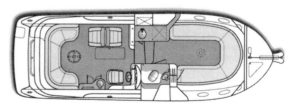

See Page 348 for Pricing Information

See Page 348 for Pricing Information

Sea Ray 290 Bowrider

Length	29'6"	Fuel	130 gals.
Beam	9'8"	Water	24 gals.
Draft, Up	2'0"	Waste	20 gals.
Draft, Down	3'1"	Hull Type	Deep-V
Weight	7,700#	Deadrise Aft	21°
Clearance	NA	Production	2001–04

Buyers continue to ask for bigger and bigger bowriders, and the Sea Ray 290 Bowrider is among the biggest of them all. With a wide 9-foot, 8-inch beam and a close to 8,000 pounds of weight, the 290 is more than big enough to handle offshore waters. Two cockpit seating plans were available: the standard layout has U-shaped seating aft, a back-to-back companion seat, and a centerline transom walk-through, while the optional seating plan includes a large sun pad aft, a starboard walk-through, and bucket seats forward. A cockpit wet bar was standard in either arrangement, as are an electric engine compartment hatch and an in-floor ski storage locker. In the bow, a table and filler cushions turn the entire bow seating area into a huge sun pad. A roomy enclosed head in the passenger-side console comes with a VacuFlush head, sink, and pullout shower. Additional features include a flip-up bolster seat, transom shower, and an extended swim platform. An expensive, good-looking runabout with plenty of sex appeal, twin 260hp MerCruiser sterndrives will cruise the 290 Bowrider at 30 knots and reach a top speed of around 45 knots.

Sea Ray 290 Sun Sport

Length	29'6"	Fuel	130 gals.
Beam	9'8"	Water	24 gals.
Draft, Up	2'2"	Waste	20 gals.
Draft, Down	3'1"	Hull Type	Deep-V
Weight	8,300#	Deadrise Aft	21°
Clearance	NA	Production	2002–Current

Classic good looks, roomy accommodations, and brisk performance characterize the Sea Ray 290 Sun Sport, a well-finished sportboat from a company with a long history in developing dayboats of this type. Built on a deep-V hull with a wide beam, the Sun Sport's rakish persona is accented by colorful graphics and a forward-sloping radar arch. Two cockpit seating plans are available: the standard seating includes a large sun pad aft, a starboard transom walk-through, and bucket seats forward, while the optional arrangement provides U-shaped seating aft, a back-to-back companion seat, and a centerline transom walk-through. A cockpit wet bar is standard, and a large lighted ski storage area is located in the cockpit sole. A lockable sliding cabin door with integral steps provides easy access to the foredeck. Below, the 290's surprisingly roomy interior includes a convertible dinette/V-berth forward, compact galley with sink and refrigerator, and an enclosed head with pullout shower and premium VacuFlush head. The 290 Sun Sport will top out at 40+ knots with a pair of 260hp MerCruiser I/Os, and twin 320hp Merc I/Os will hit a top speed of just over 45 knots.

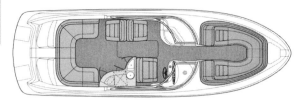

Standard Seating

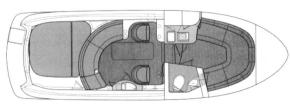

Standard Seating

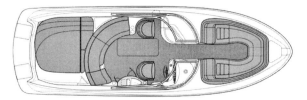

Optional Seating

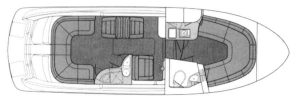

Optional Seating

See Page 348 for Pricing Information

See Page 348 for Pricing Information

RUNABOUTS

Sea Ray 310 Sun Sport

Length	31'2"	Fuel	160 gals.
Beam	9'6"	Water	20 gals.
Draft, Up	2'2"	Waste	11 gals.
Draft, Down	3'1"	Hull Type	Deep-V
Weight	8,100#	Deadrise Aft	21°
Clearance, Arch	8'10"	Production	1991–95

Considered a very stylish boat by the standards of her era, the Sea Ray 310 Sun Sport had the look and persona of a true Mediterranean-bred sportboat. She's still a distinctive boat with her reverse arch and colorful hull graphics, and the Sun Sport's sleek, low-profile appearance gave her a healthy dose of sex appeal. The Sun Sport is built on a lightweight, relatively narrow deep-V hull, and her low foredeck results in very modest cabin headroom. Because she's a dayboat and not a cruiser, the accommodations below are fairly basic. A U-shaped dinette forward—which can seat up to six—converts into a double bed, and there's a small mini-berth/storage shelf in the forepeak. The Sun Sport's small cockpit is arranged with horseshoe-shaped seating aft of the helm and twin bucket seats forward. A full-width sun pad is located over the engine compartment, and drink holders are everywhere. Note that the Sun Sport's original tubular radar arch was replaced with a more stylish fiberglass arch in 1993. Performance is excellent: she'll cruise at 30 knots with twin 350hp MerCruiser sterndrives and reach a top speed in the neighborhood of 45 knots.

World Cat 266/270 LC

Length	26'6"	Fuel	200 gals.
Beam	8'6"	Water	30 gals.
Hull Draft	12"	Transom Height	25"
Hull Weight	4,400#	Hull Type	Semi-Disp. Cat
Clearance	NA	Max HP	450
Headroom	5'10"	Production	1999–Current

Not your traditional deckboat, the World Cat 270 LC (called the 266 LC in 1999–2002) combines a huge party platform with a stable, smooth-riding catamaran hull capable of handling offshore waters. Building a deckboat on a catamaran hull makes a lot of sense; catamarans are far more stable than monohulls, and the rectangular deckboat shape fits easily on a cat's twin hulls. The comfortable, deep cockpit of the 270 LC offers lots of room to move around and plenty of storage under each bow seat. The aft U-shaped lounge converts to a huge sun pad, but the absence of a transom door means passengers have to climb over the seat to get to the swim platform. An open-air galley is to port, opposite the helm, and the head—forward in the port console—features an innovative two-part door that admits light and fresh air. Beneath the helm is a massive storage locker for skis and wakeboards. (Note the low helm windshield.) While the World Cat 270 LC is more expensive than a conventional deckboat, her ability to handle rough water is far superior to any of her monohull counterparts. A quality product, twin Honda 130hp outboards will deliver a top speed of 30+ knots.

RUNABOUTS

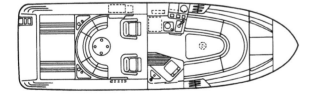

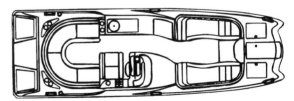

See Page 348 for Pricing Information

See Page 365 for Pricing Information

Retail Price Guide

Please read before using these prices!

Values contained in the RETAIL PRICE GUIDE are intended to provide the reader with *general price estimates only* and are not meant to represent exact market values. These prices reflect the market conditions projected by our staff to exist from November 2005 through November 2006. For price updates after January 1, 2007, call 800-832-0038.

The *Retail High* is the estimated selling price of a clean, well-maintained boat with average equipment. The *Retail Low* is the estimated selling price of a boat showing below-average maintenance, limited equipment, and high-hour engines.

A series of asterisks (******) indicates that limited resale activity prevents the editors from offering a predicted value.

The prices quoted in the following pages apply to boats found in Florida, the Atlantic East Coast, and the Gulf of Mexico. Prices in other regions *must* be adjusted as follows:

Great Lakes	+10–15%
Pacific Northwest	+10–15%
Inland Rivers & Lakes	+5–10%
California	+5–10%

Year	Power	Retail Low	Retail High
Alaskan 53 Pilothouse ******			
Alaskan 60/64 Pilothouse ******			
Alaskan 75 Pilothouse ******			
Albemarle 265/268 Express			
2004	320G I/O	63,500	73,000
2003	320G I/O	57,100	65,700
2002	320G I/O	51,400	59,100
2001	310G I/O	46,200	53,200
2000	310G I/O	42,100	48,400
1999	310G I/O	38,300	44,000
1998	310G I/O	34,800	40,100
1997	300G I/O	31,700	36,500
1996	300G I/O	28,800	33,200
1995	300G I/O	26,500	30,500
1994	300G I/O	24,400	28,100
1993	300G I/O	22,400	25,800
Albemarle 27/280 Express			
2004	T-Gas (I/B)	85,400	98,200
2004	T-Gas (I/O)	88,000	101,200
2003	T-Gas (I/B)	79,400	91,300
2003	T-Gas (I/O)	81,800	94,100
2002	T-Gas (I/B)	73,000	84,000

Year	Power	Retail Low	Retail High
2002	T-Gas (I/O)	76,100	87,500
2001	T-Gas (I/B)	67,900	78,100
2001	T-Gas (I/O)	70,700	81,400
2000	T-Gas (I/B)	63,100	72,600
2000	T-Gas (I/O)	65,800	75,700
1999	T-Gas (I/B)	58,700	67,500
1999	T-Gas (I/O)	61,200	70,400
1998	T-Gas (I/B)	54,600	62,800
1998	T-Gas (I/O)	56,900	65,400
1997	T-Gas (I/B)	50,800	58,400
1997	T-Gas (I/O)	52,900	60,800
1996	T-Gas (I/B)	47,200	54,300
1996	T-Gas (I/O)	49,200	56,600
1995	T-Gas (I/B)	43,900	50,500
1995	T-Gas (I/O)	45,700	52,600
1994	T-Gas (I/B)	40,800	47,000
1994	T-Gas (I/O)	42,500	48,900
1993	T-Gas (I/B)	38,000	43,700
1993	T-Gas (I/O)	39,600	45,500
1992	T-Gas (I/B)	35,300	40,600
1992	T-Gas (I/O)	36,800	42,300
1991	T-Gas (I/B)	32,800	37,800
1991	T-Gas (I/O)	34,200	39,300
1990	T-Gas (I/B)	30,500	35,100
1990	T-Gas (I/O)	31,800	36,600

Year	Power	Retail Low	Retail High
1989	T-Gas (I/B)	28,400	32,700
1989	T-Gas (I/O)	29,600	34,000
1988	T-Gas (I/B)	26,400	30,400
1988	T-Gas (I/O)	27,800	32,000
1987	T-Gas (I/B)	24,800	28,500
1987	T-Gas (I/O)	26,100	30,100
1986	T-Gas (I/B)	23,300	26,800
1986	T-Gas (I/O)	24,600	28,300
1985	T-Gas (I/O)	23,100	26,600
1984	T-Gas (I/O)	21,700	25,000
Albemarle 305/310 Express			
2004	T-Diesel	181,300	208,400
2003	T-Diesel	166,700	191,800
2002	T-Diesel	153,400	176,400
2001	T-Diesel	141,100	162,300
2000	T-Diesel	129,800	149,300
1999	T-Diesel	119,400	137,400
1998	T-Diesel	111,100	127,700
1997	T-Diesel	103,300	118,800
1996	T-Diesel	96,100	110,500
1995	T-Diesel	89,300	102,700
Albemarle 320 Express			
2004	T-Diesel	191,300	219,900
2003	T-Diesel	177,900	204,500

PRICES

Year	Power	Retail Low	Retail High
2002	T-Diesel	165,400	190,200
2001	T-Diesel	153,800	176,900
2000	T-Diesel	143,100	164,500
1999	T-Diesel	133,000	153,000
1998	T-Diesel	123,700	142,300
1997	T-Diesel	115,100	132,300
1996	T-Diesel	108,100	124,400
1995	T-Diesel	101,700	116,900
1994	T-Diesel	95,600	109,900
1993	T-Diesel	89,800	103,300
1992	T-Diesel	84,400	97,100
1991	T-Diesel	79,400	91,300
1990	T-Diesel	74,600	85,800

Albemarle 325 Convertible

Year	Power	Retail Low	Retail High
2003	T350D	205,600	236,400
2002	T350D	189,100	217,500
2001	T350D	174,000	200,100
2000	T350D	160,000	184,100
1999	T-Diesel	147,200	169,300
1998	T-Diesel	135,500	155,800
1997	T-Diesel	126,000	144,900
1996	T-Diesel	117,200	134,700
1995	T-Diesel	108,900	125,300
1994	T-Diesel	101,300	116,500
1993	T-Diesel	94,200	108,400
1992	T-Diesel	88,600	101,900
1991	T-Diesel	83,200	95,700
1990	T-Diesel	78,300	90,000
1989	T-Diesel	73,600	84,600

Albemarle 410 Express

Year	Power	Retail Low	Retail High
2004	T700D	474,000	545,100
2003	T660D	440,800	506,900
2002	T660D	409,900	471,400

Albin 27 Family Cruiser

Year	Power	Retail Low	Retail High
1995	S-Diesel	41,100	47,200
1994	S-Diesel	38,300	44,000
1993	S-Diesel	35,700	41,100
1992	S-Diesel	32,500	37,400
1991	S-Diesel	29,500	34,000
1990	S-Diesel	26,800	30,900
1989	S-Diesel	24,800	28,500
1988	S-Diesel	23,100	26,600
1987	S-Diesel	21,400	24,600
1986	S-Diesel	20,000	23,100
1985	S-Diesel	19,600	22,500
1984	S-Diesel	18,600	21,400
1983	S-Diesel	17,700	20,300

Albin 28 Tournament Express

Year	Power	Retail Low	Retail High
2004	S-Diesel	97,800	112,400
2003	S-Diesel	88,400	101,700
2002	S-Diesel	80,800	93,000
2001	S-Diesel	73,900	85,000
2000	S-Diesel	68,800	79,200
1999	S-Diesel	63,900	73,500
1998	S-Diesel	57,700	66,300
1997	S-Diesel	52,000	59,800
1996	S-Diesel	47,500	54,600
1995	S-Diesel	44,400	51,100
1994	S-Diesel	42,200	48,600
1993	S-Diesel	40,100	46,100

Albin 30 Family Cruiser

Year	Power	Retail Low	Retail High
2004	S315D	108,700	125,000

Albin 31 Tournament Express

Year	Power	Retail Low	Retail High
2004	T370D	202,500	232,800

Year	Power	Retail Low	Retail High
2003	T350D	186,300	214,200
2002	T350D	171,300	197,100
2001	T350D	157,600	181,300
2000	T350D	145,000	166,800
1999	T350D	133,400	153,400
1998	S300D	122,700	141,200
1997	T300D	112,900	129,900
1996	T300D	103,900	119,500
1995	T300D	95,600	109,900

Albin 32+2 Command Bridge

Year	Power	Retail Low	Retail High
2002	S370D	165,600	190,500
2001	S370D	154,200	177,400
2000	S370D	142,800	164,300
1999	S350D	132,500	152,400
1998	S300D	125,400	144,200
1997	S300D	117,700	135,300
1996	S300D	110,500	127,100
1995	S-Diesel	100,500	115,600
1995	T-Diesel	112,000	128,900
1994	S-Diesel	85,500	98,300
1994	T-Diesel	104,300	119,900
1993	S-Diesel	75,200	86,500
1993	T-Diesel	96,100	110,500
1992	S-Diesel	71,500	82,200
1992	T-Diesel	89,600	103,000
1991	S-Diesel	64,600	74,300
1991	T-Diesel	82,100	94,400
1990	S-Diesel	53,500	61,500
1990	T-Diesel	76,700	88,200
1989	S-Diesel	47,200	54,200
1989	T-Diesel	70,400	80,900

Albin 35 Convertible

Year	Power	Retail Low	Retail High
2004	T370D	262,200	301,500
2003	T370D	241,200	277,400
2002	T370D	221,900	255,200
2001	T370D	204,100	234,700
2000	T370D	189,800	218,300
1999	T350D	176,500	203,000
1998	T300D	164,200	188,800
1997	T300D	152,700	175,600
1996	T300D	142,000	163,300
1995	T300D	132,000	151,900

Albin 35 Tournament Express

Year	Power	Retail Low	Retail High
2004	T370D	256,500	294,900
2003	T370D	235,900	271,300
2002	T370D	217,100	249,600
2001	T370D	199,700	229,600
2000	T370D	185,700	213,600
1999	T350D	172,700	198,600
1998	T350D	160,600	184,700
1997	T350D	149,400	171,800
1996	T350D	138,900	159,700
1995	T350D	129,200	148,600

Albin 36 Express Trawler

Year	Power	Retail Low	Retail High
2004	S450D	227,400	261,500
2003	S450D	209,200	240,500
2002	S450D	192,400	221,300
2001	S450D	177,000	203,600
2000	S420D	162,900	187,300
1999	S420D	149,800	172,300

Albin 36 Trawler

Year	Power	Retail Low	Retail High
1993	S135D	95,000	109,200
1993	S210D	100,300	115,400
1992	S135D	86,900	100,000

Year	Power	Retail Low	Retail High
1992	S210D	91,600	105,300
1991	S135D	80,200	92,200
1991	S210D	84,900	97,700
1990	S135D	72,800	83,800
1990	S210D	77,500	89,200
1989	S135D	66,800	76,800
1989	S210D	70,900	81,600
1988	S135D	63,600	73,100
1988	S210D	67,300	77,400
1987	S135D	59,100	68,000
1986	S135D	54,800	63,000
1985	S120D	51,400	59,100
1984	S120D	48,700	56,000
1983	S120D	46,800	53,800
1982	S120D	44,800	51,500
1981	S120D	42,800	49,200
1980	S120D	41,100	47,300

Albin 40 Sundeck

Year	Power	Retail Low	Retail High
1993	T135D	137,800	158,500
1993	T210D	146,900	168,900
1992	T135D	123,700	142,300
1992	T210D	133,500	153,600
1991	T135D	113,800	130,900
1991	T210D	121,600	139,800
1990	T135D	104,700	120,400
1990	T210D	111,100	127,700
1989	T135D	92,500	106,300
1989	T210D	102,100	117,400
1988	T135D	85,800	98,700
1988	T210D	94,700	108,900
1987	T135D	82,900	95,300
1987	T210D	90,200	103,800

Albin 40 Trawler

Year	Power	Retail Low	Retail High
1993	T135D	132,100	151,900
1993	T210D	141,300	162,500
1992	T135D	118,700	136,500
1992	T210D	128,600	147,900
1991	T135D	109,600	126,100
1991	T210D	117,400	135,000
1990	T135D	101,200	116,300
1990	T210D	107,500	123,600
1989	S135D	85,000	97,800
1989	T135D	94,200	108,300
1988	S135D	79,400	91,300
1988	T135D	87,800	101,000
1987	S135D	76,500	88,000
1987	T135D	83,600	96,100

Albin 43 Sundeck

Year	Power	Retail Low	Retail High
1994	T210D	209,300	240,700
1993	T210D	190,200	218,800
1992	T210D	177,500	204,200
1991	T210D	164,100	188,700
1990	T210D	150,700	173,300
1989	T135D	127,500	146,700
1989	T210D	135,700	156,100
1988	T135D	119,100	137,000
1988	T210D	127,600	146,700
1987	T135D	110,700	127,300
1987	T210D	118,400	136,200
1986	T135D	102,200	117,600
1986	T210D	109,900	126,400
1985	T135D	94,600	108,800
1985	T210D	103,000	118,500
1984	T135D	91,500	105,200
1984	T210D	98,400	113,100

PRICES

IMPORTANT! See Page 293 for Regional Price Adjustment.

Year	Power	Retail Low	Retail High
1983	T120D	85,300	98,100
1982	T120D	80,000	92,000
1981	T120D	76,100	87,500

Albin 43 Trawler

Year	Power	Retail Low	Retail High
1994	T210D	183,500	211,000
1993	T210D	174,800	201,000
1992	T210D	163,400	187,900
1991	T210D	152,600	175,500
1990	T210D	138,900	159,700
1989	T135D	120,000	138,000
1989	T210D	128,000	147,200
1988	T135D	118,500	136,300
1988	T210D	120,000	138,000
1987	T135D	102,100	117,500
1987	T210D	110,300	126,900
1986	T135D	94,600	108,800
1986	T210D	102,900	118,300
1985	T135D	88,700	102,000
1985	T210D	96,900	111,500
1984	T135D	85,700	98,600
1984	T210D	92,400	106,300
1983	T120D	81,200	93,400
1982	T120D	77,500	89,200
1981	T120D	74,500	85,700
1980	T120D	71,600	82,300

Albin 45 Command Bridge

Year	Power	Retail Low	Retail High
2004	T450D	410,100	471,600
2003	T450D	373,100	429,100

Albin 48 Cutter

Year	Power	Retail Low	Retail High
1989	T307D	149,500	171,900
1989	T375D	156,200	179,700
1988	T307D	139,900	160,900
1988	T375D	146,700	168,700
1987	T307D	130,300	149,900
1987	T375D	137,200	157,700
1986	T255D	124,600	143,200
1985	T255D	116,900	134,400
1984	T255D	109,200	125,600
1983	T255D	101,600	116,800

Albin 49 Cockpit Trawler

Year	Power	Retail Low	Retail High
1994	T250D	223,700	257,300
1993	T250D	212,200	244,000
1992	T250D	200,000	230,000
1991	T250D	186,400	214,400
1990	T250D	168,100	193,300
1989	T135D	141,100	162,100
1989	T210D	149,100	171,500
1988	T135D	133,500	153,600
1988	T210D	141,600	162,900
1987	T135D	127,400	146,500
1987	T210D	135,500	155,900
1986	T135D	123,300	141,800
1985	T120D	114,500	131,700
1984	T120D	107,800	123,900
1983	T120D	101,700	116,900
1982	T120D	96,400	111,500
1981	T120D	93,500	107,600
1980	T120D	90,800	104,400

Albin 49 Tri-Cabin

Year	Power	Retail Low	Retail High
1993	T250D	217,800	250,500
1992	T250D	205,000	235,800
1991	T250D	190,300	218,800
1990	T250D	171,500	197,300
1989	T135D	153,400	176,400
1989	T210D	161,500	185,700
1988	T135D	144,000	165,600
1988	T210D	152,100	174,900
1987	T135D	131,300	151,000
1987	T210D	139,400	160,400
1986	T135D	126,600	145,600
1985	T120D	121,300	139,500
1984	T120D	114,300	131,400
1983	T120D	108,000	124,200
1982	T120D	103,100	118,600
1981	T120D	99,600	114,500
1980	T120D	96,700	111,200

Alden 50 Motor Yacht ****

Altima 55 Pilothouse ****

American 34 Tug

Year	Power	Retail Low	Retail High
2004	S380D	277,500	319,100
2003	S380D	258,000	296,700
2002	S370D	240,000	276,000
2001	S370D	223,200	256,600

Angler 2900 Center Console

Year	Power	Retail Low	Retail High
2004	T225 O/B	50,200	57,700
2003	T225 O/B	45,100	51,900
2002	T225 O/B	40,600	46,700
2001	T225 O/B	36,500	42,000
2000	T225 O/B	32,900	37,800

Aquarius 41 Motor Yacht ****

Aquarius 45 Motor Yacht ****

Aquasport 270 Express

Year	Power	Retail Low	Retail High
1987	T-Gas I/B	22,300	25,600
1986	T-Gas I/B	19,400	22,300
1985	T-Gas I/B	17,000	19,500
1984	T-Gas I/B	15,100	17,400

Aquasport 275 Explorer

Year	Power	Retail Low	Retail High
2004	T/225 O/B	83,200	95,600
2003	T/225 O/B	74,800	86,100
2002	T/225 O/B	67,300	77,500
2001	T/225 O/B	60,600	69,700
2000	T/225 O/B	54,500	62,700
1999	T/225 O/B	49,100	56,400

Aquasport 286/290 Express

Year	Power	Retail Low	Retail High
1990	T-Gas	35,500	40,900
1989	T-Gas	33,100	38,100
1988	T-Gas	30,600	35,200
1987	T-Gas	27,300	31,400
1986	T-Gas	25,200	29,000
1985	T-Gas	20,900	24,000
1984	T-Gas	17,200	19,800
1983	T-Gas	15,500	17,800
1982	T-Gas	13,500	15,500

Atlantic 34 Sportsman

Year	Power	Retail Low	Retail High
1992	T-Gas	63,100	72,500
1992	T-Diesel	81,200	93,400
1991	T-Gas	57,200	65,800
1991	T-Diesel	75,000	86,300
1990	T-Gas	50,900	58,600
1990	T-Diesel	69,300	79,700
1989	T-Gas	46,100	53,000
1989	T-Diesel	64,600	74,300
1988	T-Gas	43,500	50,000
1988	T-Diesel	61,500	70,700

Atlantic 37 Double Cabin

Year	Power	Retail Low	Retail High
1992	T135D	105,600	121,500
1992	T250D	115,500	132,900
1991	T135D	102,500	117,900
1991	T250D	109,900	126,400
1990	T135D	97,200	111,800
1990	T250D	103,200	118,700
1989	T135D	91,800	105,600
1989	T250D	97,200	111,800
1988	T-Diesel	88,400	101,700
1987	T-Diesel	82,200	94,500
1986	T-Diesel	77,700	89,300
1985	T-Diesel	72,800	83,800
1984	T-Diesel	67,700	77,900
1983	T-Diesel	63,100	72,600
1982	T-Diesel	58,300	67,100

Atlantic 44 Motor Yacht

Year	Power	Retail Low	Retail High
1992	T-Diesel	166,800	191,900
1991	T-Diesel	158,900	182,800
1990	T-Diesel	151,700	174,400
1989	T-Diesel	145,600	167,500
1988	T-Diesel	139,000	159,900
1987	T-Diesel	133,900	154,000
1986	T-Diesel	127,700	146,900
1985	T-Diesel	120,200	138,200
1984	T-Diesel	112,100	128,900
1983	T-Diesel	103,900	119,400
1982	T-Diesel	98,400	113,100
1981	T-Diesel	92,600	106,600
1980	T-Diesel	86,500	99,500
1979	T-Diesel	82,200	94,600
1978	T-Diesel	79,500	91,500
1977	T-Diesel	76,600	88,100

Atlantic 47 MY

Year	Power	Retail Low	Retail High
1992	T375D	221,000	254,200
1992	T450D	230,100	264,600
1991	T375D	204,500	235,100
1991	T450D	215,100	247,400
1990	T375D	193,800	222,900
1990	T450D	203,200	233,700
1989	T375D	184,500	212,200
1989	T450D	193,300	222,300
1988	T375D	176,400	202,900
1988	T450D	183,900	211,500
1987	T375D	167,100	192,200
1987	T435D	174,600	200,800
1986	T375D	157,700	181,400
1986	T435D	165,200	190,000
1985	T355D	147,700	169,900
1985	T435D	155,200	178,500
1984	T355D	137,800	158,400
1984	T410D	145,200	167,000
1983	T355D	127,100	146,200
1983	T410D	135,300	155,600
1982	T300D	114,200	131,400
1982	T410D	125,900	144,800

Azimut 36

Year	Power	Retail Low	Retail High
1998	T300D	182,500	209,900
1997	T300D	169,200	194,500
1996	T300D	155,800	179,200
1995	T300D	142,300	163,600
1994	T300D	131,300	151,000
1993	T300D	123,500	142,100

PRICES

Year	Power	Retail Low	Retail High
Azimut 39			
2004	T355D	******	******
2003	T355D	******	******
2002	T350D	258,500	297,300
2001	T350D	241,300	277,500
2000	T325D	222,300	255,600
1999	T325D	208,400	239,700
Azimut 40			
1998	T350D	211,100	242,700
1997	T350D	198,700	228,500
1996	T350D	187,300	215,400
1995	T350D	174,800	201,000
1994	T350D	162,400	186,800
1993	T350D	153,900	176,900
Azimut 42			
2004	T390D	******	******
2003	T390D	******	******
2002	T375D	328,700	378,000
2001	T375D	310,800	357,400
2000	T375D	277,800	319,500
1999	T375D	255,900	294,300
Azimut 43			
1998	T435D	266,800	306,800
1997	T435D	243,200	279,700
1996	T435D	221,500	254,800
1995	T435D	199,100	229,000
1994	T435D	178,700	205,500
1993	T435D	168,800	194,100
Azimut 46			
2004	T505D	******	******
2003	T435D	******	******
2002	T435D	437,500	503,600
2001	T435D	396,800	456,300
2000	T435D	364,800	419,500
1999	T435D	329,400	378,800
1998	T435D	299,600	344,600
1997	T435D	267,400	307,500
Azimut 50 ******			
Azimut 50/52			
2003	T660D	******	******
2002	T600D	550,500	633,000
2001	T600D	504,700	580,400
2000	T600D	459,400	528,300
1999	T600D	416,400	478,900
1998	T600D	365,100	419,900
1997	T600D	338,300	389,000
1996	T600D	320,400	368,400
Azimut 54/58			
2003	T765D	******	******
2002	T765D	******	******
2001	T765D	******	******
2000	T765D	632,300	727,200
1999	T765D	583,000	670,500
1998	T765D	516,700	594,200
1997	T765D	456,500	524,900
1996	T765D	401,000	461,100
1995	T765D	375,600	431,900
1994	T765D	355,600	409,000
1993	T765D	325,600	374,400
Azimut 55 ******			
2004	T710D	******	******
2003	T660D	******	******

Year	Power	Retail Low	Retail High
2002	T660D	******	******
2001	T660D	760,100	874,200
Azimut 62 ******			
Azimut 68 Plus ******			
Azimut 70 SeaJet ******			
Azimut 71 Motor Yacht******			
Azimut 76 Cockpit MY ******			
Azimut 78 Ultra ******			
Azimut 80 ******			
Azimut 85 Ultimate ******			
Baha 270 King Cat			
2004	T225 O/B	68,300	78,500
2003	T225 O/B	61,400	70,600
2002	T225 O/B	55,300	63,600
2001	T225 O/B	49,700	57,200
2000	T225 O/B	44,800	51,500
Baha 340 King Cat			
2004	T300G	131,100	150,700
2004	T370D	166,500	191,400
2003	T300G	117,900	135,600
2003	T370D	151,500	174,200
2002	T300G	106,100	122,100
2002	T370D	137,800	158,500
2001	T300G	96,600	111,100
2001	T370D	125,400	144,200
2000	T310G	87,900	101,100
2000	T330D	114,100	131,300
1999	T310G	80,000	92,000
1999	T330D	103,900	119,400
1998	T310G	72,800	83,700
1998	T330D	94,500	108,700
Baja 340 Islander			
2004	T250 O/B	95,000	109,200
2003	T250 O/B	85,500	98,300
2002	T250 O/B	76,900	88,400
2001	T250 O/B	70,000	80,500
2000	T250 O/B	63,700	73,200
1999	T250 O/B	57,900	66,600
Bayliner 2755 Ciera SB			
1993	S-7.4L I/O	15,300	17,700
1992	S-7.4L I/O	14,200	16,400
1991	S-7.4L I/O	13,000	15,000
1990	S-7.4L I/O	12,000	13,800
1989	S-7.4L I/O	11,000	12,600
Bayliner 2850 Contessa SB; 2855 Ciera SB			
1989	S-I/O Gas	14,800	17,100
1988	S-I/O Gas	13,300	15,300
1987	S-I/O Gas	12,300	14,100
1986	S-I/O Gas	11,300	13,000
1985	S-I/O Gas	10,200	11,800
1984	S-I/O Gas	9,700	11,200
1983	S-I/O Gas	9,200	10,600
Bayliner 2855 Ciera SB (1991-93)			
1993	S-I/O 260G	19,400	22,300
1992	S-I/O 260G	17,300	19,900
1991	S-I/O 260G	16,100	18,500
Bayliner 2855 Ciera SB (1994-99)			
1999	S300 I/O	29,300	33,700
1998	S300 I/O	27,400	31,500

Year	Power	Retail Low	Retail High
1997	S300 I/O	24,900	28,600
1996	S300 I/O	22,800	26,300
1995	S300 I/O	21,100	24,200
1994	S300 I/O	19,400	22,300
Bayliner 285 Cruiser			
2004	S300 I/O	49,900	57,300
2003	S300 I/O	45,400	52,200
2002	S300 I/O	41,300	47,500
2001	S300 I/O	37,600	43,200
2000	S300 I/O	34,200	39,300
Bayliner 2859 Classic Cruiser			
2004	S-Gas I/O	51,500	59,200
2003	S-Gas I/O	46,800	53,800
2002	S-Gas I/O	42,600	49,000
2001	S-Gas I/O	38,800	44,600
2000	S-Gas I/O	35,300	40,600
1999	S-Gas I/O	32,400	37,300
1998	S-Gas I/O	29,800	34,300
1997	S-Gas I/O	27,500	31,600
1996	S-Gas I/O	25,300	29,000
1995	S-Gas I/O	23,200	26,700
1994	S-Gas I/O	21,400	24,600
1993	S-Gas I/O	19,700	22,600
Bayliner 288 Classic Cruiser			
2004	S-Gas I/O	63,400	72,900
2003	S-Gas I/O	58,300	67,000
2002	S-Gas I/O	53,600	61,700
2001	S-Gas I/O	49,300	56,700
2000	S-Gas I/O	45,400	52,200
1999	S-Gas I/O	41,700	48,000
1998	S-Gas I/O	38,400	44,200
1997	S-Gas I/O	35,300	40,600
1996	S-Gas I/O	32,500	37,400
Bayliner 2950/2955 Avanti SB			
1990	S-Gas	19,800	22,700
1990	T-Gas	21,900	25,200
1989	S-Gas	17,600	20,300
1989	T-Gas	20,300	23,400
1988	S-Gas	16,000	18,400
1988	T-Gas	18,700	21,500
Bayliner 2950/2958 CB			
1990	T-Gas	24,100	27,700
1989	T-Gas	21,500	24,700
1988	T-Gas	19,800	22,800
Bayliner 3055 Ciera SB			
1994	S-I/O Gas	26,300	30,300
1994	T-I/O Gas	30,700	35,300
1993	S-I/O Gas	24,100	27,700
1993	T-I/O Gas	27,900	32,100
1992	S-I/O Gas	21,900	25,200
1992	T-I/O Gas	24,700	28,400
1991	S-I/O Gas	19,700	22,700
1991	T-I/O Gas	21,900	25,200
Bayliner 305 Cruiser			
2004	T300 I/O	85,600	98,400
2003	T300 I/O	77,000	88,500
2002	T300 I/O	69,300	79,700
2001	T300 I/O	62,400	71,700
2000	T300 I/O	56,100	64,500
1999	T300 I/O	50,500	58,100
Bayliner 3255 Avanti SB			
1999	T-I/O 300	55,200	63,500

Year	Power	Retail Low	Retail High
1998	T-I/O 300	49,600	57,100
1997	T-I/O 300	49,400	56,800
1996	T-I/O 300	43,000	49,500
1995	T-I/O 300	40,000	46,000
Bayliner 3258 Ciera CB			
2001	T-I/O 7.4L	71,400	82,100
2000	T-I/O 7.4L	65,000	74,800
1999	T-I/O 7.4L	58,900	67,800
1998	T-I/O 7.4L	53,400	61,400
1997	T-I/O 7.4L	50,200	57,700
1996	T-I/O 7.4L	47,800	55,000
1995	T-I/O 7.4L	43,800	50,400
Bayliner 3270/3288 MY			
1995	T-Diesel	58,300	67,000
1994	T-Diesel	52,800	60,800
1993	T-Diesel	48,200	55,400
1992	T-Gas	36,800	42,300
1992	T-Diesel	42,700	49,100
1991	T-Gas	34,700	39,900
1991	T-Diesel	39,500	45,400
1990	T-Gas	33,300	38,300
1990	T-Diesel	37,600	43,200
1989	T-Gas	32,000	36,800
1989	T-Diesel	35,800	41,100
1988	T-Gas	30,900	35,500
1988	T-Diesel	34,200	39,300
1987	T-Gas	29,300	33,700
1987	T-Diesel	32,500	37,400
1986	T-Gas	27,600	31,800
1986	T-Diesel	30,900	35,500
1985	T-Gas	26,000	29,900
1985	T-Diesel	29,300	33,700
1984	T-Gas	23,800	27,400
1984	T-Diesel	27,100	31,200
1983	T-Gas	21,500	24,800
1983	T-Diesel	24,900	28,600
1982	T-Gas	19,700	22,700
1982	T-Diesel	23,100	26,600
1981	T-Gas	18,000	20,800
1981	T-Diesel	20,900	24,000
Bayliner 3250/3255/3555 Avanti SB			
1994	T-I/O Gas	37,600	43,200
1993	T-I/O Gas	35,700	41,100
1992	T-I/O Gas	33,400	38,400
1991	T-I/O Gas	30,800	35,400
1990	T-I/O Gas	28,100	32,300
1989	T-I/O Gas	22,800	26,300
1988	T-I/O Gas	21,300	24,500
Bayliner 3388 Motor Yacht			
2000	T250D	99,200	114,000
1999	T250D	90,700	104,300
1998	T210D	79,400	91,300
1997	T210D	73,500	84,500
1996	T210D	67,100	77,200
Bayliner 3488 Avanti CB			
1999	T310G	73,400	84,400
1998	T310G	67,600	77,800
1997	T310G	62,700	72,100
1996	T310G	56,700	65,300
Bayliner 3488 Command Bridge			
2002	T260G	104,000	119,600
2001	T260G	97,500	112,100

Year	Power	Retail Low	Retail High
Bayliner 3450/3485/3785 Avanti SB			
1990	T-I/O Gas	40,300	46,400
1989	T-I/O Gas	34,800	40,100
1988	T-I/O Gas	30,600	35,200
1987	T-I/O Gas	26,300	30,300
Bayliner 3587 Motor Yacht			
1999	T-Gas	101,700	117,000
1998	T-Gas	88,600	101,900
1997	T-Gas	83,000	95,500
1996	T-Gas	75,800	87,200
1995	T-Gas	71,900	82,700
Bayliner 3685 Avanti Sunbridge			
1999	T310G	96,700	111,200
1999	T330D	124,400	143,100
1998	T310G	88,500	101,700
1998	T330D	115,500	132,900
Bayliner 3688 Motor Yacht			
1994	T-Diesel	70,600	81,100
1993	T-Diesel	66,200	76,200
1992	T-Diesel	61,500	70,700
Bayliner 3788 MY (1996-99)			
1999	T-Gas	98,500	113,300
1999	T-Diesel	114,100	131,200
1998	T-Gas	91,100	104,800
1998	T-Diesel	104,300	120,000
1997	T-Gas	86,300	99,300
1997	T-Diesel	99,300	114,200
1996	T-Gas	78,000	89,700
1996	T-Diesel	90,200	103,700
Bayliner 3788 MY (2001-02)			
2002	T310G	146,800	168,800
2002	T330D	173,600	199,700
2001	T310G	133,700	153,800
2001	T330D	158,600	182,300
Bayliner 3870/3888 Motor Yacht			
1994	T-Diesel	84,900	97,700
1993	T-Diesel	81,500	93,700
1992	T-Diesel	76,000	87,400
1991	T-Diesel	70,500	81,100
1990	T-Diesel	64,500	74,200
1989	T-Diesel	59,100	67,900
1988	T-Diesel	54,100	62,200
1987	T-Diesel	49,700	57,200
1986	T-Diesel	47,300	54,400
1985	T-Diesel	42,800	49,200
1984	T-Diesel	40,600	46,700
1983	T-Diesel	38,900	44,800
Bayliner 3988 MY			
2002	T-Diesel	188,100	216,300
2001	T-Diesel	169,700	195,200
2000	T-Diesel	153,900	177,000
1999	T-Diesel	139,400	160,300
1998	T-Diesel	123,400	141,900
1997	T-Diesel	112,200	129,000
1996	T-Diesel	104,100	119,700
1995	T-Diesel	94,200	108,300
Bayliner 4085 Avanti SB			
1999	T-Gas	113,300	130,300
1999	T-Diesel	134,800	155,100
1998	T-Gas	102,400	117,800
1998	T-Diesel	123,500	142,000
1997	T-Gas	91,600	105,400

Year	Power	Retail Low	Retail High
1997	T-Diesel	111,600	128,400
Bayliner 4087 Cockpit MY			
2001	T-Gas	139,200	160,000
2001	T-Diesel	168,600	193,900
2000	T-Gas	129,600	149,100
2000	T-Diesel	157,200	180,800
1999	T-Gas	120,200	138,200
1999	T-Diesel	140,500	161,500
1998	T-Gas	111,100	127,800
1998	T-Diesel	133,700	153,800
1997	T-Gas	99,100	114,000
1997	T-Diesel	121,800	140,000
Bayliner 4387 Aft Cabin MY			
1993	T-Gas	100,100	115,100
1993	T-Diesel	110,900	127,500
1992	T-Gas	93,700	107,700
1992	T-Diesel	102,800	118,200
1991	T-Gas	86,100	99,000
1991	T-Diesel	95,300	109,500
1990	T-Gas	78,000	89,700
1990	T-Diesel	87,200	100,300
Bayliner 4388 Mid Cabin MY			
1994	T-Diesel	111,600	128,400
1993	T-Diesel	104,800	120,500
1992	T-Diesel	97,900	112,600
1991	T-Diesel	91,600	105,300
Bayliner 4550/4588 Pilothouse MY			
1993	T-Diesel	139,800	160,800
1992	T-Diesel	128,700	148,000
1991	T-Diesel	121,300	139,500
1990	T-Diesel	111,800	128,600
1989	T-Diesel	106,400	122,400
1988	T-Diesel	100,500	115,600
1987	T-Diesel	93,200	107,100
1986	T-Diesel	87,100	100,100
1985	T-Diesel	80,900	93,100
1984	T-Diesel	77,700	89,300
Bayliner 4587 Cockpit MY			
1995	T250D	128,500	147,800
1995	T310D	138,800	159,600
1994	T250D	116,400	133,900
1994	T310D	126,400	145,400
Bayliner 4788 Pilothouse MY			
2002	T370D	337,600	388,300
2001	T370D	307,000	353,000
2000	T370D	280,100	322,200
1999	T315D	248,600	285,900
1998	T315D	226,300	260,300
1997	T315D	206,800	237,900
1996	T315D	189,200	217,600
1995	T250D	165,000	189,700
1995	T310D	177,400	204,000
1994	T250D	156,200	179,600
1994	T310D	163,700	188,300
Bayliner 5288 Pilothouse MY			
2002	T610D	574,800	661,000
2001	T610D	516,000	593,400
2000	T610D	482,800	555,300
1999	T600D	446,700	513,700
Bayliner 5788 Motor Yacht			
2002	T610D	675,600	776,900
2001	T610D	629,400	723,900

PRICES

Year	Power	Retail Low	Retail High
2000	T610D	561,500	645,800
1999	T600D	499,900	574,900
1998	T600D	440,700	506,900
1997	T600D	381,800	439,000
Benchmark 36/38			
2004	T-Diesel	******	#VALUE!
2003	T-Diesel	******	#VALUE!
2002	T450D	311,500	358,200
2001	T450D	279,400	321,300
2000	T450D	258,100	296,800
1999	T450D	235,300	270,600
1998	T450D	211,500	243,200
1997	T450D	192,800	221,700
Beneteau 42 Trawler ******			
Bertram 28 Bahia Mar			
1992	T-Gas	57,600	66,300
1992	T-Diesel	67,400	77,600
1991	T-Gas	52,200	60,100
1991	T-Diesel	61,500	70,700
1990	T-Gas	48,300	55,500
1989	T-Gas	44,500	51,200
1988	T-Gas	39,700	45,700
1987	T-Gas	36,700	42,200
1986	T-Gas	35,400	40,700
1985	T-Gas	31,500	36,200
Bertram 28 Flybridge Cruiser			
1994	T-Gas	71,600	82,400
1994	T-Diesel	83,600	96,200
1993	T-Gas	67,900	78,100
1993	T-Diesel	78,900	90,700
1992	T-Gas	62,000	71,300
1992	T-Diesel	71,300	82,000
1991	T-Gas	55,500	63,800
1991	T-Diesel	63,500	73,000
1990	T-Gas	50,300	57,800
1989	T-Gas	46,400	53,300
1988	T-Gas	42,500	48,800
1987	T-Gas	39,400	45,300
1986	T-Gas	36,400	41,900
1985	T-Gas	32,800	37,700
1984	T-Gas	31,600	36,300
1983	T-Gas	30,100	34,600
1982	T-Gas	27,300	31,400
1981	T-Gas	25,300	29,100
1980	T-Gas	21,700	24,900
Bertram 28 Moppie			
1994	T-Gas	64,300	73,900
1993	T-Gas	59,500	68,400
1992	T-Gas	55,500	63,800
1991	T-Gas	50,700	58,300
1990	T-Gas	45,700	52,500
1989	T-Gas	41,400	47,600
1988	T-Gas	37,100	42,600
1987	T-Gas	31,200	35,900
Bertram 28 SF			
1983	T-Gas	27,900	32,100
1982	T-Gas	25,300	29,100
1981	T-Gas	23,100	26,500
1980	T-Gas	18,900	21,700
Bertram 30 Flybridge Cruiser			
1985	T-Gas	45,000	51,800
1985	T-Diesel	57,100	65,700
1984	T-Gas	43,700	50,300

Year	Power	Retail Low	Retail High
1984	T-Diesel	54,800	63,100
Bertram 30 Moppie			
1997	T-Gas	87,700	100,900
1997	T-Diesel	115,300	132,600
1996	T-Gas	80,900	93,100
1996	T-Diesel	104,900	120,600
1995	T-Gas	75,000	86,200
1995	T-Diesel	97,500	112,100
1994	T-Gas	67,000	77,100
1994	T-Diesel	89,500	102,900
Bertram 31 Flybridge Cruiser			
1986	T-Gas	58,100	66,800
1983	T-Gas	41,300	47,500
1983	T-Diesel	53,200	61,200
1983	T-Gas	39,100	44,900
1983	T-Diesel	51,200	58,800
1982	T-Gas	37,500	43,200
1982	T-Diesel	49,400	56,900
1981	T-Gas	34,400	39,600
1981	T-Diesel	43,300	49,800
1980	T-Gas	31,400	36,100
1980	T-Diesel	36,500	42,000
Bertram 31 Sport Fisherman			
1982	T-Gas	32,500	37,400
1982	T-Diesel	43,800	50,300
1981	T-Gas	30,700	35,300
1981	T-Diesel	38,400	44,200
1980	T-Gas	27,200	31,300
1980	T-Diesel	31,400	36,100
Bertram 33 Flybridge Cruiser			
1992	T-Gas	95,100	109,400
1992	T-Diesel	120,300	138,400
1991	T-Gas	86,000	98,900
1991	T-Diesel	109,600	126,100
1990	T-Gas	83,600	96,100
1990	T-Diesel	102,800	118,200
1989	T-Gas	79,500	91,400
1989	T-Diesel	92,900	106,800
1988	T-Gas	73,200	84,200
1988	T-Diesel	89,000	102,300
1987	T-Gas	67,000	77,100
1987	T-Diesel	83,000	95,400
1986	T-Gas	65,100	74,800
1986	T-Diesel	80,200	92,200
1985	T-Gas	60,200	69,300
1985	T-Diesel	74,900	86,100
1984	T-Gas	55,800	64,200
1984	T-Diesel	69,300	79,700
1983	T-Gas	51,400	59,200
1983	T-Diesel	63,600	73,200
1982	T-Gas	48,000	55,200
1982	T-Diesel	58,700	67,500
1981	T-Gas	44,500	51,100
1981	T-Diesel	53,600	61,700
1980	T-Gas	39,700	45,700
1980	T-Diesel	54,300	62,400
Bertram 33 Sport Fisherman			
1992	T-Gas	94,300	108,500
1992	T-Diesel	123,300	141,800
1991	T-Gas	89,900	103,400
1991	T-Diesel	117,000	134,600
1990	T-Gas	82,700	95,100
1990	T-Diesel	110,500	127,100
1989	T-Gas	76,400	87,900

Year	Power	Retail Low	Retail High
1989	T-Diesel	99,300	114,200
1988	T-Gas	71,100	81,700
1988	T-Diesel	90,500	104,100
1987	T-Gas	68,500	78,800
1987	T-Diesel	86,600	99,700
1986	T-Gas	63,300	72,800
1986	T-Diesel	79,600	91,500
1985	T-Gas	59,000	67,800
1985	T-Diesel	76,900	88,500
1984	T-Gas	54,900	63,100
1984	T-Diesel	70,200	80,700
1983	T-Gas	51,400	59,100
1983	T-Diesel	67,200	77,200
1982	T-Gas	46,800	53,800
1982	T-Diesel	63,300	72,800
1981	T-Gas	42,900	49,400
1981	T-Diesel	57,500	66,100
1980	T-Gas	42,800	49,200
1980	T-Diesel	55,600	64,000
Bertram 35 Convertible			
1986	T-Gas	71,500	82,300
1986	T-Diesel	93,600	107,700
1985	T-Gas	68,100	78,300
1985	T-Diesel	89,900	103,400
1984	T-Gas	63,500	73,000
1984	T-Diesel	85,600	98,400
1983	T-Gas	61,200	70,400
1983	T-Diesel	82,900	95,400
1982	T-Gas	56,200	64,700
1982	T-Diesel	74,900	86,200
1981	T-Gas	54,400	62,500
1981	T-Diesel	68,400	78,700
1980	T-Gas	48,100	55,400
1980	T-Diesel	56,800	65,300
2000	T430D	247,600	284,700
1999	T430D	222,600	255,900
Bertram 36 Convertible ******			
Bertram 36 Moppie			
2000	T430D	******	******
1999	T430D	******	******
1998	T430D	******	******
1997	T330D	148,700	171,000
1996	T315D	133,800	153,900
Bertram 37 Convertible			
1993	375D	173,400	199,400
1993	450D	197,400	227,000
1993	550D	215,700	248,100
1992	375D	167,900	193,000
1992	450D	197,000	226,600
1992	550D	209,600	241,100
1991	375D	160,600	184,700
1991	450D	193,500	222,600
1990	375D	152,900	175,800
1990	450D	176,100	202,500
1989	375D	142,900	164,400
1989	450D	159,500	183,500
1988	375D	132,900	152,900
1988	450D	146,200	168,200
1987	375D	126,300	145,300
1987	435D	130,600	150,200
1987	450D	138,500	159,200
1986	375D	123,500	142,100
1986	435D	129,700	149,200

PRICES

298

Year	Power	Retail Low	Retail High
Bertram 38 III Convertible			
1986	T-Diesel	122,800	141,200
1985	T-Diesel	116,000	133,400
1984	T-Diesel	109,800	126,300
1983	T-Diesel	103,700	119,300
1982	T-Diesel	96,000	110,400
1981	T-Diesel	83,900	96,500
1980	T-Diesel	78,200	90,000
Bertram 38 Special			
1987	375D	119,000	136,800
1987	435D	127,500	146,700
1986	375D	116,700	134,300
1986	435D	125,000	143,700
Bertram 390 Convertible			
2004	480D	587,600	675,700
2003	480D	534,700	614,900
2002	480D	486,500	559,500
2001	480D	442,700	509,200
2000	480D	402,900	463,300
Bertram 42 Convertible			
1987	T-Diesel	164,400	189,100
1986	T-Diesel	158,000	181,700
1985	T-Diesel	151,000	173,600
1984	T-Diesel	144,600	166,400
1983	T-Diesel	138,700	159,500
1982	T-Diesel	130,200	149,700
1981	T-Diesel	120,900	139,100
1980	T-Diesel	112,400	129,200
Bertram 42 Motor Yacht			
1987	T-Gas	142,500	163,800
1987	T-Diesel	162,500	186,900
1986	T-Gas	135,100	155,400
1986	T-Diesel	153,500	176,500
1985	T-Gas	130,100	149,600
1985	T-Diesel	146,900	169,000
1984	T-Gas	123,900	142,500
1984	T-Diesel	143,500	165,000
1983	T-Gas	119,900	137,800
1983	T-Diesel	136,300	156,800
1982	T-Gas	113,200	130,200
1982	T-Diesel	129,700	149,200
1981	T-Gas	107,300	123,400
1981	T-Diesel	123,800	142,300
1980	T-Gas	97,000	111,600
1980	T-Diesel	113,700	130,700
Bertram 43 Convertible			
1996	565hp DD	341,600	392,900
1996	680hp MAN	372,600	428,500
1995	550hp DD	321,800	370,100
1995	665hp MAN	347,400	399,500
1994	550hp DD	304,400	350,000
1994	665hp MAN	324,700	373,400
1993	T-Diesel	304,700	350,500
1992	T-Diesel	288,300	331,500
1991	T-Diesel	273,600	314,700
1990	T-Diesel	253,100	291,100
1989	T-Diesel	238,700	274,500
1988	T-Diesel	227,100	261,100
Bertram 43 Moppie			
1996	565hp DD	299,500	344,400
1996	680hp MAN	330,300	379,800
1995	550hp DD	274,100	315,300
1995	600hp MAN	298,000	342,700

Year	Power	Retail Low	Retail High
Bertram 450 Convertible			
2004	600D	751,800	864,500
2003	560D	684,100	786,700
2002	660D	622,500	715,900
2001	660D	566,500	651,500
2000	660D	515,500	592,800
Bertram 46 Convertible (1971-87)			
1987	T-Diesel	226,000	260,000
1986	T-Diesel	211,800	243,600
1985	T-Diesel	193,900	223,000
1984	T-Diesel	189,700	218,200
1983	T-Diesel	179,300	206,200
1982	T-Diesel	161,600	185,800
1981	T-Diesel	148,900	171,200
1980	T-Diesel	132,500	152,400
Bertram 46 Convertible (1995-97)			
1997	760 DD	431,600	496,300
1997	820 MAN	441,500	507,700
1996	760 DD	408,600	469,800
1996	820 MAN	417,600	480,300
1995	735 DD	389,600	448,000
1995	820 MAN	406,900	468,000
Bertram 46 Moppie			
1996	T-Diesel	361,800	416,100
1995	T-Diesel	345,400	397,300
1994	T-Diesel	322,400	370,700
1993	T-Diesel	307,200	353,300
Bertram 46 Motor Yacht			
1987	T-Diesel	206,600	237,600
1986	T-Diesel	197,800	227,500
1985	T-Diesel	186,100	214,100
1984	T-Diesel	178,600	205,400
1983	T-Diesel	168,300	193,600
1982	T-Diesel	158,400	182,200
1981	T-Diesel	144,600	166,300
1980	T-Diesel	120,800	138,900
Bertram 50 Convertible			
1997	820D	532,400	612,300
1997	900D	554,900	638,100
1996	735D	494,700	568,900
1996	900D	529,400	608,900
1995	735D	454,000	522,100
1995	900D	489,900	563,400
1994	735D	417,700	480,300
1994	900D	468,400	538,600
1993	735D	398,200	458,000
1992	735D		
	Galley up	379,700	436,700
	Galley down	368,400	423,600
1991	735D		
	Galley up	359,700	413,700
	Galley down	348,400	400,700
1991	840D		
	Galley up	382,400	439,800
	Galley down	371,100	426,700
1990	735D		
	Galley up	336,100	386,500
	Galley down	327,400	376,500
1990	840D		
	Galley up	358,100	411,900
	Galley down	349,500	401,900
1989	735D		
	Galley up	312,100	359,000

Year	Power	Retail Low	Retail High
	Galley down	303,500	349,000
1989	840D		
	Galley up	335,300	385,600
	Galley down	326,600	375,600
1988	735D		
	Galley up	300,300	345,400
	Galley down	291,600	335,300
1987	735D	290,300	333,900
Bertram 510 Convertible			
2004	800D	******	******
2003	800D	934,800	1,075,000
2002	800D	841,300	967,500
2001	800D	757,100	870,700
2000	800D	681,400	783,600
Bertram 54 Convertible (1981-92)			
1992	T-Diesel	552,300	635,200
1991	T-Diesel	530,500	610,100
1990	T-Diesel	476,400	547,800
1989	T-Diesel	443,500	510,000
1988	T-Diesel	403,200	463,700
1987	T-Diesel	380,400	437,400
1986	T-Diesel	345,900	397,800
1985	T-Diesel	318,400	366,200
1984	T-Diesel	300,200	345,200
1983	T-Diesel	290,300	333,900
1982	T-Diesel	272,400	313,200
1981	T-Diesel	263,200	302,700
Bertram 54 Convertible (1995-03)			
2003	1200D	******	******
2002	1200D	******	******
2001	1400D	******	******
2000	1400D	******	******
2000	1350D	******	******
1999	1350D	947,000	1,089,000
1998	1350D	852,300	980,100
1997	1350D	767,000	882,100
1996	1100D	690,300	793,900
1995	1100D	621,300	714,500
Bertram 570 Convertible ******			
Bertram 58 Convertible			
1983	T-Diesel	347,100	399,100
1982	T-Diesel	331,000	380,700
1981	T-Diesel	311,500	358,200
1980	T-Diesel	287,900	331,100
Bertram 58 Motor Yacht			
1986	T-Diesel	400,900	461,100
1985	T-Diesel	380,900	438,000
1984	T-Diesel	357,500	411,100
1983	T-Diesel	337,000	387,600
1982	T-Diesel	316,400	363,900
1981	T-Diesel	295,200	339,500
1980	T-Diesel	277,800	319,500
Bertram 60 Convertible			
2004	1400 Cat	******	******
2003	1400 Cat	******	******
2002	1400 Cat	******	******
2001	1400 Cat	1,273,500	1,464,500
2000	1400 Cat	1,191,900	1,370,600
1999	1350 DD	1,123,600	1,292,200
1999	1400 Cat	1,144,000	1,315,700
1998	1350 Cat	1,079,600	1,241,600
1998	1450 DD	1,054,700	1,212,900
1997	1300 Cat	1,004,900	1,155,600

PRICES

IMPORTANT! See Page 293 for Regional Price Adjustment.

Year	Power	Retail Low	Retail High
1997	1450 DD	982,900	1,130,300
1996	1250 Cat	924,000	1,062,600
1996	1400 DD	900,400	1,035,400
1995	1250 Cat	850,600	978,200
1995	1400 DD	836,900	962,400
1994	T-Diesel	788,300	906,500
1993	T-Diesel	742,900	854,400
1992	T-Diesel	713,400	820,400
1991	T-Diesel	676,700	778,200
1990	T-Diesel	628,400	722,700

Bertram 630 Convertible ****

Bertram 670 Convertible ****

Black Watch 30 Flybridge

Year	Power	Retail Low	Retail High
1996	T-Gas	104,300	120,000
1996	T300 D	116,600	134,000
1995	T-Gas	95,100	109,300
1995	T300 D	106,500	122,500
1994	T-Gas	79,500	91,500
1994	T300 D	95,200	109,400
1993	T-Gas	71,700	82,400
1993	T300 D	88,800	102,100
1992	T-Gas	65,400	75,200
1992	T300 D	73,600	84,700
1991	T-Diesel	59,500	68,400
1991	T300 D	72,500	83,400
1990	T-Gas	55,200	63,500
1990	T300 D	67,900	78,100
1989	T-Gas	48,600	55,900
1989	T300 D	60,800	69,900

Black Watch 30 SF

Year	Power	Retail Low	Retail High
1995	T-Gas	78,300	90,100
1995	T300 D	92,100	105,900
1994	T-Gas	67,100	77,200
1994	T300 D	81,100	93,200
1993	T-Gas	60,300	69,400
1993	T300 D	74,700	85,900
1992	T-Gas	54,000	62,100
1992	T300 D	67,900	78,100
1991	T-Gas	47,900	55,100
1991	T300 D	64,300	73,900
1990	T-Gas	45,800	52,600
1990	T300 D	59,100	67,900
1989	T-Gas	39,900	45,800
1989	T300 D	52,500	60,300
1988	T-Gas	33,800	38,900
1988	T300 D	45,600	52,400
1987	T-Gas	29,600	34,000
1987	T300 D	41,700	47,900
1986	T-Gas	27,100	31,200
1986	T300 D	38,100	43,900

Black Watch 36 Flybridge

Year	Power	Retail Low	Retail High
1995	T300 D	138,700	159,500
1994	T-Gas	99,500	114,400
1994	T300 D	124,400	143,100
1993	T-Gas	94,500	108,700
1993	T300 D	115,800	133,200
1992	T-Gas	86,500	99,500
1992	T300 D	103,600	119,200
1991	T-Gas	79,900	91,900
1991	T300 D	99,200	114,100

Blackfin 27 Combi

Year	Power	Retail Low	Retail High
1992	OB*	31,100	35,800
1992	T-Gas	44,700	51,400

Year	Power	Retail Low	Retail High
1991	OB*	29,400	33,800
1991	T-Gas	40,900	47,000
1990	OB*	26,400	30,400
1990	T-Gas	38,200	44,000
1989	OB*	23,900	27,500
1989	T-Gas	33,700	38,800
1988	OB*	21,500	24,800
1988	T-Gas	30,600	35,200
1987	OB*	20,400	23,500
1987	T-Gas	30,400	34,900
1986	OB*	18,200	21,000
1986	T-Gas	27,200	31,300
1985	OB*	17,000	19,600
1985	T-Gas	25,400	29,200

Blackfin 27 Fisherman

Year	Power	Retail Low	Retail High
1991	OB*	28,600	32,900
1991	T-Gas	40,500	46,600
1990	OB*	25,800	29,700
1990	T-Gas	37,300	42,900
1989	OB*	23,800	27,400
1989	T-Gas	34,000	39,200
1988	OB*	21,400	24,600
1988	T-Gas	31,300	35,900
1987	OB*	19,800	22,800
1987	T-Gas	29,400	33,800
1986	OB*	17,600	20,300
1986	T-Gas	26,600	30,600
1985	OB*	16,400	18,900
1985	T-Gas	24,200	27,800

Blackfin 27 Sportsman

Year	Power	Retail Low	Retail High
1998	T-Gas	59,800	68,700
1998	T-Diesel	81,200	93,300
1997	T-Gas	53,800	61,800
1997	T-Diesel	74,700	85,900
1996	T-Gas	48,900	56,300
1995	T-Gas	44,500	51,200

Blackfin 29 Combi

Year	Power	Retail Low	Retail High
1998	T330 D	108,500	124,800
1997	T-Gas	76,300	87,700
1997	T330 D	98,600	113,400
1996	T-Gas	71,700	82,500
1996	T330 D	91,700	105,500
1995	T-Gas	65,500	75,400
1995	T330 D	81,100	93,300
1994	T-Gas	64,500	74,200
1994	T300 D	78,800	90,600
1993	T-Gas	59,700	68,700
1993	T300 D	73,100	84,000
1992	T-Gas	53,600	61,600
1992	T300 D	65,800	75,700
1991	T-Gas	51,600	59,400
1991	T-Diesel	63,600	73,100
1990	T-Gas	51,500	59,200
1990	T-Diesel	60,100	69,100
1989	T-Gas	43,100	49,600
1989	T-Diesel	53,900	62,000
1988	T-Gas	38,700	44,500
1988	T-Diesel	48,400	55,600
1987	T-Gas	36,800	42,300
1987	T-Diesel	45,600	52,500
1986	T-Gas	34,800	40,000
1986	T-Diesel	43,100	49,600
1985	T-Gas	32,400	37,300
1985	T-Diesel	41,300	47,500
1984	T-Gas	29,600	34,100

Year	Power	Retail Low	Retail High
1984	T-Diesel	39,000	44,800
1983	T-Gas	28,200	32,400
1983	T-Diesel	36,900	42,400

Blackfin 29 Flybridge

Year	Power	Retail Low	Retail High
1998	T-Gas	92,100	105,900
1998	T330 D	115,200	132,400
1997	T-Gas	84,800	97,500
1997	T330 D	107,800	124,000
1996	T-Gas	81,400	93,600
1996	T330 D	100,200	115,200
1995	T-Gas	77,500	89,100
1995	T330 D	92,900	106,900
1994	T-Gas	76,200	87,600
1994	T300 D	88,100	101,300
1993	T-Gas	71,300	82,000
1993	T300 D	84,800	97,500
1992	T-Gas	66,400	76,300
1992	T300 D	76,600	88,100
1991	T-Gas	58,500	67,200
1991	T-Diesel	71,000	81,700
1990	T-Gas	53,900	62,000
1990	T-Diesel	67,400	77,500
1989	T-Gas	49,000	56,400
1989	T-Diesel	61,400	70,700
1988	T-Gas	45,100	51,800
1988	T-Diesel	56,300	64,700
1987	T-Gas	42,300	48,700
1987	T-Diesel	53,300	61,300
1986	T-Gas	36,200	41,600
1986	T-Diesel	48,300	55,500

Blackfin 31 Combi

Year	Power	Retail Low	Retail High
1997	T-Gas	106,100	122,000
1997	T300 D	129,300	148,700
1996	T-Gas	93,800	107,800
1996	T300 D	119,400	137,300
1995	T-Gas	87,800	100,900
1995	T300 D	111,000	127,700
1994	T-Gas	79,600	91,600
1994	T300 D	107,100	123,200
1993	T-Gas	75,500	86,900
1993	T300 D	96,600	111,100

Blackfin 32 Combi

Year	Power	Retail Low	Retail High
1992	T-Gas	74,500	85,700
1992	T-Diesel	96,800	111,300
1991	T-Gas	68,900	79,300
1991	T-Diesel	89,800	103,300
1990	T-Gas	60,600	69,700
1990	T-Diesel	81,600	93,900
1989	T-Gas	56,000	64,400
1989	T-Diesel	74,900	86,100
1988	T-Gas	54,400	62,600
1988	T-Diesel	72,800	83,700

Blackfin 32 SF

Year	Power	Retail Low	Retail High
1991	T-Gas	68,200	78,500
1991	300D	88,600	101,800
1991	375D	101,000	116,100
1990	T-Gas	64,000	73,600
1990	300D	82,100	94,400
1990	375D	94,900	109,200
1989	T-Gas	59,400	68,300
1989	300D	74,700	85,900
1989	375D	88,900	102,200
1988	T-Gas	54,100	62,200
1988	300D	72,000	82,900

PRICES

Year	Power	Retail Low	Retail High
1988	375D	81,200	93,400
1987	T-Gas	50,300	57,800
1987	300D	67,700	77,800
1987	375D	75,900	87,300
1986	T-Gas	47,500	54,600
1986	300D	65,600	75,500
1986	375D	72,300	83,200
1985	T-Gas	45,000	51,800
1985	300D	61,300	70,500
1985	355D	68,100	78,300
1984	T-Gas	38,600	44,400
1984	300D	53,300	61,400
1984	355D	60,700	69,800
1983	T-Gas	35,900	41,200
1983	300D	49,600	57,100
1983	355D	54,600	62,800
1982	T-Gas	32,900	37,800
1982	300D	46,100	53,000
1981	T-Gas	30,900	35,500
1981	300D	44,500	51,200
1980	T-Gas	28,200	32,400
1980	T-Diesel	37,800	43,500

Blackfin 33 Combi (1979-84)

Year	Power	Retail Low	Retail High
1984	OB*	19,900	22,900
1984	T-Gas	30,900	35,500
1984	T-Diesel	38,900	44,700
1983	OB*	18,300	21,100
1983	T-Gas	28,500	32,800
1983	T-Diesel	35,500	40,900
1982	OB*	16,200	18,600
1982	T-Gas	26,900	31,000
1982	T-Diesel	33,000	38,000
1981	OB*	14,700	16,900
1981	T-Gas	24,800	28,500
1981	T-Diesel	30,900	35,500
1980	OB*	14,000	16,100
1980	T-Gas	23,200	26,700
1980	T-Diesel	29,700	34,100

Blackfin 33 Combi

Year	Power	Retail Low	Retail High
1998	T375 D	168,700	194,000
1997	T375 D	155,400	178,700
1996	T-Gas	109,900	126,400
1996	T-Diesel	142,900	164,300
1995	T-Gas	102,900	118,400
1995	T-Diesel	133,200	153,200
1994	T-Gas	89,600	103,100
1994	T-Diesel	129,100	148,500

Blackfin 33 Convertible

Year	Power	Retail Low	Retail High
1999	T435D	******	******
1998	T375D	173,600	199,700
1997	T375D	160,400	184,500
1996	T-Gas	114,600	131,700
1996	T375D	151,800	174,600
1995	T-Gas	114,100	131,200
1995	T375D	147,200	169,300
1994	T-Gas	98,600	113,400
1994	T320D	131,100	150,800
1994	T425D	138,900	159,700
1993	T-Gas	90,400	104,000
1993	T320D	122,800	141,200
1993	T425D	131,900	151,700
1992	T-Gas	85,700	98,600
1992	T320D	116,800	134,300
1992	T425D	130,400	150,000
1991	T-Gas	76,900	88,500

Year	Power	Retail Low	Retail High
1991	T320D	107,600	123,800
1991	T425D	119,500	137,400
1990	T-Gas	70,200	80,800
1990	T-Diesel	104,400	120,100

Blackfin 36 Combi

Year	Power	Retail Low	Retail High
1988	485D	123,500	142,100
1987	485D	120,200	138,300
1986	450D	116,600	134,100

Blackfin 38 Combi

Year	Power	Retail Low	Retail High
1998	485D	267,100	307,200
1998	550D	283,100	325,500
1997	485D	257,500	296,100
1997	550D	275,700	317,000
1996	485D	249,900	287,400
1996	550D	265,100	304,800
1995	485D	232,800	267,800
1995	550D	248,800	286,100
1994	485D	215,900	248,200
1994	550D	229,300	263,700
1993	485D	204,800	235,500
1993	550D	217,700	250,400
1992	485D	193,500	222,500
1992	550D	204,200	234,900
1991	485D	181,500	208,800
1991	550D	192,000	220,800
1990	485D	153,500	176,500
1990	550D	163,500	188,000
1989	485D	141,900	163,200
1989	550D	149,500	171,900

Blackfin 36 Convertible

Year	Power	Retail Low	Retail High
1988	485D	132,300	152,200
1987	485D	127,000	146,100
1986	450D	122,300	140,700

Blackfin 38 Convertible

Year	Power	Retail Low	Retail High
1998	550D	281,900	324,200
1998	660D	309,100	355,500
1997	550D	273,800	314,800
1997	660D	301,300	346,400
1996	485D	266,000	305,900
1996	550D	275,900	317,300
1995	485D	242,000	278,300
1995	550D	258,500	297,200
1994	485D	228,800	263,200
1994	550D	242,100	278,400
1993	485D	219,100	252,000
1993	550D	226,800	260,900
1992	485D	202,400	232,800
1992	550D	210,300	241,800
1991	485D	189,400	217,800
1991	550D	195,900	225,300
1990	485D	166,300	191,300
1990	550D	175,600	201,900
1989	485D	145,700	167,500
1989	550D	149,900	172,300

Blue Seas 31

Year	Power	Retail Low	Retail High
1991	S-Diesel	82,100	94,500
1990	S-Diesel	77,000	88,600
1989	S-Diesel	73,600	84,700
1988	S-Diesel	70,500	81,000

Boston Whaler 27 Offshore

Year	Power	Retail Low	Retail High
1998	O/B*	47,400	54,500
1997	O/B*	44,500	51,100
1996	O/B*	41,700	47,900

Year	Power	Retail Low	Retail High
1995	O/B*	38,900	44,800
1994	O/B*	36,100	41,600
1993	O/B*	32,800	37,700
1992	O/B*	29,000	33,400
1991	O/B*	27,300	31,500

Boston Whaler 270 Outrage

Year	Power	Retail Low	Retail High
2004	T225 O/B	96,600	111,000
2003	T225 O/B	86,900	99,900
2002	T225 O/B	79,100	90,900

Boston Whaler 275 Conquest

Year	Power	Retail Low	Retail High
2004	T225 O/B	118,400	136,100
2003	T225 O/B	106,500	122,500
2002	T225 O/B	96,900	111,500
2001	T225 O/B	88,200	101,400

Boston Whaler 28/290 Outrage

Year	Power	Retail Low	Retail High
2003	T225 O/B	120,300	138,300
2002	T225 O/B	109,400	125,800
2001	T225 O/B	99,600	114,500
2000	T225 O/B	90,600	104,200
1999	T225 O/B	82,400	94,800

Boston Whaler 28/295 Conquest

Year	Power	Retail Low	Retail High
2003	T225 O/B	133,200	153,100
2002	T225 O/B	121,200	139,300
2001	T225 O/B	110,300	126,800
2000	T225 O/B	100,300	115,400
1999	T225 O/B	91,300	105,000

Boston Whaler 305 Conquest

Year	Power	Retail Low	Retail High
2004	T225 O/B	160,400	184,400

Boston Whaler 31 SF

Year	Power	Retail Low	Retail High
1992	T-Gas	70,000	80,500
1992	T-Diesel	81,000	93,200
1991	T-Gas	60,700	69,800
1991	T-Diesel	71,900	82,700
1990	T-Gas	53,700	61,700
1990	T-Diesel	64,400	74,100
1989	T-Gas	44,400	51,000
1989	T-Diesel	56,500	65,000
1988	T-Gas	39,300	45,200
1988	T-Diesel	50,700	58,300

Boston Whaler 320 Outrage

Year	Power	Retail Low	Retail High
2004	T225 O/B	151,200	173,800
2003	T225 O/B	137,500	158,200

Boston Whaler 34/350 Defiance

Year	Power	Retail Low	Retail High
2002	T355 D	261,200	300,300
2001	T355 D	237,600	273,300
2000	T355 D	216,300	248,700
1999	T340 D	196,800	226,300

Bristol 42 Trawler

Year	Power	Retail Low	Retail High
1981	T-Diesel	76,600	88,100
1980	T-Diesel	74,500	85,700

Cabo 31 Express

Year	Power	Retail Low	Retail High
2004	385D	255,900	294,200
2003	385D	235,400	270,700
2002	385D	216,500	249,000
2001	385D	199,200	229,100
2000	385D	183,300	210,800
1999	350D	170,400	196,000
1998	350D	158,500	182,300
1997	350D	149,000	171,400
1996	350D	140,100	161,100
1995	350D	131,600	151,400

PRICES

IMPORTANT! See Page 293 for Regional Price Adjustment.

PRICES

Year	Power	Retail Low	Retail High
Cabo 35 Express			
2004	450D	366,800	421,800
2003	450D	337,400	388,000
2002	435D	310,400	357,000
2001	435D	285,600	328,400
2000	435D	265,600	305,400
1999	435D	247,000	284,100
1998	435D	229,700	264,200
1997	435D	213,600	245,700
1996	435D	200,800	230,900
1995	375D	188,700	217,100
1994	375D	177,400	204,000
1993	375D	166,800	191,800
Cabo 35 Flybridge			
2004	450D	389,300	447,600
2003	450D	358,100	411,800
2002	435D	329,500	378,900
2001	435D	303,100	348,600
2000	435D	281,900	324,200
1999	435D	262,100	301,500
1998	435D	243,800	280,400
1997	435D	226,700	260,700
1996	435D	213,100	245,100
1995	375D	200,300	230,400
1994	375D	188,300	216,600
1993	375D	178,900	205,700
1992	375D	169,900	195,400
Cabo 40 Express			
2004	700D	566,700	651,700
2003	700D	521,300	599,500
Cabo 40 Flybridge			
2004	700D	612,300	704,100
Cabo 43 Flybridge			
2004	800D	741,200	852,300
2003	800D	696,700	801,200
2002	800D	654,900	753,100
2002	800D	615,600	707,900
Cabo 45 Express			
2004	800D	723,400	831,900
2003	800D	672,700	773,600
2002	800D	632,300	727,200
2001	800D	594,400	683,600
2000	800D	558,700	642,600
1999	800D	525,200	604,000
1998	800D	493,700	567,800
1997	800D	464,100	533,700
Cabo 47/48 Flybridge			
2004	800D	984,500	1,132,100
2003	800D	915,500	1,052,900
2002	800D	851,400	979,200
2001	800D	791,800	910,600
2000	800D	736,400	846,900
Californian 34 LRC			
1983	T85D	37,300	42,900
1983	T210D	45,300	52,200
1982	T85D	36,500	42,000
1982	T210D	44,500	51,200
1981	T85D	35,200	40,500
1981	T210D	42,500	48,900
1980	T85D	33,200	38,200
1980	T210D	40,500	46,600
Californian 35 Convertible			
1987	T-Diesel	59,000	67,900
1986	T-Diesel	52,400	60,300
1985	T-Diesel	48,100	55,400
Californian 35 Motor Yacht			
1987	T-Gas	59,500	68,400
1987	T-Diesel	70,400	81,000
1986	T-Gas	52,000	59,800
1986	T-Diesel	62,600	72,000
1985	T-Gas	43,900	50,500
1985	T-Diesel	53,600	61,700
Californian 38 Convertible			
1987	T-Diesel	80,800	92,900
1986	T-Diesel	75,800	87,100
1985	T-Diesel	70,900	81,500
1984	T-Diesel	63,600	73,200
Californian 38 LRC			
1984	T-Diesel	60,700	69,800
1983	T-Diesel	58,700	67,600
1982	T-Diesel	56,800	65,300
1981	T-Diesel	54,200	62,400
1980	T-Diesel	51,600	59,400
Californian 38 Motor Yacht			
1987	T-Diesel	84,400	97,100
1986	T-Diesel	80,400	92,500
1985	T-Diesel	76,400	87,900
1984	T-Diesel	72,400	83,200
1983	T-Diesel	68,400	78,600
Californian 39 SL ******			
Californian 42 Convertible			
1989	T375D	134,400	154,600
1989	T485D	145,000	166,700
1988	T375D	123,400	142,000
1988	T485D	132,200	152,000
1987	T375D	114,600	131,800
1987	T485D	122,300	140,600
1986	T375D	107,100	123,200
1986	T450D	112,900	129,900
Californian 42 LRC			
1984	T-Diesel	77,100	88,700
1983	T-Diesel	74,700	85,900
1982	T-Diesel	72,200	83,000
1981	T-Diesel	69,700	80,200
1980	T-Diesel	65,400	75,200
Californian 43 Cockpit MY			
1987	T-Diesel	100,900	116,100
1986	T-Diesel	95,000	109,300
1985	T-Diesel	89,500	102,900
1984	T-Diesel	83,600	96,100
1983	T-Diesel	80,200	92,200
Californian 44 Veneti			
1989	T-Diesel	105,500	121,300
1988	T-Diesel	100,400	115,400
Californian 45 Motor Yacht			
1991	T375D	210,300	241,900
1991	T485D	222,000	255,300
1990	T375D	201,500	231,700
1990	T485D	211,400	243,100
1989	T375D	184,800	212,500
1989	T485D	194,500	223,600
1988	T375D	170,200	195,700
1988	T450D	177,400	204,000
Californian 48 Cockpit MY			
1989	T-Diesel	191,700	220,500
1988	T-Diesel	181,900	209,200
1987	T-Diesel	167,300	192,400
1986	T-Diesel	164,900	189,600
Californian 48 Convertible			
1989	T-Diesel	170,400	195,900
1988	T-Diesel	160,600	184,700
1987	T-Diesel	145,200	166,900
1986	T-Diesel	138,900	159,800
Californian 48 Motor Yacht			
1991	T375D	224,000	257,600
1991	T485D	232,800	267,700
1990	T375D	212,900	244,900
1990	T485D	223,000	256,400
1989	T375D	196,900	226,500
1989	T485D	206,900	237,900
1988	T375D	181,000	208,100
1988	T450D	188,300	216,500
1987	T375D	169,600	195,100
1987	T450D	176,300	202,700
1986	T375D	166,900	191,900
1985	T375D	164,400	189,000
Californian 52 Cockpit MY			
1991	T375D	239,000	274,900
1991	T485D	254,000	292,100
1990	T375D	231,200	265,900
1990	T485D	245,300	282,200
Californian 55 Cockpit MY			
1991	T485D	274,200	315,300
1991	T550D	283,400	325,900
1990	T485D	255,000	293,200
1990	T550D	265,300	305,100
1989	T485D	231,500	266,200
1989	T550D	240,900	277,100
1988	T450D	222,100	255,400
1988	T550D	230,900	265,500
1987	T450D	214,800	247,000
1987	T550D	222,100	255,400
1986	T450D	206,800	237,800
1986	T550D	214,400	246,500
Camano 28/31			
2004	S-Diesel	158,500	182,200
2003	S-Diesel	147,400	169,500
2002	S-Diesel	137,000	157,600
2001	S-Diesel	127,400	146,600
2000	S-Diesel	118,500	136,300
1999	S-Diesel	110,200	126,800
1998	S-Diesel	102,500	117,900
1997	S-Diesel	95,300	109,600
1996	S-Diesel	89,600	103,000
1995	S-Diesel	84,200	96,900
1994	S-Diesel	79,200	91,000
1993	S-Diesel	74,400	85,600
1992	S-Diesel	70,700	81,300
1991	S-Diesel	67,200	77,200
1990	S-Diesel	63,800	73,400
Camargue 48 YF			
1993	T-Diesel	193,000	222,000
1992	T-Diesel	182,000	209,300
1991	T-Diesel	172,900	198,900
1990	T-Diesel	163,300	187,800
1989	T-Diesel	160,200	184,300

Year	Power	Retail Low	Retail High
1988	T-Diesel	156,000	179,400
1987	T-Diesel	150,700	173,300
Cape Dory 28 FB			
1995	S-Diesel	64,700	74,400
1994	S-Diesel	63,200	72,600
1993	S-Diesel	59,800	68,800
1992	S-Diesel	56,300	64,800
1991	S-Diesel	50,700	58,300
1990	S-Diesel	44,500	51,200
1990	T-Diesel	80,400	92,400
1989	S-Diesel	39,600	45,600
1988	S-Diesel	36,100	41,600
1987	S-Diesel	33,200	38,200
1986	S-Diesel	31,300	36,000
1985	S-Diesel	30,100	34,600
Cape Dory 33 FB			
1994	T-Diesel	125,400	144,200
1993	T-Diesel	116,600	134,100
1992	T-Diesel	108,400	124,700
1991	T-Diesel	101,900	117,200
1990	T-Diesel	95,800	110,200
1989	T-Diesel	90,000	103,500
1988	T-Diesel	84,600	97,300
Carolina Classic 28			
2004	T-Gas JS	114,300	131,500
2004	T-Diesel	157,300	180,900
2003	T-Gas JS	103,900	119,500
2003	T-Diesel	143,000	164,500
2002	T-Gas JS	94,500	108,700
2002	T-Diesel	130,000	149,500
2001	T-Gas JS	87,100	100,100
2001	T-Diesel	118,900	136,700
2000	T-Gas JS	82,300	94,600
2000	T-Diesel	112,200	129,000
1999	T-Gas JS	75,200	86,400
1999	T-Diesel	94,300	108,400
1998	T-Gas JS	69,000	79,300
1998	T-Diesel	87,900	101,100
1997	T-Gas JS	63,500	73,000
1997	T-Diesel	81,500	93,800
1996	T-Gas JS	57,900	66,600
1996	T-Diesel	76,100	87,500
1995	T-Gas JS	51,600	59,400
1995	T-Diesel	68,300	78,600
1994	T-Gas JS	48,600	55,900
1994	T-Diesel	61,900	71,200
Carolina Classic 32			
2004	T440D	198,700	228,500
Carolina Classic 35			
2004	T480 D	319,800	367,800
2003	T480 D	290,700	334,400
2002	T480 D	264,300	304,000
2001	T450 D	240,100	276,100
2000	T450 D	226,100	260,100
1999	T450 D	213,400	245,400
1998	T450 D	199,000	228,800
Carver 27/530/300 Montego			
1993	T-I/O Gas	28,200	32,500
1992	T-I/O Gas	26,000	30,000
1991	T-I/O Gas	24,500	28,200
1990	T-I/O Gas	22,800	26,300
1989	T-I/O Gas	21,600	24,900
1988	T-I/O Gas	20,500	23,600

Year	Power	Retail Low	Retail High
1987	T-I/O Gas	19,100	21,900
1986	T-I/O Gas	17,400	20,000
Carver 27/630/300 Santego			
1993	T-I/O 5.0L	31,700	36,400
1992	T-I/O 5.0L	29,100	33,400
1991	T-I/O 5.0L	26,900	30,900
1990	T-I/O 5.0L	25,300	29,100
1989	T-I/O 5.0L	23,100	26,500
1988	T-I/O 5.0L	22,000	25,300
Carver 280 Sedan			
1998	T-I/O 4.3L	48,300	55,600
1997	T-I/O 4.3L	44,100	50,700
1996	T-I/O 4.3L	40,100	46,200
1995	T-I/O 4.3L	35,300	40,600
1994	S-I/O 5.7L	30,700	35,300
1993	T-I/O 4.3L	28,000	32,200
1992	S-I/O 5.7L	25,800	29,700
1991	T-I/O 4.3L	24,200	27,800
Carver 28 Mariner/Voyager			
1990	T-Gas	32,200	37,000
1989	T-Gas	28,300	32,500
1988	T-Gas	24,900	28,700
1987	T-Gas	23,300	26,800
1986	T-Gas	21,600	24,900
1985	T-Gas	20,500	23,600
1984	T-Gas	20,000	23,000
1983	T-Gas	19,100	21,900
Carver 28 Riviera			
1989	T-Gas	25,100	28,800
1988	T-Gas	23,200	26,700
1987	T-Gas	21,500	24,800
1986	T-Gas	20,400	23,400
1985	T-Gas	19,300	22,200
1984	T-Gas	18,100	20,800
1983	T-Gas	16,900	19,500
Carver 280 Mid Cabin Exp			
1998	S-I/O 7.4L	42,400	48,800
1997	S-I/O 7.4L	37,900	43,600
1996	S-I/O 7.4L	33,500	38,500
1995	S-I/O 7.4L	29,800	34,200
1994	S-I/O 7.4L	26,200	30,200
1993	S-I/O 7.4L	24,500	28,200
1992	S-I/O 7.4L	20,600	23,700
1991	S-I/O 7.4L	18,900	21,800
1990	S-I/O 7.4L	17,300	19,900
1989	S-I/O 7.4L	16,200	18,600
1988	S-I/O 7.4L	15,000	17,300
Carver 2866 Santa Cruz			
1982	T-I/O Gas	14,900	17,100
1982	T-Gas	16,100	18,500
1981	T-I/O Gas	13,100	15,100
1981	T-Gas	14,300	16,500
1980	T-I/O Gas	11,900	13,700
1980	T-Gas	13,100	15,100
Carver 28 Sedan			
1993	T-Gas	43,000	49,500
1992	T-Gas	39,900	45,900
1991	T-Gas	37,300	43,000
Carver 28/300/325/326 Aft Cabin			
2001	T-Gas	102,400	117,800
2000	T-Gas	93,300	107,300
1999	T-Gas	81,800	94,100

Year	Power	Retail Low	Retail High
1998	T-Gas	75,300	86,600
1997	T-Gas	69,900	80,400
1996	T-Gas	62,500	71,900
1995	T-Gas	56,900	65,400
1994	T-Gas	54,000	62,100
1993	T-Gas	49,500	56,900
1992	T-Gas	45,200	52,000
1991	T-Gas	42,100	48,400
Carver 29 Monterey			
1986	T-Gas	19,800	22,800
1985	T-Gas	18,400	21,200
Carver 30 Allegra			
1990	T235 I/O	22,900	26,300
Carver 30/634/340 Santego			
1994	T-Gas	48,000	55,200
1993	T-I/O Gas	39,600	45,500
1993	T-Gas	43,700	50,200
1992	T-I/O Gas	38,000	43,700
1992	T-Gas	40,100	46,100
1991	T-I/O Gas	35,800	41,200
1991	T-Gas	38,000	43,700
1990	T-I/O Gas	33,100	38,100
1990	T-Gas	35,300	40,600
1989	T-I/O Gas	31,000	35,700
1989	T-Gas	33,100	38,100
1988	T-I/O Gas	26,700	30,700
1988	T-Gas	28,900	33,200
Carver 310 Mid-Cabin Express			
1997	T-I/O 5.7L	55,200	63,500
1996	T-I/O 5.7L	50,300	57,800
1995	T-I/O 5.7L	46,900	54,000
Carver 310 Santego			
1998	T-I/O 5.7L	62,300	71,600
1997	T-I/O 5.7L	56,700	65,200
1996	T-I/O 4.3L	45,100	51,800
1996	T-VD/5.7L	50,900	58,600
1995	T-I/O 4.3L	42,900	49,300
1995	T-VD/5.7L	44,300	50,900
1994	T-I/O 4.3L	39,100	44,900
1994	T-VD/5.7L	40,500	46,600
Carver 32 Aft Cabin			
1990	T-Gas	37,100	42,700
1989	T-Gas	34,800	40,000
1988	T-Gas	33,200	38,200
1987	T-Gas	30,500	35,100
1986	T-Gas	28,400	32,700
1985	T-Gas	26,200	30,200
1984	T-Gas	25,400	29,200
1983	T-Gas	23,900	27,500
Carver 32 Convertible			
1993	T-Gas	49,600	57,000
1992	T-Gas	45,200	51,900
1991	T-Gas	41,300	47,500
1990	T-Gas	36,900	42,400
1989	T-Gas	33,600	38,600
1988	T-Gas	31,900	36,700
1987	T-Gas	30,800	35,500
1986	T-Gas	29,700	34,100
1985	T-Gas	28,100	32,300
1984	T-Gas	26,400	30,300
Carver 32 Montego			
1991	T-Gas	38,300	44,100

PRICES

Year	Power	Retail Low	Retail High
1990	T-Gas	36,800	42,300
1989	T-Gas	35,200	40,500
1988	T-Gas	33,100	38,100
1987	T-Gas	30,400	35,000
Carver 320 Voyager			
1999	T-Gas	84,400	97,100
1998	T-Gas	74,800	86,000
1997	T-Gas	68,500	78,800
1996	T-Gas	60,200	69,200
1995	T-Gas	53,400	61,400
1994	T-Gas	45,800	52,600
Carver 32/330 Mariner			
1996	T-Gas	72,300	83,200
1995	T-Gas	65,200	74,900
1994	T-Gas	57,500	66,100
1993	T-Gas	53,500	61,500
1992	T-Gas	50,500	58,100
1991	T-Gas	47,300	54,400
1990	T-Gas	43,100	49,500
1989	T-Gas	39,500	45,400
1988	T-Gas	35,900	41,300
1987	T-Gas	32,900	37,800
1986	T-Gas	31,700	36,500
1985	T-Gas	29,900	34,400
Carver 33 Mariner			
1984	T-Gas	26,400	30,300
1983	T-Gas	25,200	29,000
1982	T-Gas	24,000	27,600
1981	T-Gas	22,200	25,500
1980	T-Gas	20,400	23,400
Carver 33 Voyager			
1981	T-Gas	20,400	23,500
1980	T-Gas	19,000	21,900
Carver 33 Super Sport ******			
Carver 33/350 MY			
1994	T-Gas	103,400	118,900
1993	T-Gas	95,100	109,400
1992	T-Gas	87,500	100,600
1991	T-Gas	80,500	92,600
Carver 34/350 Voyager			
1994	T-Gas	70,000	80,500
1994	T210 D	86,700	99,800
1993	T-Gas	66,600	76,600
1993	T210 D	82,800	95,200
1992	T-Gas	63,800	73,300
1992	T210 D	79,400	91,400
Carver 34/638/380 Santego			
2002	T-Gas	185,400	213,200
2001	T-Gas	168,700	194,000
2000	T-Gas	153,500	176,500
1999	T-Gas	139,700	160,600
1998	T-Gas	127,100	146,200
1997	T-Gas	116,900	134,500
1996	T-Gas	107,600	123,700
1995	T-Gas	99,000	113,800
1994	T-Gas	91,000	104,700
1993	T-Gas	83,700	96,300
1992	T-Gas	77,000	88,600
1991	T-Gas	70,900	81,500
1990	T-Gas	65,200	75,000
1989	T-Gas	59,300	68,200

Year	Power	Retail Low	Retail High
Carver 350 Mariner			
2001	T5.7L Gas	132,000	151,800
2000	T5.7L Gas	122,000	140,300
1999	T5.7L Gas	112,100	128,900
1998	T5.7L Gas	103,700	119,300
1997	T5.7L Gas	95,200	109,500
Carver 355/356 MY			
2003	T-Gas	228,900	263,200
2002	T-Gas	208,200	239,500
2001	T-Gas	189,500	217,900
2000	T-Gas	172,400	198,300
1999	T-Gas	156,900	180,500
1998	T-Gas	144,400	166,000
1997	T-Gas	132,800	152,700
1996	T-Gas	122,200	140,500
1995	T-Gas	112,400	129,300
Carver 35 Monterey/538 Montego/380 Exp			
1994	T-Gas	69,300	79,700
1993	T-Gas	64,800	74,500
1992	T-Gas	61,400	70,700
1991	T-Gas	59,100	68,000
1990	T-Gas	56,300	64,800
Carver 36 Aft Cabin			
1989	T-Gas	61,500	70,700
1988	T-Gas	56,400	64,800
1987	T-Gas	52,200	60,100
1986	T-Gas	49,000	56,400
1985	T-Gas	45,000	51,800
1984	T-Gas	43,000	49,500
1983	T-Gas	39,800	45,700
1982	T-Gas	37,000	42,500
Carver 36 Mariner (1984-88)			
1988	T-Gas	48,600	55,800
1987	T-Gas	45,900	52,800
1986	T-Gas	43,700	50,200
1985	T-Gas	42,100	48,400
1984	T-Gas	41,200	47,400
Carver 36 Mariner (Current)			
2004	T320G	213,400	245,400
Carver 360 Sport Sedan			
2004	T320G	229,100	263,500
2003	T320G	208,300	239,500
Carver 366 MY			
2004	T320G	231,500	266,200
2004	T280D	262,100	301,400
2003	T320G	208,300	239,600
2003	T280D	235,800	271,200
2002	T320G	187,500	215,600
2002	T280D	212,300	244,100
Carver 36/370 Aft Cabin MY			
1996	T-Gas	117,300	134,900
1996	T-Diesel	140,500	161,600
1995	T-Gas	107,000	123,100
1995	T-Diesel	131,300	151,000
1994	T-Gas	102,900	118,300
1994	T-Diesel	121,600	139,900
1993	T-Gas	93,100	107,000
1993	T-Diesel	119,700	137,700
1992	T-Gas	89,200	102,600
1992	T-Diesel	105,100	120,900
1991	T-Gas	81,300	93,500
1991	T-Diesel	93,500	107,500

Year	Power	Retail Low	Retail High
1990	T-Gas	73,400	84,500
1990	T-Diesel	85,400	98,200
Carver 370/374 Voyager			
2002	T-Gas	182,400	209,800
2002	T330 D	221,700	255,000
2001	T-Gas	164,000	188,600
2001	T330 D	202,900	233,400
2000	T-Gas	146,800	168,800
2000	T330 D	184,600	212,300
1999	T-Gas	130,800	150,400
1999	T315 D	166,000	191,000
1998	T-Gas	119,400	137,300
1998	T315 D	147,800	169,900
1997	T-Gas	110,500	127,100
1997	T315 D	135,100	155,400
1996	T-Gas	99,000	113,900
1996	T250 D	122,500	140,900
1995	T-Gas	90,400	103,900
1995	T250 D	114,200	131,300
1994	T-Gas	79,500	91,400
1994	T210 D	98,600	113,400
1993	T-Gas	75,700	87,000
1993	T210 D	94,100	108,200
Carver 38 Santego			
1990	T-Gas	66,200	76,100
1989	T-Gas	63,000	72,500
1988	T-Gas	58,700	67,500
Carver 38 Super Sport ******			
Carver 38/390 Aft Cabin			
1995	T-Gas	118,100	135,800
1995	T-Diesel	142,700	164,100
1994	T-Gas	110,400	126,900
1994	T-Diesel	131,300	151,000
1993	T-Gas	104,400	120,100
1993	T-Diesel	125,300	144,100
1992	T-Gas	98,500	113,300
1992	T-Diesel	118,700	136,600
1991	T-Gas	92,500	106,400
1991	T-Diesel	111,000	127,600
1990	T-Gas	86,500	99,500
1990	T-Diesel	104,400	120,100
1989	T-Gas	79,400	91,300
1989	T-Diesel	96,000	110,400
1988	T-Gas	72,100	83,000
1988	T-Diesel	88,300	101,500
1987	T-Gas	66,800	76,800
1987	T-Diesel	81,100	93,300
Carver 396 MY			
2004	T370G	323,100	371,500
2004	T370D	372,300	428,100
2003	T370G	290,700	334,400
2003	T370D	338,700	389,600
2002	T370G	261,700	300,900
2002	T370D	308,300	354,500
2001	T370G	238,100	273,800
2001	T330D	280,500	322,600
2000	T380G	216,700	249,200
2000	T330D	255,300	293,600
Carver 390/400/404 Cockpit MY			
2002	T-Gas	200,200	230,300
2002	T370 D	246,600	283,600
2001	T-Gas	182,300	209,700
2001	T370 D	227,700	261,800
2000	T-Gas	167,100	192,200

PRICES

Year	Power	Retail Low	Retail High
2000	T370 D	208,900	240,200
1999	T-Gas	154,400	177,600
1999	T370 D	197,300	226,900
1998	T-Gas	145,000	166,700
1998	T315 D	176,400	202,900
1997	T-Gas	132,800	152,700
1997	T315 D	161,300	186,200
1996	T-Gas	119,100	136,900
1996	T315 D	150,300	172,900
1995	T-Gas	107,400	123,500
1995	T315 D	132,500	152,400
1994	T-Gas	97,100	111,600
1994	T300 D	114,600	131,800
1993	T-Gas	90,700	104,300
1993	T300 D	108,800	125,100
Carver 405/406 Aft Cabin MY			
2002	T-Gas	245,900	282,800
2002	T330D	271,700	312,500
2001	T-Gas	210,600	242,200
2001	T330D	253,200	291,200
2000	T-Gas	193,600	222,700
2000	T330D	228,600	262,900
1999	T-Gas	182,000	209,300
1999	T330D	213,600	245,700
1998	T-Gas	167,500	192,600
1998	T320D	196,800	226,300
1997	T-Gas	148,400	170,700
1997	T315D	182,100	209,400
Carver 410 Sport Sedan			
2003	T-Gas	******	******
2003	T375D	******	******
2002	T-Gas	240,800	276,500
2002	T375D	269,600	310,000
Carver 42 Cockpit MY			
1988	T-Gas	85,300	98,100
1988	T-Diesel	103,300	118,800
1987	T-Gas	78,900	90,700
1987	T-Diesel	95,300	109,600
1986	T-Gas	73,600	84,600
1986	T-Diesel	89,500	102,900
Carver 42 Motor Yacht			
1991	T-Gas	99,400	114,400
1991	T-Diesel	116,100	133,500
1990	T-Gas	94,100	108,200
1990	T-Diesel	110,700	127,300
1989	T-Gas	89,200	102,600
1989	T-Diesel	106,400	122,400
1988	T-Gas	84,400	97,000
1988	T-Diesel	100,500	115,600
1987	T-Gas	79,500	91,500
1987	T-Diesel	94,600	108,800
1986	T-Gas	74,700	85,900
1986	T-Diesel	88,700	102,000
1985	T-Gas	69,900	80,400
1985	T-Diesel	81,100	93,300
Carver 42 Mariner			
2004	T385G	394,500	453,600
2004	T330D	439,700	505,600
Carver 430 Cockpit MY			
1997	T-Gas	160,500	184,500
1997	T-Diesel	184,500	212,200
1996	T-Gas	140,200	161,300
1996	T-Diesel	164,200	188,800

Year	Power	Retail Low	Retail High
1995	T-Gas	133,400	153,500
1995	T-Diesel	157,000	180,500
1994	T-Gas	133,100	153,000
1994	T-Diesel	149,400	171,800
1993	T-Gas	125,500	144,300
1993	T-Diesel	140,500	161,600
1992	T-Gas	119,000	136,800
1992	T-Diesel	134,400	154,600
1991	T-Gas	113,500	130,500
1991	T-Diesel	128,900	148,200
Carver 440/445 Aft Cabin			
1999	T450D	297,900	342,600
1998	T-Gas	245,300	282,100
1998	T420 D	271,100	311,700
1997	T-Gas	209,900	241,400
1997	T420 D	245,100	281,900
1996	T-Gas	187,600	215,700
1996	T420 D	216,200	248,600
1995	T-Gas	159,400	183,300
1995	T-Diesel	195,100	224,400
1994	T-Gas	140,300	161,300
1994	T-Diesel	170,800	196,400
1993	T-Gas	130,500	150,100
1993	T-Diesel	157,300	180,900
Carver 444 Cockpit MY			
2004	T370 D	476,800	548,300
2003	T370 D	433,800	498,900
2002	T370 D	394,800	454,000
2001	T370 D	363,200	417,700
Carver 450 Voyager			
2004	T450D	562,400	646,700
2003	T450D	506,100	582,000
2002	T450D	455,500	523,800
2001	T450D	414,500	476,700
2000	T450D	377,200	433,800
1999	T450D	343,200	394,700
Carver 455/456 Aft Cabin MY			
2000	T430D	377,000	433,600
1999	T340D	341,500	392,800
1998	T-Gas	264,000	303,700
1998	T340D	302,000	347,300
1997	T-Gas	239,600	275,500
1997	T340D	284,600	327,300
1996	T-Gas	212,900	244,800
1996	T340D	249,000	286,400
Carver 466 Motor Yacht			
2004	T480D	531,200	610,800
2003	T480D	478,000	549,700
2002	T480D	430,200	494,800
2001	T480D	387,200	445,300
Carver 500/504 Cockpit MY			
2000	T480D	393,900	453,000
1999	T450D	362,700	417,200
1998	T420D	328,400	377,700
1997	T420D	299,300	344,200
1996	T420D	263,700	303,300
Carver 506 MY			
2004	T480D	636,500	731,900
2003	T480D	572,800	658,700
2002	T480D	521,200	599,400
2001	T480D	474,300	545,500
2000	T480D	431,600	496,400

Year	Power	Retail Low	Retail High
Carver 530 Voyager			
2004	T480D	763,800	878,300
2003	T480D	687,400	790,500
2002	T480D	618,600	711,400
2001	T480D	556,800	640,300
2000	T480D	501,100	576,200
1999	T480D	451,000	518,600
1998	T480D	405,900	466,800
Carver 564 Cockpit MY			
2004	T480D	846,700	973,700
2003	T480D	762,000	876,300
2002	T480D	685,800	788,700
Carver 570 Voyager			
2004	T660D	935,000	1,075,200
2004	T480D	875,200	1,006,400
2003	T635D	832,100	956,900
2003	T480D	778,900	895,700
2002	T635D	740,600	851,700
2002	T480D	693,200	797,200
2001	T635D	659,100	758,000
2001	T480D	616,900	709,500
Carver 59 Marquis ******			
Cavileer 53 Convertble			
2004	T825D	885,600	1,018,400
2003	T825D	805,800	926,700
2002	T825D	733,300	843,300
2001	T825D	674,600	775,900
2000	T825D	620,700	713,800
Celebrity 285/290/310 SC			
1996	T210 I/O	32,400	37,200
1995	T210 I/O	29,800	34,200
1994	T190 I/O	27,700	31,800
1993	T190 I/O	25,700	29,600
1992	T190 I/O	23,900	27,500
1991	T185 I/O	22,200	25,600
1990	T185 I/O	20,700	23,800
1989	T185 I/O	19,200	22,100
Century 2900 Center Console			
2004	T250/OB	85,300	98,000
2003	T250/OB	76,700	88,200
2002	T250/OB	69,000	79,400
2001	T250/OB	62,100	71,500
2000	T250/OB	55,900	64,300
Century 2900 Walkaround			
2004	T250/OB	91,200	104,800
2003	T250/OB	82,000	94,300
2002	T250/OB	73,800	84,900
2001	T250/OB	66,400	76,400
Century 300 Grande			
1989	T260/I/O	25,400	29,200
1988	T260/I/O	23,900	27,500
1987	T260/I/O	22,300	25,600
1986	T260/I/O	20,500	23,500
1985	T260/I/O	18,700	21,500
1984	T260/I/O	17,400	20,100
Century 3000 Center Console			
1999	T250/OB	57,900	66,600
1998	T250/OB	50,700	58,300
1997	T250/OB	45,400	52,300
1996	T250/OB	40,700	46,800
1995	T250/OB	36,400	41,900

PRICES

Year	Power	Retail Low	Retail High
1994	T250/OB	33,000	37,900
Century 3000 Sport Cabin			
2002	T250/OB	76,500	87,900
2001	T250/OB	70,000	80,500
2000	T250/OB	64,700	74,400
1999	T250/OB	60,400	69,500
1998	T250/OB	53,700	61,700
1997	T250/OB	47,200	54,300
Century 3100/3200 Center Console			
2004	T250/OB	94,700	108,900
2003	T250/OB	85,200	98,000
2002	T250/OB	76,700	88,200
2001	T250/OB	69,000	79,300
2000	T250/OB	62,100	71,400
1999	T250/OB	55,500	64,300
Century 3100/3200 Walkaround			
2004	T250/OB	108,500	124,700
2003	T250/OB	97,600	112,200
2002	T250/OB	87,800	101,000
2001	T250/OB	79,000	90,900
2000	T250/OB	71,100	81,800
Chaparral Signature 26/27/270			
2000	S-I/O 7.4L	38,900	44,700
1999	S-I/O 7.4L	34,500	39,600
1998	S-I/O 7.4L	31,300	36,000
1997	S-I/O 7.4L	28,300	32,600
1996	S-I/O 7.4L	24,400	28,100
1995	S-I/O 7.4L	21,300	24,500
1994	S-I/O 7.4L	18,400	21,100
1993	S-I/O 7.4L	16,900	19,500
1992	S-I/O 7.4L	15,500	17,800
Chaparral Signature 270			
2004	T225 I/O	55,700	64,000
2003	T225 I/O	50,100	57,600
Chaparral Signature 27/278 XLC			
1991	S-I/O 7.4L	14,200	16,300
1990	S-I/O 7.4L	13,400	15,500
1989	S-I/O 7.4L	12,700	14,600
1988	S-I/O 7.4L	11,800	13,600
1987	S-I/O 7.4L	11,300	13,000
1986	S-I/O 7.4L	10,700	12,300
1985	S-I/O 7.4L	10,300	11,800
1984	S-I/O 7.4L	10,000	11,500
Chaparral 280 SSi			
2004	T260 I/O	66,600	76,500
2003	T260 I/O	60,600	69,600
2002	T260 I/O	55,100	63,400
2001	T260 I/O	50,700	58,300
2000	T280 I/O	46,600	53,600
1999	T280 I/O	42,900	49,300
Chaparral 285 SSi			
2004	T260 I/O	71,600	82,300
2003	T260 I/O	65,100	74,900
2002	T260 I/O	59,200	68,100
2001	T260 I/O	54,500	62,700
2000	T280 I/O	50,100	57,700
1999	T280 I/O	46,100	53,000
Chaparral Signature 28/29			
2000	S-I/O 7.4L	46,600	53,500
1999	S-I/O 7.4L	39,600	45,600
1998	S-I/O 7.4L	36,300	41,800
1998	T-I/O 4.3L	38,100	43,900
1997	S-I/O 7.4L	34,900	40,200
1997	T-I/O 4.3L	37,300	42,900
1996	S-I/O 7.4L	32,300	37,200
1996	T-I/O 4.3L	34,000	39,200
1995	S-I/O 7.4L	29,600	34,100
1995	T-I/O 4.3L	31,800	36,600
1994	S-I/O 7.4L	29,000	33,400
1994	T-I/O 4.3L	30,500	35,100
1993	S-I/O 7.4L	25,600	29,400
1993	T-I/O 4.3L	26,500	30,500
1992	S-I/O 7.4L	22,600	26,000
1992	T-I/O 4.3L	23,600	27,100
1991	S-I/O 7.4L	20,100	23,100
1991	T-I/O 4.3L	21,100	24,300
Chaparral 280/290			
2004	T200 I/O	86,500	99,400
2003	T190 I/O	78,700	90,500
2002	T190 I/O	71,600	82,300
2001	T190 I/O	65,100	74,900
Chaparral Signature 300			
2003	T-I/O 5.0L	83,200	95,600
2002	T-I/O 5.0L	75,700	87,000
2001	T-I/O 5.0L	68,800	79,200
2000	T-I/O 5.0L	62,600	72,100
1999	T-I/O 5.0L	57,000	65,600
1998	T-I/O 5.0L	51,900	59,700
Chaparral Signature 30/31			
1997	T-I/O Gas	48,900	56,200
1996	T-I/O Gas	45,600	52,400
1995	T-I/O Gas	41,200	47,400
1994	T-I/O Gas	36,900	42,400
1993	T-I/O Gas	32,200	37,100
1992	T-I/O Gas	29,000	33,400
1991	T-I/O Gas	28,000	32,300
1990	T-I/O Gas	25,000	28,800
Chaparral Signature 310			
2004	T280 I/O	121,500	139,700
Chaparral 32 Laser			
1991	T260 I/O	27,400	31,500
1990	T260 I/O	25,700	29,600
1989	T260 I/O	24,200	27,800
1988	T260 I/O	22,700	26,100
Chaparral Signature 330			
3004	T300 I/O	146,800	168,800
2003	T300 I/O	132,100	151,900
Chaparral Signature 350			
2004	T300 I/O	173,200	199,100
2003	T300 I/O	155,800	179,200
2002	T300 I/O	141,800	163,100
2001	T300 I/O	129,000	148,400
CHB 42 Sundeck			
1987	T135D	100,000	115,000
1987	T225D	95,000	109,200
1986	T135D	90,200	103,700
1986	T225D	85,700	98,600
1985	T135D	81,400	93,600
1985	T225D	78,100	89,900
1984	T135D	75,000	86,300
1984	T225D	72,000	82,800
1983	T135D	69,100	79,500
1983	T225D	66,400	76,300
CHB 45 Sedan			
1985	T120D	103,300	118,800
1984	T120D	99,200	114,100
1983	T120D	95,200	109,500
1982	T120D	91,400	105,100
1981	T120D	87,700	100,900
1980	T120D	84,200	96,900
Cheoy Lee 32 Trawler			
1986	S-Diesel	57,600	66,200
1985	S-Diesel	53,700	61,800
1984	S-Diesel	49,900	57,400
1983	S-Diesel	46,000	52,900
1982	S-Diesel	43,000	49,400
1981	S-Diesel	41,500	47,700
1980	S-Diesel	39,100	45,000
Cheoy Lee 35 Trawler			
1986	S-Diesel	61,500	70,800
1985	S-Diesel	57,700	66,300
1984	S-Diesel	55,000	63,200
1983	S-Diesel	51,000	58,700
1982	S-Diesel	47,900	55,100
1981	S-Diesel	45,500	52,400
1980	S-Diesel	43,200	49,600
Cheoy Lee 40 LRC			
1986	T-Diesel	134,500	154,700
1985	T-Diesel	125,900	144,800
1984	T-Diesel	118,800	136,700
1983	T-Diesel	110,800	127,400
1982	T-Diesel	102,800	118,300
1981	T-Diesel	95,600	110,000
1980	T-Diesel	88,500	101,800
Cheoy Lee 46 Trawler			
1981	T-Diesel	134,500	154,600
1980	T-Diesel	127,200	146,200
Cheoy Lee 48 Motor Yacht			
1986	T-Diesel	157,000	180,600
1985	T-Diesel	149,100	171,500
1984	T-Diesel	142,700	164,100
1983	T-Diesel	137,100	157,700
1982	T-Diesel	130,900	150,600
1981	T-Diesel	125,700	144,600
Cheoy Lee 48 Sport Yacht			
1986	T-Diesel	167,600	192,700
1985	T-Diesel	159,300	183,200
1984	T-Diesel	152,900	175,900
1983	T-Diesel	146,300	168,300
1982	T-Diesel	135,500	155,800
1981	T-Diesel	129,500	148,900
1980	T-Diesel	123,400	141,900
Cheoy Lee 50 SF			
1990	T-Diesel	274,900	316,200
1989	T-Diesel	256,700	295,300
1988	T-Diesel	240,700	276,800
1987	T-Diesel	234,900	270,100
Cheoy Lee 50 Trawler			
1980	T-Diesel	167,900	193,100
Cheoy Lee 47 Efficient MY			
1994	T-Diesel	******	******
1993	T-Diesel	******	******
1992	T-Diesel	******	******
1991	T-Diesel	248,700	286,000

PRICES

Year	Power	Retail Low	Retail High
1990	T-Diesel	232,100	266,900
1989	T-Diesel	214,300	246,500
1988	T-Diesel	198,500	228,200
1987	T-Diesel	186,200	214,200
1986	T-Diesel	175,200	201,500
1985	T-Diesel	167,200	192,300
1984	T-Diesel	160,400	184,400
Cheoy Lee 52 Efficient MY			
1994	T-Diesel	******	******
1993	T-Diesel	******	******
1992	T-Diesel	******	******
1991	T-Diesel	278,100	319,900
1990	T-Diesel	259,500	298,400
1989	T-Diesel	239,700	275,600
1988	T-Diesel	221,900	255,200
1987	T-Diesel	208,200	239,500
1986	T-Diesel	196,000	225,400
1985	T-Diesel	187,000	215,000
1984	T-Diesel	179,300	206,200
Cheoy Lee 55 Long Range MY			
1996	T-Diesel	******	******
1995	T-Diesel	******	******
1994	T-Diesel	******	******
1993	T-Diesel	******	******
1992	T-Diesel	437,300	502,900
1991	T-Diesel	405,700	466,600
1990	T-Diesel	367,300	422,400
1989	T-Diesel	343,700	395,300
1988	T-Diesel	331,600	381,400
1987	T-Diesel	313,800	360,800
1986	T-Diesel	299,000	343,900
1985	T-Diesel	290,600	334,200
1984	T-Diesel	282,200	324,600
1983	T-Diesel	263,500	303,000
1982	T-Diesel	252,700	290,600
1981	T-Diesel	237,100	272,600
Cheoy Lee 55 Trawler			
1986	T-Diesel	281,200	323,300
1985	T-Diesel	262,300	301,700
1984	T-Diesel	249,400	286,800
1983	T-Diesel	241,700	278,000
1982	T-Diesel	232,500	267,400
1981	T-Diesel	225,000	258,800
1980	T-Diesel	216,300	248,800
Cheoy Lee 58 Sport Fisherman			
1990	T-Diesel	354,300	407,500
1989	T-Diesel	320,100	368,100
1988	T-Diesel	299,500	344,400
1987	T-Diesel	287,600	330,800
1986	T-Diesel	274,400	315,500
Cheoy Lee 62 Trawler			
1983	T-Diesel	415,900	478,300
1982	T-Diesel	399,300	459,100
1981	T-Diesel	381,500	438,700
1980	T-Diesel	356,300	409,800
Cheoy Lee 65 Pilothouse ******			
Cheoy Lee 66 Fast MY			
1987	T-Diesel	366,400	421,300
1986	T-Diesel	354,400	407,600
1985	T-Diesel	342,600	394,000
1984	T-Diesel	325,900	374,700
Cheoy Lee 66 Long Range MY			
2002	T-Diesel	******	******
2001	T-Diesel	******	******
2000	T-Diesel	******	******
1999	T-Diesel	******	******
1998	T-Diesel	******	******
1997	T-Diesel	******	******
1996	T-Diesel	******	******
1995	T-Diesel	******	******
1994	T-Diesel	******	******
1993	T-Diesel	******	******
1992	T-Diesel	600,700	690,800
1991	T-Diesel	570,400	656,000
1990	T-Diesel	553,700	636,800
1989	T-Diesel	538,000	618,700
1988	T-Diesel	515,400	592,700
1987	T-Diesel	488,800	562,100
1986	T-Diesel	464,500	534,200
1985	T-Diesel	450,600	518,200
1984	T-Diesel	433,400	498,400
1983	T-Diesel	415,700	478,100
1982	T-Diesel	403,900	464,500
1981	T-Diesel	395,300	454,600
1980	T-Diesel	387,300	445,400
Cheoy Lee 66 Sport Yacht			
1987	T-Diesel	393,900	452,900
1986	T-Diesel	386,900	444,900
1985	T-Diesel	376,300	432,800
1984	T-Diesel	367,200	422,300
Cheoy Lee 68 Sport MY ******			
Cheoy Lee 70 SF ******			
Chris Craft 258/268/27 Concept			
1996	S-I/O 5.0L	25,800	29,700
1995	S-I/O 5.0L	24,200	27,900
1994	S-I/O 5.0L	22,200	25,600
1993	S-I/O 5.0L	19,900	22,900
1992	S-I/O 5.0L	17,700	20,400
Chris Craft 272/282/30 Crowne			
1997	T-I/O Gas	42,400	48,700
1996	T-I/O Gas	39,100	44,900
1995	T-I/O Gas	36,700	42,200
1994	T-I/O Gas	34,000	39,100
1993	T-I/O Gas	31,400	36,100
1992	T-I/O Gas	29,300	33,700
1991	T-I/O Gas	26,700	30,700
Chris Craft 28 Corsair			
2004	T300 I/O	85,300	98,000
2003	T300 I/O	76,700	88,200
Chris Craft 28 Launch			
2004	T300 I/O	79,500	91,400
2003	T300 I/O	71,500	82,200
Chris Craft 280/284 Amerosport			
1990	T-I/O Gas	22,400	25,800
1989	T-I/O Gas	21,000	24,200
1988	T-I/O Gas	19,300	22,200
1987	T-I/O Gas	18,200	20,900
Chris Craft 280/281			
1986	S-Gas	17,400	20,000
1986	T-Gas	20,300	23,300
1985	S-Gas	16,200	18,700
1985	T-Gas	18,800	21,600
1984	S-Gas	14,900	17,200
1984	T-Gas	17,500	20,100
1983	S-Gas	13,600	15,600
1983	T-Gas	16,200	18,700
1982	S-Gas	12,900	14,900
1982	T-Gas	15,600	17,900
1981	S-Gas	12,300	14,100
1981	T-Gas	14,200	16,400
1980	S-Gas	11,700	13,400
1980	T-Gas	13,600	15,600
Chris Craft 292 Sunbridge			
1989	T-Gas	24,100	27,800
1988	T-Gas	22,300	25,700
1987	T-Gas	21,200	24,300
1986	T-Gas	19,900	22,900
Chris Craft 300/308 Express Cruiser			
2003	T-I/O 5.0L	91,300	104,900
2002	T-I/O 5.0L	82,100	94,400
2001	T-I/O 5.0L	73,900	85,000
2000	T-I/O 5.0L	66,500	76,500
1999	T-I/O 5.0L	59,900	68,800
Chris Craft 315 Sport Sedan			
1990	T-Gas	34,800	40,000
1990	T-Diesel	42,600	49,000
1989	T-Gas	31,300	36,000
1989	T-Diesel	40,000	46,000
1988	T-Gas	29,500	33,900
1988	T-Diesel	38,000	43,700
1987	T-Gas	29,500	34,000
1987	T-Diesel	37,300	42,900
1986	T-Gas	27,800	32,000
1986	T-Diesel	36,800	42,300
1985	T-Gas	26,400	30,400
1985	T-Diesel	34,800	40,000
1984	T-Gas	25,300	29,100
1984	T-Diesel	32,500	37,400
1983	T-Gas	23,300	26,800
1983	T-Diesel	29,900	34,400
Chris Craft 320/328 Express Cruiser			
2004	T280 I/O	141,200	162,300
2003	T280 I/O	127,000	146,100
2002	T280 I/O	114,300	131,500
2001	T280 I/O	102,900	118,300
2000	T280 I/O	93,600	107,700
1999	T280 I/O	85,200	98,000
1998	T280 I/O	77,500	89,200
1997	T280 I/O	70,500	81,100
Chris Craft 320 Amerosport Sedan			
1990	T270G	36,200	41,600
1990	T350G	40,100	46,100
1989	T270G	32,300	37,100
1989	T350G	36,200	41,600
1988	T270G	30,000	34,500
1988	T350G	33,400	38,400
1987	T270G	27,200	31,300
1987	T350G	30,000	34,500
Chris Craft 320/322 Amerosport Exp.			
1990	T270G	33,000	38,000
1990	T350G	36,900	42,400
1989	T270G	30,800	35,400
1989	T350G	34,100	39,200
1988	T270G	29,100	33,500
1988	T350G	32,500	37,300
1987	T270G	27,000	31,000
1987	T350G	29,700	34,200

PRICES

Year	Power	Retail Low	Retail High
Chris Craft 332 Express			
1986	T260G	29,200	33,600
1986	T340G	32,400	37,300
1985	T260G	27,100	31,100
1985	T340G	30,300	34,800
1984	T260G	24,900	28,700
1984	T340G	27,600	31,800
1983	T260G	22,800	26,200
1983	T340G	25,500	29,300
1982	T260G	21,700	25,000
1982	T340G	24,400	28,100
1981	T260G	20,700	23,800
1981	T340G	23,400	26,900
Chris Craft 333 Sedan			
1987	T-Gas	37,100	42,700
1986	T-Gas	35,000	40,200
1985	T-Gas	32,800	37,700
1984	T-Gas	30,100	34,600
1983	T-Gas	27,900	32,100
1982	T-Gas	25,800	29,700
1981	T-Gas	25,200	29,000
Chris Craft 336 Mid-Cabin Exp.			
1987	T260G	33,000	37,900
1987	T340G	35,800	41,200
1986	T260G	31,400	36,100
1986	T340G	34,700	39,900
1985	T260G	29,200	33,600
1985	T340G	32,500	37,300
1984	T260G	26,500	30,500
1984	T340G	29,200	33,600
1983	T260G	23,700	27,300
1983	T340G	27,200	31,300
Chris Craft 33/34 Crowne			
1997	T-I/O 5.7L	53,500	61,600
1997	T-IB 7.4L	56,500	64,900
1996	T-I/O 5.7L	48,500	55,800
1996	T-IB 7.4L	51,100	58,800
1995	T-I/O 5.7L	42,400	48,800
1995	T-IB 7.4L	47,300	54,400
1994	T-I/O 5.7L	39,800	45,800
1994	T-IB 7.4L	44,100	50,800
1993	T-I/O 5.7L	37,200	42,800
1993	T-IB 7.4L	40,700	46,800
Chris Craft 350 Catalina DC			
1987	T-Gas	42,400	48,700
1986	T-Gas	39,800	45,800
1985	T-Gas	38,000	43,700
1984	T-Gas	36,100	41,500
1983	T-Gas	34,300	39,400
1982	T-Gas	32,400	37,200
1981	T-Gas	30,500	35,100
1980	T-Gas	29,200	33,600
Chris Craft 36 Roamer ******			
Chris Craft 360 Convertible			
1986	T-Gas	54,400	62,600
1986	T-Diesel	70,900	81,600
1985	T-Gas	50,100	57,700
1985	T-Diesel	65,400	75,300
1984	T-Gas	47,700	54,800
1984	T-Diesel	62,700	72,100
1983	T-Gas	44,600	51,300
1983	T-Diesel	58,700	67,500
1982	T-Gas	40,600	46,800
1982	T-Diesel	56,300	64,700
1981	T-Gas	39,400	45,300
1981	T-Diesel	50,400	58,000
1980	T-Gas	36,000	41,400
1980	T-Diesel	46,200	53,100
Chris Craft 362 Catalina			
1987	T-Gas	43,900	50,500
1986	T-Gas	42,100	48,400
Chris Craft 360 Express; 370 Amerosport			
1992	T-Gas	59,300	68,200
1991	T-Gas	53,600	61,600
1990	T-Gas	48,900	56,200
1989	T-Gas	44,700	51,400
1988	T-Gas	41,900	48,200
Chris Craft 372 Catalina DC			
1990	T-Gas	58,400	67,100
1989	T-Gas	53,200	61,200
1988	T-Gas	48,500	55,800
Chris Craft 380 Continental			
1997	T-Gas	78,600	90,400
1996	T-Gas	73,600	84,600
1995	T-Gas	68,500	78,800
1994	T-Gas	62,000	71,400
1993	T-Gas	57,700	66,400
Chris Craft 380 Corinthian			
1986	T-Gas	63,000	72,500
1986	T-Diesel	71,200	81,900
1985	T-Gas	59,200	68,100
1985	T-Diesel	66,800	76,800
1984	T-Gas	55,300	63,700
1984	T-Diesel	62,300	71,600
1983	T-Gas	51,300	59,100
1983	T-Diesel	57,800	66,500
1982	T-Gas	48,000	55,200
1982	T-Diesel	54,400	62,600
1981	T-Gas	44,500	51,100
1981	T-Diesel	50,400	57,900
1980	T-Gas	40,900	47,100
1980	T-Diesel	46,900	54,000
Chris Craft 381 Catalina DC			
1989	T-Gas	76,600	88,100
1989	T-Diesel	89,000	102,300
1988	T-Gas	72,200	83,000
1988	T-Diesel	82,700	95,200
1987	T-Gas	66,900	76,900
1987	T-Diesel	76,200	87,600
1986	T-Gas	62,200	71,500
1986	T-Diesel	70,800	81,500
1985	T-Gas	58,200	66,900
1985	T-Diesel	66,200	76,100
1984	T-Gas	54,800	63,000
1984	T-Diesel	62,100	71,500
1983	T-Gas	50,600	58,200
1983	T-Diesel	57,400	66,000
1982	T-Gas	47,700	54,800
1982	T-Diesel	54,500	62,700
1981	T-Gas	44,000	50,600
1981	T-Diesel	50,900	58,500
1980	T-Gas	41,600	47,800
1980	T-Diesel	48,600	55,900
Chris Craft 382/392 Sport Sedan			
1990	T-Gas	81,600	93,900
1990	T-Diesel	102,600	118,000
1989	T-Gas	73,600	84,600
1989	T-Diesel	93,900	108,000
1988	T-Gas	67,600	77,700
1988	T-Diesel	86,200	99,100
1987	T-Gas	65,300	75,100
1987	T-Diesel	79,900	91,900
1986	T-Gas	62,800	72,200
1986	T-Diesel	75,900	87,300
1985	T-Gas	57,600	66,300
1985	T-Diesel	72,000	82,800
Chris Craft 410 Motor Yacht			
1986	T-Gas	77,600	89,300
1986	T-Diesel	94,200	108,400
1985	T-Gas	73,900	85,000
1985	T-Diesel	87,900	101,000
1984	T-Gas	70,000	80,500
1984	T-Diesel	82,800	95,200
1983	T-Gas	66,800	76,800
1983	T-Diesel	78,300	90,000
1982	T-Gas	63,700	73,200
1982	T-Diesel	73,200	84,200
1981	T-Gas	60,400	69,500
1981	T-Diesel	71,900	82,700
1980	T-Gas	59,000	67,900
1980	T-Diesel	68,900	79,300
Chris Craft 412 Amerosport Exp.			
1990	T-Gas	70,800	81,400
1990	T-Diesel	88,400	101,700
1989	T-Gas	67,200	77,300
1989	T-Diesel	81,700	93,900
1988	T-Gas	61,500	70,700
1988	T-Diesel	75,400	86,800
1987	T-Gas	56,800	65,400
1987	T-Diesel	69,800	80,300
Chris Craft 42 Convertible SF			
1990	T-Diesel	140,600	161,600
1989	T-Diesel	131,500	151,200
1988	T-Diesel	122,900	141,300
1987	T-Diesel	114,300	131,400
1986	T-Diesel	108,900	125,200
1985	T-Diesel	104,700	120,400
1984	T-Diesel	101,200	116,400
1983	T-Diesel	98,000	112,700
1982	T-Diesel	91,300	105,000
1981	T-Diesel	84,000	96,600
1980	T-Diesel	79,400	91,300
Chris Craft 421 Continental			
1994	T-Gas	84,300	97,000
1994	T-Diesel	110,300	126,800
1993	T-Gas	78,700	90,500
1993	T-Diesel	103,600	119,200
Chris Craft 425/426/427 Catalina DC			
1990	T-Gas	115,400	132,800
1990	T-Diesel	129,500	149,000
1989	T-Gas	108,100	124,300
1989	T-Diesel	122,200	140,500
1988	T-Gas	102,100	117,400
1988	T-Diesel	116,800	134,300
1987	T-Gas	96,800	111,300
1987	T-Diesel	110,800	127,400
1986	T-Gas	89,900	103,400
1986	T-Diesel	103,500	119,000
1985	T-Gas	84,100	96,700
1985	T-Diesel	95,800	110,200

Year	Power	Retail Low	Retail High
Chris Craft 43 Roamer			
2004	T440D	492,400	566,200
2003	T440D	448,000	515,200
Chris Craft 480 Catalina			
1989	T-Diesel	150,500	173,100
1988	T-Diesel	140,300	161,400
1987	T-Diesel	137,300	157,900
1986	T-Diesel	133,100	153,100
1985	T-Diesel	128,100	147,400
Chris Craft 482 Convertible			
1988	T-Diesel	174,200	200,300
1987	T-Diesel	165,400	190,300
1986	T-Diesel	156,900	180,500
1985	T-Diesel	145,800	167,700
Chris Craft 460 Motor Yacht			
1986	T-Diesel	173,800	199,800
1985	T-Diesel	167,200	192,300
Chris Craft 500 Motor Yacht			
1989	T-Diesel	219,900	252,900
1988	T-Diesel	211,900	243,700
1987	T-Diesel	206,700	237,700
1986	T-Diesel	197,100	226,700
1985	T-Diesel	187,100	215,200
Chris Craft 501 Motor Yacht			
1990	T-Diesel	273,500	314,500
1989	T-Diesel	262,800	302,200
1988	T-Diesel	246,900	284,000
1987	T-Diesel	235,500	270,800
Cobalt 272			
2000	S300 I/O	38,800	44,600
1999	S300 I/O	35,300	40,600
1998	S300 I/O	32,100	36,900
1997	S300 I/O	29,200	33,600
1996	S300 I/O	26,800	30,900
1995	S330 I/O	24,700	28,400
1994	S330 I/O	22,700	26,100
1993	S330 I/O	20,900	24,000
Cobalt 282			
2004	S425 I/O	72,400	83,200
2003	S425 I/O	65,800	75,700
2002	S425 I/O	59,900	68,900
Cobalt 292			
2002	S425 I/O	70,700	81,300
2001	S425 I/O	64,300	73,900
2000	S415 I/O	58,500	67,300
1999	S415 I/O	53,200	61,200
Cobalt 293			
2004	S425 I/O	91,400	105,100
2003	S425 I/O	83,100	95,600
2002	S425 I/O	75,600	87,000
2001	S425 I/O	68,800	79,200
2000	S415 I/O	62,600	72,000
1999	S415 I/O	57,000	65,500
1998	S415 I/O	51,900	59,600
1997	S415 I/O	47,200	54,300
Cobalt 343			
2004	T375 I/O	188,700	217,000
Cobalt 360			
2004	T375 I/O	224,100	257,700
2003	T375 I/O	201,600	231,900

Year	Power	Retail Low	Retail High
2002	T375 I/O	181,500	208,700
Cobia 260/270 Walkaround			
2004	T200 O/B	65,700	75,500
2003	T200 O/B	59,100	68,000
2002	T200 O/B	53,200	61,200
2001	T200 O/B	47,800	55,000
2000	T200 O/B	43,100	49,500
1999	T200 O/B	38,700	44,600
1998	T200 O/B	34,900	40,100
1997	T200 O/B	31,400	36,100
Cobia 254/264/274 Center Console			
2002	T200 O/B	49,600	57,000
2001	T200 O/B	44,600	51,300
2000	T200 O/B	40,100	46,200
1999	T200 O/B	36,100	41,500
1998	T200 O/B	32,500	37,400
1997	T200 O/B	29,200	33,600
Cobia 274 Center Console			
2004	T200 O/B	60,100	69,100
2003	T200 O/B	54,000	62,200
Cobia 312 Sport Cabin			
2004	T250 O/B	86,700	99,700
2003	T250 O/B	78,000	89,700
Cobia 314 Center Console			
2004	T250 O/B	83,200	95,600
2003	T250 O/B	74,800	86,100
Compass 55 Pilothouse ******			
Conch 27			
2004	T200 O/B	66,300	76,200
2003	T200 O/B	60,300	69,300
2002	T200 O/B	54,900	63,100
2001	T200 O/B	49,900	57,400
2000	T200 O/B	45,400	52,200
1999	T200 O/B	41,300	47,500
1998	T200 O/B	37,600	43,200
1997	T200 O/B	34,200	39,400
1996	T200 O/B	31,100	35,800
1995	T200 O/B	28,300	32,600
1994	T200 O/B	25,800	29,600
1993	T200 O/B	23,400	27,000
1992	T200 O/B	21,300	24,500
1991	T200 O/B	19,400	22,300
Contender 27 Open			
2004	T200 O/B	72,600	83,400
2003	T200 O/B	67,500	77,600
2002	T200 O/B	62,700	72,200
2001	T200 O/B	58,300	67,100
2000	T200 O/B	54,300	62,400
1999	T200 O/B	51,000	58,700
1998	T200 O/B	47,900	55,100
1997	T200 O/B	45,100	51,800
1996	T200 O/B	42,400	48,700
1995	T200 O/B	39,800	45,800
Contender 31 Fish Around ******			
Contender 31 Open			
2004	T225 O/B	110,600	127,100
2003	T225 O/B	102,800	118,200
2002	T225 O/B	95,600	110,000
2001	T225 O/B	88,900	102,300
2000	T225 O/B	82,700	95,100
1999	T225 O/B	77,700	89,400

Year	Power	Retail Low	Retail High
1998	T225 O/B	73,100	84,000
1997	T225 O/B	68,700	79,000
1996	T225 O/B	64,500	74,200
1995	T225 O/B	60,700	69,800
Contender 35 Express ******			
Contender 36 Open			
2004	T250 O/B	129,800	149,200
2003	T250 O/B	120,700	138,800
2002	T250 O/B	112,200	129,100
2001	T250 O/B	104,400	120,000
Contender 36 Cuddy ******			
Cranchi 33 Endurance ******			
Cranchi 34 Zaffiro ******			
Cranchi 36/37 Smeraldo ******			
Cranchi 38/40 Atlantique ******			
Cranchi 39 Endurance ******			
Cranchi 40/41 Mediterranee ******			
Cranchi 41 Endurance ******			
Cranchi 48 Atlantique ******			
Cranchi 50 Mediterranee ******			
Crownline 270 Bowrider			
2004	S300 I/O	54,300	62,400
2003	S300 I/O	48,800	56,200
Crownline 270 CR			
2004	S320 I/O	58,600	67,300
Crownline 275 CCR ******			
Crownline 288 Bowrider			
2004	T250 I/O	69,900	80,300
2003	T250 I/O	62,200	71,500
2002	T250 I/O	55,300	63,600
2001	T250 I/O	49,200	56,600
Crownline 290 CR			
2004	T250 I/O	77,600	89,200
2003	T250 I/O	69,800	80,300
2002	T250 I/O	62,800	72,200
2001	T250 I/O	56,500	65,000
2000	T250 I/O	50,900	58,500
1999	T250 I/O	45,800	52,600
Crownline 330 CR			
2000	T310 I/O	82,600	95,000
1999	T310 I/O	76,000	87,400
1998	T310 I/O	70,000	80,500
1997	T310 I/O	65,300	75,200
1996	T310 I/O	59,100	68,000
Cruisers 2870 Express; 280 Express			
2004	S375 I/O	76,300	87,700
2004	T225 I/O	81,700	93,900
2003	S375 I/O	68,600	78,900
2003	T225 I/O	73,500	84,500
2002	S375 I/O	61,800	71,000
2002	T220 I/O	66,100	76,100
2001	S375 I/O	55,600	63,900
2001	T220 I/O	59,500	68,400
2000	S300 I/O	50,000	57,500
2000	T220 I/O	53,600	61,600
1999	S300 I/O	45,000	51,800
1999	T220 I/O	48,200	55,400

PRICES

Year	Power	Retail Low	Retail High
1998	S300 I/O	40,500	46,600
1998	T220 I/O	43,400	49,900
Cruisers 2870/2970 Rogue			
1995	T-I/O 5.7L	33,400	38,400
1994	T-I/O 5.7L	30,700	35,300
1993	T-I/O 5.7L	28,700	33,000
1992	T-I/O 5.7L	26,600	30,600
1991	T-I/O 5.7L	24,500	28,200
1990	T-I/O 5.7L	22,500	25,900
Cruisers 288/298 Villa Vee; 2980 Esprit			
1990	T-Gas	28,900	33,200
1989	T-Gas	27,100	31,200
1988	T-Gas	25,000	28,700
1987	T-Gas	23,300	26,800
1986	T-Gas	22,200	25,600
1985	T-Gas	21,200	24,300
1984	T-Gas	20,100	23,100
1983	T-Gas	18,900	21,700
1982	T-Gas	17,900	20,600
1981	T-Gas	16,800	19,400
1980	T-Gas	15,700	18,100
Cruisers 286/2860/3000 Rogue			
1989	T260 I/Os	18,200	21,000
1988	T260 I/Os	17,000	19,500
1987	T260 I/Os	15,600	17,900
Cruisers 296 Avanti Vee			
1987	T-Gas	23,400	26,900
1986	T-Gas	21,900	25,200
1985	T-Gas	20,700	23,900
1984	T-Gas	19,600	22,600
Cruisers 297 Elegante; 2970 Esprit			
1991	T-Gas	30,300	34,800
1990	T-Gas	28,100	32,400
1989	T-Gas	25,900	29,800
1988	T-Gas	23,700	27,300
1987	T-Gas	22,600	26,000
1986	T-Gas	21,500	24,700
Cruisers 300 Express ******			
Cruisers 3070 Rogue			
1994	T-I/O Gas	35,000	40,300
1993	T-I/O Gas	32,800	37,800
1992	T-I/O Gas	30,300	34,900
1991	T-I/O Gas	27,800	32,000
1990	T-I/O Gas	25,900	29,800
Cruisers 3075 Express			
2003	T260 I/O	87,600	100,700
2002	T260 I/O	78,800	90,600
2001	T260 I/O	70,900	81,500
2000	T260 I/O	63,800	73,400
1999	T260 I/O	57,400	66,000
1998	T260 I/O	52,300	60,100
1997	T260 I/O	47,500	54,700
Cruisers 3020/3120 Aria			
1997	T-I/O 5.7L	45,400	52,300
1996	T-I/O 5.7L	40,700	46,800
1995	T-I/O 5.7L	37,400	43,000
1994	T-I/O Gas	34,300	39,500
1993	T-I/O Gas	31,500	36,200
1992	T-I/O Gas	28,700	33,100
Cruisers 3175 Rogue			
1998	T260 I/O	51,900	59,700

Year	Power	Retail Low	Retail High
1997	T260 I/O	46,500	53,400
1996	T260 I/O	41,400	47,600
1995	T260 I/O	38,500	44,300
Cruisers 3160/3260 Esprit			
1990	T-Gas	27,900	32,100
1989	T-Gas	25,800	29,700
1988	T-Gas	24,200	27,900
Cruisers 3170/3270 Esprit			
1994	T-Gas	42,000	48,300
1993	T-Gas	38,800	44,600
1992	T-Gas	35,600	40,900
1991	T-Gas	33,200	38,100
1990	T-Gas	31,000	35,600
1989	T-Gas	28,900	33,200
1988	T-Gas	26,700	30,700
Cruisers 3275 Express; 320 Express			
2004	T320 I/O	109,100	125,400
2003	T320 I/O	99,200	114,000
2002	T320 I/O	89,200	102,600
Cruisers 336 Ultra Vee/3360 Espirit			
1988	T260G	32,400	37,300
1988	T350G	35,000	40,300
1987	T260G	29,800	34,200
1987	T350G	32,400	37,300
1986	T260G	27,100	31,200
1986	T350G	29,200	33,600
1985	T260G	25,500	29,300
1985	T350G	27,600	31,800
1984	T260G	23,900	27,500
1984	T350G	26,000	29,900
1983	T260G	22,800	26,200
1983	T350G	24,900	28,700
Cruisers 337/3370 Esprit			
1994	T-Gas	49,600	57,100
1993	T-Gas	47,000	54,100
1992	T-Gas	44,500	51,200
1991	T-Gas	42,400	48,800
1990	T-Gas	40,300	46,300
1989	T-Gas	37,800	43,400
1988	T-Gas	35,200	40,400
1987	T-Gas	32,500	37,400
1986	T-Gas	29,500	33,900
Cruisers 3375 Esprit			
2000	T300 I/O	101,800	117,000
1999	T300 I/O	91,600	105,300
1998	T300 I/O	82,400	94,800
1997	T300 I/O	74,200	85,300
1996	T300 I/O	66,700	76,800
Cruisers 338 Chateau Vee; 3380 Esprit			
1994	T-Gas	55,000	63,200
1993	T-Gas	52,400	60,300
1992	T-Gas	49,400	56,800
1991	T-Gas	46,200	53,200
1990	T-Gas	43,100	49,600
1989	T-Gas	39,500	45,400
1988	T-Gas	36,300	41,800
1987	T-Gas	33,800	38,800
1986	T-Gas	31,600	36,400
1985	T-Gas	30,200	34,800
Cruisers 3470 Express; 340 Express			
2004	T320 VD	149,800	172,200
2004	T320 I/O	147,500	169,600

Year	Power	Retail Low	Retail High
2003	T320 VD	136,200	156,600
2003	T320 I/O	134,100	154,200
2002	T320 VD	123,900	142,500
2002	T320 I/O	122,000	140,300
2001	T320 VD	112,700	129,700
2001	T320 I/O	111,000	127,700
Cruisers 3570/3575 Esprit			
2001	T7.4L	122,800	141,200
1999	T7.4L	98,600	113,400
1998	T7.4L	86,600	99,600
1997	T7.4L	78,300	90,100
1996	T7.4L	67,900	78,100
1995	T7.4L	60,200	69,300
Cruisers 3580/3585 Flybridge			
1999	T-VD/7.4L	103,500	119,100
1998	T-VD/7.4L	91,000	104,600
1997	T-VD/7.4L	81,800	94,100
1996	T-VD/7.4L	74,800	86,000
Cruisers 3672 Express; 370 Express			
2004	T370 VD	199,900	229,900
2003	T370 VD	181,800	209,000
2002	T375 VD	163,600	188,100
2001	T310 VD	147,200	169,300
2000	T310 VD	132,500	152,400
Cruisers 375 MY			
2004	T-Gas	229,200	263,600
2004	T370D	275,600	317,000
2003	T-Gas	206,600	237,600
2003	T370D	247,900	285,100
2002	T-Gas	189,800	218,300
2002	T370D	226,500	260,500
2001	T-Gas	171,800	197,600
2001	T370D	207,000	238,000
2000	T-Gas	121,400	139,600
2000	T370D	156,900	180,400
1999	T-Gas	111,000	127,700
1999	T370D	145,800	167,700
1998	T-Gas	103,000	118,500
1998	T-Diesel	126,600	145,600
1997	T-Gas	92,000	105,800
1997	T-Diesel	115,600	133,000
1996	T-Gas	84,600	97,300
1996	T-Diesel	106,400	122,300
1995	T-Gas	77,900	89,600
1995	T-Diesel	97,900	112,600
Cruisers 3670/3675/3775 Esprit			
1995	T7.4L	70,700	81,300
1994	T7.4L	66,000	75,900
1993	T7.4L	61,400	70,600
1992	T7.4L	56,800	65,300
1991	T7.4L	50,900	58,600
1990	T7.4L	45,700	52,600
1989	T7.4L	41,700	48,000
Cruisers 3870 Express			
2003	T370G	204,800	235,500
2002	T370G	184,300	211,900
2001	T370G	165,800	190,700
2000	T370G	150,900	173,600
1999	T380G	137,300	157,900
1998	T380G	125,000	143,700
1997	T380G	113,700	130,800
Cruisers 3850/3950 Aft Cabin MY			
1997	T-Gas	121,800	140,100

Year	Power	Retail Low	Retail High
1997	T-Diesel	143,600	165,100
1996	T-Gas	106,700	122,700
1996	T-Diesel	126,900	145,900
1995	T-Gas	94,700	108,900
1995	T-Diesel	118,200	136,000
1994	T-Gas	88,200	101,500
1994	T-Diesel	105,200	121,000
1993	T-Gas	83,200	95,600
1993	T-Diesel	96,800	111,300
1992	T-Gas	78,600	90,500
1992	T-Diesel	92,800	106,700
1991	T-Gas	74,100	85,200
1991	T-Diesel	89,400	102,800
Cruisers 400 Express			
2004	T375G	244,500	281,200
2004	T370D	297,800	342,500
2003	T375G	222,300	255,600
2003	T370D	270,800	311,400
Cruisers 405 Express MY			
2004	T370D	382,500	439,800
2003	T370D	344,200	395,800
Cruisers 4270 Express			
2003	T440D	332,100	381,900
2002	T440D	302,200	347,500
2001	T420D	275,000	316,200
2000	T420D	250,200	287,800
1999	T420D	227,700	261,800
1998	T420D	207,200	238,300
1997	T420D	188,500	216,800
Cruisers 4280/4285 Express Bridge			
1995	T-Diesel	130,300	149,900
1994	T-Diesel	120,200	138,200
1993	T-Diesel	108,800	125,200
1992	T-Gas	79,300	91,300
1992	T-Diesel	99,800	114,700
1991	T-Gas	75,500	87,100
1991	T-Diesel	94,100	108,200
1990	T-Gas	71,100	81,800
1990	T-Diesel	88,100	101,400
1989	T-Gas	68,000	78,200
1989	T-Diesel	84,400	97,100
1988	T-Gas	63,400	72,900
1988	T-Diesel	80,800	93,000
Cruisers 440 Express			
2004	T440D	421,500	484,700
2003	T440D	383,200	440,600
Cruisers 4450 Express MY			
2003	T480D	394,700	453,900
2002	T480D	355,200	408,500
2001	T480D	319,700	367,600
2000	T480D	287,700	330,800
Cruisers 455 Express MY			
2004	T480D	502,500	577,800
Cruisers 500 Express ******			
Cruisers 5000 Sedan Sport			
2003	T710D	593,200	682,100
2002	T660D	539,800	620,700
2001	T660D	491,200	564,900
2000	T660D	451,900	519,700
1999	T660D	415,700	478,100
1998	T625D	382,500	439,800

Year	Power	Retail Low	Retail High
Cruisers 540 Express			
2004	T715D	863,500	993,000
2003	T800D	785,000	902,700
2002	T800D	714,300	821,500
2001	T800D	650,000	747,500
CT 35 Trawler			
1992	S-Diesel	85,000	97,700
1991	S-Diesel	80,700	92,900
1990	S-Diesel	76,700	88,200
1989	S-Diesel	72,900	83,800
1988	S-Diesel	69,900	80,400
1987	S-Diesel	67,100	77,200
1986	S-Diesel	64,500	74,100
1985	S-Diesel	61,900	71,200
1984	S-Diesel	59,400	68,300
1983	S-Diesel	57,000	65,600
1982	S-Diesel	54,700	63,000
1981	S-Diesel	52,500	60,400
1980	S-Diesel	50,400	58,000
Davis 47 Flybridge SF			
1993	T-Diesel	285,000	327,700
1992	T-Diesel	276,100	317,500
1991	T-Diesel	268,500	308,800
1990	T-Diesel	260,400	299,500
1989	T-Diesel	242,600	279,000
1988	T-Diesel	235,500	270,900
1987	T-Diesel	218,400	251,200
1986	T-Diesel	205,900	236,800
Davis 61 Flybridge SF			
1993	T-Diesel	711,700	818,400
1992	T-Diesel	677,900	779,600
1991	T-Diesel	637,200	732,800
1990	T-Diesel	596,500	686,000
1989	T-Diesel	575,000	661,200
1988	T-Diesel	555,200	638,400
1987	T-Diesel	523,300	601,800
DeFever 40 Offshore Cruiser			
1991	T-Diesel	118,500	136,300
1990	T-Diesel	109,200	125,600
1989	T-Diesel	99,900	114,900
1988	T-Diesel	93,800	107,900
1987	T-Diesel	87,800	100,900
1986	T-Diesel	81,600	93,800
1985	T-Diesel	77,200	88,800
DeFever 41 Trawler			
1988	S-Diesel	122,700	141,100
1988	T-Diesel	132,600	152,500
1987	S-Diesel	114,700	131,900
1987	T-Diesel	124,700	143,400
1986	S-Diesel	108,400	124,700
1986	T-Diesel	117,700	135,300
1985	S-Diesel	100,700	115,800
1985	T-Diesel	109,200	125,600
1984	S-Diesel	91,400	105,200
1984	T-Diesel	99,900	114,900
1983	S-Diesel	82,100	94,400
1983	T-Diesel	90,600	104,100
DeFever 43 Trawler ******			
DeFever 44 Trawler			
2004	T-Diesel	******	******
2003	T-Diesel	******	******
2002	T-Diesel	******	******

Year	Power	Retail Low	Retail High
2001	T-Diesel	******	******
2000	T-Diesel	352,300	405,100
1999	T-Diesel	331,100	380,800
1998	T-Diesel	311,200	357,900
1997	T-Diesel	292,600	336,500
1996	T-Diesel	275,000	316,300
1995	T-Diesel	258,500	297,300
1994	T-Diesel	243,000	279,400
1993	T-Diesel	228,400	262,700
1992	T-Diesel	214,700	246,900
1991	T-Diesel	201,800	232,100
1990	T-Diesel	189,700	218,200
1989	T-Diesel	178,300	205,100
1988	T-Diesel	167,600	192,800
1987	T-Diesel	157,600	181,200
1986	T-Diesel	148,100	170,300
1985	T-Diesel	139,200	160,100
1984	T-Diesel	130,900	150,500
1983	T-Diesel	123,000	141,500
1982	T-Diesel	115,600	133,000
1981	T-Diesel	108,700	125,000
DeFever 47 POC Motor Yacht			
1992	T-Diesel	253,900	292,000
1991	T-Diesel	241,300	277,500
1990	T-Diesel	224,800	258,500
1989	T-Diesel	206,200	237,100
1988	T-Diesel	197,200	226,800
1987	T-Diesel	178,600	205,400
1986	T-Diesel	163,900	188,500
DeFever 48 Trawler			
2004	T-Diesel	******	******
2003	T-Diesel	******	******
2002	T-Diesel	******	******
2001	T-Diesel	******	******
2000	T-Diesel	******	******
1999	T-Diesel	******	******
1998	T-Diesel	******	******
1991	T-Diesel	245,200	282,000
1990	T-Diesel	227,200	261,300
1989	T-Diesel	214,300	246,500
1988	T-Diesel	215,800	248,100
1987	T-Diesel	206,800	237,800
1986	T-Diesel	196,900	226,500
1985	T-Diesel	187,000	215,100
1984	T-Diesel	173,500	199,500
1983	T-Diesel	162,700	187,200
1982	T-Diesel	151,800	174,600
1981	T-Diesel	147,100	169,100
1980	T-Diesel	141,400	162,700
DeFever 49 Cockpit MY			
2004	T-Diesel	******	******
2003	T-Diesel	******	******
2002	T-Diesel	457,700	526,400
2001	T-Diesel	431,800	496,500
2000	T-Diesel	382,100	439,400
1999	T-Diesel	361,200	415,400
DeFever 49 Pilothouse (Hard Chine)			
1990	T-Diesel	246,400	283,400
1989	T-Diesel	234,000	269,100
1988	T-Diesel	214,600	246,800
1987	T-Diesel	198,700	228,500
1986	T-Diesel	191,100	219,700
1985	T-Diesel	178,800	205,700
1984	T-Diesel	169,200	194,600

PRICES

IMPORTANT! See Page 293 for Regional Price Adjustment.

Year	Power	Retail Low	Retail High
1983	T-Diesel	161,000	185,200
1982	T-Diesel	155,300	178,600
1981	T-Diesel	149,500	171,900
1980	T-Diesel	142,700	164,200
DeFever 49 Pilothouse (Soft Chine)			
2002	T-Diesel	448,000	515,300
2001	T-Diesel	412,500	474,400
2000	T-Diesel	392,700	451,600
1999	T-Diesel	370,800	426,500
1998	T-Diesel	357,100	410,700
1997	T-Diesel	348,600	400,900
1996	T-Diesel	332,900	382,800
1995	T-Diesel	311,600	358,400
1994	T-Diesel	305,700	351,600
1993	T-Diesel	289,700	333,200
1992	T-Diesel	273,300	314,300
1991	T-Diesel	259,700	298,700
1990	T-Diesel	248,700	286,100
1989	T-Diesel	229,700	264,200
1988	T-Diesel	218,500	251,300
1987	T-Diesel	204,100	234,700
1986	T-Diesel	192,700	221,700
1985	T-Diesel	180,400	207,500
1984	T-Diesel	172,200	198,000
1983	T-Diesel	162,400	186,800
1982	T-Diesel	158,000	181,700
1981	T-Diesel	153,300	176,300
1980	T-Diesel	149,400	171,800
1980	T-Diesel	145,700	167,600
DeFever 52 Offshore Cruiser			
1991	T-Diesel	409,400	470,900
1990	T-Diesel	390,700	449,300
1989	T-Diesel	372,000	427,800
1988	T-Diesel	358,900	412,800
1987	T-Diesel	345,800	397,600
1986	T-Diesel	332,700	382,600
1985	T-Diesel	317,400	365,000
1984	T-Diesel	307,200	353,300
1983	T-Diesel	282,200	324,500
1982	T-Diesel	263,600	303,100
1981	T-Diesel	251,000	288,700
1980	T-Diesel	237,600	273,200
DeFever 53 POC Motor Yacht			
1989	T-Diesel	291,700	335,400
1988	T-Diesel	283,700	326,300
1987	T-Diesel	271,100	311,800
1986	T-Diesel	260,800	299,900
DeFever 57 POC Yachtfisher			
1989	T-Diesel	357,900	411,600
1988	T-Diesel	339,000	389,900
1987	T-Diesel	318,500	366,200
1986	T-Diesel	290,100	333,600
DeFever 57 POC Motor Yacht			
1991	T-Diesel	407,800	468,900
1990	T-Diesel	397,000	456,500
1989	T-Diesel	382,300	439,600
1988	T-Diesel	362,100	416,400
1987	T-Diesel	340,100	391,200
DeFever 60 Offshore Cruiser ******			
Donzi 28/26 ZF			
2003	T200 O/B	60,100	69,100
2002	T200 O/B	54,000	62,200
2001	T200 O/B	48,600	55,900
2000	T200 O/B	43,800	50,300
1999	T200 O/B	39,400	45,300
Donzi Z27 Express			
2000	S-I/O 7.4L	41,200	47,400
1999	S-I/O 7.4L	37,000	42,500
1998	S-I/O 7.4L	33,100	38,000
1997	S-I/O 7.4L	30,600	35,200
1996	S-I/O 7.4L	27,300	31,400
1995	S-I/O 7.4L	25,700	29,600
Donzi 29 ZF Open			
2004	T225 O/B	80,700	92,800
2003	T225 O/B	73,400	84,400
Donzi 30 ZF			
2000	T225 O/B	63,200	72,600
1999	T225 O/B	56,800	65,400
1998	T225 O/B	51,100	58,800
Donzi 32 ZF			
2004	T225 O/B	99,300	114,200
2003	T225 O/B	90,300	103,800
2002	T225 O/B	81,200	93,400
2001	T225 O/B	73,100	84,100
2000	T225 O/B	65,800	75,700
Donzi Z32 Express			
2000	T-I/O 7.4L	88,300	101,500
1999	T-I/O 7.4L	78,400	90,200
1998	T-I/O 7.4L	67,700	77,900
1997	T-I/O 7.4L	60,100	69,100
1996	T-I/O 7.4L	53,900	62,000
Donzi 35 ZF Cuddy			
2004	T225 O/B	103,900	119,500
2003	T225 O/B	94,500	108,600
2002	T225 O/B	85,000	97,800
2001	T225 O/B	76,500	88,000
2000	T225 O/B	69,600	80,100
1999	T225 O/B	63,300	72,800
1998	T225 O/B	57,600	66,300
Donzi 38 ZSF ******			
Donzi 39 ZSC			
2004	T425G	288,600	331,900
2003	T425G	262,400	301,700
2002	T425G	236,100	271,500
2001	T425G	212,500	244,400
Donzi 54 Convertible ******			
Donzi Z 65 Convertible			
2004	T-Diesel	******	******
2003	T-Diesel	******	******
2002	T-Diesel	******	******
2001	T-Diesel	2,144,000	2,465,600
2000	T-Diesel	1,980,400	2,277,400
1999	T-Diesel	1,826,200	2,100,100
1998	T-Diesel	1,699,900	1,954,900
1997	T-Diesel	1,574,200	1,810,300
1996	T-Diesel	1,436,300	1,651,800
1995	T-Diesel	1,341,800	1,543,100
1994	T-Diesel	1,253,400	1,441,400
1993	T-Diesel	1,145,100	1,316,900
1992	T-Diesel	1,057,100	1,215,600
1991	T-Diesel	1,016,300	1,168,700
1990	T-Diesel	956,600	1,100,100
1989	T-Diesel	893,700	1,027,800
1988	T-Diesel	817,900	940,600
1987	T-Diesel	739,400	850,300
Donzi 72 SF ******			
Doral 270 Prestancia			
1995	S-I/O 5.7L	24,500	28,200
1994	T-I/O 4.3L	22,800	26,200
1993	T-I/O 4.3L	21,000	24,200
1992	T-I/O 4.3L	19,800	22,800
1991	T-I/O 4.3L	18,900	21,700
1990	T-I/O 4.3L	17,500	20,100
1989	T-I/O 4.3L	16,600	19,100
Doral 270 SC			
2002	S-I/O 5.7L	46,900	54,000
2001	S-I/O 5.7L	42,000	48,300
2000	S-I/O 5.7L	37,700	43,400
1999	S-I/O 5.7L	34,300	39,400
1998	S-I/O 5.7L	30,800	35,400
1997	S-I/O 5.7L	27,400	31,500
1996	S-I/O 5.7L	25,000	28,800
Doral 28 Prestancia			
2004	T225 I/O	95,200	109,400
2003	T225 I/O	85,600	98,500
Doral 31 Intrigue			
2004	T300 I/O	111,600	128,300
Doral 300 Prestancia			
1995	T-I/O 5.7L	36,200	41,700
1994	T-I/O 5.7L	32,300	37,200
1993	T-I/O 5.7L	29,800	34,200
1992	T-I/O 5.7L	26,900	31,000
1991	T-I/O 5.7L	26,100	30,000
1990	T-I/O 5.7L	24,600	28,300
1989	T-I/O 5.7L	23,200	26,600
Doral 300 SC/SE			
2001	T-I/O 5.7L	65,400	75,300
2000	T-I/O 5.7L	59,000	67,900
1999	T-I/O 5.7L	52,800	60,800
1998	T-I/O 5.7L	46,300	53,300
1997	T-I/O 5.7L	41,500	47,800
1996	T-I/O 5.7L	37,500	43,200
Doral 31 Intrigue			
2004	T300 I/O	111,600	128,300
2003	T280 I/O	100,400	115,500
2002	T280 I/O	90,300	103,900
2001	T280 I/O	81,300	93,500
Doral 33 Elegante			
2004	T320 I/O	128,400	147,600
2003	T320 I/O	115,500	132,800
2002	T320 I/O	104,000	119,600
2001	T320 I/O	93,600	107,600
Doral 350 Boca Grande			
1992	T-Gas	48,700	56,100
1991	T-Gas	44,700	51,500
1990	T-Gas	41,600	47,900
Doral 350 SC			
1999	T-I/O 7.4L	81,400	93,700
1998	T-I/O 7.4L	74,600	85,700
1997	T-I/O 7.4L	68,500	78,800
1996	T-I/O 7.4L	63,300	72,800
Doral 36 Boca Grande			
2004	T375 I/O	174,500	200,600

Year	Power	Retail Low	Retail High
2003	T375 I/O	155,300	178,600
2002	T375 I/O	138,200	158,900
2001	T375 I/O	123,000	141,400
2000	T375 I/O	109,400	125,900
1999	T310 I/O	97,400	112,000
1998	T310 I/O	86,700	99,700

Dyer 29			
2004	S-Gas	135,400	155,700
2004	S-Gas	124,500	143,200
2002	S-Gas	114,600	131,700
2001	S-Gas	105,400	121,200
2000	S-Gas	98,000	112,700
1999	S-Gas	91,100	104,800
1998	S-Gas	84,800	97,500
1997	S-Gas	78,800	90,700
1996	S-Gas	73,300	84,300
1995	S-Gas	68,200	78,400
1994	S-Gas	63,400	72,900
1993	S-Gas	58,900	67,800
1992	S-Gas	55,400	63,700
1991	S-Gas	52,100	59,900
1990	S-Gas	49,000	56,300
1989	S-Gas	46,000	52,900
1988	S-Gas	43,300	49,700
1987	S-Gas	41,100	47,300
1986	S-Gas	39,000	44,900
1985	S-Gas	37,100	42,600
1984	S-Gas	35,200	40,500
1983	S-Gas	33,500	38,500
1982	S-Gas	31,800	36,600
1981	S-Gas	30,200	34,700
1980	S-Gas	28,700	33,000

Eagle 32 Trawler			
2004	S-Diesel	177,000	203,500
2003	S-Diesel	165,400	190,200
2002	S-Diesel	154,500	177,700
2001	S-Diesel	139,100	159,900
2000	S-Diesel	132,800	152,700
1999	S-Diesel	128,400	147,600
1998	S-Diesel	120,400	138,500
1997	S-Diesel	113,300	130,300
1996	S-Diesel	107,000	123,100
1995	S-Diesel	103,200	118,700
1994	S-Diesel	97,700	112,400
1993	S-Diesel	94,000	108,100
1992	S-Diesel	91,300	105,000
1991	S-Diesel	88,200	101,400
1990	S-Diesel	85,200	98,000
1989	S-Diesel	82,700	95,100
1988	S-Diesel	80,600	92,800
1987	S-Diesel	78,300	90,100
1986	S-Diesel	76,400	87,900
1985	S-Diesel	72,600	83,500

Eagle 40 Pilothouse Trawler			
2004	S-Diesel	275,400	316,700
2003	S-Diesel	257,400	296,000
2002	S-Diesel	240,600	276,700
2001	S-Diesel	216,200	248,600
2000	S-Diesel	201,800	232,100
1999	S-Diesel	193,400	222,400
1998	S-Diesel	187,300	215,500
1997	S-Diesel	177,600	204,300
1996	S-Diesel	169,500	195,000
1995	S-Diesel	162,100	186,400
1994	S-Diesel	151,500	174,300

Eagle 53 PH Trawler ******			

Egg Harbor 33 Sedan (1971-81)			
1981	T-Gas	33,600	38,600
1981	T-Diesel	44,300	50,900
1980	T-Gas	32,000	36,900
1980	T-Diesel	37,400	43,000

Egg Harbor 33 Sedan (1982-89)			
1989	T-Gas	55,400	63,700
1989	T-Diesel	70,400	81,000
1988	T-Gas	51,500	59,200
1988	T-Diesel	65,800	75,600
1987	T-Gas	49,000	56,300
1987	T-Diesel	60,500	69,500
1986	T-Gas	46,100	53,000
1986	T-Diesel	56,200	64,600
1985	T-Gas	43,200	49,600
1985	T-Diesel	53,000	61,000
1984	T-Gas	41,200	47,300
1984	T-Diesel	51,300	59,000
1983	T-Gas	38,400	44,200
1983	T-Diesel	49,400	56,800
1982	T-Gas	36,300	41,800
1982	T-Diesel	46,900	54,000

Egg Harbor 34/35 Convertible			
1997	T-Gas	131,700	151,500
1997	T-Diesel	162,900	187,300
1996	T-Gas	113,900	131,000
1996	T-Diesel	137,300	157,800
1995	T-Gas	106,700	122,700
1995	T-Diesel	125,300	144,000
1994	T-Gas	88,000	101,200
1994	T-Diesel	109,700	126,200
1993	T-Gas	78,500	90,300
1993	T-Diesel	96,900	111,500
1990	T-Gas	67,700	77,900
1990	T-Diesel	86,700	99,700

Egg Harbor 35 Predator			
2004	T440D	297,400	342,000
2003	T440D	267,600	307,800
2002	T440D	******	******
2001	T440D	******	******
2000	T440D	******	******

Egg Harbor 35 Sport Fisherman			
1989	T-Gas	60,900	70,100
1989	T-Diesel	76,600	88,100
1988	T-Gas	56,500	65,000
1988	T-Diesel	71,900	82,700
1987	T-Gas	54,000	62,100
1987	T-Diesel	69,200	79,600

Egg Harbor 36 Sedan			
1985	T-Gas	49,800	57,300
1985	T-Diesel	60,800	69,900
1984	T-Gas	42,500	48,900
1984	T-Diesel	54,700	62,900
1983	T-Gas	41,500	47,700
1983	T-Diesel	52,600	60,500
1982	T-Gas	38,700	44,500
1982	T-Diesel	49,700	57,200
1981	T-Gas	35,600	41,000
1981	T-Diesel	44,800	51,600
1980	T-Gas	31,800	36,600
1980	T-Diesel	38,600	44,400

Egg Harbor 37 Convertible			
1989	T-Gas	83,300	95,800
1989	T-Diesel	106,000	121,900
1988	T-Gas	78,000	89,700
1988	T-Diesel	97,100	111,700
1987	T-Gas	69,900	80,400
1987	T-Diesel	87,400	100,500
1986	T-Gas	67,400	77,500
1986	T-Diesel	83,800	96,300
1985	T-Gas	64,900	74,600
1985	T-Diesel	81,000	93,100

Egg Harbor 37 Sport Yacht			
2004	T440D	383,900	441,400
2003	T440D	349,300	401,700
2002	T420D	317,900	365,500
2001	T420D	289,200	332,600

Egg Harbor 38 Convertible			
1997	T420D	235,000	270,200
1996	T-Diesel	206,900	238,000
1995	T-Diesel	179,600	206,500
1994	T-Diesel	150,600	173,200
1993	T-Gas	106,100	122,000
1993	T-Diesel	128,600	147,900
1990	T-Gas	94,900	109,100
1990	T-Diesel	113,000	129,900

Egg Harbor 40 Motor Yacht			
1986	T-Gas	91,500	105,200
1986	T-Diesel	107,900	124,100
1985	T-Gas	90,200	103,700
1985	T-Diesel	103,300	118,800
1984	T-Gas	85,000	97,700
1984	T-Diesel	98,000	112,700
1983	T-Gas	81,700	94,000
1983	T-Diesel	91,500	105,200
1982	T-Gas	71,200	81,900
1982	T-Diesel	83,000	95,400

Egg Harbor 40 Sedan			
1986	T-Gas	84,700	97,400
1986	T-Diesel	106,800	122,900
1985	T-Gas	79,500	91,500
1985	T-Diesel	99,900	114,900
1984	T-Gas	69,500	79,900
1984	T-Diesel	90,800	104,400
1983	T-Gas	65,700	75,500
1983	T-Diesel	86,100	99,000
1982	T-Gas	56,900	65,400
1982	T-Diesel	76,800	88,300
1981	T-Gas	52,500	60,400
1981	T-Diesel	69,000	79,300
1980	T-Gas	49,600	57,000
1980	T-Diesel	64,700	74,400

Egg Harbor 41 Conv.			
1989	375D	126,100	145,000
1989	485D	137,000	157,600
1988	375D	120,400	138,500
1988	485D	129,500	149,000
1987	375D	112,800	129,800
1987	485D	120,400	138,500
1986	355D	104,300	120,000
1986	450D	113,400	130,400
1985	355D	98,700	113,600
1985	450D	107,800	124,000

PRICES

313

Year	Power	Retail Low	Retail High
1984	355D	88,400	101,700
1984	450D	94,100	108,300
Egg Harbor 42 Convertible			
1997	420D	266,700	306,700
1997	550D	298,800	343,600
1996	485D	252,400	290,300
1995	485D	224,600	258,300
1994	435D	194,700	223,900
1994	485D	204,900	235,700
1993	425D	176,100	202,500
1993	485D	189,000	217,300
1990	375D	150,500	173,100
1990	485D	159,200	183,000
Egg Harbor 42 Sport Yacht ******			
Egg Harbor 43 Sport Fisherman			
1989	375D	133,800	153,900
1989	485D	144,200	165,900
1988	375D	125,300	144,100
1988	485D	133,600	153,600
1987	355D	114,900	132,100
1987	485D	123,200	141,600
1986	355D	115,200	132,500
1986	485D	121,000	139,200
Egg Harbor 48 SF			
1986	540D	151,500	174,300
1986	675D	163,500	188,000
1985	500D	137,300	157,900
1985	675D	150,000	172,500
1984	500D	125,200	144,000
1984	675D	143,700	165,300
1983	T-Diesel	123,800	142,400
1982	T-Diesel	114,700	131,900
1981	T-Diesel	107,800	124,000
1980	T-Diesel	101,500	116,800
Egg Harbor 52 Sport Yacht			
2004	T800D	834,500	959,600
2003	T800D	759,300	873,300
2002	T760D	691,000	794,700
2001	T760D	628,800	723,100
2000	T760D	572,200	658,000
1999	T760D	520,700	598,800
1998	T760D	473,800	544,900
1997	T760D	431,200	495,900
Egg Harbor 54 Convertible			
1989	735D	295,500	339,800
1988	735D	278,900	320,800
Egg Harbor 58 Convertible			
1997	900D	613,600	705,700
1997	1250D	679,600	781,600
1996	900 DD	568,200	653,500
1995	900 DD	524,800	603,500
1995	1110 DD	553,500	636,600
1995	1250 Cat	570,000	655,500
1990	900D	373,600	429,600
1990	1080D	385,000	442,700
Egg Harbor 60 Convertible			
1989	900D	356,300	409,800
1989	1080D	377,500	434,100
1988	900D	342,700	394,100
1988	1080D	358,300	412,100
1987	870D	318,500	366,200
1987	1000D	339,200	390,100

Year	Power	Retail Low	Retail High
1986	870D	291,600	335,400
1986	1000D	306,500	352,500
Ellis 36 Express ******			
Endeavour 36 TrawlerCat			
2004	T125D	203,400	233,900
2003	T125D	187,100	215,100
2002	T125D	172,100	197,900
2001	T100D	158,300	182,100
2000	T100D	145,700	167,500
1999	T100D	134,000	154,100
1998	T100D	123,300	141,800
Fairline 40 Phantom			
2004	T370D	449,700	517,100
Fairline 40 Targa			
2004	T300D	331,300	381,000
2003	T300D	301,200	346,300
2002	T300D	274,000	315,200
2001	T260D	249,400	286,800
2000	T260D	226,900	261,000
Fairline 43 Phantom			
2004	T480D	465,900	535,700
2003	T480D	423,900	487,500
2002	T480D	385,800	443,600
2001	T480D	351,000	403,700
2000	T480D	319,400	367,400
Fairline 43 Squadron			
1997	T-Diesel	248,800	286,100
1996	T-Diesel	219,600	252,600
1995	T-Diesel	196,500	226,000
1994	T-Diesel	******	******
Fairline 46 Phantom			
2004	T480D	545,200	626,900
2003	T480D	507,000	583,000
2002	T480D	471,500	542,200
2001	T480D	438,500	504,300
2000	T480D	407,800	469,000
1999	T480D	379,200	436,100
Fairline 47/50 Squadron			
1997	T600D	409,200	470,600
1996	T550D	356,300	409,800
1995	T550D	309,300	355,800
1994	T550D	******	******
1993	T550D	******	******
Fairline 48 Targa			
2002	T430D	454,700	522,900
2001	T430D	411,600	473,300
2000	T420D	376,900	433,400
1999	T420D	344,000	395,600
1998	T420D	308,700	355,000
Fairline 50 Phantom			
2004	T675D	704,500	810,100
2003	T675D	634,000	729,100
2002	T675D	570,600	656,200
Fairline 52 Squadron			
2002	T700D	737,100	847,600
2001	T600D	666,700	766,700
2000	T600D	602,900	693,300
1999	T600D	542,500	623,900
1998	T600D	484,000	556,600

Year	Power	Retail Low	Retail High
Fairline 52 Targa			
2004	T715D	625,700	719,500
2003	T715D	569,300	654,700
Fairline 55 Squadron			
2004	T715D	952,300	1,095,100
2003	T715D	866,500	996,500
2002	T700D	788,600	906,800
2001	T660D	717,600	825,200
2000	T660D	660,200	759,200
1999	T660D	607,300	698,500
1998	T660D	558,800	642,600
1997	T660D	514,100	591,200
1996	T660D	472,900	543,900
Fairline 56/59 Squadron			
1999	T600D	652,600	750,400
1998	T600D	580,000	667,000
1997	T600D	515,200	592,500
1996	T600D	471,400	542,100
1995	T600D	410,100	471,600
1994	T600D	******	******
1993	T600D	******	******
Fairline 58 Squadron			
2004	T800D	1,115,500	1,282,800
2003	T800D	1,015,100	1,167,300
2002	T700D	923,700	1,062,300
2001	T660D	840,600	966,700
Fairline 62 Squadron			
2002	T1050D	1,192,800	1,371,700
2001	T1050D	1,085,400	1,248,200
2000	T1050D	987,700	1,135,900
1999	T1050D	898,800	1,033,600
Fairline 62 Targa ******			
Fairline 62/65 Squadron			
2003	T1400D	******	******
2002	T1400D	1,344,500	1,546,200
2001	T1400D	1,213,600	1,395,600
2000	T1400D	1,129,000	1,298,400
1999	T1000D	1,028,800	1,183,200
1998	T1000D	938,000	1,078,700
1997	T1000D	845,300	972,100
1996	T1000D	739,400	850,400
1995	T1000D	655,800	754,200
1994	T1000D	******	******
1993	T1000D	******	******
1992	T1000D	******	******
1991	T1000D	******	******
Fairline 74 Squadron ******			
Ferretti 46/480 MY ******			
Ferretti 48 MY			
1998	T435D	461,000	530,100
1997	T435D	428,700	493,000
1996	T435D	398,700	458,500
1995	T435D	374,700	431,000
1994	T435D	352,300	405,100
Ferretti 500 MY ******			
Ferretti 50 MY ******			
Ferretti 530 MY ******			
Ferretti 55 MY ******			
Ferretti 57 MY ******			

Year	Power	Retail Low	Retail High
Ferretti 590 MY ******			
Ferretti 60 MY ******			
Ferretti 620 MY ******			
Ferretti 185 MY ******			
Ferretti 680 MY ******			
Ferretti 72 MY ******			
Ferretti 225 MY ******			
Ferretti 760 MY ******			
Ferretti 80/810 MY ******			
Ferretti 80 Raised PH ******			
Fleming 55 Pilothouse			
2004	T450D	1,060,000	1,219,000
2003	T450D	1,007,000	1,158,000
2002	T450D	956,600	1,100,100
2001	T450D	908,800	1,045,100
2000	T435D	863,300	992,800
1999	T435D	820,200	943,200
1998	T435D	779,100	896,000
1997	T435D	740,200	851,200
1996	T435D	703,200	808,700
1995	T-Diesel	668,000	768,200
1994	T-Diesel	634,600	729,800
1993	T-Diesel	602,900	693,300
1992	T-Diesel	572,700	658,600
1991	T-Diesel	544,100	625,700
1990	T-Diesel	516,900	594,400
1989	T-Diesel	491,000	564,700
1988	T-Diesel	466,500	536,500
1987	T-Diesel	443,200	509,600
Fleming 75 Pilothouse MY			
2004	T800D	2,875,400	3,306,700
2003	T800D	2,760,300	3,174,400
2002	T800D	2,649,900	3,047,400
2001	T800D	2,543,900	2,925,500
Formula 27 PC			
2004	T260 I/O	89,800	103,300
2003	T260 I/O	81,700	93,900
2002	T260 I/O	73,500	84,500
2001	T260 I/O	66,100	76,100
2000	T260 I/O	59,500	68,400
1999	T260 I/O	53,600	61,600
1998	T260 I/O	48,200	55,400
1997	T250 I/O	43,400	49,900
1996	T250 I/O	39,000	44,900
1995	T250 I/O	35,100	40,400
1994	T250 I/O	31,600	36,400
Formula 28 PC			
1987	T-I/O Gas	21,500	24,700
1986	T-I/O Gas	20,300	23,400
1985	T-I/O Gas	18,900	21,700
Formula 280 Bowrider			
2004	T260 I/O	71,200	81,800
2003	T260 I/O	64,000	73,600
2002	T260 I/O	57,600	66,300
2001	T260 I/O	51,900	59,600
2000	T260 I/O	46,700	53,700
1999	T260 I/O	42,000	48,300
1998	T260 I/O	37,800	43,500

Year	Power	Retail Low	Retail High
Formula 280 Sun Sport			
2004	T260 I/O	74,200	85,300
2003	T260 I/O	66,700	76,700
2002	T260 I/O	60,100	69,100
2001	T260 I/O	54,000	62,200
2000	T260 I/O	49,200	56,600
1999	T260 I/O	44,700	51,500
1998	T260 I/O	40,700	46,800
1997	T250 I/O	37,000	42,600
1996	T250 I/O	33,700	38,800
1995	T250 I/O	30,700	35,300
1994	T250 I/O	27,900	32,100
Formula 29 PC			
1992	T-I/O Gas	38,800	44,600
1991	T-I/O Gas	36,100	41,600
1990	T-I/O Gas	33,400	38,500
1989	T-I/O Gas	30,300	34,800
1988	T-I/O Gas	28,100	32,400
Formula 31 PC (1993-04)			
2004	T320 I/O	133,200	153,100
2004	T320 I/O	119,800	137,800
2002	T320 I/O	107,800	124,000
2001	T320 I/O	97,100	111,600
2000	T320 I/O	88,300	101,600
1999	T310 I/O	80,400	92,400
1998	T310 I/O	73,100	84,100
1997	T310 I/O	66,500	76,500
1996	T330 I/O	60,500	69,600
1995	T330 I/O	55,100	63,400
1994	T330 I/O	50,100	57,700
1993	T330 I/O	45,600	52,500
Formula 31 PC (Current) ******			
Formula 31 SC Express			
1985	T-Gas	30,800	35,400
1984	T-Gas	28,100	32,300
1983	T-Gas	25,800	29,700
1982	T-Gas	23,600	27,100
1981	T-Gas	21,800	25,100
Formula 330 Sun Sport			
2004	T320 I/O	131,200	150,800
2004	T320 I/O	118,000	135,700
2002	T320 I/O	106,200	122,200
2001	T320 I/O	95,600	109,900
2000	T320 I/O	87,000	100,000
1999	T310 I/O	79,200	91,000
1998	T310 I/O	72,000	82,800
1997	T310 I/O	65,500	75,400
1996	T330 I/O	59,600	68,600
Formula 34 PC (1991-2002)			
2002	T-I/O Gas	128,100	147,300
2001	T-I/O Gas	119,600	137,500
2000	T-I/O Gas	108,800	125,100
1999	T-I/O Gas	99,100	114,000
1998	T-I/O Gas	91,000	104,700
1997	T-I/O Gas	84,200	96,800
1996	T-I/O Gas	71,400	82,100
1995	T-I/O Gas	66,400	76,400
1994	T-I/O Gas	57,100	65,700
1993	T-I/O Gas	50,800	58,400
1992	T-I/O Gas	45,800	52,700
1991	T-I/O Gas	42,200	48,600

Year	Power	Retail Low	Retail High
Formula 34 PC (Current)			
2004	T320 I/O	164,300	188,900
Formula 35 PC			
1989	T-Gas	44,600	51,200
1988	T-Gas	40,100	46,200
1987	T-Gas	37,300	42,900
1986	T-Gas	34,300	39,400
Formula 36 PC			
1995	T-Gas	88,800	102,200
1994	T-Gas	81,200	93,400
1993	T-Gas	72,300	83,100
1992	T-Gas	63,300	72,800
1991	T-Gas	58,500	67,300
1990	T-Gas	52,900	60,800
Formula 37 PC			
2004	T420 I/O	242,700	279,100
2003	T420 I/O	218,400	251,100
2002	T420 I/O	196,500	226,000
2001	T375 I/O	176,900	203,400
2000	T375 I/O	159,200	183,100
1999	T375 I/O	143,300	164,800
Formula 370 Super Sport			
2004	T425 I/O	248,700	286,000
2003	T425 I/O	223,800	257,400
2002	T375 I/O	201,400	231,600
2001	T375 I/O	181,300	208,400
Formula 40 PC			
2004	T420D	312,400	359,200
2004	T420G	287,400	330,500
2003	T420D	284,200	326,900
2003	T420G	258,600	297,400
Formula 400 Super Sport			
2004	T-Diesel	332,400	382,200
2004	T-Gas	317,400	365,000
2003	T-Diesel	302,400	347,800
2003	T-Gas	285,600	328,500
2002	T-Diesel	275,200	316,500
2002	T-Gas	259,900	298,900
2001	T-Diesel	250,400	288,000
2001	T-Gas	236,500	272,000
2000	T-Diesel	227,900	262,100
2000	T-Gas	215,200	247,500
1999	T-Diesel	207,400	238,500
1999	T-Gas	195,800	225,200
Formula 41 PC			
2004	Gas	282,800	325,300
2004	T480D	362,100	416,400
2003	Gas	252,100	289,900
2003	T480D	322,500	370,900
2002	T-Gas	219,500	252,400
2002	T450D	274,800	316,000
2001	T-Gas	201,900	232,200
2001	T450D	245,400	282,200
2000	T-Gas	176,500	203,000
2000	T450D	224,000	257,600
1999	T-Gas	157,700	181,300
1999	T450D	202,300	232,700
1998	T-Gas	140,300	161,300
1998	T420D	180,100	207,100
1997	T-Gas	129,000	148,400
1997	T420D	147,700	169,900
1996	T-Gas	118,700	136,500

PRICES

Year	Power	Retail Low	Retail High
1996	T420D	135,900	156,300
Formula 47/48 ******			
Fountain 29 Center Console			
2004	T200 O/B	88,600	101,800
2003	T200 O/B	79,700	91,700
2002	T200 O/B	71,700	82,500
2001	T200 O/B	64,500	74,200
2000	T200 O/B	58,100	66,800
1999	T200 O/B	52,300	60,100
1998	T200 O/B	47,600	54,700
1997	T200 O/B	43,300	49,800
1996	T200 O/B	39,400	45,300
1995	T200 O/B	35,800	41,200
1994	T200 O/B	32,600	37,500
1993	T200 O/B	29,700	34,100
Fountain 29 SF Cruiser			
2004	T200 O/B	92,600	106,400
2003	T200 O/B	83,300	95,800
2002	T200 O/B	75,000	86,200
2001	T200 O/B	67,500	77,600
2000	T200 O/B	60,700	69,800
1999	T200 O/B	54,600	62,800
1998	T200 O/B	49,700	57,200
1997	T200 O/B	45,200	52,000
1996	T200 O/B	41,200	47,300
1995	T200 O/B	37,400	43,100
1994	T200 O/B	34,100	39,200
1993	T200 O/B	31,000	35,700
Fountain 31 Center Console			
2004	T225 O/B	101,800	117,000
2003	T225 O/B	91,600	105,300
2002	T225 O/B	82,400	94,800
2001	T225 O/B	74,200	85,300
2000	T225 O/B	66,700	76,800
1999	T225 O/B	60,100	69,100
1998	T225 O/B	54,100	62,200
1997	T225 O/B	49,200	56,600
1996	T225 O/B	44,800	51,500
1995	T225 O/B	40,700	46,800
1994	T225 O/B	37,100	42,600
1993	T225 O/B	33,700	38,800
1992	T225 O/B	31,000	35,700
1991	T225 O/B	28,500	32,800
1990	T225 O/B	26,200	30,200
1989	T225 O/B	24,100	27,800
Fountain 31 SF Cruiser			
2004	T225 O/B	111,800	128,500
2003	T225 O/B	100,600	115,700
2002	T225 O/B	90,500	104,100
2001	T225 O/B	81,500	93,700
2000	T225 O/B	73,300	84,300
1999	T225 O/B	66,000	75,900
1998	T225 O/B	59,400	68,300
1997	T225 O/B	54,000	62,100
1996	T225 O/B	49,200	56,500
1995	T225 O/B	44,700	51,400
1994	T225 O/B	40,700	46,800
1993	T225 O/B	37,100	42,600
1992	T225 O/B	34,100	39,200
Fountain 34 Center Console			
2004	3/225 O/B	152,800	175,700
2003	3/225 O/B	139,000	159,900
Fountain 38 Center Console			

Year	Power	Retail Low	Retail High
2004	3/225 O/B	170,200	195,700
2003	3/225 O/B	153,100	176,100
2002	3/225 O/B	139,300	160,300
2001	3/225 O/B	126,800	145,800
Fountain 38 Express Cruiser			
2004	T425G I/O	224,300	257,900
2003	T425G I/O	201,800	232,100
2002	T425G I/O	181,600	208,900
Fountain 38 SF Cruiser ******			
Fountain 48 Express Cruiser ******			
Four Winns 278 Vista			
1998	T-I/O 5.0L	35,700	41,100
1997	T-I/O 5.0L	31,900	36,700
1996	T-I/O 5.0L	28,400	32,600
1995	T-I/O 5.0L	24,900	28,700
1994	T-I/O 5.0L	21,900	25,200
Four Winns 280 Horizon			
2004	T260 I/O	66,500	76,400
2003	T260 I/O	59,100	68,000
2002	T260 I/O	52,600	60,500
2001	T250 I/O	46,800	53,900
2000	T250 I/O	41,700	47,900
Four Winns 285 Express			
1993	T-I/O Gas	30,100	34,700
1992	T-I/O Gas	26,200	30,100
1991	T-I/O Gas	24,200	27,800
Four Winns 285 Sundowner			
2004	T260 I/O	67,500	77,600
2003	T260 I/O	60,700	69,800
2002	T260 I/O	54,600	62,800
2001	T260 I/O	49,200	56,500
2000	T260 I/O	44,200	50,900
Four Winns 285 Vista			
1990	T-I/O 200	25,100	28,800
1990	S-I/O 300	22,500	25,800
1989	T-I/O 200	23,000	26,500
1988	T-I/O 200	21,100	24,300
Four Winns 288 Vista			
2004	T270 I/O	85,700	98,500
Four Winns 298 Vista			
2004	T280 I/O	96,300	110,700
2003	T280 I/O	86,600	99,600
2002	T280 I/O	78,000	89,700
2001	T280 I/O	70,200	80,700
2000	T280 I/O	63,100	72,600
1999	T280 I/O	56,800	65,300
Four Winns 315/325 Express			
1993	T-I/O Gas	38,800	44,600
1993	T-Gas	41,900	48,200
1992	T-I/O Gas	34,200	39,300
1992	T-Gas	37,300	42,900
1991	T-I/O Gas	30,100	34,600
1991	T-Gas	33,200	38,200
1990	T-I/O Gas	28,600	32,900
1989	T-I/O Gas	26,200	30,100
1988	T-I/O Gas	24,700	28,400
Four Winns 328 Vista			
2004	T280 I/O	135,400	155,700
2003	T280 I/O	121,800	140,100
2002	T280 I/O	109,600	126,100

Year	Power	Retail Low	Retail High
2001	T280 I/O	99,800	114,700
2000	T280 I/O	90,800	104,400
1999	T280 I/O	82,600	95,000
Four Winns 348 Vista			
2004	T320 I/B	153,400	176,400
2003	T320 I/B	138,000	158,700
2002	T320 I/B	124,200	142,800
2001	T320 I/B	111,800	128,600
Four Winns 365 Express			
1994	T-Gas	66,800	76,800
1993	T-Gas	62,600	72,000
1992	T-Gas	57,500	66,200
1991	T-Gas	52,500	60,400
Four Winns 378 Vista			
2004	T420G	247,600	284,700
2003	T420G	222,800	256,200
2002	T420G	200,500	230,600
Glastron GS 279 Sport Cruiser			
2004	S320 I/O	47,500	54,600
2003	S320 I/O	42,200	48,600
2002	S320 I/O	37,600	43,200
Grady-White 265 Express			
2004	T225 O/B	80,100	92,100
2003	T225 O/B	72,000	82,900
2002	T225 O/B	64,800	74,600
2001	T225 O/B	58,300	67,100
2000	T225 O/B	52,500	60,400
Grady-White 263/273 Chase			
2004	T225 O/B	66,700	76,700
2003	T225 O/B	60,000	69,000
2002	T225 O/B	54,000	62,100
2001	T225 O/B	48,600	55,900
2000	T225 O/B	43,700	50,300
1999	T225 O/B	39,800	45,700
1998	T225 O/B	36,200	41,600
1997	T225 O/B	32,900	37,900
1996	T225 O/B	30,300	34,800
1995	T225 O/B	27,900	32,000
1994	T225 O/B	25,600	29,500
Grady-White 268 Islander			
2002	T225 O/B	69,800	80,200
2001	T225 O/B	63,500	73,000
2000	T225 O/B	57,800	66,400
1999	T225 O/B	52,500	60,400
1998	T225 O/B	47,800	55,000
1997	T225 O/B	44,000	50,600
1996	T225 O/B	40,500	46,500
1995	T225 O/B	37,200	42,800
Grady-White 270 Islander			
2004	T225 O/B	85,600	98,400
2003	T225 O/B	77,000	88,500
Grady-White 272 Sailfish			
2000	T225 O/B	56,100	64,500
1999	T225 O/B	51,000	58,700
1998	T225 O/B	46,400	53,400
1997	T225 O/B	42,200	48,600
1996	T225 O/B	38,400	44,200
1995	T225 O/B	35,000	40,200
1994	T225 O/B	31,800	36,600
Grady-White 282 Sailfish			
2004	T225 O/B	103,500	119,000

PRICES

Year	Power	Retail Low	Retail High
2003	T225 O/B	93,100	107,100
2002	T225 O/B	83,800	96,400
2001	T225 O/B	75,400	86,700
Grady-White 283 Release			
2004	T225 O/B	84,700	97,400
2003	T225 O/B	76,200	87,600
2002	T225 O/B	69,300	79,700
Grady White 280/300 Marlin			
2004	T225 O/B	131,500	151,200
2003	T225 O/B	118,300	136,100
2002	T225 O/B	106,500	122,400
2001	T225 O/B	95,800	110,200
2000	T225 O/B	87,200	100,300
1999	T225 O/B	79,300	91,200
1998	T225 O/B	72,200	83,000
1997	T225 O/B	65,700	75,500
1996	T225 O/B	59,800	68,700
1995	T225 O/B	55,000	63,200
1994	T225 O/B	50,600	58,200
1993	T225 O/B	46,500	53,500
1992	T225 O/B	42,800	49,200
1991	T225 O/B	39,400	45,300
1990	T225 O/B	36,200	41,700
1989	T225 O/B	33,300	38,300
Grady-White 306 Bimini			
2004	T225 O/B	114,700	131,900
2003	T225 O/B	103,200	118,700
2002	T225 O/B	92,900	106,800
2001	T225 O/B	83,600	96,100
2000	T225 O/B	75,200	86,500
1999	T225 O/B	67,700	77,800
1998	T225 O/B	60,900	70,100
Grady-White 330 Express			
2004	T250 O/B	182,300	209,600
2003	T250 O/B	164,000	188,600
2002	T250 O/B	147,600	169,800
2001	T250 O/B	132,800	152,800
Grand Banks 32 Sedan			
1996	S-Diesel	151,200	173,900
1995	S-Diesel	140,900	162,000
1994	S-Diesel	129,600	149,100
1993	S-Diesel	119,200	137,000
1992	S-Diesel	112,100	129,000
1991	S-Diesel	107,400	124,100
1990	S-Diesel	101,500	116,700
1989	S-Diesel	99,300	114,200
1988	S-Diesel	96,800	111,300
1987	S-Diesel	93,000	107,000
1986	S-Diesel	88,900	102,200
1985	S-Diesel	86,900	99,900
1984	S-Diesel	84,700	97,400
1983	S-Diesel	82,100	94,400
1982	S-Diesel	80,300	92,400
1981	S-Diesel	77,400	89,000
1980	S-Diesel	74,300	85,400
Grand Banks 36 Classic			
2003	T210D	329,800	379,200
2002	T210D	314,100	361,200
2001	T210D	289,500	332,900
2000	T210D	273,900	315,000
1998	S-Diesel	245,700	282,500
1998	T-Diesel	264,600	304,300
1997	S-Diesel	237,900	273,600
1997	T-Diesel	257,300	295,900
1996	S-Diesel	230,000	264,500
1996	T-Diesel	252,000	289,800
1995	S-Diesel	233,900	269,000
1995	T-Diesel	243,900	280,500
1994	S-Diesel	222,300	255,600
1994	T-Diesel	238,800	274,700
1993	S-Diesel	223,300	256,800
1993	T-Diesel	231,800	266,600
1992	S-Diesel	206,200	237,100
1992	T-Diesel	219,900	252,900
1991	S-Diesel	193,400	222,400
1991	T-Diesel	206,700	237,700
1990	S-Diesel	173,600	199,700
1990	T-Diesel	185,800	213,600
1989	S-Diesel	153,000	175,900
1989	T-Diesel	165,200	190,000
1988	S-Diesel	134,000	154,100
1988	T-Diesel	145,300	167,100
1987	S-Diesel	119,200	137,100
1987	T-Diesel	129,800	149,300
1986	S-Diesel	109,600	126,000
1986	T-Diesel	119,200	137,100
1985	S-Diesel	103,600	119,100
1985	T-Diesel	112,500	129,400
1984	S-Diesel	99,100	114,000
1984	T-Diesel	107,300	123,400
1983	S-Diesel	96,000	110,400
1983	T-Diesel	103,600	119,100
1982	S-Diesel	91,800	105,600
1982	T-Diesel	98,600	113,400
1981	S-Diesel	89,200	102,600
1981	T-Diesel	96,200	110,600
1980	S-Diesel	84,600	97,300
1980	T-Diesel	91,700	105,400
Grand Banks 36 Europa			
1998	S-Diesel	255,400	293,700
1998	T-Diesel	274,200	315,400
1997	S-Diesel	243,100	279,500
1997	T-Diesel	263,600	303,100
1996	S-Diesel	238,600	274,400
1996	T-Diesel	260,900	300,100
1995	S-Diesel	242,100	278,400
1995	T-Diesel	252,300	290,100
1994	S-Diesel	230,600	265,200
1994	T-Diesel	248,000	285,200
1993	S-Diesel	235,100	270,300
1993	T-Diesel	245,200	282,000
1992	S-Diesel	217,800	250,500
1992	T-Diesel	232,700	267,600
1991	S-Diesel	197,100	226,600
1991	T-Diesel	211,000	242,700
1990	S-Diesel	175,100	201,400
1990	T-Diesel	188,500	216,800
1989	S-Diesel	157,700	181,300
1989	T-Diesel	170,900	196,500
1988	S-Diesel	139,900	160,900
1988	T-Diesel	150,800	173,400
Grand Banks 36 Motor Yacht			
1998	S-Diesel	232,300	267,100
1998	T-Diesel	250,800	288,500
1997	S-Diesel	219,900	252,800
1997	T-Diesel	239,900	275,900
1996	S-Diesel	214,200	246,300
1996	T-Diesel	236,600	272,100
1995	S-Diesel	219,300	252,200
1995	T-Diesel	229,400	263,800
Grand Banks 36 Sedan			
1998	S-Diesel	224,000	257,600
1998	T-Diesel	245,600	282,400
1997	S-Diesel	203,500	234,100
1997	T-Diesel	224,000	257,600
1996	S-Diesel	192,300	221,200
1996	T-Diesel	211,800	243,500
1995	S-Diesel	175,000	201,200
1995	T-Diesel	195,200	224,500
1994	S-Diesel	167,000	192,100
1994	T-Diesel	189,700	218,200
1993	S-Diesel	160,100	184,100
1993	T-Diesel	178,300	205,000
1992	S-Diesel	147,100	169,200
1992	T-Diesel	164,500	189,200
1991	S-Diesel	138,600	159,400
1991	T-Diesel	150,100	172,700
1990	S-Diesel	133,300	153,300
1990	T-Diesel	144,300	166,000
1989	S-Diesel	123,900	142,400
1989	T-Diesel	134,500	154,600
1988	S-Diesel	113,900	131,000
1988	T-Diesel	122,200	140,600
1987	S-Diesel	106,600	122,600
1987	T-Diesel	114,700	131,900
1986	S-Diesel	99,700	114,600
1986	T-Diesel	107,400	123,500
1985	S-Diesel	93,400	107,500
1985	T-Diesel	101,300	116,500
1984	S-Diesel	87,200	100,300
1984	T-Diesel	94,500	108,700
Eastbay 38 Express			
2004	T350D	******	******
2003	T375D	360,500	414,500
2002	T375D	328,000	377,200
2001	T375D	298,500	343,300
2000	T375D	271,600	312,400
1999	T-Diesel	******	******
1998	T-Diesel	******	******
1997	T-Diesel	******	******
1996	T-Diesel	******	******
1995	T-Diesel	******	******
1994	T-Diesel	******	******
Grand Banks 42 Classic			
2004	T450D	******	******
2003	T450D	514,700	591,900
2002	T450D	481,000	553,200
2001	T450D	436,100	501,500
2000	T375D	416,900	479,400
1999	T350D	400,900	461,000
1998	T350D	384,200	441,800
1997	T375D	372,900	428,800
1996	T375D	358,400	412,100
1995	T375D	342,100	393,400
1994	T300D	325,900	374,800
1993	T300D	311,300	358,000
1992	T300D	298,500	343,300
1991	T300D	284,700	327,400
1991	T135D	262,400	301,700
1990	T135D	250,300	287,800
1989	T135D	236,100	271,600
1988	T135D	218,500	251,300
1987	T135D	203,700	234,200
1986	T135D	187,500	215,600

PRICES

Year	Power	Retail Low	Retail High
1985	T135D	175,100	201,400
1984	T135D	169,200	194,500
1983	T135D	164,000	188,600
1982	T135D	157,200	180,800
1981	T135D	150,300	172,800
1980	T135D	144,200	165,800
Grand Banks 42 Europa			
2004	T450D	******	******
2003	T450D	******	******
2002	T450D	500,800	575,900
2001	T450D	450,800	518,400
2000	T375D	430,500	495,000
1999	T350D	410,500	472,100
1998	T350D	388,400	446,600
1997	T375D	374,300	430,400
1996	T375D	362,200	416,600
1991	T135D	261,600	300,800
1990	T135D	247,800	285,000
1989	T135D	234,600	269,800
1988	T135D	221,800	255,100
1987	T135D	208,400	239,700
1986	T135D	192,800	221,700
1985	T135D	173,900	200,000
1984	T135D	174,800	201,100
1983	T135D	171,300	197,000
1982	T135D	163,600	188,100
1981	T135D	155,300	178,600
1980	T135D	148,600	170,900
Grand Banks 42 Motor Yacht			
2002	T210D	472,100	542,900
2001	T210D	425,000	488,800
2000	T210D	401,100	461,300
1999	T210D	389,200	447,600
1998	T210D	379,500	436,400
1997	T210D	369,700	425,200
1996	T210D	353,900	407,000
1995	T135D	334,400	384,600
1994	T135D	314,400	361,600
1993	T135D	296,600	341,100
1992	T135D	287,200	330,200
1991	T135D	270,500	311,100
1990	T135D	244,100	280,700
1989	T135D	229,800	264,200
1988	T135D	208,500	239,700
1987	T135D	196,500	226,000
Grand Banks 42 Sports Cruiser			
1991	T135D	228,000	262,200
1991	T375D	267,400	307,600
1990	T135D	211,300	243,000
1990	T375D	239,300	275,200
1989	T135D	194,600	223,800
1989	T375D	225,200	259,000
Eastbay 40/43 Flybridge ******			
Eastbay 43 Express ******			
Eastbay 43 HX ******			
Eastbay 43 SX ******			
Grand Banks 46 Classic			
2004	T465D	653,400	751,400
2003	T420D	607,600	698,800
2002	T420D	565,100	649,800
2001	T420D	525,500	604,400
2000	T375D	494,000	568,100
1999	T375D	464,300	534,000
1998	T375D	436,500	502,000
1997	T375D	410,300	471,800
1996	T375D	385,700	443,500
1995	T375D	366,400	421,300
1994	T375D	348,100	400,300
1993	T375D	330,700	380,300
1992	T375D	314,100	361,200
1991	T375D	298,400	343,200
1990	T375D	283,500	326,000
1989	T-Diesel	269,300	309,700
1988	T-Diesel	255,800	294,200
1987	T-Diesel	243,000	279,500
Grand Banks 46 Europa			
2004	420D	648,400	745,600
2003	420D	603,000	693,400
2002	420D	560,800	644,900
2001	420D	521,500	599,700
2000	T375D	490,200	563,700
1999	T375D	460,800	529,900
1998	T375D	433,100	498,100
1997	T375D	407,100	468,200
1996	T375D	382,700	440,100
1995	T375D	359,700	413,700
1994	T375D	338,200	388,900
1993	T375D	317,900	365,600
Grand Banks 46 Motor Yacht			
2001	T375D	******	******
2000	T375D	******	******
1999	T375D	******	******
1998	T375D	435,200	500,500
1997	T375D	420,400	483,400
1996	T375D	405,300	466,100
1995	T375D	386,500	444,400
1994	T375D	371,100	426,700
1993	T375D	353,800	406,900
1992	T375D	341,500	392,700
1991	T375D	325,300	374,100
1990	T375D	311,700	358,500
Eastbay 47 Flybridge ******			
Grand Banks 49 Classic			
1999	T375D	610,900	702,600
1998	T375D	578,400	665,100
1997	T375D	557,100	640,600
1996	T375D	532,100	611,900
1995	T375D	503,600	579,200
1994	T375D	466,100	536,100
1993	T375D	432,200	497,000
1992	T375D	409,100	470,500
1991	T375D	374,500	430,700
1990	T375D	346,000	397,900
1989	T-Diesel	319,700	367,700
1988	T-Diesel	299,500	344,400
1987	T-Diesel	285,000	327,800
1986	T-Diesel	275,300	316,500
1985	T-Diesel	270,300	310,900
1984	T-Diesel	262,900	302,400
1983	T-Diesel	255,500	293,900
1982	T-Diesel	268,300	308,500
1981	T-Diesel	253,600	291,600
1980	T-Diesel	239,600	275,500
Eastbay 49 HX			
2004	660D	938,200	1,078,900
2003	660D	853,700	981,800
2002	660D	776,900	893,400
2001	435D	707,000	813,000
2000	435D	643,300	739,800
1999	435D	585,400	673,200
Grand Banks 49 Motor Yacht			
1999	T375D	585,100	672,900
1998	T375D	556,100	639,500
1997	T375D	530,600	610,300
1996	T375D	507,600	583,800
1995	T375D	478,900	550,800
1994	T375D	439,500	505,400
1993	T375D	404,400	465,100
1992	T375D	386,300	444,300
1991	T375D	350,700	403,300
1990	T375D	320,000	368,000
1989	T-Diesel	293,400	337,400
1988	T-Diesel	277,100	318,600
1987	T-Diesel	257,600	296,300
1986	T-Diesel	238,700	274,500
Grand Banks 52 Europa ******			
Eastbay 54 SX ******			
Eastbay 58 Flybridge ******			
Grand Banks 58 Motor Yacht ******			
Grand Banks 64 Aleutian ******			
Gulfstar 38 Motor Cruiser			
1984	T-Diesel	66,200	76,100
1983	T-Diesel	60,800	70,000
1982	T-Diesel	55,500	63,800
1981	T-Diesel	50,800	58,400
1980	T-Diesel	47,500	54,600
Gulfstar 44 Motor Cruiser			
1980	T-Diesel	95,500	109,800
Gulfstar 44 Motor Yacht			
1986	T-Diesel	128,800	148,200
1985	T-Diesel	124,200	142,800
Gulfstar 44 Widebody MY			
1988	T-Diesel	154,000	177,100
1987	T-Diesel	147,300	169,400
1986	T-Diesel	142,200	163,600
Gulfstar 48 Motor Yacht			
1983	T-Diesel	131,400	151,100
1982	T-Diesel	128,200	147,400
1981	T-Diesel	125,400	144,200
Gulfstar 49 Motor Yacht			
1987	T375D	185,000	212,800
1987	T435D	192,300	221,200
1986	T355D	171,600	197,400
1986	T350D	179,000	205,800
1985	T350D	158,900	182,700
1985	T435D	165,600	190,500
1984	T350D	147,600	169,700
Gulfstar 55 MY			
1988	650D	288,700	332,000
1987	650D	268,400	308,700
Gulfstar 63 Cockpit MY			
1988	735D	410,200	471,700
1987	735D	381,400	438,700
Gulfstar 63 MY			
1988	735D	401,400	461,600

PRICES

Year	Power	Retail Low	Retail High
1987	735D	373,300	429,200
Hampton 540/560 Sedan ******			
Hampton 558 Pilothouse ******			
Hampton 680 Pilothouse ******			
Hatteras 32 Flybridge			
1986	T-Gas	50,500	58,100
1986	T-Diesel	73,400	84,400
1985	T-Gas	47,900	55,100
1985	T-Diesel	71,700	82,400
1984	T-Gas	45,900	52,800
1984	T-Diesel	64,700	74,500
1983	T-Gas	43,900	50,500
1983	T-Diesel	61,600	70,800
1982	T-Gas	40,500	46,500
1982	T-Diesel	58,900	67,800
Hatteras 36 Convertible			
1987	T-Gas	76,500	88,000
1987	T-Diesel	100,300	115,400
1986	T-Gas	68,700	79,100
1986	T-Diesel	92,100	106,000
1985	T-Gas	66,700	76,700
1985	T-Diesel	85,400	98,200
1984	T-Gas	64,400	74,100
1984	T-Diesel	81,100	93,300
1983	T-Gas	61,400	70,700
1983	T-Diesel	77,600	89,200
Hatteras 36 Sedan Cruiser			
1987	T-Gas	70,800	81,400
1987	T-Diesel	95,900	110,300
1986	T-Gas	64,900	74,600
1986	T-Diesel	87,700	100,900
Hatteras 36 Sport Fisherman			
1986	T-Gas	65,300	75,100
1986	T-Diesel	83,800	96,400
1985	T-Gas	60,300	69,300
1985	T-Diesel	79,200	91,100
1984	T-Gas	56,500	65,000
1984	T-Diesel	73,900	85,000
1983	T-Gas	54,000	62,100
1983	T-Diesel	67,900	78,100
Hatteras 37 Convertible			
1983	T-Diesel	84,800	97,500
1982	T-Diesel	80,800	92,900
1981	T-Diesel	72,400	83,300
1980	T-Diesel	66,100	76,000
Hatteras 38 Convertible			
1993	T-Diesel	178,100	204,800
1992	T-Diesel	168,600	193,900
1991	T-Diesel	161,200	185,300
1990	T-Diesel	149,900	172,400
1989	T-Diesel	138,000	158,700
1988	T-Diesel	131,900	151,700
Hatteras 39 Convertible			
1998	485D	261,300	300,600
1997	485D	246,000	282,900
1996	485D	223,900	257,500
1995	485D	211,900	243,700
1994	485D	199,400	229,400
Hatteras 39 Sport Express			
1998	485D	224,800	258,600
1997	485D	209,400	240,800
1996	485D	195,600	225,000
1995	485D	185,200	213,000
Hatteras 40 Motor Yacht			
1997	T-Diesel	262,000	301,300
1996	T-Diesel	243,600	280,100
1995	T-Diesel	237,600	273,300
1994	T-Diesel	229,000	263,300
1993	T-Diesel	219,600	252,600
1992	T-Diesel	200,900	231,000
1991	T-Diesel	180,900	208,100
1990	T-Gas	147,200	169,300
1990	T-Diesel	171,100	196,800
1989	T-Gas	135,000	155,200
1989	T-Diesel	161,600	185,900
1988	T-Gas	129,800	149,300
1988	T-Diesel	150,500	173,100
1987	T-Gas	120,400	138,500
1987	T-Diesel	141,100	162,200
1986	T-Gas	112,500	129,400
1986	T-Diesel	130,400	150,000
Hatteras 41 Convertible			
1991	535D	214,400	246,500
1990	485D	194,400	223,600
1990	535D	206,000	236,900
1989	485D	173,900	200,000
1989	535D	184,900	212,600
1988	485D	155,800	179,100
1988	535D	166,200	191,200
1987	485D	148,100	170,300
1986	450D	139,900	160,900
Hatteras 42 Cockpit MY			
1997	T-Diesel	286,000	329,000
1996	T-Diesel	265,900	305,800
1995	T-Diesel	253,300	291,200
1994	T-Diesel	243,300	279,800
1993	T-Diesel	230,200	264,700
Hatteras 42 LRC			
1985	T-Diesel	140,100	161,100
1984	T-Diesel	133,000	152,900
1983	T-Diesel	123,100	141,600
1982	T-Diesel	120,800	139,000
1981	T-Diesel	116,300	133,700
1980	T-Diesel	113,300	130,300
Hatteras 43 Conv. (1979-84)			
1984	T-Diesel	136,500	157,000
1983	T-Diesel	128,200	147,500
1982	T-Diesel	118,600	136,400
1981	T-Diesel	111,900	128,600
1980	T-Diesel	107,500	123,600
Hatteras 43 Conv. (1991-98)			
1998	T-Diesel	384,200	441,900
1997	T-Diesel	359,900	413,900
1996	T-Diesel	342,000	393,300
1995	T-Diesel	313,200	360,200
1994	T-Diesel	287,900	331,100
1993	T-Diesel	268,800	309,200
1992	T-Diesel	249,100	286,500
1991	T-Diesel	229,900	264,400
Hatteras 43 Double Cabin			
1984	T280D	126,200	145,100
1984	T390D	136,200	156,600
1983	T280D	119,500	137,400
1983	T390D	126,800	145,900
1982	T280D	112,100	128,900
1982	T390D	119,500	137,400
1981	T280D	105,500	121,300
1981	T390D	113,500	130,500
1980	T-Diesel	108,800	125,100
Hatteras 43 Motor Yacht			
1987	T320D	158,500	182,300
1987	T340D	166,200	191,100
1986	T300D	149,500	172,000
1986	T340D	156,600	180,100
1985	T300D	143,100	164,600
1985	T340D	150,200	172,800
1984	T300D	137,400	158,000
1984	T340D	143,800	165,400
Hatteras 43 Sport Express			
1998	T-Diesel	297,200	341,800
1997	T-Diesel	279,100	321,000
1996	T-Diesel	259,700	298,700
Hatteras 45 Convertible			
1991	T-Diesel	251,900	289,700
1990	T-Diesel	237,000	272,600
1989	T-Diesel	220,400	253,500
1988	T-Diesel	195,900	225,200
1987	T-Diesel	185,100	212,800
1986	T-Diesel	173,000	198,900
1985	T-Diesel	164,300	189,000
1984	T-Diesel	154,600	177,800
Hatteras 46 Conv. (1974-85)			
1985	650D	177,600	204,200
1984	650D	173,000	199,000
1983	650D	168,100	193,300
1982	650D	156,800	180,300
1981	435D	134,000	154,100
1980	435D	127,300	146,400
Hatteras 46 Conv. (1992-95)			
1995	720D	341,300	392,500
1995	780D	359,900	413,900
1994	720D	324,500	373,200
1994	780D	337,900	388,500
1993	T-Diesel	313,100	360,100
1992	T-Diesel	295,900	340,300
Hatteras 48 Cockpit MY (1981-85)			
1985	T280D	177,500	204,100
1985	T425D	194,900	224,100
1984	T280D	172,200	198,100
1984	T425D	190,600	219,200
1983	T280D	163,500	188,000
1983	T425D	180,900	208,000
1982	T280D	152,500	175,400
1982	T425D	169,600	195,100
1981	T280D	144,300	165,900
1981	T425D	161,400	185,600
Hatteras 48 Cockpit MY (1993-96)			
1996	T-Diesel	431,700	496,500
1995	T-Diesel	408,500	469,800
1994	T-Diesel	384,400	442,000
1993	T-Diesel	360,100	414,100
Hatteras 48 Convertible			
1991	T-Diesel	321,900	370,200
1990	T-Diesel	316,200	363,600
1989	T-Diesel	309,800	356,200
1988	T-Diesel	284,800	327,600

PRICES

PRICES

Year	Power	Retail Low	Retail High
1987	T-Diesel	267,600	307,700

Hatteras 48 LRC

Year	Power	Retail Low	Retail High
1981	T-Diesel	179,300	206,200
1980	T-Diesel		

Hatteras 48 Motor Yacht (1981-84)

Year	Power	Retail Low	Retail High
1984	T280D	176,000	202,400
1984	T425D	196,100	225,500
1983	T280D	163,200	187,700
1983	T425D	179,900	206,900
1982	T280D	152,700	175,600
1982	T425D	171,300	197,000
1981	T280D	141,500	162,800
1981	T425D	160,200	184,200

Hatteras 48 Motor Yacht (1990-96)

Year	Power	Retail Low	Retail High
1996	T-Diesel	429,400	493,800
1995	T-Diesel	414,600	476,800
1994	T-Diesel	399,000	458,800
1993	T-Diesel	378,500	435,200
1992	T-Diesel	352,900	405,800
1991	T-Diesel	315,400	362,800
1990	T535D	275,000	316,300
1990	T720D	294,700	338,900

Hatteras 50 Conv. (1980-83)

Year	Power	Retail Low	Retail High
1983	T-Diesel	194,300	223,400
1982	T-Diesel	186,300	214,300
1981	T-Diesel	168,300	193,600
1980	T-Diesel	162,400	186,800

Hatteras 50 Conv. (1991-Current)

Year	Power	Retail Low	Retail High
2004	800D	******	******
2003	800D	836,900	962,500
2002	800D	767,800	883,000
2002	1400D	882,300	1,014,700
2001	800D	708,300	814,600
2001	1400D	813,400	935,400
2000	800D	647,000	744,100
2000	1400D	760,600	874,600
1999	800D	609,300	700,700
1999	1400D	736,800	847,400
1998	900D	568,300	653,600
1998	1150D	618,500	711,300
1997	870D	544,300	625,900
1997	1094D	585,700	673,500
1996	780D	470,000	540,500
1996	870D	513,800	590,800
1995	780D	421,800	485,100
1995	870D	462,100	531,500
1994	780D	417,700	480,400
1994	870D	451,900	519,700
1993	780D	404,600	465,300
1993	870D	432,000	496,800
1992	780D	389,000	447,400
1992	870D	410,100	471,600
1991	780D	363,500	418,000
1991	870D	382,900	440,300

Hatteras 50 Sport Deck MY

Year	Power	Retail Low	Retail High
1998	T-Diesel	517,600	595,300
1997	T-Diesel	486,800	559,800
1996	T-Diesel	455,500	523,800

Hatteras 52 Cockpit MY

Year	Power	Retail Low	Retail High
1999	800Cat	666,200	766,100
1998	800Cat	624,500	718,200
1997	T-Diesel	590,300	678,800
1996	T-Diesel	561,600	645,900

Year	Power	Retail Low	Retail High
1995	T-Diesel	524,200	602,900
1994	T-Diesel	494,600	568,800
1993	T-Diesel	464,000	533,600
1992	T-Diesel	441,900	508,200
1991	T-Diesel	411,600	473,400
1990	T-Diesel	383,200	440,700

Hatteras 52 Convertible

Year	Power	Retail Low	Retail High
1991	T-Diesel	354,000	407,100
1990	T-Diesel	339,200	390,100
1989	T-Diesel	323,700	372,300
1988	T-Diesel	299,300	344,200
1987	T-Diesel	267,900	308,100
1986	T-Diesel	248,900	286,200
1985	T-Diesel	234,200	269,400
1984	T-Diesel	226,100	260,000

Hatteras 52 Motor Yacht

Year	Power	Retail Low	Retail High
1996	T-Diesel	564,900	649,600
1995	T-Diesel	531,400	611,100
1994	T-Diesel	499,900	574,900
1993	T-Diesel	469,600	540,100

Hatteras 53 Convertible

Year	Power	Retail Low	Retail High
1980	T-Diesel	168,300	193,500

Hatteras 53 EDMY

Year	Power	Retail Low	Retail High
1988	T-Diesel	324,100	372,800
1987	T-Diesel	310,500	357,100
1986	T-Diesel	299,200	344,100
1985	T-Diesel	278,200	320,000
1984	T-Diesel	268,400	308,700
1983	T-Diesel	253,600	291,600

Hatteras 53 Motor Yacht

Year	Power	Retail Low	Retail High
1988	T-Diesel	318,700	366,500
1987	T-Diesel	305,500	351,300
1986	T-Diesel	288,800	332,100
1985	T-Diesel	271,800	312,600
1984	T-Diesel	259,300	298,200
1983	T-Diesel	244,900	281,700
1982	T-Diesel	230,200	264,800
1981	T-Diesel	220,700	253,800
1980	T-Diesel	214,100	246,200

Hatteras 53 Yacht Fisherman

Year	Power	Retail Low	Retail High
1987	T-Diesel	265,600	305,400
1986	T-Diesel	263,200	302,700
1981	T-Diesel	188,400	216,700
1980	T-Diesel	179,400	206,400
1985	T-Diesel	371,000	426,700

Hatteras 54 Conv. (1991-98)

Year	Power	Retail Low	Retail High
1998	1110 DD	802,300	922,600
1998	1350Cat	817,200	939,800
1997	1075D	746,800	858,800
1997	1310D	774,500	890,700
1996	1040D	682,300	784,600
1996	1206D	717,900	825,600
1995	1040D	633,400	728,500
1995	1206D	662,100	761,400
1994	870D	577,700	664,400
1994	1040D	611,700	703,400
1993	870D	549,200	631,500
1993	1040D	577,500	664,100
1992	870D	499,300	574,200
1992	1040D	536,700	617,300
1991	870D	486,200	559,200
1991	1040D	514,800	592,000

Hatteras 54 Conv. (Current)

Year	Power	Retail Low	Retail High
2004	800D	1,020,000	1,173,000
2003	800D	918,000	1,055,700
2002	800D	826,200	950,100

Hatteras 54 EDMY

Year	Power	Retail Low	Retail High
1992	T-Diesel	538,400	619,200
1991	T-Diesel	500,100	575,100
1990	T-Diesel	455,100	523,400
1989	T-Diesel	408,800	470,100

Hatteras 54 Motor Yacht

Year	Power	Retail Low	Retail High
1988	T-Diesel	382,200	439,600
1987	T-Diesel	374,400	430,600
1986	T-Diesel	362,300	416,700
1985	T-Diesel	350,900	403,500

Hatteras 55 Conv. (1980-89)

Year	Power	Retail Low	Retail High
1989	T-Diesel	379,200	436,100
1988	T-Diesel	356,700	410,200
1987	T-Diesel	339,300	390,200
1986	T-Diesel	309,000	355,400
1985	T-Diesel	294,200	338,300
1984	T-Diesel	287,000	330,000
1983	T-Diesel	270,700	311,300
1982	T-Diesel	262,000	301,300
1981	T-Diesel	238,900	274,800
1980	T-Diesel	228,300	262,600

Hatteras 55 Conv. (1999-02) ******

Hatteras 56 Motor Yacht

Year	Power	Retail Low	Retail High
1985	T-Diesel	348,100	400,300
1984	T-Diesel	338,400	389,100
1983	T-Diesel	327,100	376,200
1982	T-Diesel	321,200	369,400
1981	T-Diesel	310,800	357,500
1980	T-Diesel	302,800	348,300

Hatteras 58 Cockpit MY

Year	Power	Retail Low	Retail High
1981	T-Diesel	254,500	292,700
1980	T-Diesel	247,300	284,400

Hatteras 58 Convertible

Year	Power	Retail Low	Retail High
1994	1040D	684,100	786,700
1994	1350D	772,800	888,700
1993	1040D	633,700	728,800
1993	1350D	724,200	832,900
1992	1040D	569,100	654,400
1992	1350D	646,700	743,700
1991	1040D	538,100	618,900
1991	1350D	613,400	705,500
1990	1040D	509,700	586,100
1990	1350D	575,200	661,500

Hatteras 58 LRC

Year	Power	Retail Low	Retail High
1981	T-Diesel	371,500	427,200
1980	T-Diesel	367,700	422,900

Hatteras 58 MY (1977-81)

Year	Power	Retail Low	Retail High
1981	T-Diesel	268,900	309,300
1980	T-Diesel	260,200	301,700

Hatteras 58 Motor Yacht (1985-87)

Year	Power	Retail Low	Retail High
1987	T-Diesel	466,300	536,200
1986	T-Diesel	458,800	527,600
1985	T-Diesel	450,600	518,200

Hatteras 58 YF

Year	Power	Retail Low	Retail High
1982	T-Diesel	287,000	330,100
1981	T-Diesel	279,500	321,400

Year	Power	Retail Low	Retail High
1980	T-Diesel	272,300	313,200

Hatteras 60 Convertible (1977-86)

Year	Power	Retail Low	Retail High
1986	840D	442,000	508,300
1985	650D	400,200	460,300
1985	840D	429,000	493,400
1984	650D	371,100	426,800
1984	840D	401,600	461,900
1983	650D	356,700	410,200
1983	840D	384,100	441,700
1982	650D	336,700	387,200
1982	840D	354,300	407,400
1981	650D	320,000	368,000
1980	650D	315,100	362,400

Hatteras 60 Convertible (Current)

Year	Power	Retail Low	Retail High
2004	T1400Cat	******	******
2003	T1400Cat	1,544,800	1,776,600
2002	T1400Cat	1,404,400	1,615,100
2001	T1400Cat	1,314,400	1,511,600
2000	T1400Cat	1,239,600	1,425,500
1999	T1400Cat	1,136,800	1,307,300
1998	T1350Cat	1,039,600	1,195,500

Hatteras 60 EDMY

Year	Power	Retail Low	Retail High
1997	870D	910,600	1,047,100
1996	870D	837,700	963,400
1995	870D	770,700	886,300
1994	870D	716,700	824,200
1993	870D	666,600	766,500
1992	870D	619,900	712,900
1991	870D	576,500	663,000

Hatteras 60 Motor Yacht

Year	Power	Retail Low	Retail High
1990	T-Diesel	570,100	655,600
1989	T-Diesel	553,600	636,600
1988	T-Diesel	537,600	618,200

Hatteras 61 Cockpit MY

Year	Power	Retail Low	Retail High
1985	T-Diesel	461,400	530,700
1984	T-Diesel	444,100	510,700
1983	T-Diesel	436,900	502,400
1982	T-Diesel	421,700	484,900
1981	T-Diesel	410,000	471,600

Hatteras 61 Motor Yacht

Year	Power	Retail Low	Retail High
1985	T-Diesel	460,400	529,500
1984	T-Diesel	444,300	511,000
1983	T-Diesel	435,100	500,400
1982	T-Diesel	417,400	480,000
1981	T-Diesel	406,800	467,800

Hatteras 63 Cockpit MY

Year	Power	Retail Low	Retail High
1987	T-Diesel	577,300	663,900
1986	T-Diesel	559,300	643,200
1985	T-Diesel	537,200	617,800

Hatteras 63 Motor Yacht

Year	Power	Retail Low	Retail High
1987	T-Diesel	576,800	663,400
1986	T-Diesel	558,900	642,700

Hatteras 6300 Raised Pilothouse

Year	Power	Retail Low	Retail High
2004	1500D	******	******
2003	1500D	1,792,000	2,060,800
2002	1400D	1,629,100	1,873,500
2001	1400D	1,521,100	1,749,200
2000	1400D	1,420,300	1,633,300

Hatteras 64 Motor Yacht

Year	Power	Retail Low	Retail High
1981	T-Diesel	356,700	410,200
1980	T-Diesel	350,800	403,400

Hatteras 65 Convertible (1987-99)

Year	Power	Retail Low	Retail High
1999	1400Cat	1,358,200	1,562,000
1998	1350D	1,293,900	1,488,000
1998	1450D	1,291,700	1,485,500
1997	1310D	1,188,000	1,366,200
1997	1400D	1,196,800	1,376,400
1996	1040D	1,028,200	1,182,500
1996	1350D	1,147,200	1,319,300
1995	1040D	934,800	1,075,100
1995	1350D	1,064,000	1,223,600
1994	1035D	904,000	1,039,600
1994	1350D	1,013,100	1,165,100
1993	1035D	886,200	1,019,100
1993	1350D	966,000	1,110,900
1992	1035D	852,500	980,400
1992	1350D	930,700	1,070,300
1991	1035D	782,100	899,400
1991	1235D	812,100	933,900
1990	1035D	716,200	823,600
1990	1235D	728,700	838,000
1989	1035D	679,900	781,900
1989	1235D	695,200	799,500
1988	1035D	655,300	753,600
1988	1235D	674,200	775,400
1987	1035D	628,100	722,300
1987	1235D	641,700	738,000

Hatteras 65 Conv. (2002-04)

Year	Power	Retail Low	Retail High
2004	1400Cat	******	******
2003	1400Cat	1,976,100	2,272,500
2002	1400Cat	1,796,500	2,065,900
2001	1400Cat	1,703,800	1,959,400
2000	1400Cat	1,547,000	1,779,000

Hatteras 65 LRC

Year	Power	Retail Low	Retail High
1986	T-Diesel	571,900	657,600
1985	T-Diesel	541,900	623,200
1984	T-Diesel	520,600	598,700
1983	T-Diesel	503,000	578,500
1982	T-Diesel	493,400	567,400
1981	T-Diesel	486,500	559,500

Hatteras 65 Motor Yacht

Year	Power	Retail Low	Retail High
1996	T-Diesel	1,018,500	1,171,300
1995	T-Diesel	959,700	1,103,700
1994	T-Diesel	891,400	1,025,100
1993	T-Diesel	831,100	955,700
1992	T-Diesel	777,900	894,600
1991	T-Diesel	723,400	831,900
1990	T-Diesel	666,600	766,500
1989	T-Diesel	623,500	717,000
1988	T-Diesel	616,800	709,400

Hatteras 67 Cockpit MY

Year	Power	Retail Low	Retail High
1991	T-Diesel	736,300	846,800
1990	T-Diesel	693,400	797,400
1989	T-Diesel	659,400	758,400
1988	T-Diesel	637,400	733,000

Hatteras 67 EDCMY

Year	Power	Retail Low	Retail High
1997	T1075D	******	******
1997	T1310D	******	******
1996	T870D	******	******
1996	T1040D	******	******
1995	T870D	******	******
1995	T1040D	******	******
1994	T870D	919,300	1,057,100
1994	T1040D	945,600	1,087,500

Year	Power	Retail Low	Retail High
1993	T870D	881,200	1,013,400
1993	T1040D	911,600	1,048,400
1992	T870D	827,700	951,900
1992	T1040D	859,400	988,400
1991	T870D	769,600	885,100
1991	T1040D	794,700	913,900

Hatteras 68 Cockpit MY

Year	Power	Retail Low	Retail High
1987	T-Diesel	572,400	658,300
1986	T-Diesel	559,500	643,400

Hatteras 68 Convertible ******

Hatteras 70 Cockpit MY

Year	Power	Retail Low	Retail High
1998	T1075D	******	******
1998	T1310D	******	******
1997	T1075D	1,205,400	1,386,200
1997	T1310D	1,218,200	1,400,900
1996	T870D	1,140,400	1,311,400
1996	T1040D	1,169,400	1,344,800
1995	T870D	1,059,000	1,217,900
1995	T1040D	1,089,000	1,252,400
1994	T870D	1,023,300	1,176,800
1994	T1040D	1,052,900	1,210,900
1993	T870D	987,600	1,135,700
1993	T1040D	1,015,400	1,167,700
1992	T870D	920,300	1,058,400
1992	T1040D	938,200	1,079,000
1991	T870D	847,100	974,900
1991	T1040D	874,800	1,006,100
1990	T870D	781,700	898,900
1990	T1040D	804,300	924,900
1989	T870D	774,200	890,300
1988	T870D	719,400	827,300

Hatteras 70 Convertible

Year	Power	Retail Low	Retail High
2004	1400D	******	******
2004	1800D	******	******
2003	1400D	2,221,700	2,555,000
2003	1800D	2,455,100	2,823,300
2002	1400D	2,019,800	2,322,700
2002	1800D	2,231,900	2,566,700
2001	1400D	1,849,400	2,126,900
2001	1800D	2,045,400	2,352,200
2000	1400D	1,742,300	2,003,700
2000	1800D	1,946,900	2,238,900
1999	1400D	1,631,400	1,876,100
1999	1800D	1,836,600	2,112,100
1998	1350D	1,519,000	1,746,800
1998	1800D	1,711,000	1,967,600

Hatteras 70 EDMY

Year	Power	Retail Low	Retail High
1983	T-Diesel	601,400	691,600
1982	T-Diesel	587,300	675,400
1981	T-Diesel	572,800	658,700
1980	T-Diesel	559,700	643,600

Hatteras 70 Motor Yacht (1971-81)

Year	Power	Retail Low	Retail High
1981	T-Diesel	538,700	619,600
1980	T-Diesel	513,000	590,000

Hatteras 70 Motor Yacht (1988-93)

Year	Power	Retail Low	Retail High
1993	T870D	998,700	1,148,600
1993	T1040D	1,022,400	1,175,800
1992	T870D	956,000	1,099,400
1992	T1040D	973,600	1,119,600
1991	T870D	880,200	1,012,200
1991	T1040D	905,200	1,041,000
1990	T870D	820,700	943,900
1990	T1040D	843,000	969,400

PRICES

Year	Power	Retail Low	Retail High
1989	T870D	783,200	900,700
1988	T870D	750,300	862,800

Hatteras 70 Sport Deck MY

Year	Power	Retail Low	Retail High
1998	T1110D	1,326,400	1,525,400
1998	T1350D	1,352,600	1,555,500
1997	T1075D	1,261,300	1,450,500
1997	T1310D	1,292,100	1,486,000
1996	T870D	1,165,900	1,340,800
1996	T1040D	1,221,900	1,405,200
1995	T870D	1,112,800	1,279,800
1995	T1040D	1,158,600	1,332,400

Hatteras 72 Motor Yacht

Year	Power	Retail Low	Retail High
1992	T-Diesel	981,600	1,128,900
1991	T-Diesel	920,900	1,059,000
1990	T-Diesel	882,700	1,015,100
1989	T-Diesel	840,600	966,700
1988	T-Diesel	800,500	920,600
1987	T-Diesel	773,400	889,400
1986	T-Diesel	725,900	834,700
1985	T-Diesel	710,000	816,500
1984	T-Diesel	683,700	786,200
1983	T-Diesel	652,000	749,900

Hatteras 74 Cockpit MY

Year	Power	Retail Low	Retail High
1999	T1400Cat	1,608,300	1,849,500
1998	T1350D	1,577,200	1,813,800
1997	T1350D	1,504,100	1,729,700
1996	T1350D	1,421,600	1,634,900

Hatteras 74 Sport Deck MY

Year	Power	Retail Low	Retail High
1999	T1400Cat	1,688,900	1,942,200
1998	T1350D	1,651,200	1,898,900
1997	T1350D	1,560,700	1,794,800
1996	T1350D	1,497,000	1,721,500

Hatteras 75 Cockpit MY

Year	Power	Retail Low	Retail High
2004	1400D	******	******
2003	1400D	******	******
2002	1400D	2,381,300	2,738,500
2001	1400D	2,284,600	2,627,300
2000	1400D	2,191,000	2,519,600

Hatteras 77 Cockpit MY

Year	Power	Retail Low	Retail High
1986	T-Diesel	926,600	1,065,600
1985	T-Diesel	876,100	1,007,500
1984	T-Diesel	847,700	974,900
1983	T-Diesel	789,300	907,700

Hatteras 80 MY ******

Henriques 28 Express Fish

Year	Power	Retail Low	Retail High
2004	T200D	135,500	155,800
2003	T200D	123,300	141,800
2002	T200D	112,200	129,000
2001	T200D	102,100	117,400
2000	T200D	93,900	108,000
1999	T200D	86,400	99,300
1998	T200D	79,500	91,400
1997	T200D	73,900	85,000
1996	T200D	68,700	79,000
1995	T200D	63,900	73,500
1994	T200D	59,400	68,400

Henriques 35 Express

Year	Power	Retail Low	Retail High
2004	T370D	240,600	276,600
2003	T370D	221,300	254,500
2002	T370D	203,600	234,100
2001	T370D	187,300	215,400
2000	T370D	172,300	198,200
1999	T370D	158,500	182,300

Henriques 35 Flybridge

Year	Power	Retail Low	Retail High
2004	T440D	288,300	331,500
2003	T440D	268,100	308,300
2002	T440D	249,300	286,700

Henriques 35 Maine Coaster SF

Year	Power	Retail Low	Retail High
2000	S420D	144,900	166,600
1999	S420D	133,000	153,000
1998	S420D	122,100	140,400
1997	S420D	116,800	134,400
1996	T-Diesel	111,200	127,900
1995	T-Diesel	104,400	120,100
1994	T-Diesel	98,100	112,800
1993	T-Diesel	91,800	105,600
1992	T-Diesel	84,600	97,200
1991	T-Diesel	79,800	91,800
1990	T-Diesel	78,400	90,100
1989	T-Diesel	74,400	85,600
1988	T-Diesel	69,300	79,700
1987	T-Diesel	62,600	72,000
1986	T-Diesel	56,500	64,900
1985	T-Diesel	51,500	59,200
1984	T-Diesel	45,900	52,800
1983	T-Diesel	44,600	51,300
1982	T-Diesel	43,200	49,700
1981	T-Diesel	41,100	47,300
1980	T-Diesel	39,800	45,700

Henriques 38 El Bravo

Year	Power	Retail Low	Retail High
2004	T480D	324,200	372,800
2003	T480D	298,200	343,000
2002	T450D	274,400	315,500
2001	T450D	252,400	290,300
2000	T450D	234,700	269,900
1999	T450D	218,300	251,000
1998	T450D	203,000	233,500
1997	T450D	188,800	217,100
1996	T420D	175,600	201,900
1995	T375D	163,300	187,800
1994	T375D	151,900	174,600
1993	T375D	141,200	162,400
1992	T-Diesel	131,300	151,000
1991	T-Diesel	122,100	140,500

Henriques 38 Sport Fisherman

Year	Power	Retail Low	Retail High
2004	T450D	348,400	400,600
2003	T450D	320,500	368,600
2002	T450D	294,800	339,100
2001	T450D	271,200	311,900
2000	T450D	252,300	290,100
1999	T450D	234,600	269,800
1998	T450D	218,200	250,900
1997	T450D	202,900	233,300
1996	T420D	188,700	217,000
1995	T375D	175,500	201,800
1994	T375D	163,200	187,700
1993	T375D	151,800	174,500
1992	T-Diesel	141,100	162,300
1991	T-Diesel	131,300	150,900
1990	T-Diesel	122,100	140,400
1989	T-Diesel	113,500	130,500
1988	T-Diesel	105,600	121,400

Henriques 42 Convertible ******

Henriques 44 Sport Fisherman

Year	Power	Retail Low	Retail High
2004	T660D	******	******
2003	T660D	523,100	601,500
2002	T660D	476,000	547,400
2001	T610D	433,100	498,100
2000	T600D	394,100	453,300
1999	T600D	362,600	417,000
1998	T550D	333,600	383,600
1997	T550D	306,900	352,900
1996	T550D	282,300	324,700
1995	T550D	259,800	298,700
1994	T550D	239,000	274,800
1993	T550D	219,800	252,800
1992	T-Diesel	202,300	232,600
1991	T-Diesel	186,100	214,000
1990	T-Diesel	171,200	196,900
1989	T-Diesel	157,500	181,100
1988	T-Diesel	144,900	166,600
1987	T-Diesel	133,300	153,300
1986	T-Diesel	122,600	141,000
1985	T-Diesel	112,800	129,700
1984	T-Diesel	103,800	119,400
1983	T-Diesel	95,500	109,800

Heritage East 36 Sundeck

Year	Power	Retail Low	Retail High
2004	S220D	172,400	198,200
2003	S220D	162,000	186,300
2002	S220D	152,300	175,100
2001	S220D	143,100	164,600
2000	S220D	134,600	154,700
1999	S220D	126,500	145,500
1998	S220D	120,100	138,200
1997	S220D	114,100	131,300

Heritage East 42 Sundeck

Year	Power	Retail Low	Retail High
2004	T-220D	337,500	388,100
2003	T-220D	317,200	364,800

Hi-Star 44 Convertible

Year	Power	Retail Low	Retail High
1992	T-Diesel	150,300	172,900
1991	T-Diesel	143,700	165,300
1990	T-Diesel	142,500	163,900
1989	T-Diesel	135,800	156,200
1988	T-Diesel	129,200	148,600
1987	T-Diesel	122,000	140,300
1986	T-Diesel	114,700	131,900

Hi-Star 48 Convertible

Year	Power	Retail Low	Retail High
1992	T-Diesel	171,100	196,700
1991	T-Diesel	162,600	187,000
1990	T-Diesel	154,600	177,800
1989	T-Diesel	149,100	171,500
1988	T-Diesel	140,700	161,800
1987	T-Diesel	132,800	152,800
1986	T-Diesel	127,400	146,500

Hi-Star 48 Motor Yacht

Year	Power	Retail Low	Retail High
1992	T-Diesel	192,500	221,400
1991	T-Diesel	185,100	212,900
1990	T-Diesel	175,900	202,200
1989	T-Diesel	167,800	193,000
1988	T-Diesel	160,600	184,600
1987	T-Diesel	152,900	175,800
1986	T-Diesel	146,300	168,200

Hi-Star 55 Yacht Fisherman

Year	Power	Retail Low	Retail High
1992	T-Diesel	231,900	266,700
1991	T-Diesel	217,600	250,300
1990	T-Diesel	207,100	238,100
1989	T-Diesel	199,700	229,700
1988	T-Diesel	188,700	217,000
1987	T-Diesel	178,500	205,200

PRICES

Year	Power	Retail Low	Retail High
1986	T-Diesel	169,800	195,300
Hi-Star 55 Pilothouse ******			
Hinckley Talaria 29C			
2004	S440D	207,600	238,800
2003	S370D	188,800	217,100
2002	S370D	173,600	199,700
Hinckley Tararia 29R ******			
Hinckley 36 Picnic Boat			
2004	S440 Jet	394,400	453,500
2004	S440 Jet	366,700	421,800
2002	S350 Jet	341,100	392,200
2001	S350 Jet	317,200	364,800
2000	S350 Jet	298,200	342,900
1999	S350 Jet	280,300	322,300
1998	S350 Jet	263,400	303,000
1997	S350 Jet	247,600	284,800
1996	S350 Jet	232,800	267,700
1995	S350 Jet	218,800	251,600
Hinkley Talaria 40 ******			
Hinckley Talaria 42 ******			
Hinckley Talaria 44			
2004	T440 Jet	******	******
2003	T440 Jet	845,200	971,900
2002	T440 Jet	786,000	903,900
2001	T440 Jet	738,800	849,700
2000	T440 Jet	694,500	798,700
1999	T440 Jet	652,800	750,700
Hinckley Talaria 44 FB ******			
Horizon 62 MY ******			
Horizon 70 MY (1998-2003)			
2003	T1350	1,585,600	1,823,400
2002	T1350	1,458,700	1,677,500
2001	T1350	1,342,000	1,543,300
2000	T1350	1,234,600	1,419,800
1999	T1350	1,135,900	1,306,300
1998	T1350	******	******
Horizon 70 MY (Current) ******			
Horizon 76 MY			
2004	T1400 D	1,925,000	2,213,700
2003	T1400 D	1,771,000	2,036,600
2002	T1400 D	1,629,300	1,873,700
2001	T1400 D	1,498,900	1,723,800
Hunt 29 Surfhunter			
2004	S310D	146,400	168,300
Hunt 33 Express			
2004	S370D	225,200	259,000
2003	S370D	193,100	222,100
2002	S370D	171,800	197,600
2001	S370D	157,800	181,400
2000	S370D	146,700	168,700
1999	S355D	136,400	156,900
Hunt 36 Harrier			
2004	T370D	326,500	375,400
Hydra-Sports 2550/2750 WA			
1998	T225/OB	42,800	49,200
1997	T225/OB	39,900	45,900
1996	T225/OB	36,300	41,700
1995	T225/OB	32,500	37,400
1994	T225/OB	28,800	33,200
1993	OB*	20,400	23,400
1992	OB*	18,800	21,600
1991	OB*	16,600	19,100
Hydra-Sports 2796/2800 Center Console			
2004	T225/OB	80,500	92,500
2003	T225/OB	71,600	82,300
2002	T225/OB	63,700	73,300
2001	T225/OB	56,700	65,200
2000	T225/OB	50,500	58,000
Hydra-Sports 2800 Walkaround			
2004	T225/OB	92,400	106,200
2003	T225/OB	82,200	94,500
2002	T225/OB	73,100	84,100
2001	T225/OB	65,100	74,900
Hydra-Sports 2800/3100 SF			
1998	T225 O/B	55,400	63,700
1997	T225 O/B	50,400	57,900
1996	T225 O/B	45,800	52,700
1995	T225 O/B	41,700	48,000
1994	T225 O/B	37,900	43,600
1993	T225 O/B	34,500	39,700
1992	T225 O/B	31,400	36,100
Hydra-Sports 3000 CC			
2000	T225/OB	63,900	73,500
1999	T225/OB	58,500	67,300
1998	T225/OB	51,000	58,600
1997	T225/OB	46,100	53,000
Hydra-Sports 3300 CC ******			
Hydra-Sports 3300 SF			
1992	T250 O/B	40,600	46,700
1991	T250 O/B	36,100	41,500
1990	T250 O/B	32,100	36,900
1989	T250 O/B	28,800	33,200
Independence 45 Trawler			
2000	S-Diesel	457,700	526,400
2000	T-Diesel	499,500	574,500
1999	S-Diesel	424,100	487,700
1999	T-Diesel	461,600	530,800
1998	S-Diesel	393,100	452,100
1998	T-Diesel	411,200	472,900
1997	S-Diesel	367,000	422,000
1997	T-Diesel	384,600	442,300
1996	S-Diesel	344,200	395,900
1996	T-Diesel	361,800	416,100
1995	S-Diesel	314,600	361,700
1995	T-Diesel	331,900	381,700
1994	S-Diesel	288,100	331,400
1994	T-Diesel	303,900	349,500
1993	S-Diesel	272,600	313,500
1993	T-Diesel	292,100	335,900
1992	S-Diesel	251,200	288,900
1992	T-Diesel	266,500	306,400
1991	S-Diesel	230,500	265,100
1991	T-Diesel	245,100	281,900
1990	S-Diesel	213,900	246,000
1990	T-Diesel	227,900	262,000
1989	S-Diesel	207,200	238,200
1989	T-Diesel	220,500	253,600
1988	S-Diesel	199,000	228,800
1988	T-Diesel	211,100	242,800
1987	S-Diesel	190,700	219,300
1987	T-Diesel	202,100	232,400
1986	S-Diesel	187,000	215,000
1985	S-Diesel	181,800	209,100
Intrepid 289 Center Console			
2003	T225 O/B	74,500	85,600
2002	T225 O/B	67,000	77,100
2001	T225 O/B	60,300	69,300
2000	T225 O/B	54,900	63,100
1999	T225 O/B	49,900	57,400
1998	T225 O/B	45,400	52,200
1997	T225 O/B	41,300	47,500
Intrepid 289 Walkaround			
2003	T225 O/B	80,100	92,100
2002	T225 O/B	72,000	82,900
2001	T225 O/B	64,800	74,600
2000	T225 O/B	59,000	67,800
1999	T225 O/B	53,700	61,700
1998	T225 O/B	48,800	56,200
1997	T225 O/B	44,400	51,100
Intrepid 30 Cuddy			
1996	T225 O/B	52,300	60,100
1995	T225 O/B	47,500	54,700
1994	T225 O/B	43,300	49,800
1993	T225 O/B	39,800	45,800
1992	T225 O/B	36,600	42,100
1991	T225 O/B	33,700	38,700
1990	T225 O/B	31,000	35,600
1989	T225 O/B	28,500	32,800
1988	T225 O/B	26,200	30,200
1987	T225 O/B	24,400	28,000
1986	T225 O/B	22,700	26,100
1985	T225 O/B	21,100	24,200
1984	T225 O/B	19,600	22,500
Intrepid 300 Center Console			
2004	T250 O/B	97,800	112,400
Intrepid 310 Walkaround ******			
Intrepid 322 Cuddy			
2003	T250 O/B	98,700	113,500
2002	T250 O/B	88,800	102,100
2001	T250 O/B	79,900	91,900
2000	T250 O/B	71,900	82,700
1999	T250 O/B	64,700	74,400
1998	T250 O/B	58,200	67,000
1997	T250 O/B	52,400	60,300
1996	T250 O/B	47,200	54,200
Intrepid 323 Cuddy			
2004	T250 O/B	113,200	130,100
Intrepid 33 Cuddy			
1996	T250 O/B	54,500	62,600
1995	T250 O/B	50,100	57,600
1994	T250 O/B	46,100	53,000
1993	T250 O/B	42,400	48,800
Intrepid 339 Center Console			
2001	T250 O/B	91,700	105,400
2000	T250 O/B	84,200	96,900
1999	T250 O/B	75,400	86,700
1998	T250 O/B	69,800	80,300
1997	T250 O/B	65,100	74,800
1996	T250 O/B	59,900	68,900
Intrepid 339 Walkaround			
2001	T250 O/B	99,700	114,600
2000	T250 O/B	90,600	104,200

PRICES

Year	Power	Retail Low	Retail High
1999	T250 O/B	81,500	93,700
1998	T250 O/B	75,800	87,100
1997	T250 O/B	71,000	81,600
1996	T250 O/B	65,600	75,500
1995	T250 O/B	60,300	69,400
Intrepid 348 Walkaround			
2004	T250 O/B	140,500	161,500
2003	T250 O/B	126,400	145,400
2002	T250 O/B	113,800	130,800
Intrepid 356 Cuddy			
2001	T250 O/B	110,500	127,000
2000	T250 O/B	100,500	115,600
1999	T250 O/B	91,500	105,200
1998	T250 O/B	83,200	95,700
1997	T250 O/B	75,700	87,100
1996	T250 O/B	69,700	80,100
1995	T250 O/B	64,100	73,700
1994	T250 O/B	59,000	67,800
Intrepid 366 Cuddy			
2003	T250 O/B	132,400	152,200
2002	T250 O/B	120,400	138,500
2001	T250 O/B	109,600	126,000
2000	T250 O/B	99,700	114,700
1999	T250/OB	90,700	104,400
Intrepid 370 Cuddy			
2004	3-250 O/B	184,500	212,100
2003	3-250 O/B	166,000	190,900
Intrepid 377 Walkaround			
2004	3-250 O/B	209,800	241,200
2003	3-250 O/B	188,800	217,100
2002	3-250 O/B	169,900	195,400
2001	3-250 O/B	152,900	175,800
2000	3-250 O/B	139,100	160,000
Intrepid 395 Walkaround			
2000	T450D	261,500	300,800
1999	T450D	245,200	282,000
1998	T420D	217,200	249,800
1997	T420D	195,200	224,500
Island Gypsy 30 Sedan			
1985	S-Diesel	40,300	46,400
1985	T-Diesel	43,800	50,400
1984	S-Diesel	38,600	44,400
1984	T-Diesel	41,900	48,200
1983	S-Diesel	36,600	42,100
1983	T-Diesel	39,900	45,900
1982	S-Diesel	35,300	40,600
1982	T-Diesel	38,600	44,400
1981	S-Diesel	33,400	38,400
1981	T-Diesel	36,000	41,400
1980	S-Diesel	32,000	36,900
1980	T-Diesel	34,600	39,800
Island Gypsy 32 Europa			
2000	S-Diesel	140,300	161,300
2000	T-Diesel	150,100	172,600
1999	S-Diesel	125,500	144,300
1999	T-Diesel	134,100	154,200
1998	S-Diesel	120,700	138,800
1998	T-Diesel	134,100	154,200
1997	S-Diesel	116,000	133,400
1997	T-Diesel	125,600	144,500
1996	S-Diesel	112,400	129,300
1996	T-Diesel	122,400	140,800
1995	S-Diesel	105,000	120,800
1995	T-Diesel	115,600	132,900
1994	S-Diesel	95,600	110,000
1994	T-Diesel	105,200	121,000
1993	S-Diesel	88,500	101,800
1993	T-Diesel	88,100	101,400
1992	S-Diesel	83,600	96,200
1992	T-Diesel	90,100	103,600
1991	S-Diesel	77,500	89,100
1991	T-Diesel	83,400	95,900
1990	S-Diesel	72,400	83,300
1990	T-Diesel	79,000	90,900
1989	S-Diesel	66,800	76,800
1989	T-Diesel	73,300	84,300
1988	S-Diesel	59,300	68,200
1988	S-Diesel	63,500	73,000
1987	S-Diesel	51,300	59,000
1987	T-Diesel	55,300	63,500
1986	S-Diesel	47,700	54,800
1986	T-Diesel	50,800	58,500
1985	S-Diesel	45,700	52,600
1985	T-Diesel	48,900	56,200
1984	S-Diesel	42,900	49,400
1984	T-Diesel	45,800	52,700
1983	S-Diesel	41,200	47,400
1983	T-Diesel	44,900	51,600
1982	S-Diesel	39,900	45,900
1982	T-Diesel	44,000	50,600
1981	S-Diesel	39,100	44,900
1981	T-Diesel	42,800	49,200
Island Gypsy 32 Fisherman			
1996	S-Diesel	94,600	108,800
1996	T-Diesel	101,900	117,200
1995	S-Diesel	82,700	95,200
1995	T-Diesel	93,800	107,800
1994	S-Diesel	74,500	85,700
1994	T-Diesel	85,700	98,600
1993	S-Diesel	69,000	79,300
1993	T-Diesel	80,100	92,100
1992	S-Diesel	62,800	72,200
1992	T-Diesel	75,800	87,100
1991	S-Diesel	58,300	67,000
1991	T-Diesel	71,800	82,500
1990	S-Diesel	53,100	61,100
1990	T-Diesel	64,300	74,000
1989	S-Diesel	47,900	55,000
1989	T-Diesel	59,500	68,400
1988	S-Diesel	40,100	46,100
1988	T-Diesel	48,900	56,300
1987	S-Diesel	34,500	39,700
1987	T-Diesel	40,100	46,100
Island Gypsy 32 Sedan			
1994	S-Diesel	91,800	105,500
1994	T-Diesel	101,200	116,400
1993	S-Diesel	84,800	97,500
1993	T-Diesel	91,100	104,800
1992	S-Diesel	80,100	92,100
1992	T-Diesel	86,500	99,500
1991	S-Diesel	74,200	85,400
1991	T-Diesel	80,100	92,100
1990	S-Diesel	69,900	80,300
1990	T-Diesel	75,800	87,200
1989	S-Diesel	64,600	74,200
1989	T-Diesel	70,500	81,100
1988	S-Diesel	56,600	65,100
1988	T-Diesel	60,600	69,700
1987	S-Diesel	49,400	56,800
1987	T-Diesel	52,700	60,600
1986	S-Diesel	46,200	53,200
1986	T-Diesel	49,000	56,400
1985	S-Diesel	43,800	50,300
1985	T-Diesel	46,500	53,500
1984	S-Diesel	40,400	46,400
1984	T-Diesel	41,700	48,000
1983	S-Diesel	37,100	42,600
1983	T-Diesel	39,900	45,900
1982	S-Diesel	34,200	39,300
1982	T-Diesel	37,100	42,600
1981	S-Diesel	32,000	36,900
1981	T-Diesel	34,900	40,200
Island Gypsy 36 Aft Cabin			
1990	S-Diesel	87,600	100,700
1990	T-Diesel	93,600	107,700
1989	S-Diesel	83,300	95,800
1989	T-Diesel	88,800	102,100
1988	S-Diesel	79,600	91,600
1988	T-Diesel	83,300	95,800
Island Gypsy 36 Classic			
2002	T210D	234,700	269,900
2001	T210D	221,900	255,200
2000	T210D	212,500	244,400
1999	T210D	202,400	232,800
1998	T210D	192,700	221,600
1997	T210D	184,800	212,500
1996	T210D	173,600	199,700
1995	T210D	164,800	189,600
Island Gypsy 36 Europa			
1999	T210 D	194,400	223,600
1998	T210 D	185,400	213,200
1997	T210 D	177,000	203,500
1996	T210 D	166,900	192,000
1995	T-Diesel	158,700	182,600
1994	T-Diesel	142,900	164,400
1994	S-Diesel	118,400	136,100
1993	T-Diesel	126,700	145,700
1993	S-Diesel	105,000	120,800
1992	T-Diesel	112,900	129,800
1992	S-Diesel	97,000	111,600
1991	T-Diesel	104,600	120,300
1991	S-Diesel	92,000	105,900
1990	T-Diesel	99,500	114,500
1990	S-Diesel	85,800	98,600
1989	T-Diesel	92,700	106,600
1989	S-Diesel	79,500	91,400
1988	T-Diesel	85,800	98,600
1988	S-Diesel	75,300	86,600
Island Gypsy 36 Motor Yacht			
2002	T210D	225,700	259,600
2001	T210D	210,200	241,700
2000	T210D	199,300	229,200
1999	T210D	190,600	219,200
1998	T210D	185,000	212,800
1997	T210D	175,100	201,300
1996	T210D	163,000	187,400
1995	T210D	150,500	173,100
Island Gypsy 36 Quad Cabin			
1994	S-Diesel	116,700	134,200
1994	T-Diesel	124,800	143,600

Year	Power	Retail Low	Retail High
1993	S-Diesel	107,100	123,200
1993	T-Diesel	115,900	133,200
1992	S-Diesel	99,600	114,500
1992	T-Diesel	107,100	123,200
1991	S-Diesel	93,300	107,300
1991	T-Diesel	100,800	115,900
1990	S-Diesel	87,600	100,700
1990	T-Diesel	94,500	108,700
1989	S-Diesel	81,700	93,900
1989	T-Diesel	87,900	101,100
1988	S-Diesel	76,000	87,500
1988	T-Diesel	81,100	93,200
1987	S-Diesel	70,400	81,000
1987	T-Diesel	75,400	86,800
1986	S-Diesel	65,500	75,300
1986	T-Diesel	69,800	80,300
1985	S-Diesel	59,800	68,800
1985	T-Diesel	64,200	73,800
1984	S-Diesel	57,100	65,700
1984	T-Diesel	61,000	70,100
1983	S-Diesel	52,600	60,600
1983	T-Diesel	56,500	65,000
1982	S-Diesel	48,800	56,100
1982	T-Diesel	52,600	60,600
1981	S-Diesel	45,400	52,200
1981	T-Diesel	49,300	56,700
1980	S-Diesel	43,200	49,600
1980	T-Diesel	46,500	53,500

Island Gypsy 40 Classic

Year	Power	Retail Low	Retail High
1998	T300D	241,800	278,000
1997	T300D	224,000	257,600
1996	T300D	210,400	242,000
1995	T135D	179,800	206,800
1995	T300D	197,500	227,100
1994	T135D	170,700	196,300
1994	T300D	181,200	208,300
1993	T135D	161,500	185,800

Island Gypsy 40 Europa

Year	Power	Retail Low	Retail High
1998	T210D	226,300	260,300
1997	T210D	212,900	244,800
1996	T210D	193,700	222,700
1995	T210D	183,400	210,900

Island Gypsy 40 Flush Aft Deck

Year	Power	Retail Low	Retail High
1994	T135D	157,700	181,300
1994	T375D	181,200	208,400
1993	T135D	149,300	171,700
1993	T375D	172,700	198,600
1992	T135D	144,600	166,300
1992	T375D	167,900	193,100
1991	T135D	142,200	163,500
1991	T375D	159,900	183,900
1990	T135D	135,300	155,600
1990	T375D	151,700	174,400
1989	T135D	127,000	146,100
1989	T375D	143,400	165,000
1988	T135D	117,500	135,200
1988	T375D	130,200	149,700
1987	T135D	108,000	124,300
1987	T375D	114,400	131,500
1986	T135D	95,800	110,100

Island Gypsy 40 Motor Cruiser

Year	Power	Retail Low	Retail High
1994	T135D	153,000	175,900
1994	T375D	170,600	196,200
1993	T135D	146,100	168,000

Year	Power	Retail Low	Retail High
1993	T375D	163,600	188,100
1992	T135D	138,300	159,100
1992	T375D	155,300	178,600
1991	T135D	128,600	147,900
1991	T375D	145,600	167,500
1990	T135D	123,800	142,400
1990	T375D	139,900	160,900
1989	T135D	115,700	133,100
1989	T375D	131,900	151,700
1988	T135D	107,700	123,900
1988	T375D	122,000	140,300
1987	T135D	99,600	114,600
1987	T375D	112,100	128,900
1986	T135D	91,600	105,400
1986	T375D	104,600	120,300

Island Gypsy 44 Flush Aft Deck

Year	Power	Retail Low	Retail High
2002	T-Diesel	******	******
2001	T-Diesel	******	******
1996	T300D	******	******
1995	T300D	******	******
1995	T135D	******	******
1994	T300D	******	******
1994	T135D	******	******
1993	T300D	175,700	202,100
1993	T135D	193,900	223,000
1992	T300D	166,600	191,600
1992	T135D	182,400	209,700
1991	T375D	157,500	181,100
1991	T135D	174,500	200,700
1990	T375D	154,100	177,200
1990	T135D	168,400	193,700
1989	T375D	142,900	164,300
1989	T135D	161,500	185,800
1988	T375D	134,800	155,000
1987	T135D	121,800	140,100
1986	T135D	111,600	128,400
1985	T135D	107,000	123,000
1984	T135D	101,600	116,900
1983	T135D	98,500	113,300
1982	T135D	96,500	111,000
1981	T120D	93,100	107,100
1980	T120D	90,300	103,800

Island Gypsy 44 Motor Cruiser

Year	Power	Retail Low	Retail High
2001	T-Diesel	******	******
1996	T370D	******	******
1995	T370D	******	******
1995	T375D	******	******
1994	T135D	******	******
1994	T300D	******	******
1993	T135D	******	******
1993	T300D	******	******
1992	T135D	172,000	197,800
1992	T375D	191,400	220,100
1991	T135D	164,300	189,000
1991	T375D	184,100	211,800
1990	T135D	156,100	179,500
1990	T375D	176,300	202,700
1989	T135D	154,200	177,400
1989	T375D	168,600	193,900
1988	T135D	137,400	158,000
1987	T375D	156,100	179,500
1986	T135D	132,000	151,800
1985	T135D	120,900	139,000
1984	T135D	114,400	131,500
1983	T135D	105,300	121,100

Islander 34 Convertible

Year	Power	Retail Low	Retail High
2002	T-315D	******	******
2001	T-315D	212,500	244,300
2000	T-315D	193,200	222,100
1999	T-315D	175,300	201,500
1998	T-315D	157,700	181,400
1997	T-315D	141,900	163,200
1996	T-315D	127,700	146,900
1995	T-315D	115,000	132,200
1994	T-315D	103,500	119,000
1993	T-315D	93,100	107,100

Jefferson 31 Marlago

Year	Power	Retail Low	Retail High
2003	T200 O/B	75,600	86,900
2002	T200 O/B	68,000	78,200
2001	T200 O/B	61,200	70,400
2000	T200 O/B	55,700	64,000
1999	T200 O/B	50,700	58,300
1998	T200 O/B	46,100	53,000
1997	T200 O/B	41,900	48,200
1996	T200 O/B	38,200	43,900

Jefferson 35 Marlago

Year	Power	Retail Low	Retail High
2004	T225 O/B	96,400	110,800
2003	T225 O/B	86,700	99,700
2002	T225 O/B	78,000	89,700
2001	T225 O/B	70,200	80,800
2000	T225 O/B	63,200	72,700
1999	T225 O/B	56,900	65,400
1998	T225 O/B	51,200	58,900
1997	T225 O/B	46,100	53,000
1996	T225 O/B	41,400	47,700
1995	T225 O/B	37,300	42,900
1994	T225 O/B	33,600	38,600

Jefferson 37 Convertible

Year	Power	Retail Low	Retail High
1994	T300D	111,200	127,900
1993	T300D	104,400	120,100
1992	T300D	97,700	112,300
1991	T300D	91,400	105,200
1990	T300D	86,300	99,200
1989	T300D	83,900	96,500
1988	T300D	81,300	93,500

Jefferson 37 Sundeck

Year	Power	Retail Low	Retail High
1994	T300D	122,100	140,400
1994	T375D	134,100	154,200
1993	T300D	115,100	132,400
1993	T375D	126,400	145,300
1992	T300D	107,900	124,100
1992	T375D	119,300	137,200
1991	T300D	101,000	116,100
1991	T375D	111,400	128,100
1990	T300D	97,100	111,700
1990	T375D	104,700	120,400
1989	T300D	88,400	101,600
1989	T375D	98,300	113,000
1988	T300D	83,800	96,300
1988	T375D	93,100	107,000

Jefferson 42 Sundeck

Year	Power	Retail Low	Retail High
1989	T210D	127,000	146,100
1989	T375D	141,900	163,200
1988	T210D	115,900	133,300
1988	T320D	129,600	149,100
1987	T200D	108,300	124,500
1987	T320D	121,000	139,100
1986	T200D	100,800	115,900

PRICES

Year	Power	Retail Low	Retail High
1986	T320D	113,500	130,500
1985	T200D	96,700	111,200
1985	T300D	110,400	127,000
Jefferson 42 Viscount Sundeck			
1999	T330D	233,300	268,300
1999	T370D	245,200	282,000
1998	T330D	216,200	248,600
1998	T370D	229,600	264,100
1997	T315D	205,000	235,800
1997	T370D	218,400	251,200
1996	T300D	192,700	221,700
1996	T375D	205,800	236,700
1995	T300D	183,000	210,500
1995	T375D	194,600	223,800
1994	T300D	166,100	191,000
1994	T375D	177,000	203,500
1993	T300D	158,200	181,900
1993	T375D	168,400	193,700
1992	T300D	146,800	168,900
1992	T375D	157,000	180,600
1991	T300D	140,700	161,800
1991	T375D	148,000	170,200
1990	T300D	129,500	149,000
1990	T375D	135,700	156,100
Jefferson 43 Marlago SD			
2001	T450D	291,400	335,100
2000	T315D	258,500	297,300
2000	T420D	276,000	317,400
1999	T315D	245,400	282,200
1999	T420D	260,500	299,500
1998	T315D	235,000	270,300
1998	T420D	249,700	287,100
1997	T315D	217,700	250,400
1997	T420D	231,900	266,700
1996	T300D	204,700	235,400
1996	T425D	228,600	262,900
1995	T300D	187,000	215,100
1995	T425D	211,800	243,600
1994	T300D	172,000	197,800
1994	T425D	197,000	226,500
1993	T300D	167,200	192,300
1993	T425D	184,300	212,000
1992	T300D	152,500	175,400
1992	T425D	170,700	196,400
1991	T300D	145,600	167,400
1991	T425D	160,400	184,400
Jefferson 45 Motor Yacht			
1989	T200D	133,300	153,300
1989	T320D	146,900	169,000
1988	T200D	123,400	141,900
1988	T320D	135,300	155,600
1987	T200D	114,600	131,800
1987	T320D	124,000	142,600
1986	T200D	106,400	122,400
1986	T320D	115,900	133,300
1985	T200D	100,100	115,200
1985	T320D	108,900	125,300
1984	T200D	93,700	107,800
1984	T320D	102,600	118,000
1983	T200D	87,900	101,100
1983	T320D	97,600	112,200
1982	T200D	82,100	94,400
1982	T320D	91,100	104,800
Jefferson 46 Marlago SD			

Year	Power	Retail Low	Retail High
2001	T450D	314,100	361,200
2000	T430D	293,600	337,600
1999	T430D	279,500	321,500
1998	T430D	268,000	308,200
1997	T375D	248,300	285,600
1996	T375D	232,300	267,200
1995	T300D	204,400	235,100
1995	T375D	221,900	255,200
1994	T300D	192,000	220,800
1994	T375D	213,400	245,400
1993	T300D	183,700	211,300
1993	T375D	197,500	227,200
1992	T300D	168,700	194,000
1992	T375D	180,100	207,100
1991	T300D	162,100	186,400
1991	T375D	170,500	196,100
Jefferson 46 Sundeck			
1989	T200D	141,300	162,500
1989	T375D	155,700	179,100
1988	T200D	131,200	150,900
1988	T375D	143,800	165,300
1987	T200D	120,200	138,200
1987	T375D	130,900	150,500
1986	T200D	111,300	128,000
1986	T375D	120,700	138,900
1985	T200D	103,700	119,300
1985	T375D	113,200	130,100
Jefferson 48 Rivanna Sundeck			
2001	T420D	391,300	449,900
2000	T420D	349,900	402,400
1999	T450D	329,400	378,900
1998	T450D	316,500	363,900
1997	T420D	299,200	344,100
1996	T300D	267,400	307,500
1996	T425D	291,800	335,600
1995	T300D	246,900	283,900
1995	T425D	269,200	309,600
1994	T300D	236,600	272,100
1994	T425D	256,000	294,400
1993	T300D	220,100	253,200
1993	T425D	236,600	272,100
1992	T300D	211,000	242,700
1992	T425D	223,200	256,700
1991	T300D	200,100	230,100
1991	T425D	210,500	242,100
1990	T300D	189,200	217,600
1990	T425D	200,100	230,100
Jefferson 50 Rivanna SE			
2004	480D	500,500	575,500
Jefferson 52 Marquessa MY (Std.)			
2001	600D	537,500	618,100
2000	600D	486,200	559,200
1999	550D	457,800	526,500
1998	550D	443,400	509,900
1997	550D	421,300	484,500
1996	550D	391,000	449,600
1995	550D	366,200	421,200
1994	550D	346,200	398,100
1993	550D	315,600	362,900
1992	550D	291,700	335,400
1991	550D	273,400	314,400
1990	550D	251,200	288,900
1989	550D	242,000	278,300
Jefferson 52 Monticello MY			

Year	Power	Retail Low	Retail High
1989	T-Diesel	223,000	256,400
1988	T-Diesel	205,100	235,900
1987	T-Diesel	188,700	217,000
1986	T-Diesel	173,600	199,600
Jefferson 52 Rivanna CMY			
2001	450D	******	******
2000	450D	******	******
1999	450D	******	******
1998	450D	372,300	428,100
1997	450D	342,500	393,800
1996	450D	315,100	362,300
1995	435D	289,900	333,300
1994	435D	266,700	306,700
1993	435D	245,300	282,100
Jefferson 5300 International			
2002	T635D	547,000	629,000
2001	T635D	503,200	578,700
2000	T635D	462,900	532,400
1999	T600D	425,900	489,800
1998	T600D	391,800	450,600
Jefferson 56 Marquessa CMY			
2001	600D	493,200	567,100
2000	600D	458,600	527,400
1999	550D	426,500	490,500
1998	550D	396,700	456,200
1997	550D	368,900	424,200
1996	550D	343,100	394,500
1995	550D	319,000	366,900
1994	550D	296,700	341,200
1993	550D	275,900	317,300
1992	550D	256,600	295,100
1991	550D	238,700	274,500
Jefferson 56 Rivanna CMY ******			
Jefferson 57 Pilothouse			
2004	635D	900,100	1,035,100
2003	635D	837,000	962,600
2002	635D	778,400	895,200
2001	600D	724,000	832,600
Jefferson 60 Marquessa CMY			
2004	635D	873,400	1,004,400
2003	635D	812,200	934,100
2002	635D	755,400	868,700
2001	635D	702,500	807,900
2000	600D	653,300	751,300
1999	600D	607,600	698,700
Jefferson 60 Marquessa MY			
1992	T-Diesel	445,000	511,800
1991	T-Diesel	433,700	498,800
1990	T-Diesel	406,900	467,900
1989	T-Diesel	390,900	449,500
1988	T-Diesel	361,900	416,200
1987	T-Diesel	348,000	400,200
Jersey 36 Dawn Convertible			
1992	T-Gas	97,700	112,300
1992	T-Diesel	115,500	132,800
1991	T-Gas	89,700	103,200
1991	T-Diesel	107,700	123,800
1990	T-Gas	80,700	92,900
1990	T-Diesel	98,700	113,500
1989	T-Gas	74,700	85,900
1989	T-Diesel	89,700	103,200
1988	T-Gas	68,800	79,100

PRICES

Year	Power	Retail Low	Retail High
1988	T-Diesel	83,700	96,300
1987	T-Gas	63,600	73,200
1987	T-Diesel	78,800	90,600
1986	T-Gas	57,500	66,200
1986	T-Diesel	72,700	83,600
Jersey 40 Dawn Convertible			
1988	T-Diesel	112,200	129,000
1987	T-Diesel	101,300	116,500
1986	T-Diesel	94,500	108,700
1985	T-Diesel	84,100	96,700
1984	T-Diesel	76,700	88,300
1983	T-Diesel	70,900	81,500
1982	T-Diesel	66,500	76,500
1981	T-Diesel	61,500	70,700
1980	T-Diesel	56,900	65,500
Jersey 42 Dawn Convertible			
1992	T-Diesel	207,400	238,600
1991	T-Diesel	194,700	223,900
1990	T-Diesel	180,300	207,400
1989	T-Diesel	161,000	185,100
Jersey 47 Dawn Convertible			
1992	T-Diesel	215,800	248,200
1991	T-Diesel	210,000	241,500
1990	T-Diesel	199,600	229,500
1989	T-Diesel	190,200	218,800
1988	T-Diesel	179,600	206,600
1987	T-Diesel	162,100	186,500
Johnson 56/58 Motor Yacht			
2004	800D	******	******
2003	800D	******	******
2002	800D	******	******
2001	800D	754,500	867,600
2000	800D	701,600	806,900
1999	800D	652,500	750,400
1998	735D	606,800	697,900
1997	735D	564,400	649,000
1996	735D	524,800	603,600
1995	735D	488,100	561,300
1994	735D	453,900	522,000
1993	735D	422,200	485,500
1992	735D	392,600	451,500
Johnson 63/65 MY			
2002	T1150 MTU	******	******
2001	T1150 MTU	******	******
2000	T1150 MTU	1,038,500	1,194,200
1999	T1150 MTU	984,500	1,132,200
1998	T1100 MAN	941,400	1,082,600
1997	T1100 MAN	896,700	1,031,200
1996	T1100 MAN	859,800	988,800
1995	T1100 MAN	803,000	923,400
1994	T1100 MAN	744,700	856,400
1993	T1100 MAN	690,000	793,500
1992	T735D	601,700	692,000
1991	T735D	560,200	644,200
1990	T735D	534,600	614,800
Johnson 70 MY ******			
Jupiter 27 Open			
2004	T225 O/B	88,300	101,500
2003	T225 O/B	79,400	91,300
2002	T225 O/B	71,500	82,200
2001	T225 O/B	64,300	74,000
2000	T225 O/B	58,500	67,300
1999	T225 O/B	53,300	61,300

Year	Power	Retail Low	Retail High
1998	T225 O/B	48,500	55,700
Jupiter 31 Open			
2004	T250 O/B	118,300	136,000
2003	T250 O/B	107,600	123,800
2002	T250 O/B	97,900	112,600
2001	T250 O/B	89,100	102,500
2000	T250 O/B	82,000	94,300
1999	T250 O/B	75,400	86,700
1998	T250 O/B	69,400	79,800
1996	T250 O/B	63,800	73,400
1995	T225 O/B	58,700	67,500
1994	T225 O/B	54,600	62,800
1993	T225 O/B	50,800	58,400
1992	T225 O/B	47,200	54,300
1991	T225 O/B	43,900	50,500
1990	T225 O/B	40,800	47,000
1989	T225 O/B	38,000	43,700
Jupiter 35 Conv. ******			
Kha Shing 40 Sundeck			
1995	T-Diesel	******	******
1995	T-Diesel	******	******
1994	T-Diesel	******	******
1994	T-Diesel	******	******
1993	T-Diesel	******	******
1993	T-Diesel	******	******
1992	T150D	134,900	155,100
1992	T250D	148,600	170,900
1991	T150D	132,100	152,000
1991	T250D	143,900	165,500
1990	T150D	126,200	145,200
1990	T250D	134,600	154,800
1989	T150D	120,700	138,800
1989	T250D	128,300	147,600
1988	T150D	113,200	130,200
1988	T250D	120,100	138,100
1987	T150D	103,700	119,300
1987	T250D	110,700	127,300
1986	T165D	96,900	111,400
1986	T260D	104,000	119,600
1985	T165D	88,900	102,300
1985	T260D	96,100	110,500
1984	T165D	85,100	97,900
1984	T260D	92,500	106,400
1983	T165D	81,200	93,400
1983	T260D	88,700	102,000
1982	T165D	78,200	90,000
1982	T260D	85,800	98,700
1981	T165D	76,100	87,600
1981	T260D	82,800	95,200
1980	T165D	71,200	81,900
1980	T260D	79,100	91,000
Krogen 36 Manatee			
1991	S-Diesel	99,800	114,700
1990	S-Diesel	95,400	109,700
1989	S-Diesel	93,200	107,200
1988	S-Diesel	91,700	105,500
1987	S-Diesel	90,000	103,600
1986	S-Diesel	85,000	97,800
1985	S-Diesel	80,500	92,500
1984	S-Diesel	78,300	90,000
Krogen 39 Trawler			
2004	S-Diesel	423,500	487,000
2003	S-Diesel	393,800	452,900
2002	S-Diesel	366,200	421,200

Year	Power	Retail Low	Retail High
2001	S-Diesel	340,600	391,700
2000	S-Diesel	320,200	368,200
1999	S-Diesel	300,900	346,100
1998	S-Diesel	282,900	325,300
Krogen 42 Trawler			
1998	S-Diesel	327,200	376,300
1997	S-Diesel	308,900	355,200
1996	S-Diesel	294,600	338,800
1995	S-Diesel	270,000	310,500
1994	S-Diesel	249,800	287,300
1993	S-Diesel	232,100	266,900
1992	S-Diesel	212,500	244,400
1991	S-Diesel	201,100	231,300
1990	S-Diesel	191,300	220,000
1989	S-Diesel	181,600	208,900
1988	S-Diesel	173,600	199,600
1987	S-Diesel	165,600	190,400
1986	S-Diesel	159,100	183,000
1985	S-Diesel	152,700	175,700
1984	S-Diesel	142,000	163,300
1983	S-Diesel	135,200	155,500
1982	S-Diesel	127,800	147,000
1981	S-Diesel	121,000	139,100
1980	S-Diesel	114,300	131,400
Krogen 44 Trawler			
2004	S-Diesel	588,400	676,600
Krogen 48 North Sea Trawler			
2004	S-Diesel	******	******
2003	S-Diesel	******	******
2002	S-Diesel	595,500	684,800
2001	S-Diesel	547,800	630,000
2000	S-Diesel	504,000	579,600
1999	S-Diesel	463,700	533,200
1998	S-Diesel	426,600	490,600
1997	S-Diesel	392,400	451,300
1996	S-Diesel	361,000	415,200
1995	S-Diesel	332,200	382,000
Krogen 48 Whaleback			
2003	S-Diesel	******	******
2002	S-Diesel	593,000	682,000
2001	S-Diesel	560,900	645,000
2000	S-Diesel	541,500	622,700
1999	S-Diesel	520,100	598,100
1998	S-Diesel	475,200	546,500
1997	S-Diesel	442,900	509,300
1996	S-Diesel	405,100	465,900
1995	S-Diesel	357,500	411,200
1994	S-Diesel	318,900	366,800
1993	S-Diesel	298,400	343,100
1992	S-Diesel	276,100	317,600
Krogen Express 49 ******			
Krogen 52 Express ******			
Krogen 54 Trawler ******			
Krogen 58 Trawler			
2004	S-Diesel	1,215,000	1,397,200
2003	S-Diesel	1,117,800	1,285,400
2002	S-Diesel	1,028,300	1,182,600
2001	S-Diesel	946,100	1,088,000
LaBelle 40 MY			
1988	T200D	110,400	127,000
1987	T200D	105,100	120,900
1986	T200D	97,800	112,400

PRICES

IMPORTANT! See Page 293 for Regional Price Adjustment.

Year	Power	Retail Low	Retail High
1985	T200D	90,900	104,500
1984	T200D	85,700	98,500
1983	T200D	80,200	92,300
LaBelle 43 Motor Yacht			
1988	T-Diesel	124,500	143,200
1987	T-Diesel	115,600	132,900
1986	T-Diesel	107,500	123,600
1985	T-Diesel	100,000	115,000
1984	T-Diesel	93,300	107,400
1983	T-Diesel	88,100	101,400
LaBelle 44 CPMY			
1988	T200D	141,400	162,600
1987	T200D	136,300	156,800
1986	T200D	128,800	148,200
1985	T200D	120,500	138,500
1984	T200D	114,700	131,900
1983	T200D	109,800	126,200
Lagoon 43 ******			
Larson 270 Cabrio			
2001	S310 I/O	40,900	47,000
2000	S310 I/O	36,900	42,500
1999	S310 I/O	33,600	38,600
1998	S310 I/O	27,900	32,100
1997	S300 I/O	23,900	27,500
1996	S300 I/O	21,300	24,400
Larson 270 Mirado; 270 Cabrio			
1993	S-I/O Gas	17,000	19,600
1993	T-I/O Gas	18,900	21,700
1992	S-I/O Gas	15,800	18,100
1992	T-I/O Gas	17,600	20,300
1991	S-I/O Gas	14,300	16,400
1991	T-I/O Gas	15,800	18,100
1990	S-I/O Gas	13,200	15,200
1990	T-I/O Gas	14,600	16,900
1989	S-I/O Gas	12,400	14,300
1989	T-I/O Gas	13,900	16,000
Larson 274 Cabrio			
2004	S300 I/O	52,800	60,700
2003	S300 I/O	46,900	54,000
2002	S300 I/O	41,800	48,000
Larson 280/290 Cabrio			
2001	T260 I/O	60,200	69,200
2001	S320 I/O	51,600	59,300
2000	T260 I/O	54,100	62,300
2000	S320 I/O	46,400	53,400
1999	T260 I/O	48,700	56,000
1999	S310 I/O	41,700	48,000
1998	T260 I/O	43,800	50,400
1998	S310 I/O	37,600	43,200
1997	T260 I/O	39,400	45,400
1997	S310 I/O	33,800	38,900
1996	T250 I/O	35,500	40,800
1996	S300 I/O	30,400	35,000
1995	T250 I/O	31,900	36,700
1995	S300 I/O	27,400	31,500
1994	T250 I/O	28,700	33,100
1994	S300 I/O	24,600	28,300
Larson 300/310 Cabrio			
1998	T260 I/O	50,700	58,300
1997	T260 I/O	46,300	53,200
1996	T260 I/O	41,500	47,700
1995	T260 I/O	37,800	43,500
1994	T250 I/O	35,300	40,600
1993	T250 I/O	31,900	36,700
1992	T250 I/O	29,800	34,300
1991	T250 I/O	27,600	31,800
Larson 310 Cabrio			
2004	T280 I/O	103,400	118,900
2003	T280 I/O	93,000	107,000
Larson 330 Cabrio			
2004	T280 I/O	123,200	141,600
2003	T280 I/O	112,100	128,900
2002	T280 I/O	102,000	117,300
2001	T280 I/O	92,800	106,700
2000	T280 I/O	84,400	97,100
1999	T280 I/O	76,800	88,400
Larson 370 Cabrio			
2004	T370 I/O	176,500	202,900
Lazzara 68 MY ******			
Lazzara 76 Motor Yacht			
2004	T-Diesel	******	******
2003	T-Diesel	******	******
2002	T-Diesel	2,331,500	2,681,300
2001	T-Diesel	2,178,000	2,504,800
2000	T-Diesel	2,056,400	2,364,800
1999	T-Diesel	1,950,000	2,242,500
1998	T-Diesel	1,866,300	2,146,300
1997	T-Diesel	1,806,900	2,078,000
1996	T-Diesel	1,714,800	1,972,100
1995	T-Diesel	1,615,700	1,858,100
1994	T-Diesel	1,531,200	1,760,900
1993	T-Diesel	1,451,900	1,669,600
Lazzara 80 Cockpit MY ******			
Lazzara 80 SC Skylounge ******			
Lazzara 80 E MY ******			
Legacy 28 Express			
2004	S315D	145,600	167,400
2003	S300D	133,900	154,000
2002	S300D	123,200	141,700
2001	S300D	113,300	130,300
2000	S250D	105,400	121,200
1999	S250D	98,000	112,700
Legacy 34 Express			
2004	T315D	******	******
2003	T300D	264,900	304,600
2002	T300D	246,300	283,300
2001	T330D	229,100	263,400
2000	T330D	213,000	245,000
1999	T270D	198,100	227,800
1998	T270D	184,200	211,900
1997	T270D	171,300	197,000
1996	T270D	159,300	183,200
Legacy 40 Sedan			
2004	T440D	******	******
2003	T440D	392,900	451,800
2002	S450D	361,400	415,600
2001	S450D	332,500	382,400
2000	S450D	309,200	355,600
1999	S420D	287,600	330,700
1998	S420D	267,400	307,600
1997	S420D	248,700	286,000
1996	S375D	231,300	266,000
1995	S375D	215,100	247,400
Legacy 40 Express			
2004	T440D	******	******
2003	T440D	442,300	508,600
2002	T370D	406,900	467,900
2001	T370D	374,300	430,500
2000	T370D	348,100	400,300
1999	T370D	323,700	372,300
1998	T370D	301,100	346,200
Lien Hwa 47 CPMY			
1999	S250D	******	******
1998	T375D	******	******
1997	T375D	255,200	293,500
1996	T375D	239,700	275,700
1995	T375D	219,300	252,100
1994	T375D	204,300	234,900
1993	T375D	188,200	216,500
1992	T375D	174,200	200,300
1991	T375D	165,400	190,200
1990	T375D	155,800	179,200
1989	T375D	149,300	171,700
1988	S250D	142,000	163,300
Litton 41 Trawler ******			
Lord Nelson 37 Victory Tug			
1989	S-Diesel	169,000	194,300
1988	S-Diesel	162,200	186,500
1987	S-Diesel	155,700	179,100
1986	S-Diesel	149,500	171,900
1985	S-Diesel	143,500	165,000
1984	S-Diesel	137,700	158,400
1983	S-Diesel	132,100	152,100
Luhrs 280 Open ******			
Luhrs 290 (1986-88)			
1988	T-Gas	23,400	26,900
1987	T-Gas	22,500	25,900
1986	T-Gas	19,900	22,900
Luhrs 290 (1989-90)			
1990	T-Gas	27,700	31,900
1989	T-Gas	25,500	29,400
Luhrs 290 Open			
2002	T-Gas	90,600	104,200
2002	T-Diesel	121,100	139,300
2001	T-Gas	80,900	93,000
2001	T-Diesel	108,900	125,300
2000	T-Gas	72,900	83,900
2000	T-Diesel	97,400	112,100
1999	T-Gas	68,500	78,800
1999	T-Diesel	91,500	105,200
1998	T-Gas	63,700	73,200
1998	T-Diesel	86,000	98,900
1997	T-Gas	54,500	62,700
1997	T-Diesel	69,200	79,600
1996	T-Gas	49,200	56,600
1996	T-Diesel	60,500	69,600
1995	T-Gas	44,600	51,300
1995	T-Diesel	57,500	66,100
1994	T-Gas	41,000	47,100
1994	T-Diesel	51,200	58,900
1993	T-Gas	37,100	42,600
1993	T-Diesel	47,400	54,500
1992	T-Gas	32,400	37,300
1992	T-Diesel	42,600	49,000

PRICES

Year	Power	Retail Low	Retail High
Luhrs 30 Alura			
1990	S-Gas	23,700	27,300
1989	S-Gas	20,800	24,000
1988	S-Gas	18,900	21,800
1987	S-Gas	17,300	19,900
1986	S-Gas	16,000	18,400
Luhrs 30 Open			
2004	T320G	125,300	144,000
2004	T315D	150,400	172,900
Luhrs 300 Express			
1996	T270G	55,800	64,200
1996	T170D	71,000	81,600
1995	T270G	50,500	58,100
1995	T170D	66,000	75,900
1994	T270G	46,900	54,000
1994	T170D	59,300	68,200
1993	T260G	44,000	50,600
1993	T170D	55,600	63,900
1992	T260G	40,200	46,200
1992	T170D	50,700	58,300
1991	T260G	30,200	34,700
1991	T170D	37,500	43,100
Luhrs 32 Convertible			
2002	T325G	112,700	129,600
2002	T315D	156,500	180,000
2001	T325G	110,600	127,200
2001	T300D	146,500	168,500
Luhrs 32 Open			
2002	T-Gas	116,800	134,300
2002	T-Diesel	158,900	182,800
2001	T-Gas	105,700	121,600
2001	T-Diesel	140,600	161,700
2000	T-Gas	96,500	110,900
2000	T-Diesel	133,000	153,000
1999	T-Gas	89,700	103,100
1999	T-Diesel	124,200	142,800
1998	T-Gas	82,900	95,400
1998	T-Diesel	115,200	132,500
1997	T-Gas	78,800	90,600
1997	T-Diesel	105,900	121,800
1996	T-Gas	71,400	82,100
1996	T-Diesel	93,300	107,300
1995	T-Gas	61,600	70,900
1995	T-Diesel	83,700	96,300
1994	T-Gas	53,900	62,000
1994	T-Diesel	77,900	89,600
Luhrs 320 Convertible			
1999	T-Gas	93,000	106,900
1999	T-Diesel	126,800	145,800
1998	T-Gas	86,400	99,400
1998	T-Diesel	112,000	128,800
1997	T-Gas	79,000	90,900
1997	T-Diesel	105,900	121,800
1996	T-Gas	72,000	82,900
1996	T-Diesel	93,300	107,300
1995	T-Gas	61,900	71,100
1995	T-Diesel	83,100	95,500
1994	T-Gas	53,100	61,000
1994	T-Diesel	76,000	87,400
1993	T-Gas	49,100	56,400
1993	T-Diesel	68,200	78,400
1992	T-Gas	46,000	53,000
1992	T-Diesel	61,800	71,000
1991	T-Gas	43,000	49,500
1991	T-Diesel	55,200	63,500
1990	T-Gas	37,000	42,500
1990	T-Diesel	51,200	58,800
1989	T-Gas	33,900	39,000
1989	T-Diesel	45,300	52,100
1988	T-Gas	29,900	34,300
1988	T-Diesel	41,100	47,300
Luhrs 34 Convertible			
2003	T320G	160,300	184,300
2003	T-315D	199,500	229,400
2002	T375G	152,300	175,100
2002	T300D	183,500	211,000
2001	T310D	138,500	159,300
2001	T300D	168,800	194,100
2000	T310G	126,100	145,000
2000	T300D	153,600	176,700
Luhrs 340 SF			
1987	T-Gas	37,100	42,700
1987	T-Diesel	44,200	50,800
1986	T-Gas	33,400	38,400
1986	T-Diesel	39,900	45,800
1985	T-Gas	31,600	36,300
1985	T-Diesel	36,800	42,300
1984	T-Gas	29,700	34,200
1984	T-Diesel	34,300	39,500
1983	T-Gas	25,700	29,600
1983	T-Diesel	31,900	36,700
Luhrs 3400 Motor Yacht			
1992	T-Gas	52,300	60,100
1991	T-Gas	46,300	53,200
1990	T-Gas	40,800	47,000
Luhrs 342 Convertible			
1989	T-Gas	45,200	52,000
1989	T-Diesel	54,700	62,900
1988	T-Gas	42,900	49,400
1988	T-Diesel	51,100	58,800
1987	T-Gas	39,300	45,200
1987	T-Diesel	47,800	55,000
1986	T-Gas	35,700	41,100
1986	T-Diesel	41,200	47,400
Luhrs 3420 Motor Yacht			
1993	T-Gas	52,300	60,100
1992	T-Gas	49,200	56,500
1991	T-Gas	43,500	50,100
Luhrs Alura 35			
1989	T-Gas	36,800	42,300
1989	T-Diesel	46,000	52,900
1988	T-Gas	34,500	39,700
1988	T-Diesel	42,000	48,300
Luhrs 350 Convertible			
1996	T-Gas	108,600	124,800
1996	T-Diesel	125,300	144,000
1995	T-Gas	99,900	114,800
1995	T-Diesel	116,500	134,000
1994	T-Gas	91,900	105,700
1994	T-Diesel	108,300	124,600
1993	T-Gas	84,500	97,200
1993	T-Diesel	100,700	115,900
1992	T-Gas	77,800	89,400
1992	T-Diesel	93,700	107,700
1991	T-Gas	71,500	82,300
1991	T-Diesel	87,100	100,200
1990	T-Gas	65,800	75,700
1990	T-Diesel	81,000	93,200
Luhrs 36 Convertible			
2004	T-Gas	211,900	243,600
2004	T420D	265,300	305,000
2003	T-Gas	192,800	221,700
2003	T420D	244,000	280,600
2002	T-Gas	175,400	201,700
2002	T420D	224,500	258,200
2001	T-Gas	159,600	183,600
2001	T420D	206,500	237,500
2000	T-Gas	146,900	168,900
2000	T420D	192,100	220,900
1999	T-Gas	135,100	155,400
1999	T420D	178,600	205,400
1998	T-Gas	124,300	142,900
1998	T420D	166,100	191,000
Luhrs 36 Open			
2004	T-Gas	207,900	239,000
2004	T420D	261,300	300,400
2003	T-Gas	189,100	217,500
2003	T420D	240,300	276,400
2002	T-Gas	172,100	197,900
2002	T-420D	221,100	254,300
2001	T-Gas	156,600	180,100
2001	T420D	203,400	233,900
2000	T-Gas	144,100	165,700
2000	T420D	189,200	217,600
1999	T-Gas	132,600	152,400
1999	T420D	175,900	202,300
1998	T-Gas	121,900	140,200
1998	T420D	163,600	188,200
1997	T-Gas	113,400	130,400
1997	T420D	152,200	175,000
Luhrs 380/40 Convertible			
2003	T420D	277,800	319,400
2002	T420D	252,700	290,700
2001	T420D	230,000	264,500
2000	T420D	211,600	243,300
1999	T420D	194,700	223,900
1998	T420D	179,100	206,000
1997	T420D	164,800	189,500
1996	T420D	151,600	174,300
1995	T420D	141,000	162,100
1994	T420D	131,100	150,800
1993	T485D	121,900	140,200
1992	T485D	113,400	130,400
1991	T485D	105,400	121,300
1990	T485D	98,000	112,800
1989	T485D	91,200	104,900
Luhrs 380/40 Open			
2004	T420D	******	******
2003	T420D	298,400	343,200
2002	T420D	273,800	314,800
2001	T420D	249,100	286,500
2000	T420D	226,700	260,700
1999	T420D	208,500	239,800
1998	T420D	191,900	220,600
1997	T420D	176,500	203,000
1996	T420D	162,400	186,700
1995	T420D	149,400	171,800
1994	T420D	138,900	159,800
1993	T485D	129,200	148,600
1992	T485D	120,200	138,200

PRICES

Year	Power	Retail Low	Retail High
1991	T485D	111,700	128,500
Luhrs 400 Convertible			
1990	T-Gas	79,600	91,600
1990	T-Diesel	95,500	109,800
1989	T-Gas	69,500	79,900
1989	T-Diesel	87,900	101,000
1988	T-Gas	63,900	73,400
1988	T-Diesel	81,900	94,200
1987	T-Gas	59,900	68,700
1987	T-Diesel	76,700	88,200
Luhrs 41 Convertible			
2004	T535D	448,000	515,200
Luhrs 44 Convertible			
2004	T500D	485,200	557,900
2003	T500D	436,600	502,100
Luhrs 50 Convertible			
2003	T900D	******	******
2002	T900D	718,400	826,200
2001	T900D	651,700	749,400
2000	T800D	588,400	676,700
1999	T800D	529,200	608,600
Magnum 40 Sport ******			
Magnum 53 Sport ******			
Magnum 63 Sport ******			
Mainship Pilot 30			
2004	S315D	108,600	124,800
2004	S315D	97,700	112,400
2002	S230D	87,900	101,100
2001	S230D	79,100	91,000
2000	S230D	71,200	81,900
1999	S230D	64,100	73,700
1998	S230D	57,700	66,300
Mainship Pilot 30 Sedan			
2004	S315D	123,200	141,600
2004	S315D	110,800	127,500
2002	S230D	99,700	114,700
2001	S230D	89,800	103,200
2000	S230D	80,800	92,900
Mainship 30 Sedan			
1983	S124D	23,200	26,700
1982	S124D	21,500	24,800
1981	S124D	19,800	22,800
Mainship 31 Sedan Bridge			
1999	T-Gas	81,100	93,300
1998	T-Gas	74,300	85,500
1997	T-Gas	67,900	78,100
1996	T-Gas	61,700	71,000
1995	T-Gas	56,000	64,400
1994	T-Gas	52,200	60,000
Mainship 34			
1982	S-Diesel	36,800	42,300
1981	S-Diesel	34,900	40,100
1980	S-Diesel	32,900	37,800
Mainship 34 II			
1982	S-Diesel	33,600	38,700
1981	S-Diesel	32,000	36,800
1980	S-Diesel	30,800	35,400
Mainship 34 III			
1988	S-Diesel	47,900	55,100

Year	Power	Retail Low	Retail High
1987	S-Diesel	46,100	53,000
1986	S-Diesel	44,400	51,100
1985	S-Diesel	42,100	48,400
1984	S-Diesel	40,500	46,600
1983	S-Diesel	38,200	43,900
Mainship 34 Motor Yacht			
1999	T320G	******	******
1998	T320G	101,400	116,600
1997	T340G	95,700	110,100
1996	T340G	89,500	102,900
Mainship 34 Pilot			
2004	S370D	155,400	178,700
2003	S370D	141,400	162,600
2002	S300D	128,600	147,900
2001	S300D	117,100	134,600
2000	S300D	107,700	123,800
1999	S300D	99,100	113,900
Mainship 34 Pilot Sedan			
2004	S370D	161,200	185,300
2003	S370D	146,600	168,600
2002	S300D	133,400	153,500
2001	S300D	121,400	139,600
2000	S300D	111,700	128,500
1999	S300D	102,800	118,200
Mainship 34 Trawler ******			
Mainship 35 Convertible			
1994	T-Gas	68,100	78,400
1993	T-Gas	63,800	73,400
1992	T-Gas	58,200	66,900
1991	T-Gas	53,000	61,000
1990	T-Gas	48,500	55,800
1989	T-Gas	44,500	51,100
1988	T-Gas	41,100	47,200
Mainship 35 Open; 36 Express			
1994	T-Gas	66,500	76,500
1993	T-Gas	60,500	69,500
1992	T-Gas	56,000	64,400
1991	T-Gas	51,600	59,300
1990	T-Gas	48,200	55,400
Mainship 35 Open; 36 Sedan Bridge			
1992	T-Gas	62,200	71,600
1991	T-Gas	56,500	65,000
1990	T-Gas	50,900	58,600
Mainship 350/390 Trawler			
2004	S-Diesel	224,500	258,100
2004	T-240D	242,300	278,600
2003	S-Diesel	204,200	234,900
2003	T-240D	220,400	253,500
2002	S-Diesel	185,900	213,700
2002	T-240D	200,600	230,700
2001	S-Diesel	169,100	194,500
2001	T-230D	182,500	209,900
2000	S-Diesel	155,600	178,900
2000	T-230D	167,900	193,100
1999	S-Diesel	143,100	164,600
1999	T-200	154,500	177,700
1998	S-Diesel	131,700	151,400
1998	T-Diesel	142,100	163,500
1997	S-Diesel	121,100	139,300
1997	T-Diesel	130,800	150,400
1996	S-Diesel	111,500	128,200
1996	T-Diesel	120,300	138,300

Year	Power	Retail Low	Retail High
Mainship 36 Double Cabin			
1989	T-Gas	66,700	76,700
1989	T-Diesel	84,900	97,700
1988	T-Gas	61,400	70,600
1988	T-Diesel	75,800	87,200
1987	T-Gas	54,300	62,500
1987	T-Diesel	68,400	78,700
1986	T-Gas	52,100	59,900
1986	T-Diesel	61,700	71,000
1985	T-Gas	48,600	55,900
1985	T-Diesel	56,200	64,600
1984	T-Gas	44,800	51,600
1984	T-Diesel	52,400	60,300
Mainship 36 Sedan			
1988	T-Gas	53,100	61,100
1987	T-Gas	47,100	54,100
1986	T-Gas	43,000	49,500
Mainship 37 Motor Yacht			
1998	T-320G	130,500	150,100
1997	T-320G	116,800	134,300
1996	T-340G	105,400	121,300
1995	T-340G	96,100	110,500
Mainship 39 Express			
1993	T380G	76,600	88,100
1992	T380G	70,600	81,100
1991	T-360G	65,600	75,500
1990	T-360G	61,900	71,200
1989	T-360G	57,900	66,600
Mainship 40 Double Cabin			
1988	T-Gas	76,500	88,000
1988	T-Diesel	90,900	104,600
1987	T-Gas	72,600	83,500
1987	T-Diesel	85,800	98,700
1986	T-Gas	68,500	78,800
1986	T-Diesel	80,400	92,500
1985	T-Gas	60,700	69,800
1985	T-Diesel	72,500	83,400
1984	T-Gas	55,200	63,400
1984	T-Diesel	66,200	76,100
Mainship 40 Motor Cruiser			
1984	T-Diesel	77,100	88,700
1983	T-Diesel	74,600	85,800
1982	T-Diesel	70,900	81,600
1981	T-Diesel	67,800	78,000
1980	T-Diesel	66,900	77,000
Mainship 40 Sedan Bridge			
1999	T-320G	127,700	146,900
1998	T-320G	119,300	137,200
1997	T-320G	110,700	127,400
1996	T-340G	101,500	116,800
1995	T-340G	90,500	104,100
1994	T-340G	85,500	98,300
1993	T-340G	81,600	93,800
Mainship 400 Trawler			
2004	S370D	264,500	304,100
2003	S315D	240,600	276,700
Mainship 41 Convertible			
1992	T-Gas	88,100	101,400
1992	T-Diesel	114,300	131,500
1991	T-Gas	82,000	94,300
1991	T-Diesel	103,800	119,300
1990	T-Gas	75,700	87,000

PRICES

Year	Power	Retail Low	Retail High
1990	T-Diesel	96,700	111,200
1989	T-Gas	71,200	81,900
1989	T-Diesel	90,400	103,900
Mainship 41 Grand Salon			
1990	T-Gas	69,300	79,700
1990	T-Diesel	90,500	104,100
1989	T-Gas	62,700	72,100
1989	T-Diesel	81,400	93,600
Mainship 430 Trawler			
2004	T370D	428,900	493,200
2003	T315D	390,200	448,800
2002	T315D	355,100	408,400
2001	T300D	323,200	371,600
2000	T300D	294,100	338,200
1999	T300D	267,600	307,700
Mainship 47 Motor Yacht			
1999	T-Diesel	335,900	386,300
1998	T-Diesel	312,800	359,700
1997	T-Diesel	291,600	335,300
1996	T-Diesel	272,700	313,600
1995	T-Diesel	254,000	292,100
1994	T-Diesel	237,400	273,000
1993	T-Diesel	222,400	255,700
1991	T-Diesel	198,600	228,400
1990	T-Diesel	179,900	206,900
Mako 260B/270B/273B WA			
1994	T200 O/B	27,800	31,900
1993	T200 O/B	25,500	29,400
1992	T200 O/B	23,500	27,000
1991	T200 O/B	21,600	24,800
1990	T200 O/B	19,900	22,900
Mako 282 Center Console			
2003	T255 O/B	53,500	61,500
2002	T255 O/B	47,600	54,800
2001	T255 O/B	42,800	49,300
2000	T255 O/B	38,400	44,100
1999	T255 O/B	35,400	40,700
1998	T255 O/B	33,400	38,500
1997	T255 O/B	29,300	33,700
1996	T255 O/B	25,200	29,000
1995	T255 O/B	22,700	26,100
Mako 286 Inboard			
1995	T-Gas	50,700	58,300
1994	T-Gas	47,800	55,000
1993	T-Gas	44,700	51,400
1992	T-Gas	41,600	47,900
1991	T-Gas	37,000	42,500
1990	T-Gas	31,500	36,300
1989	T-Gas	29,200	33,600
1988	T-Gas	27,400	31,500
1987	T-Gas	24,700	28,400
1986	T-Gas	22,300	25,700
1985	T-Gas	20,300	23,400
Mako 293 Walkaround			
2003	T250 O/B	82,400	94,700
2002	T250 O/B	74,100	85,200
2001	T250 O/B	66,700	76,700
2000	T250 O/B	60,700	69,800
1999	T250 O/B	55,200	63,500
1998	T250 O/B	50,200	57,800
1997	T250 O/B	45,700	52,600
1996	T250 O/B	41,600	47,800
1995	T250 O/B	38,300	44,000

Year	Power	Retail Low	Retail High
1994	T250 O/B	35,200	40,500
1993	T250 O/B	32,400	37,200
Mako 295 Center Console			
1997	T250 O/B	40,900	47,100
1996	T250 O/B	36,200	41,700
Mako 295 Side Console Cuddy			
1999	T250 O/B	57,400	66,000
1998	T250 O/B	48,800	56,100
1997	T250 O/B	43,300	49,800
1996	T250 O/B	38,700	44,500
1995	T250 O/B	34,700	40,000
1994	T250 O/B	31,700	36,500
1993	T250 O/B	28,400	32,600
Make 314 Cuddy			
2004	T250 O/B	96,700	111,200
2003	T250 O/B	87,000	100,000
2002	T250 O/B	78,300	90,000
Mako 333 Express			
2000	T250 O/B	83,400	95,900
1999	T250 O/B	75,000	86,300
1998	T250 O/B	67,500	77,600
1997	T250 O/B	60,700	69,900
Marine Trader 34 DC			
2004	S-Diesel	******	******
2003	S-Diesel	******	******
2002	S-Diesel	138,500	159,300
2001	S-Diesel	129,800	149,200
2000	S-Diesel	123,300	141,700
1999	S-Diesel	116,300	133,800
1998	S-Diesel	109,900	126,400
1997	S-Diesel	102,100	117,400
1996	S-Diesel	96,700	111,200
1995	S-Diesel	89,100	102,500
1994	S-Diesel	86,300	99,200
1993	S-Diesel	82,600	95,000
1992	S-Diesel	75,900	87,300
1991	S-Diesel	72,300	83,100
1990	S-Diesel	66,500	76,500
1989	S-Diesel	62,100	71,500
1988	S-Diesel	57,900	66,500
1987	S-Diesel	54,400	62,600
1986	S-Diesel	52,100	59,900
1985	S-Diesel	49,100	56,500
1984	S-Diesel	46,700	53,700
1983	S-Diesel	44,300	51,000
1982	S-Diesel	42,100	48,400
1981	S-Diesel	40,000	46,000
1980	S-Diesel	38,000	43,700
Marine Trader 34 Sedan			
2004	S-Diesel	******	******
2003	S-Diesel	******	******
2002	S-Diesel	137,100	157,700
2001	S-Diesel	129,400	148,800
2000	S-Diesel	122,300	140,700
1999	S-Diesel	114,700	131,900
1998	S-Diesel	108,100	124,300
1997	S-Diesel	99,800	114,700
1996	S-Diesel	93,800	107,800
1995	S-Diesel	89,000	102,400
1994	S-Diesel	86,200	99,200
1993	S-Diesel	83,000	95,500
1992	S-Diesel	76,000	87,400
1991	S-Diesel	70,500	81,100

Year	Power	Retail Low	Retail High
1990	S-Diesel	66,100	76,000
1989	S-Diesel	59,900	68,900
1988	S-Diesel	57,400	66,000
1987	S-Diesel	53,700	61,800
1986	S-Diesel	50,800	58,500
1985	S-Diesel	48,700	56,000
1984	S-Diesel	46,400	53,400
1983	S-Diesel	44,100	50,800
1982	S-Diesel	41,900	48,200
1981	S-Diesel	39,700	45,700
1980	S-Diesel	37,800	43,500
Marine Trader 36 Double Cabin			
1993	S-Diesel	97,200	111,800
1993	T-Diesel	105,500	121,300
1992	S-Diesel	92,600	106,500
1992	T-Diesel	100,300	115,300
1991	S-Diesel	86,400	99,400
1991	T-Diesel	94,300	108,400
1990	S-Diesel	80,700	92,800
1990	T-Diesel	87,800	101,000
1989	S-Diesel	74,400	85,600
1989	T-Diesel	81,400	93,700
1988	S-Diesel	68,000	78,200
1988	T-Diesel	75,100	86,400
1987	S-Diesel	61,600	70,900
1987	T-Diesel	68,700	79,000
1986	S-Diesel	57,400	66,000
1986	T-Diesel	63,800	73,300
1985	S-Diesel	52,700	60,600
1985	T-Diesel	59,300	68,200
1984	S-Diesel	49,900	57,400
1984	T-Diesel	56,600	65,100
1983	S-Diesel	47,600	54,800
1983	T-Diesel	52,800	60,800
1982	S-Diesel	44,700	51,400
1982	T-Diesel	50,600	58,200
1981	S-Diesel	43,200	49,700
1981	T-Diesel	47,600	54,800
1980	S-Diesel	40,600	46,700
1980	T-Diesel	45,100	51,900
Marine Trader 36 Sedan			
1993	S-Diesel	96,800	111,300
1993	T-Diesel	105,300	121,100
1992	S-Diesel	92,100	106,000
1992	T-Diesel	100,000	115,000
1991	S-Diesel	85,900	98,800
1991	T-Diesel	93,100	107,000
1990	S-Diesel	80,900	93,000
1990	T-Diesel	88,100	101,300
1989	S-Diesel	74,500	85,600
1989	T-Diesel	81,600	93,800
1988	S-Diesel	68,000	78,200
1988	T-Diesel	75,200	86,500
1987	S-Diesel	62,300	71,600
1987	T-Diesel	69,400	79,800
1986	S-Diesel	58,000	66,700
1986	T-Diesel	64,400	74,100
1985	S-Diesel	54,900	63,200
1985	T-Diesel	61,700	71,000
1984	S-Diesel	50,400	58,000
1984	T-Diesel	57,200	65,800
1983	S-Diesel	48,200	55,400
1983	T-Diesel	53,400	61,400
1982	S-Diesel	45,200	51,900
1982	T-Diesel	51,200	58,900

PRICES

PRICES

Year	Power	Retail Low	Retail High
1981	S-Diesel	43,700	50,200
1981	T-Diesel	48,200	55,400
1980	S-Diesel	40,700	46,800
1980	T-Diesel	45,200	51,900
Marine Trader 36 Sundeck			
1993	S-Diesel	102,400	117,800
1993	T-Diesel	111,000	127,600
1992	S-Diesel	97,700	112,300
1992	T-Diesel	105,700	121,500
1991	S-Diesel	91,300	105,000
1991	T-Diesel	99,400	114,300
1990	S-Diesel	85,500	98,300
1990	T-Diesel	92,800	106,800
1989	S-Diesel	79,600	91,600
1989	T-Diesel	87,000	100,000
1988	S-Diesel	73,000	84,000
1988	T-Diesel	80,400	92,500
1987	S-Diesel	66,500	76,400
1987	T-Diesel	73,800	84,800
1986	S-Diesel	62,100	71,400
1986	T-Diesel	68,700	79,000
1985	S-Diesel	54,700	63,000
1985	T-Diesel	61,300	70,500
Marine Trader 38 Double Cabin			
2004	S-Diesel	204,400	235,000
2004	T-Diesel	222,900	256,400
2003	S-Diesel	185,800	213,700
2003	T-Diesel	202,800	233,200
2002	S-Diesel	180,600	207,700
2002	T-Diesel	196,800	226,300
2001	S-Diesel	171,600	197,400
2001	T-Diesel	185,800	213,700
2000	S-Diesel	165,000	189,700
2000	T-Diesel	178,600	205,400
1999	S-Diesel	153,300	176,300
1999	T-Diesel	168,600	194,000
1998	S-Diesel	140,100	161,100
1998	T-Diesel	153,700	176,800
1997	S-Diesel	132,600	152,500
1997	T-Diesel	146,200	168,200
1996	S-Diesel	128,500	147,700
1996	T-Diesel	140,400	161,400
1995	S-Diesel	124,800	143,600
1995	T-Diesel	134,800	155,000
1994	S-Diesel	120,500	138,600
1994	T-Diesel	129,800	149,300
1993	S-Diesel	113,800	130,900
1993	T-Diesel	124,000	142,600
1992	S-Diesel	106,700	122,700
1992	T-Diesel	115,200	132,500
1991	S-Diesel	100,400	115,400
1991	T-Diesel	108,800	125,200
1990	S-Diesel	92,900	106,900
1990	T-Diesel	101,700	117,000
1989	S-Diesel	85,800	98,700
1989	T-Diesel	93,700	107,800
1988	S-Diesel	82,800	95,200
1988	T-Diesel	89,400	102,800
1987	S-Diesel	75,300	86,700
1987	T-Diesel	83,600	96,200
1986	S-Diesel	68,700	79,000
1986	T-Diesel	77,600	89,200
1985	S-Diesel	64,900	74,600
1985	T-Diesel	73,800	84,900
1984	S-Diesel	61,800	71,100

Year	Power	Retail Low	Retail High
1984	T-Diesel	69,700	80,100
1983	S-Diesel	57,400	66,000
1983	T-Diesel	65,300	75,100
1982	S-Diesel	53,100	61,000
1982	T-Diesel	61,000	70,100
1981	S-Diesel	50,400	58,000
1981	T-Diesel	57,900	66,600
1980	S-Diesel	47,900	55,100
1980	T-Diesel	55,000	63,300
Marine Trader 38 Sedan			
1994	S-Diesel	120,500	138,500
1994	T-Diesel	129,900	149,400
1993	S-Diesel	115,900	133,300
1993	T-Diesel	124,200	142,900
1992	S-Diesel	111,400	128,100
1992	T-Diesel	119,000	136,900
1991	S-Diesel	106,800	122,900
1991	T-Diesel	113,300	130,200
1990	S-Diesel	103,400	118,900
1990	T-Diesel	109,300	125,700
1989	S-Diesel	97,700	112,400
1989	T-Diesel	102,900	118,400
1988	S-Diesel	91,300	105,000
1988	T-Diesel	96,500	111,000
1987	S-Diesel	83,600	96,100
1987	T-Diesel	88,700	102,100
Tradewinds 39 Sundeck			
1994	T135D	135,400	155,800
1993	T135D	128,300	147,500
1992	T135D	121,200	139,300
1991	T135D	115,900	133,300
1990	T135D	108,700	125,000
1989	T135D	102,100	117,500
Marine Trader 40 Double Cabin			
1986	S-Diesel	81,500	93,700
1986	T-Diesel	90,000	103,500
1985	S-Diesel	75,300	86,600
1985	T-Diesel	83,000	95,500
1984	S-Diesel	70,600	81,200
1984	T-Diesel	77,600	89,300
1983	S-Diesel	57,400	66,100
1983	T-Diesel	72,900	83,900
1982	S-Diesel	55,000	63,300
1982	T-Diesel	69,800	80,300
1981	S-Diesel	51,200	58,900
1981	T-Diesel	66,800	76,800
1980	S-Diesel	56,700	65,200
1980	T-Diesel	63,600	73,100
Marine Trader 40 Sedan			
1986	S-Diesel	76,300	87,700
1986	T-Diesel	84,400	97,000
1985	S-Diesel	69,700	80,200
1985	T-Diesel	77,000	88,600
1984	S-Diesel	65,300	75,100
1984	T-Diesel	71,900	82,700
1983	S-Diesel	62,200	71,600
1983	T-Diesel	68,200	78,400
1982	S-Diesel	59,200	68,100
1982	T-Diesel	66,000	75,900
1981	S-Diesel	56,300	64,800
1981	T-Diesel	62,200	71,600
1980	S-Diesel	52,600	60,500
1980	T-Diesel	58,500	67,300

Year	Power	Retail Low	Retail High
Marine Trader 40 Sundeck			
2004	S-Diesel	******	******
2004	T-Diesel	******	******
2003	S-Diesel	******	******
2003	T-Diesel	******	******
2002	S-Diesel	206,700	237,800
2002	T-Diesel	219,600	252,600
2001	S-Diesel	207,500	238,600
2001	T-Diesel	221,600	254,900
2000	S-Diesel	191,800	220,600
2000	T-Diesel	204,900	235,700
1999	S-Diesel	174,600	200,800
1999	T-Diesel	185,700	213,600
1998	S-Diesel	163,200	187,700
1998	T-Diesel	175,400	201,800
1997	S-Diesel	149,000	171,300
1997	T-Diesel	161,000	185,200
1996	S-Diesel	139,000	159,900
1996	T-Diesel	150,700	173,300
1995	S-Diesel	131,000	150,600
1995	T-Diesel	143,100	164,600
1994	S-Diesel	124,200	142,800
1994	T-Diesel	139,000	159,800
1993	S-Diesel	120,000	138,000
1993	T-Diesel	130,200	149,800
1992	S-Diesel	116,300	133,800
1992	T-Diesel	125,400	144,200
1991	S-Diesel	111,900	128,700
1991	T-Diesel	118,900	136,800
1990	S-Diesel	105,500	121,300
1990	T-Diesel	111,900	128,700
1989	S-Diesel	99,200	114,100
1989	T-Diesel	104,800	120,500
1988	S-Diesel	93,900	108,000
1988	T-Diesel	99,600	114,600
1987	S-Diesel	88,500	101,800
1987	T-Diesel	94,400	108,500
1986	S-Diesel	83,400	95,900
1986	T-Diesel	90,400	104,000
1985	S-Diesel	79,700	91,600
1985	T-Diesel	85,800	98,700
1984	S-Diesel	76,700	88,200
1984	T-Diesel	83,900	96,500
1983	S-Diesel	74,000	85,100
1983	T-Diesel	80,700	92,900
Tradewinds 43 Motor Yacht			
1997	T-Diesel	188,200	216,400
1996	T-Diesel	173,600	199,700
1995	T-Diesel	157,600	181,200
1994	T-Diesel	149,000	171,400
1993	T-Diesel	143,200	164,700
1992	T-Diesel	135,100	155,300
1991	T-Diesel	130,000	149,600
1990	T-Diesel	123,200	141,700
1989	T-Diesel	117,000	134,500
1988	T-Diesel	108,600	125,000
1987	T-Diesel	101,000	116,100
1986	T-Diesel	93,900	108,000
Marine Trader 44 Tri Cabin			
1988	S-Diesel	110,700	127,300
1988	T-Diesel	118,600	136,400
1987	T-Diesel	111,400	128,100
1986	T-Diesel	104,900	120,700
1985	T-Diesel	97,800	112,400
1984	T-Diesel	90,500	104,100

Year	Power	Retail Low	Retail High
1983	T-Diesel	84,000	96,700
1982	T-Diesel	79,800	91,700
1981	T-Diesel	74,000	85,100
1980	T-Diesel	70,300	80,900
Marine Trader 46 Double Cabin			
1999	T135D	259,700	298,700
1998	T135D	235,500	270,800
1997	T135D	216,400	248,800
1996	T135D	202,200	232,600
1995	T135D	187,400	215,500
1994	T135D	177,200	203,800
1993	T135D	168,400	193,700
1992	T135D	157,500	181,200
1991	T135D	150,600	173,200
1990	T135D	144,100	165,700
Tradewinds 47 MY (1989-97)			
1997	T135D	219,900	252,900
1996	T135D	207,400	238,600
1995	T135D	193,800	222,900
1994	T135D	183,900	211,500
1993	T135D	173,900	200,000
1992	T135D	165,500	190,400
1991	T135D	157,000	180,500
1990	T135D	146,700	168,700
1989	T135D	142,100	163,400
Tradewinds 47 MY (1986-88)			
1988	T135D	136,300	156,800
1987	T135D	128,200	147,400
1986	T135D	119,300	137,200
Med 48 Morocco MY			
1991	T375D	179,500	206,400
1990	T375D	171,500	197,200
1989	T375D	162,500	186,900
1988	T375D	147,000	169,000
1987	T375D	140,300	161,400
1986	T375D	134,200	154,300
1985	T375D	127,300	146,500
1984	T375D	120,000	138,000
Marine Trader 49 Pilothouse			
1993	T-Diesel	207,400	238,500
1992	T-Diesel	195,300	224,600
1991	T-Diesel	180,800	207,900
1990	T-Diesel	169,400	194,900
1989	T-Diesel	158,800	182,600
1988	T-Diesel	148,800	171,100
1987	T-Diesel	139,400	160,400
1986	T-Diesel	131,600	151,400
1985	T-Diesel	126,600	145,600
1984	T-Diesel	122,300	140,700
1983	T-Diesel	118,000	135,700
1982	T-Diesel	116,100	133,500
1981	T-Diesel	111,700	128,400
1980	T-Diesel	108,000	124,300
Marine Trader 50 Motor Yacht			
1994	T-Diesel	246,300	283,300
1993	T-Diesel	238,200	274,000
1992	T-Diesel	221,200	254,300
1991	T-Diesel	207,800	239,000
1990	T-Diesel	196,100	225,500
1989	T-Diesel	185,800	213,700
1988	T-Diesel	172,000	197,800
1987	T-Diesel	156,900	180,400
1986	T-Diesel	143,100	164,600
1985	T-Diesel	136,400	156,800
1984	T-Diesel	127,600	146,800
1983	T-Diesel	125,900	144,800
1982	T-Diesel	120,600	138,700
1981	T-Diesel	116,300	133,800
1980	T-Diesel	111,400	128,100
Marinette 28 Express			
1989	T-Gas	19,600	23,200
1988	T-Gas	18,800	22,500
1987	T-Gas	17,800	21,300
1986	T-Gas	17,200	20,400
1985	T-Gas	16,400	19,500
1984	T-Gas	15,600	18,600
1983	T-Gas	14,800	17,600
1982	T-Gas	13,900	16,700
1981	T-Gas	13,400	16,000
1980	T-Gas	12,900	15,400
Marinette 29 Sedan			
1989	T-Gas	23,000	27,300
1988	T-Gas	20,300	24,200
1987	T-Gas	18,400	21,900
1986	T-Gas	17,600	21,000
1985	T-Gas	16,800	20,100
Marinette 32 Sedan			
1990	T-IB/260G	44,000	50,600
1989	T-IB/260G	41,500	47,700
1988	T-IB/260G	40,500	46,600
1987	T-IB/260G	38,700	44,500
1986	T-IB/260G	36,800	42,400
1985	T-IB/260G	34,900	40,100
1984	T-IB/260G	33,000	38,000
1983	T-IB/260G	31,100	35,800
1982	T-IB/260G	28,700	33,000
1981	T-IB/260G	27,000	31,100
1980	T-IB/260G	25,000	28,800
Marinette 37 MY			
1991	T-IB/7.4L	87,400	100,600
1990	T-IB/7.4L	81,000	93,100
1989	T-IB/7.4L	75,700	87,100
1988	T-IB/7.4L	70,900	81,500
Marinette 41 MY			
1994	T-IB/7.4L	125,400	144,200
1993	T-IB/7.4L	118,200	135,900
1992	T-IB/7.4L	111,500	128,200
1991	T-IB/7.4L	104,800	120,500
1990	T-IB/7.4L	98,300	113,000
1989	T-IB/7.4L	91,900	105,700
1988	T-IB/7.4L	107,400	123,500
1987	T-IB/7.4L	78,500	90,200
Marlin 350 Sportfish			
2004	T250 O/B	122,500	140,800
2003	T250 O/B	111,400	128,100
2002	T250 O/B	101,400	116,600
2001	T250 O/B	92,300	106,100
2000	T250 O/B	84,000	96,600
1999	T250 O/B	76,400	87,900
1998	T250 O/B	69,500	79,900
1997	T250 O/B	63,900	73,500
1996	T250 O/B	58,800	67,700
1995	T250 O/B	54,100	62,200
1994	T250 O/B	49,800	57,300
1993	T250 O/B	46,300	53,200
1992	T250 O/B	43,100	49,500
1991	T250 O/B	40,000	46,000
Marlow 65 Explorer			
2004	T800D	1,270,000	1,460,500
2003	T800D	1,193,800	1,372,800
2002	T800D	1,122,100	1,290,400
2001	T800D	1,054,800	1,213,000
Maryland 37 ******			
Maxum 2700 SE			
2004	S320 I/O	61,100	70,200
2003	S320 I/O	54,900	63,200
2002	S320 I/O	49,400	56,900
2001	S320 I/O	44,500	51,200
Maxum 2700/2800 SCR; 2900 SE			
2004	S320 I/O	69,700	80,100
2004	T190 I/O	73,600	84,600
2003	S320 I/O	62,700	72,100
2003	T190 I/O	66,200	76,100
2002	S320 I/O	56,400	64,900
2002	T190 I/O	59,600	68,500
2001	S310 I/O	50,800	58,400
2001	T190 I/O	53,600	61,700
2000	S310 I/O	45,700	52,500
2000	T190 I/O	48,200	55,500
1999	S310 I/O	41,100	47,300
1999	T190 I/O	43,400	49,900
1998	S310 I/O	37,000	42,500
1998	T190 I/O	39,500	45,400
1997	S310 I/O	33,700	38,700
1997	T190 I/O	35,900	41,300
1996	S310 I/O	30,600	35,200
1996	T190 I/O	32,700	37,600
1995	S300 I/O	27,900	32,100
1995	T180 I/O	29,800	34,200
1994	S300 I/O	25,400	29,200
1994	T180 I/O	27,100	31,100
1993	S300 I/O	23,100	26,500
1993	T180 I/O	24,600	28,300
Maxum 3000 SCR			
2001	T260 I/O	66,600	76,600
2000	T260 I/O	60,100	69,100
1999	T260 I/O	54,300	62,400
1998	T260 I/O	48,100	55,300
1997	T260 I/O	42,700	49,100
Maxum 3100 SE			
2004	T260 I/O	93,400	107,400
2003	T260 I/O	84,000	96,600
2002	T260 I/O	75,600	87,000
Maxum 3200 SCR			
1998	T-260 I/O	60,000	69,000
1997	T-280 I/O	55,600	63,900
1996	T-250 I/O	49,300	56,700
1995	T-250 I/O	42,700	49,100
1994	T-250 I/O	36,600	42,100
Maxum 3300 SE			
2004	T320 I/O	121,900	140,100
2003	T320 I/O	109,700	126,100
2002	T320 I/O	98,700	113,500
2001	T320 I/O	88,800	102,100
2000	T310 I/O	79,900	91,900
1999	T310 I/O	71,900	82,700
Maxum 3500 Sport Yacht			
2004	T370G	167,800	192,900

PRICES

Year	Power	Retail Low	Retail High
2003	T370G	151,000	173,600
2002	T380G	135,900	156,300
2001	T380G	122,300	140,600

Maxum 3700 SCR

Year	Power	Retail Low	Retail High
2001	T380G	143,500	165,000
2000	T380G	129,100	148,500
1999	T380G	116,200	133,600
1998	T380G	104,600	120,300

Maxum 3700 Sport Yacht

Year	Power	Retail Low	Retail High
2004	T370G	158,700	182,500
2003	T370G	142,800	164,200

Maxum 3900/4100 SCR

Year	Power	Retail Low	Retail High
1999	T310G	122,600	141,000
1999	T330D	153,100	176,100
1998	T310G	101,200	116,400
1998	T330D	132,300	152,200
1997	T310G	91,900	105,700
1997	T315D	122,300	140,600
1996	T310G	81,600	93,800
1996	T315D	111,300	128,000

Maxum 4100 SCA

Year	Power	Retail Low	Retail High
2001	T330D	219,100	252,000
2000	T330D	194,800	224,100
1999	T330D	176,000	202,400
1998	T330D	157,800	181,500
1997	T330D	145,500	167,300

Maxum 4100 SCB

Year	Power	Retail Low	Retail High
2001	T330D	211,000	242,700
2000	T330D	188,500	216,800
1999	T330D	171,100	196,800
1998	T330D	153,900	177,000
1997	T330D	142,300	163,600

Maxum 4200 Sport Yacht

Year	Power	Retail Low	Retail High
2004	T450D	364,200	418,800
2003	T450D	327,700	376,900
2002	T450D	295,000	339,200

Maxum 4600 SCB

Year	Power	Retail Low	Retail High
2001	T450D	263,000	302,400
2000	T370D	226,000	259,900
1999	T370D	204,800	235,600
1998	T370D	188,800	217,200
1997	T370D	176,200	202,700

McKinna 47 Sedan

Year	Power	Retail Low	Retail High
2001	330D	315,900	363,200
2000	330D	287,400	330,500
1999	330D	261,500	300,800

McKinna 48 PH

Year	Power	Retail Low	Retail High
2000	T450D	418,000	480,700
1999	T450D	388,700	447,100
1998	T450D	370,200	425,800
1997	T375D	340,800	391,900
1996	T375D	308,300	354,500
1995	T375D	285,800	328,700
1994	T375D	262,200	301,500
1993	T375D	243,700	280,300
1992	T375D	225,300	259,100
1991	T375D	210,700	242,300

McKinna 57 Pilothouse

Year	Power	Retail Low	Retail High
2002	T600D	606,600	697,600
2001	T600D	551,200	633,900
2000	T600D	527,000	606,000

Year	Power	Retail Low	Retail High
1999	T600D	504,300	580,000
1998	T600D	477,800	549,500
1997	T600D	447,000	514,100

McKinna 60 Express ******

McKinna 65 Pilothouse

Year	Power	Retail Low	Retail High
2004	T800D	1,350,000	1,552,500
2003	T800D	1,242,000	1,428,300
2002	T800D	1,142,600	1,314,000
2001	T800D	1,051,200	1,208,900
2000	T800D	967,100	1,112,200

Med 56 Montechristo MY

Year	Power	Retail Low	Retail High
1991	T485D	291,900	335,700
1990	T485D	282,200	324,600
1989	T485D	268,300	308,600
1988	T485D	256,100	294,500
1987	T485D	242,600	279,000
1986	T485D	229,800	264,300
1985	T485D	216,900	249,400
1984	T485D	203,400	233,900

Mediterranean 38 Convertible

Year	Power	Retail Low	Retail High
2004	T-Diesel	258,400	297,200
2003	T-Diesel	229,600	264,000
2002	T-Diesel	218,000	250,700
2001	T-Diesel	208,500	239,800
2000	T-Diesel	194,400	223,600
1999	T-Diesel	177,600	204,300
1998	T-Diesel	171,000	196,600
1997	T-Diesel	163,700	188,300
1996	T-Diesel	154,500	177,700
1995	T-Diesel	148,400	170,700
1994	T-Diesel	142,900	164,400
1993	T-Diesel	134,700	154,900
1992	T-Diesel	123,100	141,600
1991	T-Diesel	114,000	131,100
1990	T-Diesel	110,600	127,100
1989	T-Diesel	105,100	120,900
1988	T-Diesel	101,600	116,800
1987	T-Diesel	96,500	111,000
1986	T-Diesel	91,700	105,400
1985	T-Diesel	87,100	100,200

Mediterranean 38 Express

Year	Power	Retail Low	Retail High
2004	T440D	******	******
2003	T440D	******	******
2002	T420D	228,600	262,900
2001	T420D	206,800	237,800
2000	T420D	200,400	230,400
1999	T420D	179,400	206,400

Mediterranean 54 Convertible

Year	Power	Retail Low	Retail High
2004	800 CAT	******	******
2003	800 CAT	******	******
2002	800 CAT	623,900	717,500
2001	800 CAT	570,300	655,800
2000	800 CAT	538,100	618,800
1999	800 CAT	514,700	591,900
1998	DD 6V92	423,800	487,400
1998	DD 8V92	474,800	546,000
1997	DD 6V92	399,100	459,000
1997	DD 8V92	448,000	515,200
1996	DD 6V92	377,400	434,000
1996	DD 8V92	424,000	487,600
1995	DD 6V92	349,300	401,700
1995	DD 8V92	392,900	451,800
1994	DD 6V92	332,200	382,000

Year	Power	Retail Low	Retail High
1994	DD 8V92	376,100	432,500

Midnight Express 39 SF ******

Meridian 341 Sedan (2003-04)

Year	Power	Retail Low	Retail High
2004	T260G	150,200	172,700
2004	T250D	181,200	208,300
2003	T260G	135,100	155,400
2003	T250D	164,800	189,600

Meridian 341 Sedan (Current) ******

Meridian 368 MY ******

Meridian 381 Sedan

Year	Power	Retail Low	Retail High
2004	T320G	202,300	232,600
2004	T270D	229,500	263,900
2003	T320G	182,000	209,300
2003	T270D	208,800	240,100

Meridian 408 MY

Year	Power	Retail Low	Retail High
2004	T330D	322,500	370,800
2003	T330D	293,400	337,400

Meridian 411 Sedan

Year	Power	Retail Low	Retail High
2004	T330D	219,600	252,500
2003	T330D	199,800	229,800

Meridian 459 Cockpit MY

Year	Power	Retail Low	Retail High
2004	T330D	375,000	431,200
2003	T330D	341,200	392,400

Meridian 540 Pilothouse

Year	Power	Retail Low	Retail High
2004	T535D	728,900	838,200
2003	T535D	663,200	762,700

Meridian 580 Pilothouse

Year	Power	Retail Low	Retail High
2004	T635D	885,600	1,018,400
2003	T635D	805,800	926,700

Midnight Express 30 SF ******

Midnight Lace 40 Express

Year	Power	Retail Low	Retail High
1994	T-Diesel	166,500	191,400
1993	T-Diesel	155,600	178,900
1992	T-Diesel	144,500	166,200
1991	T-Diesel	134,600	154,800

Midnight Lace 44 Express

Year	Power	Retail Low	Retail High
1989	T-Diesel	134,300	154,400
1988	T-Diesel	123,500	142,000
1987	T-Diesel	116,000	133,500
1986	T-Diesel	109,000	125,400
1985	T-Diesel	103,500	119,000
1984	T-Diesel	99,700	114,600
1983	T-Diesel	95,900	110,300
1982	T-Diesel	94,100	108,200
1981	T-Diesel	91,200	104,900
1980	T-Diesel	90,500	104,100

Midnight Lace 52 Express

Year	Power	Retail Low	Retail High
1989	T-Diesel	176,600	203,100
1988	T-Diesel	163,500	188,000
1987	T-Diesel	154,200	177,400
1986	T-Diesel	143,600	165,200
1985	T-Diesel	136,200	156,600
1984	T-Diesel	131,200	150,900
1983	T-Diesel	127,500	146,600
1982	T-Diesel	122,500	140,900

Mikelson 42 Sedan

Year	Power	Retail Low	Retail High
1993	T-Diesels	******	******
1992	T-Diesels	******	******
1991	T-Diesels	193,000	221,900

PRICES

IMPORTANT! See Page 293 for Regional Price Adjustment.

Year	Power	Retail Low	Retail High
1990	T-Diesels	179,400	206,400
1989	T-Diesels	166,900	191,900
1988	T-Diesels	155,200	178,500
1987	T-Diesels	144,300	166,000
1986	T-Diesels	134,200	154,400
Mikelson 43 Sportfisher			
2004	T450D	481,200	553,300
2003	T450D	437,800	503,500
2002	T450D	398,400	458,200
2001	T430D	362,600	417,000
2000	T420D	333,600	383,600
1999	T420D	306,900	352,900
1998	T420D	282,300	324,700
1997	T420D	259,700	298,700
Mikelson 50 Sportfisher			
2004	T450D	724,500	833,100
2003	T450D	666,500	766,500
2002	T450D	613,200	705,100
2001	T435D	564,100	648,700
2000	T435D	519,000	596,800
1999	T435D	477,500	549,100
1998	T435D	439,300	505,200
1997	T435D	404,100	464,700
1996	T435D	371,800	427,600
1995	T435D	345,700	397,600
1994	T435D	321,500	369,800
1993	T435D	299,000	343,900
1992	T435D	278,100	319,800
Mikelson 59 Nomad			
2004	T635D	1,178,000	1,354,700
Mikelson 60 Sportfisher			
1997	T735D	599,200	689,100
1996	T735D	567,900	653,100
1995	T735D	519,800	597,800
1994	T735D	477,200	548,700
1993	T735D	444,900	511,600
1992	T735D	391,700	450,500
Mikelson 61 Pilothouse SF			
2004	T800D	1,227,800	1,411,900
2003	T800D	1,129,500	1,299,000
2002	T800D	1,039,200	1,195,000
2001	T800D	956,000	1,099,400
2000	T800D	879,500	1,011,500
Mikelson 64 Sportfisher ******			
Mikelson 70 Sportfisher ******			
Mikelson 72/78 SF ******			
Monk 36 Trawler			
2004	S220D	221,300	254,400
2003	S220D	205,800	236,600
2002	S220D	191,400	220,100
2001	S220D	178,000	204,700
2000	S220D	165,500	190,300
1999	S220D	153,900	177,000
1998	S-Diesel	144,700	166,400
1997	S-Diesel	136,000	156,400
1996	S-Diesel	127,800	147,000
1995	S-Diesel	120,200	138,200
1994	S-Diesel	112,900	129,900
1993	S-Diesel	106,200	122,100
1992	S-Diesel	100,800	116,000
1991	S-Diesel	95,800	110,200
1990	S-Diesel	91,000	104,700

Year	Power	Retail Low	Retail High
1989	S-Diesel	86,500	99,400
1988	S-Diesel	82,100	94,500
1987	S-Diesel	78,000	89,700
1986	S-Diesel	74,100	85,200
1985	S-Diesel	70,400	81,000
1984	S-Diesel	66,900	76,900
1983	S-Diesel	63,500	73,100
1982	S-Diesel	60,400	69,400
Monterey 265/276 Cruiser			
1999	S310 I/O	41,400	47,600
1998	S310 I/O	36,700	42,200
1997	S310 I/O	32,400	37,200
1996	S300 I/O	27,200	31,300
1995	S300 I/O	24,700	28,400
1994	S300 I/O	22,100	25,400
1993	S300 I/O	20,300	23,400
Monterey 282 Cruiser			
2004	T250 I/O	84,200	96,800
2003	T250 I/O	75,700	87,100
2002	T250 I/O	68,200	78,400
2001	T190 I/O	61,300	70,500
Monterey 296 Cruiser			
2000	T250 I/O	56,700	65,200
2000	T250 I/O	51,500	59,300
1999	T250 I/O	46,900	53,900
1998	T250 I/O	42,700	49,100
1997	T250 I/O	38,800	44,700
1996	T250 I/O	35,300	40,600
1995	T250 I/O	32,100	37,000
1994	T250 I/O	29,300	33,600
1993	T225 I/O	26,600	30,600
Monterey 298 Sport Cruiser			
2004	T320 I/O	77,500	89,100
2003	T320 I/O	69,700	80,200
Monterey 298 Super Sport			
2004	T320 I/O	80,100	92,100
2003	T320 I/O	72,000	82,900
2002	T320 I/O	64,800	74,600
2001	T320 I/O	58,300	67,100
Monterey 302 Cruiser			
2004	T260 I/O	100,400	115,400
2003	T260 I/O	90,300	103,900
2002	T260 I/O	81,300	93,500
2001	T250 I/O	73,100	84,100
2000	T250 I/O	66,600	76,500
Monterey 322 Cruiser			
2004	T320 I/O	115,400	132,700
2003	T320 I/O	103,800	119,400
2002	T320 I/O	93,400	107,400
2001	T320 I/O	84,100	96,700
2000	T310 I/O	76,500	88,000
1999	T310 I/O	69,600	80,100
1998	T310 I/O	63,300	72,900
Monterey 350 Sport Yacht ******			
Nautique 42 Cockpit MY ******			
Navigator 3300 FB Sedan			
1995	T200D	89,300	102,600
1994	T200D	82,600	95,000
1993	T200D	76,100	87,600
Navigator 336 FB Express			
1992	T318D	52,400	60,300

Year	Power	Retail Low	Retail High
1991	T318D	46,400	53,400
1990	T318D	40,500	46,600
1989	T318D	36,700	42,300
Navigator 42 Classic			
2001	T318D	260,500	299,500
2000	T318D	240,300	276,400
1999	T318D	220,300	253,300
1998	T318D	204,800	235,600
1997	T318D	182,200	209,500
1996	T318D	167,000	192,000
Navigator 4300 FB Sedan			
1994	T318D	150,000	172,500
1992	T318D	130,800	150,400
1991	T318D	118,300	136,100
1990	T318D	102,500	117,900
Navigator 44 Classic			
2004	T318D	423,500	487,000
2003	T318D	385,300	443,100
2002	T318D	350,700	403,300
Navigator 48 Classic			
2004	T318D	522,800	601,200
2003	T318D	475,700	547,100
2002	T318D	432,900	497,800
2001	T318D	393,900	453,000
2000	T318D	362,400	416,800
1999	T318D	333,400	383,400
1998	T318D	306,700	352,700
1997	T318D	282,200	324,500
Navigator 50 Classic ******			
Navigator 53 Classic			
2004	T370D	576,000	662,400
2003	T370D	524,100	602,700
2002	T370D	476,900	548,500
2001	T370D	434,000	499,100
2000	T370D	399,300	459,200
1999	T370D	367,300	422,400
1998	T370D	337,900	388,600
1997	T370D	310,900	357,500
1996	T370D	286,000	328,900
1995	T370D	263,100	302,600
Navigator 5300 Pilothouse ******			
Navigator 56 Classic			
2004	T370D	665,400	765,200
2003	T370D	605,500	696,300
2002	T370D	551,000	633,600
2001	T370D	501,400	576,600
2000	T370D	******	******
Navigator 5600 Pilothouse ******			
Navigator 58 Classic ******			
Navigator 61 Motor Yacht			
2004	T715D	860,400	989,500
2003	T715D	783,000	900,500
2002	T675D	712,500	819,400
2001	T675D	648,400	745,700
2000	T675D	596,500	686,000
1999	T675D	548,800	631,100
Navigator 63 Classic ******			
Nordhavn 35 Coastal Pilot ******			

PRICES

IMPORTANT! See Page 293 for Regional Price Adjustment.

Year	Power	Retail Low	Retail High
Nordhavn 40			
2004	S140D	528,800	608,100
2003	S140D	497,000	571,600
2002	S140D	467,200	537,300
2001	S140D	439,200	505,000
2000	S140D	412,800	474,700
1999	S140D	388,000	446,300
Nordhavn 43 ******			
Nordhavn 46			
2004	S-Diesel	******	******
2003	S-Diesel	******	******
2002	S-Diesel	569,100	654,400
2001	S-Diesel	530,300	609,800
2000	S-Diesel	501,400	576,600
1999	S-Diesel	477,500	549,100
1998	S-Diesel	454,500	522,700
1997	S-Diesel	422,300	485,600
1996	S-Diesel	395,100	454,400
1995	S-Diesel	363,100	417,600
1994	S-Diesel	338,500	389,300
1993	S-Diesel	318,900	366,800
1992	S-Diesel	303,500	349,000
1991	S-Diesel	300,200	345,200
1990	S-Diesel	290,600	334,200
1989	S-Diesel	285,100	327,800
Nordhavn 47 ******			
Nordhavn 50 ******			
2004	S-Diesel	855,000	983,200
2003	S-Diesel	803,700	924,200
2002	S-Diesel	755,400	868,800
2001	S-Diesel	710,100	816,600
2000	S-Diesel	667,500	767,600
1999	S-Diesel	627,400	721,600
1998	S-Diesel	589,800	678,300
1997	S-Diesel	554,400	637,600
Nordhavn 57 ******			
Nordhavn 62 ******			
Nordic 26 Tug			
1998	S-Diesel	84,600	97,300
1997	S-Diesel	77,000	88,600
1996	S-Diesel	69,500	80,000
1995	S-Diesel	66,400	76,400
1994	S-Diesel	64,500	74,200
1993	S-Diesel	62,100	71,400
1992	S-Diesel	58,400	67,200
1991	S-Diesel	55,000	63,300
1990	S-Diesel	51,600	59,400
1989	S-Diesel	49,500	56,900
1988	S-Diesel	45,500	52,400
1987	S-Diesel	43,300	49,800
1986	S-Diesel	41,000	47,200
1985	S-Diesel	38,100	43,800
1984	S-Diesel	36,300	41,800
1983	S-Diesel	35,000	40,200
1982	S-Diesel	34,400	39,600
1981	S-Diesel	32,900	37,900
1980	S-Diesel	32,600	37,500
Nordic 32 Tug			
2004	S-Diesel	216,500	248,900
2003	S-Diesel	203,500	234,000
2002	S-Diesel	191,200	219,900
2001	S-Diesel	179,800	206,700

Year	Power	Retail Low	Retail High
2000	S-Diesel	169,000	194,300
1999	S-Diesel	158,800	182,700
1998	S-Diesel	149,300	171,700
1997	S-Diesel	140,300	161,400
1996	S-Diesel	131,900	151,700
1995	S-Diesel	125,300	144,100
1994	S-Diesel	119,100	136,900
1993	S-Diesel	113,100	130,100
1992	S-Diesel	107,400	123,600
1991	S-Diesel	102,100	117,400
1990	S-Diesel	97,000	111,500
1989	S-Diesel	92,100	105,900
1988	S-Diesel	87,500	100,600
1987	S-Diesel	83,100	95,600
1986	S-Diesel	79,000	90,800
Nordic 37 Tug			
2004	S330D	331,200	380,800
2003	S330D	311,300	358,000
2002	S330D	292,600	336,500
2001	S330D	275,000	316,300
2000	S330D	261,300	300,500
1999	S330D	248,200	285,500
1998	S330D	235,800	271,200
Nordic 42 Tug			
2004	T450D	435,400	500,700
2003	T450D	409,200	470,600
2002	T450D	384,700	442,400
2001	S330D	361,600	415,800
2000	S330D	343,500	395,000
1999	S330D	326,300	375,300
1998	S330D	310,000	356,500
1997	S330D	294,500	338,700
1996	S330D	279,800	321,800
Nordic 480 Motor Yacht			
1991	T-Diesel	262,800	302,200
1990	T-Diesel	244,400	281,000
1989	T-Diesel	235,000	270,300
1988	T-Diesel	225,100	258,800
1987	T-Diesel	214,100	246,200
1986	T-Diesel	203,900	234,500
1985	T-Diesel	190,600	219,200
North Coast 31 SF			
1990	T-Gas	47,500	54,600
1990	T-Diesel	77,300	88,800
1989	T-Gas	43,100	49,500
1989	T-Diesel	71,600	82,300
1988	T-Gas	40,200	46,200
1988	T-Diesel	65,700	75,600
Nova 36 Sundeck			
1990	T135D	78,900	90,700
1989	T135D	75,100	86,300
1988	T135D	72,100	82,900
1987	T135D	70,000	80,600
1986	T135D	66,800	76,900
1985	T135D	63,300	72,800
Nova 40 Sundeck			
1990	T135D	99,900	114,900
1989	T135D	96,200	110,600
1988	T135D	92,800	106,700
1987	T135D	87,700	100,900
1986	T135D	84,100	96,800
1985	T135D	80,900	93,100
1984	T135D	77,500	89,100

Year	Power	Retail Low	Retail High
Nova 42 Sundeck			
1990	T135D	116,500	134,000
1989	T135D	113,200	130,200
1988	T135D	109,500	126,000
1987	T135D	104,900	120,600
1986	T135D	101,500	116,700
1985	T135D	97,200	111,800
Nova 44 Sundeck			
1990	T135D	123,800	142,400
1989	T135D	120,800	138,900
1988	T135D	117,200	134,800
1987	T135D	112,300	129,100
1986	T135D	109,000	125,400
1985	T135D	105,300	121,100
Nova Embassy 44 SD			
1992	375D	184,500	212,100
1991	375D	171,500	197,300
1990	375D	159,500	183,500
1989	375D	150,000	172,500
1988	375D	141,000	162,100
1987	375D	132,500	152,400
Novatec 46/48 Sundeck ******			
Novatec 50 Cockpit MY			
2004	450D	433,500	498,500
2003	450D	394,400	453,600
2002	450D	358,900	412,800
2001	450D	326,600	375,600
2000	450D	300,500	345,600
1999	450D	276,400	317,900
1998	T375D	254,300	292,500
1997	T375D	234,000	269,100
1996	T375D	215,300	247,600
Novatec 55 Cockpit MY			
2004	T660D	785,400	903,200
2003	T660D	714,700	821,900
2002	T660D	650,300	747,900
2001	T660D	591,800	680,600
2000	T660D	544,500	626,100
1999	T660D	500,900	576,000
1998	T660D	460,800	530,000
Novatec 66 MY ******			
Novatec 80 MY ******			
Ocean Alexander 38 DC			
1987	T135D	100,200	115,300
1986	T135D	91,800	105,500
1985	T135D	84,600	97,300
1984	T135D	79,100	91,000
Ocean Alexander 390 Sundeck			
1999	T220D	240,900	277,100
1998	T220D	221,700	254,900
1997	T220D	203,900	234,500
1996	T220D	187,600	215,800
1995	T220D	174,500	200,600
1994	T220D	162,300	186,600
1993	T220D	150,900	173,500
1992	T210D	140,300	161,400
1991	T210D	130,500	150,100
1990	T210D	121,400	139,600
1989	T210D	112,900	129,800
1988	T210D	105,000	120,700
1987	T210D	97,600	112,300

PRICES

Year	Power	Retail Low	Retail High
1986	T210D	******	******

Ocean Alexander 40 DC

Year	Power	Retail Low	Retail High
1989	T-Diesel	122,700	141,100
1988	T-Diesel	116,100	133,500
1987	T-Diesel	107,100	123,200
1986	T-Diesel	100,200	115,200
1985	T-Diesel	96,600	111,100
1984	T-Diesel	91,000	104,700
1983	T-Diesel	87,300	100,400
1982	T-Diesel	82,300	94,700
1981	T-Diesel	77,500	89,200
1980	T-Diesel	74,700	85,900

Ocean Alexander 40 Sedan

Year	Power	Retail Low	Retail High
1989	T-Diesel	122,300	140,700
1988	T-Diesel	115,600	132,900
1987	T-Diesel	109,500	126,000
1986	T-Diesel	104,500	120,200
1985	T-Diesel	95,900	110,300
1984	T-Diesel	86,300	99,300
1983	T-Diesel	81,200	93,300

Ocean Alexander 42 Sedan

Year	Power	Retail Low	Retail High
1994	T375D	197,800	227,500
1993	T375D	188,100	216,300
1992	T250D	162,500	186,900
1992	T375D	180,100	207,100
1991	T250D	154,200	177,400
1991	T375D	170,800	196,500
1990	T250D	147,300	169,400
1990	T375D	163,000	187,400
1989	T250D	140,400	161,500
1989	T375D	155,300	178,600
1988	T250D	134,900	155,100
1988	T375D	148,900	171,200
1987	T250D	129,600	149,000
1987	T375D	143,100	164,600

Ocean Alexander 422 Sport Sedan

Year	Power	Retail Low	Retail High
2001	T420D	354,800	408,000
2000	T420D	318,000	365,700
1999	T420D	295,600	340,000
1998	T420D	276,700	318,300
1997	T375D	248,200	285,500
1996	T375D	236,500	272,000
1995	T375D	218,900	251,700
1994	T375D	202,100	232,400

Ocean Alexander 423 Classico

Year	Power	Retail Low	Retail High
2002	T220D	379,300	436,200
2001	T220D	338,200	389,000
2000	T210D	308,600	354,900
1999	T210D	292,700	336,700
1998	T210D	272,700	313,600
1997	T210D	260,700	299,800
1996	T210D	244,500	281,200
1995	T210D	229,100	263,500
1994	T210D	213,200	245,200
1993	T210D	199,300	229,200

Ocean Alexander 426 Classico

Year	Power	Retail Low	Retail High
2002	T220D	362,400	416,800
2001	T220D	335,100	385,400
2000	T220D	305,700	351,600
1999	T220D	290,500	334,000
1998	T220D	271,400	312,100
1997	T220D	264,400	304,100
1996	T220D	246,300	283,200

Year	Power	Retail Low	Retail High
1995	T220D	233,200	268,200
1994	T220D		

Ocean Alexander 420/440 Sundeck

Year	Power	Retail Low	Retail High
1999	T220D	248,600	285,800
1999	T375D	270,400	311,000
1998	T220D	237,800	273,500
1998	T375D	257,600	296,200
1997	T220D	220,300	253,300
1997	T375D	242,300	278,600
1996	T250D	212,100	243,900
1996	T375D	230,800	265,400
1995	T250D	199,900	229,900
1995	T375D	219,800	252,700
1994	T250D	187,600	215,800
1994	T375D	203,500	234,000
1993	T250D	178,100	204,800
1993	T375D	192,100	220,900
1992	T250D	169,600	195,000
1992	T375D	183,800	211,400
1991	T250D	158,600	182,400
1991	T375D	172,600	198,500
1990	T250D	151,600	174,300
1990	T375D	165,100	189,800
1989	T250D	141,300	162,500
1989	T375D	155,500	178,900
1988	T250D	137,700	158,400
1988	T375D	151,300	174,000
1987	T250D	129,200	148,500
1987	T375D	142,500	163,900

Ocean Alexander 43 Double Cabin

Year	Power	Retail Low	Retail High
1985	T-Diesel	121,700	140,000
1984	T-Diesel	112,200	129,000
1983	T-Diesel	104,300	120,000
1982	T-Diesel	98,000	112,700
1981	T-Diesel	92,200	106,000
1980	T-Diesel	88,200	101,400

Ocean Alexander 430/460 Classico MKI

Year	Power	Retail Low	Retail High
2004	T220D	******	******
2003	T220D	******	******
2002	T220D	418,300	481,000
2001	T220D	377,100	433,700
2000	T220D	344,600	396,300

Ocean Alexander 450 Classico Sedan

Year	Power	Retail Low	Retail High
2004	T220D	******	******
2003	T220D	******	******
2002	T220D	366,200	421,100
2001	T220D	337,900	388,600
2000	T210D	305,500	351,300

Ocean Alexander 456 Classico

Year	Power	Retail Low	Retail High
2002	T220D	401,200	461,400
2002	T375D	438,300	504,100
2001	T220D	371,300	427,000
2001	T375D	406,200	467,100
2000	T220D	337,400	388,000
2000	T375D	366,400	421,300
1999	T220D	309,000	355,300
1999	T375D	331,000	380,600
1998	T220D	302,000	347,400
1998	T375D	331,600	381,400
1997	T220D	285,100	327,800
1997	T375D	305,800	351,700
1996	T220D	266,400	306,400
1996	T375D	286,700	329,700
1995	T220D	258,200	296,900

Year	Power	Retail Low	Retail High
1995	T375D	274,400	315,600
1994	T210D	244,800	281,600
1994	T375D	266,100	306,000
1993	T210D	235,900	271,300
1993	T375D	252,600	290,500
1992	T210D	223,300	256,800
1992	T375D	238,000	273,700

Ocean Alexander 48 Yachtsman

Year	Power	Retail Low	Retail High
1991	T375D	249,400	286,800
1990	T375D	227,000	261,100
1989	T375D	204,000	234,600
1988	T375D	185,500	213,400
1987	T375D	166,600	191,600

Ocean Alexander 480 Sport Sedan

Year	Power	Retail Low	Retail High
2001	T420D	467,400	537,500
2000	T420D	427,000	491,100
1999	T420D	394,500	453,700
1998	T420D	371,400	427,100
1997	T420D	347,600	399,800
1996	T375D	330,200	379,800
1995	T375D	298,800	343,600
1994	T375D	275,100	316,400
1993	T375D	256,400	294,900

Ocean Alexander 48/50 Sedan

Year	Power	Retail Low	Retail High
1991	T-Diesel	272,700	313,600
1990	T-Diesel	248,400	285,700
1989	T-Diesel	229,500	263,900
1988	T-Diesel	209,900	241,400

Ocean Alexander 486 Classico

Year	Power	Retail Low	Retail High
2002	T420D	565,900	650,800
2001	T420D	513,200	590,200
2000	T420D	467,700	537,900
1999	T420D	437,800	503,500
1998	T420D	422,100	485,400
1997	T420D	395,100	454,300
1996	T-Diesel	368,500	423,800
1995	T-Diesel	342,700	394,100
1994	T-Diesel	317,700	365,300
1993	T-Diesel	289,900	333,400

Ocean Alexander 50 PH MK I

Year	Power	Retail Low	Retail High
1985	T-Diesel	233,400	268,400
1984	T-Diesel	208,000	239,200
1983	T-Diesel	193,800	222,800
1982	T-Diesel	179,700	206,700
1981	T-Diesel	166,000	191,000
1980	T-Diesel	152,200	175,100

Ocean Alexander 50 PH MK II

Year	Power	Retail Low	Retail High
1990	T-Diesel	324,100	372,800
1989	T-Diesel	306,400	352,400
1988	T-Diesel	286,300	329,300
1987	T-Diesel	266,500	306,500
1986	T-Diesel	247,500	284,700
1985	T-Diesel	238,400	274,100
1984	T-Diesel	211,800	243,500

Ocean Alexander 51/53 Sedan

Year	Power	Retail Low	Retail High
1998	T550D	******	******
1997	T550D	******	******
1996	T485D	******	******
1995	T400D	******	******
1995	T735D	412,700	474,600
1994	T400D	325,500	374,400
1994	T735D	388,600	446,900
1993	T400D	316,700	364,200

PRICES

IMPORTANT! See Page 293 for Regional Price Adjustment.

Year	Power	Retail Low	Retail High
1993	T735D	370,000	425,600
1992	T400D	300,000	345,000
1992	T735D	353,400	406,400
1991	T400D	297,300	341,900
1991	T735D	345,700	397,500
1990	T400D	284,900	327,600
1990	T735D	332,500	382,400
1989	T400D	277,200	318,800
1989	T735D	317,300	364,900
Ocean Alexander 520/540 PH			
2002	T420D	******	******!
2001	T420D	526,500	605,500
2000	T420D	491,200	564,900
1999	T420D	460,300	529,400
1998	T-Diesel	430,900	495,500
1997	T-Diesel	405,100	465,900
1996	T-Diesel	379,100	435,900
1995	T-Diesel	348,700	401,000
1994	T-Diesel	325,700	374,600
1993	T-Diesel	307,900	354,100
1992	T-Diesel	297,300	341,900
1991	T-Diesel	286,200	329,100
1990	T-Diesel	277,700	319,400
Ocean Alexander 548 PH			
2002	T660D	833,900	959,000
2001	T660D	760,200	874,200
2000	T660D	706,700	812,800
1999	T660D	654,000	752,100
1998	T550D	605,100	695,900
1997	T550D	556,400	639,800
1996	T550D	513,400	590,400
Ocean Alexander 60 MY			
1987	T-Diesel	400,600	460,700
1986	T-Diesel	369,500	424,900
1985	T-Diesel	340,400	391,500
1984	T-Diesel	308,800	355,100
1983	T-Diesel	297,000	341,600
Ocean Alexander 600 Classico MK I			
2004	T660D	******	******
2003	T660D	******	******
2002	T660D	1,003,600	1,154,100
2001	T660D	917,900	1,055,600
Ocean Alexander 610 Pilothouse			
2003	T660D	******	******
2002	T660D	950,500	1,093,100
2001	T660D	876,400	1,007,800
2000	T660D	823,300	946,800
1999	T660D	769,100	884,400
1998	T735D	713,200	820,200
1997	T735D	653,500	751,500
Ocean Alexander 600/630 MY			
2003	T800D	******	******
2002	T800D	1,177,900	1,354,600
2001	T800D	1,079,900	1,241,900
2000	T800D	1,015,100	1,167,400
1999	T800D	935,500	1,075,900
1998	T735D	859,200	988,100
1997	T735D	792,400	911,300
1996	T735D	750,000	862,500
1995	T735D	701,700	806,900
1994	T735D	676,000	777,400
1993	T735D	635,300	730,600
1992	T735D	599,000	688,900
Ocean Alexander 63 MY			
1992	T735D	627,500	721,700
1991	T735D	581,300	668,500
1990	T735D	551,200	633,900
1989	T735D	518,900	596,800
1988	T735D	477,700	549,400
1987	T735D	456,200	524,700
1986	T735D	426,700	490,700
Ocean Alexander 64 PH ******			
Ocean Alexander 66 MY			
1992	T735D	687,700	790,900
1991	T735D	663,500	763,000
1990	T735D	628,300	722,500
1989	T735D	582,100	669,400
1988	T735D	525,600	604,400
1987	T735D	459,900	528,800
1986	T735D	432,300	497,200
Ocean Master 27 Center Console			
2004	T200 O/B	******	******
2003	T200 O/B	83,500	96,100
2002	T200 O/B	76,100	87,600
2001	T200 O/B	70,000	80,500
2000	T200 O/B	65,800	75,700
1999	T200 O/B	60,600	69,700
1998	T200 O/B	55,600	63,900
1997	T200 O/B	51,400	59,100
1996	T200 O/B	46,600	53,600
1995	T200 O/B	42,600	48,900
1994	T200 O/B	38,300	44,000
1993	T200 O/B	36,800	42,300
1992	T200 O/B	33,600	38,600
1991	T200 O/B	31,200	35,900
1990	T200 O/B	29,400	33,800
1989	T200 O/B	26,400	30,400
1988	T200 O/B	25,100	28,900
1987	T200 O/B	24,600	28,300
Ocean Master 31 Center Console			
2004	T225 O/B	120,100	138,100
2003	T225 O/B	110,200	126,700
2002	T225 O/B	99,800	114,700
2001	T225 O/B	94,800	109,100
2000	T225 O/B	90,100	103,700
1999	T225 O/B	83,100	95,600
1998	T225 O/B	76,400	87,900
1997	T225 O/B	70,100	80,600
1996	T225 O/B	64,900	74,700
1995	T225 O/B	60,900	70,000
1994	T225 O/B	55,500	63,800
1993	T225 O/B	52,900	60,900
1992	T225 O/B	51,500	59,200
1991	T225 O/B	49,000	56,400
1990	T225 O/B	45,800	52,700
1989	T225 O/B	43,000	49,400
1988	T225 O/B	39,000	44,800
1987	T225 O/B	36,700	42,200
1986	T225 O/B	34,900	40,100
1985	T225 O/B	33,500	38,500
1984	T200 O/B	33,300	38,400
1983	T200 O/B	32,800	37,700
1982	T200 O/B	32,300	37,200
1981	T200 O/B	32,000	36,800
1980	T200 O/B	31,400	36,100
Ocean Master 31 Walkaround			
2004	T225 O/B	******	******
2003	T225 O/B	113,800	130,900
2002	T225 O/B	103,600	119,100
2001	T225 O/B	96,600	111,100
2000	T225 O/B	90,600	104,200
1999	T225 O/B	83,100	95,600
1998	T225 O/B	75,300	86,600
1997	T225 O/B	70,100	80,600
1996	T225 O/B	62,400	71,800
1995	T225 O/B	59,300	68,200
1994	T225 O/B	54,000	62,100
1993	T225 O/B	51,600	59,400
1992	T225 O/B	49,300	56,800
1991	T225 O/B	47,500	54,600
1990	T225 O/B	43,300	49,800
1989	T225 O/B	40,500	46,600
1988	T225 O/B	37,100	42,600
1987	T225 O/B	34,700	40,000
1986	T225 O/B	33,000	37,900
1985	T225 O/B	32,100	36,900
1984	T200 O/B	31,300	36,000
1983	T200 O/B	30,900	35,600
1982	T200 O/B	30,600	35,200
1981	T200 O/B	30,300	34,800
1980	T200 O/B	29,700	34,200
Ocean Master 34 Center Console			
2004	T250 O/B	******	******
2003	T250 O/B	******	******
2002	T250 O/B	112,100	128,900
2001	T250 O/B	101,900	117,200
2000	T250 O/B	96,300	110,800
1999	T250 O/B	86,900	99,900
1998	T250 O/B	80,100	92,100
1997	T250 O/B	71,700	82,400
1996	T250 O/B	64,000	73,600
Ocean 29 Super Sport			
1992	T-Gas	49,500	56,900
1992	T-Diesel	67,200	77,300
1991	T-Gas	46,500	53,500
1991	T-Diesel	63,200	72,700
1990	T-Gas	43,700	50,200
1990	T-Diesel	59,400	68,300
Ocean 32 Super Sport			
1992	T-Gas	65,300	75,100
1992	T-Diesel	79,400	91,300
1991	T-Gas	59,300	68,200
1991	T-Diesel	71,700	82,500
1990	T-Gas	55,100	63,400
1990	T-Diesel	65,100	74,900
1989	T-Gas	50,100	57,600
1989	T-Diesel	58,200	66,900
Ocean 35 SF			
1992	T-Gas	71,300	82,000
1992	T-Diesel	82,900	95,300
1991	T-Gas	61,400	70,600
1991	T-Diesel	74,300	85,400
1990	T-Gas	58,100	66,900
1990	T-Diesel	70,800	81,400
Ocean 35 Super Sport			
1994	T-Diesel	110,500	127,100
1993	T-Diesel	103,400	118,900
1992	T-Gas	81,200	93,400
1992	T-Diesel	95,500	109,800
1991	T-Gas	73,300	84,300

PRICES

IMPORTANT! See Page 293 for Regional Price Adjustment.

Year	Power	Retail Low	Retail High
1991	T-Diesel	87,700	100,800
1990	T-Gas	67,100	77,200
1990	T-Diesel	78,800	90,700
1989	T-Gas	62,400	71,800
1989	T-Diesel	73,100	84,000
1988	T-Gas	58,500	67,300
1988	T-Diesel	69,400	79,800
Ocean 38 SS (1984-91)			
1991	T-Diesel	114,900	132,200
1990	T-Gas	84,900	97,600
1990	T-Diesel	109,000	125,400
1989	T-Gas	79,800	91,800
1989	T-Diesel	101,400	116,600
1988	T-Gas	75,000	86,200
1988	T-Diesel	96,400	110,900
1987	T-Gas	70,200	80,800
1987	T-Diesel	90,700	104,300
1986	T-Gas	65,200	75,000
1986	T-Diesel	82,800	95,300
1985	T-Gas	59,800	68,800
1985	T-Diesel	79,600	91,500
1984	T-Gas	56,100	64,500
1984	T-Diesel	76,000	87,400
Ocean 38 SS (1992-95)			
1995	T-Diesel	173,000	198,900
1994	T-Diesel	161,800	186,100
1993	T-Diesel	148,900	171,200
1992	T-Diesel	134,600	154,800
Ocean 40 Sport Fish			
2004	T420D	329,500	378,900
2003	T420D	303,100	348,600
2002	T420D	278,800	320,700
2001	T420D	256,500	295,000
2000	T420D	236,000	271,400
1999	T420D	217,100	249,700
Ocean 40 Super Sport			
2004	T420D	359,800	413,700
2003	T420D	327,400	376,500
2002	T420D	297,900	342,600
2001	T420D	271,100	311,800
2000	T420D	249,400	286,800
1999	T420D	229,400	263,900
1998	T420D	211,100	242,700
1997	T420D	194,200	223,300
Ocean 40+2 Trawler			
1980	T-Diesel	60,500	69,500
Ocean 42 Sunliner			
1985	T-Diesel	100,700	115,800
1984	T-Diesel	95,200	109,500
1983	T-Diesel	89,100	102,500
1982	T-Diesel	82,900	95,400
1981	T-Diesel	78,200	89,900
Ocean 42 Super Sport (1980-83)			
1983	T-Diesel	93,500	107,600
1982	T-Diesel	87,300	100,400
1981	T-Diesel	80,500	92,500
1980	T-Diesel	75,200	86,500
Ocean 42 Super Sport (1991-95)			
1995	485D	235,900	271,300
1994	435D	209,300	240,700
1994	485D	221,200	254,400
1993	425D	197,300	226,900
1993	485D	206,800	237,900
1992	425D	193,200	222,200
1992	485D	201,400	231,700
1991	425D	177,500	204,100
1991	485D	186,000	213,900
Ocean 43 Super Sport			
2004	T480D	449,000	516,300
2003	T480D	408,500	469,800
2002	T480D	371,800	427,500
2001	T480D	338,300	389,100
2000	T480D	311,200	357,900
Ocean 44 Motor Yacht			
1999	T485D	361,200	415,300
1998	T485D	332,300	382,100
1997	T485D	305,700	351,500
1996	T485D	281,200	323,400
1995	T485D	261,500	300,800
1994	T485D	243,200	279,700
1993	T485D	226,200	260,100
1992	T485D	210,300	241,900
Ocean 44 Super Sport			
1991	T485D	179,100	205,900
1990	T485D	176,900	203,500
1989	T485D	166,800	191,900
1988	T485D	156,700	180,300
1987	T485D	147,700	169,900
1986	T485D	137,700	158,400
1985	T485D	128,800	148,100
Ocean 45 Super Sport			
1999	T485D	336,400	386,900
1998	T485D	314,100	361,300
1997	T485D	295,900	340,300
1996	T485D	273,000	314,000
Ocean 46 Sunliner			
1986	T-Diesel	142,400	163,800
1985	T-Diesel	133,200	153,100
1984	T-Diesel	126,000	144,900
1983	T-Diesel	118,100	135,800
Ocean 46 SS (1983-85)			
1985	T485D	146,000	167,900
1984	T485D	139,900	160,900
1983	T485D	136,100	156,500
Ocean 46 SS (Current) ******			
Ocean 48 Cockpit MY			
1999	T485D	382,900	440,300
1998	T485D	348,400	400,700
1997	T485D	317,000	364,600
1996	T485D	288,500	331,800
1995	T485D	265,400	305,200
1994	T485D	244,200	280,800
Ocean 48 Motor Yacht			
1994	T485D	321,100	369,200
1993	T485D	292,900	336,900
1992	T485D	263,100	302,500
1991	T485D	239,500	275,400
1990	T485D	220,900	254,000
1989	T485D	203,500	234,100
Ocean 48 Sport Fish			
2001	T660D	459,700	528,600
2000	T660D	419,800	482,800
1999	T660D	393,500	452,600
1998	T625D	362,600	417,000
1997	T625D	322,500	370,900
Ocean 48 SS (1986-90)			
1990	T485D	226,300	260,200
1989	T485D	215,500	247,800
1988	T485D	201,700	232,000
1987	T485D	188,500	216,800
1986	T485D	174,400	200,600
Ocean 48 SS (1991-94)			
1995	T550D	305,400	351,200
1994	T550D	287,300	330,300
1993	T485D	263,500	303,000
1992	T485D	244,100	280,700
1991	T485D	233,100	268,100
Ocean 48 SS (1995-2003)			
2003	660D	593,000	682,000
2003	825D	621,500	714,800
2002	660D	549,100	631,400
2002	800D	575,500	661,800
2001	660D	500,400	575,500
2001	800D	523,500	602,000
2000	660D	467,800	538,000
2000	800D	497,100	571,700
1999	660D	429,400	493,800
1999	800D	485,500	558,300
1998	625D	388,900	447,200
1998	800D	457,100	525,700
1997	625D	363,000	417,500
1997	800D	431,300	496,000
1996	625D	333,300	383,300
1996	760D	389,400	447,800
1995	625D	320,000	368,000
1995	760D	373,400	429,400
Ocean 50 Super Sport (1982–85			
1985	T-Diesel	161,500	185,700
1984	T-Diesel	147,400	169,500
1983	T-Diesel	135,100	155,400
1982	T-Diesel	124,200	142,900
Ocean 50 SS (Current) ******			
Ocean 52 Super Sport			
2004	800 CAT	751,200	863,800
2003	800 CAT	683,500	786,100
2002	800 CAT	622,000	715,300
2001	800 CAT	566,000	650,900
Ocean 53 Motor Yacht			
1991	T760D	312,100	358,900
1990	T735D	288,000	331,300
1989	T735D	274,800	316,100
1988	T735D	264,000	303,600
Ocean 53 Super Sport			
1999	800 CAT	523,400	601,900
1999	820 MAN	529,300	608,700
1998	800 CAT	509,300	585,700
1998	820 MAN	514,600	591,800
1997	800 CAT	490,400	564,000
1997	820 MAN	494,600	568,800
1996	760D	432,700	497,700
1996	820D	460,100	529,100
1995	760D	409,300	470,700
1995	820D	430,500	495,100
1994	760D	380,600	437,700
1994	820D	399,800	459,800

PRICES

Year	Power	Retail Low	Retail High
1993	760D	356,700	410,200
1993	820D	375,700	432,000
1992	735D	334,700	384,900
1992	820D	351,700	404,500
1991	735D	307,600	353,700
1991	820D	322,900	371,300
Ocean 55 Sunliner			
1986	T-Diesel	223,800	257,300
1985	T-Diesel	215,700	248,000
1984	T-Diesel	208,200	239,400
1983	T-Diesel	202,000	232,300
Ocean 55 Super Sport			
1990	T735D	295,500	339,800
1989	T735D	280,300	322,300
1988	T735D	256,700	295,200
1987	T710D	238,600	274,400
1986	T570D	230,800	265,400
1985	T570D	215,300	247,500
1984	T570D	199,200	229,100
1983	T600D	189,400	217,800
1982	T600D	181,000	208,100
1981	T600D	169,800	195,300
Ocean 56 Cockpit MY			
1992	T485D	315,700	363,000
1991	T485D	296,400	340,800
Ocean 56 Super Sport			
2002	1050 MAN	859,900	988,800
2001	1050 MAN	778,400	895,200
2000	1050 MAN	719,700	827,600
1999	1050 MAN	655,600	753,900
Ocean 57 Odyssey			
2004	T800D	989,000	1,137,300
Ocean 57 Super Sport			
2004	1015D	983,400	1,130,900
2003	1015D	894,800	1,029,100
Ocean 58 Super Sport			
1993	1080 DD	478,700	550,500
1993	1100 MAN	497,700	572,400
1992	1050 MAN	475,200	546,500
1992	1080 DD	446,000	512,900
1991	1050 MAN	461,300	530,500
1991	1080 DD	434,000	499,100
1990	1050 MAN	406,000	466,900
1990	1050 MAN	394,400	453,500
Ocean 60 Super Sport			
2001	1350D	1,026,600	1,180,700
2000	1350D	921,300	1,059,500
1999	1350D	871,900	1,002,700
1998	1350D	832,100	956,900
1997	1350D	775,300	891,600
1996	1350D	727,200	836,200
Ocean 62 Super Sport			
2004	T1400D	1,450,000	1,667,500
2003	T1350D	1,319,500	1,517,400
2002	T1350D	1,200,700	1,380,800
Ocean 63 Super Sport			
1991	1050 DD	524,100	602,700
1991	1050 MAN	541,500	622,700
1990	1050 DD	505,600	581,400
1990	1050 MAN	523,400	601,900
1989	1050 DD	480,800	553,000

Year	Power	Retail Low	Retail High
1989	1050 MAN	499,000	573,800
1988	1050 DD	439,600	505,600
1987	1050 DD	412,600	474,500
1986	1050 DD	385,800	443,700
Ocean 65 Odyssey ******			
Ocean 66 Super Sport			
1999	1200 MAN	922,500	1,060,900
1998	1200 MAN	864,700	994,400
1997	1200 MAN	795,900	915,200
1997	1350 CAT	829,800	954,200
1996	1200 MAN	719,000	826,900
1995	1110 DD	637,500	733,100
1995	1200 MAN	677,500	779,100
1994	1080 DD	640,500	736,500
1994	1100 MAN	671,700	772,500
1993	1040 DD	598,500	688,300
1993	1100 MAN	643,000	739,500
Ocean 70 Super Sport			
2004	T1500D	******	******
2003	T1400D	******	******
2003	T1800D	******	******
2002	T1400D	1,747,600	2,009,800
2002	1800D	1,912,500	2,199,400
2001	T1400D	1,601,100	1,841,300
2001	1800D	1,752,100	2,014,900
2000	T1400D	1,536,200	1,766,600
2000	1800D	1,682,400	1,934,700
Offshore 48 Pilothouse			
2001	T435D	546,600	628,600
2000	T420D	502,800	578,300
1999	T420D	462,600	532,000
Offshore 48 Sedan			
2001	T435D	500,400	575,400
2000	T435D	460,300	529,400
1999	T435D	423,500	487,000
1998	T435D	389,600	448,100
1997	T435D	358,400	412,200
1996	T435D	329,800	379,200
1995	T375D	306,700	352,700
1994	T375D	285,200	328,000
1993	T375D	265,200	305,000
1992	T375D	246,700	283,700
1991	T375D	229,400	263,800
1990	T375D	215,600	248,000
1989	T375D	202,700	233,100
1988	T375D	190,500	219,100
1987	T375D	179,100	206,000
Offshore 48 Cockpit MY			
1999	T435D	427,800	492,000
1998	T435D	399,400	459,400
1997	T435D	377,900	434,600
1996	T435D	352,500	405,300
1995	T375D	336,100	386,500
1994	T375D	320,400	368,500
1993	T375D	292,200	336,000
1992	T375D	271,700	312,500
1991	T375D	253,900	292,000
1990	T375D	238,900	274,800
1989	T375D	223,600	257,200
1988	T375D	213,600	245,700
1987	T375D	206,000	236,900
1986	T375D	197,700	227,400
1985	T375D	192,000	220,900

Year	Power	Retail Low	Retail High
Offshore 52 Sedan			
1999	T420D	542,300	623,600
1998	T420D	498,900	573,700
1997	T450D	459,000	527,800
1996	T450D	422,200	485,600
1995	T485D	392,700	451,600
1994	T485D	365,200	420,000
1993	T485D	339,600	390,600
1992	T485D	315,800	363,200
1991	T485D	293,700	337,800
Offshore 52/54 Pilothouse			
2004	T450D	800,800	920,900
2003	T450D	713,800	820,900
2002	T450D	673,700	774,800
2001	T450D	647,700	744,800
2000	T450D	602,700	693,100
1999	T450D	560,500	644,600
1998	T420D	521,300	599,500
Offshore 55 Pilothouse			
2004	T660D	******	******
2003	T660D	******	******
2002	T660D	957,400	1,101,000
2001	T660D	869,400	999,800
2000	T660D	820,000	943,000
1999	T660D	762,300	876,600
1998	T660D	693,200	797,200
1997	T550D	641,400	737,600
1996	T550D	583,100	670,600
1995	T-Diesel	561,200	645,400
1994	T-Diesel	515,900	593,300
1993	T-Diesel	487,800	561,000
1992	T-Diesel	454,300	522,400
1991	T-Diesel	440,000	506,000
1990	T-Diesel	425,200	489,000
Offshore 58/62 Flush Deck MY			
2002	T660D	******	******
2001	T660D	******	******
2000	T660D	******	******
1999	T660D	******	******
1998	T660D	775,100	891,400
1997	T550D	728,700	838,000
1996	T550D	688,000	791,300
1995	T550D	655,100	753,300
1994	T550D	617,700	710,400
Offshore 58/62 Pilothouse			
2004	T660D	1,080,000	1,242,000
2003	T660D	993,600	1,142,600
2002	T660D	914,100	1,051,200
2001	T660D	840,900	967,100
2000	T660D	782,100	899,400
1999	T660D	727,300	836,400
1998	T660D	676,400	777,900
1997	T550D	629,000	723,400
1996	T550D	585,000	672,800
1995	T550D	549,900	632,400
1994	T550D	516,900	594,500
Offshore 80 Voyager ******			
Osprey 30			
2004	T188 D	144,500	166,100
2003	T188 D	131,400	151,200
2002	T188 D	119,600	137,600
2001	T188 D	108,800	125,200
2000	T188 D	99,000	113,900

Year	Power	Retail Low	Retail High
1999	T188 D	90,100	103,600

Pace 36 Sport Fisherman

Year	Power	Retail Low	Retail High
1992	T-Gas	79,100	91,000
1992	T-Diesel	91,300	105,000
1991	T-Gas	73,500	84,600
1991	T-Diesel	85,800	98,700
1990	T-Gas	68,000	78,200
1990	T-Diesel	80,900	93,000
1989	T-Gas	61,500	70,800
1989	T-Diesel	75,100	86,400
1988	T-Gas	55,400	63,700
1988	T-Diesel	69,600	80,000

Pace 40 Sport Fisherman

Year	Power	Retail Low	Retail High
1992	T-Diesel	118,100	135,800
1991	T-Diesel	110,700	127,300
1990	T-Diesel	103,900	119,500
1989	T-Diesel	98,400	113,200
1988	T-Diesel	92,200	106,100

Pace 48 Sport Fisherman

Year	Power	Retail Low	Retail High
1992	T-Diesel	184,800	212,500
1991	T-Diesel	171,800	197,500
1990	T-Diesel	158,700	182,600
1989	T-Diesel	146,800	168,800
1988	T-Diesel	137,200	157,800
1987	T-Diesel	126,000	144,900

Pacemaker 34 Convertible

Year	Power	Retail Low	Retail High
1992	T-Gas	72,300	83,100
1992	T-Diesel	88,000	101,200
1991	T-Gas	64,300	74,000
1991	T-Diesel	77,300	88,900
1990	T-Gas	59,600	68,500
1990	T-Diesel	69,300	79,700
1989	T-Gas	54,800	63,100
1989	T-Diesel	65,100	74,900
1988	T-Gas	48,500	55,800
1988	T-Diesel	60,600	69,700

Pacemaker 37 SF ******

Pacific Mariner 65 Motor Yacht

Year	Power	Retail Low	Retail High
2004	T825D	1,429,200	1,643,500
2004	T825D	1,314,800	1,512,000
2002	T800D	1,209,600	1,391,100
2001	T800D	1,124,900	1,293,700
2000	T800D	1,046,200	1,203,100
1999	T800D	973,000	1,118,900
1998	T800D	914,600	1,051,800
1997	T800D	859,700	988,700

Pacific Seacraft 38T Fast Trawler

Year	Power	Retail Low	Retail High
2004	S370D	******	******
2003	S370D	******	******
2002	S350D	351,800	404,600
2001	S350D	316,900	364,500
2000	S350D	289,700	333,100
1999	S350D	257,200	295,700

Pacific Trawler 40

Year	Power	Retail Low	Retail High
2004	S220D	******	******
2003	S220D	******	******
2002	S220D	303,300	348,800
2001	S220D	266,000	305,900
2000	S220D	241,900	278,200

Pacifica 44 Sport Fisherman

Year	Power	Retail Low	Retail High
1992	485D	205,800	236,600
1991	485D	188,800	217,200

Year	Power	Retail Low	Retail High
1990	485D	173,600	199,600
1989	485D	160,300	184,400
1988	485D	150,400	173,000
1987	485D	141,700	162,900
1986	450D	136,500	157,000
1985	450D	128,000	147,200
1984	450D	119,600	137,500
1983	450D	110,800	127,500
1982	T-Diesel	108,100	124,300
1981	T-Diesel	102,000	117,400
1980	T-Diesel	93,200	107,200

Packet Craft 360 Express ******

PDQ 32/34 Passagemaker

Year	Power	Retail Low	Retail High
2004	T100D	214,500	246,600
2003	T100D	201,600	231,800
2002	T75D	189,500	217,900
2001	T75D	178,100	204,800
2000	T75D	167,400	192,500

Pearson True North 33

Year	Power	Retail Low	Retail High
2004	S440D	224,500	258,100

Pearson 34 Convertible

Year	Power	Retail Low	Retail High
1991	T320D	86,100	99,100
1990	T320D	82,200	94,500
1989	T320D	77,200	88,800

Pearson 38 Convertible

Year	Power	Retail Low	Retail High
1991	T375D	121,900	140,200
1990	T375D	111,000	127,700
1989	T375D	103,000	118,500
1988	T375D	99,200	114,100
1987	T375D	92,100	106,000

Pearson 38 Double Cabin

Year	Power	Retail Low	Retail High
1991	T-Gas	102,500	117,900
1991	T-Diesel	121,200	139,400
1990	T-Gas	73,000	83,900
1990	T-Diesel	85,800	98,600
1989	T-Gas	68,200	78,400
1989	T-Diesel	78,800	90,700
1988	T-Gas	61,800	71,100
1988	T-Diesel	72,400	83,300

Pearson True North 38

Year	Power	Retail Low	Retail High
2004	S440D	273,500	314,500
2003	S440D	251,600	289,300
2002	S440D	231,400	266,200

Pearson 43 Motor Yacht

Year	Power	Retail Low	Retail High
1986	T-Gas	79,600	91,500
1986	T-Diesel	87,800	101,000
1985	T-Gas	73,900	85,000
1985	T-Diesel	81,400	93,700
1984	T-Gas	68,800	79,200
1984	T-Diesel	75,800	87,100

Phoenix 27 Tournament

Year	Power	Retail Low	Retail High
1999	T-Gas	60,500	69,600
1999	T200 D	73,900	85,000
1998	T-Gas	52,700	60,700
1998	T200 D	70,300	80,800
1997	T-Gas	51,100	58,700
1997	T200 D	66,100	76,000
1996	T-Gas	48,800	56,200
1996	T200 D	61,900	71,200
1995	T-Gas	47,400	54,500
1995	T200 D	60,700	69,800
1994	T-Gas	44,700	51,500

Year	Power	Retail Low	Retail High
1994	T200 D	58,200	66,900
1993	T-Gas	43,700	50,300
1993	T200 D	57,000	65,500
1992	T-Gas	42,300	48,700
1992	T200 D	54,600	62,700
1991	T-Gas	39,700	45,700
1991	T200 D	49,600	57,000
1990	T-Gas	34,000	39,100
1990	T200 D	44,000	50,600

Phoenix 27 Weekender

Year	Power	Retail Low	Retail High
1994	T-Gas	43,400	49,900
1994	T-Diesel	55,000	63,300
1993	T-Gas	39,600	45,500
1993	T-Diesel	50,000	57,500
1992	T-Gas	37,100	42,700
1992	T-Diesel	45,800	52,700
1991	T-Gas	36,500	42,000
1991	T-Diesel	42,600	49,000
1990	T-Gas	32,400	37,300
1990	T-Diesel	40,000	46,000
1989	T-Gas	29,800	34,300
1989	T-Diesel	37,300	42,900
1988	T-Gas	26,700	30,700
1988	T-Diesel	34,400	39,600
1987	T-Gas	25,400	29,200
1987	T-Diesel	33,700	38,800
1986	T-Gas	23,600	27,200
1986	T-Diesel	31,600	36,300
1985	T-Gas	22,500	25,800
1985	T-Diesel	29,500	34,000
1984	T-Gas	20,700	23,800
1984	T-Diesel	27,800	31,900
1983	T-Gas	18,900	21,800
1983	T-Diesel	25,400	29,200
1982	T-Gas	17,700	20,300
1982	T-Diesel	23,000	26,500
1981	T-Gas	16,200	18,700
1981	T-Diesel	20,500	23,600
1980	T-Gas	15,000	17,300
1980	T-Diesel	19,000	21,800

Phoenix 29 Convertible

Year	Power	Retail Low	Retail High
1987	T-Gas	32,400	37,200
1987	T-Diesel	41,500	47,700
1986	T-Gas	30,800	35,400
1986	T-Diesel	37,700	43,400
1985	T-Gas	28,900	33,300
1985	T-Diesel	34,900	40,100
1984	T-Gas	28,100	32,300
1984	T-Diesel	34,300	39,500
1983	T-Gas	26,000	29,900
1983	T-Diesel	31,300	36,000
1982	T-Gas	23,400	26,900
1982	T-Diesel	29,000	33,400
1981	T-Gas	21,700	24,900
1981	T-Diesel	26,700	30,700
1980	T-Gas	19,600	22,600
1980	T-Diesel	24,200	27,900

Phoenix 29 SFX Convertible

Year	Power	Retail Low	Retail High
1999	T-Gas	77,200	88,800
1999	T200 D	96,300	110,800
1998	T-Gas	71,100	81,800
1998	T200 D	85,500	98,400
1997	T-Gas	64,200	73,900
1997	T200 D	81,900	94,200
1996	T-Gas	65,400	75,200

PRICES

PRICES

Year	Power	Retail Low	Retail High
1996	T200 D	79,500	91,400
1995	T-Gas	60,800	69,900
1995	T200 D	76,400	87,900
1994	T-Gas	58,800	67,700
1994	T200 D	70,700	81,300
1993	T-Gas	55,900	64,300
1993	T200 D	66,900	77,000
1992	T-Gas	52,600	60,400
1992	T200 D	63,100	72,600
1991	T-Gas	46,100	53,000
1991	T200 D	58,600	67,400
1990	T-Gas	42,000	48,300
1990	T200 D	55,000	63,200
1989	T-Gas	38,700	44,500
1989	T200 D	50,000	57,500
1988	T-Gas	34,300	39,500
1988	T200 D	42,900	49,300

Phoenix Blackhawk 909

Year	Power	Retail Low	Retail High
1987	T-Gas	31,800	36,600
1987	T-Diesel	39,600	45,600
1986	T-Gas	28,400	32,700
1986	T-Diesel	36,200	41,700
1985	T-Gas	25,100	28,900
1985	T-Diesel	32,900	37,800

Phoenix 32 Tournament

Year	Power	Retail Low	Retail High
1999	T350D	161,500	185,700
1998	T350D	152,100	174,900
1997	T350D	142,200	163,600

Phoenix 33/34 SFX Convertible

Year	Power	Retail Low	Retail High
1999	T-Gas	149,100	171,400
1999	T385D	188,900	217,300
1998	T-Gas	124,000	142,700
1998	T375D	176,600	203,100
1997	T-Gas	118,900	136,700
1997	T375D	164,800	189,600
1996	T-Gas	113,700	130,700
1996	T375D	151,800	174,600
1995	T-Gas	109,500	125,900
1995	T-Diesel	149,000	171,300
1994	T-Gas	107,200	123,300
1994	T-Diesel	144,200	165,800
1993	T-Gas	103,500	119,000
1993	T-Diesel	135,800	156,200
1992	T-Gas	100,400	115,500
1992	T-Diesel	135,200	155,500
1991	T-Gas	89,200	102,600
1991	T-Diesel	121,800	140,100
1990	T-Gas	82,500	94,900
1990	T-Diesel	116,100	133,500
1989	T-Gas	71,000	81,600
1989	T-Diesel	99,900	114,900
1988	T-Gas	62,700	72,200
1988	T-Diesel	90,000	103,500
1987	T-Gas	57,800	66,500
1987	T-Diesel	82,200	94,500

Phoenix 33/34 Tournament

Year	Power	Retail Low	Retail High
1999	T-Gas	125,800	144,700
1999	T385D	177,600	204,300
1998	T-Gas	110,700	127,300
1998	T375D	165,300	190,000
1997	T-Gas	107,900	124,100
1997	T375D	158,400	182,200
1996	T-Gas	103,000	118,400
1996	T375D	150,600	173,200

Year	Power	Retail Low	Retail High
1995	T-Gas	101,300	116,500
1995	T-Diesel	143,000	164,500
1994	T-Gas	101,000	116,200
1994	T-Diesel	138,200	158,900
1993	T-Gas	97,000	111,500
1993	T-Diesel	131,300	151,100
1992	T-Gas	91,200	104,900
1992	T-Diesel	124,700	143,400
1991	T-Gas	83,500	96,100
1991	T-Diesel	120,200	138,200
1990	T-Gas	76,500	88,000
1990	T-Diesel	112,000	128,800

Phoenix 37/38 SFX Convertible

Year	Power	Retail Low	Retail High
1999	435D	268,300	308,500
1999	480D	276,600	318,100
1998	420D	247,200	284,300
1998	485D	258,700	297,500
1997	420D	234,800	270,000
1997	485D	246,800	283,800
1996	420D	222,300	255,700
1996	485D	234,200	269,400
1995	375D	206,600	237,600
1995	485D	222,200	255,600
1994	375D	193,400	222,400
1994	485D	205,800	236,700
1993	375D	184,100	211,700
1993	485D	196,900	226,500
1992	375D	169,700	195,100
1992	485D	182,300	209,600
1991	375D	151,100	173,700
1991	485D	160,300	184,400
1990	375D	135,200	155,500
1990	485D	149,600	172,100
1989	375D	115,400	132,700
1989	485D	124,700	143,500

Phoenix 38 Convertible

Year	Power	Retail Low	Retail High
1988	375D	105,100	120,900
1988	485D	114,100	131,200
1987	375D	99,200	114,100
1987	450D	106,700	122,700
1986	375D	94,900	109,100
1986	450D	98,800	113,600
1985	355D	90,000	103,500
1985	410D	92,800	106,700
1984	355D	81,500	93,800
1984	410D	87,800	100,900
1983	300D	78,600	90,400
1983	410D	84,300	96,900
1982	300D	71,000	81,700
1982	410D	80,500	92,600

Pilgrim 40

Year	Power	Retail Low	Retail High
1989	S-Diesel	119,400	137,400
1988	S-Diesel	114,300	131,500
1987	S-Diesel	109,200	125,600
1986	S-Diesel	103,400	118,900
1985	S-Diesel	101,100	116,200
1984	S-Diesel	99,100	114,000

Post 42 Sport Fisherman (1975-83)

Year	Power	Retail Low	Retail High
1983	310D	95,500	109,800
1983	450D	111,600	128,400
1982	310D	93,600	107,600
1982	450D	107,100	123,200
1981	310D	93,600	107,600
1981	410D	101,300	116,500

Year	Power	Retail Low	Retail High
1980	310D	86,200	99,200
1980	410D	95,300	109,600

Post 42 SF (Current)

Year	Power	Retail Low	Retail High
2004	T430D	492,300	566,100
2003	T430D	447,900	515,100
2002	T430D	407,600	468,800
2001	T430D	370,900	426,600
2000	T430D	341,300	392,500
1999	T430D	314,000	361,100
1998	T430D	288,800	332,200
1997	T430D	265,700	305,600

Post 43 SF (1984-89)

Year	Power	Retail Low	Retail High
1989	T485D	182,900	210,300
1988	T450D	171,800	197,600
1987	T450D	160,400	184,500
1986	T450D	149,400	171,800
1985	T450D	137,800	158,500
1984	T450D	131,700	151,400

Post 43 SF (1995-96)

Year	Power	Retail Low	Retail High
1996	T550D	277,000	318,500
1995	T550D	257,300	295,900

Post 44 Sport Fisherman

Year	Power	Retail Low	Retail High
1994	T550	248,200	285,500
1993	T550	226,900	260,900
1992	T550	209,000	240,400
1991	T550	195,200	224,400
1990	T550	185,900	213,800

Post 46 Sport Fisherman

Year	Power	Retail Low	Retail High
1996	T550D	342,000	393,300
1995	T550D	314,600	361,800
1994	T550D	289,400	332,800
1993	T550D	266,300	306,200
1992	T550D	247,600	284,800
1991	T550D	230,300	264,800
1990	T550D	214,200	246,300
1989	T550D	199,200	229,000
1988	T485D	187,200	215,300
1987	T485D	176,000	202,400
1986	T485D	165,400	190,200
1985	T450D	157,100	180,700
1984	T450D	149,300	171,700
1983	T450D	141,800	163,100
1982	T450D	134,700	154,900
1981	T450D	128,000	147,200
1980	T450D	121,600	139,800

Post 47 Sport Fisherman

Year	Power	Retail Low	Retail High
2004	T680 MAN	701,200	806,300
2003	T680 MAN	638,000	733,800
2002	T680 MAN	580,600	667,700
2001	T680 MAN	534,200	614,300
2000	T680 MAN	491,400	565,100
1999	T680 MAN	452,100	519,900
1998	T680 MAN	420,500	483,500
1997	T550 DD	391,000	449,700

Post 50 Sport Fisherman

Year	Power	Retail Low	Retail High
2004	T860 MAN	908,700	1,045,000
2003	T860 MAN	826,900	950,900
2002	T820 MAN	752,400	865,300
2001	T820 MAN	684,700	787,400
2000	T820 MAN	629,900	724,400
1999	T820 MAN	579,500	666,500
1998	T820 MAN	533,200	613,200
1997	T735 DD	490,500	564,100

Year	Power	Retail Low	Retail High
1996	T735 DD	456,200	524,600
1995	T735 DD	424,200	487,900
1994	T735 DD	398,800	458,600
1993	T735 DD	374,900	431,100
1992	T735 DD	352,400	405,200
1991	T735 DD	331,200	380,900
1990	T735 DD	311,300	358,000
1989	T735 DD	292,700	336,600
Post 56 Convertible			
2004	T1300D	******	******
2003	T1300D	******	******
2002	T1300D	1,086,400	1,249,400
2001	T1300D	990,700	1,139,300
Powerplay 33 Sportfish			
2004	T250 O/B	117,300	134,800
2003	T250 O/B	105,500	121,400
2002	T250 O/B	95,000	109,200
2001	T250 O/B	86,400	99,400
2000	T250 O/B	78,600	90,400
1999	T250 O/B	71,500	82,300
1998	T250 O/B	65,100	74,900
President 35 Double Cabin			
1992	T225D	97,900	112,500
1991	T225D	93,000	107,000
1990	T225D	88,300	101,600
1989	T225D	83,900	96,500
1988	T225D	79,700	91,700
1987	T225D	75,700	87,100
President 35 Sedan			
1992	T350G	75,500	86,800
1992	T225D	82,500	94,800
1991	T350G	70,900	81,600
1991	T225D	78,300	90,100
1990	T350G	67,400	77,500
1990	T225D	74,400	85,600
1989	T350G	63,300	72,800
1989	T225D	70,700	81,300
1988	T350G	60,200	69,200
1988	T225D	67,100	77,200
1987	T350G	56,500	65,000
1987	T225D	63,800	73,400
President 37 Sedan			
1991	T350G	******	******
1991	T275D	******	******
1990	T350G	******	******
1990	T275D	******	******
1989	T350G	83,400	95,900
1989	T275D	108,500	124,700
1988	T350G	78,300	90,100
1988	T275D	103,000	118,500
1987	T350G	73,600	84,700
1987	T275D	96,800	111,400
1986	T350G	69,200	79,600
1986	T275D	92,000	105,800
President 37 Sundeck			
1992	T350G	******	******
1992	T275D	******	******
1991	T350G	******	******
1991	T275D	******	******
1990	T350G	92,800	106,700
1990	T275D	119,100	137,000
1989	T350G	88,400	101,600
1989	T275D	113,500	130,500

Year	Power	Retail Low	Retail High
1988	T350G	83,000	95,500
1988	T275D	107,800	123,900
1987	T350G	78,100	89,800
1987	T275D	101,300	116,500
1986	T350G	73,400	84,400
1986	T275D	96,200	110,700
President 41 DC			
1989	T135D	110,200	126,700
1989	T275D	117,500	135,100
1988	T135D	104,600	120,300
1988	T275D	111,600	128,300
1987	T135D	99,400	114,300
1987	T275D	106,000	121,900
1986	T135D	94,400	108,600
1986	T275D	100,700	115,800
1985	T135D	89,700	103,200
1985	T275D	95,700	110,000
1984	T135D	85,200	98,000
1984	T225D	90,900	104,500
1983	T135D	81,000	93,100
1983	T225D	86,300	99,300
1982	T135D	76,900	88,500
1982	T225D	82,000	94,300
President 42 Trawler ****			
President 43 DC			
1990	T135D	132,700	152,700
1990	T275D	142,100	163,500
1989	T135D	125,700	144,500
1989	T275D	134,200	154,400
1988	T135D	117,000	134,600
1988	T275D	124,800	143,600
1987	T135D	110,000	126,500
1987	T275D	117,000	134,600
1986	T135D	102,200	117,500
1986	T275D	109,300	125,700
1985	T135D	95,300	109,700
1985	T225D	102,400	117,300
1984	T135D	88,200	101,400
1984	T225D	95,300	109,700
Pro-Line 27 Walk			
2004	T200 O/B	65,500	75,300
2003	T200 O/B	58,900	67,700
2002	T200 O/B	53,000	61,000
2001	T200 O/B	47,700	54,900
2000	T200 O/B	42,900	49,400
1999	T200 O/B	38,600	44,400
1998	T200 O/B	34,800	40,000
Pro-Line 27/29 Express			
2004	T200 O/B	63,800	73,300
2003	T200 O/B	57,400	66,000
2002	T200 O/B	51,600	59,400
2001	T200 O/B	46,500	53,400
Pro-Line 27 Sport			
2004	T200 O/B	61,200	70,300
2003	T200 O/B	55,000	63,300
2001	T200 O/B	49,500	57,000
2000	T200 O/B	44,600	51,300
Pro-Line 2700 Sportsman			
1999	T200 O/B	40,500	46,600
1998	T200 O/B	36,900	42,400
1997	T200 O/B	33,600	38,600
1996	T200 O/B	30,500	35,100
1995	T200 O/B	27,800	32,000

Year	Power	Retail Low	Retail High
1994	T200 O/B	25,300	29,100
1993	T200 O/B	23,000	26,500
Pro-Line 2810 Walkaround			
2000	T225 O/B	51,700	59,400
1999	T225 O/B	46,500	53,500
1998	T225 O/B	41,800	48,100
1997	T225 O/B	37,600	43,300
Pro-Line 2950 Mid-Cabin			
1999	T225 O/B	49,300	56,600
1999	T I/O Gas	53,500	61,600
1998	T225 O/B	44,300	51,000
1998	T I/O Gas	48,400	55,700
1997	T225 O/B	39,900	45,900
1997	T I/O Gas	42,900	49,300
1996	T225 O/B	36,300	41,700
1996	T I/O Gas	40,300	46,300
1995	T225 O/B	33,000	38,000
1995	T I/O Gas	37,300	42,900
1994	T225 O/B	30,000	34,600
1994	T I/O Gas	35,400	40,700
1993	T225 O/B	27,300	31,400
1993	T I/O Gas	31,600	36,400
1992	T225 O/B	24,900	28,600
1992	T I/O Gas	28,200	32,400
Pro-Line 30/31 Express			
2004	T225 O/B	86,900	99,900
2003	T225 O/B	78,200	89,900
2002	T225 O/B	70,300	80,900
2001	T225 O/B	63,300	72,800
2000	T225 O/B	57,000	65,500
Pro-Line 30/31 Sport			
2004	T225 O/B	79,300	91,100
2003	T225 O/B	71,300	82,000
2002	T225 O/B	64,200	73,800
2001	T225 O/B	57,800	66,400
2000	T225 O/B	52,000	59,800
Pro-Line 30/31 Walk			
2004	T225 O/B	87,600	100,700
2003	T225 O/B	78,800	90,600
2002	T225 O/B	70,900	81,500
2001	T225 O/B	63,800	73,400
2000	T225 O/B	57,400	66,000
Pro-Line 3250 Exp; 32 Express			
2002	T320G I/O	117,700	135,300
2001	T320G I/O	107,100	123,100
2000	T310G I/O	97,400	112,000
1999	T310G I/O	88,600	102,000
1998	T310G I/O	80,700	92,800
1997	T310G I/O	73,400	84,400
Pro-Line 33 Express			
2004	T370G I/B	157,500	181,100
2004	T315D I/B	******	******
2003	T370G I/B	141,700	163,000
2003	T315D I/B	******	******
2002	T370G I/B	127,500	146,700
2002	T315D I/B	******	******
2001	T310G I/B	114,800	132,000
2001	T350D I/B	154,700	177,900
2000	T310G I/B	104,400	120,100
2000	T350D I/B	142,300	163,600
1999	T310G I/B	95,000	109,300
1999	T350D I/B	130,900	150,500

PRICES

Year	Power	Retail Low	Retail High
Pro-Line 33/34 Walk			
2004	T250 O/B	122,700	141,100
2003	T250 O/B	110,400	126,900
Pro-Line 3400 Bimini Cuddy			
1999	T250 O/B	56,200	64,600
1998	T250 O/B	50,200	57,800
1997	T250 O/B	45,000	51,800
1996	T250 O/B	39,300	45,300
Pro-Line 3400 Super Sport			
2001	T250 O/B	85,100	97,800
2000	T250 O/B	74,800	86,100
1999	T250 O/B	67,600	77,800
1998	T250 O/B	61,900	71,200
PT 35 Sedan			
1990	T-Diesel	90,300	103,900
1989	T-Diesel	85,900	98,800
1988	T-Diesel	79,500	91,400
1987	T-Diesel	74,400	85,600
1986	T-Diesel	70,200	80,700
1985	T-Diesel	64,400	74,100
1984	T-Diesel	60,200	69,200
PT 35 Sundeck			
1990	T-Diesel	94,100	108,200
1989	T-Diesel	87,500	100,600
1988	T-Diesel	82,300	94,600
1987	T-Diesel	77,400	89,000
1986	T-Diesel	71,400	82,100
1985	T-Diesel	65,500	75,300
1984	T-Diesel	60,200	69,200
PT 38 Double Cabin			
1985	S-Diesel	66,600	76,600
1985	T-Diesel	74,000	85,100
1984	S-Diesel	60,600	69,700
1984	T-Diesel	68,200	78,500
1983	S-Diesel	57,500	66,100
1983	T-Diesel	65,700	75,600
1982	S-Diesel	54,600	62,800
1982	T-Diesel	61,500	70,700
1981	S-Diesel	50,700	58,300
1981	T-Diesel	57,700	66,400
1980	S-Diesel	46,900	53,900
1980	T-Diesel	53,900	61,900
PT 41 Double Cabin			
1984	T-Diesel	74,000	85,100
1983	T-Diesel	69,500	79,900
1982	T-Diesel	66,500	76,500
1981	T-Diesel	63,600	73,200
1980	T-Diesel	60,600	69,700
PT 42 Cockpit MY			
1990	T-Diesel	129,700	149,100
1989	T-Diesel	123,000	141,400
1988	T-Diesel	115,200	132,500
1987	T-Diesel	108,300	124,600
1986	T-Diesel	99,800	114,700
1985	T-Diesel	92,400	106,200
1984	T-Diesel	86,200	99,200
PT 52 Cockpit MY			
1990	T-Diesel	219,000	251,800
1989	T-Diesel	200,400	230,500
1988	T-Diesel	187,900	216,100
1987	T-Diesel	179,600	206,500
1986	T-Diesel	174,100	200,200

Year	Power	Retail Low	Retail High
Pursuit 2650 Cuddy; 2655 Express			
1994	T200 O/B	27,500	31,600
1994	S330 I/O	25,900	29,800
1993	T200 O/B	26,100	30,000
1993	S330 I/O	23,800	27,300
1992	S200 O/B	24,800	28,500
1992	S330 I/O	22,600	26,000
1991	T200 O/B	23,500	27,100
1991	S330 I/O	21,400	24,700
1990	T200 O/B	22,300	25,700
1990	S330 I/O	20,400	23,400
1989	T200 O/B	21,200	24,400
1989	S330 I/O	19,300	22,200
Pursuit 2655 Center Console			
1996	T200 O/B	40,700	46,800
1995	T200 O/B	36,600	42,100
1994	T200 O/B	32,800	37,700
1993	T200 O/B	29,400	33,800
1992	T200 O/B	26,300	30,200
Pursuit 2670 Cuddy Console			
2004	T225 O/B	65,400	75,200
2003	T225 O/B	59,500	68,400
2002	T225 O/B	54,100	62,200
Pursuit 2670 Denali			
2004	T225 O/B	72,300	83,100
2003	T225 O/B	66,500	76,400
Pursuit 27 Open; 2700 Express			
1993	T260G	39,100	44,900
1992	T260G	36,700	42,200
1991	T260G	34,500	39,700
1990	T260G	32,800	37,700
1989	T270G	31,100	35,800
1988	T270G	29,600	34,000
1987	T270G	28,100	32,300
1986	T270G	26,700	30,700
1985	T270G	25,600	29,500
1984	T270G	24,600	28,300
1983	T270G	23,600	27,200
Pursuit 2800 Open			
1992	T200 O/B	36,500	41,900
1991	T200 O/B	34,300	39,400
1990	T200 O/B	32,200	37,000
1989	T200 O/B	30,300	34,800
Pursuit 2855 Express Fish			
1995	T200 O/B	45,900	52,800
1994	T200 O/B	42,700	49,100
1993	T200 O/B	39,700	45,600
Pursuit 2860/2865 Denali			
2004	S375G I/O	80,500	92,500
2003	S375G I/O	73,200	84,200
2002	S375G I/O	66,600	76,600
2001	S310G I/O	60,600	69,700
2000	S310G I/O	55,800	64,100
1999	S310G I/O	51,300	59,000
1998	S310G I/O	47,200	54,300
1997	S310G I/O	43,400	49,900
Pursuit 2870 Center Console			
2004	T225 O/B	86,700	99,700
2003	T225 O/B	78,000	89,700
2002	T225 O/B	70,200	80,700
2001	T225 O/B	63,200	72,600
2000	T225 O/B	57,500	66,100

Year	Power	Retail Low	Retail High
1999	T225 O/B	52,300	60,100
1998	T225 O/B	47,600	54,700
1997	T225 O/B	43,300	49,800
Pursuit 2870 Offshore CC			
2002	T225 O/B	74,500	85,600
2001	T225 O/B	67,700	77,900
2000	T225 O/B	61,600	70,900
1999	T225 O/B	56,100	64,500
1998	T225 O/B	51,000	58,700
1997	T225 O/B	46,400	53,400
1996	T225 O/B	42,300	48,600
Pursuit 2870 Walkaround			
2004	T225 O/B	93,400	107,400
2003	T225 O/B	84,000	96,600
2002	T225 O/B	75,600	87,000
2001	T225 O/B	68,000	78,300
2000	T225 O/B	61,900	71,200
1999	T225 O/B	56,300	64,800
1998	T225 O/B	51,300	59,000
1997	T225 O/B	46,600	53,600
1996	T225 O/B	42,400	48,800
Pursuit 3000 Express			
2003	T320G	108,500	124,700
2003	T250D	143,200	164,600
2002	T320G	98,700	113,500
2002	T250D	131,700	151,500
2001	T320G	90,800	104,400
2001	T250D	121,200	139,300
2000	T320G	83,500	96,100
2000	T250D	112,700	129,600
1999	T320G	76,800	88,400
1999	T250D	104,800	120,500
1998	T320G	70,700	81,300
1998	T225D	97,400	112,100
Pursuit 3000 Offshore			
2004	T-Gas	130,500	150,000
2004	T315D	181,400	208,600
2003	T-Gas	117,400	135,000
2003	T315D	163,200	187,700
2002	T-Gas	105,700	121,500
2002	T315D	146,900	168,900
2001	T-Gas	95,100	109,400
2001	T315D	132,200	152,000
2000	T-Gas	86,500	99,500
2000	T315D	120,300	138,300
1999	T-Gas	78,700	90,500
1999	T315D	109,500	125,900
1998	T-Gas	71,600	82,400
1998	T-Diesel	99,600	114,600
1997	T-Gas	65,200	75,000
1997	T-Diesel	90,600	104,200
1996	T-Gas	59,300	68,200
1996	T-Diesel	82,500	94,900
1995	T-Gas	54,000	62,100
1995	T-Diesel	75,000	86,300
Pursuit 3070 Center Console			
2004	T250 O/B	118,400	136,100
2003	T250 O/B	106,500	122,500
2002	T250 O/B	95,900	110,200
2001	T250 O/B	86,300	99,200
Pursuit 3070 Offshore CC			
2004	T250 O/B	131,200	150,800
2003	T250 O/B	118,000	135,700

PRICES

344

Year	Power	Retail Low	Retail High
2002	T250 O/B	106,200	122,200
2001	T250 O/B	95,600	109,900
2000	T250 O/B	87,000	100,000
1999	T250 O/B	79,200	91,000

Pursuit 3070 Express ****

Pursuit 3100 Express

Year	Power	Retail Low	Retail High
1997	T300G	75,500	86,800
1996	T300G	69,400	79,900
1995	T300G	63,900	73,500
1994	T300G	58,800	67,600
1993	T300G	54,100	62,200

Pursuit 3100 Offshore

Year	Power	Retail Low	Retail High
2004	T330G	119,300	137,100
2004	T315D	163,400	187,900

Pursuit 3250 Express

Year	Power	Retail Low	Retail High
1993	T-Gas	74,300	85,400
1993	T-Diesel	93,900	108,000
1992	T-Gas	69,700	80,200
1992	T-Diesel	85,400	98,200
1991	T-Gas	62,100	71,400
1991	T-Diesel	77,800	89,400
1990	T-Gas	55,800	64,100
1990	T-Diesel	71,800	82,600

Pursuit 3370 Offshore

Year	Power	Retail Low	Retail High
2004	T300 O/B	158,600	182,400

Pursuit 3400 Express Fish

Year	Power	Retail Low	Retail High
2003	T375G	168,600	193,800
2003	T370D	210,000	241,500
2002	T375G	153,400	176,400
2002	T370D	191,100	219,700
2001	T370G	139,600	160,500
2001	T370D	173,900	199,900
2000	T370G	128,400	147,700
2000	T370D	159,900	183,900
1999	T320G	116,800	134,400
1999	T370D	147,100	169,200
1998	T320G	107,500	123,600
1998	T370D	136,800	157,400
1997	T320G	97,800	112,500
1997	T370D	127,300	146,400

Pursuit 3800 Express

Year	Power	Retail Low	Retail High
2004	T480D	366,500	421,400
2003	T480D	337,100	387,700
2002	T480D	310,200	356,700

Pursuit 3480 CC ****

Queenship 68 Raised Pilothouse ****

Rampage 28 Sportsman

Year	Power	Retail Low	Retail High
1993	T-Gas	48,200	55,500
1993	T-Diesel	59,900	68,900
1992	T-Gas	43,900	50,500
1992	T-Diesel	55,000	63,200
1991	T-Gas	41,100	47,300
1991	T-Diesel	50,800	58,400
1990	T-Gas	35,100	40,300
1990	T-Diesel	43,200	49,700
1989	T-Gas	33,300	38,300
1988	T-Gas	29,600	34,100
1987	T-Gas	28,100	32,300
1986	T-Gas	25,600	29,500

Rampage 30 Express

Year	Power	Retail Low	Retail High
2004	T-Gas	165,300	190,000

Year	Power	Retail Low	Retail High
2004	T315D	207,700	238,800
2003	T-Gas	150,400	172,900
2003	T315D	189,000	217,300
2002	T-Gas	136,800	157,400
2002	T300D	171,900	197,700
2001	T-Gas	124,500	143,200
2001	T300D	156,500	179,900
2000	T-Gas	113,300	130,300
2000	T300D	142,400	163,700
1999	T-Gas	103,100	118,600
1999	T300D	129,600	149,000

Rampage 31 Sport Fisherman

Year	Power	Retail Low	Retail High
1993	T-Gas	66,000	75,900
1993	T300 D	84,100	96,800
1992	T-Gas	60,000	69,000
1992	T300 D	74,000	85,100
1991	T-Gas	57,100	65,700
1991	T300 D	68,600	78,900
1990	T-Gas	50,100	57,600
1990	T300 D	64,900	74,700
1989	T-Gas	46,400	53,300
1989	T300 D	62,600	71,900
1988	T-Gas	40,800	47,000
1988	T300 D	60,800	70,000
1987	T-Gas	39,100	45,000
1987	T300 D	52,400	60,300
1986	T-Gas	34,600	39,800
1986	T300 D	47,700	54,800
1985	T-Gas	33,200	38,200
1985	T300 D	41,800	48,100

Rampage 33 Express ****

Rampage 33 Sport Fisherman

Year	Power	Retail Low	Retail High
1993	T-Gas	77,800	89,400
1993	T300 D	96,300	110,700
1992	T-Gas	72,900	83,800
1992	T300 D	90,000	103,500
1991	T-Gas	69,900	80,400
1991	T300 D	85,500	98,300
1990	T-Gas	67,200	77,300
1990	T300 D	81,400	93,600

Rampage 36 Sport Fisherman

Year	Power	Retail Low	Retail High
1993	T375 D	138,600	159,400
1992	T375 D	128,300	147,600
1991	T375 D	117,100	134,700
1990	T375 D	109,900	126,400
1989	T375 D	105,200	121,000

Rampage 38 Express

Year	Power	Retail Low	Retail High
2004	T480D	358,900	412,700
2003	T480D	326,500	375,500
2002	T480D	297,200	341,700
2001	T480D	270,400	311,000
2000	T450D	246,100	283,000
1999	T450D	223,900	257,500

Rampage 40 Sport Fisherman

Year	Power	Retail Low	Retail High
1990	T-Diesel	151,200	173,800
1989	T-Diesel	139,900	160,900
1988	T-Diesel	126,100	145,000

Rampage 45 Convertible

Year	Power	Retail Low	Retail High
2004	T800D	876,900	1,008,400
2003	T800D	797,900	917,500
2002	T800D	726,100	835,000

Regal 260 Valenti; 272 Commodore

Year	Power	Retail Low	Retail High
1996	S300 I/O	27,100	31,100
1996	T190 I/O	28,700	33,000
1995	S300 I/O	24,600	28,300
1995	T190 I/O	26,100	30,000
1994	S300 I/O	22,400	25,800
1994	T190 I/O	23,700	27,300
1993	S300 I/O	20,400	23,400
1993	T180 I/O	21,600	24,800
1992	S300 I/O	18,500	21,300
1992	T180 I/O	19,600	22,600
1991	S300 I/O	16,900	19,400
1991	T180 I/O	17,900	20,500

Regal 2660/2765 Commodore

Year	Power	Retail Low	Retail High
2004	S375 I/O	64,900	74,600
2004	T220 I/O	69,600	80,000
2003	S375 I/O	58,400	67,100
2003	T220 I/O	62,600	72,000
2002	S320 I/O	52,500	60,400
2002	T190 I/O	56,300	64,800
2001	S310 I/O	47,300	54,400
2001	T190 I/O	50,700	58,300
2000	S310 I/O	42,500	48,900
2000	T190 I/O	45,600	52,500
1999	S310 I/O	38,300	44,000
1999	T190 I/O	41,000	47,200

Regal 265/270/276 Commodore

Year	Power	Retail Low	Retail High
1993	S310 I/O	22,200	25,600
1992	S310 I/O	20,800	23,900
1991	S300 I/O	19,200	22,100
1990	S300 I/O	18,300	21,000

Regal 2760/2860 Commodore

Year	Power	Retail Low	Retail High
2004	T220 I/O	84,600	97,200
2003	T220 I/O	76,100	87,500
2002	T220 I/O	68,500	78,800
2001	T210 I/O	61,600	70,900
2000	T210 I/O	56,100	64,500
1999	T210 I/O	51,000	58,700

Regal Ventura 8.3 SC

Year	Power	Retail Low	Retail High
1997	S300 I/O	24,600	28,200
1997	T190 I/O	27,900	32,000
1996	S300 I/O	22,300	25,700
1996	T190 I/O	25,300	29,100
1995	S300 I/O	20,500	23,600
1995	T190 I/O	23,300	26,800
1994	S300 I/O	18,900	21,700
1994	T180 I/O	21,400	24,700
1993	S300 I/O	17,400	20,000
1993	T180 I/O	19,700	22,700
1992	S300 I/O	16,000	18,400
1992	T180 I/O	18,100	20,900

Regal 277XL/280/290/300

Year	Power	Retail Low	Retail High
1994	T-I/O 5.7L	33,800	38,900
1993	T-I/O 5.7L	30,600	35,200
1992	T-I/O 5.7L	29,200	33,500
1991	T-I/O 5.7L	26,900	30,900
1990	T-I/O 5.7L	24,500	28,200
1989	T-I/O 5.7L	22,000	25,300
1988	T-I/O 5.7L	20,600	23,700
1987	T-I/O 5.7L	17,300	19,900
1986	T-I/O 5.7L	15,900	18,300
1985	T-I/O 5.7L	14,700	16,900
1984	T-I/O 5.7L	14,000	16,200

PRICES

Year	Power	Retail Low	Retail High
1983	T-I/O 5.7L	13,000	15,000
1982	T-I/O 5.7L	12,100	13,900

Regal 2800/2900 LSR

Year	Power	Retail Low	Retail High
2004	S375 I/O	63,000	72,400
2003	S375 I/O	56,000	64,400
2002	S375 I/O	49,900	57,300
2001	S310 I/O	44,400	51,000
2000	S310 I/O	39,500	45,400
1999	S310 I/O	35,100	40,400

Regal 292/2960/3060 Commodore

Year	Power	Retail Low	Retail High
2003	T260 I/O	85,200	97,900
2002	T260 I/O	76,600	88,100
2001	T260 I/O	69,000	79,300
2000	T260 I/O	62,800	72,200
1999	T260 I/O	57,100	65,700
1998	T260 I/O	52,000	59,800
1997	T260 I/O	47,300	54,400
1996	T260 I/O	43,000	49,500
1995	T260 I/O	39,100	45,000

Regal 3060 Commodore

Year	Power	Retail Low	Retail High
2004	T260 I/O	102,300	117,600

Regal 320 Commodore

Year	Power	Retail Low	Retail High
1992	T260 I/O	38,600	44,400
1991	T260 I/O	36,100	41,500
1990	T260 I/O	33,600	38,700
1989	T260 I/O	31,100	35,800
1988	T260 I/O	28,600	32,900

Regal Ventura 9.8; 322/3260 Commodore

Year	Power	Retail Low	Retail High
2004	T320 I/B	151,300	173,900
2004	T300 I/O	144,300	165,900
2003	T320 I/B	136,100	156,500
2003	T300 I/O	129,800	149,300
2002	T320 I/B	122,500	140,900
2002	T300 I/O	116,800	134,400
2001	T310 I/B	110,200	126,800
2001	T310 I/O	105,100	120,900
2000	T310 I/B	100,300	115,400
2000	T310 I/O	95,700	110,000
1999	T310 I/B	91,300	105,000
1999	T310 I/O	87,100	100,100
1998	T310 I/B	83,100	95,500
1998	T310 I/O	79,200	91,100
1997	T310 I/B	75,600	86,900
1997	T310 I/O	72,100	82,900
1996	T310 I/B	68,800	79,100
1996	T310 I/O	65,600	75,400
1995	T310 I/B	63,300	72,800
1995	T310 I/O	60,300	69,400
1994	T310 I/B	58,200	66,900
1994	T310 I/O	55,500	63,800
1993	T310 I/B	53,500	61,600
1993	T310 I/O	50,500	58,100

Regal 3350 Sport Cruiser ******

Regal 3560 Commodore

Year	Power	Retail Low	Retail High
2004	T370 I/B	185,600	213,400
2004	T375 I/O	179,500	206,400
2003	T370 I/B	167,000	192,000
2003	T375 I/O	161,500	185,700

Regal 360 Commodore

Year	Power	Retail Low	Retail High
1990	T340G	60,100	69,100
1989	T340G	55,900	64,200
1988	T340G	51,900	59,700

Year	Power	Retail Low	Retail High
1987	T340G	48,300	55,600
1986	T340G	44,900	51,700
1985	T340G	42,200	48,600

Regal 380/400/402 Commodore

Year	Power	Retail Low	Retail High
1999	T310G	130,200	149,700
1998	T310G	117,100	134,700
1997	T310G	106,600	122,600
1996	T310G	97,000	111,500
1995	T310G	89,200	102,600
1994	T310G	82,100	94,400
1993	T310G	75,500	86,800
1992	T310G	69,500	79,900
1991	T340G	63,900	73,500

Regal 3860 Commodore

Year	Power	Retail Low	Retail High
2004	T-Gas	243,600	280,100
2004	T370D	293,500	337,500
2003	T-Gas	219,200	252,100
2003	T-370D	264,100	303,700
2002	T-Gas	197,300	226,900
2002	T-370D	240,300	276,400

Regal 3880 Commodore

Year	Power	Retail Low	Retail High
2004	T-Gas	250,400	287,900
2004	T370D	301,800	347,000
2003	T-Gas	227,800	262,000
2003	T370D	274,600	315,800
2002	T-Gas	207,300	238,400
2002	T330D	249,900	287,400
2001	T-gas	188,600	216,900
2001	T330D	227,400	261,500

Regal 4160/4260 Commodore

Year	Power	Retail Low	Retail High
2004	T450D	343,500	395,000
2003	T450D	316,000	363,400
2002	T370D	284,400	327,000
2001	T370D	255,900	294,300
2000	T370D	230,300	264,900

Regulator 32 Center Console

Year	Power	Retail Low	Retail High
2004	T250 O/B	131,900	151,600
2003	T250 O/B	120,000	138,000
2002	T250 O/B	109,200	125,600
2001	T250 O/B	100,400	115,500
2000	T250 O/B	92,400	106,300
1999	T250 O/B	85,000	97,800

Rinker 270 Fiesta Vee

Year	Power	Retail Low	Retail High
2004	S250 I/O	50,300	57,800
2003	S250 I/O	44,700	51,400
2002	S250 I/O	39,800	45,800
2001	S250 I/O	35,400	40,700
2000	S250 I/O	31,500	36,200
1999	S250 I/O	28,000	32,300

Rinker 272 Captiva Bowrider

Year	Power	Retail Low	Retail High
2002	S320 I/O	32,200	37,000
2001	S320 I/O	28,600	32,900
2000	S320 I/O	25,500	29,300
1999	S310 I/O	22,700	26,100

Rinker 272 Captiva Cuddy

Year	Power	Retail Low	Retail High
2002	S320 I/O	33,300	38,200
2001	S320 I/O	29,600	34,000
2000	S320 I/O	26,300	30,300
1999	S310 I/O	23,400	26,900

Rinker 280 Fiesta Vee

Year	Power	Retail Low	Retail High
1999	T190 I/O	38,300	44,000

Year	Power	Retail Low	Retail High
1998	T190 I/O	35,700	41,000
1997	T190 I/O	33,200	38,200
1996	T180 I/O	30,900	35,500
1995	T180 I/O	27,900	32,100
1994	T180 I/O	25,700	29,600
1993	T180 I/O	23,400	27,000

Rinker 282 Captiva Bowrider

Year	Power	Retail Low	Retail High
2004	S320 I/O	44,300	50,900
2003	S320 I/O	39,800	45,800

Rinker 282 Captiva Cuddy

Year	Power	Retail Low	Retail High
2004	S320 I/O	46,900	53,900
2003	S320 I/O	42,200	48,500

Rinker 290/300 Fiesta Vee

Year	Power	Retail Low	Retail High
2004	T260 I/O	74,500	85,600
2003	T260 I/O	67,000	77,100

Rinker 300 Fiesta Vee

Year	Power	Retail Low	Retail High
1997	T250 I/O	46,700	53,700
1996	T250 I/O	41,900	48,200
1995	T250 I/O	37,500	43,100
1994	T260 I/O	35,300	40,600
1993	T260 I/O	32,400	37,200
1992	T260 I/O	29,600	34,100
1991	T260 I/O	26,900	31,000
1990	T260 I/O	24,000	27,600

Rinker 310/312/320 Fiesta Vee

Year	Power	Retail Low	Retail High
2004	T260 I/O	93,900	107,900
2003	T260 I/O	84,500	97,100
2002	T260 I/O	76,000	87,400
2001	T240 I/O	68,400	78,700
2000	T240 I/O	61,600	70,800

Rinker 330/340/342 Fiesta Vee

Year	Power	Retail Low	Retail High
2004	T300 I/O	118,000	135,700
2003	T300 I/O	106,200	122,100
2002	T300 I/O	95,500	109,900
2001	T260 I/O	86,000	98,900
2000	T260 I/O	77,400	89,000
1999	T260 I/O	69,600	80,100
1998	T260 I/O	62,700	72,100

Rinker 360 Fiesta Vee ******

Rinker 410 Fiesta Vee

Year	Power	Retail Low	Retail High
2004	T420G	270,000	310,500

Riviera 3000 Offshore

Year	Power	Retail Low	Retail High
2003	T260D	141,200	162,300
2002	T260D	131,300	151,000
2001	T260D	122,100	140,400
2000	T260D	113,500	130,600

Riviera 33 Conv. (1992-98)

Year	Power	Retail Low	Retail High
1997	T210D	124,200	142,800
1996	T210D	115,500	132,800
1995	T210D	107,400	123,500
1994	T210D	99,900	114,800
1993	T210D	92,900	106,800
1992	T210D	86,400	99,300

Riviera 33 Conv. (Current) ******

Riviera 34 Convertible

Year	Power	Retail Low	Retail High
2002	T370D	203,000	233,400
2001	T370D	186,700	214,700
2000	T350D	173,600	199,700
1999	T330D	161,500	185,700
1998	T315D	150,200	172,700

Year	Power	Retail Low	Retail High
1997	T315D	139,700	160,600
Riviera 36 Convertible			
2002	T370 Cum.	234,800	270,000
2001	T370 Cum.	216,000	248,400
2000	T350 Cum.	200,800	231,000
1999	T330 Cum.	186,800	214,800
1998	T315 Cum.	173,700	199,800
1997	T315 Cum.	161,500	185,800
1996	T315 Cum.	150,200	172,800
1995	T315 Cum.	141,200	162,400
1994	T300 Cum.	132,700	152,700
1993	T300 Cum.	124,800	143,500
Riviera 37 Convertible			
2004	T330D	288,400	331,600
2003	T330D	265,300	305,100
2002	T330D	244,100	280,700
2001	T315D	224,500	258,200
Riviera 39 Convertible			
1999	T450D	264,500	304,100
1998	T420D	243,300	279,800
1997	T420D	223,800	257,400
1996	T375D	205,900	236,800
1995	T375D	191,500	220,200
1994	T375D	178,100	204,800
Riviera 40 Convertible			
2004	T430D	418,400	481,100
2003	T430D	384,900	442,600
2002	T470D	354,100	407,200
2001	T470D	325,800	374,600
Riviera 4000 Offshore			
2003	T450D	361,200	415,300
2002	T450D	332,300	382,100
2001	T450D	305,700	351,500
2000	T450D	281,200	323,400
1999	T450D	258,700	297,500
1998	T435D	238,000	273,700
Riviera 42 Conv. (1992-94) ******			
Riviera 42 Conv. (Current)			
2004	T4800D	522,300	600,600
Riviera 43 Convertible			
2003	T430D	485,000	557,700
2002	T430D	446,200	513,100
2001	T430D	410,500	472,000
2000	T450D	377,600	434,300
1999	T450D	347,400	399,500
1998	T420D	319,600	367,600
1997	T420D	294,000	338,100
Riviera 47 Convertible			
2004	T700D	723,000	831,400
2003	T660D	657,900	756,600
Riviera 48 Convertible			
2002	T800D	615,900	708,300
2001	T800D	565,900	650,800
2000	T660D	479,900	551,900
1999	T660D	449,800	517,300
1998	T660D	417,000	479,600
1997	T435D	368,300	423,600
1996	T435D	336,000	386,500
1995	T435D	309,000	355,400
1994	T435D	286,200	329,100
1993	T435D	265,000	304,700

Year	Power	Retail Low	Retail High
Riviera 51 Convertible ******			
Riviera 58 Conv. (Closed Bridge)			
2004	T1400D	1,280,300	1,472,300
2003	T1400D	1,165,000	1,339,800
Rivolta 38 ******			
Roughwater 37			
1988	S-Diesel	55,400	63,700
1987	S-Diesel	52,600	60,500
1986	S-Diesel	49,900	57,400
1985	S-Diesel	47,400	54,600
1984	S-Diesel	45,100	51,800
1983	S-Diesel	42,800	49,200
1982	S-Diesel	40,700	46,800
1981	S-Diesel	38,600	44,400
Roughwater 41			
1985	S-Diesel	76,000	87,400
1984	S-Diesel	72,200	83,000
1983	S-Diesel	68,500	78,800
1982	S-Diesel	65,100	74,900
1981	S-Diesel	61,900	71,100
1980	S-Diesel	58,800	67,600
Roughwater 42			
1989	T-Diesel	******	******
1988	T-Diesel	******	******
1987	T-Diesel	91,800	105,600
1986	T-Diesel	84,000	96,600
Rybo Runner 30 Center Console			
1989	Seadrive	32,300	37,100
1989	T-Gas	45,800	52,700
1988	Seadrive	31,400	36,100
1988	T-Gas	42,500	48,900
1987	Seadrive	30,000	34,600
1987	T-Gas	39,900	45,900
1986	Seadrive	27,700	31,900
1986	T-Gas	35,000	40,300
1985	Seadrive	25,500	29,300
1985	T-Gas	32,100	36,900
1984	Seadrive	22,800	26,300
1984	T-Gas	29,400	33,800
1983	Seadrive	20,200	23,300
1983	T-Gas	27,400	31,600
Sabreline 34			
2002	T220D	233,800	268,900
2001	T220D	215,100	247,400
2000	T220D	197,900	227,600
1999	T220D	184,000	211,700
1998	T220D	171,200	196,800
1997	T220D	159,200	183,100
1996	T210D	148,000	170,200
1995	T210D	139,100	160,000
1994	T210D	130,800	150,400
1993	T210D	122,900	141,400
1992	T210D	115,600	132,900
1991	T210D	108,600	124,900
Sabreline 36 Aft Cabin			
1998	T-Diesel	202,700	233,200
1997	T-Diesel	188,500	216,800
1996	T-Diesel	175,300	201,600
1995	T-Diesel	164,800	189,500
1994	T-Diesel	154,900	178,200
1993	T-Diesel	145,600	167,500
1992	T-Diesel	136,900	157,400

Year	Power	Retail Low	Retail High
1991	T-Diesel	128,700	148,000
1990	T-Diesel	122,200	140,600
1989	T-Diesel	116,100	133,500
Sabreline 36 Express			
2003	T315D	248,900	286,200
2002	T315D	228,900	263,300
2001	T315D	210,600	242,200
2000	T315D	195,900	225,300
1999	T300D	182,200	209,500
1998	T300D	169,400	194,800
1997	T300D	157,500	181,200
1996	T300D	146,500	168,500
Sabreline 38 Express ******			
Sabreline 42 Express			
2004	T440D	479,400	551,300
Sabreline 42 Sedan			
2004	T440D	497,900	572,500
2003	T440D	458,000	526,700
2002	T420D	421,400	484,600
2001	T420D	387,700	445,800
Sabreline 43 Aft Cabin			
2004	T370D	614,500	706,600
2003	T370D	565,300	650,100
2002	T370D	520,100	598,100
2001	T370D	478,500	550,200
2000	T350D	445,000	511,700
1999	T350D	413,800	475,900
1998	T350D	384,800	442,600
1997	T350D	357,900	411,600
1996	T350D	332,800	382,800
Sabreline 47 Aft Cabin			
2004	T465D	706,700	812,700
2003	T465D	650,100	747,600
2002	T420D	598,100	687,800
2001	T420D	550,200	632,800
2000	T420D	511,700	588,500
1999	T420D	475,900	547,300
1998	T420D	442,600	509,000
1997	T350D	411,600	473,400
San Juan 38 ******			
Scout 260/280 Abaco			
2004	T200 O/B	83,500	96,000
2003	T200 O/B	75,100	86,400
2002	T200 O/B	67,600	77,700
2001	T200 O/B	61,500	70,700
2000	T200 O/B	56,000	64,400
Scout 280 Sportfish			
2004	T200 O/B	77,500	89,100
2003	T200 O/B	69,700	80,200
2002	T200 O/B	62,700	72,100
2001	T200 O/B	57,100	65,600
Sea Ray 270 Amberjack			
1990	T260 I/O	22,100	25,400
1989	T260 I/O	20,200	23,300
1988	T260 I/O	18,400	21,200
1987	T260 I/O	15,800	18,200
1986	T260 I/O	14,800	17,000
Sea Ray 270 Sundancer (1982-88)			
1988	T-I/O Gas	20,000	23,000
1987	T-I/O Gas	18,300	21,100
1986	T-I/O Gas	16,800	19,300

PRICES

347

IMPORTANT! See Page 293 for Regional Price Adjustment.

Year	Power	Retail Low	Retail High
1985	T-I/O Gas	15,700	18,100
1984	T-I/O Gas	14,700	16,900
1983	T-I/O Gas	14,100	16,300
1982	T-I/O Gas	13,600	15,700
Sea Ray 270 Sundancer (1992-93)			
1993	S-I/O Gas	22,600	26,000
1993	T-I/O Gas	24,100	27,800
1992	S-I/O Gas	21,000	24,200
1992	T-I/O Gas	22,100	25,400
Sea Ray 270 Sundancer (1994-97)			
1997	S330 I/O	31,900	36,700
1996	S330 I/O	29,600	34,100
1995	S330 I/O	26,800	30,800
1994	S330 I/O	23,500	27,000
Sea Ray 270 Sundancer (1998-2001)			
2001	S300 I/O	46,500	53,400
2001	T190 I/O	49,100	56,400
2000	S300 I/O	41,800	48,100
2000	T190 I/O	44,100	50,800
1999	S300 I/O	37,600	43,300
1999	T190 I/O	39,700	45,700
1998	S300 I/O	33,800	38,900
1998	T190 I/O	35,700	41,100
Sea Ray 270 Sundeck			
2004	S320 I/O	51,000	58,600
2003	S320 I/O	45,900	52,700
2002	S320 I/O	41,300	47,500
Sea Ray 270 Weekender			
1993	S300 I/O	19,200	22,100
1992	S300 I/O	16,500	19,000
Sea Ray 270/290 Sundancer (1990-93)			
1993	S300 I/O	23,000	26,400
1993	T175 I/O	24,000	27,700
1992	S300 I/O	20,000	23,100
1992	T175 I/O	20,900	24,000
1991	S300 I/O	17,700	20,300
1991	T175 I/O	18,200	20,900
1990	S300 I/O	15,200	17,500
1990	T175 I/O	15,900	18,300
Sea Ray 280 Bowrider			
2001	S300 I/O	52,500	60,300
2001	T260 I/O	61,000	70,100
2000	S300 I/O	47,700	54,900
2000	T260 I/O	55,500	63,800
1999	S300 I/O	43,400	49,900
1999	T260 I/O	50,500	58,000
1998	S300 I/O	39,500	45,400
1998	T260 I/O	45,900	52,800
1997	S300 I/O	36,000	41,400
1997	T250 I/O	41,800	48,100
1996	S300 I/O	32,700	37,600
1996	T250 I/O	38,000	43,700
Sea Ray 280 Sun Sport			
2001	S300 I/O	55,500	63,800
2001	T260 I/O	61,000	70,100
2000	S300 I/O	50,500	58,000
2000	T260 I/O	55,500	63,800
1999	S300 I/O	45,900	52,800
1999	T260 I/O	50,500	58,000
1998	S300 I/O	41,800	48,000
1998	T260 I/O	45,900	52,800
1997	S300 I/O	38,000	43,700

Year	Power	Retail Low	Retail High
1997	T250 I/O	41,800	48,100
1996	S300 I/O	34,600	39,800
1996	T250 I/O	38,000	43,700
Sea Ray 280 Sundancer (1989-91)			
1991	T230 I/O	25,800	29,700
1990	T230 I/O	23,300	26,800
1989	T230 I/O	20,800	24,000
Sea Ray 280 Sundancer (Current)			
2004	S375 I/O	86,800	99,800
2004	T260 I/O	96,400	110,800
2003	S375 I/O	78,100	89,800
2003	T260 I/O	86,700	99,700
2002	S375 I/O	70,300	80,800
2002	T260 I/O	78,000	89,700
2001	S375 I/O	63,200	72,700
2001	T260 I/O	70,200	80,800
Sea Ray 290 Amberjack			
2004	T260 I/O	100,400	115,400
2003	T260 I/O	90,300	103,900
2002	T260 I/O	81,300	93,500
2001	T260 I/O	73,100	84,100
2000	T260 I/O	66,600	76,500
1999	T260 I/O	60,600	69,700
1998	T260 I/O	55,100	63,400
Sea Ray 290 Bowrider			
2004	T260 I/O	94,500	108,600
2003	T260 I/O	85,000	97,800
2002	T260 I/O	76,500	88,000
2001	T260 I/O	68,800	79,200
Sea Ray 290 Sun Sport			
2004	T260 I/O	97,500	112,100
2003	T260 I/O	87,700	100,900
2002	T260 I/O	78,900	90,800
Sea Ray 290 Sundancer (1994-97)			
1997	S330 I/O	44,000	50,600
1997	T190 I/O	46,000	52,900
1996	S330 I/O	40,400	46,500
1996	T190 I/O	42,300	48,600
1995	S330 I/O	36,000	41,400
1995	T190 I/O	37,200	42,800
1994	S310 I/O	30,000	34,500
1994	T190 I/O	31,100	35,800
Sea Ray 290 Sundancer (1998-2001)			
2001	T260 I/O	75,400	86,700
2000	T260 I/O	66,500	76,500
1999	T260 I/O	61,300	70,500
1998	T260 I/O	55,900	64,300
Sea Ray 300 Express Cruiser			
1981	T330 I/B	19,800	22,800
1980	T330 I/B	19,100	22,000
Sea Ray 300 Sedan Bridge (1976-81)			
1981	T330 I/B	20,500	23,600
1980	T330 I/B	19,800	22,800
Sea Ray 300 Sedan Bridge (1985-87)			
1987	T260 VD	29,100	33,500
1986	T260 VD	27,300	31,400
1985	T260 VD	25,400	29,200
Sea Ray 300 Sundancer (1985-89)			
1989	T260 I/O	29,600	34,100
1988	T260 I/O	27,600	31,700
1987	T260 I/O	25,700	29,600

Year	Power	Retail Low	Retail High
1986	T260 I/O	24,500	28,100
1985	T260 I/O	23,500	27,000
Sea Ray 300 Sundancer (1992-93)			
1993	T-I/O 5.7L	34,100	39,300
1993	T-VD/5.7L	35,800	41,100
1992	T-I/O 5.7L	31,900	36,700
1992	T-VD/5.7L	33,200	38,100
Sea Ray 300 Sundancer (1994-97)			
1997	T260 I/O	59,900	68,900
1996	T260 I/O	52,200	60,000
1995	T260 I/O	47,200	54,300
1994	T260 I/O	39,900	45,900
Sea Ray 300 Sundancer (Current)			
2004	T260 I/O	112,300	129,100
2003	T260 I/O	101,000	116,200
2002	T260 I/O	90,900	104,600
2001	T260 I/O	81,800	94,100
Sea Ray 300 Weekender (1991-95)			
1995	T-I/O 5.7L	39,800	45,800
1995	T-VD/5.7L	42,300	48,700
1994	T-I/O 5.7L	32,100	36,900
1994	T-VD/5.7L	34,100	39,300
1993	T-I/O 5.7L	29,800	34,300
1993	T-VD/5.7L	31,900	36,700
1992	T-I/O 5.7L	27,500	31,600
1992	T-VD/5.7L	29,000	33,400
1991	T-I/O 5.7L	24,200	27,800
1991	T-VD/5.7L	26,300	30,200
Sea Ray 300 Weekender (1975-81)			
1981	T228 I/B	18,600	21,400
1980	T228 I/B	18,000	20,700
Sea Ray 300 Weekender (1985-89)			
1989	T260 I/O	27,600	31,800
1988	T260 I/O	25,500	29,300
1987	T260 I/O	24,300	27,900
1986	T260 I/O	22,100	25,500
1985	T260 I/O	21,700	25,000
Sea Ray 300/305 Sedan Bridge (1988-89)			
1989	T260 VD	34,400	39,500
1988	T260 VD	31,000	35,700
Sea Ray 310 Amberjack			
1994	T310 I/B	51,200	58,900
1993	T310 I/B	48,000	55,200
1992	T310 I/B	43,800	50,300
1991	T310 I/B	39,100	45,000
Sea Ray 310 Sport Bridge			
1993	T-Gas	48,300	55,600
1993	T-Diesel	62,100	71,400
1992	T-Gas	43,000	49,400
1992	T-Diesel	57,300	65,900
Sea Ray 310 Sun Sport			
1995	T415G	42,600	50,500
1994	T350G	36,800	43,600
1993	T350G	32,600	38,300
1992	T330G	28,600	33,900
1991	T330G	24,400	27,900
Sea Ray 310 Sundancer (1982-83)			
1983	T-IB 7.4L	21,700	24,900
1982	T-IB 7.4L	18,700	21,500
1981	T-IB 7.4L	17,200	19,800

Sea Ray 310 Sundancer (1998-02)

Year	Power	Retail Low	Retail High
2002	T260 I/O	105,800	121,700
2001	T260 I/O	96,300	110,700
2000	T260 I/O	87,600	100,800
1999	T260 I/O	79,700	91,700
1998	T260 I/O	72,500	83,400

Sea Ray 310/330 EC (1990-95)

Year	Power	Retail Low	Retail High
1995	T-I/O 7.4L	53,200	61,200
1995	T-IB/7.4L	55,300	63,600
1994	T-I/O 7.4L	48,900	56,300
1994	T-IB/7.4L	50,900	58,500
1993	T-I/O 7.4L	45,000	51,800
1993	T-IB/7.4L	46,800	53,800
1992	T-I/O 7.4L	41,400	47,600
1992	T-IB/7.4L	43,100	49,500
1991	T-I/O 7.4L	38,100	43,800
1991	T-IB/7.4L	39,600	45,600
1990	T-I/O 7.4L	35,000	40,300
1990	T-IB/7.4L	36,400	41,900

Sea Ray 310/330 Sundancer (1990-94)

Year	Power	Retail Low	Retail High
1994	T-I/O 7.4L	54,000	62,200
1994	T-VD/7.4L	55,100	63,300
1993	T-I/O 7.4L	48,700	56,000
1993	T-VD/7.4L	50,300	57,800
1992	T-I/O 7.4L	44,400	51,100
1992	T-VD/7.4L	47,600	54,700
1991	T-I/O 7.4L	40,600	46,700
1991	T-VD/7.4L	44,400	51,100
1990	T-I/O 7.4L	36,400	41,800
1990	T-VD/7.4L	40,100	46,100

Sea Ray 320 Sundancer

Year	Power	Retail Low	Retail High
2004	T300 I/B	152,300	175,100
2004	T260 I/O	141,300	162,400
2003	T300 I/B	137,000	157,600
2003	T260 I/O	127,100	146,200

Sea Ray 330 Sundancer (1995-99)

Year	Power	Retail Low	Retail High
1999	T300 I/O	86,500	99,500
1999	T300 VD	92,300	106,100
1998	T300 I/O	77,300	88,900
1998	T300 VD	84,000	96,600
1997	T300 I/O	70,300	80,900
1997	T300 VD	76,400	87,900
1996	T300 I/O	64,000	73,600
1996	T310 VD	69,500	80,000
1995	T300 I/O	58,200	67,000
1995	T310 VD	63,300	72,800

Sea Ray 330 Express; 340 Amberjack

Year	Power	Retail Low	Retail High
2003	T370G	173,400	199,400
2002	T370G	157,700	181,400
2001	T370G	143,500	165,100
2000	T310G	132,100	151,900
1999	T310G	121,500	139,700
1998	T310G	111,800	128,500
1997	T310G	102,800	118,200

Sea Ray 340 EC

Year	Power	Retail Low	Retail High
1989	T340G	39,800	45,700
1988	T340G	35,700	41,000
1987	T340G	32,500	37,300
1986	T340G	29,200	33,600
1985	T340G	26,600	30,700
1984	T340G	24,600	28,300

Sea Ray 340 Sedan Bridge

Year	Power	Retail Low	Retail High
1987	T340G	37,300	42,900
1986	T340G	35,100	40,300
1985	T340G	32,800	37,700
1984	T340G	31,100	35,800
1983	T340G	29,400	33,800

Sea Ray 340 Sport Fisherman

Year	Power	Retail Low	Retail High
1987	T-IB/340G	32,000	36,800
1986	T-IB/340G	29,500	34,000
1985	T-IB/340G	27,300	31,400
1984	T-IB/340G	25,500	29,400

Sea Ray 340 Sundancer (1984-89)

Year	Power	Retail Low	Retail High
1989	T340G	44,400	51,100
1988	T340G	39,100	45,000
1987	T340G	35,600	41,000
1986	T340G	31,800	36,600
1985	T340G	29,700	34,100
1984	T340G	27,500	31,600

Sea Ray 340 Sundancer (1999-2002)

Year	Power	Retail Low	Retail High
2002	T320 G	139,900	160,800
2001	T320 G	128,700	148,000
2000	T310 G	118,400	136,100
1999	T310 G	108,900	125,200

Sea Ray 340 Sundancer (Current)

Year	Power	Retail Low	Retail High
2004	T-VD 370G	178,000	204,700
2003	T-VD 370G	161,900	186,200

Sea Ray 340/345 Sedan Bridge

Year	Power	Retail Low	Retail High
1989	T-Gas	47,500	54,600
1988	T-Gas	41,700	47,900

Sea Ray 350 Express Bridge

Year	Power	Retail Low	Retail High
1994	T-VD/7.4L	63,000	72,500
1993	T-VD/7.4L	57,200	65,800
1992	T-VD/7.4L	51,000	58,700

Sea Ray 355T Sedan

Year	Power	Retail Low	Retail High
1983	T-Diesels	36,500	41,900
1982	T-Diesels	34,600	39,800
1981	T-Diesels	32,900	37,800
1980	T-Diesels	31,200	35,900

Sea Ray 350/370 EC (1990-95)

Year	Power	Retail Low	Retail High
1995	T 310G I/B	83,400	95,900
1994	T 310G I/B	73,000	84,000
1993	T 310G I/B	66,200	76,100
1992	T300G I/B	61,600	70,800
1991	T300G I/B	57,600	66,200
1990	T300G I/B	51,800	59,600

Sea Ray 350/370 Sundancer (1990-94)

Year	Power	Retail Low	Retail High
1994	T-VD 310G	79,600	91,500
1993	T-VD 310G	70,400	80,900
1992	T-VD 300G	65,500	75,300
1991	T-VD 300G	60,700	69,800
1990	T-VD 300G	55,000	63,300

Sea Ray 360 Aft Cabin

Year	Power	Retail Low	Retail High
1987	T-Gas	55,700	64,100
1987	T-Diesel	64,100	73,700
1986	T-Gas	48,800	56,100
1986	T-Diesel	57,900	66,500
1985	T-Gas	44,500	51,200
1985	T-Diesel	52,900	60,900
1984	T-Gas	41,700	48,000
1984	T-Diesel	48,800	56,100
1983	T-Gas	38,300	44,100
1983	T-Diesel	45,300	52,100

Sea Ray 360 EC

Year	Power	Retail Low	Retail High
1983	T350G	31,600	36,400
1982	T350G	29,500	33,900
1981	T350G	27,800	32,000
1980	T350G	26,200	30,100

Sea Ray 360 Sedan SF

Year	Power	Retail Low	Retail High
1982	T-IB 7.4L	35,400	40,700
1981	T-IB 7.4L	30,700	35,400

Sea Ray 360 Sundancer

Year	Power	Retail Low	Retail High
2004	T370G	231,200	265,800
2003	T370G	210,300	241,900
2002	T370G	191,400	220,100

Sea Ray 370 Express Cruiser

Year	Power	Retail Low	Retail High
2000	T-Gas	165,800	190,700
2000	T340D	196,200	225,600
1999	T-Gas	147,900	170,100
1999	T340D	175,600	201,900
1998	T-Gas	130,600	150,300
1998	T340D	155,000	178,300
1997	T-Gas	117,600	135,200
1997	T340D	143,500	165,000

Sea Ray 370 Sedan Bridge

Year	Power	Retail Low	Retail High
1997	T-Gas	132,800	152,700
1997	T-Diesel	163,400	187,900
1996	T-Gas	122,100	140,500
1996	T-Diesel	150,300	172,800
1995	T-Gas	112,400	129,200
1995	T-Diesel	138,300	159,000
1994	T-Gas	103,400	118,900
1994	T-Diesel	127,200	146,300
1993	T-Gas	95,100	109,400
1993	T-Diesel	117,000	134,600
1992	T-Gas	87,500	100,600
1992	T-Diesel	107,600	123,800
1991	T-Gas	80,500	92,600
1991	T-Diesel	99,000	113,900

Sea Ray 370 Sundancer (1995-99)

Year	Power	Retail Low	Retail High
1999	T-VD/7.4L	151,700	174,500
1999	T-Diesel	191,600	220,300
1998	T-VD/7.4L	141,300	162,600
1998	T-Diesel	169,500	194,900
1997	T-VD/7.4L	124,400	143,100
1997	T-Diesel	150,600	173,200
1996	T-VD/7.4L	115,000	132,300
1996	T-Diesel	136,300	156,700
1995	T-VD/7.4L	103,600	119,100
1995	T-Diesel	124,300	142,900

Sea Ray 370/380 Aft Cabin

Year	Power	Retail Low	Retail High
2001	T-Gas	217,700	250,400
2001	T340D	250,200	287,700
2000	T-Gas	197,300	226,900
2000	T340D	226,700	260,700
1999	T-Gas	177,500	204,100
1999	T340D	202,900	233,300
1998	T-Gas	159,600	183,500
1998	T340D	189,100	217,400
1997	T-Gas	148,400	170,600
1997	T340D	176,300	202,700

Sea Ray 380 Aft Cabin (1989-91)

Year	Power	Retail Low	Retail High
1991	T-Gas	92,300	106,100
1991	T-Diesel	108,800	125,100

PRICES

Year	Power	Retail Low	Retail High
1990	T-Gas	85,000	97,800
1990	T-Diesel	99,500	114,500
1989	T-Gas	77,800	89,400
1989	T-Diesel	91,600	105,400
Sea Ray 380 Sundancer			
2003	T370G	238,700	274,500
2003	T340D	279,000	320,800
2002	T370G	217,200	249,800
2002	T340D	253,800	291,900
2001	T370G	197,600	227,300
2001	T340D	231,000	265,600
2000	T310G	181,800	209,100
2000	T340D	212,500	244,400
1999	T310G	167,300	192,400
1999	T340D		
Sea Ray 390 EC			
1991	T-Gas	83,000	95,400
1991	T-Diesel	107,300	123,400
1990	T-Gas	78,000	89,700
1990	T-Diesel	100,800	116,000
1989	T-Gas	73,300	84,300
1989	T-Diesel	94,800	109,000
1988	T-Gas	68,900	79,300
1988	T-Diesel	89,100	102,500
1987	T-Gas	64,800	74,500
1987	T-Diesel	83,700	96,300
1986	T-Gas	60,900	70,000
1986	T-Diesel	78,700	90,500
1985	T-Gas	57,200	65,800
1985	T-Diesel	74,000	85,100
1984	T-Gas	53,800	61,900
1984	T-Diesel	69,600	80,000
Sea Ray 390 MY			
2004	T370G	366,100	421,000
2004	T446D	421,700	484,900
2003	T370G	333,100	383,100
2003	T446D	383,700	441,300
Sea Ray 390 Sedan SF			
1986	T-Gas	52,700	60,600
1986	T-Diesel	68,000	78,200
1985	T-Gas	50,400	57,900
1985	T-Diesel	65,200	74,900
1984	T-Gas	47,600	54,700
1984	T-Diesel	56,600	65,100
1983	T-Gas	44,100	50,800
1983	T-Diesel	53,900	62,000
Sea Ray 390 Sundancer			
2004	T370G	267,900	308,000
2004	T340D	324,500	373,100
Sea Ray 400 EC			
1999	T-Gas	174,500	200,600
1999	T-Diesel	218,500	251,200
1998	T-Gas	160,500	184,600
1998	T-Diesel	201,000	231,100
1997	T-Gas	147,600	169,800
1997	T-Diesel	184,900	212,600
1996	T-Gas	135,800	156,200
1996	T-Diesel	170,100	195,600
1995	T-Gas	125,000	143,700
1995	T-Diesel	156,500	180,000
1994	T-Gas	115,000	132,200
1994	T-Diesel	144,000	165,600
1993	T-Gas	105,800	121,600
1993	T-Diesel	132,400	152,300
1992	T-Gas	97,300	111,900
1992	T-Diesel	121,800	140,100
Sea Ray 400 Sedan Bridge			
2003	T-Gas	311,200	357,800
2003	T-Diesel	358,600	412,300
2002	T-Gas	283,100	325,600
2002	T-Diesel	326,300	375,200
2001	T-Gas	257,700	296,300
2001	T-Diesel	296,900	341,500
2000	T-Gas	237,000	272,600
2000	T-Diesel	273,200	314,100
1999	T-Gas	218,100	250,800
1999	T-Diesel	251,300	289,000
1998	T-Gas	200,600	230,700
1998	T-Diesel	231,200	265,900
1997	T-Gas	184,600	212,300
1997	T-Diesel	212,700	244,600
1996	T-Gas	169,800	195,300
1996	T-Diesel	195,700	225,000
Sea Ray 400 Sundancer			
1999	T-Gas	207,900	239,000
1999	T350D	251,300	288,900
1998	T-Gas	191,200	219,900
1998	T350D	231,100	265,800
1997	T-Gas	175,900	202,300
1997	T350D	212,700	244,600
Sea Ray 410 EC			
2003	T370D	307,800	353,900
2002	T340D	283,100	325,600
2001	T340D	260,500	299,600
2000	T340D	239,600	275,600
1999	T340D	220,500	253,500
Sea Ray 410 Sundancer			
2003	T370D	327,600	376,700
2002	T340D	301,300	346,600
2001	T340D	277,200	318,800
2000	T340D	255,000	293,300
Sea Ray 410/415/440 Aft Cabin			
1991	T-Gas	119,000	136,800
1991	T-Diesel	144,500	166,200
1990	T-Gas	111,700	128,500
1990	T-Diesel	131,400	151,100
1989	T-Gas	104,500	120,200
1989	T-Diesel	120,900	139,000
1988	T-Gas	90,700	104,400
1988	T-Diesel	106,200	122,100
1987	T-Gas	82,100	94,400
1987	T-Diesel	97,400	112,000
1986	T-Gas	76,100	87,500
1986	T-Diesel	90,100	103,700
Sea Ray 420 Aft Cabin			
2002	T-Gas	323,400	371,900
2002	T-Diesel	373,000	428,900
2001	T-Gas	297,500	342,100
2001	T-Diesel	346,800	398,900
2000	T-Gas	273,700	314,700
2000	T-Diesel	319,100	367,000
1999	T-Gas	251,800	289,600
1999	T-Diesel	293,600	337,600
1998	T-Gas	231,600	266,400
1998	T-Diesel	270,100	310,600
1997	T-Gas	213,100	245,100
1997	T-Diesel	248,500	285,700
1996	T-Gas	196,000	225,500
1996	T-Diesel	228,600	262,900
Sea Ray 420 Sedan Bridge			
2004	T450D	435,400	500,700
Sea Ray 420 Sundancer			
2004	T450D	406,700	467,700
2003	T450D	370,000	425,600
Sea Ray 420/440 Sundancer			
1995	T375D	174,700	200,900
1994	T375D	161,000	185,100
1993	T375D	150,800	173,400
1992	T375D	136,700	157,200
1991	T375D	123,300	141,800
1990	T375D	112,100	128,900
1989	T375D	104,800	120,500
Sea Ray 430/440 Convertible			
1991	T-Diesel	135,600	156,000
1990	T-Diesel	123,200	141,700
1989	T-Diesel	108,500	124,800
1988	T-Diesel	103,300	118,800
Sea Ray 440 Express Bridge			
1998	T340D	280,800	322,900
1997	T340D	257,500	296,100
1996	T340D	230,300	264,900
1995	T350 D	204,200	234,900
1994	T350 D	173,100	199,000
1993	T375 D	160,800	185,000
Sea Ray 450 Express Bridge			
2004	T450D	511,200	587,800
2003	T450D	470,300	540,800
2002	T430D	432,600	497,500
2001	T430D	398,000	457,700
2000	T430D	370,200	425,700
1999	T420D	344,200	395,900
1998	T420D	320,100	368,200
Sea Ray 450 Sundancer			
1999	T407D	275,700	317,000
1998	T407D	260,100	299,100
1997	T407D	241,000	277,100
1996	T375D	217,200	249,800
1995	T375D	200,600	230,600
Sea Ray 460 Convertible			
1988	375D	132,200	152,000
1988	550D	148,200	170,500
1987	375D	123,200	141,700
1987	550D	137,300	157,900
Sea Ray 460 Express Cruiser			
1989	T375D	121,900	140,100
1989	T550D	135,700	156,000
1988	T375D	112,600	129,500
1988	T550D	124,400	143,100
1987	T375D	103,000	118,500
1987	T550D	112,600	129,500
1986	T375D	96,800	111,300
1986	T550D	105,000	120,700
1985	T375D	93,700	107,700
1985	T550D	101,100	116,300
Sea Ray 460 Sundancer			
2003	T450D	438,900	504,700
2002	T450D	403,700	464,300

PRICES

Year	Power	Retail Low	Retail High
2001	T450D	371,400	427,200
2000	T430D	341,700	393,000
1999	T430D	314,400	361,500
Sea Ray 480 Motor Yacht			
2004	T640D	593,400	682,400
2003	T640D	545,900	627,800
2002	T640D	502,200	577,500
2001	T640D	462,000	531,300
Sea Ray 480 Sedan Bridge			
2004	T640D	644,500	741,100
2003	T640D	592,900	681,800
2002	T640D	545,500	627,300
2001	T640D	501,800	577,100
2000	T640D	466,700	536,700
1999	T640D	434,000	499,100
1998	T640D	403,600	464,200
Sea Ray 480/500 Sundancer			
2000	T535D	460,300	529,300
2000	T735D	512,300	589,100
1999	T535D	423,400	486,900
1999	T735D	471,300	542,000
1998	T535D	389,500	448,000
1998	T600D	433,600	498,600
1997	T535D	358,400	412,100
1997	T600D	398,900	458,700
1996	T485D	329,700	379,200
1996	T735D	367,000	422,000
1995	T485D	306,600	352,600
1995	T735D	341,300	392,500
1994	T485D	285,200	327,900
1994	T735D	317,400	365,000
1993	T485D	265,200	305,000
1993	T735D	295,200	339,400
1992	T485D	246,600	283,600
1992	T735D	274,500	315,700
1991	T485D	229,400	263,800
1991	T735D	255,300	293,600
1990	T485D	213,300	245,300
1990	T735D	237,400	273,000
Sea Ray 500 Sedan Bridge (1989-95)			
1995	T735D	364,800	419,500
1994	T735D	337,200	387,800
1993	T650D	310,200	356,700
1992	T650D	286,500	329,500
1991	T650D	268,600	308,900
1990	T650D	250,100	287,600
1989	T650D	234,600	269,800
Sea Ray 500 Sedan Bridge (Curr.) ******			
Sea Ray 500 Sundancer			
2004	T640D	697,400	802,000
2003	T640D	634,600	729,800
Sea Ray 510 Sundancer			
2003	T640D	664,800	764,500
2002	T640D	611,600	703,300
2001	T640D	562,600	647,000
2000	T640D	517,600	595,300
Sea Ray 540 Cockpit MY			
2003	T640D	865,600	995,400
2002	T640D	796,300	915,800
2001	T640D	732,600	842,500
Sea Ray 540 Sundancer			
2001	T640D	672,600	773,500

Year	Power	Retail Low	Retail High
2000	T640D	579,000	665,800
1999	T640D	518,900	596,700
1998	T640D	467,500	537,700
Sea Ray 550 Sedan Bridge (1992-98)			
1998	T735D	584,000	671,600
1997	T735D	543,900	625,500
1996	T735D	509,100	585,500
1995	T735D	474,600	545,800
1994	T735D	435,300	500,500
1993	T650D	411,600	473,300
1992	T650D	396,000	455,400
Sea Ray 550 Sedan Bridge (Curr.) ******			
Sea Ray 550 Sundancer			
2004	T765D	862,400	991,700
2003	T765D	793,400	912,400
2002	T765D	729,900	839,400
Sea Ray 560 Sedan Bridge			
2004	T1000D	******	******
2003	T1000D	******	******
2002	T776D	827,200	951,200
2001	T776D	756,900	870,400
2000	T776D	663,100	762,500
1999	T776D	581,200	668,400
1998	T660D	495,600	570,000
1998	T776D	509,300	585,700
Sea Ray 580 Super Sun Sport			
2002	T776D	827,100	951,200
2001	T776D	739,800	850,700
2000	T776D	683,400	786,000
1999	T776D	607,600	698,700
1998	T776D	536,600	617,100
1997	T776D	475,400	546,800
Sea Ray 630 Sun Sport			
2001	T1300D	1,003,500	1,154,000
2000	T1300D	874,200	1,005,300
1999	T1300D	804,000	924,600
1998	T1300D	713,400	820,400
1997	T1040D	648,400	745,600
1996	T1040D	591,400	680,100
1995	T1040D	555,500	638,900
1994	T1040D	528,600	607,900
1993	T1040D	496,100	570,500
1992	T1040D	465,700	535,600
1991	T1040D	447,900	515,000
Sea Ray 630 Sundancer			
1999	T1040D	886,200	1,019,100
1998	T1040D	777,800	894,500
1997	T1040D	683,100	785,600
1996	T1040D	649,600	747,100
1995	T1040D	601,000	691,200
Sea Ray 650 Cockpit MY			
1996	T-Diesel	785,400	903,200
1995	T-Diesel	761,800	876,100
1994	T-Diesel	707,600	813,800
1993	T-Diesel	666,800	766,900
1992	T-Diesel	634,400	729,600
Sea Sport 27 Seamaster ******			
Sea Sport 3200 Pacific ******			
Sea Vee 340 Open			
2004	T225 O/B	102,300	117,600
2003	T225 O/B	93,000	107,000

Year	Power	Retail Low	Retail High
2002	T225 O/B	84,700	97,400
2001	T225 O/B	77,000	88,600
SeaCraft 32 Center Console			
2004	T250 O/B	85,000	97,700
2003	T250 O/B	78,200	89,900
2002	T250 O/B	71,900	82,700
2001	T250 O/B	66,200	76,100
2000	T250 O/B	60,800	70,000
Sealine F37 Flybridge			
2004	T260D	******	******
2003	T260D	287,700	330,800
2002	T260D	263,900	303,500
2001	T260D	245,400	282,200
2000	T260D	228,200	262,500
Sealine S37 Sports Cruiser			
2003	T-Diesel	******	******
2002	T-Diesel	203,700	234,200
2001	T-Diesel	184,700	212,400
2000	T-Diesel	161,500	185,800
1999	T-Diesel	145,300	167,100
1998	T-Diesel	134,400	154,600
1997	T-Diesel	123,400	142,000
1996	T-Diesel	112,000	128,800
Sealine C39 Coupe			
2004	T310D	295,400	339,700
2003	T310D	271,700	312,500
Sealine C39 Coupe ******			
Sealine S41/43 Sports Yacht ******			
Sealine F42/5 Flybridge			
2004	T480D	503,900	579,500
2003	T480D	462,300	531,600
Sealine F43 Flybridge			
2004	T370D	434,900	500,200
2003	T370D	402,700	463,100
2002	T370D	372,900	428,800
2001	T370D	330,700	380,300
2000	T370D	304,800	350,600
1999	T370D	275,300	316,600
1998	T370D	253,800	291,900
1997	T370D	230,200	264,700
1996	T370D	201,600	231,800
1995	T-Diesel	189,600	218,100
1994	T-Diesel	******	******
1993	T-Diesel	******	******
1992	T-Diesel	******	******
1991	T-Diesel	******	******
Sealine 44 Flybridge; 420 Statesman			
2002	T370D	******	******
2001	T370D	333,000	383,000
2000	T370D	313,100	360,000
1999	T370D	273,700	314,800
1998	T370D	259,500	298,400
1997	T370D	233,400	268,400
1996	T370D	211,000	242,700
1995	T370D	196,400	225,900
Sealine 450 Statesman			
1997	T380D	291,300	335,100
1996	T380D	263,100	302,500
1995	T-Diesel	******	******
1994	T-Diesel	******	******
1993	T-Diesel	******	******

PRICES

351

PRICES

Year	Power	Retail Low	Retail High
1992	T-Diesel	******	******
1991	T-Diesel	******	******
Sealine T46 Motor Yacht			
2003	T480D	568,000	653,200
2002	T480D	521,100	599,300
2001	T450D	464,700	534,400
2000	T450D	411,000	472,700
1999	T450D	376,400	432,900
Sealine T47 Motor Yacht			
2004	T480D	649,800	747,200
2003	T480D	601,600	691,900
2002	T480D	557,100	640,600
2001	T480D	497,600	572,200
2000	T480D	458,100	526,900
Sealine S48 Sports Yacht			
2004	T480D	633,800	728,800
2003	T480D	586,800	674,900
2002	T480D	543,400	624,900
Sealine T51 Motor Yacht			
2004	T660D	******	******
2003	T660D	******	******
2002	T600D	762,300	876,700
2001	T600D	694,000	798,100
2000	T600D	640,200	736,200
1999	T600D	560,600	644,700
1998	T600D	489,800	563,300
Sealine T60 MY ******			
Selene 36 Trawler ******			
Selene 43 Pilothouse ******			
Selene 47 Pilothouse ******			
Selene 53 Pilothouse ******			
Seamaster 48 Motor Yacht			
1989	T-Diesel	158,800	182,600
1988	T-Diesel	148,600	170,900
1987	T-Diesel	138,300	159,000
1986	T-Diesel	131,100	150,800
1985	T-Diesel	123,400	141,900
1984	T-Diesel	116,200	133,700
1983	T-Diesel	108,500	124,800
Shamrock 270 Mackinaw			
2004	S330G	79,800	91,700
2004	S315D	101,300	116,400
2003	S330G	72,600	83,500
2003	S315D	92,100	106,000
2002	S300G	66,000	75,900
2002	S315D	83,800	96,400
2001	S300G	60,100	69,100
2001	S230D	76,300	87,700
2000	S300G	54,700	62,900
2000	S230D	69,400	79,800
Shamrock 270 Open			
2004	T330G	59,300	68,100
2003	T330G	53,900	62,000
2002	T300G	49,100	56,400
2001	T300G	44,600	51,300
2000	T300G	41,100	47,200
Shamrock 290 Walkaround			
2004	T330G	106,700	122,700
2003	T300G	97,000	111,600
2002	T300G	88,300	101,600

Year	Power	Retail Low	Retail High
2001	T300G	80,400	92,400
2000	T300G	73,900	85,000
1999	T300G	66,500	76,600
Shamrock 31 Grand Slam			
1994	T-Gas	61,800	71,000
1994	T-Diesel	80,200	92,200
1993	T-Gas	56,100	64,600
1993	T-Diesel	74,300	85,400
1992	T-Gas	53,100	61,100
1992	T-Diesel	66,100	76,000
1991	T-Gas	51,600	59,400
1991	T-Diesel	62,300	71,600
1990	T-Gas	51,100	58,800
1990	T-Diesel	60,700	69,900
1989	T-Gas	46,700	53,700
1989	T-Diesel	56,200	64,700
1988	T-Gas	44,700	51,500
1988	T-Diesel	54,000	62,100
1987	T-Gas	42,000	48,300
1987	T-Diesel	51,700	59,500
Silhouette 42			
1991	T-Diesel	110,100	126,600
1990	T-Diesel	104,000	119,600
1989	T-Diesel	98,800	113,700
1988	T-Diesel	91,600	105,300
1987	T-Diesel	85,400	98,200
Silverton 271 Express			
1997	S250 I/O	30,800	35,400
1996	S250 I/O	27,600	31,700
1995	S250 I/O	25,100	28,900
Silverton 29 Sportcruiser			
1987	T-Gas	21,900	25,100
1986	T-Gas	20,100	23,100
1985	T-Gas	18,300	21,100
Silverton 30X Express			
1989	T-Gas	28,400	32,700
1988	T-Gas	26,700	30,700
Silverton 31 Convertible (1976-87)			
1987	T-Gas	27,500	31,600
1986	T-Gas	25,700	29,600
1985	T-Gas	23,900	27,500
1984	T-Gas	22,700	26,100
1983	T-Gas	21,600	24,800
1982	T-Gas	19,800	22,800
1981	T-Gas	18,600	21,400
1980	T-Gas	16,800	19,400
Silverton 31 Convertible (1991-95)			
1995	T5.7L	50,200	57,700
1994	T5.7L	46,500	53,500
1993	T5.7L	43,300	49,800
1992	T5.7L	39,300	45,200
1991	T5.7L	35,700	41,100
Silverton 31 Gulfstream			
1986	T270G	23,200	26,700
1986	T350G	26,000	30,000
1985	T270G	21,400	24,700
1985	T350G	24,400	28,000
1984	T270G	20,300	23,300
1984	T350G	22,600	26,000
1983	T270G	19,900	22,900
1983	T350G	21,600	24,900
1982	T270G	19,300	22,200

Year	Power	Retail Low	Retail High
1982	T350G	21,000	24,200
1981	T270G	18,100	20,900
1981	T350G	20,500	23,500
1980	T270G	15,800	18,200
1980	T350G	19,300	22,200
Silverton 310 Express			
2000	T250 I/O	72,000	82,800
1999	T250 I/O	65,500	75,300
1998	T250 I/O	59,600	68,500
1997	T250 I/O	54,200	62,400
1996	T235 I/O	49,300	56,800
1995	T235 I/O	44,900	51,600
1994	T235 I/O	40,900	47,000
Silverton 312 Sedan Cruiser			
1999	T2500 I/O	58,300	67,100
1998	T2500 I/O	53,100	61,000
1997	T2500 I/O	48,300	55,500
1996	T235 I/O	43,900	50,500
1995	T235 I/O	40,400	46,500
1994	T235 I/O	37,200	42,800
Silverton 322 Motor Yacht			
2001	T320G	113,600	130,700
2000	T320G	103,400	118,900
1999	T320G	94,100	108,200
1998	T320G	85,600	98,500
Silverton 330 Sport Bridge			
2004	T320G	145,200	166,900
2003	T320G	133,500	153,600
2002	T320G	122,800	141,300
2001	T320G	113,000	130,000
2000	T320G	104,000	119,600
1999	T320G	95,600	110,000
Silverton 34 Conv. (1978-88)			
1988	T-Gas	37,400	43,100
1987	T-Gas	35,200	40,400
1986	T-Gas	32,700	37,600
1985	T-Gas	31,000	35,700
1984	T-Gas	28,700	33,000
1983	T-Gas	25,800	29,700
1982	T-Gas	24,500	28,200
1981	T-Gas	22,700	26,100
1980	T-Gas	21,300	24,500
Silverton 34 Conv. (1989-90)			
1990	T-Gas	44,000	50,600
1989	T-Gas	38,900	44,700
Silverton 34 Conv. (1991-95)			
1995	T-Gas	72,600	83,500
1994	T-Gas	71,000	81,600
1993	T-Gas	65,600	75,500
1992	T-Gas	59,700	68,600
1991	T-Gas	55,300	63,700
Silverton 34 Conv. (Current)			
2004	T320G	157,800	181,400
Silverton 34 Express (1987-89)			
1989	T-Gas	38,200	43,900
1988	T-Gas	35,400	40,700
1987	T-Gas	33,700	38,700
Silverton 34 Express (1990-94)			
1994	T-Gas	73,800	84,800
1993	T-Gas	66,300	76,300
1992	T-Gas	59,100	68,000

Year	Power	Retail Low	Retail High
1991	T-Gas	53,800	61,900
1990	T-Gas	48,500	55,800
Silverton 34 Motor Yacht			
1996	T320G	84,200	96,800
1995	T300G	77,400	89,100
1994	T300G	72,000	82,800
1993	T300G	67,000	77,000
Silverton 34 Sedan			
1980	T-Gas	24,300	28,800
Silverton 35 Motor Yacht			
2004	T385G	213,400	245,400
2003	T385G	194,100	223,300
Silverton 351 Sedan			
2001	T320G	143,300	164,700
2000	T320G	130,400	149,900
1999	T320G	118,600	136,400
1998	T300G	107,900	124,100
1997	T300G	98,200	113,000
Silverton 352 Motor Yacht			
2002	T370G	152,400	175,200
2002	T250D	193,700	222,700
2001	T320G	138,600	159,400
2001	T250D	176,200	202,700
2000	T320G	126,200	145,100
2000	T250D	160,400	184,400
1999	T320G	114,800	132,000
1999	T300D	145,900	167,800
1998	T320G	104,500	120,100
1998	T300D	132,800	152,700
1997	T320G	95,100	109,300
1997	T300D	120,900	139,000
Silverton 360 Express			
2000	T320G	103,500	119,000
1999	T320G	94,100	108,300
1998	T320G	85,700	98,500
1997	T320G	77,900	89,600
1996	T320G	70,900	81,600
1995	T300G	64,500	74,200
Silverton 362 Sedan			
1998	T320G	87,400	100,600
1997	T320G	80,400	92,500
1996	T320G	74,000	85,100
1995	T320G	68,100	78,300
1994	T320G	62,600	72,000
Silverton 37 Conv. (1980-89)			
1989	T-Gas	57,000	65,600
1989	T-Diesel	72,800	83,700
1988	T-Gas	53,900	62,000
1988	T-Diesel	65,800	75,700
1987	T-Gas	48,800	56,100
1987	T-Diesel	61,400	70,700
1986	T-Gas	45,600	52,400
1986	T-Diesel	57,000	65,600
1985	T-Gas	43,000	49,500
1985	T-Diesel	53,200	61,200
1984	T-Gas	39,900	45,900
1984	T-Diesel	49,400	56,800
1983	T-Gas	38,000	43,600
1982	T-Gas	36,700	42,200
1981	T-Gas	35,400	40,700
1980	T-Gas	34,200	39,300

Year	Power	Retail Low	Retail High
Silverton 37 Conv. (1990-2001)			
2001	T-Gas	140,500	161,500
2001	T350D	188,700	217,000
2000	T-Gas	124,100	142,700
2000	T350D	166,700	191,700
1999	T-Gas	116,100	133,500
1999	T350D	156,400	179,800
1998	T-Gas	104,900	120,600
1998	T350D	142,000	163,300
1997	T-Gas	98,700	113,500
1997	T350D	130,000	149,600
1996	T-Gas	94,300	108,500
1996	T350D	123,500	142,000
1995	T-Gas	89,500	103,000
1995	T350D	116,900	134,500
1994	T-Gas	87,700	100,900
1994	T350D	112,100	129,000
1993	T-Gas	85,100	97,900
1993	T350D	106,400	122,300
1992	T-Gas	78,000	89,700
1992	T350D	99,300	114,200
1991	T-Gas	67,300	77,400
1991	T350D	90,900	104,500
1990	T-Gas	64,100	73,700
Silverton 37 Motor Yacht			
1989	T-Gas	63,000	72,500
1989	T-Diesel	76,600	88,100
1988	T-Gas	56,900	65,400
1988	T-Diesel	68,600	78,900
Silverton 372/392 Motor Yacht			
2001	T-Gas	163,800	188,300
2000	T-Gas	152,500	175,400
1999	T-Gas	139,200	160,100
1998	T-Gas	130,700	150,400
1997	T-Gas	122,500	140,900
1996	T-Gas	114,800	132,000
Silverton 38 Express			
1994	T-Gas	79,900	91,900
1994	T-Diesel	112,900	129,800
1993	T-Gas	74,900	86,100
1993	T-Diesel	102,600	118,000
1992	T-Gas	69,100	79,400
1992	T-Diesel	92,500	106,400
1991	T-Gas	65,300	75,100
1991	T-Diesel	85,200	98,000
1990	T-Gas	60,200	69,200
1990	T-Diesel	77,200	88,800
Silverton 38 Convertible			
2004	T385G	210,800	247,400
2003	T385G	191,200	225,100
Silverton 38 Sport Bridge ******			
Silverton 39 Motor Yacht			
2004	T-Gas	256,900	295,400
2004	T-Diesel	296,900	341,400
2003	T-Gas	233,700	268,800
2003	T-Diesel	273,100	314,100
2002	T-Gas	212,700	244,600
2002	T-Diesel	251,200	288,900
Silverton 40 Aft Cabin			
1990	T-Gas	75,000	86,300
1990	T-Diesel	96,000	110,400
1989	T-Gas	69,500	79,900

Year	Power	Retail Low	Retail High
1989	T-Diesel	87,900	101,100
1988	T-Gas	64,500	74,200
1988	T-Diesel	81,200	93,400
1987	T-Gas	59,600	68,600
1987	T-Diesel	75,000	86,300
1986	T-Gas	56,400	64,900
1986	T-Diesel	70,200	80,700
1985	T-Gas	53,800	61,900
1985	T-Diesel	65,200	74,900
1984	T-Gas	50,500	58,100
1984	T-Diesel	60,100	69,100
1983	T-Gas	47,700	54,900
1983	T-Diesel	55,500	63,800
1982	T-Gas	43,600	50,100
1982	T-Diesel	50,800	58,400
Silverton 40 Convertible			
1990	T-Gas	74,600	85,800
1990	T-Diesel	91,700	105,400
1989	T-Gas	68,400	78,600
1989	T-Diesel	85,400	98,200
1988	T-Gas	62,600	72,000
1988	T-Diesel	77,400	89,000
1987	T-Gas	56,400	64,800
1987	T-Diesel	68,900	79,200
1986	T-Gas	51,100	58,700
1986	T-Diesel	62,700	72,100
1985	T-Gas	45,700	52,600
1985	T-Diesel	56,300	64,700
Silverton 402/422 Motor Yacht			
2001	T-Gas	199,000	228,900
2001	T-Diesel	246,700	283,700
2000	T-Gas	166,600	191,600
2000	T-Diesel	212,600	244,500
1999	T-Gas	152,400	175,300
1999	T-Diesel	194,500	223,700
1998	T-Gas	148,100	170,400
1998	T-Diesel	184,400	212,100
1997	T-Gas	139,700	160,700
1997	T-Diesel	177,300	203,900
1996	T-Gas	130,700	150,400
1996	T-Diesel	168,900	194,300
Silverton 41 Aft Cabin			
1995	T-Gas	128,900	148,300
1995	T-Diesel	162,400	186,800
1994	T-Gas	119,500	137,400
1994	T-Diesel	150,800	173,500
1993	T-Gas	114,000	131,100
1993	T-Diesel	145,000	166,700
1992	T-Gas	107,900	124,100
1992	T-Diesel	133,700	153,800
1991	T-Gas	103,400	119,000
1991	T-Diesel	123,800	142,400
Silverton 41 Convertible			
1999	T-Gas	149,500	172,000
1999	T450D	206,700	237,700
1998	T-Gas	140,000	161,000
1998	T450D	190,400	218,900
1997	T-Gas	133,700	153,700
1997	T420D	172,400	198,300
1996	T-Gas	124,600	143,300
1996	T420D	159,700	183,600
1995	T-Gas	116,700	134,200
1995	T435D	145,500	167,300
1994	T-Gas	112,600	129,500

PRICES

Year	Power	Retail Low	Retail High
1994	T425D	139,600	160,500
1993	T-Gas	106,300	122,200
1993	T375D	133,300	153,200
1992	T-Gas	97,800	112,500
1992	T375D	123,700	142,300
1991	T-Gas	92,500	106,400
1991	T375D	113,400	130,400

Silverton 410 Sport Bridge

Year	Power	Retail Low	Retail High
2004	T-Gas	276,800	318,300
2004	T-Diesel	321,800	370,000
2003	T-Gas	251,800	289,600
2003	T-Diesel	292,800	336,700
2002	T-Gas	229,200	263,600
2002	T-Diesel	266,400	306,400
2001	T-Gas	208,500	239,800
2001	T-Diesel	242,400	278,800

Silverton 42 Convertible

Year	Power	Retail Low	Retail High
2004	T-Gas	270,000	310,500
2004	T-350D	306,700	352,700
2003	T-Gas	245,700	282,500
2003	T-350D	279,000	320,900
2002	T-Gas	223,500	257,100
2002	T-350D	253,900	292,000
2001	T-Gas	203,400	233,900
2001	T-350D	231,100	265,700
2000	T-Gas	185,100	212,900
2000	T350 D	210,300	241,800

Silverton 43 Motor Yacht

Year	Power	Retail Low	Retail High
2004	T355D	341,200	392,300
2003	T355D	310,400	357,000
2002	T355D	285,600	328,500
2001	T355D	262,800	302,200

Silverton 442 CPMY

Year	Power	Retail Low	Retail High
2001	T-Gas	210,100	241,600
2001	T-Diesel	243,700	280,200
2000	T-Gas	193,600	222,700
2000	T-Diesel	224,900	258,700
1999	T-Gas	175,400	201,700
1999	T-Diesel	204,300	235,000
1998	T-Gas	169,500	195,000
1998	T-Diesel	195,800	225,100
1997	T-Gas	163,500	188,100
1997	T-Diesel	185,800	213,600
1996	T-Gas	152,500	175,400
1996	T-Diesel	177,400	204,000

Silverton 453 Motor Yacht

Year	Power	Retail Low	Retail High
2004	T430D	394,500	453,600
2003	T430D	362,900	417,300
2002	T350D	337,500	388,100
2001	T350D	313,900	360,900
2000	T350D	291,900	335,700
1999	T350D	271,400	312,200

Silverton 46 Motor Yacht

Year	Power	Retail Low	Retail High
1997	T485D	274,400	315,600
1996	T485D	260,600	299,700
1995	T485D	244,000	280,600
1994	T485D	229,600	264,100
1993	T485D	215,800	248,200
1992	T485D	198,000	227,700
1991	T-Diesel	179,500	206,500
1990	T-Diesel	167,200	192,300
1989	T-Diesel	150,700	173,300

Silverton 48 Convertible

Year	Power	Retail Low	Retail High
2004	T715D	553,800	636,800

Skipjack 30 Flybridge

Year	Power	Retail Low	Retail High
2004	T330D	224,500	258,100
2003	T330D	206,500	237,500
2002	T315D	190,000	218,500
2001	T315D	174,800	201,000
2000	T315D	162,500	186,900
1999	T315D	151,100	173,800
1998	T315D	140,600	161,700
1997	T315D	130,700	150,300

Skipjack 35 Sport Cruiser

Year	Power	Retail Low	Retail High
1995	T-Diesel	126,300	145,300
1994	T-Diesel	119,100	136,900
1993	T-Diesel	112,000	128,800
1992	T-Diesel	104,600	120,300
1991	T-Diesel	98,000	112,700
1990	T-Diesel	91,400	105,200

Solo 43 ******

Southern Cross 44 SF

Year	Power	Retail Low	Retail High
1990	T-Diesel	170,000	195,500
1989	T-Diesel	163,900	188,500
1988	T-Diesel	157,800	181,500
1987	T-Diesel	151,500	174,300

Southern Cross 52 SF

Year	Power	Retail Low	Retail High
1990	T-Diesel	244,400	281,100
1989	T-Diesel	234,400	269,600
1988	T-Diesel	223,900	257,500
1987	T-Diesel	213,800	245,900
1986	T-Diesel	201,300	231,600

Southern Cross 53 CPMY

Year	Power	Retail Low	Retail High
1989	T-Diesel	277,500	319,100
1988	T-Diesel	263,300	302,800
1987	T-Diesel	247,900	285,000
1986	T-Diesel	236,600	272,100

Stamas 270 Express

Year	Power	Retail Low	Retail High
2004	T225 O/B	87,600	100,700
2003	T225 O/B	78,800	90,600
2002	T225 O/B	70,900	81,500
2001	T225 O/B	64,500	74,200
2000	T225 O/B	58,700	67,500
1999	T225 O/B	53,400	61,400
1998	T225 O/B	48,600	55,900
1997	T225 O/B	44,200	50,900

Stamas 270 Tarpon

Year	Power	Retail Low	Retail High
2004	T225 O/B	81,300	93,400
2003	T225 O/B	73,100	84,100
2002	T225 O/B	65,800	75,700
2001	T225 O/B	59,900	68,900
2000	T225 O/B	54,500	62,700
1999	T225 O/B	49,600	57,000
1998	T225 O/B	45,100	51,900
1997	T225 O/B	41,000	47,200

Stamas 288 Liberty

Year	Power	Retail Low	Retail High
1994	T-I/O	41,700	48,000
1993	T200 O/B	38,200	43,900
1993	T-I/O	39,200	45,100
1992	T200 O/B	35,900	41,200
1992	T-I/O	36,800	42,400
1991	T200 O/B	33,700	38,800
1991	T-I/O	34,600	39,800

Year	Power	Retail Low	Retail High
1990	T200 O/B	31,700	36,400
1990	T-I/O	32,500	37,400
1989	T200 O/B	29,800	34,200
1989	T-I/O	30,600	35,200
1988	T200 O/B	28,000	32,200
1988	T-I/O	28,800	33,100
1987	T200 O/B	26,300	30,300
1987	T-I/O	27,000	31,100

Stamas 290 Express

Year	Power	Retail Low	Retail High
2004	T250 O/B	112,300	129,100
2003	T250 O/B	101,000	116,200
2002	T225 O/B	90,900	104,600
2001	T225 O/B	82,700	95,100
2000	T225 O/B	75,300	86,600
1999	T225 O/B	68,500	78,800
1998	T225 O/B	62,300	71,700
1997	T225 O/B	56,700	65,200
1996	T225 O/B	52,200	60,000
1995	T225 O/B	48,000	55,200
1994	T225 O/B	44,200	50,800
1993	T225 O/B	40,600	46,700
1992	T225 O/B	37,400	43,000

Stamas 290 Tarpon

Year	Power	Retail Low	Retail High
2004	T225 O/B	94,500	108,600
2003	T225 O/B	85,000	97,800
2002	T225 O/B	76,500	88,000
2001	T225 O/B	68,900	79,200
2000	T225 O/B	62,600	72,000
1999	T225 O/B	57,000	65,600
1998	T225 O/B	51,900	59,700
1997	T225 O/B	47,200	54,300
1996	T225 O/B	42,900	49,400
1995	T225 O/B	39,100	44,900

Stamas 310 Express

Year	Power	Retail Low	Retail High
2004	T300 I/B	108,500	124,700
2004	T300 O/B	122,500	140,800
2003	T300 I/B	98,700	113,500
2002	T225 O/B	111,400	128,100
2002	T260 I/B	89,800	103,300
2002	T225 O/B	101,400	116,600
2001	T260 I/B	81,700	94,000
2001	T225 O/B	92,300	106,100
2000	T260 I/B	74,400	85,500
2000	T225 O/B	84,000	96,600
1999	T260 I/B	68,400	78,700
1999	T225 O/B	77,200	88,800
1998	T260 I/B	62,900	72,400
1998	T225 O/B	71,100	81,700
1997	T250 I/B	57,900	66,600
1997	T225 O/B	65,400	75,200
1996	T250 I/B	53,300	61,200
1996	T225 O/B	60,100	69,200
1995	T250 I/B	49,000	56,300
1995	T225 O/B	55,300	63,600
1994	T250 I/B	45,100	51,800
1994	T225 O/B	50,900	58,500
1993	T250 I/B	41,500	47,700
1993	T225 O/B	46,800	53,800

Stamas 310 Tarpon

Year	Power	Retail Low	Retail High
2004	T225 O/B	108,700	125,000
2003	T225 O/B	98,900	113,700
2002	T225 O/B	90,000	103,500
2001	T225 O/B	81,900	94,200
2000	T225 O/B	74,500	85,700

PRICES

IMPORTANT! See Page 293 for Regional Price Adjustment.

Year	Power	Retail Low	Retail High
1999	T225 O/B	67,800	78,000
Stamas 32 Continental			
1987	T-Gas	34,500	39,700
1986	T-Gas	32,500	37,400
1985	T-Gas	30,100	34,600
1984	T-Gas	28,400	32,600
1983	T-Gas	26,600	30,600
1982	T-Gas	25,300	29,100
Stamas 32 Sport Fisherman			
1987	T-Gas	38,900	44,700
1986	T-Gas	36,600	42,000
1985	T-Gas	33,800	38,900
1984	T-Gas	31,900	36,700
1983	T-Gas	29,900	34,400
1982	T-Gas	28,500	32,800
1981	T-Gas	26,600	30,600
1980	T-Gas	23,400	26,900
Stamas 32 Sport Sedan			
1987	T-Gas	41,200	47,400
1986	T-Gas	38,700	44,500
1985	T-Gas	35,800	41,200
1984	T-Gas	33,800	38,900
1983	T-Gas	31,700	36,500
1982	T-Gas	30,200	34,700
1981	T-Gas	28,100	32,400
1980	T-Gas	24,800	28,500
Stamas 320 Express			
2004	T320G	144,300	165,900
2004	T225 O/B	154,800	178,000
2004	T240D	179,500	206,400
Stamas 340 Express			
2004	T320G I/B	195,600	224,900
2004	T370D I/B	254,900	293,100
2003	T320G I/B	177,900	204,600
2003	T370D I/B	231,900	266,700
2002	T320G I/B	161,900	186,200
2002	T370D I/B	211,000	242,700
Stamas 360/370 Express			
2004	T-Gas	218,500	251,200
2004	T370D		
2003	T-Gas	198,800	228,600
2003	T370D	272,300	313,100
2002	T-Gas	180,900	208,000
2002	T370D	247,700	284,900
2001	T-Gas	164,600	189,300
2001	T370D	225,400	259,300
2000	T-Gas	149,800	172,300
2000	T370D	205,100	235,900
1999	T-Gas	136,300	156,800
1999	T-Diesel	186,700	214,700
1998	T-Gas	124,000	142,600
1998	T-Diesel	169,900	195,400
1997	T-Gas	112,900	129,800
1997	T-Diesel	154,600	177,800
1996	T-Gas	102,700	118,100
1996	T-Diesel	140,700	161,800
1995	T-Gas	93,500	107,500
1995	T-Diesel	128,000	147,200
1994	T-Gas	85,000	97,800
1994	T-Diesel	116,500	134,000
1993	T-Gas	77,400	89,000
1993	T-Diesel	106,000	121,900
1992	T-Gas	70,400	81,000

Year	Power	Retail Low	Retail High
1992	T-Diesel	96,400	110,900
Stratos 2700 Center Console			
1998	T200 O/B	34,100	39,200
1997	T200 O/B	31,000	35,600
1996	T200 O/B	28,200	32,400
1995	T200 O/B	25,600	29,500
1994	T200 O/B	23,300	26,800
1993	T200 O/B	21,200	24,400
1992	T200 O/B	19,300	22,200
Stratos 2700 Walkaround			
1996	T200 O/B	30,300	34,800
1995	T200 O/B	27,500	31,700
1994	T200 O/B	25,000	28,800
1993	T200 O/B	22,800	26,200
1992	T200 O/B	20,700	23,800
Stratos 3300 Center Console			
1998	T225 O/B	45,500	52,300
1997	T225 O/B	40,700	46,800
1996	T225 O/B	35,900	41,300
1995	T225 O/B	31,700	36,500
1994	T225 O/B	28,500	32,800
1993	T225 O/B	26,000	29,900
1992	T225 O/B	24,400	28,100
Sunseeker 37 Sport Fish			
2004	3/250 O/B	281,200	323,300
Sunseeker 44 Camargue			
2002	T480D	370,600	426,200
2001	T480D	340,900	392,100
2000	T435D	313,600	360,700
1999	T435D	288,500	331,800
1998	T435D	265,500	305,300
Sunseeker 44 Manhattan			
2001	T435D	476,600	548,100
2000	T435D	438,500	504,200
1999	T435D	403,400	463,900
1998	T435D	371,100	426,800
Sunseeker 47 Camargue			
1999	T435D	320,300	368,400
1998	T435D	294,700	338,900
1997	T435D	271,100	311,800
1996	T435D	249,400	286,900
Sunseeker 48 Manhattan			
1999	T435D	414,000	476,100
1998	T435D	380,900	438,000
1997	T435D	354,200	407,400
1996	T435D	329,400	378,900
Sunseeker 50 Camargue ******			
Sunseeker 51 Camargue			
1998	T600D	437,200	502,800
1997	T600D	403,600	464,200
1996	T600D	364,400	419,100
1995	T625D	337,900	388,600
1994	T625D	302,300	347,700
Sunseeker 53 Portofino			
2004	T715D	730,500	840,000
Sunseeker 55 Camargue			
1996	T760D	432,600	497,500
1995	T760D	398,600	458,400
1994	T760D	367,100	422,200

Year	Power	Retail Low	Retail High
Sunseeker 56 Manhattan ******			
Sunseeker 56 Predator ******			
Sunseeker 58/60 Predator			
2002	T800D	946,100	1,088,000
2001	T800D	850,800	978,500
2000	T800D	779,400	896,300
1999	T800D	715,700	823,000
1998	T800D	641,900	738,200
1997	T800D	567,600	652,700
Sunseeker 58/62 Manhatten			
1999	T760D	780,600	897,700
1998	T760D	724,100	832,700
1997	T760D	664,700	764,400
1996	T760D	597,400	687,100
1995	T760D	535,900	616,300
1994	T760D	543,700	625,300
Sunseeker 60 Renegede ******			
Sunseeker 61 Predator ******			
Sunseeker 63 Predator			
1999	T1200D	819,900	942,900
1998	T1100D	773,700	889,800
1997	T1100D	714,000	821,100
1996	T1100D	652,400	750,300
1995	T1100D	590,000	678,500
Sunseeker Manhattan 64 ******			
Sunseeker 74 Manhattan ******			
Sunseeker Predator 75 ******			
Sunseeker Predator 80 ******			
Symbol 41 Sundeck			
1989	T210D	133,400	153,400
1988	T210D	125,300	144,200
1987	T210D	117,800	135,500
1986	T210D	110,800	127,400
1985	T210D	104,100	119,700
1984	T210D	97,900	112,500
Symbol 42 Classic Trawler ******			
Symbor 42 MY ******			
Symbol 44 MKII Sundeck ******			
1989	T375D	149,100	171,400
1988	T375D	140,100	161,100
1987	T375D	131,700	151,500
1986	T375D	123,800	142,400
1985	T375D	116,400	133,800
1984	T375D	109,400	125,800
Symbol 44 MY			
1986	T-Diesel	138,300	159,000
1985	T-Diesel	128,600	147,900
1984	T-Diesel	119,600	137,500
1983	T-Diesel	111,200	127,900
Symbol 45 Pilothouse Trawler			
2004	S450D	424,600	488,200
2003	S450D	390,600	449,200
Symbol 50 Pilothouse ******			
Symbol 51 Yachtfisher ******			
Symbol 54/58 Pilothouse ******			

PRICES

Year	Power	Retail Low	Retail High
Symbol 55 Pilothouse ******			
Symbol 55 Yachtfisher ******			
Symbol 62/64 Pilothouse *****			
Thompson 3100 Santa Cruz ******			
Tiara 2700 Continental			
1986	T260 I/O	23,500	27,000
1985	T260 I/O	22,400	25,700
1984	T260 I/O	20,900	24,100
1983	T260 I/O	19,500	22,400
1982	T260 I/O	17,700	20,400
Tiara 2700 Open			
1993	T260G	40,800	46,900
1992	T260G	38,400	44,100
1991	T260G	36,100	41,500
1990	T260G	33,900	39,000
1989	T260G	31,800	36,600
1988	T270G	29,900	34,400
1987	T270G	28,100	32,400
Tiara 2900 Coronet			
2004	T320G	121,800	140,000
2003	T320G	110,800	127,400
2002	T320G	100,800	115,900
2001	T320G	91,700	105,500
2000	T320G	83,500	96,000
1999	T320G	76,000	87,400
1998	T320G	69,100	79,500
1997	T-Gas	62,900	72,300
Tiara 2900 Open			
2004	T320G	143,600	165,100
2003	T320G	130,600	150,200
2002	T320G	118,900	136,700
2001	T320G	108,200	124,400
2000	T320G	99,500	114,400
1999	T320G	91,500	105,300
1998	T320G	84,200	96,900
1997	T320G	77,500	89,100
1996	T320G	71,300	82,000
1995	T260G	65,600	75,400
1994	T260G	60,300	69,400
1993	T260G	55,500	63,800
Tiara 3100 Convertible			
1992	T-Gas	64,200	73,800
1991	T-Gas	59,900	68,900
1990	T-Gas	56,100	64,500
1989	T-Gas	50,700	58,300
1988	T-Gas	48,400	55,700
1987	T-Gas	46,600	53,600
1986	T-Gas	42,200	48,500
1985	T-Gas	40,400	46,500
1984	T-Gas	37,800	43,400
1983	T-Gas	35,100	40,400
1982	T-Gas	32,100	37,000
Tiara 3100 Open (1979-91)			
1991	T-Gas	57,200	65,800
1991	T-Diesel	78,800	90,600
1990	T-Gas	53,000	60,900
1990	T-Diesel	72,000	82,800
1989	T-Gas	49,400	56,800
1989	T-Diesel	64,700	74,400
1988	T-Gas	45,200	52,000
1988	T-Diesel	57,700	66,400
1987	T-Gas	44,300	50,900

Year	Power	Retail Low	Retail High
1987	T-Diesel	51,900	59,700
1986	T-Gas	40,100	46,100
1986	T-Diesel	48,100	55,300
1985	T-Gas	37,500	43,100
1985	T-Diesel	44,600	51,200
1984	T-Gas	35,900	41,300
1984	T-Diesel	38,500	44,200
1983	T-Gas	28,200	32,400
1983	T-Diesel	32,100	36,900
1982	T-Gas	26,300	30,200
1981	T-Gas	23,400	26,900
1980	T-Gas	21,100	24,300
Tiara 3100 Open (1992-04)			
2004	T-Gas	182,200	209,500
2004	T330D	214,000	246,100
2003	T-Gas	165,800	190,600
2003	T330D	194,700	223,900
2002	T-Gas	150,800	173,500
2002	T330D	177,200	203,700
2001	T-Gas	137,300	157,800
2001	T330D	161,200	185,400
2000	T-Gas	124,900	143,600
2000	T300D	146,700	168,700
1999	T-Gas	113,600	130,700
1999	T300D	133,500	153,500
1998	T-Gas	103,400	118,900
1998	T300D	121,500	139,700
1997	T-Gas	94,100	108,200
1997	T300D	110,500	127,100
1996	T-Gas	85,600	98,500
1996	T-Diesel	100,600	115,700
1995	T-Gas	77,900	89,600
1995	T-Diesel	91,500	105,300
1994	T-Gas	70,900	81,500
1994	T-Diesel	83,300	95,800
1993	T-Gas	64,500	74,200
1993	T-Diesel	75,800	87,200
1992	T-Gas	58,700	67,500
1992	T-Diesel	69,000	79,300
Tiara 3200 Open			
2004	T385G	234,300	269,400
2004	T310D	275,300	316,500
Tiara 3300 Flybridge			
1992	T-Gas	79,500	91,400
1992	T-Diesel	92,600	106,500
1991	T-Gas	71,800	82,600
1991	T-Diesel	86,400	99,400
1990	T-Gas	61,700	71,000
1990	T-Diesel	79,900	91,900
1989	T-Gas	57,400	66,000
1989	T-Diesel	75,300	86,600
1988	T-Gas	52,600	60,500
1988	T-Diesel	70,200	80,700
1987	T-Gas	50,500	58,000
1987	T-Diesel	67,400	77,500
1986	T-Gas	48,000	55,200
1986	T-Diesel	64,300	74,000
Tiara 3300 Open			
1997	T-Gas	101,300	116,500
1997	T-Diesel	130,000	149,500
1996	T-Gas	91,900	105,700
1996	T-Diesel	118,900	136,800
1995	T-Gas	85,200	98,000
1995	T-Diesel	109,300	125,700
1994	T-Gas	77,000	88,500

Year	Power	Retail Low	Retail High
1994	T-Diesel	100,400	115,500
1993	T-Gas	73,100	84,100
1993	T-Diesel	95,900	110,300
1992	T-Gas	72,000	82,800
1992	T-Diesel	87,500	100,600
1991	T-Gas	62,700	72,100
1991	T-Diesel	78,900	90,800
1990	T-Gas	58,700	67,500
1990	T-Diesel	76,000	87,400
1989	T-Gas	54,500	62,700
1989	T-Diesel	70,800	81,400
1988	T-Gas	50,700	58,300
1988	T-Diesel	63,700	73,300
Tiara 3500 Express			
2002	T435D	273,100	314,100
2001	T435D	252,300	290,100
2000	T435D	236,700	272,200
1999	T435D	226,100	260,000
1998	T435D	203,200	233,700
1997	T435D	190,000	218,500
1996	T435D	177,300	203,900
1995	T435D	166,300	191,200
Tiara 3500 Open			
2004	T385G	221,400	254,600
2004	T370D	276,900	318,400
2003	T385G	201,400	231,600
2003	T370D	251,900	289,700
2002	T385G	183,300	210,800
2002	T370D	229,300	263,600
2001	T320G	166,800	191,800
2001	T370D	208,600	239,900
2000	T320G	151,800	174,500
2000	T370D	189,800	218,300
1999	T320G	138,100	158,800
1999	T370D	172,700	198,700
1998	T320G	125,700	144,500
1998	T370D	157,200	180,800
Tiara 3600 Convertible			
1995	T-Gas	139,000	159,900
1995	T-Diesel	172,500	198,400
1994	T-Gas	125,500	144,300
1994	T-Diesel	167,700	192,900
1993	T-Gas	125,000	143,800
1993	T-Diesel	158,700	182,500
1992	T-Gas	107,100	123,200
1992	T-Diesel	139,400	160,400
1991	T-Gas	97,800	112,500
1991	T-Diesel	128,200	147,400
1990	T-Gas	88,900	102,300
1990	T-Diesel	117,200	134,800
1989	T-Gas	82,100	94,400
1989	T-Diesel	115,200	132,500
1988	T-Gas	81,000	93,100
1988	T-Diesel	107,300	123,400
1987	T-Gas	76,600	88,200
1987	T-Diesel	101,900	117,200
Tiara 3600 Open (1985-96)			
1996	T-Gas	140,100	161,100
1996	T-Diesel	178,200	204,900
1995	T-Gas	127,100	146,200
1995	T-Diesel	162,900	187,300
1994	T-Gas	116,100	133,500
1994	T-Diesel	156,200	179,600
1993	T-Gas	115,700	133,100

PRICES

Year	Power	Retail Low	Retail High
1993	T-Diesel	146,600	168,600
1992	T-Gas	104,300	120,000
1992	T-Diesel	138,100	158,800
1991	T-Gas	95,600	109,900
1991	T-Diesel	126,400	145,400
1990	T-Gas	87,900	101,100
1990	T-Diesel	118,400	136,100
1989	T-Gas	80,100	92,100
1989	T-Diesel	108,000	124,200
1988	T-Gas	78,000	89,800
1988	T-Diesel	103,800	119,400
1987	T-Gas	75,400	86,700
1987	T-Diesel	94,900	109,100
1986	T-Gas	69,900	80,400
1986	T-Diesel	93,100	107,000
1985	T-Gas	66,300	76,200
1985	T-Diesel	86,000	99,000
Tiara 3600 Open (Current) ******			
Tiara 3600 Sovran			
2004	T385G	261,200	300,300
2004	T450D	335,300	385,500
Tiara 3700 Open			
2000	T435D	261,800	301,000
1999	T435D	240,800	276,900
1998	T435D	221,500	254,800
1997	T435D	203,800	234,400
1996	T435D	189,500	218,000
1995	T435D	176,300	202,700
Tiara 3800 Open			
2004	T480 D	417,700	480,300
2003	T450 D	380,100	437,100
2002	T450 D	345,800	397,700
2001	T450 D	314,700	361,900
2000	T450 D	286,400	329,400
Tiara 4000 Express			
2003	T450D	425,600	489,400
2002	T450D	387,200	445,300
2001	T450D	352,400	405,300
2000	T435D	324,200	372,800
1999	T435D	298,300	343,000
1998	T435D	274,400	315,600
1997	T435D	252,400	290,300
1996	T435D	232,200	267,100
1995	T435D	216,000	248,400
1994	T435D	200,900	231,000
Tiara 4100 Open			
2002	T450D	412,900	474,800
2001	T450D	375,700	432,100
2000	T435D	345,600	397,500
1999	T435D	318,000	365,700
1998	T435D	292,500	336,400
1997	T435D	269,100	309,500
1996	T435D	247,600	284,700
Tiara 4200 Open			
2004	T525D	574,500	660,600
2004	T660D	616,300	708,700
2003	T535D	522,700	601,200
2003	T660D	560,800	644,900
Tiara 4300 Convertible			
2002	T660D	580,800	668,000
2001	T660D	530,700	610,400
2000	T660D	490,100	563,600
1999	T570D	461,200	530,400
1998	T550D	399,900	459,900
1997	T550D	375,600	431,900
1996	T550D	339,600	390,500
1995	T550D	315,000	362,200
1994	T550D	291,800	335,600
1993	T550D	260,500	299,600
1992	T550D	236,400	271,800
1991	T550D	223,700	257,300
1990	T550D	213,300	245,300
Tiara 4300 Open			
2002	T660D	488,700	562,100
2001	T660D	441,200	507,400
2000	T660D	411,200	472,800
1999	T550D	375,600	431,900
1998	T550D	338,200	388,900
1997	T550D	321,500	369,700
1996	T550D	295,000	339,300
1995	T550D	273,400	314,500
1994	T550D	253,700	291,700
1993	T535D	240,300	276,300
1992	T535D	226,100	260,000
1991	T535D	212,400	244,300
Tiara 4400 Sovran			
2004	T535D	608,000	699,200
2004	T660D	632,200	727,000
2003	T535D	553,200	636,200
2003	T660D	575,300	661,500
Tiara 5000 Express			
2003	T800D	855,000	983,200
2002	T800D	786,600	904,500
2001	T800D	723,600	832,200
2000	T800D	665,700	765,600
1999	T800D	612,500	704,300
Tiara 5000 Open			
2003	T800D	824,500	948,100
2002	T800D	758,500	872,300
Tiara 5200 Sovran Salon			
2004	T800D	975,000	1,121,200
2003	T800D	906,700	1,042,700
Tides 27			
2000	S300D	109,800	126,300
2000	T170D	118,900	136,800
1999	S300D	97,700	112,300
1999	T170D	106,000	121,900
1998	S300D	91,300	105,000
1998	T170D	98,900	113,700
1997	S300D	85,800	98,700
1997	T170D	93,100	107,100
1996	S300D	78,300	90,100
1996	T170D	89,000	102,300
1995	S300D	69,800	80,300
1995	T170D	79,500	91,400
1994	S300D	59,800	68,700
1994	T170D	68,700	79,000
1993	S300D	55,000	63,300
1993	T170D	60,800	70,000
1992	S300D	52,900	60,900
1992	T170D	57,600	66,200
1991	S300D	49,200	56,600
1991	T170D	53,500	61,500
1990	S300D	47,000	54,000
1990	T170D	50,600	58,200
1989	S300D	45,700	52,500
1989	T170D	50,300	57,900
1988	S300D	44,800	51,500
1988	T170D	49,800	57,300
1987	S300D	43,800	50,400
1987	T170D	49,300	56,700
Tollycraft 30 Sedan			
1984	T-Gas	34,400	39,600
1983	T-Gas	31,900	36,700
1982	T-Gas	29,400	33,800
1981	T-Gas	26,900	30,900
1980	T-Gas	25,000	28,700
Tollycraft 30 Sport Cruiser			
1992	T-Gas	46,900	54,000
1991	T-Gas	43,500	50,100
1990	T-Gas	41,000	47,200
1989	T-Gas	37,800	43,500
1988	T-Gas	36,100	41,500
1987	T-Gas	33,900	39,000
1986	T-Gas	32,300	37,200
1985	T-Gas	30,200	34,800
Tollycraft 34 Convertible Sedan			
1986	T-Gas	54,600	62,800
1985	T-Gas	50,500	58,000
1984	T-Gas	46,400	53,400
1983	T-Gas	42,900	49,400
1982	T-Gas	39,500	45,400
1981	T-Gas	37,100	42,700
Tollycraft 34 Sport Sedan			
1993	T-Gas	85,500	98,300
1992	T-Gas	79,900	91,900
1991	T-Gas	73,400	84,400
1990	T-Gas	68,900	79,200
1989	T-Gas	63,900	73,500
1988	T-Gas	60,600	69,700
1987	T-Gas	57,700	66,400
Tollycraft 34 Sundeck			
1988	T-Gas	66,700	76,700
1988	T-Diesel	75,300	86,600
1987	T-Gas	61,100	70,200
1987	T-Diesel	68,900	79,300
1986	T-Gas	54,400	62,600
1986	T-Diesel	62,400	71,700
Tollycraft 34 Tri-Cabin			
1985	T-Gas	48,900	56,300
1985	T-Diesel	55,200	63,500
1984	T-Gas	46,500	53,500
1984	T-Diesel	52,900	60,900
1983	T-Gas	42,500	48,900
1983	T-Diesel	48,900	56,200
1982	T-Gas	40,200	46,300
1982	T-Diesel	46,000	52,900
1981	T-Gas	37,900	43,600
1981	T-Diesel	42,500	48,900
1980	T-Gas	33,900	39,000
1980	T-Diesel	36,800	42,300
Tollycraft 37 Convertible			
1985	T-Gas	64,600	74,300
1985	T-Diesel	80,400	92,500
1984	T-Gas	59,700	68,600
1984	T-Diesel	74,300	85,400
1983	T-Gas	56,000	64,400
1983	T-Diesel	68,800	79,100

PRICES

Year	Power	Retail Low	Retail High
1982	T-Gas	53,000	60,900
1982	T-Diesel	63,400	72,900
1981	T-Gas	50,400	57,900
1981	T-Diesel	59,000	67,900
1980	T-Gas	47,300	54,400
1980	T-Diesel	55,900	64,300

Tollycraft 39 Sport Yacht

Year	Power	Retail Low	Retail High
1991	T-Gas	106,700	122,700
1991	T-Diesel	119,800	137,800
1990	T-Gas	101,400	116,600
1990	T-Diesel	113,900	131,000

Tollycraft 40 Sport Sedan

Year	Power	Retail Low	Retail High
1995	T-Diesel	202,900	233,400
1994	T-Diesel	184,600	212,300
1993	T-Gas	147,100	169,200
1993	T-Diesel	173,700	199,700
1992	T-Gas	138,600	159,400
1992	T-Diesel	162,100	186,500
1991	T-Gas	125,600	144,500
1991	T-Diesel	152,900	175,900
1990	T-Gas	116,600	134,100
1990	T-Diesel	143,600	165,200
1989	T-Gas	111,800	128,600
1989	T-Diesel	137,800	158,400
1988	T-Gas	96,800	111,300
1988	T-Diesel	123,700	142,300
1987	T-Gas	92,900	106,900
1987	T-Diesel	114,200	131,300

Tollycraft 40 Sundeck

Year	Power	Retail Low	Retail High
1993	T-Gas	148,500	170,700
1993	T-Diesel	178,600	205,400
1992	T-Gas	137,500	158,100
1992	T-Diesel	166,700	191,800
1991	T-Gas	128,600	147,900
1991	T-Diesel	158,300	182,100
1990	T-Gas	118,900	136,700
1990	T-Diesel	146,100	168,000
1989	T-Gas	108,400	124,700
1989	T-Diesel	132,500	152,400
1988	T-Gas	107,000	123,100
1988	T-Diesel	126,300	145,300
1987	T-Gas	104,400	120,100
1987	T-Diesel	121,600	139,800
1986	T-Gas	97,800	112,500
1986	T-Diesel	116,600	134,100
1985	T-Gas	95,200	109,500
1985	T-Diesel	112,300	129,200

Tollycraft 43 Motor Yacht

Year	Power	Retail Low	Retail High
1986	T-Diesel	128,000	147,200
1985	T-Diesel	122,800	141,200
1984	T-Diesel	116,100	133,500
1983	T-Diesel	109,900	126,400
1982	T-Diesel	104,300	120,000
1981	T-Diesel	99,200	114,100
1980	T-Diesel	96,700	111,200

Tollycraft 44/45 Cockpit MY

Year	Power	Retail Low	Retail High
1996	T-Diesel	247,100	284,200
1995	T-Diesel	235,100	270,400
1994	T-Diesel	218,400	251,100
1993	T-Gas	175,000	201,200
1993	T-Diesel	208,700	240,000
1992	T-Gas	167,900	193,100
1992	T-Diesel	197,300	226,900
1991	T-Gas	153,900	177,000

Year	Power	Retail Low	Retail High
1991	T-Diesel	181,800	209,100
1990	T-Gas	146,100	168,000
1990	T-Diesel	173,100	199,100
1989	T-Gas	137,000	157,600
1989	T-Diesel	162,300	186,600
1988	T-Gas	129,200	148,600
1988	T-Diesel	152,000	174,800
1987	T-Gas	122,400	140,800
1987	T-Diesel	145,300	167,200
1986	T-Gas	114,600	131,900
1986	T-Diesel	143,900	165,500

Tollycraft 48 Convertible

Year	Power	Retail Low	Retail High
1985	300D	162,600	187,000
1985	550D	184,600	212,300
1984	300D	152,200	175,100
1984	550D	178,800	205,600
1983	300D	145,700	167,600
1983	550D	168,700	194,100
1982	300D	133,600	153,600
1982	550D	159,800	183,800

Tollycraft 48 MY

Year	Power	Retail Low	Retail High
1998	T435D	438,900	504,700
1997	T435D	408,200	469,400
1996	T435D	383,700	441,200
1995	T435D	360,600	414,700
1994	T435D	339,000	389,900
1993	T-Diesel	318,700	366,500
1992	T-Diesel	302,700	348,100
1991	T-Diesel	287,600	330,700
1986	T-Diesel	273,200	314,200
1985	T-Diesel	259,500	298,500
1984	T-Diesel	246,600	283,500
1983	T-Diesel	234,200	269,400
1982	T-Diesel	222,500	255,900
1981	T-Diesel	211,400	243,100
1980	T-Diesel	200,800	230,900

Tollycraft 53 Motor Yacht

Year	Power	Retail Low	Retail High
1994	T550D	506,400	582,400
1993	T550D	474,800	546,000
1992	T550D	456,100	524,500
1991	T550D	437,200	502,800
1990	T550D	415,200	477,500
1989	T550D	397,500	457,100
1988	T550D	384,200	441,900

Tollycraft 57 Motor Yacht

Year	Power	Retail Low	Retail High
1998	T760D	815,800	938,200
1997	T760D	776,300	892,800
1996	T-Diesel	729,000	838,400
1995	T-Diesel	676,600	778,100
1994	T-Diesel	609,400	700,800
1993	T-Diesel	557,800	641,400
1992	T-Diesel	543,100	624,600
1991	T-Diesel	500,500	575,600
1990	T-Diesel	468,600	538,900
1989	T-Diesel	457,200	525,800

Tollycraft 61 Motor Yacht

Year	Power	Retail Low	Retail High
1992	T735D	607,400	698,600
1991	T735D	579,400	666,300
1990	T735D	552,000	634,800
1989	T735D	522,500	600,900
1988	T735D	495,400	569,700
1987	T650D	468,000	538,200
1986	T550D	444,200	510,900
1985	T550D	403,200	463,700

Year	Power	Retail Low	Retail High
1984	T550D	388,900	447,300
1983	T550D	377,400	434,100

Tollycraft 65 Cockpit MY

Year	Power	Retail Low	Retail High
1998	T760D	1,023,500	1,177,000
1997	T760D	964,000	1,108,700
1996	T665D	891,900	1,025,700
1995	T665D	833,400	958,400
1994	T665D	775,200	891,500
1993	T665D	728,000	837,200

Topaz 29 Sport Fisherman

Year	Power	Retail Low	Retail High
1988	T-Gas	34,200	39,400
1988	T-Diesel	41,800	48,100
1987	T-Gas	32,200	37,000
1987	T-Diesel	38,000	43,700
1986	T-Gas	30,800	35,400
1986	T-Diesel	35,900	41,300
1985	T-Gas	27,700	31,900
1985	T-Diesel	32,900	37,800
1984	T-Gas	25,300	29,100
1984	T-Diesel	31,200	35,800
1983	T-Gas	24,200	27,800
1983	T-Diesel	30,100	34,600

Topaz 32 Royale

Year	Power	Retail Low	Retail High
2002	T-Diesel	242,800	279,200
2001	T-Diesel	221,200	254,400
2000	T-Diesel	193,800	222,900
1999	T-Diesel	181,100	208,300
1991	T-Diesel	101,500	116,700
1990	T-Diesel	91,000	104,700

Topaz 32 Sportfisherman

Year	Power	Retail Low	Retail High
1991	T-Diesel	94,300	108,400
1990	T-Diesel	85,600	98,400
1989	T-Diesel	80,700	92,800
1988	T-Diesel	74,200	85,400
1987	T-Diesel	68,700	79,000
1986	T-Diesel	65,700	75,500

Topaz 36 Sportfisherman

Year	Power	Retail Low	Retail High
1985	T-Diesel	73,600	84,700
1984	T-Diesel	70,200	80,700
1983	T-Diesel	66,000	75,900
1982	T-Diesel	60,400	69,500
1981	T-Diesel	53,900	62,000
1980	T-Diesel	48,800	56,100

Topaz 37 Sportfisherman

Year	Power	Retail Low	Retail High
2002	T-Diesel	******	******
2001	T-Diesel	******	******
2000	T-Diesel	******	******
1991	T-Diesel	129,000	148,400
1990	T-Diesel	122,500	140,900
1989	T-Diesel	115,200	132,500
1988	T-Diesel	108,700	125,100
1987	T-Diesel	102,500	117,900
1986	T-Diesel	96,100	110,500

Topaz 38 Flybridge SF

Year	Power	Retail Low	Retail High
1987	T-Diesel	108,500	124,800
1986	T-Diesel	103,200	118,700
1985	T-Diesel	95,300	109,600

Topaz 39 Royale

Year	Power	Retail Low	Retail High
1991	T-Diesel	161,300	185,500
1990	T-Diesel	148,300	170,500
1989	T-Diesel	141,200	162,400
1988	T-Diesel	133,500	153,600

PRICES

Year	Power	Retail Low	Retail High
Topaz 44 Flybridge SF			
1989	T-Diesel	171,000	196,700
1988	T-Diesel	154,600	177,700
1987	T-Diesel	139,800	160,700
Trojan 8.6 Meter Mid-Cabin			
1990	T-Gas	31,100	35,800
1989	T-Gas	29,000	33,300
1988	T-Gas	27,400	31,500
1987	T-Gas	25,800	29,600
Trojan 32 Sedan			
1992	T-Gas	56,200	64,700
1991	T-Gas	51,600	59,300
1990	T-Gas	47,500	54,600
1989	T-Gas	44,000	50,600
1988	T-Gas	41,000	47,100
1987	T-Gas	38,700	44,500
1986	T-Gas	36,300	41,800
1985	T-Gas	33,900	39,000
1984	T-Gas	32,300	37,200
1983	T-Gas	30,600	35,200
1982	T-Gas	29,400	33,800
1981	T-Gas	28,800	33,100
1980	T-Gas	27,500	31,700
Trojan 10 Meter Express			
1989	T-Gas	48,200	55,400
1988	T-Gas	45,000	51,800
1987	T-Gas	42,400	48,800
1986	T-Gas	39,800	45,700
1985	T-Gas	37,900	43,600
1984	T-Gas	36,000	41,400
1983	T-Gas	33,900	38,900
1982	T-Diesel	31,600	36,400
1981	T-Gas	30,000	34,600
Trojan 10 Meter Mid-Cabin			
1992	T-Gas	64,900	74,700
1991	T-Gas	60,600	69,700
1990	T-Gas	56,800	65,300
1989	T-Gas	53,500	61,600
1988	T-Gas	50,300	57,800
1987	T-Gas	46,500	53,400
1986	T-Gas	43,200	49,700
Trojan 10 Meter Sedan			
1989	T-Gas	55,900	64,300
1988	T-Gas	52,700	60,600
1987	T-Gas	48,400	55,700
1986	T-Gas	44,700	51,500
1985	T-Gas	41,000	47,100
1984	T-Gas	37,800	43,500
1983	T-Gas	36,200	41,700
1982	T-Gas	34,100	39,200
Trojan 10.8 Meter Express			
1992	T-Gas	79,800	91,800
1991	T-Gas	74,300	85,400
Trojan 10.8 Meter Sedan			
1992	T-Gas	74,200	85,400
1991	T-Gas	70,700	81,300
1990	T-Gas	66,600	76,600
1989	T-Gas	62,500	71,800
1988	T-Gas	58,800	67,700
1987	T-Gas	54,800	63,000
1986	T-Gas	50,200	57,700
Trojan 350/360 Express			
2002	T-IB/7.4L	145,400	167,300
2001	T-IB/7.4L	130,400	149,900
2000	T-IB/7.4L	123,300	141,800
1999	T-IB/7.4L	112,700	129,600
1997	T-IB/7.4L	101,800	117,100
1996	T-IB/7.4L	95,400	109,700
1995	T-IB/7.4L	88,900	102,300
Trojan 36 Convertible			
1989	T-Gas	63,500	73,000
1988	T-Gas	59,300	68,200
1987	T-Gas	55,800	64,100
1986	T-Gas	52,800	60,700
1985	T-Gas	49,800	57,300
1984	T-Gas	48,400	55,700
1983	T-Gas	46,600	53,600
1982	T-Gas	44,200	50,800
1981	T-Gas	41,800	48,000
1980	T-Gas	38,100	43,900
Trojan 36 Tri Cabin			
1987	T-Gas	61,700	70,900
1986	T-Gas	55,900	64,300
1985	T-Gas	50,100	57,600
1984	T-Gas	45,700	52,600
1983	T-Gas	41,500	47,800
1982	T-Gas	38,600	44,400
1981	T-Gas	37,400	43,000
1980	T-Gas	36,200	41,600
Trojan 11 Meter Express (1983-89)			
1989	T-Gas	66,400	76,300
1989	T-Diesel	91,600	105,400
1988	T-Gas	62,500	71,900
1988	T-Diesel	85,600	98,400
1987	T-Gas	58,700	67,500
1987	T-Diesel	79,500	91,500
1986	T-Gas	55,900	64,300
1986	T-Diesel	76,800	88,300
1985	T-Gas	53,200	61,200
1985	T-Diesel	73,500	84,500
1984	T-Gas	50,400	58,000
1984	T-Diesel	70,200	80,700
1983	T-Gas	48,200	55,500
1983	T-Diesel	65,200	75,000
Trojan 11 Meter Express (1990-92)			
1992	T-Gas	89,400	102,800
1992	T-Diesel	125,300	144,200
1991	T-Gas	81,700	94,000
1991	T-Diesel	114,900	132,100
1990	T-Gas	75,600	86,900
1990	T-Diesel	106,000	121,900
Trojan 11 Meter Sedan			
1988	T-Gas	66,900	77,000
1988	T-Diesel	89,000	102,300
1987	T-Gas	61,500	70,700
1987	T-Diesel	82,900	95,400
1986	T-Gas	57,100	65,700
1986	T-Diesel	79,000	90,900
1985	T-Gas	51,600	59,400
1985	T-Diesel	71,900	82,700
Trojan 370/390/400 Express			
2002	T-Gas	181,500	208,700
2001	T-Gas	161,000	185,200
2000	T-Gas	148,600	170,900
(continued)			
1999	T-Gas	140,500	161,600
1998	T-Gas	128,200	147,400
1997	T-Gas	121,600	139,800
1996	T-Gas	115,500	132,800
1995	T-Gas	105,400	121,200
1994	T-Gas	99,500	114,400
1993	T-Gas	93,200	107,200
Trojan 12 Meter Convertible			
1992	T-Gas	111,800	128,600
1992	T-Diesel	136,400	156,800
1991	T-Gas	101,700	117,000
1991	T-Diesel	129,800	149,300
1990	T-Gas	97,400	112,000
1990	T-Diesel	121,000	139,200
1989	T-Gas	88,000	101,200
1989	T-Diesel	108,000	124,300
1988	T-Gas	83,500	96,100
1988	T-Diesel	100,700	115,800
1987	T-Gas	76,200	87,600
1987	T-Diesel	92,600	106,600
1986	T-Gas	70,800	81,500
1986	T-Diesel	85,600	98,400
Trojan 12 Meter Express			
1992	T375D	135,100	155,400
1992	T550D	154,000	177,200
1991	T375D	127,100	146,100
1991	T550D	144,600	166,300
1990	T375D	119,600	137,600
1990	T450D	128,100	147,400
1989	T375D	112,700	129,600
1989	T450D	120,100	138,200
Trojan 12 Meter MY			
1992	T375D	147,000	169,000
1991	T375D	134,400	154,500
1990	T375D	124,300	142,900
1989	T375D	113,900	131,000
1988	T375D	105,300	121,100
1987	T375D	99,300	114,200
Trojan 40 MY			
1984	T-Gas	72,200	83,100
1984	T-Diesel	90,900	104,500
1983	T-Gas	66,800	76,800
1983	T-Diesel	84,200	96,900
1982	T-Gas	64,400	74,000
1982	T-Diesel	79,500	91,400
1981	T-Gas	60,200	69,200
1981	T-Diesel	74,000	85,200
1980	T-Gas	58,300	67,100
1980	T-Diesel	68,600	78,900
Trojan 13 Meter Express			
1990	T450D	147,600	169,700
1990	T735D	176,900	203,500
1989	T450D	138,500	159,200
1989	T735D	166,800	191,900
1988	T450D	130,400	150,000
1988	T735D	155,600	178,900
1987	T450D	122,400	140,800
1987	T735D	144,400	166,000
1986	T450D	114,900	132,200
1986	T550D	128,800	148,200
1985	T450D	109,600	126,000
1985	T550D	117,600	135,200
1984	T450D	104,700	120,500
1984	T550D	112,200	129,100

PRICES

Year	Power	Retail Low	Retail High
Trojan 44 Motor Yacht			
1984	T-Gas	93,800	107,900
1984	T-Diesel	113,600	130,600
1983	T-Gas	88,200	101,500
1983	T-Diesel	106,200	122,100
1982	T-Gas	84,600	97,300
1982	T-Diesel	99,400	114,300
1981	T-Gas	80,200	92,200
1981	T-Diesel	94,400	108,600
1980	T-Gas	75,300	86,600
1980	T-Diesel	90,100	103,700
Trojan 440 Express			
2002	T450D	374,500	430,700
2001	T450D	334,400	384,600
2000	T450D	301,900	347,200
1999	T450D	287,700	330,900
1998	T450D	261,800	301,100
1997	T450D	239,700	275,600
1996	T420D	221,600	254,800
1995	T420D	200,400	230,400
Trojan 14 Meter Convertible			
1992	485D	230,400	264,900
1992	735D	263,300	302,800
1991	485D	212,800	244,700
1991	735D	246,800	283,800
1990	485D	197,500	227,100
1990	735D	224,900	258,600
1989	485D	175,500	201,800
1989	735D	200,200	230,200
1988	450D	159,100	182,900
1988	735D	186,500	214,500
Trophy 2802 Walkaround			
2001	T225/OB	51,400	59,100
2000	T225/OB	46,200	53,200
1999	T225/OB	41,600	47,800
1998	T225/OB	37,400	43,100
1997	T225/OB	33,700	38,700
Trophy 2902 Walkaround			
2004	T225 O/B	66,700	76,700
2003	T225 O/B	60,000	69,000
Uniflite 28 Mega			
1984	T-Gas	25,400	29,200
1983	T-Gas	24,000	27,600
1982	T-Gas	22,700	26,100
1981	T-Gas	21,300	24,500
1980	T-Gas	20,000	23,000
Uniflite 28 Salty Dog			
1984	T-Gas	24,400	28,100
1983	T-Gas	23,100	26,500
1982	T-Gas	21,500	24,700
1981	S-Gas	16,400	18,900
1981	T-Gas	20,400	23,500
1980	S-Gas	14,600	16,800
1980	T-Gas	17,500	20,100
Uniflite 32 Sport Sedan			
1984	T-Gas	35,800	41,100
1983	T-Gas	32,200	37,100
1982	T-Gas	29,800	34,300
1981	T-Gas	28,000	32,200
1980	T-Gas	26,200	30,200
Uniflite 34 Sport Sedan			
1984	T-Gas	39,200	45,100
(Uniflite 34 Sport Sedan cont.)			
1984	T-Diesel	47,700	54,900
1983	T-Gas	36,200	41,600
1983	T-Diesel	45,300	52,100
1982	T-Gas	34,800	40,000
1982	T-Diesel	42,800	49,300
1981	T-Gas	32,900	37,800
1981	T-Diesel	39,700	45,600
1980	T-Gas	30,700	35,300
1980	T-Diesel	36,400	41,800
Uniflite 36 Double Cabin			
1984	T-Gas	49,200	56,500
1984	T-Diesel	55,700	64,100
1983	T-Gas	44,800	51,500
1983	T-Diesel	51,300	59,100
1982	T-Gas	42,600	49,000
1982	T-Diesel	48,100	55,300
1981	T-Gas	40,400	46,500
1981	T-Diesel	45,900	52,800
1980	T-Gas	38,200	44,000
1980	T-Diesel	43,700	50,300
Uniflite 36 Sport Sedan			
1984	T-Gas	49,000	56,300
1984	T-Diesel	57,800	66,500
1983	T-Gas	46,300	53,300
1983	T-Diesel	55,500	63,800
1982	T-Gas	44,200	50,900
1982	T-Diesel	52,000	59,800
1981	T-Gas	41,100	47,300
1981	T-Diesel	50,200	57,700
1980	T-Gas	37,900	43,600
1980	T-Diesel	44,300	51,000
Uniflite 37 Coastal Cruiser			
1984	S-Diesel	68,000	78,200
1984	T-Diesel	76,300	87,800
1983	S-Diesel	63,800	73,400
1983	T-Diesel	71,600	82,300
1982	S-Diesel	58,800	67,600
1982	T-Diesel	66,000	75,900
1981	S-Diesel	53,000	60,900
1981	T-Diesel	59,500	68,400
1980	S-Diesel	49,900	57,400
1980	T-Diesel	55,000	63,300
Uniflite 38 Convertible			
1984	T-Diesel	92,000	105,800
1983	T-Diesel	85,000	97,800
1982	T-Diesel	80,100	92,200
1981	T-Diesel	75,800	87,100
1980	T-Diesel	70,000	80,500
Uniflite 42 Convertible			
1984	T-Diesel	114,400	131,600
1983	T-Diesel	108,500	124,800
1982	T-Diesel	103,100	118,500
1981	T-Diesel	96,000	110,400
1980	T-Diesel	89,500	102,900
Uniflite 42 Double Cabin			
1984	T-Gas	90,800	104,400
1984	T-Diesel	109,900	126,300
1983	T-Gas	88,000	101,200
1983	T-Diesel	105,600	121,400
1982	T-Gas	84,500	97,100
1982	T-Diesel	101,400	116,600
1981	T-Gas	82,300	94,700
1981	T-Diesel	97,900	112,600
(Uniflite 42 Double Cabin cont.)			
1980	T-Gas	76,700	88,200
1980	T-Diesel	90,800	104,400
Uniflite 46 Motor Yacht			
1984	T-Diesel	174,100	200,300
1983	T-Diesel	163,900	188,500
1982	T-Diesel	156,400	179,900
1981	T-Diesel	152,500	175,400
Uniflite 48 Convertible			
1984	T-Diesel	170,700	196,300
1983	T-Diesel	163,700	188,300
1982	T-Diesel	153,200	176,200
1981	T-Diesel	144,200	165,800
1980	T-Diesel	137,200	157,800
Uniflite 48 Yachtfisherman			
1984	T-Diesel	135,500	155,900
1983	T-Diesel	128,100	147,400
1982	T-Diesel	122,200	140,500
1981	T-Diesel	117,800	135,400
1980	T-Diesel	111,800	128,600
Venture 34 Center Console			
2004	T250 O/B	147,500	169,600
2003	T250 O/B	134,200	154,300
2002	T250 O/B	122,100	140,400
2001	T250 O/B	111,100	127,800
2000	T250 O/B	102,200	117,500
1999	T250 O/B	94,000	108,100
1998	T250 O/B	86,500	99,500
1997	T250 O/B	79,600	91,500
Viking 35 Convertible			
1991	T-Gas	91,700	105,400
1991	T-Diesel	117,500	135,200
1990	T-Gas	89,200	102,600
1990	T-Diesel	115,200	132,500
1989	T-Gas	82,800	95,300
1989	T-Diesel	111,700	128,500
1988	T-Gas	78,700	90,600
1988	T-Diesel	106,000	121,900
1987	T-Gas	75,200	86,500
1987	T-Diesel	101,900	117,200
1986	T-Gas	74,400	85,600
1986	T-Diesel	99,500	114,400
1985	T-Gas	70,000	80,500
1985	T-Diesel	90,200	103,800
1984	T-Gas	65,900	75,800
1984	T-Diesel	78,800	90,600
1983	T-Gas	63,000	72,500
1983	T-Diesel	71,600	82,300
1982	T-Gas	58,000	66,700
1982	T-Diesel	66,600	76,600
1981	T-Gas	53,300	61,300
1981	T-Diesel	63,700	73,300
1980	T-Gas	50,400	58,000
1980	T-Diesel	60,100	69,100
Viking 35 Sportfisherman			
1986	T350G	62,800	72,300
1986	T375D	81,100	93,200
1985	T350G	58,500	67,200
1985	T375D	74,600	85,800
1984	T350G	53,500	61,500
1984	T375D	68,100	78,300
Viking 38 Convertible			
1995	T485D	232,300	267,200
1994	T485D	222,500	255,900

IMPORTANT! See Page 293 for Regional Price Adjustment.

Year	Power	Retail Low	Retail High
1993	T485D	213,800	245,900
1992	T485D	204,700	235,400
1991	T485D	193,200	222,200
1990	T485D	180,900	208,100
Viking 38 Flybridge			
1997	T350D	228,500	262,800
1996	T350D	201,600	231,900
1995	T350D	179,400	206,300
Viking 40 Flybridge			
2002	T370D	381,600	438,800
2001	T370D	340,100	391,100
2000	T370D	296,700	341,200
Viking V40 Express			
1999	T430D	261,900	301,200
1998	T430D	239,600	275,500
1997	T420D	214,800	247,000
1996	T420D	189,400	217,900
1995	T420D	167,900	193,100
Viking 40 Sedan			
1982	T-Gas	85,400	98,200
1982	T-Diesel	102,300	117,700
1981	T-Gas	80,400	92,500
1981	T-Diesel	96,700	111,200
1980	T-Gas	75,500	86,800
1980	T-Diesel	87,500	100,600
Viking 41 Convertible			
1989	T-Gas	142,900	164,300
1989	T-Diesel	187,900	216,100
1988	T-Gas	136,900	157,400
1988	T-Diesel	175,500	201,800
1987	T-Gas	131,500	151,300
1987	T-Diesel	163,200	187,700
1986	T-Gas	119,900	137,700
1986	T-Diesel	148,100	170,400
1985	T-Gas	111,900	128,700
1985	T-Diesel	138,900	159,800
1984	T-Gas	106,300	122,200
1984	T-Diesel	131,600	151,400
1983	T-Gas	99,900	114,900
1983	T-Diesel	124,900	143,600
Viking Sport Cruiser 42/43 Flybridge			
1999	T420D	328,500	377,800
1998	T420D	297,400	342,000
1997	T420D	263,100	302,600
1996	T420D	236,900	272,400
1995	T420D	215,400	247,800
Viking 43 Convertible			
2002	680hp MAN	520,000	598,000
2001	680hp MAN	471,500	542,200
2000	680hp MAN	439,000	504,800
1999	680hp MAN	416,200	478,700
1998	625hp DD	359,600	413,600
1998	680hp MAN	393,400	452,500
1997	625hp DD	342,800	394,200
1997	680hp MAN	368,200	423,400
1996	625hp DD	320,800	369,000
1996	600hp MAN	338,100	388,800
1995	550hp DD	298,800	343,600
1995	600hp MAN	312,400	359,300
1994	T-Diesel	277,700	319,300
1993	T-Diesel	251,500	289,200
1992	T-Diesel	225,100	258,900
1991	T-Diesel	210,400	242,000

Year	Power	Retail Low	Retail High
1990	T-Diesel	201,600	231,800
Viking 43 Double Cabin			
1982	T-Gas	93,300	107,300
1982	T-Diesel	111,600	128,400
1981	T-Gas	90,600	104,200
1981	T-Diesel	106,400	122,400
1980	T-Gas	87,300	100,400
1980	T-Diesel	101,200	116,300
Viking 43 Open			
2002	680 MAN	505,900	581,700
2001	680 MAN	454,600	522,700
2000	680 MAN	423,600	487,100
1999	680 MAN	397,900	457,600
1998	625hp DD	353,000	405,900
1998	680 MAN	376,100	432,500
1997	625hp DD	334,600	384,800
1997	680 MAN	358,600	412,400
1996	550 DD	313,800	360,800
1996	600 MAN	330,700	380,300
1995	550 DD	295,400	339,700
1995	600 MAN	311,900	358,700
1994	T-Diesel	281,700	324,000
Viking 44 Motor Yacht			
1990	T485D	217,200	249,700
1989	T485D	208,300	239,500
1988	T485D	195,300	224,600
1987	T450D	181,400	208,600
1986	T450D	170,400	196,000
1985	T375D	158,200	181,900
1984	T375D	151,800	174,600
1983	T375D	145,500	167,300
1982	T375D	139,100	159,900
Viking 45 Conv. (1987-93)			
1993	T550D	271,100	311,800
1992	T550D	254,800	293,000
1991	T550D	240,500	276,600
1990	T550D	225,000	258,800
1989	T550D	208,300	239,600
1988	T485D	192,900	221,900
1987	T485D	181,500	208,700
Viking 45 Conv. (Current)			
2004	T800D	766,800	881,800
2003	T800D	705,400	811,200
Viking Sport Cruiser 45 Flybridge			
2004	T480D	560,000	644,000
2003	T480D	509,600	586,000
2002	T480D	463,700	533,200
2001	T480D	422,000	485,300
2000	T480D	384,000	441,600
Viking 45 Open			
2004	T800D	729,800	839,200
Viking Sport Cruiser 45/46 Flybridge			
2000	T430D	403,500	464,000
1999	T430D	382,600	440,000
1998	T430D	357,000	410,600
1997	T430D	329,600	379,000
1996	T430D	292,000	335,800
1995	T430D	266,300	306,300
Viking 46 Convertible			
1985	T565D	179,400	206,300
1984	T565D	173,300	199,300
1983	T500D	166,900	192,000

Year	Power	Retail Low	Retail High
1982	T500D	158,100	181,800
1981	T500D	150,000	172,500
Viking 47 Convertible			
2002	T680D	654,500	752,700
2001	T680D	595,600	684,900
2000	T680D	542,000	623,300
1999	T680D	493,200	567,200
1998	T680D	453,700	521,800
1997	T680D	417,400	480,000
1996	T680D	384,000	441,600
1995	T680D	353,300	406,300
1994	T680D	325,000	373,800
Viking 48 Conv. (1985-90)			
1990	T735D	289,400	332,800
1989	T735D	274,900	316,100
1988	T735D	261,100	300,300
1987	T710D	250,700	288,300
1986	T710D	240,700	276,800
1985	T710D	231,000	265,700
Viking 48 Conv. (Current)			
2004	T860D	810,900	932,500
2003	T860D	737,900	848,600
2002	T860D	671,500	772,200
Viking 48 MY			
1988	T735D	274,500	315,600
1987	T735D	260,700	299,800
1986	T735D	247,700	284,800
Viking Sport Cruiser 48/50 Flybridge			
1999	T435D	456,000	524,400
1998	T435D	417,800	480,500
1997	T435D	374,600	430,800
1996	T435D	340,100	391,200
1995	T435D	313,100	360,000
1994	T435D	285,700	328,500
Viking 50 Cockpit MY			
1989	T-Diesel	242,300	278,700
1988	T-Diesel	223,300	256,900
1987	T-Diesel	209,800	241,300
1986	T-Diesel	192,300	221,200
1985	T-Diesel	179,600	206,600
1984	T-Diesel	173,300	199,300
1983	T-Diesel	166,900	191,900
Viking 50 Convertible			
2001	820D	708,600	814,900
2001	1050D	753,800	866,900
2000	820D	647,500	744,600
2000	1050D	688,600	791,900
1999	820D	607,000	698,000
1999	1050D	647,100	744,100
1998	820D	562,700	647,200
1998	1200D	625,000	718,700
1997	820D	542,500	623,900
1997	1200D	593,200	682,200
1996	820D	514,000	591,100
1995	820D	471,300	542,000
1994	820D	439,700	505,600
1993	735D	389,400	447,800
1993	820D	418,200	480,900
1992	735D	374,200	430,400
1992	820D	396,900	456,400
1991	735D	359,500	413,500
Viking Sport Cruiser 50 Flybridge			

PRICES

Year	Power	Retail Low	Retail High
2004	T480D	703,400	808,900
2003	T480D	633,000	728,000
2002	T480D	569,700	655,200
2001	T480D	512,700	589,600
Viking V50 Express			
2002	T480D	687,000	790,000
2001	T480D	618,300	711,000
2000	T480D	556,400	639,900
1999	T480D	500,800	575,900
Viking 50 Motor Yacht			
1993	T735D	443,300	509,800
1992	T735D	416,600	479,100
1991	T485D	388,900	447,200
1990	T485D	373,900	430,000
Viking 50 Open			
2003	T820D	762,400	876,700
2003	T1050D	836,900	962,400
2002	T800D	705,900	811,800
2002	T1050D	774,900	891,100
2001	T800D	638,400	734,200
2001	T1050D	700,200	805,200
2000	T800D	590,600	679,200
2000	T1050D	648,400	745,700
1999	T800D	548,100	630,300
1999	T1050D	605,200	695,900
Viking 52 Convertible			
2004	T1300D	1,232,400	1,417,200
2003	T1050D	1,121,400	1,289,700
2002	T1050D	1,020,500	1,173,600
Viking Sport Cruiser 52 Flybridge			
2002	T615D	731,500	841,200
2001	T615D	658,000	756,800
2000	T610D	590,300	678,900
1999	T610D	523,300	601,800
1998	T610D	463,900	533,500
1997	T610D	419,200	482,100
Viking V55 Express			
2002	T800D	769,200	884,600
2001	T800D	693,400	797,400
2000	T800D	624,900	718,600
1999	T800D	551,800	634,600
1998	T680D	466,200	536,100
1997	T680D	424,500	488,200
1996	T680D	396,200	455,700
1995	T680D	364,100	418,700
Viking 53 Convertible			
1998	T820D	627,700	721,800
1998	T1200D	687,600	790,700
1997	T820D	592,500	681,300
1997	T1200D	656,300	754,700
1996	T820D	561,100	645,200
1996	T1200D	635,500	730,800
1995	T820D	545,100	626,900
1994	T820D	515,000	592,300
1993	T820D	494,100	568,200
1992	T820D	459,800	528,700
1991	T820D	426,000	489,900
1990	T820D	402,400	462,700
Viking Sport Cruiser 53/56 Flybridge			
2002	T615D	882,000	1,014,400
2001	T615D	789,900	908,400
2000	T610D	703,000	808,400

Year	Power	Retail Low	Retail High
1999	T610D	631,200	725,900
1998	T610D	577,100	663,700
1997	T610D	522,500	600,900
1996	T610D	475,900	547,300
1995	T610D	442,200	508,500
Viking 54 Sports Yacht			
2001	T820D	797,300	916,900
2001	T1050D	849,200	976,600
2000	T820D	735,900	846,200
2000	T1050D	788,600	906,900
1999	T820D	661,100	760,300
1999	T1050D	718,600	826,400
1998	T820D	609,000	700,300
1998	T1200D	666,100	766,000
1997	T820D	603,400	693,900
1997	T1200D	663,900	763,500
1996	T820D	579,600	666,500
1995	T820D	548,400	630,700
1994	T820D	502,000	577,300
1993	T820D	478,800	550,600
1992	T820D	457,500	526,200
Viking 55 Convertible			
2003	T1300D	******	******
2002	T1300D	1,133,500	1,303,500
2001	T1050D	1,055,500	1,213,800
2000	T1050D	971,300	1,117,000
1999	T1050D	893,900	1,028,000
1998	T1050D	823,900	947,500
Viking 55 Motor Yacht			
1991	T735D	445,100	511,800
1990	T735D	421,400	484,600
1989	T735D	403,300	463,800
1988	T735D	368,400	423,700
1987	T735D	326,200	375,100
Viking 56 Convertible			
2004	T1480D	1,627,000	1,871,000
Viking 57 Convertible			
1991	T1080D	542,200	623,500
1990	T1080D	524,200	602,900
1989	T1080D	508,900	585,300
Viking Sport Cruiser 57 Flybridge ******			
Viking 57 Motor Yacht			
1995	T760D	663,000	762,400
1994	T820D	616,500	709,000
1993	T735D	573,400	659,400
1992	T735D	539,000	619,800
1991	T735D	506,600	582,600
Viking 58 Convertible			
2000	T1200D		
	Open Bridge	919,400	1,057,300
	Closed Bridge	996,100	1,145,600
1999	T1200D		
	Open Bridge	857,000	985,600
	Closed Bridge	944,400	1,086,000
1998	T1150D		
	Open Bridge	779,900	896,900
	Closed Bridge	878,500	1,010,300
1997	T1200D	760,100	874,100
1996	T1200D	722,500	830,900
1995	T1200D	680,600	782,700
1994	T1100D	643,900	740,500
1993	T1100D	628,800	723,100

Year	Power	Retail Low	Retail High
1992	T1100D	616,400	708,900
1991	T1100D	585,600	673,500
Viking V58 Express ******			
Viking 60 Cockpit Sport Yacht			
2001	T820D	938,200	1,078,900
2001	T1200D	1,012,700	1,164,700
2000	T820D	881,700	1,014,000
2000	T1200D	951,500	1,094,300
1999	T820D	802,200	922,600
1999	T1200D	863,100	992,500
1998	T820D	752,800	865,700
1998	T1200D	814,800	937,000
1997	T820D	727,300	836,400
1997	T1200D	787,000	905,100
1996	T820D	684,000	786,600
1996	T1200D	746,800	858,800
1995	T820D	671,700	772,400
1994	T820D	651,000	748,700
Viking Sport Cruiser 60 Flybridge			
2001	T800D	903,700	1,039,200
2000	T800D	842,200	968,600
1999	T800D	763,800	878,300
1998	T800D	682,900	785,300
1997	T800D	606,800	697,900
1996	T800D	547,800	630,000
Viking 61 Conv. (Open Bridge)			
2004	T1480D	1,698,000	1,952,700
2003	T1480D	1,545,100	1,776,900
2002	T1480D	1,421,500	1,634,800
2001	T1300D	1,307,800	1,504,000
Viking Sport Cruiser 61 Flybridge			
2004	T800D	1,209,900	1,391,300
2003	T800D	1,101,000	1,266,100
Viking 63 Cockpit MY			
1991	T735D	******	******
1990	T735D	504,200	579,900
1989	T735D	472,700	543,600
1988	T735D	441,200	507,400
1987	T735D	411,500	473,300
Viking 63 Motor Yacht			
1991	T735D	589,400	677,800
1990	T735D	541,000	622,200
1989	T735D	512,100	588,900
1988	T735D	481,800	554,100
1987	T735D	460,200	529,200
Viking 65 Cockpit MY			
1994	T-Diesel	817,500	940,100
1993	T-Diesel	766,500	881,500
1992	T-Diesel	722,300	830,600
1991	T-Diesel	671,600	772,400
Viking 65 Conv. (Open Bridge)			
2004	T1480 D	******	******
2004	T1800 D	******	******
2003	T1480 D	******	******
2004	T1800 D	******	******
2002	T1480 D	1,780,000	2,047,000
2002	T1800 D	1,988,900	2,287,200
2001	T1480 D	1,634,700	1,879,900
2001	T1800 D	1,807,700	2,078,900
2000	T1350 D	1,547,300	1,779,300
2000	T1800 D	1,717,500	1,975,100
1999	T1350 D	1,421,800	1,635,100

PRICES

IMPORTANT! See Page 293 for Regional Price Adjustment.

Year	Power	Retail Low	Retail High
1999	T1800 D	1,592,500	1,831,300
Viking Sport Cruiser 65 Express			
2002	T1300 D	1,434,600	1,649,800
2001	T1300 D	1,295,100	1,489,300
2000	T1300 D	1,147,200	1,319,200
Viking 65 MY (1991-95)			
1995	T1000D	900,100	1,035,100
1994	T1000D	869,100	999,400
1993	T1000D	837,500	963,100
1992	T900D	802,100	922,400
1991	T900D	761,200	875,300
Viking Sport Cruiser 65 MY			
2004	T1050D	1,718,700	1,976,500
2003	T1050D	1,564,000	1,798,600
2002	T1050D	1,423,200	1,636,700
2001	T1050D	1,295,100	1,489,400
2000	T1050D	1,191,500	1,370,200
1999	T1050D	1,096,200	1,260,600
Viking V65 Express			
2004	T1050D	1,622,300	1,865,600
2003	T1050D	1,476,200	1,697,700
2002	T1050D	1,343,400	1,544,900
2001	T1050D	1,222,500	1,405,800
2000	T1050D	1,124,700	1,293,400
1999	T1050D	1,034,700	1,189,900
Viking Sport Cruiser 68 Motor Yacht			
2003	T1200D	1,865,000	2,144,700
2002	T1200D	1,697,100	1,951,700
2001	T1200D	1,544,400	1,776,000
2000	T1200D	1,420,800	1,633,900
1999	T1200D	1,307,100	1,503,200
1998	T1200D	1,202,600	1,383,000
Viking 72 Cockpit MY			
1994	T1050D	955,400	1,098,700
1993	T1050D	926,800	1,065,900
1992	T1050D	866,000	995,900
1991	T1050D	805,100	925,900
1990	T1050D	754,000	867,100
Viking 72 Convertible ****			
Viking 72 Motor Yacht			
1994	T-Diesel	1,027,500	1,181,600
1993	T-Diesel	966,000	1,110,900
1992	T-Diesel	919,000	1,056,800
1991	T-Diesel	829,600	954,100
1990	T-Diesel	764,600	879,300
1989	T-Diesel	719,400	827,300
Viking Sport Cruiser 72 MY ****			
Vista 43 Motor Yacht			
1994	T375	199,000	228,900
1993	T375	184,400	212,100
1992	T375	173,200	199,200
1991	T375	162,100	186,400
1990	T375	149,300	171,700
1989	T375	139,700	160,700
1988	T375	128,700	148,000
1987	T375	117,200	134,800
Vista 46 Motor Yacht			
1988	T375	149,200	171,600
1987	T375	137,400	158,000
1986	T375	128,600	147,900
1985	T355	120,500	138,600

Year	Power	Retail Low	Retail High
1984	T355	113,800	130,900
Vista 48/50 Sport Fisherman			
1992	425D	215,500	247,800
1992	735D	233,100	268,100
1991	425D	195,300	224,600
1991	735D	214,200	246,400
1990	425D	179,500	206,400
1990	735D	198,400	228,200
1989	425D	161,900	186,200
1989	735D	179,500	206,400
1988	375D	144,800	166,600
1988	650D	165,700	190,500
1987	375D	138,600	159,400
1987	650D	157,500	181,200
1986	375D	129,100	148,500
1986	650D	148,000	170,300
Vista 49 Motor Yacht			
1994	T375	235,700	271,100
1993	T375	224,000	257,600
1992	T375	210,100	241,600
1991	T375	196,600	226,100
1990	T375	183,300	210,800
1989	T375	169,700	195,200
1988	T375	158,300	182,000
1987	T375	149,200	171,600
Vista 52 Motor Yacht			
1994	T375	256,300	294,700
1993	T375	236,100	271,500
1992	T375	229,500	264,000
1991	T375	215,500	247,800
1990	T375	201,200	231,400
1989	T375	186,600	214,600
1988	T375	175,100	201,300
1987	T375	165,500	190,300
1986	T375	156,200	179,600
1985	T355	147,200	169,200
1984	T355	139,800	160,800
Vitesse 48 PH ****			
Wellcraft 270 Coastal			
2004	T225 O/B	85,600	98,400
2004	S375 I/O	62,400	71,700
2003	T225 O/B	77,000	88,500
2003	S375 I/O	56,100	64,500
2002	T225 O/B	69,300	79,700
2002	S330 I/O	50,500	58,100
2001	T225 O/B	62,400	71,700
2001	S330 I/O	45,400	52,300
Wellcraft 2700/2800 Martinique			
1999	S310 I/O	43,500	50,100
1998	S310 I/O	40,300	46,400
1997	S330 I/O	37,200	42,800
1996	S330 I/O	33,200	38,200
1995	S330 I/O	29,900	34,400
1994	S330 I/O	27,300	31,400
Wellcraft 2800 Coastal			
1994	T-Gas	36,000	41,400
1993	T-Gas	31,500	36,300
1992	T-Gas	29,200	33,500
1991	T-Gas	26,800	30,800
1990	T-Gas	23,600	27,200
1989	T-Gas	21,800	25,100
1988	T-Gas	20,200	23,300
1987	T-Gas	18,900	21,700

Year	Power	Retail Low	Retail High
1986	T-Gas	18,200	20,900
Wellcraft 2800 Martinique			
2002	T190 I/O	59,400	68,300
2001	T190 I/O	53,400	61,500
Wellcraft 2800 Monte Carlo			
1989	T-I/O Gas	21,000	24,100
1988	T-I/O Gas	19,400	22,300
1987	T-I/O Gas	17,700	20,400
1986	T-I/O Gas	16,700	19,200
Wellcraft 287 Prima			
1993	S-I/O Gas	24,500	28,200
1992	S-I/O Gas	22,900	26,300
1991	S-I/O Gas	21,200	24,400
1990	S-I/O Gas	19,600	22,600
Wellcraft 29 Scarab Sport			
2004	T225 O/B	74,600	85,700
2003	T225 O/B	66,300	76,300
2002	T225 O/B	59,000	67,900
2001	T225 O/B	52,500	60,400
Wellcraft 290 Coastal			
2004	T225 O/B	89,600	103,000
2003	T225 O/B	80,600	92,700
2002	T225 O/B	72,500	83,400
2001	T225 O/B	66,000	75,900
2000	T225 O/B	60,100	69,100
1999	T225 O/B	54,600	62,800
Wellcraft 2900 Express			
1987	T-Gas	19,800	22,800
1986	T-Gas	18,700	21,500
1985	T-Gas	17,000	19,600
1984	T-Gas	15,900	18,300
1983	T-Gas	14,800	17,000
1982	T-Gas	14,300	16,400
1981	T-Gas	13,700	15,800
1980	T-Gas	13,200	15,200
Wellcraft 2900 Sport Bridge			
1986	T-Gas	22,800	26,200
1985	T-Gas	21,700	24,900
1984	T-Gas	20,000	23,000
1983	T-Gas	18,200	20,900
Wellcraft 30 Scarab Sport			
1993	T225 O/B	18,400	21,100
1992	T225 O/B	17,300	19,800
1991	T225 O/B	16,200	18,700
1990	T225 O/B	15,200	17,500
1989	T225 O/B	14,300	16,500
1988	T200 O/B	13,500	15,500
1987	T200 O/B	12,600	14,600
1986	T200 O/B	11,900	13,700
1985	T200 O/B	11,200	12,900
1984	T200 O/B	10,500	12,100
1983	T200 O/B	9,900	11,400
1982	T200 O/B	9,300	10,700
1981	T200 O/B	8,700	10,000
1980	T200 O/B	8,200	9,400
Wellcraft 3000 Martinique			
2003	T260 I/O	84,800	97,500
2002	T260 I/O	76,300	87,700
2001	T260 I/O	68,600	78,900
2000	T260 I/O	62,500	71,800
1999	T260 I/O	56,800	65,400

PRICES

Year	Power	Retail Low	Retail High
1998	T260 I/O	51,700	59,500
Wellcraft 3000 Monaco			
1992	T245 I/O	33,400	38,400
1991	T245 I/O	30,600	35,200
1990	T240 I/O	28,400	32,600
1989	T240 I/O	26,200	30,100
Wellcraft 302 Scarab Sport			
2000	T225 O/B	48,000	55,200
1999	T225 O/B	43,600	50,200
1998	T225 O/B	39,700	45,500
1997	T225 O/B	36,100	41,500
1996	T225 O/B	32,900	37,800
1995	T225 O/B	29,900	34,400
1994	T225 O/B	27,200	31,300
Wellcraft 310 Flybridge Sedan			
1983	T-Gas	25,300	29,100
1982	T-Gas	23,600	27,100
1981	T-Gas	21,900	25,100
Wellcraft 3100 Express			
1985	T350G	28,300	32,600
1984	T350G	24,900	28,700
1983	T350G	22,700	26,100
1982	T350G	21,000	24,100
1981	T350G	19,200	22,100
1980	T350G	18,100	20,900
Wellcraft 32 CCF			
2004	T250 O/B	77,900	89,500
2003	T250 O/B	70,100	80,600
2002	T250 O/B	63,000	72,500
2001	T250 O/B	56,700	65,300
Wellcraft 3200 Coastal			
1986	T260	31,300	36,000
1985	T260	28,600	32,800
1984	T260	25,900	29,800
Wellcraft 3200 Martinique			
2000	T310 I/O	75,300	86,600
1999	T310 I/O	68,500	78,800
1998	T310 I/O	62,300	71,700
1997	T310 I/O	57,300	66,000
1996	T300 I/O	52,800	60,700
1995	T300 I/O	48,500	55,800
1994	T300 I/O	44,600	51,300
Wellcraft 3200 Sedan Bridge			
1986	T-Gas	33,400	38,400
1985	T-Gas	29,900	34,400
Wellcraft 3200 St. Tropez			
1993	T300G	45,200	51,900
1992	T300G	42,500	48,800
1991	T300G	39,900	45,900
1989	T300G	37,500	43,100
1988	T300G	35,300	40,500
1987	T300G	33,100	38,100
1986	T300G	31,100	35,800
1985	T300G	29,300	33,700
Wellcraft 33 St. Tropez			
1992	T260G	37,400	43,100
1991	T260G	35,200	40,500
1990	T260G	33,100	38,000
Wellcraft 330 Coastal			
2004	T-Gas	158,900	182,700
2003	T-Diesel	202,300	232,600

Year	Power	Retail Low	Retail High
2003	T-Gas	143,000	164,400
2003	T-Diesel	184,000	211,700
2002	T-Gas	128,700	148,000
2002	T-Diesel	167,500	192,600
2001	T-Gas	115,800	133,200
2001	T-Diesel	154,100	177,200
2000	T-Gas	105,400	121,200
2000	T-Diesel	141,700	163,000
1999	T-Gas	95,900	110,300
1999	T-Diesel	130,400	150,000
1998	T-Gas	87,200	100,300
1998	T-Diesel	120,000	138,000
1997	T-Gas	79,400	91,300
1997	T-Diesel	110,400	126,900
1996	T-Gas	72,200	83,100
1996	T-Diesel	101,500	116,800
1995	T-Gas	66,500	76,400
1995	T-Diesel	93,400	107,400
1994	T-Gas	61,100	70,300
1994	T-Diesel	85,900	98,800
1993	T-Gas	56,200	64,700
1993	T-Diesel	79,000	90,900
1992	T-Gas	51,700	59,500
1992	T-Diesel	72,700	83,600
1991	T-Gas	47,600	54,700
1991	T-Diesel	66,900	76,900
1990	T-Gas	43,800	50,400
1990	T-Diesel	61,500	70,800
1989	T-Gas	40,300	46,300
1989	T-Diesel	56,600	65,100
Wellcraft 3300 Martinique			
2003	T310G	******	******
2002	T310G	104,700	120,400
2001	T310G	94,000	108,100
Wellcraft 3300 Sport Bridge			
1992	T-Gas	48,500	55,800
1991	T-Gas	43,200	49,700
Wellcraft 34 Scarab Super Sport			
1992	T250 O/B	27,200	31,300
1991	T250 O/B	25,900	29,800
1990	T250 O/B	24,500	28,200
1989	T250 O/B	23,200	26,700
1988	T250 O/B	21,700	24,900
1987	T250 O/B	20,200	23,300
Wellcraft 34 Triumph			
1993	T-Gas	55,600	63,900
1992	T-Gas	50,700	58,300
1991	T-Gas	46,800	53,800
1990	T-Gas	43,900	50,500
Wellcraft 3400 Gran Sport			
1992	T-Gas	55,400	63,700
1991	T-Gas	50,600	58,200
1990	T-Gas	46,700	53,700
1989	T-Gas	41,400	47,600
1988	T-Gas	38,100	43,800
1987	T-Gas	35,900	41,200
1986	T-Gas	33,700	38,700
1985	T-Gas	32,000	36,800
1984	T-Gas	30,400	34,900
Wellcraft 35 CCF			
2004	T250 O/B	108,200	124,400
2003	T250 O/B	97,300	111,900
2002	T250 O/B	87,600	100,700

Year	Power	Retail Low	Retail High
2001	T250 O/B	78,800	90,700
Wellcraft 350 Coastal			
2003	T360D	227,800	261,900
2002	T360D	209,500	241,000
2001	T370D	192,800	221,700
2000	T370D	177,300	203,900
Wellcraft 3500 Corsair			
1993	T-Gas	56,700	65,200
1992	T-Gas	51,900	59,700
Wellcraft 3600 Martinique			
2000	T385G	117,600	135,200
1999	T385G	107,000	123,100
1998	T380G	97,400	112,000
1997	T330G	88,600	101,900
1996	T330G	81,500	93,800
1995	T330G	75,000	86,200
1994	T330G	69,000	79,300
Wellcraft 37 Corsica			
1991	T-Gas	66,000	75,900
1990	T-Gas	59,900	68,900
1989	T-Gas	54,800	63,000
Wellcraft 3700 Cozumel			
1989	T-Gas	62,200	71,600
1988	T-Gas	57,400	66,000
Wellcraft 3700 Martinique			
2002	T310G	145,500	167,300
2001	T310G	132,000	151,800
Wellcraft 38 Excalibur			
2002	T425 I/O	174,500	200,600
2001	T425 I/O	157,000	180,600
2000	T385 I/O	142,900	164,300
1999	T385 I/O	130,000	149,500
1998	T385 I/O	118,300	136,100
1997	T385 I/O	107,600	123,800
1996	T385 I/O	98,000	112,700
Wellcraft 390 Coastal ******			
Wellcraft 400 Coastal			
2003	T480D	328,700	378,000
2002	T480D	299,100	343,900
2001	T430D	272,100	313,000
2000	T430D	250,400	287,900
1999	T430D	230,300	264,900
Wellcraft 43 Portofino			
1997	T-Gas	150,100	172,600
1997	T-Diesel	188,600	216,800
1996	T-Gas	136,500	157,000
1996	T-Diesel	171,600	197,300
1995	T-Gas	124,200	142,900
1995	T-Diesel	156,100	179,600
1994	T-Gas	114,300	131,500
1994	T-Diesel	143,600	165,200
1993	T-Gas	105,200	120,900
1993	T-Diesel	132,100	152,200
1992	T-Gas	96,700	111,300
1992	T-Diesel	121,600	139,800
1991	T-Gas	89,000	102,400
1991	T-Diesel	111,800	128,600
1990	T-Gas	81,900	94,200
1990	T-Diesel	102,900	118,500
1989	T-Gas	75,300	86,600
1989	T-Diesel	94,700	108,900

PRICES

Year	Power	Retail Low	Retail High
1988	T-Gas	69,300	79,700
1988	T-Diesel	87,100	100,100
1987	T-Gas	63,700	73,300
1987	T-Diesel	80,100	92,100
Wellcraft 43 San Remo			
1990	T-Gas	83,800	96,400
1990	T-Diesel	99,800	114,800
1989	T-Gas	78,800	90,700
1989	T-Diesel	93,700	107,800
1988	T-Gas	76,000	87,500
1988	T-Diesel	89,900	103,400
Wellcraft 45 Excalibur			
2001	T415G	223,000	256,400
2000	T415G	202,900	233,300
1999	T415G	184,600	212,300
1998	T415G	168,000	193,200
1997	T415G	154,600	177,700
1996	T415G	142,200	163,500
1995	T415G	130,800	150,400
Wellcraft 46 Cockpit MY			
1995	T-Diesel	189,000	217,400
1994	T-Diesel	173,900	200,000
1993	T-Diesel	160,000	184,000
1992	T-Diesel	147,200	169,300
1991	T-Diesel	135,400	155,700
1990	T-Diesel	124,600	143,300
West Bay 4500 Pilothouse ******			
West Bay 52 Sonship ******			

Year	Power	Retail Low	Retail High
West Bay 58 Sonship ******			
West Bay 68 Sonship ******			
West Bay 78 Sonship ******			
Whitewater 28 Center Console ******			
Willard 30 Sedan Trawler			
2004	S-Diesel	188,600	216,800
2003	S-Diesel	179,100	206,000
2002	S-Diesel	170,200	195,700
2001	S-Diesel	161,700	185,900
2000	S-Diesel	155,200	178,500
1999	S-Diesel	149,000	171,300
1998	S-Diesel	143,000	164,500
1997	S-Diesel	137,300	157,900
1996	S-Diesel	131,800	151,600
1995	S-Diesel	126,500	145,500
1994	S-Diesel	121,500	139,700
1993	S-Diesel	116,600	134,100
1992	S-Diesel	111,900	128,700
1991	S-Diesel	107,500	123,600
1990	S-Diesel	103,200	118,600
1989	S-Diesel	99,000	113,900
1988	S-Diesel	95,100	109,300
World Cat 266/270 LC			
2004	No Power	43,500	50,000
2003	No Power	39,500	45,500
2002	No Power	36,000	41,400

Year	Power	Retail Low	Retail High
2001	No Power	32,700	37,600
2000	No Power	29,800	34,300
1999	No Power	27,100	31,200
World Cat 266/270 SC			
2004	T200 O/B	69,300	79,700
2003	T200 O/B	62,400	71,700
2002	T200 O/B	56,100	64,600
2001	T200 O/B	50,500	58,100
2000	T200 O/B	45,500	52,300
1999	T200 O/B	40,900	47,000
1998	T200 O/B	36,800	42,300
World Cat 270 TE			
2004	T200 O/B	65,300	75,100
2003	T200 O/B	58,800	67,600
2002	T200 O/B	52,900	60,800
2001	T200 O/B	47,600	54,700
2000	T200 O/B	42,800	49,300
1999	T200 O/B	38,500	44,300
1998	T200 O/B	34,700	39,900
World Cat 270 Express Cabin			
2004	T200 O/B	72,300	83,200
2003	T200 O/B	65,100	74,900
World Cat 330 TE ******			
Yellowfin 31			
2004	T225 O/B	109,500	125,900
2003	T225 O/B	98,500	113,300
2002	T225 O/B	88,600	101,900
2001	T225 O/B	79,800	91,700

PRICES

365

Index